Ultimate Guide to
Medical Schools

Third Edition

Josh Fischman and the staff of U.S.News & World Report

Foreword by Bernadine Healy, M.D.

Anne McGrath, Editor

Robert Morse, Director of Data Research

Brian Kelly, Series Editor

SOURCEBOOKS, INC.
NAPERVILLE, ILLINOIS

Published by Sourcebooks, Inc.
P.O. Box 4410
Naperville, Illinois 60567-4410
(630) 961-3900 FAX: (630) 961-2168
www.sourcebooks.com

Third Edition
Printed and bound in the United States of America
CHG   10 9 8 7 6 5 4 3 2 1

Table of Contents

Foreword

On Being a Doctor

by Bernadine Healy, M.D.

Medicine is a way of life. It is a way of knowing and thinking, of seeing the world, and of feeling about people. No one
is born a doctor, and the long road to becoming one requires
unrelenting study, discipline, and the cultivation of unique
talents and skills. But whatever the domain of medical pursuit and however removed from the bedside one's work may
ultimately be, its ethos and raison d'être stems from that
one enduring relationship: physician and patient.

In our time, this most personal of human services has
burgeoned into a $1.5 trillion enterprise employing one in
ten Americans. It is a growth propelled by the endless fron-
tier of medical discovery, translating into better ways to care
for people. In that sense, a medical career is the intellectual

journey of a lifetime. In a field where the sands shift so quickly and one technology is swept away by another, medical school is not about teaching you all the facts you'll ever need to know. Rather, it is the place in which students are slowly converted from lay people into doctors.

This conversion takes time, with and beyond the books, journals, and professorial pronouncements. Ultimately, one becomes a doctor from an immersion in the unpredictable, varied, and complex ways in which patients fall ill, and the momentous efforts of people and technology to make them well. It comes from learning the secrets of the body, the passages of life from birth to death, the tortured times and the peaceful times of human souls, and the uplifting (and carefully harnessed) power of the physician to make a difference every step along the way. For the best of students, by the time they walk across the stage and accept their medical diploma, doctorhood has seeped into the marrow of their bones, the depth of their hearts. Whatever their chosen line of work, they will always see the world through the lens of a doctor.

That lens is broad. Medicine embraces a continuum of knowledge and practice from the micro to macro level—from the medical scientist in the laboratory, to the doctor at the bedside, to the public health specialist tracking down the latest epidemic anywhere in the world. And along that broad spectrum, one can carve out a professional life of research, teaching, practice or administration, or some combination of all four. There is a place for generalists and specialists, writers and policy wonks, computer jocks and business gurus—all part of a medical community doing something that is in its ultimate purpose about helping another human being.

That the profession helps human beings in a profound and measurable way is in fact why young people dream of being a doctor, and it is the single most common reason medical school applicants give for pursing a medical career. Indeed, it is that perspective that ultimately overrides some of the negative sides of a career in medicine, which in today's world can discourage even the strongest-hearted premed. For medicine as we know it today brings its own set of hassles: managed care, increasing government regulations, and malpractice premiums (and massive malpractice awards), on top of discouraging medical school debt averaging nearly $100,000 at a time when physician's incomes are relatively stagnant.

Although there are two applicants for every medical school slot, and the quality of prospective students is thought to be as good as ever, there is widespread belief among medical school educators that because of these strains, fewer students are interested in applying to medical school now than a decade ago, a phenomenon masked by the dramatic increase in female applicants. But the reality is that no profession—and nothing worth pursuing in life—is free from its own set of hassles. The reward-to-hassle ratio is what counts. It is something each prospective doctor must sort out for himself or herself.

And the rewards of today's medicine are many. The expanding knowledge base is truly compelling and ever changing to the betterment of patient and doctor. There is virtually no illness we cannot make better, if not cure, and with improved drugs and technology and emerging knowledge of human genomes, we see more tailored treatment of individual patients with better results. As for the doctor's personal life, the hours today are more reasonable and controllable than in the past. The solo doc is becoming a rare breed; large group practices and clinics enable medical practitioners to escape the direct brunt of administrative hassles while at the same time gaining camaraderie and an enriched practice environment. Medicine is a tough and fulfilling career, immutably purpose driven, value laden, intellectually stimulating, and emotionally gratifying. But it is a profession that demands the right stuff of those who serve.

Certain deeply held personal qualities are essential; without them, from my perspective as a former medical school dean, students quite simply need not apply. Think hard about them, for they are the essence of the art and the science of being a doctor.

Compassion and generosity. Kindness goes beyond "bedside manner." It is reflected in generosity of time and self, and sensitivity to the unique circumstance of any given situation. Making an extra stop by the room of a lonely patient; giving a worried family member your home phone number; being calm and measured with an ornery, angry, or noncompliant patient. Sickness can bring out the best in people but also the worst, and a physician can lighten a patient's load by being a source of hope, caring, and cheerleading—along with providing technical expertise.

Hard work and grit. It takes a lot of stamina to be part of a world that is always on call in some fashion. The stress might come from a rather mundane struggle with an insurance company for an extra day in the hospital or a needed MRI, or from perseverance against an engulfing bureaucracy. But stress most especially comes from the challenge of caring for the very sick. This demands the courage to make tough medical decisions, and in the face of risk and uncertainty, to proceed with

a risky operation, or embark on a drastic course of medical therapy. It takes grit to confront one's inevitable failures and learn from them—without becoming timid because of them. In their hearts, doctors must live with the confidence that at the end of the day, they did the best they could, and tirelessly so.

Scholarship and good sense. With medical practice reborn almost every day in new knowledge and emerging technology, new approaches are an essential part of medicine, disseminated in hospital corridors, medical rounds, mortality and morbidity conferences, journal clubs, and national medical gatherings. The wise and learned physicians are those who can sift through the flood of new knowledge and the latest evidence to make it apply to any given patient. That's why we teach medicine at the bedside and through individual case studies of real people. And that's why we respect reasoned judgment that often comes out with different advice. Should that 30-year-old woman with a newly discovered benign heart tumor have prompt heart surgery, as is the practice? Of course—but she is six months pregnant and with surgery, risks losing the baby, so dare we wait? The PSA is intermittently elevated in a 55-year-old man. Do you watch, or biopsy? Yes, a lumpectomy is the conventional wisdom for this precancerous change detected by mammogram, but this patient wants a mastectomy as an alternative because she has a breast cancer gene running through her family. Do we go along? The hyperactive child is driving his family to distraction with behaviors that another family could manage better. Do you medicate?

Medical wisdom is about knowing when conventional practice guidelines apply, particularly in the context of the unlimited variables that confound any given patient's illness or circumstance.

The best decisions come from the marriage of scholarship and good sense.

Integrity and trust. Despite the variability of human illness, one of the great insights of medicine is that with regard to reaction to their disease, most patients are fundamentally the same. Though they may show it differently, they share the same fears and vulnerabilities; and have the same needs for comfort, support, and trust. The physician is the focus of that trust, and that is a heavy responsibility. Never give advice that you yourself would not take—or you would not recommend to a loved one. Imagine you are the patient, particularly when the going gets tough. Matters of privacy, conflicts of interest, participation of patients in research trials—these are all issues of trust. Underpinning this essential quality of being a doctor is a quiet reverence for what it means to be a doctor and what it feels like to care—in the deepest sense—for a patient in your charge. The late Dr. George Crile, Jr., a pioneering Cleveland surgeon and son of one of the founders of the Cleveland Clinic, wrote a short passage in his book on cancer back in 1955 that captures the quiet reverence of a profession that has the ability to restore health or even life, and always to relieve human suffering. His words mean as much now as they did then:

No physician, sleepless and worried about a patient, can return to the hospital in the midnight hours without feeling the importance of his faith. The dim corridor is silent; the doors are closed. At the end of the corridor in the glow of the desk lamp, the nurse watches over those who sleep or lie lonely and wait behind closed doors. No physician entering the hospital in these quiet hours can help feeling that the medical institution of which he is a part is in essence religious, that it is built on trust. No physician can fail to be proud that he is part of his patient's faith.

The student who understands that faith is the one who is ready to embark on life as doctor.

Dr. Healy graduated from Harvard Medical School and spent much of her career caring for patients and teaching and researching at the Johns Hopkins School of Medicine and the Cleveland Clinic Foundation. She served as the dean of the College of Medicine and Public Health at Ohio State University, president of the American Red Cross, and was the first woman to be the director of the National Institutes of Health. Currently she writes health and medical columns for U.S.News & World Report, where she speaks to some twenty million "patients."

Introduction

There are certainly easier careers than medicine. You'll struggle through difficult science courses, indenture yourself for a *long* decade of school and training, and lose countless hours of sleep. The reward? You may end up owing $100,000, being mired in paperwork that robs you of time for patients (or for a life outside of work), and holding a job that leaves you a ripe target for malpractice lawsuits.

And it spite of it all, medicine could be the best choice you ever make. You could be the person who turns pain and suffering into relief and hope. You might solve the mystery of an illness that has stumped generations of doctors. Your colleagues will be extraordinary people. You will see babies safely born, and you will save people's lives.

"I think I have the best job on Earth," said Ronald Drusin, a doctor and associate dean at Columbia University's College of Physicians and Surgeons. "Half of my time, I deal with students and help make sure they get the best education. And half the time I'm in practice as a cardiologist, working at our heart transplant center. So I get to see miracles everyday."

"I can't put into words how wonderful this job is," said Cynthia Romero, a family practice doctor in Virginia Beach, Virginia. "I spend my time seeing my patients as people, not just handing out medications. I get to know them, see them again and again and help them to live a healthy lifestyle. And I can see that it makes a big difference in my community."

It sounds ideal—and idyllic. But before you rush into medical school, stop and think about whether the vision of the profession you carry in your head matches today's reality. Medicine has always demanded a lot of physicians, even in the pre-HMO days of small practices and house calls. For many years, however, it has been changing in ways that doctors simply don't like. Lawrence Klein, an internist who enjoys his private practice in Washington, D.C., feels frustrated that increasing bureaucracy and financial pressures steal time from his patients. After all, seeing patients and giving them good care is what drew him to medicine in the first place. Would he go to medical school today? "Yes, but I'd think about it a bit more."

He'd consider, for example, the skyrocketing malpractice insurance premiums now hitting doctors—price hikes that insurers blame on outrageous jury awards in malpractice cases. "It's a dangerous situation for everyone," said Donald Palmisano, former president of the American Medical Association. "The costs are forcing doctors to close practices." Indeed, physicians in Pennsylvania, West Virginia, Connecticut, and many other states have held protest marches to plead for relief.

Klein would also factor in the pressure that hospitals, practice groups, and HMOs exert on doctors to bring in more revenue by seeing more patients and seeing them faster. And he would certainly think about one unfortunate consequence of rising health care costs: Employers, looking for the best deals, are switching health plans frequently—every two years, in many cases—and that means that patients have to switch doctors, too. As a result of these switches and the hurried patient visits, many physicians find it impossible to build the long-term relationships they feel are so essential to effective patient care. Indeed, fewer med school graduates are even going into primary care, opting instead for specialties such as radiology where they believe they will be insulated from these forces.

Because of the time, vast sums of money, and effort involved, it's important to take a hard look at yourself—your motives, your goals, your personality—before embarking on this course. One undergrad at the University of Virginia, after slogging through organic chemistry and other premed courses, getting top marks, and prepping for and acing the all-important Medical College Admissions Test (MCAT), began collecting school applications. Then, she remembers, she was sitting in the school library one night and looking across the table at a bunch of med students hunched over their books. "That's all they ever do: work," she said to her best friend. "That's not a life. It's a huge sacrifice. And I don't think I can do that." She didn't.

At least she realized her mismatch early.

"Sometimes we have alums who stop med school after two or three years," said Carol Baffi-Dugan, director of health profession advising at Tufts University. "It's not often, but when it happens, it's the saddest thing. They've got debt coming out of their ears. And they've devoted an incredible amount of time and energy learning skills that are not really transferable."

So how can you give yourself a reality test before medical school tests you? The Association of American Medical Colleges poses several general questions, such as: Do I care deeply about other people, their problems, and their pain? Do I enjoy helping people with my skills and knowledge? Do I enjoy learning and gaining new understanding? Do I often dig deeper into a subject than my teacher requires? Surely, your response in all cases ought to be a well-considered and resounding "yes" if you're about to start writing tuition checks. But a "yes" could just as easily foreshadow a brilliant career in social work.

So as you go about measuring your reservoir of empathy and intellectual drive, check your motives, too. "People want to go into medicine for all sorts of reasons," said a student at Columbia's College of Physicians and Surgeons. "Sometimes it's money or prestige. And that's just stupid. Look, you'll always make a comfortable living as a doctor. But there's got to be something more for you to be happy." Larry Sullivan, the prehealth professions advisor at Avila University in Kansas City, Kansas, often sees students who "have 'inherited' the idea of being a doctor. It comes from pressure from their family, or their peers." This, said Baffi-Dugan, is "one of the biggest pitfalls: the idea that 'it's going to make my parents happy.'" Still others want to practice because they've always watched ER on television and think that medicine is dramatic and exciting. They don't consider how little independence doctors often have in real life and how difficult a workplace the health care system can be.

It's also worth considering whether or not you have some specific strengths that seem to stand out in the profession. Admissions directors and advisors agree that good doctors come in a whole range of personality types. "Is every good doctor an extrovert? No," said Baffi-Dugan. But beyond an honest desire to help sick people, good doctors do share some important characteristics, chief among them self-discipline, an ability to think clearly and make decisions in a crisis, and conscientiousness.

A mix of great attention to detail and a desire to strive for high-quality work proves extremely valuable in medical school, too. In an unpublished study of 610 Belgian medical students over six years of their education, across the board, conscientiousness predicted the strongest performance in medical school. This finding mirrors an earlier study of 176 English med students, in which teacher references, student personality statements, and personality scores were all compared to see what factor best predicted med school performance, and the winner was conscientiousness.

Why does care and thoroughness mean so much? "You have to have remarkable perseverance to get through medical school," said psychologist Cheryl Weinstein of Harvard Medical School, who studies learning and learning disabilities. "If you are reasonably intelligent and can learn facts, you can get through the MCAT. If you have high intelligence and love science you are likely to get the references. But once you have to start spending the long hours, once you have to sustain attention and be able to plan and attend, if you don't have [perseverance] you will be found out." Ask yourself: Are you someone who meticulously proofreads a paper before handing it in, not relying on the caprices of computerized spelling and grammar programs to do your work? Did you work extra hours as a hospital volunteer because there was work that needed to be done? And when former professors or former employers write your recommendations, will they note that assignments and projects were never late?

> *"You have to have remarkable perseverance to get through medical school."*

Perhaps the most practical way to research the depth of your commitment is to actually watch what real doctors do. Marilyn Becker, director of admissions for the University of Minnesota Medical School, said that her picks usually have some serious experience in a medical setting before med school, often in a community clinic, a doctor's office, or a hospital. Applicants are strongly encouraged to get this sort of exposure, perhaps part-time while they're in college or over the summers. Sullivan said that Avila University makes such work a part of a course called Introduction to Health Care Careers. More typically, students arrange it on their own. In college, Virginia Beach doctor Cynthia Romero set herself up with what she calls "mini rotations" by asking different doctors if she could shadow them for a week or more. (And she did this even though she already had more than a passing familiarity with the profession: Her mother is a physician.)

Romero liked what she saw, but for others, work experience can be a jolting reality check. "People volunteered in hospitals and realized they didn't have the patience to see patients," Romero

recalled. "Or they couldn't handle the pressure, or they couldn't stand seeing sick children. Some got really upset at the sight of blood." That's a fairly safe sign that you should bail out.

Those who stay the course but aren't truly enthusiastic are easy to identify when you meet them, said Charles Bardes, admissions director at Weill Medical College at Cornell University. "That's why you can't get into medical school without an interview," he notes. What are the signs of true commitment to an activity mentioned in an application? "Did they do this work in a perfunctory way, say for just one hour per week? Were they involved in the leadership of this activity, or did they just show up?" he said. "We try and get a feel for all this when we interview the students." Nor is Becker impressed by someone who emphasizes his or her family's illustrious medical past as qualification—two doctor-uncles, a grandfather on the faculty of a renowned med school—rather than a personal passion for the profession.

One student at Columbia remembers that he felt it was really important to take time off after college to put to rest any doubts about his career direction. He worked as a chef for a while, and then as a high school teacher. Not only did he gain confidence in his decision to go to med school, but "now I have some sense of professionalism," he said. "Being a doctor is a position of responsibility. You need a solid sense of yourself. School won't teach you that."

Assuming that all this soul searching reveals you're meant to be in medicine, this book is your step-by-step guide to getting there. The first chapter offers snapshots of what you'll experience as a first-year med student, followed by a discussion in Chapter 2 of how to choose a medical school that meets your particular needs. Chapter 3 profiles the life and academics at five very different types of medical schools. In Chapter 4, you'll learn how to fine-tune your application so that your first-choice school chooses you. Chapter 5 is a primer on that all-important topic: financing your education. And Chapter 6 explores second chances, telling you what to do if you don't get accepted the first time.

Beginning on page 77, you'll find a series of exclusive lists that allow you to compare medical schools on all kinds of key attributes: which are the hardest and easiest to get into, for example, and which ones leave graduates with the most and least debt. Finally, in the directory at the back of the book, you'll find detailed information on the country's medical schools, including schools offering the D.O. degree in osteopathy. This alternative medical degree involves a slightly different course of training, which is described in Chapter 2.

As you go through the extensive—some would say excruciating—application process, bear in mind that the interview, recommendation letters, and work experiences act as a final filter. They separate good students who *like* the idea of being a doctor from those who really would *be* a good doctor. Assuming that you possess all of the right qualifications, your best chance of making it through this sieve is to do what Harvard's Weinstein, and several ancient philosophers, suggest: "Know thyself." Perhaps friends, parents, mentors, school counselors, or trusted doctors will be able to ask you all the right questions to help you make this important decision. Regardless, there is only one person who can give the right answer. You.

Chapter One

A Med Student's First Year

Let's say you make it through your premed coursework, do well on the MCATs, and actually get into medical school. What happens next? Rachel Sobel was a young medical writer when she decided that the world she'd been covering as a journalist was something she wanted to experience firsthand. She'd majored in the history of science at Harvard and finished her premed coursework shortly after college. In 2002 she enrolled at the University of California, San Francisco School of Medicine (UCSF). "The process of becoming a physician is exhilarating," she said. "You will learn more about yourself and the world around you than you ever have." When she started school, Sobel also chronicled her experiences as a new med student. Here's her report from the front lines.

Fall, Year One

Meet Mr. Danovic

Sirens were blaring when the paramedics wheeled in John Danovic. The twenty-nine-year-old motorcyclist, who had just been laid off from his trucking job, had been drinking. He got hit by a car and thrown from his bike. Blood oozed from wounds in his scalp and chest, and a broken bone was jutting out of one arm.

The scene could have come straight out of any ER, but the case of John Danovic unfolded before my eyes in a lecture hall, not a hospital. The "blood" was actually a viscous burgundy concoction, and the team of doctors and nurses attending to the actor playing Mr. Danovic were my professors.

Welcome to my first lecture at medical school.

Med school isn't famous for its drama, nor is it known for its openness to change. Yet as the Mr. Danovic lecture reveals, change is afoot. Indeed, there is something of a revolution underway, transforming the first years of medical education. Many schools are dramatically revamping their curricula to prepare future physicians for an increasingly fragmented health care system in which any body of biomedical knowledge is bound to be quickly outdated.

Medical education has been virtually unchanged since the early twentieth century, when educators first standardized training. The "2+2" curriculum devoted the first two years to basic science lectures and the last two years to hospital training. Most med schools still use that general framework, but at UCSF and several other places, the first two years would be unrecognizable to a physician who graduated even five years ago.

Forget lectures from 8 a.m. until 5 p.m. Professors here have trimmed away esoteric hard science, keeping only what's essential to patient care. The reasoning is that you don't have to be a biochemist to be a skillful internist. In place of all that lab time, new disciplines are now considered essential to medical training, such as psychology, ethics, and even anthropology. For example, a patient assaulted by a gang (a real victim, unlike Mr. Danovic) talked to us about the psychological dimensions of healing.

David Irby, vice dean of education at UCSF, told me that the school's overhaul was driven in part by studies saying that newly minted M.D.s were unprepared to navigate today's health care system. There was also a widespread sense that medical school, rather than being an inspiring experience, had become a deadening one. Why did education have to be a boring exercise in memorization?

Mr. Danovic's case teaches that it can be otherwise. From him we learned the proper way to insert a chest tube (over the rib so you don't hit the nerves or vessels) and to recognize the signs of shock. Making the material more clinically relevant is not only more compelling but also more practical: According to Irby, study after study suggests that human memory is better wired for narrative than for rote learning.

Another major change taking place in medical training is an increased emphasis on cooperation, which grew out of the frequent observation that new doctors had great difficulty working in teams. You can imagine twenty- and thirty-somethings scoffing at the nursery school notion of cooperative learning, but in fact it's instilled so subtly that it's the way we're learning to think about how medicine works. Grades are pass/fail, which discourages competition. Half our classes take place in small groups, where the only way to learn is from one another. Picture a class where everyone doffs their shirts (women wear sports bras) and students draw on each other with Mr. Sketch markers to learn the complex intertwining of nerves, arteries, and veins of the arm. Being half-naked with classmates in "surface anatomy" isn't exactly a breeding ground for cutthroat rivalry.

Speaking of anatomy, I know my Uncle Peter will ask me over winter break how it went. Before I left for California, he regaled me with tales from his own medical school days—and reminded me to get there early for anatomy to get the best cadaver. I'm bracing for the next "In my day..." speech. But at UCSF, we learn from already dissected cadavers, and there is no competition to get the best one. Instead of spending hours trying to dig out, say, the renal artery, the idea is to save time and learn first from an intact specimen. To be sure, students still do a lot of memorizing. (For the eight wrist bones, remember: Some Lovers Try Positions That They Can't Handle: scaphoid, lunate, triquetrum, pisiform....You get the idea.) And budding surgeons can take a dissection elective, on, say, the abdomen or the pelvis.

No one knows if this new approach will prove better than the old one. Other schools that have made similar switches admit to growing pains. The ultimate measure is whether this generation of M.D.s will be better doctors in the modern health care system. On that, we'll have to wait to hear from the real Mr. Danovic.

Winter, Year One

The Art of Listening

One of my first epiphanies at med school came not from a gray-haired professor nor from *Gray's Anatomy* but from a fellow classmate. During our orientation in the fall, Jane (not her real name) told our entering class at UCSF about her heart surgery just a few weeks earlier.

Jane was a teenager when she first noticed an odd fluttering sensation inside her chest. The doctor did a quick exam and chalked it up to palpitations from too much caffeine. Later, while in college, Jane was getting ready for bed when her heart began racing and her room suddenly started spinning. Different symptoms, different doctor, but the same cursory approach: In this case, the diagnosis was anxiety.

Not until a recent checkup—six years after her initial complaint—did a keen physician find what was really wrong. He took a meticulous history and then listened to her heart with a stethoscope. Medicine's fancy term for this is auscultation: basically, listening to the body's various sounds. According to Jane, this physician "wasn't just going through the motions." He placed the stethoscope on her chest, closed his eyes, and listened for a long time. It paid off. The doc discovered a dangerous murmur, and further tests showed a two-inch hole in the wall between two chambers of her heart. Left untreated, such a defect could have caused heart and lung failure.

I was reminded of Jane's ordeal when I heard that the U.S. Medical Licensing Examination Committee had approved a new requirement for all medical students: a clinical-skills exam. The new test measures two things: communication skills and the ability to gather information through the physical exam. Students will interview and examine a series of "patients" (all actors) and complete a write-up for each one.

Many students were miffed that we would have to shell out an extra $1,000 or more to get licensed—not pocket change, considering that our average debt will close in on $100,000 by graduation. What's more, most schools already offer their own clinical-skills exams. Still, the new test sets important priorities. After all, isn't this what we came to school for, to learn the art of bedside diagnosis?

Kanu Chatterjee, a UCSF cardiologist who is legendary at performing physical examinations, has seen these vital skills atrophy in the profession over time. The repercussions, he says, include not only missed diagnoses but also the erosion of the patient–doctor relationship. Chatterjee trained in the 1950s when a physician's main diagnostic tool was a stethoscope. Now younger doctors rely more on sophisticated technology. He doesn't blame them; there is limited teaching time and technology is powerful. Still, he says, the physical exam "is the only tool to really get to know your patient."

A physical exam includes everything from inspecting a patient's appearance to palpating the abdomen to finding various pulses. As straightforward as that sounds, it is not easy. Last quarter, one of my professors played a recording of aberrant heart sounds during a lecture. I could not identify most of them. He played them again. Was that the abnormal "gallop"? I desperately clung to some fleeting rumble. Or was I just deluding myself into hearing something—anything?

My classmates and I got into medical school based in large part on our aptitude for science. But the art of physical diagnosis calls upon an entirely new sensibility: a heightened ability to listen, and look, and feel. Textbooks and flashcards can't teach these skills. They require practice, more practice, and an entirely new awareness of our own bodies to nourish the senses we have long neglected at the library.

An equally essential part of the bedside exam, obvious as it may seem, is good communication.

In fact, educators who pushed for the new licensing exam say part of the rationale is to weed out poor communicators and encourage schools to emphasize this competency in training. They cite a growing body of literature suggesting that the rising rate of malpractice complaints is linked to poor interpersonal skills.

This quarter, Jane and I took an in-house clinical-skills test. When our grader, a doctor from a nearby hospital, told a colleague she was going to be an evaluator, the colleague quipped: "They still teach that stuff?" Jane looked at me and said: "I can think of a few reasons why."

Spring, Year One

My future life?

The red-headed lady doesn't want her toddler to know she smokes. The man sitting next to her suffered two heart attacks this year and says it's time to quit. Another man, who has asthma, wants cleaner lungs. And in the corner, a transgendered woman undergoing hormone therapy vows to cut back on her two-pack-a-day habit because the combination puts her at increased risk for blood clots.

The motives for quitting might have been familiar, but clearly this was no ordinary smoking cessation meeting. It took place near the end of my first year as a medical student at a shelter in the squalid Tenderloin district of San Francisco, and its participants were a group of determined homeless people. Yes, they had unfathomable troubles to deal with, such as finding work and somewhere permanent to sleep, but they also had an unbending desire to take care of their own health.

The participants inspired not only each other but also the medical students who led the meetings each week. Medical school coursework is rigorous, yet many of us still squeeze in time to volunteer during the classroom years. At UCSF, for example, students set up pediatric health fairs in underserved areas, teach science to high schoolers, and coordinate bone marrow drives, among other things. It is here that we continue to cultivate what brought many of us into medicine in the first place: a desire to serve others through improving health care.

After the first two medical school years, where classroom learning dominates, in the final two years students are immersed in clinical experience and get to funnel all of their idealism, passion, and brain cells into taking care of patients. Enthusiastic friends who are in those years tell me, "you finally get to do what you came here for." Yet, at the same time, students are charged with figuring out their next step—their choice of specialty—and it is quite a complex decision. A new sense of pragmatism emerges.

During my first year, when I was on the wards for a few days during our winter "clinical interlude," I simply wasn't used to the new rhetoric about career choice. A third-year student told me in casual conversation that he wanted to specialize in radiology because of the "great lifestyle." I was shocked at first because I at least expected him to mention something intrinsically attractive about the field, such as its visual elegance or the satisfaction of nailing down diagnoses through images.

But then I began to hear more about this "ROAD to happiness"—radiology, ophthalmology, anesthesia, dermatology. The hours are good and the pay is at the top of the profession. These specialties are so popular that others are getting short shrift. For example, in 2002, less than half of all family practice residencies were filled by recent U.S. graduates.

Indeed, a recent study reported that lifestyle factors, such as adequate time for hobbies and family and control of weekly work hours, are a major reason for recent shifts in specialty career choices. The proportion of students who ranked anesthesiology as their first career choice, for example, went up more than fivefold in the last six years. At the same time, family practice applications have dropped 40 percent and the popularity of general surgery has also significantly declined.

There are many possible reasons why. One explanation is that more and more women are going into medicine and they are choosing more family-friendly fields. Another is that some students quickly become jaded in the modern medical climate. And who could blame them? Their role models are weary. A fourth-year student at an East Coast medical school told me that the attending physicians on his primary care rotation spent the whole time trying to convince him not to go into their field. The sacrifices such specialties call for, the student said, just aren't as appealing during these days of managed care pressures, high malpractice costs, and lower reimbursement rates.

Medical schools are concerned. Harvard's associate dean for student affairs, Nancy Oriol, believes that much of the growing acclaim of "lifestyle specialties" is simply urban legend passed around by students who haven't actually experienced these careers. She advises her students to pick their specialty based on their gut love of the field and then carve out the lifestyle they want once they begin practicing. "If you start off saying 'what are the lifestyle specialties?' then you may miss the ones you really love," she says. In almost every field, Oriol contends, a doctor can find a position that fits his or her choice of hours. There are surgeons who work part time, she says,

How med school works

Though schools vary widely in the courses they teach, most of this variation is grafted on top of a basic curriculum: two years of medical science followed by two years of clinical practice. This is followed by an apprenticeship period, or residency, that lasts from three to seven years. Here's a general outline:

Years One and Two: Coursework covers these topics: anatomy and embryology, physiology, biochemistry, histology, neuroscience, medical genetics, pharmacology, microbiology, pathology, and immunology. These first two years may also include courses on sexuality, nutrition, health care delivery, ethics, and other subjects.

Years Three and Four: You start clinical rotations in hospitals, usually beginning with surgery, family medicine, pediatrics, neuroscience, and obstetrics and gynecology. As you gain experience in patient care, these are followed by more rotations with advanced responsibility. You can also take elective courses in areas such as end-of-life care, psychiatry, or public and community health. Year four is also when students apply for residencies at various hospitals around the country in particular medical specialties. You graduate at the end of four years, and you can put an M.D. or D.O. after your name.

Year Five Postgraduate: You begin the first year of your residency, sometimes called an internship, taking primary responsibility for patient care while being supervised yourself by experienced doctors. Depending on the program—surgery, for instance, is very time-consuming—residencies can last as long as seven years.

Beyond Year Five: There's a lot of hard work involved in residency programs. After completing them successfully and passing national medical exams and state licensing tests, you are a full-fledged physician.

and there are academicians in radiology and dermatology who work all the time.

I recently spoke with a friend who is graduating from the University of Pennsylvania medical school. He is going into pediatrics, as did about one-sixth of the Penn class that graduated a year before him. Pediatrics is, on average, the lowest-paying field. "The majority of people," he observes, "still end up doing what their heart has told them to do from the beginning."

Now that I've finished my first year and have some perspective on it, I count my blessings: how privileged I am to be studying medicine and starting to work in the field. I know that in my training there will be elation and frustration, excitement and exhaustion—as there has been for many of my predecessors. Still, in the whirlwind events of a day during my training, I hope to always find meaning in the simple wonders of medicine—like the wonder I witnessed in the Tenderloin, as that group of homeless people threw away their lighters and cigarettes to begin a tough journey toward healthier living.

Chapter Two

Which Is the Right School for You?

There are essentially two ways to choose a medical school. There's the cynical approach: "You don't really have much choice," said one student. That is, you'll apply to the very few schools that might take you, and if you're lucky "get into one or maybe two. And there you go." This view gets some support from many medical school admissions officers, although they phrase it a little more diplomatically: All schools offer a similarly fine education because of medicine's rigid accreditation requirements. (Still, their own schools are better than most, these officers hasten to add.) So what does it matter where you go, in the end?

Then there's the smarter approach. It won't make getting in any easier, but it greatly improves your odds of thriving if you make it. "Schools really aren't created equal," said Lucy Wall, assistant dean for admissions at the University of Wisconsin medical school. "There are differences in teaching methods and curriculum, some schools are more research oriented, public schools can be very different environments than private schools....There are lots of things to consider." A school's location can make a huge difference in the kind of experience you have, both academically and in terms of your quality of life. An institution's

---

"Schools really aren't created equal....There are lots of things to consider."

---

reputation—whether it's viewed as a topflight research school or the place to go to become a primary care physician—can influence your chances of getting the residency slot you want after graduation. And since the learning environment is greatly affected by the other students and the campus culture, the most important consideration may be "that gut feeling you get about a school, how comfortable you feel there," said Lauren Oshman, a former president of the American Medical Student Association and a graduate of Baylor College of Medicine in Houston.

Take Fernanda Musa's experience as a first-year student at Columbia University's College of Physicians and Surgeons in New York City. Musa wanted to attend a big-city institution doing cutting-edge research ("our teachers are some of the top names in their fields") where she would see the greatest variety of patients and conditions. Columbia was the perfect fit, she said. "The school culture is so happy. We're a really close, supportive group. We study together, and we also go out to concerts and bars. Most first-year students live

together in Bard Hall, and that's where we get this great sense of community." Jessica Vorpahl, when she came to the University of Wisconsin a few years ago as a student interested in family practice, felt equally thrilled about her Midwestern, primary-care oriented, smaller-town school: "There's absolutely no better place. I'm totally convinced."

The hard numbers—your overall grade point average, your all-important science GPA, and your score on the Medical College Admissions Test—will narrow the field considerably by telling you which schools are within your reach. (See Chapter 4 for tips on figuring out the extent of your reach, then check out the directory at the back of this book for a sense of the numbers needed for entry at each school.) But your proper place in the field will depend on more, much more, than collections of statistics. Examining how the school teaches students (Does it rely on huge lectures? Will you get clinical experience early on or not until the latter half of your med school career?), what its curricular strengths are, what specialties graduates go on to practice, and how current students feel about the school will give you the best chance of finding, like Vorpahl, "no better place."

Consider the school culture

At the University of Iowa's Carver College of Medicine, students from all four years are grouped into small "learning communities" and interact both in class and out. First-year students relish the contact with upperclassmen, who are founts of invaluable advice about choosing courses and figuring out ways to fit all your hospital rotations into a tight schedule.

At more traditionally organized schools, such as the University of Chicago Pritzker School of Medicine, older students can disappear from sight once they start their clinical rotations. "Insanely competitive" is the phrase one student from the University of Alabama School of Medicine used to describe classmates. While the med school at Johns Hopkins University also has a reputation for intense competition, many students there protest that this is a myth—though they concede that, as a group, they tend to drive themselves hard and aren't exactly famous for kicking back and relaxing. At Yale, on the other hand, a policy of optional exams and no grades (students get evaluations from faculty) seems to create a less-pressured atmosphere, aided by the school schedule, which mandates a few weekday afternoons off.

Clearly, getting a feel for the ambience of a school requires some on-the-ground reporting. When you visit campus for your interview—which every med school requires—you'll be taken on a guided tour set up by the admissions office and designed to impress. Figure out how to break away and do some independent poking around. One way to gather information is to visit a school early in the application process—before you're called in. Medical school admission offices aren't set up for drop-in visits the way college admissions offices are, so you may not get a lot of help from them. But you can contact alumni from your college at a particular med school, and they should be able to find you people to talk with and places to stay. Once you're on campus, don't be shy about buttonholing a few students and asking them some pointed questions:

What is student life like outside the classroom? Columbia students might tell you about the school's P & S Club, a student-run group central to most medical students' social lives that one day is running a wine tasting and another is producing *West Side Story* with students in the starring roles. One student at Iowa reports that in Iowa City, "the world stops for college athletics. This place is overwhelmed by Hawkeye fever, and it's a lot of fun. Everyone goes to football and basketball games. At hospitals, you even see doctors with Hawkeye lapel pins next to their name badges." Hopkins students, in contrast, say they have to work to find extracurricular activities in Baltimore; the fun is there, but you need to dig for it. At Northwestern University's Feinberg School of Medicine, as at Columbia, a social life is easy to come by. First-year students at Northwestern live together in Lake Shore Center, which leads to impromptu gatherings, study support, and therapeutic venting sessions.

How intense is the competition? Often a lot less so than you might think. Sure, there are people at Hopkins who are intensely competitive, said one student, "but it hasn't affected me." Study groups and note-sharing are more the norm. A student at Case Western Reserve University School of Medicine said, "I had heard students at Case were kind of snobby and I was concerned that might lead to competition, but that's definitely not the case!" At Alabama, too, the "insanity" is more exception than rule. "The students are very helpful if you ask," said an Alabama student. "I think there are really only a few people who don't like to help others, and nobody likes them anyway."

Many new med students may *fear* competition because they remember, all too clearly, how fiercely they fought to get into medical school in the first place. But the reality is that once admitted, students feel a kinship with each other—that they're in this often-grueling, often-exhilarating experience together, said Jack Snarr, former associate dean for student programs at Northwestern. They want to do well so as to get into a good residency program, but aren't willing to do it by hurting others. "I know what I want to score on an exam, because I know what I'm capable of. But I don't want to get that score by withholding information from another student," said a student at Wright State University School of Medicine in Dayton, Ohio.

How accessible are the professors? Try to get input from a number of people because opinions may differ a lot within schools: Students who hang back may find they have very little contact with faculty, while more assertive students have no complaints. A lecture format, which predominates during the first years of school at the University of Chicago, for example, will probably make it more difficult to get to know faculty, especially if the school and the lectures are large. In the faculty-led small discussion and problem-solving groups that pepper the first years at Cornell University's Weill Medical College in New York City, by contrast, even the shyest students are soon known by name. At the University of Minnesota Medical School at Duluth, where entering class sizes hover around 50 rather than the more typical 100 to 150, faculty and administration "really feel more like family," said one student. "People have open-door policies, and you can just walk in and discuss something if you have a problem or are confused by something."

Yet even at schools like Chicago, professors have office hours. Find out whether they keep them, and whether those who go up and knock on the door are welcome or treated as nuisances. Keep in mind that even though medical schools list particular faculty members as "course directors" in their catalogs, at some schools you may see that professor only at the first lecture and then spend the rest of the semester dealing with assistants.

How welcoming is the school and the student body to people of different backgrounds? You can often tell a lot by just walking around with your eyes open. How diverse does the population seem to be? How much a part of things are the minority students? "We do OK on women here," said Philip Farrell, former dean at Wisconsin. "But we don't do so well on minorities."

Nor do a good many other medical schools, but finding and encouraging would-be minority doctors is a goal that some are now getting serious about. Wisconsin has initiated "pipeline" programs to try and remedy the shortage, running summer science and math workshops for disadvantaged and minority high school students. Some med schools, such as Columbia and the University of California–San Francisco, have tried to build special support networks for minority students to reduce feelings of isolation and deal with any academic troubles. At UCSF, for example, the Medical Scholars Program was started because some underrepresented minority students found a few of the science courses to be tough going. Students who want help can meet twice a week in small workshops to discuss coursework, problem-solving skills, and better ways of organizing their study time. The workshops also serve as social hubs, where students meet one another and forge friendships.

If you can't manage to get to a school in person, some virtual exploration might be in order. Student perspectives can be found on the website of the Student Doctor Network (www.studentdoctor.net), a volunteer not-for-profit group that collects questionnaires about medical schools from premed students who have visited them. "Really laid back, friendly and enjoyable. Interviews were conversational. I had to explain my nontraditional stuff, which I expected (I'm 25). Really got me excited about the school," wrote one visitor to the University of Michigan–Ann Arbor. Another visitor to the same school, however, had this to say: "I got the real picture from some of the students. They told me most people are sons of doctors, or their parents are wealthy benefactors of the school. Lots of Ivy Leaguers too over there, not much room for people without money."

Obviously, opinions can differ, and you're sure to get conflicting information. But complaints can clue you in to areas that bear further investigation. The SDN site also features chat rooms where you can quiz students at schools of interest. You can also trade impressions with premeds and med students at another online community, www.medschoolchat.com.

Weigh the location

Beyond student culture, one of the most important features of a school to consider is its address. Location affects the kinds of patients you'll see, the range of diseases you'll be trained in, and the emphasis the school puts on different medical specialties—not to mention whether or not your significant other will have to give up his or her job and follow you out of state.

"An urban setting exposes you to a wide variety of patients, simply because that's the population. And that's going to make you a more well-rounded clinician." said Charles Bardes, admissions director at Cornell, which sits on the east side of Manhattan. It's important, he said, for applicants comparing schools to get a sense of the patient populations when they're visiting campus. "Walk up and down the hospital halls, and talk to students." If the school has a spectrum of hospitals, he said, there will in all likelihood be a spectrum of patients. A student at Cornell, for instance, might spend time in a hospital where a number of patients are elderly and have brittle bones, then move on to a hospital in a poor neighborhood and

> *"An urban setting exposes you to a wide variety of patients, simply because that's the population."*

see pregnant teenagers and children affected by lead poisoning. And because the school is affiliated with the world-renowned Memorial Sloan-Kettering Cancer Center, the student might well see more rare cancers than the average medical student—and the latest in treatment.

But don't take this to mean that all noncity schools will offer you an all-white or otherwise one-dimensional experience. Even though Wisconsin is located in the small city of Madison, for example, it sends students to training sites across the state. They can spend weeks seeing patients in small towns like Chippewa Falls, where many people have adequate health insurance and are easily available for follow-up care. But they can also go to Milwaukee, which has a large Latino population, and where patient care might involve surmounting language barriers that don't exist in Chippewa Falls. That said, schools like Minnesota–Duluth and Iowa, in rural states, do tend to focus more on family practice medicine because that specialty is much in demand in these areas.

Connor Shannon was the son of a doctor and he knew, very early, that he wanted to be an M.D., too. So after graduating from the University of Colorado, he trained as an emergency medical technician, spent a couple of years working, and applied to 25 medical schools. Because his science background was relatively weak, which in turn "made me not do so well on the MCATs," he was rejected by 23 schools and waitlisted by the remaining two.

In the months that followed, Shannon got to know several doctors with the "other" medical degree—a doctor of osteopathy or D.O.—and began to suspect he might be chasing the wrong kind of training. "I liked [the D.O.s'] bedside manner better," he said. Shannon went to—and loved—the Chicago College of Osteopathic Medicine at Midwestern University.

Many medical school advisors recommend applying to a combination of D.O. and M.D. schools right from the start. "Both produce well-trained doctors," said Carol Baffi-Dugan,

program director for health professions advising at Tufts University. Curricula at both cover the same basic scientific principles of medicine, and osteopaths are licensed in all 50 states in surgery, internal medicine, and every other medical discipline.

Where the two schools of medicine differ is in philosophy. Doctors of osteopathy "treat people, not just symptoms," says Karen Nichols, dean of the Chicago College of Osteopathic Medicine. "The course list looks exactly the same, but the M.D.'s focus is on discreet organs. The osteopathic focus is that all of those pieces are interrelated. You can't affect one with out affecting another." That means more than paying simple lipservice to the idea of the "whole" patient: It means examining his or her environment, family, and general situation in life, too. Michael Kuchera, a D.O., described the emphasis as being on health rather than disease. Not surprisingly, more than 65 percent of the 52,000 licensed osteopaths in the United States are primary care

physicians—in family practice or pediatrics, for example. The American Association of Colleges of Osteopathic Medicine provides a description of osteopathic training, as well as short profiles of 20 schools, on its website (www.aacom.org). The D.O. programs and their contact information are listed in the Directory section of this book.

Beyond their other medical studies, osteopathic students get 200 hours of training in "osteopathic manipulative medicine," a hands-on technique for diagnosis and healing. Limited motion in the lower ribs, for instance, can cause pain in the stomach that seems a lot like irritable bowel syndrome. Identifying the muscle strain in the ribs through manipulation, and then treating it, can relieve the stomach distress. An osteopath learns to apply specific amounts of pressure on a body part, attempting to relax it or stimulate it. While such an approach might have raised eyebrows in the profession a decade or two ago, these days no one—except perhaps the crustiest old M.D.s—dismisses it as New Age nonsense. Manipulative medicine is based on the not-terribly-heretical idea that structures in the body influence function, and that a problem in the structure of one body part can cause problems in the function of other parts.

Don't think of applying to D.O. schools as a fallback plan. Some of them accept a greater percentage of applicants than do M.D. schools, but many are just as selective. And all D.O. schools are searching for a particular kind of person. "Students have to understand the osteopathic schools are not looking for people who couldn't get into M.D. schools," said Nichols. "I want them to understand the osteopathic philosophy, to have spent time with a D.O. so they can get a strong letter of recommendation." And as for Connor Shannon, he decided that his rejections were a good thing because they allowed him to land where he was always meant to be.

Indeed, public institutions supported by state money generally emphasize medical training targeted to state and local needs. While it's possible to be trained in ophthalmology or oncology at the University of Washington in Seattle, for example, there's a definite push to turn out primary care docs who will stay in the Northwestern corner of the country and practice. Wisconsin offers many more opportunities to learn about rural health care than does Columbia. At SUNY Downstate Medical Center College of Medicine in Brooklyn, students get exposure to a high-risk obstetrics program because there are so many high-risk pregnancies in that community.

Another way state schools fulfill state objectives is by educating their own residents, and doing so relatively cheaply. "The first issue I usually ask students to think about when thinking about schools is where they live," said John Friede, the health professions advisor at Villanova University in Philadelphia.

"Staying in-state can often mean real savings, and getting out of school with less debt." Pennsylvania residents who choose Pennsylvania State University College of Medicine pay about $32,000 per year in tuition, for instance. The school charges students from out of state an extra $12,000 per year. If Pennsylvania residents go to Duluth to study medicine, they pay $35,000 for the first year, while the Minnesota locals pay $28,000. The next year, Minnesota residents' tuition drop to $19,000, while out-of-staters stay above $23,000. Likewise, leaving state for a private institution could mean tuition bills of $30,000–40,000 a year. (See Chapter 5 for other strategies for financing your education.)

You'll probably find that staying close to home gives you a better chance of getting in, too. Recently, for example, the University of California–San Diego School of Medicine had about 3,000 in-state applicants and admitted 120; of about 1,100 applicants from out-of-state, it took just 2. Wisconsin's med school is committed to taking 80 to 90 percent of its students from the Badger State. Finally, of course, a school's location can mean a great deal for your personal life. One of the reasons Columbia worked so well for one student is that her family members, who lived in Brazil, found it easy to fly up and visit her on the East Coast; a California school would have called for a longer, more expensive trip.

> *"Staying in-state can often mean real savings, and getting out of school with less debt."*

Put prestige in perspective

You might be tempted to pay any amount of money to get your M.D. from a great medical school—a really, really great school. Someplace you've always heard about, like Harvard, or Stanford, or Cornell, or Johns Hopkins, whose name alone says "first-rate education."

Not so fast, cautions Bardes. As admissions director at Cornell, he can certainly brag about a top-notch faculty and state-of-the-art facilities. He just can't say that Cornell's strengths add up to a quality of education that's significantly better than most others. "The quality range in medical schools is much narrower than in other types of schools," he said. Andrew Frantz, associate dean of admissions at Columbia, which usually scores near the top in the annual *U.S.News & World Report* ranking of med schools, agreed: "For maybe 90 percent of the schools, the quality seems very tight, and very high." Or as Delores Brown, associate dean for admissions at Northwestern's med school, put it: "For medical training, there is no bad school."

Why would medicine produce such a tight bunch? There are a few reasons. Bardes points out that because the public has a life-and-death interest in highly skilled physicians, the accreditation process for medical schools is unusually elaborate and demanding. That process, overseen by both the Association of American Medical Colleges and the American Medical Association, examines everything from the technology at student clinical sites to the teaching qualifications of the faculty to the curriculum content, ensuring that it covers not just the scientific basis of medicine but also behavioral and socioeconomic aspects. The resulting accreditation reports for any given school are as bulky as a Los Angeles telephone directory. "They ask a lot of questions and want very specific answers," said Wisconsin's Farrell, hefting his school's report off his desk. "There are about 120 certification standards in here. With us, they liked our faculty development program and our mentoring program for students. But they thought we had too many lectures and not enough self-directed study."

Another equalizer? The national standardized tests students must take during their four years in school. Passing the initial U.S. Medical Licensing Examination, which tests knowledge of basic medical science, is required for promotion from the second to the third year, and students have to pass further stages of the test during their final two years in order to graduate. Obviously, failure doesn't just hurt the student: A pattern of failures reflects badly on the school and may jeopardize its accreditation.

Schools that do enjoy an aura of prestige tend to be the ones with the big research programs, said Thomas Langhorne, the prehealth professions advisor at Binghamton University in New York. "These are schools with lots of Nobel Prize winners, or researchers that make discoveries about diseases, or get big grants, and so they get a lot of press," he said. "You read the names 'Harvard' and 'Stanford' a lot. But these are things that, to me, don't have a lot to do with your training to be a physician."

It's not that a strong and active research program is irrelevant; in fact, the research might well enhance your academic experience. If you find yourself drawn to the study of glaucoma or the genetics of antibiotic resistance, for example, it should be relatively easy at a school pulling in lots of grants in these areas to get funding for a short research project, often working alongside a faculty member. The research may also inform course content—indeed, the experts may be teaching the classes. At a smaller school with less research money—say, a state school focused on primary care—you'll have fewer opportunities to "follow your nose" and go in unexpected directions. And anyone who tells you that having Harvard or Cornell on a résumé won't open a few extra doors simply isn't being honest.

In certain cases, however, a great research reputation might actually be a career handicap, said Phyllis Guze, former president of the Association of Program Directors in Internal Medicine—the people who run residency programs and thus hire med school graduates for their first job. "You can come from a school with a stellar academic reputation, and depending on the residency you're applying for, that's not going to help you," she said. If she were looking at applicants for an inner-city hospital residency without a big research component, a Stanford résumé wouldn't be the top one on her pile. "It's a school noted for great scholarship and academic physicians," she said, "so why would the student be interested in this kind of hospital? Program directors really think about things like this."

Rather than focusing on reputation, advisors and med school faculty suggest taking a hard look at the concrete—and the metal and the electronics. Good facilities are a harbinger of a good educational experience. Wisconsin's new health sciences building, for

"The quality range in medical schools is much narrower than in other types of schools."

instance, has Ethernet jacks at every classroom desk, so if a lecturer is using a PowerPoint presentation, students can download it right onto their laptops. The University of Pittsburgh School of Medicine is going totally wireless, so students can do the same thing even when sprawled out in a hallway.

Pittsburgh also has installed high-resolution cameras and monitors that cover every inch of its anatomy lab. Typically, when new students are dissecting a cadaver and people at one table find something interesting, like the heart, "a buzz goes through the room and 150 students line up to look," said John Mahoney, the school's associate dean for medical education. "That takes forever and number 150 probably can't see anything. But with our cameras, an image immediately shows up over every dissecting table, so all students have to do is look up for a great view." Features like these indicate that the school is investing in education, and not neglecting students to pay hospital debts.

One aspect of a school's reputation that should matter to you a lot is how well-regarded it is among residency directors who aim to hire the most skilled doctors they can find. Examining the school's record on residency matches will give you a good idea. In general, academic hospitals—those closely affiliated with a university—tend to be more sought after because they are better teaching environments than stand-alone hospitals. And how many of the students get into their top choices? At most schools, 90 percent of graduates get into their first-, second-, or

---

"You read the names 'Harvard' and 'Stanford' a lot. But these are things that, to me, don't have a lot to do with your training to be a physician."

---

third-choice program. If the school reports a lower number, that should be a warning.

There are other signs of trouble, and they have to do with money. If a school is strapped, count on it: You'll be affected. In the late 1990s, for instance, MCP-Hahnemann University School of Medicine in Philadelphia was in dire straits because its hospitals were hemorrhaging money. Morale among faculty was low and researchers had trouble getting the school to pay their bills on time. Since then, Hahnemann has merged with another Philly school to form the Drexel University College of Medicine. There's new management, new money flowing in, new technology, new ownership arrangements for the hospitals, and much more happiness on campus. So check the local newspapers for stories about financial worries. You might even call a broker. If a school or medical center has floated bond issues, agencies like Moody's rate those bonds based on the financial soundness of the institution issuing them.

What and how you'll learn

A school's curriculum and the style faculty use to teach it are crucial elements of your decision, even though the topics covered during the first and second years are pretty much the same wherever you go. Anatomy and embryology, physiology, biochemistry, histology, neuroscience, genetics, pharmacology, microbiology, pathology, and immunology—all are basic science areas that every budding doctor needs to cover.

What varies is the way in which they are taught; many schools present the facts in tried-and-true large lectures, while others emphasize small-group discussions that center around solving problems. Some schools use a mix of the two styles. At Harvard and Pittsburgh, two institutions that rely heavily on "problem-based learning," or PBL, a group of first-year students studying anatomy or immunology or microbiology will meet for, say, 90 minutes to discuss a hypothetical patient with specific symptoms—Mr. X has come to his family doctor complaining of fever and chills—and brainstorm ways to figure out what's wrong. If the course is microbiology, someone might suggest an infection. Then the question becomes: What kind of infection? Everyone goes off to research possible conditions and appropriate diagnostic tests, and the group meets again and again during the week, eventually arriving at a solution: Mr. X has a staph infection. The idea is that by teaching themselves how to solve problems, students are better equipped for the real world. "When they present to you one specific disease and you talk about it in PBL, it really sticks with you," noted a Pittsburgh student.

A microbiology lecture on staph, in contrast, might present a list of germs, symptoms they can cause, and antibiotics that might kill them.

Not everyone is a believer in PBL. One Columbia student pointed out that while it gives students the needed information, it can also take a lot of extra time. "It's great when everyone in the group comes in with a different knowledge base and can exchange information. But the first year of med school is *not* like that. People actually know very little. So you end up spending an awful lot of time running around to the library, looking up basic things. It's not efficient at all." The Columbia faculty agrees with him for the most part and has emphasized lectures, adopting PBL techniques in just a few courses. One University of Chicago med student added that she got more with less fuss out of the science lectures that dominate at her school: "You need to have the basic sciences down first in order to do something good later. It might not seem interesting but we can't help patients without it."

Another variation is the way schools serve up the required topics. For example, many are moving away from courses that cover discrete subjects such as microbiology or pharmacology as overviews of the entire body, moving instead toward interdisciplinary "organ-based" courses that examine all aspects of, say, the kidneys. Students learn about kidney anatomy, microbiology, immunology, and the drugs that affect this organ. Next, they might move on to the heart and circulatory system, then go on to the nervous system, and so on throughout the body. "I think it helps you put things together and see how the body actually works," said a Duluth student. Her school, along with Brown, Yale, the University of Texas Medical Branch at Galveston, and many others, have switched to this way of teaching.

The amount of time spent helping patients—or at the very least seeing patients—is an increasingly important variable, too. For a large part of the last century, the basic science courses during the

> *"You need to have the basic sciences down first in order to do something good later."*

first years of med school kept students in large lecture halls or with their noses buried in textbooks. Then, in the third year, they'd enter the hospital for clinical training and encounter their first real patients. Often they were ill-prepared. "Our faculty was getting worried that students weren't making the connections between science and patient care that they could be making," said Donald Innes, associate dean for curriculum at the University of Virginia's medical school. That concern was shared nationwide, said Robert Eaglen of the Liaison Committee on Medical Education, the curriculum guidance arm of the Association of American Medical Colleges. Medical schools across the country began revamping their first-year curriculum so that student–patient encounters would occur early on.

It's a welcome change for many students. "I want the science backed up by experience," said one student at the University of New Mexico, explaining that the promise of early and plentiful experience with patients drew him to that school. As a supplement to time in class, New Mexico places first-year students in local clinics where they work with supervising physicians in actual practice. "Having a real face behind these medical problems is really helpful," said the student. Moreover, students learn early how to interact with patients—a skill you can't get from a textbook, said Scott Obenshain, New Mexico's former associate dean for undergraduate medical education. The

---

"Our faculty was getting worried that students weren't making the connections between science and patient care that they could be making."

---

contact is helpful to patients, too—which is why New Mexico originally started making it happen. "We're in a rural area and we have a great call for physicians who have general skills, rather than specialists," said Obenshain. Case Western pairs students in their first month of school with expectant mothers at local clinics. The students work as patient advocates until these mothers give birth.

Some schools simulate patient interaction instead. Virginia, for instance, uses "standardized patients" in first-year lecture classes. These are not real patients, but people who have been trained to complain of symptoms that are signs of a particular illness. Students learn to take medical histories from working with them and progress to giving them physical exams.

Most schools also now require that first-year students "shadow" practicing physicians on their rounds, perhaps once a week or once a month. But beware: Not all shadowing experiences are equally useful. "Applicants really should ask if shadowing is an active or passive experience," said Cornell's

Bardes, who believes that just sitting around watching the doctor work doesn't do much good. A more active role, which Cornell asks of its students, is to function as a patient advocate or a kind of social worker in a medical clinic, talking to the patient and making sure any concerns are addressed by the medical team. "Not only does that get the student involved with the patient," Bardes said, "it also involves the student with the doctors and nurses directly, and helps the student understand that care is a team effort."

New topics are also shouldering their way into the mix. At Pritzker in Chicago, first-years take a course called Introduction to Clinical Medicine, which gets away from science and into interpersonal relationships and ethics; at Iowa, this course is called Foundations of Clinical Practice. UCSF offers an introduction to pain treatment. And Emory, in Atlanta, teaches Complementary Medical Practices as an elective, in which students visit acupuncture studios and Chinese herbalists. Other schools have added complementary medicine to the curriculum, too, as doctors begin to realize how many of their patients take herbs and supplements.

Finally, although medical students often joke that "C equals M.D." (meaning that you can count on being a doctor as long as you don't flunk out), it's worth considering the way schools on your list handle grades. The traditional "ABC" system may be the most comfortable one for you if you like getting fairly specific feedback about how firm a grasp you have of the material. Some students at Yale, in fact, say that school's relaxed no-grade approach can cause people to slip far behind unless they are highly motivated and disciplined.

On the other hand, many students find that simple pass/fail grades relieve some of the pressure that comes with a letter system. One student at Case Western noted that grading policies helped him choose between Case in Cleveland and Ohio State in Columbus. Ohio State was a lot cheaper and "in a town that felt more like home." Yet he decided on Case largely because the first two years of the program are graded pass/fail. To him, that meant the likelihood that Case "might be more humane than the rest," and that there would be more cooperation with other students. Indeed, he reports that his time in school was filled with fun as well as work, and much of the credit goes to his fellow students. "So I'll take my Case Western degree and smile."

Chapter Three

Inside Five Top Schools

There's more than one way to become a doctor—146 ways, in fact, if you count all of the accredited medical schools in the country. (Turn to the Directory for details.) The five top schools profiled in this chapter each typify a different approach to the teaching of medicine. All place highly in the annual *U.S.News & World Report* rankings. Two are public schools, one in a small Midwestern city (the University of Wisconsin in Madison) and the other in a dense, urban West Coast setting (the University of Washington in Seattle). Both of these schools try to meet local needs by turning out world-class primary care doctors, but they do so in very different ways.

The remaining three are private institutions. Duke University, in the Southeast, has an accelerated program of science courses for first-year students, setting them up to do complex research. At Yale University in the Northeast, students don't take exams unless they want to, yet are required to write a thesis. Then there is Johns Hopkins University in the mid-Atlantic, a research power-house whose students serve urban Baltimore when they are not busy in the school's labs.

Of course, each school boasts features that defy the limits of any stereotype: Washington, for instance, creates family doctors while also pulling in more research money than most other schools in the nation. That's why any school you're inter-ested in merits a closer look. To give you a head start, here are profiles, including student and fac-ulty viewpoints, of each member of this medical Fab Five.

University of Wisconsin School of Medicine and Public Health

- Madison, Wisconsin
- Public
- Enrollment 2007–2008 academic year: 614
- Overall rank in the 2009 *U.S. News* medical school rankings (research): 27
- Overall rank in the 2009 *U.S. News* medical school rankings (primary care): 13
- Average MCAT score: 10.4
- Average undergraduate GPA: 3.76

Stroll over to Wisconsin's anatomy department and you'll be able to talk to—or take a class from—James Thomson, the scientist who first isolated human stem cells from an embryo, a giant break-through that has raised hopes for dramatic new medical therapies and embroiled the country in an ethical debate over use of these cells. Nearly 600 of Wisconsin's other 1,100 faculty members are involved in leading medical science programs in aging, neuroscience, cancer, and other key areas. The university as a whole pulled in $770 million in research money in a recent year, making it one of the top public schools doing this kind of work. So what draws most students to Madison? Surprisingly, *not* the lure of the lab. "I came because we train some of the best primary care physicians around," said one student. It's a senti-ment fellow students echo again and again.

Philip Farrell, dean of the medical school, said there's no contradiction here, given Wisconsin's status as both a fine academic institution and a state university. "We have a superb clinical care program; that's absolutely true. It's a core part of our mission. Yet we're also part of this enormous research university." The med school has almost as many Ph.D. students as it does M.D. students; joint M.D./Ph.D. degrees in the Medical Scientist Training Program are also popular. Pioneering research programs on the connection between cancer and nutrition, and on cardiac electrophysi-ology, have spawned courses for medical students. "But yeah," Farrell said, "we produce fine, caring doctors."

This, then, is the "Wisconsin idea": While the university is tucked away on a narrow isthmus of land, almost cut off by two surrounding beautiful lakes, Mendota and Monona, the medical school itself is a statewide institution. Students do research in Madison at the highly regarded cancer center, for example, but also go to Milwaukee and work with the urban poor, or head out to small towns like Eagle River or Ashland, where they learn about rural health care issues and everyone around knows their names. Feeling a strong responsibility to make sure Wisconsin has the necessary supply of doctors, the university's Board of Regents presses Farrell to reserve 80 to 90 percent of the spots in each entering class for in-state students, many of whom will stay in the area once they get their M.D.

To fan interest in treating patients, the school pairs first- and second-year students with family practice doctors, internists, or pediatricians for a half-day each month. Students themselves run a program called MEDIC (Medical Information Center), which puts them to work advising patients at clinics in the Madison area. For at least six weeks during the third year, the school boots everyone out for rotations in small-town clinics and hospitals throughout the state. "It's not that they absolutely want to push us in that direction, but they definitely want to expose us to that," said one student interested in family practice. (The school does look beyond the Dairy State borders: It runs a summer medical clinic in Ecuador, for example.) And the exposure definitely gets results: Since 1999, about 20 percent of each graduating class has gone into family medicine residencies. Internal medicine has drawn an additional 12 to 20 percent, and the third most popular specialty has been pediatrics. In contrast, about five or six percent choose surgery, and a fraction of a percent go into neurology.

Whatever specialty students explore, they do it in close contact with their professors. Particularly at the small-town sites, there's often just one student rotating through at a time, which translates into a lot of attention from teacher-physicians. That's true on campus, too. Faculty members have a reputation for being very approachable and often

come in during the evenings to tutor students. "There's a lot of interaction with professors," one student said. "When I went to get recommendations for residency programs, there was no shortage of people I could talk to. I was on a first-name basis with a lot of them." Indeed, teaching skill, not just the number of publications or amount of grant funding brought in, is weighed more heavily

> *"When I went to get recommendations for residency programs, there was no shortage of people I could talk to."*

in promotion decisions than at most schools, and junior faculty are assigned a senior faculty mentor to help them along.

The warm, intimate feeling extends to fellow students. "I got into here, and Dartmouth, and Yale," said one third-year student. "This place seemed different. People at Madison take time out of their schedules to stop and discuss the school with you, in the classrooms and in the hallways, because they like it so much. I remember I visited one other school where I didn't see a student all day, and I know they weren't all on vacation." Students call the culture supportive, not competitive; there are even side bets in each class on how many members will end up marrying one another. And while everyone studies hard, people here "also know how to have a good time," said another student. Yet another one noted that she liked the fact that much of her class was older and brought mature, diverse perspectives to discussions about subjects such as medical ethics.

Not everything about the school gets rave reviews. There are too many basic science lectures, according to some students and faculty. Unlike schools that try to pepper the first year with small-group learning experiences, Wisconsin has retained the large-lecture format. "I'd say that small-group learning is our biggest weakness right now," said Susan Skochelak, the senior associate dean for academic affairs. Her concern is echoed by students. "There were six or seven hours of lectures per day during the first year," said one. "They don't take attendance, so you don't have to be there. But I felt that much structured time was excessive, at least for me." There are also complaints that the school buildings are old and overcrowded and that there's no student parking.

Class sizes and facilities were drastically improved in the fall of 2004, when the school's new Health Sciences Learning Center opened, giving Wisconsin one of the most modern medical school buildings in the country. Numerous classrooms and labs allow for smaller course sections and discussion groups. The school's formerly separate libraries are now consolidated here and equipped with more computer terminals as well as wireless access. The entire building, in fact, is a wireless heaven, with numerous "hot spots" where students can download course materials and medical data out of the ether. The building also houses Wisconsin's nursing and physician assistant programs, allowing for a lot of cross-pollination of ideas and staff.

Parking spaces are still going to be a problem, however. If that's a big issue for you, Madison is not going to make you happy. But everything else—the patient contact, the access to leading research if you want it, the new building, the famously rich university-made ice cream sold at the student center—makes for some of the best-trained (and happiest) future doctors around.

Duke University School of Medicine

- **Durham, North Carolina**
- **Private**
- **Enrollment 2007–2008 academic year: 404**
- **Overall rank in the 2009 U.S. News medical school rankings (research): 6**
- **Overall rank in the 2009 U.S. News medical school rankings (primary care): 41**
- **Average MCAT score: 11.5**
- **Average undergraduate GPA: 3.74**

Most medical students spend their third year of school racing around hospitals, going from cardiology units to pediatric wards to try out various clinical specialties. But by Brian Griffith's third year at Duke, he had already been there and done that. Instead, Griffith was holed up in his own little corner of a bustling microbiology lab, surrounded by rows and rows of petri dishes filled with a fungus that can cause meningitis in people with weak immune systems. Griffith was designing tests to identify genes that help the fungus become virulent.

Meanwhile, across town at a Duke clinic, Griffith's classmate Jennifer Kim was interviewing and examining 100 patients enrolled in a new study on the reliability of various blood pressure monitors. "Blood pressure is used so often for diagnosis and patient status info," said Kim, whose goal was to bring better, more reliable devices into hospitals and clinics. "I think this sort of research is key to the practice of medicine."

This notion—that research is the cornerstone of health care—dominates the Duke experience. To this end, the school packs all basic science classes into the first 11 months, running August through July, instead of spreading them across the first two years as most schools do. The science acceleration gets students into the hospital sooner—during year two instead of year three, so their third year is devoted full-time to research.

Clearly, Duke is not aiming to swell the ranks of family practice docs. Instead, the program is geared toward producing physician-scientists who can easily move between the lab bench and the bedside. "Our current body of knowledge will have nothing to do with the practice of medicine in ten years," said R. Sanders Williams, senior vice chancellor for academic affairs and former dean. "We aim to provide graduates with both the tools and the ethos of lifetime scholarship." He noted that a full 40 percent of students go on to pursue dual degrees such as an M.D./Ph.D. or an M.D. combined with a new master's degree in translational medicine, which focuses on turning basic research into clinically useful models.

The pressure can be great here, especially early on, so Duke students must hit the ground running. That early push to cover everything from physiology and neurobiology to pathology in the first year means spending all day, every day in a lecture hall and then a lab. It's difficult, say students, but doable. "We're learning the essentials, not a lot of fluff, because you don't need it," said one second-year student, adding that she felt extremely well-prepared for her clinical rotations. In fact, most students are eager to hit the wards. "I came to med school to practice medicine, to put a white coat on and get out into the hospital—not to sit in a classroom for two years," explained a student in the fourth year of a combined M.D./Ph.D. program in medical sociology and health policy.

Then it's on to the third year for research.

The school pushes this hard, said Edward Halperin, former vice dean of the med school (current dean of the University of Louisville School of Medicine), in part because of a belief that would-be doctors need to be able to interpret constantly advancing research. "Just because a study is in the *Journal of the American Medical Association* doesn't mean it's true," he said. "You

> "We aim to provide graduates with both the tools and the ethos of lifetime scholarship."

have to learn how to critically read scientific literature—*how do you read what's published and* decide when things change research to therapy? And there's no better way to assess the value of research than to do it yourself." The individualized research process requires a lot of initiative and self-motivation—much like the rest of the Duke experience—but gives students exceptional benefits. It provides an opportunity to work closely with a faculty mentor, for one thing, perhaps one of the big names you see on the covers of your textbooks. It can also be an important résumé boost when you start shopping for a residency, particularly if you've published a scientific paper or two, as both Griffith and Kim planned to do.

There are a few complaints about the pace. Some students say that the chock-full first year ignores important areas such as embryology; others say that it's particularly difficult to cover gross anatomy—and dissect a human body—in only nine weeks. (Other schools spend twice as much time teaching these skills.) Currently, Duke is in the midst of revamping its curriculum to better address changes in the field. The traditional first-year lecture courses will be regrouped into three blocks—Molecules and Cells, Normal Body, and Body and Disease—with a focus on individual organ systems rather than broad topics, and more emphasis on interaction and case-based learning. In the second year, there will be five

---

"There's no better way to assess the value of research than to do it yourself."

---

weeklong "mini courses" that cover diagnostic exercises and exposure to areas of health care like physical rehabilitation and social work. In addition, the research year will expand from eight to ten months and require a written thesis.

Already, though, both research and clinical opportunities abound throughout the relatively young and rich Duke University Medical Center, a $1.7 billion system closely affiliated with the medical school, encompassing myriad health care providers from the Duke Hospital and Clinics to the Duke Community Hospice. That range provides chances for students to gain exposure to many different areas of medicine. This is perhaps another reason why the vast majority of students here end up focusing on competitive specialties and subspecialties like dermatology, pediatrics, plastic surgery, orthopedics, and radiology, as opposed to primary care or family medicine. A good number go on to obtain coveted residencies in these areas at top institutions, including nearly a quarter at Duke itself. After they graduate, some 20 percent of Duke students

go on to hold academic positions; the remaining 80 percent pursue a wide variety of career paths, from running biotech companies to working in government health organizations. And, yes, a few do serve as physicians in small towns.

Although Duke is filled with one hyperqualified overachiever after another, students say the culture here is overwhelmingly collegial. Many tell tales of sharing notes and study charts with their whole class during the first year, perhaps because students aren't grubbing for A's. The grading system here is pass, fail, and honors; some complain that the latter designation can be arbitrary, but most say they're happy with the results. It helps that faculty are said to be very accessible. In the first year, students are assigned to an advisory dean and meet with that person and a handful of peers for lunch once a week; these gatherings let students discuss current events and schoolwide issues, or simply blow off steam. In the second year, larger groups of 25 congregate to talk about being in the hospital and share important milestones, like delivering a baby for the first time.

This collegiality was crucial, students say, when the unthinkable happened a few years back. In a case that made major headlines, a Duke surgeon infamously botched an organ transplant on a young illegal immigrant named Jesica Santillan, who eventually died. "I think we were all shocked, to say the least," recalled one student. "But we talked about it a lot [in advising groups and classes] and I think we learned from it. It made me more aware of how vigilant you have to be at all times, even with the most routine things." In the aftermath, some students say they feel more empowered to speak up to physicians if they notice a mistake or an inconsistency.

In addition to its many academic advantages, Duke, surprisingly, can also provide a relatively inexpensive medical education. The low cost of living in Durham, combined with a famously generous financial aid office, results in a much lower average debt burden: the mean for Duke grads is $74,790, compared to the national average of slightly more than $100,000. That, say students, relieves a lot of anxiety about the future. The med school offers 11 full-tuition scholarships per class; and recently, 65 out of 100 third-year students received research scholarships from sources such as the Howard Hughes Medical Institute. And despite the hard work, students say, there's plenty of time to hang out with friends and enjoy Durham Bulls minor league baseball and the university's nationally ranked basketball teams. (The comprehensive, student-produced *Duke Med School Made Ridiculously Simple* is a favorite resource for information about how you'll spend your free time, in addition to academics.)

Duke is, in short, a school of tremendous challenges but also tremendous opportunities. Said the school's dean: "Being here is about dreaming big, following your dream, and not being afraid." The fearless thrive and go on to push back the current boundaries of medicine.

Yale University School of Medicine

■ **New Haven, Connecticut**
■ **Private**
■ **Enrollment 2007–2008 academic year: 395**
■ **Overall rank in the 2009 *U.S. News* medical school rankings (research): 9**
■ **Overall rank in the 2009 *U.S. News* medical school rankings (primary care): N/A**
■ **Average MCAT score: 11.3**
■ **Average undergraduate GPA: 3.72**

When Yale students invite friends from other med schools for some weekend fun, such as skiing or a trip to the ballpark, the response is usually something along the lines of "Are you kidding?" That's because most med students spend their weekends cramming for exams. But not at Yale. Most exams here are optional, anonymous, online self-evaluations. What's more, students get two free afternoons each week. So perhaps it's not surprising that they jokingly refer to laid-back Yale as the "Utopia School of Medicine."

Officially, though, the school's approach is called "The Yale System." It aims to give med students wide latitude in constructing their own educational experiences, akin to Ph.D. programs in, say, genetics or history. And if this is utopia, it requires plenty of self-discipline. "Students must assume more than usual responsibility for their education," reads the school's literature. "Memorization of facts should be far less important than a well-rounded education in fundamental principles, training in methods of investigation, and the acquisition of the scientific habit of mind."

For the academic overachievers who populate Yale's ranks, The System can take some getting used to. It tries to transform students who have previously succeeded by being extremely competitive into team players. "Yale is full of people who are Type A personalities but are trying to be Type B," said one second-year student. The reason? Success in modern medicine depends more than ever before on collaboration. There's so much knowledge to absorb and then put into practice that doctors and researchers have to team up. "At

---

> "Yale is full of people who are Type A personalities but are trying to be Type B."

Yale, it's all about getting through this stuff together," said a student. "It's not like, 'I won't give you the answer because you'll get a better orthopedics residency.'" Said another second-year student: "Students here study for the right reasons. You take self-evaluations to see if you understand the material, not to see who got a 94 percent and who got a 97 percent." The school's size—each class is roughly 100 students—also breeds an intimate, cooperative atmosphere. For second-year students who cycle through a long series of total-immersion modules—a few weeks on the cardiovascular system followed by a few weeks of psychiatry, and so on—classes outside the lectures are invariably tiny. In labs and workshops, class size stays below 20.

But the system has its pitfalls, students say. Basic science lectures for first and second years are often poorly attended, probably due in part to lecturers not taking attendance. And because self-evaluations are optional, some students never get around to taking them, which could mean playing catch-up before taking national licensing exams.

"If one is too liberal in slacking," said a first-year student, "the system will give you enough rope to hang yourself." Still, most students learn to keep up with the curriculum; Yale's pass rate on the national exams is similar to other top-ranked med schools.

What Yale does require is a thesis, an unusual demand among medical schools. This project, usually begun during the first or second year and completed during the fourth and final year of school, may be lab research or an investigation of clinical, epidemiological, or sociological subjects. Recent papers have examined the stigma attached to AIDS in Africa and the causes of type II diabetes in lab mice. Students doing this work can tap into Yale's resources as a leading research institution (it received $300.7 million in National Institutes of Health grants in 2005), funding thesis-related research through grants and getting access to top faculty for thesis advisors. Meeting with his advisor for the first time, one third-year student remembered, "we had a fifteen-minute appointment and [the advisor] stayed for two hours. His eyes shone as he talked—I didn't think you could get that excited about basic science." Most students secure research funding for the summer between their first and second year, often for overseas projects and thesis-related work. Roughly half of each class takes an extra year to graduate, often to devote a full year to the thesis; in these cases, Yale waives fifth-year tuition.

Because of this program, Yale is known for breeding academic physicians. Even students who aren't drawn to Yale for the thesis often wind up getting hooked on research. Many publish their papers in medical journals. "Our purpose here is to turn out individuals who are going to be the leading physician-scientists in the country," said Dennis Spencer, a professor of neurosurgery and, until 2004, the school's acting dean. "We don't turn out many people who are going to do primary care." Indeed, Yale New Haven Hospital, the school's main teaching hospital, doesn't count family medicine among the residencies it offers, though a large number of Yale students do take residencies in pediatrics.

Despite the heady academic atmosphere, students are not locked in an ivory research tower. The M.D. program puts students in touch with patients early on. From the first year, all students meet weekly to practice taking medical histories from fellow students, then from actual patients—sometimes within the first few weeks of med school. This is a big help when students hit the hospital wards full-time in their third year. One third-year student said he didn't appreciate the weekly meetings until he had to tell a former drug user that he'd need regular kidney dialysis for the rest of his life—a test of interpersonal, rather than medical, skills. "By the time third-year rolls around," he said, "you spend time caring for the patient instead of figuring out how to gather information from them." Even during their time in the hospitals, students are encouraged to take control of their learning. "The structure on the wards is flat as opposed to hierarchical," one student said. "There's no objection to saying, 'I don't think that's right' to an attending [physician]. Just because they've had all this training doesn't mean they can't be challenged."

During that third year, which can be quite intense, Yale still prides itself on maintaining free afternoons. Most students don't use these to sleep in or goof off, however. Many spend the time doing volunteer work, like educating local school children on AIDS/HIV prevention or creating basic medical records for New Haven's homeless population. An annual auction, organized by students, raises tens of thousands of dollars for the homeless. With plenty of low-income residents,

> ## "We don't turn out many people who are going to do primary care."

New Haven is flush with volunteer opportunities. "You can't be isolated here," said Spencer. "You have to engage in the community." The medical school is also a short walk from Yale's main campus, which allows students to interact with other university departments.

Most of their engagement, however, is at the med school itself, where the administration seems unusually responsive to student input. When a pair of students recently developed a formula that allowed third-year students to schedule their clinical clerkships more easily, administrators agreed to adopt it. And when international students lobbied to extend financial aid to foreign students last year, the school obliged. After all, if a school urges students to take their education into their own hands, it has to face the consequences.

Johns Hopkins University School of Medicine

- Baltimore, Maryland
- Private
- Enrollment 2007–2008 academic year: 460
- Overall rank in the 2009 *U.S. News* medical school rankings (research): 2
- Overall rank in the 2009 *U.S. News* medical school rankings (primary care): 26
- Average MCAT score: 11.8
- Average undergraduate GPA: 3.85

Johns Hopkins researchers invented the implantable pacemaker, discovered restriction enzymes that let geneticists manipulate DNA, and developed CPR. The medical school received $475.3 million in National Institutes of Health funding in 2005. Hopkins surgeons routinely make newspaper headlines by, say, separating conjoined twins in intricate operations. So what is it like at the bottom of the Hopkins pecking order, as a lowly medical student? Like being taught by the best in the world, said a fourth-year student. "Even the greatest researchers there completely feel that part of their job is to train students."

And they should feel teaching is important— modern medical education was born at Hopkins. When the school opened in 1893, most medical institutions offered only lectures—future doctors never laid eyes on a live patient. But Quaker merchant Johns Hopkins stipulated that the medical school carrying his name had to be connected to a hospital with the size and means to train medical students. As a result, Hopkins students learned through hands-on experience. Eventually, this model spread throughout American medical education. Since its founding, the school has been home to over a century of influential medical educators, such as William Osler and William Halsted, inventors of the modern medical residency.

"I think that the tradition here is important," said Frank Herlong, former associate dean of student affairs. "And I think we have to be careful that it doesn't become oppressive." He gave the example of the resident who, several years ago, announced that she just wanted to be a regular old doctor, not an academic. A faculty member called her into his office to ask "Where have we failed?" Today, however, Herlong said that Hopkins students are "pluripotent"—like the human embryo's primordial stem cells, they could develop into anything, not just academic physicians. "The person who has been a leader in some small community by influencing the health care for the underserved, that person may not be famous or in the newspaper, but I hope that we would continue to embrace that," he noted. Still, more than half of Hopkins graduates spend some part of their career in academic medicine, whether as full professors or as part-timers at local medical schools. Only about 10 percent of graduates focus exclusively on primary care.

Medical education at Hopkins, overall, follows the traditional pattern: science lectures until April of the second year, then just over two years of learning by watching and doing in the hospital. But several years ago, the school reassessed first-year courses, which leapt from biochemistry to genetics to immunology with no attempt to explore the relationships between these topics. Now the curriculum starts with the molecule, builds up to cells, then to organs, and finishes with organ functions in a healthy person. Although lectures dominate in the beginning, most of the teaching in later years happens one-on-one, with a research mentor or on the wards, said pediatrician David Nichols, vice dean for education. "Teaching how to develop a bedside manner—that's really a one-on-one kind of experience," he said. "You can't teach it in a lecture and you can't read about it in a book."

Even before bedside manners are taught, however, Hopkins students begin feeling the research tug: More than 80 percent do some kind of research as an elective, most often in the summer after their first year. One fourth-year student said she came to school with a strong interest in international health. She'd been an anthropology major in college, and said there was no way anyone was getting her to sit at a lab bench for months at a stretch. "Then all of a sudden here I was working in a lab and, you know, I took a year off to do it." Her research, on how HIV lives in the body even during antiviral treatment, taught her how the lab relates to patient care—in her case, to the international HIV prevention work that she eventually wants to do.

Besides its name for fostering cutting-edge research, Hopkins also has a reputation for generating cutthroat competition. Hopkins takes only 120 of its 4,000 or so applicants every year, so its students are among the best in the country academically. But reputation isn't necessarily reality, one student said. "My experience has been that there are always a handful of people who are very, very intensely competitive and that's kind of their thing." Many students say they usually study in groups, helping each other get through the difficult science courses. And during those first few years of school, students spend a great deal of time together, in and out of class.

Professors seem to be supportive as well. After the first exam of her first year, one student recalled getting "the worst grade I've ever seen in my life." She went to see the professor and "just started bawling like an idiot." But her prof calmed her down, reassuring her that everyone goes through tough times in medical school, and she wasn't destined to fail. After talking about the situation, the student realized she had to overhaul her study habits to focus on learning, not grades. When she had to

"Even the greatest researchers there completely feel that part of their job is to train students."

explain the material to other students in study groups, she finally knew that she had it down pat.

Hopkins' urban home, Baltimore, may be known as "Charm City," but those charms are usually not immediately evident to med students. "Baltimore is a great place once you get to know it, but at first it seems maybe not the most friendly place that I've ever been," said one student. The hospital and school are wedged into a dense urban campus in rough East Baltimore, although the neighborhood has been improving in recent years. Security officers check IDs by every entrance, and the students consider the hospital campus to be safe. Eventually, they learn to navigate Baltimore's many neighborhoods, such as nightclub-packed Fell's Point and tree-lined, pet-friendly Butchers Hill, and many fall in love with the city. Washington, D.C., is less than an hour away, and students can get to New York City in a few hours. One med student noted that he spent his spare time exploring Maryland's state parks—in addition to the horse racing scene, which includes the Preakness, Baltimore's leg of the Triple Crown.

The city plays a role in students' education, too. Part of the hospital's mission is to take care of the poor. While students see many unusual cases referred from other hospitals (because Hopkins has so many top specialists), they also tackle the day-to-day health problems of their closest neighbors. Many students work on community health projects: Some teach sex education workshops in Baltimore middle schools, work on a program to introduce local high school kids to health careers, or mentor pregnant teenagers.

While students are working to change the area around the school, the school is working hard to change itself. Committees of faculty and students are discussing an overhaul of the curriculum to take effect in 2006 or 2007. As more and more conditions are treated without a hospital stay, medical students rarely see a patient with pneumonia. Doctors are spending less time with patients, which means new doctors have less time to learn clinical skills, such as listening to the way lung and heart sounds change as people get better or worse. In the next few years, the school will start using more high-tech simulations to train students, such as special mannequins that can be programmed to make different heart sounds and mimic these changes. Another major debate about the curriculum is how new research on genetics will change medical practice—for example, whether doctors should drop the old idea of a sick body as a machine that needs fixing and focus instead on each patient's genes, environment, and personal history.

In the meantime, the school is still turning out new doctors with an impressive entry on their résumés. "To be honest, the name helps a lot," a student said, but added that it was more than just a name; it was a superior education. "They set me up to do whatever I wanted to do after medical school."

University of Washington School of Medicine

- **Seattle, Washington**
- **Public**
- **Enrollment 2007–2008 academic year: 826**
- **Overall rank in the 2009 U.S. News medical school rankings (research): 6**
- **Overall rank in the 2009 U.S. News medical school rankings (primary care): 1**
- **Average MCAT score: 10.5**
- **Average undergraduate GPA: 3.68**

It's puzzling: Why would more than half the graduates of a huge school with an expansive academic research program like the University of Washington School of Medicine go into primary care? And why would so many graduates leave this urban Seattle campus to practice medicine in rural areas, many outside the state?

The answer, it seems, is WWAMI. That's the acronym for five Northwestern states—Washington, Wyoming, Alaska, Montana, and Idaho—that together make up more than a quarter of the land mass in the United States, yet have only one medical school among them. People in these states need good primary care in fields such as family medicine and pediatrics. So for thirty years, all five states have united behind that one school, UW, pooling far-flung resources, doctors, and science faculty at local colleges to bring WWAMI residents to Seattle—and get them back to WWAMI states once they've graduated.

The route many of them take is, for med students, a little unusual. One, Courtney Paterson, grew up in Bozeman, Montana, where she also went to college. After getting into UW's medical program, she spent her first year not in Seattle, but at Montana State University, where there is no med school. There she took the basic medical science courses—physiology, microbiology, and so on—with visiting faculty and the school's own science staff. Paterson then went to work for a summer at a clinic in tiny Ronan, Montana (population 1,800) which had six primary care docs and not much else. She followed the doctors around, watching how they did their work, and also did research on local rates of sexually transmitted diseases. She finally set foot on UW's campus at the beginning of her second year—the first time she'd been there since her admissions interview. "It was a little weird to have to mix with all these people who've already been here for a year when I didn't even know where the main office was yet," she said, "But I knew I wasn't alone."

Far from it. Nearly half of the 178 students in Paterson's med school class spent their first year like her, doing basic science at one of four Northwestern schools outside Seattle. More than a hundred UW students spend their first-year summers working side-by-side with local docs in underserved, rural areas. And ultimately more than 50 percent of UW graduates end up practicing medicine in a WWAMI state.

This commitment to rural primary care came about, said Paul Ramsey, the school's dean, because 37 percent of the population in the region lives in rural areas. "Over two billion people in the world have no access to a physician," he said, "Does the world really need more big city specialists?" Not from UW, which has sent graduates everywhere from Kodiak Island, Alaska, to Thermopolis, Wyoming.

Primary care "is just part of the culture" that suffuses UW and its affiliated hospitals, said Kristi Nix. Recently a pediatrics resident at a UW children's hospital in Seattle, Nix worked with both students and faculty from the med school. She said that you get a feel, watching the professors, for what it is to be a "good doctor." Nix didn't go to UW for medical school herself, and at other

"I was in a clinic taking a personal history the first week of my first year."

schools, she said, the good doctors all "have labs and see patients half-time and do research eighty hours a week. Out here, most of the docs are living lives as physicians, they're actually taking care of people—and they don't have that aggressive, 'you've got to publish' type of feeling."

Instead, faculty push clinical skills on their students early and often. In both first and second years, students take the required course Introduction to Clinical Medicine, where they are tutored in interviewing skills, usually in small groups of six or seven. "I was in a clinic taking a personal history the first week of my first year," said one student.

In their third and fourth years, when a lot of other med students are touring specialty areas in big teaching hospitals, UW students are encouraged to do their rotations outside Seattle, in more than one hundred WWAMI towns from Pocatello to Coeur d'Alene to Mountain Home. "It's just an unbeatable experience out there," said Joe Woodward, a student who did his family medicine rotation in a five-doctor clinic in eastern

Washington. The doctors there had known their patients for years. In some cases, they were delivering the babies of people they'd delivered. "I saw things I'd never see in an urban hospital with a hundred interns running around," he said.

When students do rotations as far away as Alaska, the isolation puts a premium on developing diverse medical skills. "Out there you have no

> "Sometimes specialists just take care of a problem, you know? In primary care, your job really is to take care of people."

idea what could walk in the door at any moment," said Woodward. "If you can't handle it, the patient gets choppered a hundred miles to someone who can," and the helicopter ride can, for critically injured patients, take too long.

This emphasis on primary care does have its downside. It "can be a good thing as an introduction to medicine, but it's a double-edged sword," said one student torn between hospital-based primary care and infectious diseases. She worried that UW students who don't know what they want to specialize in can easily fall into something like family medicine for lack of extensive exposure to anything else. "It's entirely possible to find yourself at the end of your third year, and you haven't rotated in any other fields." Other students say UW does offer plenty of options outside primary care for those who truly want them. "If you're proactive, it's easy to find [an advisor] in something else," said one, who

specialized in internal medicine yet made space in her schedule for classes in anesthesiology.

Many of those options come from UW's enormous research presence. In 2005, the school scored nearly $540 million in grants from the National Institutes of Health, one of the highest totals in the nation. Over 1,600 full-time faculty wend their ways through the fir trees on the shores of Lake Washington each day to the school's Pentagon-sized labyrinth of laboratories. Calling Washington home are 25 members of the Institute of Medicine, and students can also work with dozens of award-winning cancer vaccine researchers at the Fred Hutchinson Cancer Research Center a few miles from campus. Scott Sears, a recent grad now working as a general internist in Billings, Montana, earned three separate grants at UW to work with the school's collection of human and primate eyeballs, one of the largest in the country, studying ophthalmology and developmental proteins in retinas.

Still, for Paterson and so many of her classmates, the UW road will lead to WWAMI's primary needs. "When I was 16, I wanted to be a brain surgeon," she said. "When I was 18, it was obstetrics/gynecology. I was never interested in family practice until that summer" in Ronan. And after graduation, Paterson planned to head back to Montana. "Sometimes specialists just take care of a problem, you know? In primary care, your job really is to take care of people."

Chapter Four

Getting In

There are lots of good reasons for wanting to be a doctor. Maybe you think you have a healing touch, or you want to serve the community, or there's something about solving the puzzle of an illness that satisfies your mind and your soul. And there are probably some bad reasons, like doing it for the money, or because your family will be disappointed if you don't make medicine a career. But no matter what the motives, everyone has to jump over the same hurdle: medical school admissions.

It's not an easy leap. More than 37,000 people try to get in every year, yet just 18,000 succeed. And that's only the overall picture. Individual schools can be much more picky. The University of Chicago Pritzker School of Medicine recently received almost 8,000 applications for its incoming class of about 100 students. Georgetown University School of Medicine had over 10,000 applicants for about 200 spaces. You do the math.

If you want in, you'd better be *able* to do the math. This is a brainy crowd. Admissions committees are swamped with applications from students whose undergraduate grade point averages hover at 3.5 and who average a score of 28 out of 45 on the Medical College Admission Test (MCAT). Those who attend the most competitive schools consistently score well over 30. "The competition is very intense," said

---

"The competition is very intense. There are a whole bunch of applicants who, in terms of numbers, are all equally qualified."

Greg Goldmakher, a medical school advisor with AdmissionsConsultants, Inc. in Vienna, Virginia. "There are a whole bunch of applicants who, in terms of numbers, are all equally qualified."

To stand out—and get in—applicants must find ways to distinguish themselves from the rest of the premed pack. In this chapter, you'll learn how. *U.S. News* asked admissions directors at the nation's top medical schools to describe what they look for in candidates who get the green light. All of them said good grades and MCATs are a great start. But science smarts are not enough. Admissions committees are looking for unique, highly motivated people who excel in and out of the classroom. "It's a very special segment of the human race," said Andrew Frantz, associate dean of admissions at Columbia University's College of Physicians and Surgeons in New York. "They have to be intelligent, sensitive to others, compassionate, committed to finding joy in their work and they should want to be of service to others." Here are tips to best let you show those traits, along with ways to get the best test scores and grades that you can.

Making the grades

It all starts in the classroom. Science is the backbone of medicine, and no matter how caring or compassionate you may be, medical schools want to know that you can handle the academic material. You will need to complete certain science courses before you can apply to medical school and you should start taking them freshman year, if possible. By the time you apply to medical school, you should have completed one year each (including labs) of chemistry, biology, physics, and organic chemistry. In addition, medical schools often want to see a year of English and a year of math, including a semester of calculus. The American Medical Student Association (AMSA) tells premeds to head for their school's preprofessional health advisor, usually found in the career counseling office, and together plot a course for completing all of the classes.

Tip: Pace yourself. A heavy load of rigorous courses can drag down your performance in each class, so don't take more than two prerequisites a semester.

If you decide to jump on the premed track a bit later—say, well into your sophomore year—you may need to take summer classes to make up for lost time. Find a summer school that is comparable to the one you attend during the school year; admissions committees do take note of the difference. "We are troubled by someone taking one or two semesters of something like organic chemistry at a community college over the summer," said Robert Witzburg, associate dean and director of admissions at Boston University School of Medicine. But if the course is taken at a school like

The "nontraditional" student

There was a time when almost every applicant to medical school came directly from college. No longer. An ever-increasing number are taking time after they graduate to pursue other interests or get some work experience. Called "nontraditional applicants," even though their path is becoming a tradition in itself, these people are often viewed favorably, even prized, by admissions committees. Boston University's medical school admissions office says the school's nontraditional students, many of whom have put off their physician training to work in jobs serving communities without many resources, demonstrate "flexible intelligence" and an ability to interact well with patients. Henry Ralston, who was the associate dean of admissions at the University of California—San Francisco agreed—that's why he encouraged premeds to take a year off and get some experience outside of the school setting. "I prefer older students," he said.

But not all schools feel this way, cautioned Trina Denton, a nontraditional applicant who served as director of premedical affairs at AMSA, the medical student advocacy group. Some medical schools may worry that applicants who have taken time away from studying will find it hard to get back into the habit. Applicants can ask the schools they are interested in if taking time off could harm their chances of getting in—or better yet, ask for the numbers of nontraditional students in the entering class.

Some nontraditional applicants decide after finishing college that they want to apply to medical school, but have not taken the prerequisite science courses. Such applicants should consider a premed, postbaccalaureate program. You get the basic courses plus the chance to take some advanced electives. At Georgetown University, the post-baccalaureate program "gives students the courses they need so they will qualify as premed despite the fact that they may have majored in poetry," said Douglas Eagles, Associate professor and Biology department chair. Programs take one to two years and offer students some valuable structure and help when they get ready to take the MCAT and prepare their school applications. Some people find this much easier than going it all alone. And because postbaccalaureate programs can include some of the same courses a first-year med student would take, they let the admissions office see that you can really do the work—because you have.

The Association of American Medical Colleges offers a searchable database to find these programs nationwide. Go to www.aamc.org and search "postbaccalaureate programs." (For a list of several well-regarded programs, see 352.) An alternative is to take the classes on a full- or part-time basis at a local university under a nondegree-seeking status, and med schools will usually accept them. Some are more restrictive, however, so check with the schools before signing up.

the one you're already studying at, he said, "no one here is going to be bothered by that."

If you plan on using Advanced Placement courses taken during high school to fulfill these requirements, be wary. Many med schools won't accept them, and whether they do or not can depend on your other science courses. Remember, schools want to see that you can

"The ideal candidate has strong performance in science, but also has taken humanities."

handle the material. So college students who major in science and also received AP credit can demonstrate they know the basics by performing well in their upper-level science courses. Med schools are more likely to let their AP work count for a college course. But applicants who do not take more advanced college science classes may not be able to use their AP scores. If you already have an idea about the med schools you want to apply to, check with those admissions offices about their AP credit policies.

This focus on science doesn't mean you have to major in biology or physics. In fact, admissions committees look for students who have challenged themselves academically and taken a broad range of classes throughout their undergraduate years. "The ideal candidate has strong performance in science, but also has taken humanities," said Albert Kirby, former associate dean for admissions at Case Western Reserve University School of Medicine in Cleveland, Ohio. "We love students who are nonscience majors," said William Eley, executive associate

dean for medical education and former director of admissions at Emory University School of Medicine in Atlanta, Georgia. "We are looking for that breadth because it indicates involvement in the human side of medicine."

Indeed, majoring in something nonscientific might actually help you. In a crowd of biology and physics students, that history degree stands out. According to the Association of American Medical Colleges (AAMC), 52 percent of humanities and social science majors who applied were accepted to medical school in 2001. That's actually a little better than the 48 percent of successful applicants who majored in biology.

Tip: Take some humanities courses. Applicants who focus solely on science can be viewed as weaker candidates than those who have performed well across many fields.

Testing, testing

In addition to science classes, undergraduates must take the MCAT, a five-hour computerized test given by the AAMC. The MCAT is offered twice in January, and then at least once a month from April until mid-September. Typically, applicants first take the test in the spring of their junior year of college. For a detailed MCAT exam schedule or to pre-register, go to www.aamc.org/mcat. Registration usually begins 120 days before a test date. Aim to take the test early so that you will have some later test dates to fall back on if your scores are not as high as you'd like. Also, try to register early because space can be limited at certain testing sites, and slots are filled in the order they are received. The regular registration fee is $210, and can be paid with a credit card.

Unlike other standardized tests that attempt to predict a student's ability (such as the SAT), the MCAT is content-driven, testing your mastery of the basic science material covered in premed courses. The test consists of four sections: physical sciences, which includes physics and chemistry; biological sciences, which includes biology and organic chemistry; verbal reasoning; and the writing sample. You can score up to 15 points in each of the two science sections and in verbal reasoning, for a possible total score of 45. (Most med school applicants, successful and unsuccessful, score in the high 20s and low 30s.) The writing sample is graded according to an eleven-letter system that goes alphabetically from "J" (lowest) to "T" (highest).

Obviously, it's best to have completed all of the science prerequisites before you take the test. Even so, to adequately prepare, you should plan to devote at least 200 and 300 hours to studying. Many applicants, perhaps as many as three-quarters, choose to take a preparatory class to help them structure their studying and to ensure that they cover all of the material. Princeton Review and Kaplan, Inc., offer widely available courses. You get multiple classroom sessions, prep materials, and practice tests. The courses are expensive, many approaching the $2,000 mark, but if you are not satisfied with your score, the companies will refund your fee or let you take the course again. (That's not going to help you, however, if you're not satisfied with your score and not satisfied with the course itself.) There are many local prep companies, too. But prep courses certainly aren't a must; if you feel you can be both disciplined and organized in your studying, you can purchase practice tests from the AAMC and a study guide from a bookstore, and prepare on your own.

Tip: Consider prepping. Prep classes can particularly help because they provide proctored practice tests to get you used to the grueling task of sitting and answering questions for five hours straight.

Taken together, your GPA and MCAT score form the basis of the initial cut medical schools make in their applicant pool. Why? Studies have shown that performance on the MCAT and in undergraduate courses is a reliable predictor of how well an applicant will do during the first two years of medical school.

It takes about 30 days to get your scores back. If your initial MCAT score falls well below what you expected, consider taking the test again over the summer. Medical schools vary on whether they will use your highest or your most recent score, with some averaging the two. Call admissions offices to find out how they handle the second set. But be warned: Waiting for the later score to come in could slow down the admission committee's review of your application, and when schools offer admissions on a rolling basis, that may reduce your chances of getting a spot.

Apply yourself

Once you have completed an initial MCAT exam, it is time to start thinking about assembling your application. This is one-stop shopping: Most medical schools use the American Medical College Application Service (AMCAS), a division of the AAMC, to process all the paperwork. You submit one completed application online, and that includes an application form, a personal statement, transcripts from all the undergraduate schools you have attended, and other paperwork, as well as a list of schools you want to apply to. For a fee, AMCAS assembles your application file, verifies it, and

What schools want...and what they don't

Some of our most difficult applicants are the majors from technical schools who took AP English in high school and never took another humanities course. They generally don't do well in the application process.
—*Robert Witzburg, associate dean of admissions, Boston University School of Medicine*

Don't ask *me* why you should pick our school. It's a turn-off.
—*Andrew Frantz, associate dean of admissions, Columbia University College of Physicians and Surgeons in New York*

We value individuals who will bring different strengths to the class. If everyone in the class had the same background, it would be dull.
—*Albert Kirby, former associate dean for admissions, Case Western Reserve University School of Medicine in Cleveland*

Write about something you really experienced, not a two-week trip to a developing country where you saw poverty and were moved by it.
—*Henry Ralston, former associate dean of admissions, UCSF School of Medicine in San Francisco*

We are looking for people who can do lots of things well. I like to see someone who is engaged in events and issues, someone who is not just interested in medicine.
—*Gaye Sheffler, director of admissions, University of Pennsylvania School of Medicine in Philadelphia*

I do not view the goal of the essays as either to entertain me, persuade me that the applicant would be 'fun to teach,' or regale me with stories of wondrous achievements and world travel. I expect applicants to take the writing of the essays seriously.
—*Edward Halperin, vice dean, Duke University School of Medicine*

forwards it to the schools you have designated. The service also sends along your MCAT scores if you tell them to do so. (If you plan on retaking the test, you have the option to withhold your scores.)

The application, along with timelines, resources, and worksheets, is available at www.aamc.org/amcas. You should be able to get the application in early May, and the service begins accepting completed applications in early June. It stops accepting applications the night before what-

ever deadline is set by the medical schools you are applying to, and that's generally from October to mid-December. It is your responsibility to meet these deadlines.

Tip: Double check. Some schools do not use the AMCAS application and rely on some other form instead. Contact the schools you are interested in to see if you need other application materials.

After AMCAS, there's still more application paperwork to deal with. Once the service has sent a copy of your application to each of your chosen medical schools, the schools themselves may send you a "secondary application." Some schools send secondary applications to all applicants, others send them only to those who make the initial cut after a review of GPAs and MCATs. The secondary application usually asks for additional personal essays, letters of recommendation, and an application fee. AMSA recommends that applicants fill out and return secondary applications no later than two weeks after they are received to avoid paperwork pileup.

Because the competition is so steep, plan to send out about 10 to 15 applications, maximizing your chances of success. Include three or four "reach" schools—where you just might have good enough credentials to get in—two back-up schools, and five to ten schools that you have a reasonable chance of getting into. What's a reach and what's a backup? Look at the mean GPA and MCAT scores for the incoming class of each medical school, which you can find in the directory section of this book. If your numbers are higher, you can think of the school as a backup. If they are lower, consider the school a reach—and the greater the gap, the longer the reach. Close matches are just that: By the numbers, you're a good fit. (See Chapter 2 for details about other important factors—things to consider before you worry about your chances for successful admission—in choosing schools.) Of course, the rest of your application has to be strong: Good numbers are ultimately no substitute for a poor essay or lackluster recommendations.

Getting personal

The next phase of application review, if you have the grades and MCAT scores to make it past a school's cut-off points, is when the school tries to get to know you as more than a set of numbers. Admissions committees are keenly interested in learning who you are, based on what you have done and how you express yourself. Here is where

---

"It is very important in medicine to be able to extend yourself emotionally."

---

your written statements, recommendation letters, and interview come into play.

Keep in mind that medical schools receive thousands of applications from people who appear to be pretty much the same as one another. They have good grades, good MCATs, experience working in a research lab for a summer or two, have worked in a hospital shadowing a physician, and have volunteered with a community organization delivering food to homeless people. These are strong candidates, said Goldmakher—but they are not distinctive. If you want to get into an ultra-selective school, you will need to be all this and more. That could mean demonstrating a longer commitment to one of these extracurricular activities or to the pursuit of something that is entirely unrelated to medicine, but is challenging nonetheless. The depth of your involvement in a project will indicate to medical schools how important that activity was to you.

Schools really are not looking for any one type of person or set of experiences. They want individuals with traits such as leadership, compassion, commitment, enthusiasm, and competence. For example, athletics can be an excellent way to show that you can work with a team—an important trait in many fields of medicine—as well as demonstrate that you have leadership skills and the ability to make quick decisions. Athletics also demonstrate physical stamina, which can be important in certain fields, such as surgery. Admissions committees consider all of these traits, so include hobbies and talents that you are passionate about in your application even if you think they are not relevant to your interest in becoming a doctor. These outside interests reveal a lot to admissions committees about who you are and what you are capable of. Andrew Frantz from Columbia University said he is drawn to applicants with an interest in theater because acting "forces you to put yourself in another person's shoes. It is very important in medicine to be able to extend yourself emotionally."

Of course, actors and lacrosse goalies still must know something about taking care of people, in sickness and in health. "Applicants need to show that they can deal with illness," said Henry Ralston, former associate dean of admissions at the University of California–San Francisco School of Medicine. Volunteering at a hospital or nursing home, shadowing a physician, or even having personal exposure to serious illness, such as a terminally ill family member, are all avenues to gain such experience.

But even here you can find ways to set yourself apart from the typical medical school applicant and further bolster your application. Gaye Sheffler, director of admissions at the University of Pennsylvania School of Medicine, recalled one student who, along with his wife, developed a program for Hispanic residents in his community who were having difficulty accessing health care. That showed inner strength, she said, and an ability to take a project to its end, in addition to hands-on experience in the medical field.

Recommendation letter 101

Letters of recommendation should speak to these experiences or personality traits, and they should be written by people who know you well. It is better to have a letter from someone who can provide details about how you work and what kind of a person you are than one from some well-known professor who only taught you in a 250-student lecture and cannot say very much about you as an individual. If you have been engaged in a variety of activities outside of the classroom, it should not be hard to find people who can write about you in detail. Athletic coaches, employers, and volunteer work supervisors are all good sources of letters.

Tip: Choose wisely. Avoid asking for letters from people like your minister or congressman unless they can speak directly to your ability to lead, teach others, put forth the extra effort, or learn new skills.

Medical schools will want to see letters of recommendation from your college professors. Students who attend large universities may have a harder time establishing a close relationship with their teachers, especially in basic science classes with 100 or more students. The folks at AMSA suggest a way around this problem: Approach professors of larger classes near the beginning of the term to let them know that you will be applying to medical school and may ask them for a letter of recommendation at the end of the semester. Throughout the semester, attend the professor's office hours to ask questions about the material. After the class has ended and your grade has been

Countdown to med school

WHEN	WHAT YOU SHOULD DO
College freshman year	Get some medical experience
College sophomore year	Contact your premed advisor about planning coursework
	Do some community work
	Check out the nonmedical world—don't be one-dimensional
College junior year	
First semester	Take an MCAT prep course if you can afford it
	Register for the January MCAT if you want to get a head start
	Take the MCAT in January if ready; otherwise, register for the spring test
Second semester	The majority of hopefuls take the MCAT in April
	Obtain the AMCAS application and start writing your personal statement
Summer	Turn in your AMCAS application; register for your next MCAT if you're taking the test again
College senior year	
First semester	If necessary, take a final MCAT in September
	Fill out secondary applications and send them in
	Go to interviews
	Early decision applicants receive admission letters
Second semester	Regular admission applicants receive admission letters
	Graduate college and start packing for med school

determined, then make the request for the letter. Bring a copy of your résumé and perhaps your personal statement and be ready to sit down to discuss your interests and desire to become a doctor. Make sure you ask the professor if she or he can write a *strong* letter of recommendation on your behalf. If the answer is no, look elsewhere. If it is yes, send a thank-you note two weeks after you ask for the letter, both to be polite and as a gentle reminder to finish the letter in time to meet your application deadlines. (And don't forget to send along a stamped, addressed envelope.)

Your undergraduate school may have a pre-professional committee, generally made up of faculty members from different academic departments and a preprofessional advisor. They will ask you for your academic record, personal statement, letters of recommendation, employment and volunteer experience, and extracurricular activities. You may be called in for an interview as well. Using this information, the committee will write a single letter of recommendation, which you then send to all of the medical schools you are applying to.

Making a statement

The personal statement is your chance to show that you can express a point of view clearly while also explaining a little bit about yourself. It's also probably the hardest part of the application process, prompting a lot of staring at a blank computer screen, multiple drafts, and much anxiety. Here are strategies to make things easier.

Pick a topic that reveals something about you that admissions committee members would not otherwise have known. It should come from your life experiences, such as an event or person that has made a deep impression on you. And it should reflect you and your life in an honest, thoughtful way. "Tell me something I don't know, not just 'I love science and I want to help people,'" said Emory's Eley. "There are moments in life that teach. Tell us about them. It could be about being sick, or a special grandparent, or climbing a mountain."

Structure the personal statement either around a theme or as a chronology, advised Goldmakher. A thematic essay about being sick, for example, might focus on shepherding a friend or family member through illness. Admissions committees want to see that you can write and express yourself well, but they also want to get to know something about your insights and attributes. A chronological essay might focus more on a series of events or activities and how you grew or changed as a result. One example might be an essay about a year spent abroad.

Tip: Gimmicks are not impressive. Although you want your essay to stand out, avoid tricks that fall flat, such as poems, plays, or mock press releases.

Face to faces

If your written application sparks enough interest, the admissions committee will invite you to visit the school for an interview. At some schools, this will be a one-on-one with a faculty member, but at others you may sit down with a group of senior medical students and professors. Whatever the configuration, interviews have some things in common. Someone is probably going to ask you to elaborate on some experience you wrote about, or will ask you to talk about your interests in medicine or your background. Some typical questions: Why do you want to be a doctor? What makes you think you'll make a good one? What experiences in your life led to this decision? What weaknesses do you struggle against in yourself? The committee is looking for signs that you are mature, confident without being arrogant, and able to communicate well.

You can write passionately about many things in your application, but in an interview, applicants often reveal how truly meaningful an experience was. "If they are doing all of these things because they think it's what they are supposed to do, it will be a boring interview," said Eley. "If they have followed their heart, their eyes will light up, and that's what we look for."

To prepare for the interview, brush up on current events, especially those related to medicine as well as some issues like medical ethics. Goldmakher said that admissions committees generally aren't looking for one particular answer when they ask you these less personal kinds of questions. They are interested in how you think and whether you can see different points of view. He advises his clients to take a deep breath, come up with a few points they want to make, and try to express them clearly. Don't rehearse your answers too much: Admissions directors say canned answers are a good way for an applicant to get, well, canned.

Be sure to know something about the school before you arrive for the interview. It is a big turn-off to admissions committees if they ask you why you are interested in their program and it becomes clear you don't know very much about the school. Take advantage of the chance to ask about something specific to the school—and not something easily answered in the brochure. It shows you have genuine interest. After the interview, remember to send a thank-you note to the people who interviewed you as well as anyone else who helped you throughout

"If they have followed their heart, their eyes will light up, and that's what we look for."

the interview day. This is a good way to get them to remember you.

After all this, what's left? You get to sit back and wait for your acceptance letters.

Chapter Five

Finding the Money

Make no mistake: It costs an arm and a leg to become a doctor. The tab at private medical schools—for tuition, living expenses, and books—easily tops $200,000 over four years. At the George Washington University School of Medicine, for instance, the four-year budget is almost $250,000—and that's before allowing for the inevitable tuition increases. Costs are equally high for out-of-state students at public institutions. A nonresident at the University of North Carolina–Chapel Hill School of Medicine will pay nearly $250,000. Even in-state students at public medical schools can expect to spend $150,000 or more to earn an M.D. degree.

Most medical students borrow heavily to cover the bills. Total debts in excess of $100,000 are typical for new doctors, and that's not counting whatever they may have borrowed as an undergraduate. Not surprisingly, many young docs continue to feel strapped for cash even after their incomes begin to soar.

How can you limit the damage? While financial aid in the form of grants and scholarships is not as plentiful as it is for undergraduates, most schools do make modest need-based or merit-based awards to some medical students. A handful of outside scholarships are available, too—especially for members of minority groups. Uncle Sam's largesse, in the form of tax credits for the cost of higher education, can also free up some extra cash. And students who are willing to serve in the military or commit to practicing medicine in underserved communities can go to medical school practically for free—or at least have a portion of their debts forgiven.

Even if you do have to borrow a bundle, you can take some comfort in the fact that education debt is as cheap as it ever has been because interest rates are relatively low. And through your tax deductions, the federal government will chip in on the interest you do pay. Here's what you need to know to pay for your degree.

Need-based grants might help a little—very little

As you'll probably remember from your undergraduate days, anyone applying for financial aid funds handed out by the federal government has to fill out the Free Application for Federal Student Aid, also known as the FAFSA. That's where you'll start, but the truth is that most medical schools have only a modest amount of money available for need-based grants. They assume that most students will borrow to finance their degrees and will easily be able to repay their debts once they are

doctors. At the University of Missouri School of Medicine, for example, only about 50 percent of students receive need-based awards—and they average a measly $2,780 yearly, a drop in the bucket compared to tuition.

Even schools with more money available generally won't meet your full need with grants: There simply aren't enough funds available at the graduate level to fulfill the requirements of students no longer dependent on their parents. At Johns Hopkins University School of Medicine in Baltimore, for instance, the average need-based grant is $22,513; tuition runs about $40,600 for first-year students, who need an estimated $55,575 to cover everything. (The school offers over 200 endowed scholarships to help meet students' financial need.)

You may find that your eligibility for need-based aid varies dramatically from school to school. That's because medical schools, like undergraduate colleges and universities, use different formulas to calculate how big a discrepancy there is between what med school will cost and what your income and assets are. Under the formula used to hand out federal aid, for example, all graduate students are considered *independent*: supporting themselves, regardless of their age or whether they have financial help from their parents. Bottom line: Full-time students at schools using the federal formula will have significant need.

But most medical schools use their own institutional formulas, which classify many students as *dependent*. You'll provide schools with information about your parents' income and assets on additional needs-analysis forms (GAPS–FAS, CSS, and Need Access are the common ones), and the financial aid office will consider those resources to be available to pay the bills. At Johns Hopkins, parent resources are weighed on a case-by-case basis. "If someone is the son or daughter of elderly parents, we won't expect much," said Paul T. White, assistant dean for admissions and financial aid. "But there are also children well over 30 whose parents are still supporting them. We consider that," White said.

Parents' income and assets also are used in determining who is eligible for federal Scholarships for Disadvantaged Students. These are need-based awards, specifically for medical students who come from disadvantaged backgrounds, based on family income or ethnicity. The size of the award varies from school to school.

Regardless of which forms are required, be sure to get them in as soon as possible after January. Some aid is awarded on a first-come, first-served basis.

Apply with an eye on the merit money

Harvard Medical School does not award any merit scholarships. At the University of Michigan Medical School, by contrast, about one-third of each entering class receives a renewable scholarship ranging from $1,000 to $30,000 a year. At Vanderbilt School of Medicine in Tennessee, about 27 percent of students receive scholarships ranging from $1,000 to $26,000, some based solely on academic merit and extracurricular record (such as the Canby-Robinson Scholarship), others based on a combination of merit and need. The school also awards money to applicants who will diversify the student body; recipients have included not only students of color, but also students of Jewish background (not so common in the Southeast), students from Appalachian Tennessee, and one

recipient who grew up in Montana and was a cowboy, according to J. Harold Helderman, assistant dean for admissions.

Schools that do have merit money to dole out usually base their awards on the admission application. High MCAT scores and undergraduate grades are a big factor, but, like Vanderbilt, many schools are also looking to attract people with varied strengths and backgrounds. Many of the awards are endowed scholarships handed out based on the donor's wishes. One award might be reserved for residents of a certain state or county, for example, another for students studying cardiology or pediatrics.

Search for outside scholarships

Scholarships from foundations, associations, and civic organizations are not as plentiful in medicine as they are for other graduate students, and many are reserved for minority students, residents of specific states or counties, or students concentrating in specific areas of medicine. Regardless, it's well worth checking an online search engine for possibilities. (Good search engines include www.fastweb.com and www.collegenet.com. Also try the excellent listing of grants on Michigan State University's website at www.lib.msu.edu/harris23/grants/3gradinf.htm.) Check with any civic, religious, or community groups you or your family members belong to, as well. And be sure to ask your med school's financial aid officer for other leads. Shelley Corrigan at the University of Vermont College of Medicine has been able to lead students to a variety of special scholarships—including ones for people with epilepsy and diabetes.

How varied are the opportunities? Here's a sampling of scholarships:

• The Jack Kent Cooke Foundation Graduate Scholarship program (www.jackkentcooke foundation.org) makes approximately 40 awards a year to college seniors or recent grads who are pursuing graduate study. The scholarship pays for full tuition, fees, room, board, and books (up to $50,000 a year) for up to six years of graduate study. Candidates must be nominated by their undergraduate institution.

• The Medical Scientist Training Program (www.nigms.nih.gov/Training) is for students pursuing a combined M.D./Ph.D. degree at one of 41 participating medical schools, including Harvard, Stanford, Tufts, and the University of Michigan. Students accepted into the program, which is funded by the National Institutes of Health, earn full tuition plus a stipend; $21,000 to $26,000 per year is typical.

• The Nicholas Pisacano Family Practice Scholarship is awarded by the American Board of Family Practice (www.fpleaders.org/leaderfrm. html). Five awards of $7,000 per year, up to $28,000, are made to third-year med school students planning to specialize in family medicine.

• National Medical Fellowships (www.nmf-online.org) are awards of up to $10,000 for med students who have financial need and who are African American, mainland Puerto Rican, Mexican American, American Indian, or native Alaskan or Hawaiian. The group also offers numerous other merit-based fellowships and scholarships for minorities.

Get set to borrow

The average medical student borrows roughly $120,000; a third borrow more than $150,000, 4.6 percent borrow more than $200,000, according to the Association of American Medical Colleges. Ultralow interest rates will help ease the sting. And if you shop around for a lender, you may save a bit more in upfront fees.

Federal loans. Government-guaranteed Stafford loans are a staple for most medical students; a typical full-time student borrows the annual maximum of $8,500 in a "subsidized" Stafford loan plus at least a portion of the additional $12,000 allowed each year in "unsubsidized" loans, for a total of up to $20,500 per year. The federal government pays the interest on a subsidized loan while you're in school and for six months after you graduate or drop below half-time status. Interest accrues on the unsubsidized loan while you're a student, so the grand total mounts, but with both types of loan you can delay making payments until after graduation— or even until after your residency. In total, you can borrow up to $138,500 in Stafford loans to finance your education, including whatever you've already taken on as an undergraduate.

To qualify for a subsidized loan, you have to show on your FAFSA form that you have "need" (a gap between what you've got and the cost of school), which is fairly easy to do with medical school costs being so high. If your school participates in the Federal Direct Student Loan Program, you'll borrow directly from the federal government. Otherwise you can choose your own funding source using a list of preferred lenders provided by your school. While all lenders offer the same interest rate on Stafford loans, some waive the up-front origination and guarantee fees (which can run up to 4 percent of the loan amount), some reduce the interest rate in repayment if you sign up for automatic payments or make a certain number of payments on time, and some do both. Rates on these variable-rate loans change every summer, but will not exceed a cap of 7.25 percent.

Students with high financial need—the FAFSA shows that they're expected to contribute very little or nothing to their medical school education—will also qualify for a Perkins loan of up to $8,000 per year. The interest rate is a fixed 5 percent. In addition, there are no up-front origination fees. The Perkins is a subsidized loan, so no interest accrues until nine months after you graduate or drop below half-time status—or until after your residency if you qualify for a deferment (page 52).

The federal government also makes certain loans available specifically to medical students. Federal Loans for Disadvantaged Students are available to needy students from disadvantaged backgrounds, based on family income or ethnicity. The interest rate is a fixed 5 percent, with no loan fees, and interest is subsidized. Primary Care Loans, which have the same rate and no fees, go to students who agree to enter family medicine, internal medicine, pediatrics, or preventive medicine—and to practice primary care until the loan is fully repaid. There's a big catch, though: The interest rate jumps to 18 percent if you change your mind and practice in another specialty.

Private loans. If the federal loan limits leave you short, private lenders stand ready to lend you up to the full cost of your education, less any financial aid. (Some medical schools also have their own loan programs.) Interest rates tend to be only slightly higher than the rates on Stafford loans, but origination fees can be significantly higher—up to 6 percent of the loan amount—and interest begins accruing right away. Some lenders who market specifically to medical students will even lend you up to $13,000 to cover the costs of traveling to your residency interviews.

Some popular programs include MEDLOANS

Alternative Loan Program, from Sallie Mae and the Association of American Medical Colleges (www.aamc.org/programs/medloans/start.htm), Medical Access Loan, from Access Group, Inc. (www.accessgroup.org), CitiAssist Health Profession Loans, from Citibank (www.studentloan.com), and MedAchiever, from KeyBank (key.com/html/H-1.33.b7.html).

To qualify for a private loan, you need a clean credit history—or a cosigner. It's a good idea to check your credit reports for errors before you apply.

Home-equity loans. For students who own a home, a home-equity line of credit is another attractive choice. Rates are low, fees are minimal, and the interest on up to $100,000 in debt is tax deductible if you itemize. If you expect to graduate into a high-paying job, home-equity debt may be a better choice than other debt because you won't qualify to deduct the interest on government or private student loans. Interest on student loans will be fully tax deductible only if your income falls below $50,000 if you're a single taxpayer and below $100,000 if you file jointly. Remember, though, that a home-equity line of credit is secured by your home. Will you be able to make the payments when you're a struggling resident?

Find help paying the money back

At current rates, the payment on $100,000 in Stafford loan debt is roughly $1,000 a month over the standard ten-year repayment term. Those payments usually aren't manageable on a typical resident's pay of $40,000 or so a year. But there are ways to ease the burden.

Deferment and forbearance. Most medical residents with high levels of debt will qualify for an economic hardship deferment on their Stafford loans, which allows them to push off making payments for up to three years. Interest continues to accrue on unsubsidized loans (at the "in-school" rate, which is somewhat lower than the "repayment" rate that kicks in when payments are due) but does not accrue on subsidized loans. After three years, residents can continue to have their payments suspended for the remainder of their residency by requesting "forbearance," during which interest accrues on all loans at the repayment rate. You file an application for deferment or forbearance with your lender.

Flexible repayment options. The standard 10-year repayment term for Stafford loans—which for most new doctors begins after residency ends—can be stretched in various ways to reduce your monthly payments. With an extended repayment plan, for instance, you can lengthen the loan term to up to 30 years. Another option, a graduated repayment schedule that extends over 12 to 30 years, starts you off with lower payments than the standard plan would call for and then ratchets them up annually as your paycheck presumably grows. Income-contingent or income-sensitive repayment plans adjust your payment each year based on your income. In the end, you'll pay more interest over the longer payback periods, but you can always boost your payments as your income rises to pay down the loan more quickly than you're asked to.

Loan consolidation. You may also be able to reduce the interest you pay on Stafford loans by consolidating them when interest rates are low. That locks in current interest rates instead of allowing them to fluctuate annually. You may even be able to consolidate your undergraduate and early medical school loans to take advantage of low rates while you're still in school. For more details on student loan consolidation, see loanconsolidation.ed.gov at the Department of Education's web site, or www.federalconsolidation.org, a website sponsored by Access Group, Inc., a private nonprofit lender.

Student loan interest deduction. You can deduct up to $2,500 a year in student loan interest if you earn less than $50,000 as a single taxpayer or less than $100,000 if you are married and filing jointly. (You can deduct a lesser amount with income up to $65,000 filing singly or $130,000 filing jointly.)

Note to parents: You get to take this deduction on your own return if you're legally obligated to pay back the debt and you claim the student as a dependent on your tax return.

Loan repayment programs. Doctors who agree to practice certain kinds of medicine where there are shortages or who work in underserved areas of the country can qualify to have significant portions of their debt forgiven. Through the National Health Service Corps, for instance, doctors practicing primary care medicine in underserved areas can have up to $50,000 of their debt repaid by the federal government during a two-year minimum service commitment.

Many states have similar debt repayment programs for doctors who live or are licensed in the state and who practice primary care medicine in-state. Doctors in Massachusetts, for instance, can earn $20,000 a year in debt payments if they work a minimum of two years in a Massachusetts community health center. A listing of state programs is available at the website of the Association of American Medical Colleges, at http://services.aamc.org/fed_loan_pub.

The National Institutes of Health offers a debt repayment program for employees engaged in various kinds of research, including AIDS research, pediatric research, and clinical research, whose debt load is at least 20 percent of their annual salary.

M.D. researchers can have up to $35,000 per year of debt repaid during a two-year service period.

Get a job

One reason M.D. students tally up so much debt is that most cannot work part-time while earning their degree, even during summers. "There is no time to work," said Conway Jones, former coordinator of financial aid at the University of Missouri– Columbia School of Medicine. For that reason, most financial aid officers do not include a federal work-study job in financial aid packages for med students. But for students who feel they can handle it, work-study is available and can reduce the need to borrow. An award of $1,500 to $2,000 might typically cover 10 to 15 hours of work a week in the university hospital or in a lab.

In most programs, there is a summer break between the first and second years of med school, after which the academic year runs 11 or 12 months. During the first-year summer break, some students earn extra money assisting faculty with a research project or participating in a summer preceptorship in which they shadow a doctor in exchange for a stipend. At the University of California–San Francisco, for instance, students can earn $3,000 for a four- to six-week full-time summer preceptorship.

Take advantage of Uncle Sam

If your household income is modest, the federal government offers help in the form of a tax credit or tax deduction for educational expenses. Medical students who qualify will want to take advantage of the Lifetime Learning tax credit, worth $2,000 a year (20 percent of the first $10,000 you spend in tuition and fees each year). You qualify for the full credit if you file a single tax return and your income is $47,000 or less, and for a partial credit if you make up to $57,000. If you're married and filing jointly, the full credit is available when income is less than $94,000, and a partial credit is available up to $114,000. (A tax credit reduces your tax bill dollar for dollar.)

Most full-time medical students won't exceed those thresholds. (In fact, those with little or no income won't benefit at all from the credits because they won't owe any taxes to begin with.) But if you do cross the line—perhaps because you are married and your spouse earns a good income—you may still qualify for a tax deduction for your educational expenses. In 2007, students can take a deduction for up to $4,000 in tuition and fees if their incomes don't exceed $65,000 filing singly or $130,000 filing jointly. That's worth up to $1,000 to a taxpayer in the 25 percent tax bracket. Note: You can't take both the credit and the deduction.

Medical students who are willing to pay for their education with a service commitment to the military or to the National Health Service Corps can start their medical careers with little or no debt. An Armed Forces Health Professions Scholarship, for instance, pays for tuition, fees, books, and supplies, plus a living-expense stipend of about $1,200 a month. After your residency, you repay the armed forces with a year of service for each year of support you received. You can get in touch with an Army, Army Reserve, Navy, or Air Force recruiter for more information. (Anyone who is gay or lesbian will want to keep in mind the military's policy on homosexuality; one website that provides an overview is gaylife.about.com/cs/politicsactivism.)

If there's time, plan ahead

If you're looking ahead to medical school in the next couple of years and can set aside some savings, take advantage of the tax benefits of a state-sponsored 529 plan. While most investors use these plans to save for a child's undergraduate expenses, the plans generally allow you to open an account and name yourself as the beneficiary.

The primary benefit is that the earnings on your savings will be tax-free, and your state may throw in a deduction for your contributions. All 529 plans include investments that are appropriate for adults who will need to tap the money soon, such as bonds and money-market accounts.

While many of the broker-sold 529s impose up-front sales fees that would minimize or offset any tax benefits over just a year or two, many of the direct-sold plans, such as those offered by TIAA-CREF and Vanguard, do not. Several are paying a guaranteed 3 percent or so right now. Not a bad parking place for a couple of years, especially when Uncle Sam isn't claiming any of the gains.

Students on a National Health Service Corps scholarship also get a free ride that covers tuition, fees, books, and supplies, plus a stipend. The tradeoff: These students agree that, for each year of support, they'll practice a year of primary care medicine in an underserved area, which may be a rural community or even a prison. What if you renege? You'll owe the government the loan amount plus interest, and $7,500 for each month of service that you miss. This is not a commitment to make lightly.

Chapter Six

What If You Don't Get In?

Dreams have a predictable way of taking unpredictable turns. For many, the dream of med school started in childhood with a mini doctor's bag molded in black plastic, and continued through grueling college organic chemistry classes and cram sessions for the MCAT. But for all too many, what comes next is a mailbox full of rejection letters—and an uncertain future. These rude awakenings are unavoidable: Many medical schools accept fewer than 1 in 10 or 15 of those who apply.

So what happens next?

Your first priority should be to put things in perspective. "A lot of high quality kids can't make the cut," said William Harvey, who retired after spending years advising aspiring medical students at Earlham College in

Richmond, Indiana. While this sometimes can be the result of unrealistic aspirations, he notes, it may be for reasons as impersonal as that you hail from the same state as a huge number of other applicants that year.

And take heart: You do have options. You can rethink your goals altogether. You can retake your MCATs and get more science courses—perhaps a master's degree—and reapply. Or you can do what thousands of successful doctors have done: study abroad.

Trying again

Start by reassessing your goals. Are you so sure that you belong in medicine that you're really prepared to go through all this again? "The hardest thing about medical school is not getting in, it's getting through," warned Karen Nichols, dean of Midwestern University's Chicago College of Osteopathic Medicine. If an honest second look tells you "you aren't motivated by all the right reasons, you must not come." Added Nancy Nielsen, senior associate dean for medical education at the University at Buffalo School of Medicine and Biomedical Sciences: "Ask [yourself] how badly you want to be a doctor, and if the answer is 'more than anything,' consider reapplying."

That's assuming you've got the grades, of course. You may have spent your last four summers working at an inner-city clinic and every scrap of free time reading journal articles about cancer research, but if your college grades are mediocre, "you can apply till the cows come home, but you're not going to get in" to a U.S. school, said Nielsen. Even if you do have a respectable grade point average, statistics from the Association of American Medical Colleges show that repeat

applicants are less likely than first-timers to be accepted, so you may have to target less-competitive schools this go around.

Ask admissions officers at the schools that sent rejection letters to explain your shortcomings. Often, they're happy to offer insights. The University of Minnesota Medical School–Twin Cities, in fact, sends out rejections with an explicit offer: "I am very willing to speak with applicants by phone or in a personal interview and give them very, very specific information about what they can do to improve their applications," said the former director of admissions, Marilyn Becker. Good scores may have been overshadowed by weak essays, flat letters of recommendation, or an unimpressive science background. The tell-all postrejection interview "takes the mystery out of it and gives concrete ideas" about what to do next, Becker said.

If the admissions staff isn't helpful—and even if they are—pose the same question to your undergraduate advisor, said Nichols. "Ask them to be ruthless—and have thick skin." Then apply their answers to the next application. While you're tapping undergrad resources, you might also ask someone in your college admissions office to give you a mock interview. The right answer, expressed in the wrong way, can tank an acceptance. Nichols once had an applicant say, "'I would really like to go to your school because I really don't want to work that hard,'" she recalled. "What he meant was, 'Your school really understands the importance of a balanced approach.'" The end result of his poor phrasing: He didn't get in.

It's probably a given that you'll revisit your MCAT scores; taking the test again and raising your numbers will certainly be a big help. So find a study group. Take a prep class. Hire a tutor. And take as many practice tests as you can. Admissions deans further recommend looking critically at your science background and doing whatever you need to do to bolster it. Indeed, one of the best ways to upgrade your application is to get a master's degree in one of the sciences.

It pays to get work or service experience, too; exposure to the health care field will enhance an application, admissions deans say. If grades and MCAT scores are equal, "the person who has a history of volunteering has an edge," Nielsen said. Volunteering for a medical facility that interests you, such as a clinic, a pediatric cancer ward, or a nursing home, underscores your commitment to medicine and desire to learn and can also offer evidence that you've got other valued attributes. Leadership, for example, "is one quality that is highly weighted," said Gregory Vercellotti, former senior associate dean for education at the University of Minnesota. So are level-headedness and heart. The admissions committee is on the lookout for "students who have a sense of well-being and balance and can demonstrate compassion," he said.

When your new, improved application is ready to go, don't worry too much that your rejection will taint it. "Given the number of applications and number of students who have to try more than once, there's nothing really adverse about a second application," said Vercellotti. Indeed, it's worth remembering that some people are accepted on the third or occasionally the fourth try.

Looking abroad

During Peter Burke's first two years of college, he was "a student athlete, with more emphasis on 'athlete,'" he said. Though he "got serious" by junior year and worked for a few years as a lab technician after graduation, his early history hurt him when he decided on medical school. "I was always having to explain my first two years in college," he said—and American medical schools were not forgiving. So he joined more than 8,000 Americans currently taking an alternate "offshore" route and went to The American University of the Caribbean School of Medicine, located in St. Maarten.

Many aspiring doctors look at the offshore schools as a poor substitute for U.S. institutions, but the reality is that more than 25 percent of doctors practicing in the United States today got their education outside of the country, according to some sources. Some 43,000, or 6 percent, of these doctors are United States citizens. "There are a number of international schools that are worth looking at," said former Earlham advisor Harvey. (For a list of foreign schools that educate significant numbers of American students, see page 361.)

Look carefully, though, because the quality of overseas programs varies enormously. Some of the most highly regarded schools in Europe are just as selective as U.S. medical schools and are not known for training Americans who failed to make the cut stateside. Besides AUC, foreign schools that do take large numbers of U.S. citizens—and that have track records for turning out solid doctors—include St. George's University School of Medicine in Grenada, Tel Aviv University Sackler School of Medicine in Israel, and Ross University School of Medicine in Dominica (which is now owned by DeVry University).

How do you determine which schools are worth your time and money? Separating the winners from the losers is a chore made both easier and harder by the Internet, which will probably be your first route to campus. Building an impressive website is much easier than building a high-quality faculty or campus; on the other hand, the Web can be a source of expert advice and an insider's point of view.

Approach your search with a similarly critical eye, advised Harvey. The overseas medical schools that cater to Americans follow a curriculum essentially the same as that of U.S. schools—two years of basic sciences followed by two years

---

"There are a number of international schools that are worth looking at."

---

of clinical rotations in hospitals—in preparation for the same set of licensing exams all U.S. doctors-to-be must pass. But you may find considerable variation in the quality of the faculty (Where did they train? What kind of research are they engaged in? Will you be taught by full-time professors or part-time local practitioners?) and how accessible they are. While a dedicated, permanent staff is ideal, some students note that they have had excellent courses taught by gifted U.S. professors enjoying the adventure of a year in an exotic locale.

The faculty/student ratio will provide a clue as to how likely you are to get professors' attention; in the U.S., ratios range from 13.6 faculty members per student at Mayo Medical School to 1 professor for every 31 students at the New York College of Osteopathic Medicine. Anyone considering a European or other medical school that doesn't teach in English will want to find out whether there's an English-language program and if foreign students have the same access to faculty as native students do.

To assess how well schools prep students for the U.S. Medical Licensing Examination (USMLE), compare their students' pass rates on "Step 1," the portion of the exam taken after second year, and "Step 2," generally taken during the last clinical year of medical school or around graduation. Pass rates vary. For example, Tel Aviv's Sackler School's recent pass rate for Step 1 was 98 percent; St. George's in Grenada had a 90 percent pass rate. Lesser schools have lower rates—sometimes much lower. As is true for American medical schools, too, you'll want to find out what type of clinical experience you can expect, and how early. Ask what kind of support services students have available: stress management? counseling? help with study skills?

A number of offshore schools have come and gone in the last several years, particularly in Mexico, Central America, and the Caribbean. So focus from the start on schools with a history. Indeed, before you invest in a place, make sure the place has invested in itself. Be wary of a school operating in rented space—some marginal schools have been known to hold classes in hotels or even private homes—because, as the AAIMG website cautions, "the school that rents a few classrooms has little incentive to remain open during hard times."

Make a visit before you commit so you can gauge quality and viability by sitting in on classes, quizzing students, and checking out the library and labs. While a listing in the "World Directory of Medical Schools," published by the World Health Organization, doesn't guarantee that a school is worthy, being included is considered a good sign. Another tip: The U.S. Department of Education Federal School Code Search (www.fafsa.ed.gov/

FOTWWebApp/FSLookupServlet) lets you plug in a foreign institution's code number and find out if it can receive and distribute American financial aid.

Find out, too, who the school considers a worthy candidate. At Ross University School of Medicine in Dominica, the class admitted in January 2007 had an average undergraduate GPA of 3.4. And whereas "most U.S. schools are looking at [MCAT scores of] 27 and above, our average was 21," said Andrew Serenyi, director of marketing for the school. At American University of the Caribbean, the incoming classes often include "people who are nurses, paramedics and EMTs; career transfers; people who are young, didn't study well in college and didn't get the grades that they needed; and people who are waitlisted," said Susan Atchley, professor of immunology and director of community services. "They judge you based on what you are doing now instead of on what you did as an 18-year-old," said Burke, who was 28 when he arrived at AUC in September 2000. "But then you have to prove yourself. My class started with 180 [students] and is now about 90. If you're not meeting the criteria you'll get weeded out of the system."

Many students attending offshore schools return to the United States after the second year to do their clinical rotations in U.S. hospitals; before applying to any overseas school, ask if the school is affiliated with clinical sites in the United States. Students often find residencies in the States, too, through the same match system as do their stateside peers (students pick schools and schools pick students and the computer matches them up). The website of the Educational Commission for Foreign Medical Graduates (www.ecfmg.org) walks students through the required steps to a U.S. residency.

The chances of making a match are good for students from reputable international programs who have strong USMLE scores. While some 15,000 students graduate from U.S. medical schools each year, there are about 22,200 postgraduate residency positions available. Among the eligible U.S. citizens attending St. George's University Medical School who applied in a typical recent year, 99 percent landed U.S. residency positions. Students from Ross University School of Medicine have been offered residencies at such noted hospitals as Yale–New Haven Hospital, Loma Linda University Medical Center in California, Georgetown University Medical Center, and UCLA Medical Center. As you shop for a school, ask those that interest you to provide a contact list of graduates who are now practicing in the U.S., as well as a history of residency placements.

"The great equalizer is standardized tests," said Burke, who said he scored in the 95th percentile on Step 1 and in the 99th on Step 2. Before he finished his fourth year in a cardiology rotation at Providence Hospital in Southfield, Michigan, he was matched to a residency in internal medicine with the hospital. From there, he planned to move on to a cardiology fellowship.

Finding your Plan B

What do you do if, in the end, your dream is dashed? "You need to think about Plan B: a different career choice," said Harvey.

But Plan B may well be a modification of Plan A: a career in public health or another health-related field, or the pursuit of a Ph.D. in the biological sciences, for example. Carol Baffi-Dugan, who advises undergrads going into health professions at Tufts University in Massachusetts, said the first thing she asks students who have been rejected by a medical school is why they were attracted to medicine in the first place. "Sometimes a student is motivated by an incredible love of science. It may be that that student would be intellectually stimulated and more successful doing a Ph.D.," she said. "But if they say the classic, 'I want to help people and use science,' then I start to talk about the clinical health professions and the area of public health. Other health professions are playing an increasingly important role in health care delivery." She has also pointed to physician assistants, who can specialize in cardiology or surgery, or nurse practitioners, who can specialize in pediatrics. (For an introduction to a number of health care options, see Chapter 7.)

Baffi-Dugan said she hopes that the students she advises have at least been thinking about other possibilities all along. At a recent freshman orientation she told the incoming class, "Look at all areas [in medicine], even if you do decide that a M.D. degree is what you want. You will understand that medical care is a team effort [and] you'll be better prepared." You will also be more likely to make a thoughtful and heartfelt choice. No one wants "the dentist who wanted to be a doctor," Baffi-Dugan said.

Chapter Seven

Other Choices, Other Paths

So you like medicine and you like making people feel better, yet you don't want to be a doctor? Good. Though it may surprise many physicians, there are plenty of good health careers that *don't* take you through medical school. Physical therapy, physician assistant, and nursing are among some of the booming fields in the allied health professions. People working in them say the intellectual challenges, emotional rewards, and relationships with patients are often more satisfying than in the doctor's world. "I can see a patient for ten consecutive weeks, make corrections in their treatment, and see steady progress," said one physical therapist. "How many doctors can do that?"

Here we profile eight such professions, highlighting the pluses and minuses of each, the training needed, and tips on how to get into a program or school. We also list the top three schools in each field (or more in the case of a third-place tie) according to the latest *U.S News & World Report* rankings, which are based on opinion surveys of faculty and administrators at accredited schools. (Note: There are no rankings for dentistry programs.)

Physician Assistant

Health care has changed enormously over the last 20 years, and as a result, the role physician assistants play in medicine has been transformed. Treating acute illnesses is now less important than preventing them. Widespread use of routine screening and an arsenal of new drugs has made managing chronic illness a top priority. Today, there is a premium on controlling costs, and four of five Americans are enrolled in managed care plans. Health care is delivered not only by physicians but by a team of medical providers, and physician assistants have become some of the team's most sought-after players.

Physician assistants (PAs) are licensed to practice medicine under the supervision of physicians. They are nationally certified after graduating from an accredited program, usually about two years in length, and passing a certifying exam. More than half of the nation's 50,000 PAs specialize in primary care—family medicine, internal medicine, pediatrics, or obstetrics and gynecology. Over a third specialize either in surgery or emergency medicine. They see patients, take histories, evaluate tests, make diagnoses, prescribe drugs, give advice, suture cuts, perform simple surgeries such as biopsies, and more.

"I love the potpourri of family practice," said Julie Theriault, who has been a physician assistant at the Sutter Medical Group in Elk Grove, California. "I do see some complicated things, and one of the key factors in the job of a PA is knowing when to get the doctor involved. I just had a diabetic patient who was on three medications and yet her blood sugar level was still out of whack. So I called the doctor." Theriault was able to describe the patient's test results and other factors, allowing the physician to make a diagnosis and advise treatment—even though he was located in another office miles away. The ability of one highly paid doctor to supervise a number of PAs who can manage patient care on-site not only cuts costs, it also allows rural and medically vulnerable communities access to care when they may have had none before. A study of primary care providers in two Western states showed that more physician assistants were practicing in rural areas than any other type of provider, and in vulnerable minority and poor communities, physician assistants, along with family physicians and internists, provide the majority of medical services available.

Pluses. PAs end up in much the same place as primary care physicians but spend about half the time in school and probably one-fifth of the money to get there. Salaries are high, and many practices and hospitals work out flexible schedules to allow PAs to have lives outside of work. Women find the PA career—with its high skill levels, good salaries, and flexible hours—particularly rewarding: They make up nearly 60 percent of the profession.

Minuses. Some doctors worry that the huge growth in nonphysician clinicians may lead to competition—rather than cooperation—between doctors and PAs. Physician assistants estimate that they can treat 50 to 75 percent of the complaints that send patients to doctors. The ability of physician assistants to treat so many conditions, coupled with a two- to four-fold increase in the number of PAs and other nonphysician clinicians, has left doctors wondering if there may be less need for M.D.s in the future. Still, Joseph Kaplowe, physician assistant coordinator at New Britain Hospital in New Britain, Connecticut, said that's unlikely. "With so many people in the population getting into their 50s and 60s, and that being the age at which people need more health and hospital care, there will be a need for more docs *and* more PAs."

Training. Many of the first PAs were Navy medical corpsmen who had received training and experience in Vietnam, but returned home to find there were no similar positions in the civilian health care system. At the same time, the nation faced a shortage of primary care physicians, particularly in rural and inner-city communities, so PA positions were created for these veterans.

Today most PAs are trained not on the battlefield but in programs that offer a master's degree. The coursework is divided into two parts spread over two years. The preclinical curriculum during the first year includes medical science courses—topics such as pharmacology, signs and symptoms of diseases, and primary care aspects of every medical specialty. The second year consists of clinical clerkships where PA students work with physicians treating patients and managing their cases. Many programs now require a thesis or "capstone" project on a medical topic of interest such as obesity or childhood depression. Newly minted PAs must pass a national certifica-

tion exam, and then must acquire 100 hours of continuing medical education every two years and be recertified every six years.

Tips on getting started. Nationally, there are about two applicants for every opening in PA programs, and at some schools the competition is stiffer. Applicants to PA programs must complete at least two years of college-level courses in basic

"With so many people in the population getting into their 50s and 60s...there will be a need for more docs and PAs."

and behavioral sciences as prerequisites. There are 137 PA programs at various schools across the country, and for about 110 of them applications can be submitted online through a central system, at www.caspaonline.org. At this site, you can click on the schools, look at what their programs offer, and get details on requirements, prerequisites, and more. You can apply to more than one program and add to your list if your application is turned down at your first few choices.

Most PA students already hold undergraduate degrees in a wide variety of fields and have worked in health care for four years before beginning training. Kaplowe said, "the most competitive applicant for PA school is 28 or older and this is a second career for them. They have a liberal arts degree and they understand the way the world works. They'll be able to communicate better to patients, staffs, and to write clearly. The person who has a strong work ethic, who understands they will be part of a team, who understands the boundaries that they work in— he or she will be a successful PA applicant."

Top schools. master's programs, ranked for 2009: 1) University of Iowa, 2) Duke University, North Carolina, 3) Emory University, Georgia.

To find out more. The American Academy of Physician Assistants (703-836-2272; www. aapa.org) has extensive resources about schools, training, and careers on its site.

> *"The person who has a strong work ethic, who understands they will be part of a team, will be a successful PA applicant."*

Nursing

In Victorian England, nursing was routinely considered "menial employment needing neither study nor intelligence." But then came Florence Nightingale, whose lifesaving work during the Crimean War in the mid-1800s transformed the practice into a respected and highly skilled profession. Today, nurses are witnessing an explosion in demand for their services, from geriatric care in nursing homes to cutting-edge work in high-tech medical facilities. There is now a veritable "candy store" of opportunities in the field, said Patricia Rowell, former senior policy fellow at the American Nurses Association. Ruth Corcoran, former CEO of the National League for Nursing, concurred: "The job security is amazing, the salaries are very fair, and it's an opportunity to make a difference every day in work that is appreciated and needed."

This is still an intimate career, requiring empathy and close relationships with patients who may be sick or dying. In general, nurses collect and analyze data on patients' physical and psychological situations, help diagnose ailments, provide continuous care and monitoring, and offer critical support to physicians. But there's more than one kind of nurse, and they are classified by their skill levels.

First come licensed vocational or practical nurses. They are typically high school graduates with a year of nursing training from a vocational school or junior college. They work under the direction of higher-level nurses and focus on the physical care of the patient, such as monitoring vital signs, making beds, and caring for some wounds.

Above LPNs are registered nurses, and they make up the majority of the field. They are state-licensed and have earned either an associate degree in nursing from a community college or a bachelor's of science in nursing from a four-year school. Unlike LPNs, they handle medications, complex treatments, patient assessments, and plans for care. RNs can remain generalist nurses and serve in operating rooms, pediatric and maternity wards, rehabilitation centers, or psychiatric units, to name just a few places.

There are more options for students who earn postgraduate degrees, such as a master's in nursing. These are gateways to a variety of specialized paths. Nurse practitioners, for instance, see patients in primary care settings and help set up treatment plans. Clinical nursing specialists provide expert care in fields like oncology. Nurse anesthetists take care of a patient's anesthesia needs during surgery or childbirth. There's also academia: Some highly motivated baccalaureate students go directly into Ph.D. programs that prepare them for teaching and research positions.

Pluses. Many hospitals allow nurses to negotiate their work schedules, which is a boon for working parents. "If you have a child who is in school all day, you may want to work days so you can be home at night," Rowell said. If you want regular hours, you can find them in public health clinics or doctors' offices. Nursing is also a highly mobile profession, with opportunities growing overseas as well. The current nursing shortage means plenty of jobs, and salaries that keep going up.

Minuses. Nurses in some hospitals are asked to work different hours every week, or even every day. As an acute care nurse, Rowell worked three separate shifts: Days were 7 a.m. to 3:30 p.m., for five or ten days straight, followed by a couple of days off, and then a stretch of night and evening shifts. "You can't really plan anything more than a month ahead of time," she said.

Training. LPNs start with that one-year vocational training program. The first step in the RN path is usually the associate or bachelor's degree. There are 606 such bachelor's degree programs in the United States, which take four years to complete, and 909 associate degree programs, which take from two to three years. Most bachelor's degree programs require students to first apply for general undergrad admissions. After completing the school's required courses, students may then apply to the nursing program. The University of Washington's school of nursing in Seattle is a good example. It requires students to take ninety credits—usually during freshman and sophomore year—in English composition, problem-solving, statistics, art, sociology, and the sciences before they can begin the nursing program. Applicants also must maintain at least a 2.0 GPA and provide a résumé outlining health care experience (volunteer and paid), a recommendation from a health care provider, and various essays. Once admitted, nursing students take various courses ranging from anatomy to pharmacotherapeutics to ethics. There also are several required clinical practicums. Clinical nurse specialists and other advanced nursing degree candidates take more advanced courses and must do a thesis or research project.

Once students have completed their undergraduate program, there's yet another hurdle: a state license. That means passing a nationally standardized test from the National Council Licensure Examination (NCLEX). Depending on your state nursing board, additional certification may be required for clinical nurse specialists and nurse anesthetists. You can find links to those boards through the National Council of State Boards of Nursing site at www.ncsbn.org.

The cost of a nursing degree varies enormously depending on the program and the school. Community colleges are the least expensive, costing $3,000 to $5,000 per year. At the other end of the spectrum, a private, four-year college can cost more than $20,000 per year.

Tips on getting started. Preparing for a nursing program is no cakewalk. High school students should take the most rigorous college prep courses, especially in biology, chemistry, and math. They must also show excellent writing skills because documentation is a big part of nursing. Clear communication is essential because nurses assess patients and relay information to other health care providers. Each undergraduate nursing program has its own set of admission prerequisites, but there are some basic requirements: the SAT or ACT exam and high school courses in math, biology, chemistry, English, and a foreign language. The American Nurses Association also recommends courses in computer science and the behavioral and social sciences. Rowell said volunteer work in a nursing setting is key for students "to see if it's what they really want to do. We see students drop out because they had an idealized notion of what a nurse was. Try it out a bit."

Top schools. Master's, ranked for 2009: 1) University of Washington; 2) University of California–San Francisco; 3) University of Pennsylvania.

To find out more. The National Student Nurses' Association (718-210-0705; www.nsna.org/career) has information about the variety of nursing careers. So does the American Nurses Association (800-274-4ANA; www.nursingworld.org). The American Association of Colleges of Nursing (202-463-6930; www.aacn.nche. edu) has details on schools and programs.

Dentistry

Dentists roll up their sleeves, put on their surgical gloves, and get down to work in patients' mouths. They pull out painful wisdom teeth, fill cavities, and fit prosthetics where teeth used to be; some operate on cleft palates or even do cosmetic surgery. Research has linked oral health to general health, so dentists see their work as helping to keep their patients hale and hearty overall. Dentists work with their hands more than most physicians do, said Laura Neumann, of the American Dental Association, and that's a stimulating part of the job. "They work in a small space. It requires very fine motor skills," she said. Those skills are applied not only to the mouth's function, but also to its appearance. "We like to say it's an art and a science," said Neumann. "The art that goes into restoring or improving aesthetics can be both challenging and fun, and people always feel good

when you've done something like that for them." Over 80 percent of dentists are general practitioners, and most are in private practice. The rest specialize: Orthodontists correct poorly aligned teeth, for instance, while oral surgeons operate in and around the mouth. Other specialties include prosthodontics (restoring or replacing teeth) and periodontics (treating diseases of gums and other structures around the teeth).

Pluses. Dentistry can drastically improve a patient's life without placing the life-and-death stress of medicine on its practitioners. "Sometimes medical problems can be a little bit depressing," said Neumann. But in dentistry, "you tend to deal with less life-threatening situations." Plus dentists get to treat diseases directly, not just by writing prescriptions, and there's a great deal of satisfaction in that approach. Dentists earn a healthy income, and demands from work don't take over their lives. "Especially if you have your own practice or you're an associate, you can control your hours," Neumann said. That makes it an attractive career for women, she noted. She had three children—one before dental school, one during, and one just after. "I started practicing right away. I'm not going to say it was a piece of cake, but it was doable."

Minuses. In addition to learning how to pull teeth, anyone interested in private practice should be willing to learn how to manage a payroll and a small business. There's also the inescapable fact that people don't like coming to see you. But with improving technology, things have gotten much more pleasant for the patient—although they never seem to get used to the sound of the drill.

Training. Dental schools offer a D.D.S (doctor of dental surgery) or the equivalent D.M.D. (doctor of dental medicine); both degrees are universally accepted. Like med school, dental school lasts four years. The first two years, students take basic science classes—such as anatomy, microbiology, and physiology—concentrated on the head and neck. They try out techniques on synthetic models or extracted teeth. Since most dentists end up in private practice, courses on management are also part of the dental training. Students learn how to lead a dental team—which usually includes a hygienist and a dental assistant—and follow employment and tax laws.

Students may begin to see real, live patients in their second year, or sooner in some cases. That clinical experience accelerates in the third and fourth years, when they treat patients under the supervision of faculty dentists. A few schools have students rotate through community-based clinics or hospitals, but the majority of clinical work is in dental schools' own clinics.

Before they can practice, dentists have to pass a national written exam and a clinical licensing exam that may vary from state to state. In every state but Delaware, you can start practicing as soon as you get your degree, but about 20 percent of graduates go on to a residency for further training. Check your state licensing board to determine their requirements Some residencies are in dental schools, others in hospitals. The length of residency depends on the specialty. Most general practice residencies are one year, while orthodontics and periodontics take three years and oral surgery takes four years. Some oral surgeons get an M.D. as part of their residency, which takes an additional two years. Having an M.D. can make it easier to get hospital privileges. There are a variety of other programs, such as one- to two-year residencies in public health.

A public health dentist might work for a city, running dental education and screening programs.

Tips on getting started. Dentistry isn't a fallback for students who don't have high enough numbers to get into medical school. Recent entering classes of Harvard's medical and dental schools had around the same average GPA: 3.8. In addition to great grades, schools also usually require students to have

"Sometimes medical problems can be a little bit depressing," but in dentistry, "you tend to deal with less life-threatening situations."

had courses in English, biology, chemistry, and physics—these are part of an established predental curriculum, and your school's health advisor can fill you in on other details. Remember, too, that aligning teeth and making sure they look good is also an art—admissions offices take that seriously. Students should consider taking studio art classes to help with their spatial skills. And get some experience: schools want applicants to prove they care about dentistry, and part of that proof is spending time with professionals, doing "chairside observation," and shadowing dentists.

Applicants should also decide whether they are most interested in a practice or in doing research: Some dental schools focus on clinical skills, others on scientific research. Schools do try to simplify the application process by using a central service: AADSAS, the Associated American Dental Schools Application Service (www.adea.org), will send your application to all the schools you select. As part of your application, you have to take the computerized DAT, or Dental Admission Test. The test covers biology and chemistry, perceptual ability (matching shapes and judging distances), reading comprehension, and math. Registration is online at the American Dental Association's website (www.ada.org; look for their Education & Testing section), and you can schedule the test for almost any time at one of a few hundred testing centers across the country. You can spend $1,000 on a DAT prep class, it's not necessary if you buy practice tests and study on your own. Some schools also require a manual dexterity test, like carving a piece of chalk or soap to specifications.

To find out more. The American Dental Association has information on careers in dentistry and on the DAT test (312-440-2500; www.ada.org). The American Dental Education Association (1-800-353-2237; www.adea.org) publishes the *Official Guide to Dental Schools* ($35), which describes the programs at U.S. and Canadian schools and explains the application process.

Psychology

Psychologists have moved far beyond the "talking cure" during the century since Sigmund Freud set up his couch in Vienna. Therapists still talk, of course, and still try to cure. But the field has broadened significantly. Through a wide variety of psychotherapies—some short-term, some long, some directed at modifying behavior, some focused on the thinking behind that behavior— psychologists may work with clients to identify and change unhealthy or irrational attitudes that make people dissatisfied with their lives and, in some cases, utterly miserable. They may also test applicants' fitness for jobs using paper-and-pencil questionnaires, perform IQ tests, and do other kinds of assessments. Some teach and do academic research in different topics, such as a cul-

ture's effect on the way people feel. School psychologists work with students' behavior problems and may help teachers learn to manage classrooms. Psychologists may also bring their understanding of the mind to bear on physical illnesses, cooperating with physicians to help patients with stress-related ulcers or others who don't stick with their medications.

One thing all psychologists have in common is that they view distress as a complex problem, not one simply rooted in body chemistry or solved solely by antidepressants. "If you see the solutions to mental illness lying in biology, then I'd probably go to medical school," said George Stricker, a clinical psychologist retired from Adelphi University in Garden City, New York. (Unlike psychiatrists, psychologists can't prescribe drugs—except in New Mexico and Louisiana.)

Pluses. When clinical psychologist Tom Olkowski worked in a suburban Colorado school system, he evaluated children and helped them, their families, and teachers understand how the kids could learn better. "When you see a kid who's been struggling doing better in school, that's something tangible," he said. Variety is another advantage: Olkowski's psychology Ph.D. gave him the background in research and theory to work in many fields. In his 30-year career, he worked not only in schools, but also in a mental health center; written a book on the stress of moving with children; and made two videos for a real estate company on the same topic.

Minuses. Psychology can be stressful, especially when you deal with clients who may turn suicidal or violent. Olkowski cautioned that doctoral training doesn't prepare you for running a private practice, when you have to know about things like marketing and cash flow. Insurance restrictions on the number of therapy sessions with a client can add to the hassle factor. And training is expensive: Clinical psychologists often emerge from school $30,000 to $60,000 in debt.

Training. In most states, you need a doctorate in order to practice independently, without a doctorate-level psychologist supervising you. To get that doctorate, Ph.D.s used to be the only option for psychologists. But today, the Psy.D. (doctor of psychology) degree has become popular (although there are still more Ph.D. programs than Psy.D. programs). A Ph.D. has more emphasis on original research and requires an extensive dissertation. Students usually spend five years taking classes, doing research, and learning clinical skills, plus at least another year completing the dissertation. Psy.D. programs concentrate more on clinical practice and therapeutic methods. Students still learn how to do research and how to use the findings, but have to write a shorter paper to graduate. The clinical emphasis makes the Psy.D. attractive, but the Ph.D. makes it easier to get an academic job.

All doctoral students also learn the foundations of the discipline, including skills such as assessing patients using a variety of tests and how to practice ethically. Many students study statistics and research design. They also learn the cognitive, social, and biological bases of behavior, which may include classes in neurological and physiological psychology. Many states only license psychologists with doctorates from programs accredited by the American Psychological Association (most programs are APA-accredited). Graduates who want to be licensed as psychologists also have to take a national written exam and, in some states, a separate test that may cover the state's ethical codes and mental health laws. Many states also require

that psychologists practice under supervision for a while before they can get an independent license.

Are you doctorate-phobic? Consider a master's in psychology. Master's programs are short—two or three years—and thus relatively cheap. The degree allows you to do marriage and family counseling, mental health counseling, and social work. Master's programs are accredited by the Masters in Psychology Accreditation Council.

Tips on getting started. You don't have to be a psych major in college to get into graduate school, although it may be tougher to work the classes you'll need into your art history major. Most programs require undergrad courses in statistics and experimental psychology. Stricker also recommends getting some experience with emotionally troubled people to be sure you want to work with them professionally. He suggests volunteering with a peer counseling service, for example. If you plan on going to a Ph.D. program, research experience can be very helpful; try finding a professor who will let you volunteer in his or her lab. About half of the U.S. doctoral programs in psychology require applicants to take the Graduate Record Examinations. Some programs also require the psychology subject GRE, which has multiple-choice questions about experimental and natural sciences, social sciences, and general psychology, including the history of the discipline and research design. Scores on these tests are important, but schools place even more emphasis on the applicant's statement of goals, recommendations from professors, and research experience.

Doctoral students who responded to a 1999 survey funded by the Pew Charitable Trusts said one extremely important factor in picking a school was choosing an advisor you can work with. A Ph.D. student and her advisor may work together closely or meet a few times a year, depending on the school and the person, so it's important to choose someone whose style fits your own. It's also a good idea to ask about funding when you're looking at schools to find out how students there are financially supported. Ph.D. students can be carried on an advisor's research grant. But because Psy.D.s are usually offered by smaller schools that don't have a lot of research money, most Psy.D. students have to come up with loans, which means more postgrad debt.

Top schools. Doctorate programs in clinical psychology, ranked for 2009: 1) (tie) University of California–Los Angeles; University of Washington; University of Wisconsin–Madison.

To find out more. The American Psychological Association (800-374-2721; www.apa.org) has information on psychology careers and education. The APAs *Graduate Study in Psychology* (www.apa.org/books; $25.95 in print, $19.95 for three months' access to the online version) lists psychology programs in the United States and Canada, and is updated yearly. The Pew-funded survey on Ph.D. student experiences (www.phd-survey.org) has a valuable section devoted to psychology.

Physical Therapy

The human body is pretty good at self-repair, knitting torn muscles and fractured bones together after an injury. But sometimes it can't handle the workload alone. Physical therapists help the healing process by flexing stiffened muscles, stretching limbs, and teaching balance to people who have been off their feet for a while. "It's the study of movement and its application, but it's more than that," said Sue Schafer, former associate director of the School of Physical Therapy at Texas Woman's University in Dallas, Texas. It's understanding

individual needs, she said, and matching them to individual capabilities. When assessing a patient—from a hulking football player to a stroke survivor to a tiny infant—the therapist determines what structures are damaged, and what a patient needs to do to recover—given his or her particular physical limits—and then oversees the appropriate rehabilitation therapy. Techniques include exercise, massage, ultrasound, and heat therapy.

Sports medicine is one of the better known PT subfields, but therapists don't just rehab athletes. Today, for example, they are often called on to work with breast cancer patients, advising them on how to remain active while undergoing chemotherapy and radiation treatments, and also working to reduce postsurgery side effects such as painful swelling of the arms. Although they often work in tandem with occupational therapists, physical therapists focus on increasing mobility and strength and decreasing pain, while occupational therapists tackle the ability to perform specific tasks.

Pluses. Hanging out with professional sports teams and mixing with world-famous ballerinas isn't too shabby, but in reality, very few physical therapists have celeb-studded jobs. The rest relish the opportunity to work extensively one-on-one with patients and see the fruits of their labor in every step that patients make. PT's also have the flexibility to work in either a hospital or private practice, and the range of patients—from kids with cerebral palsy to senior citizens recovering from hip replacement surgery—keeps them on their toes.

Minuses. The work takes a toll on therapists' own bodies. The job can require heavy lifting—moving around large patients or large equipment—and standing or crouching for long periods of time. "It's a physical profession and eventually we have personal limitations," Schafer said. "I don't do well getting on the ground any more and that's what you have to do when you work with children." Other therapists say that the greatest frustration is patients who are not willing to do the work needed for recovery. Physical therapy often demands that patients be not only cooperative, but determined.

Training. Either a master's or doctorate is required to practice. (The Commission on Accreditation in Physical Therapy stopped recognizing baccalaureate professional degrees a few years ago, and by 2020, the American Physical Therapy Association hopes to make the profession an all-doctorate field.) Master's programs usually take two years and teach students basic sciences such as chemistry and biology as well as the psychosocial aspects of disease, intervention and treatment options, and current PT research directions. In addition to classroom work, students receive an average of fifteen weeks of field training at hospitals, rehab centers, schools, or outpatient clinics.

Doctorates, which take about three years, supplement this training with expanded work in areas like pharmacology, radiology, health care management, and pathology. They also insist on more field training—as long as a year. Graduates must pass a national exam as well as fulfill any individual state requirements, which may include additional training to maintain licensure.

Tips for getting started. To get into a PT program, applicants need some prerequisite undergrad courses, which include psychology, biology, physics, chemistry, statistics, and the humanities. A high GPA in these courses is important, as is performance on the GRE. But program directors warn that numbers alone won't get you in. Applicants need to show a knack for working with people. Work as a physical therapy assistant (an accredited aide who has completed a two-year pro-

gram) or volunteer experience at a nursing home or hospital can also make an application shine.

Top schools. Master's and doctorate programs, ranked for 2009: 1) University of Southern California; 2) (tie) University of Pittsburgh; Washington University in St. Louis; 4) University of Delaware.

To find out more. The American Physical Therapy Association (703-684-2782; www.apta.org) lists accredited programs and residency and fellowship information and offers financial aid advice.

Occupational Therapy

Most people view occupations as that thing they do from 9 to 5. Occupational therapists don't. While OT's most often help patients with temporary or permanent disabilities function smoothly in the workplace, they handle every aspect of the business of life, from inventing ways for handicapped parents to make lunches for their kids to teaching premature babies the proper movements for nursing. Retired folks don't stare into computer monitors or punch time cards every day, but they can call on occupational therapists to help them relearn how to dress and bathe themselves after a hip replacement or stroke.

As in physical therapy, the long-term goal of occupational therapy is to increase independence. But while physical therapists focus on overall strength and movement, OT's tackle obstacles to particular activities. When consulting with a patient, a therapist must break down an activity into each of its components, whether they are physical, environmental, mental, or behavioral. "Bowling isn't just picking up a ball and rolling it," explained Janet Falk-Kessler, director of Columbia

University's occupational therapy programs. "It involves everything from posture, bilateral motor coordination, aspects of vision, sound, and strength. It also has social components, like how one behaves in a bowling alley."

It's a field that requires a lot of creative problem-solving. When some of Falk-Kessler's students were working with the homebound elderly, they discovered that the Meals on Wheels packaging was too difficult to open. So the therapists created a tool specifically designed to cut the boxes.

Pluses. Not bound to hospitals, occupational therapists can ply their trade in a range of industries. Some work with architects—helping design accessible homes and buildings—while others, who are interested in mental health, can work with children and teenagers who have anxiety disorders or substance abuse problems, improving their ability to stay on task and interact better with peers and adults.

Minuses. Sometimes patients have difficulty understanding the purpose of therapy. "We're not here to take away the pain. You have to feed your dog and we have to figure out how to do that," explained one therapist. Dealing with insurance companies that offer patients only limited therapy coverage can also be frustrating.

Training. Undergraduate degrees for OT are on their way out: The Accreditation Council for Occupational Therapy Education will only recognize those programs that confer a master's or doctorate. Anyone now enrolling in an undergrad program is going to need summer coursework to finish by the deadline. The new emphasis is on the master's degree, which requires two years of classroom study, including courses in anatomy, sociology, psychology, and biology. This is followed by six to nine months of fieldwork under the guidance of a licensed therapist. Some combined baccalaureate/master's programs can shorten the amount of schooling by a year. A national certification exam is required to practice.

Tips for getting started. Proof of a commitment to community service looks stellar on any kind of application, but for almost all occupational therapy programs, it is required. To impress admissions officers, work beyond the minimum number of hours and try to volunteer in hospitals that will allow you to shadow members of the occupational therapy unit. Experience in varied settings, like homeless shelters or schools, helps demonstrate your dedication as well. There are some required undergrad courses, including biology, physiology, and psychology. Programs also examine GPAs and scores on the Graduate Record Exam.

Top schools. Master's and doctorate programs, ranked for 2009: 1) (tie) Boston University (Sargent); Washington University in St. Louis; 3) University of Southern California; .

To find out more. The American Occupational Therapy Association (301-652-2682; www.aota.org) has resources on education and snagging a job in the field. The American Occupational Therapy Foundation (301-652-6611, ext. 2550; www.aotf.org) has information on financial aid.

Social Work

When life gets tough, social workers get moving. People at high risk for AIDS, or low-income parents who are caught between the demands of work and the need to find decent child care, have traditionally been able to get counseling and practical help from social workers employed by public welfare agencies and hospitals. Today private companies, including HMOs and for-profit health service organizations, have added social workers to their payroll to advise patients and their families. While specialties aren't strictly defined in the field, most social workers build an area of expertise or gain certification in the areas of family care, public health, or mental health.

Pluses. No surprises here—the positive impact you have is a big reason for doing this job. Many social workers also praise the diversity of the work, which can range from grief counseling to supervising a homeless outreach program. Some social work positions also allow for flexible working hours; private firms, in particular, often hire counselors on a part-time basis.

Minuses. The emotional rewards typically are higher than the monetary ones, and the long, intense hours often lead to burnout.

Training. Education requirements for social workers vary in each state; call your state social work board for details. A master's degree as well as a passing score on a licensing exam are needed for most positions, especially clinical or management ones. However, some entry-level positions, such as child welfare case workers or counseling jobs in the private sector, only call for an undergraduate degree in social work. That degree, offered at many universities, involves the study of social welfare policies and methods. As part of the major, most schools require seminars on dealing with individuals and families, and an internship where students are placed in a public or private social service organization to get hands-on experience dealing with patients.

The master's degree is similar but more intense. In over 150 programs accredited by the Council on Social Work Education, students take two years of classes in social welfare policy and practice, human behavior, and research methods. Other courses may include applied psychology, sociology, and ethics. Budding social workers also need to take a 1,200-hour practicum. At the University of Illinois–Urbana-Champaign, for instance, graduate students work Monday

> *"Patients get what their policy covers, not necessarily what they need."*

through Thursday at anywhere from a school to a nursing home depending on their area of interest; the work typically includes client interviews and case evaluations. On Fridays, students attend a seminar at the school to discuss and learn from their experiences.

An increasing number of graduate schools are offering minors and dual-degree programs for students who want to demonstrate an expertise in a certain area—and get a step ahead in the job market. Columbia University started a dual-degree program in social work and international affairs that helps graduates land positions with international organizations like the United Nations. "We know that there isn't a single social problem that requires one profession to intervene," said Jeanette Takamura, dean of the university's School of Social Work. "So why should we offer one single degree?" The program at Columbia takes three years to finish, and students graduate with two master's degrees. The school also offers dual social work degrees in other areas such as urban planning and Jewish studies.

If you want to become a clinical social worker who provides mental health therapy, you need to receive still more training. Clinical social workers who work as psychotherapists, doing in-depth counseling, can receive reimbursement for their services from HMOs. Besides a master's degree, psychotherapists need two years of supervised work experience and a passing score on a clinical licensing test.

Tips on getting started. "You need to have passion if you want to be a social worker. And that

---

> *"Social workers work with some of the most seriously troubled individuals in American culture."*

---

passion can't be taught," one social work professor said. The best way to demonstrate this kind of dedication is to show it on your résumé. If you haven't been working in a related field such as teaching or nursing, volunteer experience is very important for an applicant—even as little as spending one evening each week playing cards at a nearby nursing home or one Saturday a month helping mentally-ill children. While universities do not require an undergraduate degree in social work, most schools do give preference to students who have performed well in social sciences courses like psychology and sociology. Many graduate schools of social work do not require applicants to take the Graduate Record Exam but they do want to see a high undergraduate GPA.

Top schools. Master's programs, ranked for 2009: 1) Washington University in St. Louis; 2) University of Michigan–Ann Arbor; 3) University of Chicago.

To find out more. The National Association of Social Workers (202-408-8600; www.social

workers.org) has general information and career advice The Council on Social Work Education (703-683-8080; www.cswe.org) has complete listings of accredited school programs. The Association of Social Work Boards (800-225-6880; www.aswb.org) administers the licensing exams and maintains information on each state's test and license requirements.

Speech-Language Pathology

Humans need to communicate. It's an essential characteristic of the species. But sometimes it doesn't come easy. That's where speech-language pathologists (SLP) come in. They work in hospitals, clinics, schools, corporate offices, or private practice, diagnosing speaking and communication problems and developing treatment plans. For example, children who have trouble articulating certain words and sounds can learn to talk fluently with proper training. For stroke victims who suffer aphasia—trouble speaking, comprehending, or writing language—early treatment by an SLP can help preserve and improve language skills by using verbal or visual drills and conversational role-playing.

Pluses. Good salaries and opportunities to work in a variety of settings with all kinds of patients keep SLPs happy. Those that tire of working in a hospital, for instance, can easily find another job in a school helping students with speech problems. New SLPs say they are amazed and gratified when they see a struggling student finally turn a corner.

Minuses. "It's not like giving somebody a pill," said Diane Paul-Brown of the American Speech-Language-Hearing Association. Some patients with severe disabilities may never reach normal levels, and their progress can be slow and frustrating. There are also hassles in getting compensation from schools and insurers.

Training. In almost every state, practicing speech-language pathologists must have a master's degree in the field, pass a national licensing exam, and complete a nine-month supervised fellowship. Programs are accredited by a council of the American Speech-Language-Hearing Association, and a typical master's curriculum involves four semesters and a summer of full-time study. Classes focus on specific disorders. For example, at the University of Maryland–College Park, besides a diagnostic methods course and an audiology course, all students must study aphasia, voice disorders, stuttering, child language disorders, and phonological disorders. They can also take electives such as augmentative communications (using technology to enhance innate ability). Once graduate students have a grasp of their field and its tools, they begin clinical rotations where they learn how to evaluate and diagnose actual patients and design customized courses of treatment. Some programs also require a thesis.

Tips on getting started. Aspiring undergrads can major in speech pathology or communication sciences and disorders, which gives them many of the prerequisite courses for grad school. (Some grad programs only accept applicants with these majors.) The prerequisites include anatomy and physiology of speech, anatomy and physiology of hearing, speech science, hearing science, speech and language development, phonetics, psychology of language, and acoustics.

You're not barred from becoming an SLP if you didn't major in it, however. Some students without this background do postbaccalaureate work before

> *"You need to have passion if you to want to be a social worker. And that passion can't be taught."*

applying to grad programs, while others apply anyway, and are accepted with the provision that they first take a year of make-up classes. In general, schools are looking for high GPAs and GRE scores. Students with better chances of admission usually have volunteered or worked in nursing homes and preschools.

Top schools. Master's programs, ranked for 2009: 1) University of Iowa; 2) (tie) Northwestern University, Illinois; Purdue University–West Lafayette, Indiana; University of Wisconsin–Madison.

To find out more. The American Speech-Language-Hearing Association (800-498-2071; www.asha.org) has extensive student materials with a guide to accredited programs by state.

How Do
the Schools
Stack Up?

Which are the hardest and easiest medical schools to get into?

While the number of applications to medical schools has dropped in recent years, it is still extremely hard to get in. Many of the most competitive only accept 1 in 20 of those who apply—or even fewer. Schools are ranked here from most to least selective based on a formula that combines average MCAT scores and undergraduate GPA for the Fall 2007 entering class as well as the school's acceptance rates. Average GPAs and MCATs will give you a sense of the competition.

Most to least selective

	Overall acceptance rate	Acceptance rate (men)	Acceptance rate (women)	Acceptance rate (minorities)	Average undergraduate GPA	Average composite MCAT score (scale: 1-15)	Average MCAT score, verbal reasoning (scale: 1-15)	Average MCAT score, physical sciences (scale: 1-15)	Average MCAT score, biological sciences (scale: 1-15)	Average MCAT score, writing (scale: J-T)
Washington University in St. Louis	11.1%	8.9%	14.1%	11.8%	3.88	12.5	11.7	12.8	13.0	Q
Johns Hopkins University (MD)	6.4%	6.3%	6.6%	5.7%	3.85	11.8	10.9	12.3	12.3	Q
Harvard University (MA)	4.4%	4.1%	4.8%	4.7%	3.81	11.9	11.1	12.4	12.4	R
University of California–Los Angeles (Geffen)	4.0%	4.2%	3.7%	4.6%	3.78	11.9	10.2	11.7	11.8	Q
Baylor College of Medicine (TX)	6.0%	5.7%	6.4%	6.1%	3.82	11.6	11.0	11.8	11.9	P
Columbia Univ. College of Physicians and Surgeons (NY)	4.1%	N/A	N/A	N/A	3.78	11.8	11.1	12.1	12.2	Q
University of Chicago (Pritzker)	3.9%	3.4%	4.3%	4.5%	3.79	11.6	11.0	11.8	11.9	Q
University of Pennsylvania	4.2%	3.9%	4.6%	4.1%	3.79	11.6	10.8	12.0	12.0	Q
Stanford University (CA)	3.3%	4.1%	2.4%	3.5%	3.76	11.6	11.0	12.0	12.0	Q
Vanderbilt University (TN)	5.9%	5.1%	6.9%	6.6%	3.80	11.5	10.6	11.8	12.0	Q
University of Michigan–Ann Arbor	6.8%	5.7%	8.2%	N/A	3.74	11.7	11.0	11.9	12.2	Q
Duke University (NC)	3.7%	3.2%	4.3%	6.4%	3.74	11.5	10.7	11.8	12.0	P
Brown University (Alpert) (RI)	3.5%	3.5%	3.4%	3.2%	3.66	11.7	10.8	11.6	12.0	Q
University of California–San Francisco	4.0%	3.6%	4.5%	N/A	3.73	11.4	10.7	11.6	11.8	Q
Cornell University (Weill) (NY)	4.0%	5.1%	2.9%	4.9%	3.70	11.5	11.0	11.6	11.8	P
Mayo Medical School (MN)	1.5%	1.2%	1.9%	1.6%	3.81	11.0	11.2	10.9	10.9	Q
Emory University (GA)	8.4%	8.6%	8.1%	8.6%	3.70	11.5	10.9	11.6	11.9	Q
New York University	5.7%	5.8%	5.7%	5.4%	3.76	11.2	10.5	11.5	11.7	Q
Northwestern University (Feinberg) (IL)	6.0%	6.0%	6.1%	N/A	3.71	11.4	10.6	11.8	11.8	Q
Ohio State University	8.7%	8.7%	8.7%	6.9%	3.74	11.2	10.5	11.5	11.6	O
University of Pittsburgh	7.9%	7.0%	8.9%	8.6%	3.70	11.4	10.9	11.5	11.8	P
Yale University (CT)	5.8%	5.6%	6.1%	6.5%	3.72	11.3	10.6	11.7	11.7	R
Dartmouth Medical School (NH)	5.6%	5.1%	6.1%	4.7%	3.74	11.1	10.5	11.3	11.6	Q
University of California–San Diego	5.5%	5.3%	5.8%	5.0%	3.75	11.0	10.0	11.3	11.7	Q
University of North Carolina–Chapel Hill	5.7%	5.3%	6.1%	5.4%	3.73	11.0	10.9	11.0	11.1	P
Mount Sinai School of Medicine (NY)	5.7%	5.1%	6.2%	5.8%	3.64	11.3	10.7	11.7	11.7	Q
University of Colorado–Denver	9.3%	9.3%	9.2%	5.8%	3.71	11.0	10.4	10.8	11.1	P
University of Virginia	13.0%	12.7%	13.3%	13.1%	3.70	11.1	10.7	11.3	11.4	P
Yeshiva University (Einstein) (NY)	7.3%	7.1%	7.5%	5.5%	3.73	10.8	10.3	11.0	11.0	P
Case Western Reserve University (OH)	7.6%	7.0%	8.4%	8.3%	3.62	11.2	10.7	11.5	11.5	Q
University of Southern California (Keck)	5.6%	5.2%	6.0%	5.1%	3.64	11.1	10.4	11.4	11.4	Q
St. Louis University	9.4%	8.5%	10.4%	6.5%	3.76	10.4	10.2	10.3	10.7	P
Univ. of Texas Southwestern Medical Center–Dallas	12.3%	11.8%	12.9%	14.3%	3.68	10.8	10.1	11.0	11.3	P
University of Wisconsin–Madison	7.6%	6.3%	9.3%	8.6%	3.76	10.4	9.8	10.6	10.9	P
Georgetown University (DC)	3.5%	3.3%	3.8%	N/A	3.68	10.6	10.3	10.7	10.8	N/A
University of Florida	8.2%	8.1%	8.2%	13.2%	3.70	10.6	10.0	10.7	11.0	Q
University of California–Irvine	6.1%	5.3%	6.9%	5.8%	3.65	10.7	10.0	11.0	11.0	Q
University of Cincinnati	8.2%	8.2%	8.2%	N/A	3.67	10.6	10.1	10.6	11.0	O

	Overall acceptance rate	Acceptance rate (men)	Acceptance rate (women)	Acceptance rate (minorities)	Average undergraduate GPA	Average composite MCAT score (scale: 1-15)	Average MCAT score, verbal reasoning (scale: 1-15)	Average MCAT score, physical sciences (scale: 1-15)	Average MCAT score, biological sciences (scale: 1-15)	Average MCAT score, writing (scale: J-7)
University of Iowa (Carver)	10.3%	9.7%	11.2%	7.5%	3.71	10.5	10.2	10.4	11.0	P
University of Missouri–Columbia	13.5%	12.7%	14.4%	5.3%	3.77	10.3	10.2	10.2	10.5	N/A
University of Washington	5.2%	4.6%	5.8%	3.1%	3.68	10.5	10.3	10.3	10.9	Q
Indiana University–Indianapolis	13.5%	13.1%	13.9%	N/A	3.73	10.3	10.2	10.2	10.5	P
University of Miami (Miller) (FL)	8.2%	8.9%	7.4%	7.2%	3.68	10.4	9.9	10.6	10.7	P
University of Minnesota Medical School	8.7%	7.7%	9.9%	6.9%	3.69	10.4	10.2	10.3	10.7	P
University of Rochester (NY)	7.6%	6.5%	8.7%	6.9%	3.63	10.6	10.0	10.6	11.2	Q
Stony Brook University (NY)	8.3%	8.1%	8.4%	7.4%	3.60	10.7	10.0	11.0	11.0	P
University of Maryland	7.0%	6.0%	8.0%	6.9%	3.67	10.4	10.1	10.5	10.8	P
University of Vermont	3.3%	2.8%	3.9%	2.6%	3.70	10.2	9.8	10.1	10.5	Q
Tufts University (MA)	7.2%	7.3%	7.1%	7.1%	3.60	10.6	10.3	10.7	10.9	Q
Jefferson Medical College (PA)	5.9%	5.6%	6.1%	5.9%	3.62	10.4	10.3	10.3	10.6	Q
Medical College of Wisconsin	6.8%	5.2%	8.9%	N/A	3.74	9.9	9.6	9.8	10.3	P
Wake Forest University (NC)	3.7%	3.3%	4.1%	N/A	3.64	10.3	10.3	10.2	10.5	P
Medical College of Georgia	13.5%	14.7%	12.2%	11.5%	3.70	10.1	9.9	10.1	10.5	N/A
Temple University (PA)	5.4%	4.9%	6.0%	5.4%	3.64	10.2	9.9	10.2	10.5	Q
University of Alabama–Birmingham	11.3%	13.4%	8.9%	8.3%	3.71	10.0	9.7	9.9	10.3	P
University of California–Davis	4.7%	3.5%	5.9%	3.8%	3.62	10.3	10.8	10.0	11.0	Q
Creighton University (NE)	6.3%	5.4%	7.3%	5.9%	3.67	10.0	9.7	9.9	10.2	N/A
Rush University (IL)	4.8%	4.9%	4.7%	5.2%	3.60	10.3	9.8	10.2	10.4	P
University of South Florida	7.4%	7.5%	7.3%	7.8%	3.71	9.9	9.5	9.8	10.3	P
University of Texas Health Science Center–Houston	11.5%	11.7%	11.2%	10.0%	3.70	10.0	9.8	9.9	10.3	P
University of Texas Medical Branch–Galveston	14.6%	14.8%	14.4%	14.3%	3.78	9.7	9.5	9.5	10.1	P
New York Medical College	8.0%	6.7%	9.3%	7.1%	3.60	10.3	9.9	10.3	10.6	Q
Oregon Health and Science University	4.8%	3.9%	5.8%	3.8%	3.61	10.2	10.2	9.8	10.7	P
Texas A&M Health Science Center	13.6%	13.6%	13.6%	13.9%	3.76	9.7	9.0	10.0	10.0	Q
UMDNJ-Robert Wood Johnson Medical School	10.0%	8.2%	11.7%	10.1%	3.63	10.2	9.6	10.4	10.7	P
University of Connecticut	5.8%	4.9%	6.6%	N/A	3.65	10.0	9.8	10.1	10.7	Q
University of Kentucky	8.6%	7.1%	10.8%	N/A	3.65	10.1	9.9	10.1	10.4	P
University of Massachusetts–Worcester	22.8%	21.5%	23.9%	N/A	3.59	10.5	10.3	10.4	10.6	Q
University of South Dakota (Sanford)	10.1%	8.8%	11.6%	1.1%	3.77	9.6	9.6	9.4	9.9	O
SUNY–Syracuse	8.8%	8.5%	9.0%	6.6%	3.63	10.1	9.6	10.4	10.4	P
University at Buffalo–SUNY	8.4%	7.0%	9.9%	N/A	3.62	10.1	9.6	10.2	10.5	P
University of Nebraska College of Medicine	12.1%	13.3%	10.6%	4.9%	3.73	9.7	9.7	9.4	10.0	O
University of Nevada–Reno	7.8%	N/A	N/A	N/A	3.63	10.1	9.2	9.3	10.0	Q
Loyola University Chicago (Stritch)	5.0%	4.7%	5.2%	4.0%	3.64	9.9	9.6	9.9	10.4	P
Tulane University (LA)	5.1%	4.6%	5.6%	3.5%	3.60	10.0	10.0	10.0	10.0	P
University of Illinois–Chicago	8.4%	8.6%	8.1%	9.1%	3.58	10.1	N/A	N/A	N/A	N/A
Drexel University (PA)	8.8%	8.9%	8.8%	5.1%	3.53	10.3	9.8	10.2	10.5	Q
Northeastern Ohio Universities College of Medicine	10.5%	9.6%	11.6%	N/A	3.71	9.5	9.6	9.3	9.6	P
University of Oklahoma	17.2%	19.3%	14.6%	14.5%	3.69	9.7	9.9	9.5	9.8	O
University of Tennessee Health Science Center	17.1%	17.5%	16.6%	16.0%	3.62	10.0	10.0	10.0	10.0	O
West Virginia University	5.6%	5.0%	6.3%	5.5%	3.69	9.5	9.4	9.3	9.9	P
Boston University	4.3%	3.7%	4.9%	4.7%	3.56	10.0	9.7	10.5	10.9	P
Texas Tech University Health Sciences Center	10.3%	10.4%	10.2%	9.2%	3.62	9.8	9.5	9.8	10.3	R
University of Kansas Medical Center	11.5%	10.5%	12.7%	9.2%	3.69	9.5	9.7	9.1	9.8	Q
University of Louisville (KY)	11.3%	10.3%	12.6%	7.9%	3.65	9.7	9.7	9.5	9.9	P
University of Toledo	9.1%	11.9%	5.7%	N/A	3.58	10.0	10.0	10.0	10.0	P
Wayne State University (MI)	14.1%	15.5%	12.6%	9.1%	3.57	10.1	9.4	10.3	10.6	O
University of Arizona	31.7%	26.2%	37.2%	32.3%	3.68	9.8	9.7	9.6	10.0	Q
University of Arkansas for Medical Sciences	16.1%	17.3%	14.4%	44.4%	3.62	9.8	10.0	9.4	9.9	O

Which are the hardest and easiest medical schools to get into?

	Overall acceptance rate	Acceptance rate (men)	Acceptance rate (women)	Acceptance rate (minorities)	Average undergraduate GPA	Average composite MCAT score (scale: 1-15)	Average MCAT score, verbal reasoning (scale: 1-15)	Average MCAT score, physical sciences (scale: 1-15)	Average MCAT score, biological sciences (scale: 1-15)	Average MCAT score, writing (scale: J-T)
University of South Carolina	7.5%	7.1%	8.0%	6.4%	3.66	9.5	9.7	8.9	9.8	O
University of Utah	11.0%	10.1%	13.0%	10.4%	3.64	9.7	9.7	9.3	10.2	P
Virginia Commonwealth University	7.2%	7.3%	7.2%	5.9%	3.60	9.8	9.5	9.8	10.2	P
East Tennessee State University (Quillen)	8.8%	7.8%	9.9%	7.1%	3.64	9.4	9.5	9.1	9.5	O
Rosalind Franklin University of Medicine and Science (IL)	5.1%	5.1%	5.1%	4.0%	3.55	9.7	9.0	9.9	10.3	P
George Washington University (DC)	3.0%	N/A	N/A	N/A	3.55	9.6	9.3	9.6	10.0	P
Medical University of South Carolina	14.4%	15.2%	13.6%	16.1%	3.57	9.7	9.8	9.5	9.8	O
Florida State University	15.1%	14.6%	15.5%	5.0%	3.62	9.4	9.4	9.1	9.6	P
Uniformed Services Univ. of the Health Sci. (Hebert) (MD)	14.7%	15.3%	13.6%	9.6%	3.51	9.8	9.8	9.5	10.0	P
Wright State University (OH)	6.8%	N/A	N/A	N/A	3.58	9.4	9.5	9.1	9.8	O
University of New Mexico	8.9%	8.0%	9.8%	8.4%	3.61	9.2	9.0	8.9	9.8	N/A
Michigan State University	6.3%	5.4%	7.3%	4.5%	3.51	9.5	9.3	9.3	10.0	O
University of North Dakota	28.6%	31.5%	25.8%	43.3%	3.70	9.0	8.9	8.8	9.4	N
Morehouse School of Medicine (GA)	4.5%	N/A	N/A	N/A	N/A	N/A	N/A	N/A	N/A	N/A
New York College of Osteopathic Medicine	11.8%	12.1%	11.5%	N/A	N/A	N/A	N/A	N/A	N/A	N/A
U. of North Texas Health Sci. Center	20.1%	19.9%	20.3%	19.8%	3.56	9.1	9.0	8.8	9.5	O
Eastern Virginia Medical School	6.2%	5.8%	6.7%	N/A	3.49	N/A	9.9	9.9	10.3	N/A
Oklahoma State University	22.4%	20.6%	25.1%	N/A	3.64	8.7	9.1	8.1	8.8	O
Southern Illinois University–Springfield	11.2%	10.7%	11.9%	N/A	3.52	9.1	9.3	8.7	9.3	O
East Carolina University (Brody) (NC)	12.9%	12.2%	13.6%	12.7%	3.50	9.1	8.9	8.3	9.4	P
University of Missouri–Kansas City	23.1%	24.1%	22.1%	26.3%	N/A	N/A	N/A	N/A	N/A	N/A
Coll. of Osteopathic Med. of the Pacific (Western Univ.) (CA)	15.6%	16.6%	14.8%	14.8%	3.50	9.0	8.7	9.1	9.7	P
Michigan State Univ. College of Osteopathic Medicine	11.0%	10.4%	11.6%	6.6%	3.55	8.7	8.5	8.4	9.1	O
Ohio University	4.8%	6.4%	3.9%	3.0%	3.57	8.4	8.4	7.5	8.4	O
UMDNJ–School of Osteopathic Medicine	5.5%	5.3%	5.7%	3.7%	3.47	8.9	8.6	8.8	9.3	P
Mercer University (GA)	12.3%	14.4%	10.1%	6.7%	3.52	8.5	8.9	8.0	8.6	N/A
Touro University College of Osteopathic Medicine (CA)	6.9%	N/A	N/A	N/A	3.35	9.0	8.9	8.8	9.4	Q
A.T. Still University of Health Sciences (Kirksville) (MO)	12.4%	13.8%	10.7%	10.8%	3.42	8.7	8.7	8.3	9.0	O
Lake Erie College of Osteopathic Medicine (PA)	11.5%	11.6%	11.4%	11.2%	3.40	8.7	9.0	8.2	9.0	O
Univ. of New England Col. of Osteopathic Medicine (ME)	7.1%	8.4%	5.9%	1.0%	3.41	8.5	8.8	8.0	8.8	Q
Edward Via Virginia College of Osteopathic Medicine	10.6%	10.5%	10.6%	12.6%	3.53	8.0	8.0	8.0	8.0	Q
Nova Southeastern Univ. Col. of Osteopathic Med. (FL)	17.4%	N/A	N/A	N/A	3.48	8.3	8.3	8.2	8.6	M
Howard University (DC)	5.8%	6.6%	5.3%	7.1%	3.40	8.2	7.8	8.0	8.7	O
West Virginia School of Osteopathic Medicine	18.7%	18.6%	18.9%	N/A	3.44	7.8	8.1	7.4	8.0	M
Pikeville College School of Osteopathic Medicine (KY)	14.7%	13.5%	16.3%	3.8%	3.30	7.3	7.6	7.0	7.4	O

The total cost of an M.D. degree can easily top $200,000 at the most expensive private schools once you factor in living expenses. Private medical schools are ranked here by tuition and fees for the 2007–2008 academic year, with the most expensive at the top. Public institutions follow, sorted by in-state tuition so you can easily see what you might save by sticking close to home.

Private Schools

	Tuition and fees	Room and board
Tufts University (MA)	$47,116	$11,088
Columbia University College of Physicians and Surgeons (NY)	$45,213	$11,890
Tulane University (LA)	$45,080	$12,890
George Washington University (DC)	$44,615	$20,085
University of Southern California (Keck)	$44,240	$14,610
New York University	$43,919	$10,000
New York Medical College	$43,696	$18,798
Rush University (IL)	$43,680	$9,340
Washington University in St. Louis	$43,380	$9,428
Yeshiva University (Einstein) (NY)	$43,370	$15,200
Boston University	$43,234	$11,933
Case Western Reserve University (OH)	$43,206	$17,930
Northwestern University (Feinberg) (IL)	$43,140	$12,375
Albany Medical College (NY)	$42,873	N/A
St. Louis University	$42,783	$11,988
Georgetown University (DC)	$42,764	$15,030
University of Pennsylvania	$42,706	$17,260
Drexel University (PA)	$42,030	$14,960
Harvard University (MA)	$41,861	$11,434
Duke University (NC)	$41,817	$12,240
Creighton University (NE)	$41,778	$13,500
Stanford University (CA)	$41,760	$20,700
Brown University (Alpert) (RI)	$41,184	$16,796
Jefferson Medical College (PA)	$41,101	$15,609
Cornell University (Weill) (NY)	$40,890	$10,709
Yale University (CT)	$40,770	$10,660
Dartmouth Medical School (NH)	$40,675	$9,750
Johns Hopkins University (MD)	$40,669	$14,906
University of Rochester (NY)	$40,384	$16,000
Emory University (GA)	$39,976	$22,020
University of New England College of Osteopathic Medicine (ME)	$39,520	$11,500
Vanderbilt University (TN)	$39,511	$10,260
Rosalind Franklin University of Medicine and Science (IL)	$39,472	$14,400
College of Osteopathic Medicine of the Pacific (Western University) (CA)	$39,275	$11,190
Loyola University Chicago (Stritch)	$39,215	$15,725
New York College of Osteopathic Medicine	$38,965	$21,000
University of Chicago (Pritzker)	$38,658	$15,769
Mount Sinai School of Medicine (NY)	$38,528	$15,000
Temple University (PA)	$38,502	$10,320

Who's the priciest? Who's the cheapest?

Private Schools, cont'd.

	Tuition and fees	Room and board
A.T. Still University of Health Sciences (Kirksville) (MO)	$38,000	$10,593
Wake Forest University (NC)	$37,134	$19,326
Touro University College of Osteopathic Medicine (CA)	$35,800	$14,798
Mercer University (GA)	$35,132	$13,740
Morehouse School of Medicine (GA)	$33,681	N/A
Medical College of Wisconsin	$32,515	$8,000
Pikeville College School of Osteopathic Medicine (KY)	$31,745	N/A
Edward Via Virginia College of Osteopathic Medicine	$31,000	$25,300
University of Miami (Miller) (FL)	$30,048	$22,955
Howard University (DC)	$29,846	$14,340
Mayo Medical School (MN)	$29,700	$12,375
Nova Southeastern University College of Osteopathic Medicine (FL)	$28,580	$17,050
Lake Erie College of Osteopathic Medicine (PA)	$25,950	$11,550
Baylor College of Medicine (TX)	$12,848	$19,718

Public Schools

	In-state tuition and fees	Out-of-state tuition and fees	Room and board
Texas A&M Health Science Center	$10,682	$23,782	$13,000
East Carolina University (Brody) (NC)	$11,056	$36,075	$11,019
Texas Tech University Health Sciences Center	$11,914	$25,014	$10,831
University of North Carolina–Chapel Hill	$11,919	$35,585	$27,052
University of Texas Health Science Center–Houston	$12,193	$25,293	$13,910
University of Texas Medical Branch–Galveston	$12,230	$25,330	$17,694
University of Texas Southwestern Medical Center–Dallas	$12,594	$25,694	$16,208
U. of North Texas Health Sci. Center (Texas Col. of Osteopathic Medicine)	$13,950	$29,700	$14,070
University of Massachusetts–Worcester	$14,087	N/A	$12,347
Medical College of Georgia	$14,297	$31,723	$3,611
University of Nevada–Reno	$15,077	$34,933	$9,540
University of Arkansas for Medical Sciences	$16,430	$31,962	N/A
University of New Mexico	$16,754	$42,910	$10,810
University of Arizona	$17,736	N/A	$9,500
University of Washington	$17,900	$41,904	$14,007
University of Alabama–Birmingham	$17,998	$45,238	$10,879
Oklahoma State University	$18,325	$34,686	$7,300
University of South Dakota (Sanford)	$18,436	$38,409	$20,030
West Virginia University	$19,204	$41,866	$9,080
Florida State University	$19,332	$52,160	$15,910
Stony Brook University (NY)	$19,890	$34,590	$22,800
West Virginia School of Osteopathic Medicine	$20,030	$49,273	N/A
University at Buffalo–SUNY	$20,218	$34,918	$10,707
University of Oklahoma	$20,450	$42,535	$20,116
University of Utah	$20,693	$38,529	$8,964
SUNY–Syracuse	$20,850	$35,550	$10,450
East Tennessee State University (Quillen)	$21,043	$41,993	$12,325
University of Tennessee Health Science Center	$21,095	$38,935	$13,251
University of South Florida	$21,192	$53,066	$10,200
University of Maryland	$22,316	$41,101	$18,490

	In-state tuition and fees	Out-of-state tuition and fees	Room and board
University of California–Los Angeles (Geffen)	$22,551	$34,796	$13,780
University of Wisconsin–Madison	$22,722	$33,846	$15,330
University of North Dakota	$22,873	$41,120	$9,104
University of California–San Diego	$22,959	$35,204	$12,493
University of Louisville (KY)	$23,079	$43,425	$6,618
University of South Carolina	$23,094	$60,410	$12,210
University of Florida	$23,170	$51,018	$9,640
University of California–San Francisco	$23,438	$35,683	$18,525
University of Missouri–Columbia	$23,848	$47,492	$9,000
Southern Illinois University–Springfield	$23,856	$66,160	$7,560
University of Kentucky	$23,910	$45,313	$12,370
Eastern Virginia Medical School	$24,204	$43,400	N/A
University of California–Irvine	$24,328	$36,573	$13,490
University of Nebraska College of Medicine	$24,338	$53,910	$14,400
Medical University of South Carolina	$24,713	$67,243	$10,770
University of Michigan–Ann Arbor	$24,755	$39,119	$20,052
University of Colorado–Denver	$24,828	$48,030	$14,500
University of Toledo	$24,850	$53,590	N/A
University of California–Davis	$25,155	$37,400	$13,978
Ohio University	$25,476	$35,809	$10,071
University of Kansas Medical Center	$25,476	$42,867	$18,981
University of Iowa (Carver)	$25,689	$41,719	$9,270
UMDNJ–School of Osteopathic Medicine	$25,783	$38,850	$13,650
Indiana University–Indianapolis	$25,904	$42,894	$15,168
UMDNJ–Robert Wood Johnson Medical School	$26,128	$39,195	$12,294
Wright State University (OH)	$26,393	$36,461	$11,946
University of Connecticut	$26,827	$49,463	N/A
University of Vermont	$27,143	$46,243	$10,564
Ohio State University	$27,234	$33,322	$8,320
Virginia Commonwealth University	$27,502	$41,004	$13,400
Michigan State University	$28,010	$60,890	$12,456
Michigan State University College of Osteopathic Medicine	$28,025	$60,905	$14,484
University of Missouri–Kansas City	$28,142	$55,075	$8,000
University of Cincinnati	$28,542	$47,639	$18,888
University of Illinois–Chicago	$28,572	$57,468	$12,967
Wayne State University (MI)	$28,668	$56,656	$13,450
Northeastern Ohio Universities College of Medicine	$28,794	$55,599	$10,000
University of Virginia	$31,305	$41,070	$18,730
Oregon Health and Science University	$31,538	$42,353	$17,500
University of Minnesota Medical School	$33,109	$40,423	$11,448
University of Pittsburgh	$35,990	$39,856	$14,500

Compared to what you're going to need, you may be surprised at how little you get: Medical schools assume that their students will borrow to pay the bills because they'll make enough after graduation to manage the loan payments. However, a lucky few with top scores and undergraduate grades may find a merit award on the table. Schools are ranked here by percentage of students receiving aid.

Private Schools

	% receiving aid of any kind	% receiving loans	% receiving grants/ scholarships	% receiving work-study benefits
Mayo Medical School (MN)	100%	73%	100%	0%
Morehouse School of Medicine (GA)	100%	100%	77%	0%
Pikeville College School of Osteopathic Medicine (KY)	98%	98%	72%	N/A
University of Chicago (Pritzker)	97%	76%	79%	1%
Edward Via Virginia College of Osteopathic Medicine	95%	91%	21%	0%
New York College of Osteopathic Medicine	95%	92%	34%	N/A
Howard University (DC)	95%	83%	69%	0%
Medical College of Wisconsin	95%	85%	62%	0%
Rosalind Franklin University of Medicine and Science (IL)	94%	94%	47%	6%
A.T. Still University of Health Sciences (Kirksville) (MO)	94%	94%	16%	18%
Creighton University (NE)	94%	88%	27%	0%
Nova Southeastern University College of Osteopathic Medicine (FL)	94%	88%	N/A	1%
Loyola University Chicago (Stritch)	93%	84%	73%	0%
New York Medical College	93%	91%	18%	3%
Touro University College of Osteopathic Medicine (CA)	93%	90%	18%	10%
Lake Erie College of Osteopathic Medicine (PA)	92%	90%	25%	N/A
Wake Forest University (NC)	92%	86%	68%	0%
Mercer University (GA)	91%	88%	63%	0%
University of New England College of Osteopathic Medicine (ME)	91%	89%	29%	0%
George Washington University (DC)	90%	90%	40%	0%
University of Rochester (NY)	90%	83%	45%	22%
University of Southern California (Keck)	90%	90%	40%	0%
Washington University in St. Louis	90%	51%	73%	0%
College of Osteopathic Medicine of the Pacific (Western University) (CA)	88%	86%	13%	0%
Yeshiva University (Einstein) (NY)	88%	84%	47%	0%
Rush University (IL)	88%	86%	59%	6%
Temple University (PA)	87%	87%	33%	11%
Georgetown University (DC)	87%	85%	44%	1%
University of Miami (Miller) (FL)	87%	87%	40%	0%
University of Pennsylvania	87%	69%	60%	2%
Emory University (GA)	87%	77%	66%	0%
Duke University (NC)	86%	67%	73%	0%
Yale University (CT)	85%	69%	60%	0%
Vanderbilt University (TN)	84%	69%	59%	0%
Tulane University (LA)	83%	74%	38%	0%
Albany Medical College (NY)	82%	78%	33%	16%
Case Western Reserve University (OH)	82%	79%	57%	0%
Harvard University (MA)	82%	79%	54%	2%
Mount Sinai School of Medicine (NY)	81%	77%	37%	11%

	% receiving aid of any kind	% receiving loans	% receiving grants/ scholarships	% receiving work-study benefits
Jefferson Medical College (PA)	81%	77%	46%	10%
Boston University	80%	77%	31%	0%
Columbia University College of Physicians and Surgeons (NY)	80%	67%	54%	8%
Dartmouth Medical School (NH)	80%	80%	52%	0%
Stanford University (CA)	80%	55%	71%	11%
St. Louis University	80%	79%	25%	0%
Tufts University (MA)	79%	75%	20%	1%
Baylor College of Medicine (TX)	78%	67%	47%	20%
Johns Hopkins University (MD)	78%	72%	57%	16%
Cornell University (Weill) (NY)	77%	66%	57%	16%
Brown University (Alpert) (RI)	75%	73%	45%	0%
Northwestern University (Feinberg) (IL)	75%	66%	36%	0%
New York University	69%	66%	47%	10%
Drexel University (PA)	61%	60%	23%	17%

Public Schools

	% receiving aid of any kind	% receiving loans	% receiving grants/ scholarships	% receiving work-study benefits
University of Nebraska College of Medicine	98%	90%	60%	0%
University of California–Los Angeles (Geffen)	98%	91%	98%	0%
University of Connecticut	98%	98%	45%	0%
University of South Dakota (Sanford)	98%	92%	82%	2%
West Virginia School of Osteopathic Medicine	98%	96%	16%	8%
University of Missouri–Columbia	97%	97%	80%	0%
University of North Dakota	97%	91%	62%	0%
Oklahoma State University	96%	90%	42%	23%
University of Iowa (Carver)	96%	90%	60%	1%
U. of North Texas Health Sci. Center (Texas Col. of Osteopathic Medicine)	96%	92%	65%	2%
University of Massachusetts–Worcester	95%	93%	29%	0%
Virginia Commonwealth University	95%	91%	41%	0%
West Virginia University	95%	81%	57%	0%
Indiana University–Indianapolis	94%	91%	34%	1%
University at Buffalo–SUNY	94%	80%	24%	1%
University of Arkansas for Medical Sciences	94%	91%	45%	0%
University of California–Irvine	94%	83%	72%	0%
University of Minnesota Medical School	94%	80%	65%	1%
University of Oklahoma	94%	90%	53%	0%
Southern Illinois University–Springfield	94%	93%	47%	0%
Ohio State University	94%	86%	62%	0%
University of Colorado–Denver	93%	88%	73%	1%
University of California–Davis	93%	87%	92%	0%
East Carolina University (Brody) (NC)	93%	89%	48%	0%
Oregon Health and Science University	93%	90%	80%	2%
University of South Carolina	93%	83%	42%	0%

Which schools award the most and the least financial aid?

Public Schools, cont'd.

	% receiving aid of any kind	% receiving loans	% receiving grants/ scholarships	% receiving work-study benefits
University of Kansas Medical Center	93%	87%	74%	0%
University of Vermont	92%	88%	58%	0%
East Tennessee State University (Quillen)	92%	85%	40%	0%
Michigan State University	92%	87%	64%	0%
Michigan State University College of Osteopathic Medicine	92%	88%	72%	0%
Ohio University	92%	90%	30%	2%
University of Kentucky	92%	83%	52%	9%
University of Louisville (KY)	92%	85%	34%	0%
University of Arizona	91%	77%	79%	2%
University of Washington	91%	83%	65%	0%
Eastern Virginia Medical School	90%	85%	66%	9%
University of Maryland	90%	82%	70%	0%
University of Virginia	90%	85%	67%	0%
Wright State University (OH)	90%	87%	40%	4%
University of Toledo	89%	86%	24%	16%
University of Wisconsin–Madison	89%	82%	37%	0%
University of New Mexico	89%	83%	62%	0%
University of North Carolina–Chapel Hill	89%	81%	82%	0%
University of California–San Diego	88%	81%	55%	1%
University of Cincinnati	88%	86%	40%	2%
University of South Florida	88%	85%	40%	0%
University of Texas Southwestern Medical Center–Dallas	87%	81%	65%	5%
Stony Brook University (NY)	87%	80%	32%	8%
University of Alabama–Birmingham	87%	76%	23%	0%
University of Florida	87%	78%	65%	0%
University of Pittsburgh	87%	72%	60%	0%
University of Tennessee Health Science Center	87%	82%	43%	0%
Texas Tech University Health Sciences Center	86%	83%	56%	0%
UMDNJ-Robert Wood Johnson Medical School	86%	84%	47%	7%
University of Utah	86%	86%	73%	0%
Wayne State University (MI)	86%	84%	38%	2%
Florida State University	85%	85%	33%	0%
University of Texas Medical Branch–Galveston	85%	81%	49%	3%
Texas A&M Health Science Center	84%	75%	74%	0%
University of Michigan–Ann Arbor	84%	79%	61%	0%
Northeastern Ohio Universities College of Medicine	84%	83%	33%	0%
University of California–San Francisco	82%	79%	81%	1%
Medical University of South Carolina	82%	80%	25%	3%
Medical College of Georgia	81%	77%	41%	4%
SUNY–Syracuse	80%	80%	38%	5%
University of Texas Health Science Center–Houston	80%	79%	44%	0%
Uniformed Services University of the Health Sciences (Hebert) (MD)	0%	0%	0%	0%

Which are the largest and smallest medical schools?

As you compare schools, you'll want to pay attention to the total enrollment, the size of the first-year class, and the faculty-to-student ratio. All will have an impact on the schools' personalities, the availability of professors outside of class, and the extent to which you engage with your classmates.

	Total enrollment	% in-state enrollment	Size of first-year class	Faculty-to-student ratio
Lake Erie College of Osteopathic Medicine (PA)	1,567	36%	438	0.1
University of Illinois–Chicago	1,443	74%	404	0.5
New York College of Osteopathic Medicine	1,202	85%	295	N/A
Indiana University–Indianapolis	1,175	88%	312	1.2
Wayne State University (MI)	1,161	90%	320	0.9
Drexel University (PA)	1,070	30%	288	0.5
Jefferson Medical College (PA)	999	50%	265	2.8
University of Minnesota Medical School	944	80%	246	1.7
Nova Southeastern University College of Osteopathic Medicine (FL)	916	49%	249	0.1
University of Texas Southwestern Medical Center–Dallas	909	87%	232	1.8
University of Texas Medical Branch–Galveston	882	94%	234	1.1
University of Texas Health Science Center–Houston	877	97%	244	0.8
College of Osteopathic Medicine of the Pacific (Western University) (CA)	829	61%	220	N/A
University of Washington	826	88%	198	2.5
Ohio State University	819	88%	219	2.8
Medical College of Wisconsin	795	44%	211	1.6
Michigan State University College of Osteopathic Medicine	787	90%	231	0.3
New York Medical College	786	32%	204	1.8
Georgetown University (DC)	779	0%	197	2.1
Harvard University (MA)	758	N/A	166	10.1
Rosalind Franklin University of Medicine and Science (IL)	757	25%	N/A	N/A
Yeshiva University (Einstein) (NY)	753	44%	191	3.5
Medical College of Georgia	739	99%	194	0.7
University of North Carolina–Chapel Hill	736	76%	165	1.8
Virginia Commonwealth University	734	59%	186	1.1
University of Alabama–Birmingham	716	93%	181	1.6
University of Kansas Medical Center	712	84%	186	0.8
Case Western Reserve University (OH)	711	41%	187	2.8
Temple University (PA)	707	51%	182	0.6
Tufts University (MA)	705	38%	175	2.2
George Washington University (DC)	700	0%	184	1.0
Northwestern University (Feinberg) (IL)	700	26%	179	2.7
St. Louis University	698	50%	191	0.8
A.T. Still University of Health Sciences (Kirksville) (MO)	697	21%	183	0.1
University of California–Los Angeles (Geffen)	693	94%	173	3.2
Baylor College of Medicine (TX)	681	86%	171	2.7
University of Miami (Miller) (FL)	681	76%	179	1.9
University of Southern California (Keck)	679	72%	174	1.8
Boston University	674	16%	175	2.1

Which are the largest and smallest medical schools?

	Total enrollment	% in-state enrollment	Size of first-year class	Faculty-to-student ratio
UMDNJ-Robert Wood Johnson Medical School	674	99%	162	1.4
University of Michigan–Ann Arbor	671	45%	173	2.5
New York University	670	46%	162	2.3
Uniformed Services University of the Health Sciences (Hebert) (MD)	670	6%	169	0.4
Tulane University (LA)	652	33%	177	0.6
Columbia University College of Physicians and Surgeons (NY)	645	31%	157	3.2
University of Cincinnati	634	94%	161	2.2
SUNY–Syracuse	623	86%	164	0.7
University of Oklahoma	623	92%	168	1.2
University of Maryland	621	81%	162	2.0
Medical University of South Carolina	620	93%	164	1.6
Edward Via Virginia College of Osteopathic Medicine	617	37%	162	0.1
University of Toledo	614	90%	172	0.4
University of Wisconsin–Madison	614	83%	155	1.7
University of Colorado–Denver	607	89%	157	2.5
University of Tennessee Health Science Center	605	97%	155	1.3
West Virginia School of Osteopathic Medicine	598	36%	211	0.1
University of Arkansas for Medical Sciences	596	91%	155	1.7
University of Louisville (KY)	595	83%	159	1.2
University of California–San Francisco	594	94%	147	3.1
U. of North Texas Health Sci. Center (Texas Col. of Osteopathic Medicine)	593	95%	173	0.5
Washington University in St. Louis	591	8%	123	2.6
University of Pennsylvania	585	38%	153	3.7
University of Pittsburgh	582	30%	148	3.4
University of Iowa (Carver)	576	71%	158	1.4
Texas Tech University Health Sciences Center	571	96%	143	1.0
University at Buffalo–SUNY	571	100%	147	0.7
Albany Medical College (NY)	566	42%	149	N/A
Loyola University Chicago (Stritch)	563	45%	146	1.1
University of Virginia	558	59%	143	1.7
Touro University College of Osteopathic Medicine (CA)	540	N/A	135	0.1
Rush University (IL)	536	81%	132	0.9
University of California–San Diego	521	92%	135	1.7
Oregon Health and Science University	512	59%	122	3.2
University of Florida	509	97%	134	2.5
Mount Sinai School of Medicine (NY)	506	33%	141	2.1
University of New England College of Osteopathic Medicine (ME)	501	20%	131	0.1
Creighton University (NE)	500	13%	128	0.6
Michigan State University	494	74%	156	1.2
University of Arizona	481	101%	138	1.8
Emory University (GA)	480	31%	134	3.9
University of South Florida	480	99%	124	1.2
University of Nebraska College of Medicine	476	86%	124	1.2
Stanford University (CA)	472	40%	86	1.6
Howard University (DC)	469	8%	132	0.5
Johns Hopkins University (MD)	460	23%	120	5.1
Northeastern Ohio Universities College of Medicine	455	98%	122	0.7
Wake Forest University (NC)	454	37%	122	2.1
Stony Brook University (NY)	449	96%	116	1.2
Eastern Virginia Medical School	447	67%	N/A	N/A
University of Chicago (Pritzker)	441	30%	113	2.0

	Total enrollment	% in-state enrollment	Size of first-year class	Faculty-to-student ratio
Ohio University	438	98%	110	0.2
University of Massachusetts–Worcester	435	98%	106	2.1
University of Vermont	431	32%	111	1.3
West Virginia University	421	70%	115	1.4
Vanderbilt University (TN)	417	17%	104	4.4
University of Rochester (NY)	414	43%	103	3.4
UMDNJ–School of Osteopathic Medicine	413	99%	110	0.4
University of Kentucky	413	84%	108	1.7
University of Utah	411	87%	102	2.6
Cornell University (Weill) (NY)	410	53%	105	5.3
Wright State University (OH)	409	98%	104	0.9
University of California–Irvine	408	100%	106	1.2
Duke University (NC)	404	13%	101	4.1
University of Missouri–Kansas City	401	81%	122	1.6
Yale University (CT)	395	10%	100	2.7
University of California–Davis	393	99%	106	1.6
University of Missouri–Columbia	387	98%	100	1.3
Brown University (Alpert) (RI)	372	13%	98	1.9
Florida State University	357	100%	120	0.3
Texas A&M Health Science Center	353	92%	109	2.5
Oklahoma State University	342	90%	94	0.3
University of Connecticut	320	94%	85	1.3
Dartmouth Medical School (NH)	316	8%	74	2.7
University of New Mexico	315	79%	81	2.2
University of South Carolina	315	94%	86	0.8
Pikeville College School of Osteopathic Medicine (KY)	301	51%	80	0.1
East Carolina University (Brody) (NC)	293	100%	75	1.4
Southern Illinois University–Springfield	291	100%	72	1.1
University of North Dakota	248	82%	65	0.6
Mercer University (GA)	243	100%	65	0.9
East Tennessee State University (Quillen)	240	91%	61	1.1
University of Nevada–Reno	224	90%	63	0.9
Morehouse School of Medicine (GA)	210	30%	53	1.0
University of South Dakota (Sanford)	210	98%	54	1.3
Mayo Medical School (MN)	160	22%	43	15.1

Which get the most research money? Which get the least?

How much research does the school support? One prime indicator is the amount of grant money the medical school and its affiliated hospitals are awarded by the National Institutes of Health, the federal research department devoted to medicine. Institutions with an asterisk have received grants to the medical school only.

	Amount of NIH grants in 2007, in millions	Number of NIH grants in 2007	Number of principal investigators associated with NIH-funded grants	Number of full-time faculty associated with NIH research grants
Harvard University (MA)	$1,178.5	2,746	1,909	3,858
University of Washington	$579.7	1,151	760	1,148
University of Pennsylvania	$486.8	1,159	723	1,044
Johns Hopkins University (MD)	$450.8	1,002	648	1,370
University of California–San Francisco	$442.7	1,126	671	941
University of California–Los Angeles (Geffen)	$426.7	1,385	694	2,012
Baylor College of Medicine (TX)	$413.1	1,115	716	1,409
Duke University (NC)	$369.4	669	412	635
Columbia University College of Physicians and Surgeons (NY)	$362.3	764	546	885
University of Pittsburgh	$358.3	859	572	997
Washington University in St. Louis	$347.0	715	443	892
Yale University (CT)	$320.2	858	627	1,113
University of Michigan–Ann Arbor	$320.2	789	544	833
University of California–San Diego	$293.0	579	330	496
Vanderbilt University (TN)	$285.8	792	438	1,024
Stanford University*	$259.0	681	353	393
Case Western Reserve University (OH)	$246.4	613	425	638
Cornell University (Weill) (NY)	$239.7	730	376	704
Ohio State University	$237.8	750	500	904
University of Chicago (Pritzker)	$211.7	677	344	467
Mount Sinai School of Medicine (NY)	$210.8	525	319	610
University of North Carolina–Chapel Hill	$210.1	548	358	484
Emory University (GA)	$209.6	529	350	673
Northwestern University (Feinberg) (IL)	$205.9	919	384	495
Oregon Health and Science University	$201.4	662	420	670
University of Cincinnati	$196.5	659	360	N/A
Georgetown University (DC)	$190.2	665	321	321
Mayo Medical School (MN)	$188.7	411	264	630
University of Colorado–Denver	$188.3	625	319	N/A
University of Wisconsin–Madison	$184.0	531	326	516
University of Texas Southwestern Medical Center–Dallas	$182.7	578	364	940
Boston University	$181.8	551	291	648
University of Alabama–Birmingham	$180.5	423	262	463
Yeshiva University (Einstein) (NY)	$178.2	417	265	427
University of Virginia*	$174.5	402	224	995
University of Rochester (NY)	$162.0	448	290	484
University of Minnesota Medical School	$153.2	495	276	276
University of Maryland*	$149.1	362	232	496
University of Southern California (Keck)	$143.7	268	177	376
New York University	$143.4	391	265	726
University of Iowa (Carver)	$130.9	345	238	238
Wake Forest University*	$129.0	310	191	232
University of Massachusetts–Worcester*	$119.0	410	226	473
Brown University (Alpert) (RI)	$118.3	348	237	265
University of Texas Medical Branch–Galveston	$100.8	236	159	430
University of California–Irvine	$98.9	379	152	191

	Amount of NIH grants in 2007, in millions	Number of NIH grants in 2007	Number of principal investigators associated with NIH-funded grants	Number of full-time faculty associated with NIH research grants
University of Utah	$98.6	308	163	N/A
Indiana University–Indianapolis*	$97.3	328	219	452
Medical College of Wisconsin	$92.4	214	196	N/A
University of Florida	$91.8	381	244	265
University of Illinois–Chicago	$89.1	295	156	239
University of Miami (Miller) (FL)	$88.2	245	172	423
Dartmouth Medical School (NH)	$87.9	296	168	227
Tufts University (MA)	$86.4	255	117	213
Medical University of South Carolina	$84.0	259	165	329
University of Connecticut*	$80.0	N/A	150	N/A
University of California–Davis	$75.4	286	166	332
Wayne State University*	$70.7	177	139	247
Jefferson Medical College (PA)	$70.3	303	161	269
University of Kentucky	$69.3	195	124	182
Tulane University (LA)	$66.9	154	97	202
Virginia Commonwealth University*	$61.8	283	143	322
Stony Brook University (NY)	$61.5	323	168	201
University at Buffalo–SUNY	$61.1	266	158	205
University of Texas Health Science Center–Houston	$58.2	158	95	N/A
University of South Florida	$56.7	172	79	N/A
UMDNJ-Robert Wood Johnson Medical School	$55.5	145	127	235
University of New Mexico	$54.0	126	83	79
University of Vermont*	$51.2	132	83	177
University of Kansas Medical Center	$49.9	118	83	148
University of Louisville (KY)	$46.6	177	119	174
University of Oklahoma	$43.4	178	120	N/A
Medical College of Georgia	$43.3	220	115	171
Temple University (PA)	$41.8	134	83	110
George Washington University (DC)	$38.6	99	69	257
University of Tennessee Health Science Center*	$38.1	122	98	122
Rush University (IL)	$38.0	80	66	236
Uniformed Services University of the Health Sciences (Hebert) (MD)	$34.4	67	44	44
University of Nebraska College of Medicine*	$33.6	98	80	152
Morehouse School of Medicine (GA)	$27.8	35	28	N/A
University of Missouri–Columbia	$23.9	84	46	89
Loyola University Chicago (Stritch)	$22.6	105	65	84
Drexel University*	$22.4	65	80	76
New York Medical College	$21.7	57	42	N/A
St. Louis University	$21.0	100	77	68
Howard University (DC)	$19.4	45	21	40
University of Nevada–Reno*	$18.3	42	39	N/A
West Virginia University	$17.4	49	47	87
U. of North Texas Health Sci. Center (Texas Col. of Osteopathic Medicine)	$16.0	101	42	62
Wright State University*	$15.3	42	30	N/A
Michigan State University*	$14.9	63	28	27
University of South Dakota (Sanford)	$14.2	25	17	22
University of Toledo	$13.5	63	39	125
Creighton University (NE)	$11.6	79	42	70
University of North Dakota	$10.3	17	13	39
Texas A&M Health Science Center	$8.8	37	30	69
University of South Carolina	$8.5	72	46	79
Rosalind Franklin University of Medicine and Science (IL)	$6.9	36	23	23
University of Missouri–Kansas City	$6.8	16	16	23
Southern Illinois University–Springfield*	$5.4	29	22	22
East Carolina University (Brody) (NC)	$5.3	21	19	25

Which get the most research money? Which get the least?

	Amount of NIH grants in 2007, in millions	Number of NIH grants in 2007	Number of principal investigators associated with NIH-funded grants	Number of full-time faculty associated with NIH research grants
Michigan State University College of Osteopathic Medicine	$4.9	38	29	54
Texas Tech University Health Sciences Center	$4.4	19	14	21
UMDNJ–School of Osteopathic Medicine	$3.6	15	13	15
Northeastern Ohio Universities College of Medicine	$2.5	11	8	8
Florida State University	$2.2	15	12	11
East Tennessee State University (Quillen)*	$2.0	12	12	21
Oklahoma State University	$1.1	7	7	7
Edward Via Virginia College of Osteopathic Medicine	$.9	9	8	11
College of Osteopathic Medicine of the Pacific (Western University) (CA)	$.6	6	5	5
Nova Southeastern University College of Osteopathic Medicine (FL)	$.6	2	2	2
Ohio University	$.5	1	5	9
A.T. Still University of Health Sciences (Kirksville) (MO)	$.2	1	4	6
University of New England College of Osteopathic Medicine*	$.2	3	3	4
West Virginia School of Osteopathic Medicine	$.0	0	0	0

Whose graduates have the most debt? The least?

How much should you expect to borrow? On average, medical school grads who need to take out loans start their residencies with debt of $100,000—and that's not counting any college loans. This table shows the average amount of debt incurred by borrowers in the Class of 2007, from highest to lowest.

	Average medical school debt		Average medical school debt
Drexel University (PA)	$182,684	Eastern Virginia Medical School	$134,179
Univ. of New England Col. of Osteopathic Medicine (ME)	$180,730	Case Western Reserve University (OH)	$134,100
Tulane University (LA)	$175,598	University of Rochester (NY)	$131,881
Tufts University (MA)	$171,686	Stony Brook University (NY)	$130,513
Rosalind Franklin University of Medicine and Science (IL)	$169,863	Medical University of South Carolina	$130,000
New York Medical College	$168,000	University of North Dakota	$129,975
Col. of Osteopathic Med. of the Pacific (Western Univ.) (CA)	$164,315	Wayne State University (MI)	$129,245
Michigan State University	$163,390	Howard University (DC)	$129,136
University of Chicago (Pritzker)	$162,859	University of Toledo	$128,346
Albany Medical College (NY)	$162,151	Wake Forest University (NC)	$125,852
Rush University (IL)	$159,701	Ohio State University	$125,322
Lake Erie College of Osteopathic Medicine (PA)	$159,000	University of Wisconsin–Madison	$124,950
New York College of Osteopathic Medicine	$158,600	University of Louisville (KY)	$124,604
Boston University	$158,478	Emory University (GA)	$124,138
West Virginia School of Osteopathic Medicine	$158,372	University of Texas Medical Branch–Galveston	$123,960
Loyola University Chicago (Stritch)	$157,299	University of Utah	$123,335
George Washington University (DC)	$156,752	Texas Tech University Health Sciences Center	$122,818
St. Louis University	$156,722	University of Colorado–Denver	$121,327
Michigan State University College of Osteopathic Medicine	$156,045	UMDNJ-Robert Wood Johnson Medical School	$121,096
Creighton University (NE)	$155,871	Virginia Commonwealth University	$121,056
Nova Southeastern Univ. Col. of Osteopathic Medicine (FL)	$154,676	SUNY–Syracuse	$120,442
Jefferson Medical College (PA)	$153,198	Columbia University Col. of Physicians and Surgeons (NY)	$120,050
A.T. Still University of Health Sciences (Kirksville) (MO)	$152,713	University of Oklahoma	$120,000
Temple University (PA)	$150,614	West Virginia University	$118,962
University of Miami (Miller) (FL)	$150,607	University of Nebraska College of Medicine	$118,669
Northwestern University (Feinberg) (IL)	$150,468	University of South Dakota (Sanford)	$118,438
Mercer University (GA)	$147,266	UMDNJ–School of Osteopathic Medicine	$118,039
Georgetown University (DC)	$146,000	University of Tennessee Health Science Center	$116,936
Oregon Health and Science University	$145,576	University of Pennsylvania	$116,700
University of Vermont	$145,409	University of Nevada–Reno	$114,760
Touro University College of Osteopathic Medicine (CA)	$145,200	Yale University (CT)	$114,744
Ohio University	$143,771	Florida State University	$114,543
Medical College of Wisconsin	$143,605	U. of N. TX Health Sci. Center (TX Col. of Osteopathic Med.)	$114,000
University of Southern California (Keck)	$142,961	Southern Illinois University–Springfield	$113,724
Indiana University–Indianapolis	$142,859	New York University	$112,839
Oklahoma State University	$142,791	University of Virginia	$112,634
University of Cincinnati	$139,091	University of South Florida	$112,611
Mount Sinai School of Medicine (NY)	$136,338	University of Arkansas for Medical Sciences	$112,469
University of Missouri–Columbia	$136,108	University of Maryland	$112,440
Pikeville College School of Osteopathic Medicine (KY)	$136,000	Brown University (Alpert) (RI)	$112,062
Wright State University (OH)	$135,749	Northeastern Ohio Universities College of Medicine	$112,043
University of Pittsburgh	$135,254	Yeshiva University (Einstein) (NY)	$112,000
Morehouse School of Medicine (GA)	$134,930	University of Texas Health Science Center–Houston	$111,834
University of Minnesota Medical School	$134,493	University of Kansas Medical Center	$110,840

Whose graduates have the most debt? The least?

	Average medical school debt
University of Massachusetts–Worcester	$110,722
Dartmouth Medical School (NH)	$110,343
Vanderbilt University (TN)	$110,200
University of Alabama–Birmingham	$110,040
University of Florida	$109,907
East Tennessee State University (Quillen)	$108,073
University of South Carolina	$108,000
University of Missouri–Kansas City	$107,185
University of Kentucky	$107,110
Harvard University (MA)	$106,344
University of Arizona	$104,616
Washington University in St. Louis	$100,975
University of Michigan–Ann Arbor	$100,373
University of California–Davis	$100,178
University of Connecticut	$100,000
University of Iowa (Carver)	$100,000
Cornell University (Weill) (NY)	$98,144
University of Washington	$97,604

	Average medical school debt
University at Buffalo–SUNY	$97,027
University of New Mexico	$94,639
Johns Hopkins University (MD)	$93,753
Medical College of Georgia	$93,064
University of California–Irvine	$90,597
University of Texas Southwestern Medical Center–Dallas	$90,000
Duke University (NC)	$89,335
Texas A&M Health Science Center	$87,961
University of California–Los Angeles (Geffen)	$86,564
University of California–San Francisco	$85,020
Mayo Medical School (MN)	$84,422
University of North Carolina–Chapel Hill	$83,475
Baylor College of Medicine (TX)	$81,329
East Carolina University (Brody) (NC)	$81,212
University of California–San Diego	$79,562
Stanford University (CA)	$70,235
Uniformed Services Univ. of the Health Sci. (Hebert) (MD)	$0

Which schools have the most minority students? The fewest?

If you're looking for a medical school culture that is welcoming to students from a wealth of backgrounds, one way to judge is by the percentage of minority students already there.

	% minority	American Indian	Asian-American	Black	Hispanic	White	International	Men	Women
Howard University (DC)	94%	0.2%	9.6%	71.9%	2.6%	5.5%	10.2%	49%	51%
Morehouse School of Medicine (GA)	86%	N/A	5.2%	68.1%	2.9%	14.3%	9.5%	40%	60%
University of California–Los Angeles (Geffen)	60%	0.4%	39.0%	8.8%	11.4%	35.4%	0.9%	49%	51%
University of California–San Francisco	56%	N/A	N/A	N/A	N/A	N/A	N/A	45%	55%
Baylor College of Medicine (TX)	55%	2.1%	32.3%	7.5%	12.9%	44.5%	0.7%	52%	48%
University of California–Davis	55%	0.8%	41.0%	2.5%	10.4%	43.8%	0.3%	44%	56%
Stanford University (CA)	53%	0.8%	32.4%	4.9%	14.6%	43.2%	4.0%	55%	45%
Stony Brook University (NY)	50%	0.7%	36.5%	7.6%	5.1%	49.4%	0.7%	49%	51%
University of Texas Southwestern Medical Center–Dallas	50%	0.4%	28.9%	6.5%	13.5%	43.9%	2.2%	54%	46%
UMDNJ-Robert Wood Johnson Medical School	50%	0.0%	35.3%	9.9%	4.9%	45.4%	0.0%	45%	55%
Duke University (NC)	50%	1.5%	19.3%	14.9%	2.2%	49.0%	6.9%	52%	48%
Johns Hopkins University (MD)	48%	0.9%	35.0%	8.3%	4.1%	48.9%	2.8%	52%	48%
University of Pittsburgh	48%	0.3%	33.0%	9.6%	4.8%	51.9%	0.0%	53%	47%
Northwestern University (Feinberg) (IL)	48%	1.0%	35.3%	6.4%	4.9%	43.6%	4.1%	52%	48%
Rosalind Franklin University of Medicine and Science (IL)	48%	0.0%	41.3%	5.2%	1.1%	41.5%	0.8%	54%	46%
Harvard University (MA)	47%	1.6%	26.4%	11.6%	7.9%	41.2%	6.9%	50%	50%
UMDNJ–School of Osteopathic Medicine	47%	0.0%	19.9%	19.4%	8.0%	50.6%	0.2%	41%	59%
Boston University	47%	0.7%	27.4%	10.2%	8.9%	46.7%	4.3%	45%	55%
University of Missouri–Kansas City	47%	0.2%	38.4%	5.0%	3.5%	44.9%	0.0%	42%	58%
Texas A&M Health Science Center	47%	0.6%	28.3%	3.1%	9.9%	53.3%	0.6%	46%	54%
University of California–Irvine	47%	0.5%	35.3%	1.5%	9.1%	50.7%	0.0%	51%	49%
University of California–San Diego	46%	0.4%	41.1%	1.5%	8.6%	39.5%	0.0%	53%	47%
College of Osteopathic Medicine of the Pacific (Western University) (CA)	45%	0.6%	39.6%	1.1%	4.2%	46.6%	1.6%	50%	50%
Mount Sinai School of Medicine (NY)	44%	1.2%	20.6%	6.7%	14.8%	47.6%	4.2%	48%	52%
University of Illinois–Chicago	44%	N/A	N/A	N/A	N/A	N/A	N/A	52%	48%
Drexel University (PA)	43%	0.6%	34.8%	3.6%	4.2%	50.5%	0.0%	51%	49%
Brown University (Alpert) (RI)	43%	0.3%	25.5%	8.9%	8.3%	45.7%	2.7%	45%	55%
University of Texas Medical Branch–Galveston	42%	0.7%	16.4%	9.4%	15.5%	53.2%	0.3%	51%	49%
University of Miami (Miller) (FL)	42%	0.3%	22.3%	6.6%	12.6%	55.1%	0.3%	54%	46%
University of Michigan–Ann Arbor	41%	1.3%	26.2%	8.0%	5.8%	55.3%	0.0%	51%	49%
Cornell University (Weill) (NY)	41%	1.2%	20.2%	10.0%	8.8%	56.1%	1.5%	50%	50%
Texas Tech University Health Sciences Center	41%	0.5%	25.4%	3.2%	11.9%	55.7%	0.0%	57%	43%
New York Medical College	40%	0.3%	37.5%	1.7%	0.9%	52.4%	0.5%	47%	53%
U. of North Texas Health Sci. Center (Texas Col. of Osteopathic Medicine)	40%	0.5%	27.2%	2.7%	9.9%	57.8%	0.5%	50%	50%
University of New Mexico	40%	3.8%	6.7%	1.3%	28.3%	58.4%	0.0%	47%	53%
Northeastern Ohio Universities College of Medicine	40%	0.4%	33.2%	3.7%	2.4%	58.2%	0.0%	49%	51%
University of South Florida	40%	1.0%	21.9%	5.8%	10.8%	59.0%	0.0%	47%	53%
Temple University (PA)	39%	0.4%	23.6%	7.4%	8.1%	56.4%	0.0%	53%	47%
Rush University (IL)	39%	1.1%	33.2%	2.8%	2.6%	59.3%	0.0%	48%	52%
Columbia University College of Physicians and Surgeons (NY)	39%	0.5%	17.7%	9.3%	8.7%	57.8%	2.9%	47%	53%
George Washington University (DC)	38%	N/A	N/A	N/A	N/A	N/A	N/A	44%	56%
Case Western Reserve University (OH)	38%	0.0%	25.3%	8.6%	3.1%	54.6%	3.9%	55%	45%
University of Chicago (Pritzker)	38%	0.7%	22.0%	8.4%	7.0%	53.7%	3.4%	50%	50%
University of Southern California (Keck)	38%	0.3%	23.6%	3.2%	10.6%	55.7%	2.1%	51%	49%
University of Florida	37%	0.0%	0.0%	5.2%	0.0%	56.7%	0.0%	50%	50%
University of Maryland	37%	0.0%	22.2%	12.2%	2.4%	58.5%	0.6%	42%	58%
Yale University (CT)	37%	1.0%	22.3%	6.8%	6.6%	53.9%	8.4%	47%	53%

Which schools have the most minority students? The fewest?

	% minority	American Indian	Asian	Black	Hispanic	White	International	Men	Women
Albany Medical College (NY)	36%	N/A	N/A	N/A	N/A	N/A	N/A	43%	57%
Washington University in St. Louis	36%	0.8%	27.1%	4.9%	3.4%	57.4%	3.7%	53%	47%
New York University	35%	0.6%	23.4%	4.6%	6.6%	56.6%	0.4%	51%	49%
University of Connecticut	35%	0.9%	12.2%	12.2%	2.5%	63.1%	2.2%	39%	61%
Tufts University (MA)	34%	0.6%	25.4%	3.4%	3.4%	64.8%	0.9%	54%	46%
Virginia Commonwealth University	34%	0.7%	24.9%	7.2%	1.4%	58.2%	0.3%	52%	48%
Florida State University	34%	0.8%	11.8%	12.6%	9.0%	64.4%	0.0%	40%	60%
University of Pennsylvania	34%	0.7%	15.9%	9.2%	6.3%	62.9%	1.4%	50%	50%
Michigan State University	33%	1.0%	16.0%	9.1%	6.7%	63.2%	1.0%	45%	55%
Mayo Medical School (MN)	33%	1.3%	11.3%	6.3%	5.6%	63.1%	0.0%	49%	51%
Nova Southeastern University College of Osteopathic Medicine (FL)	33%	0.8%	18.2%	3.5%	10.9%	61.2%	1.1%	50%	50%
University of Rochester (NY)	33%	0.5%	21.3%	8.2%	2.9%	64.5%	0.0%	48%	52%
University at Buffalo–SUNY	33%	0.5%	27.8%	3.2%	1.1%	65.0%	0.0%	47%	53%
Jefferson Medical College (PA)	32%	0.5%	22.6%	1.9%	3.5%	67.9%	3.6%	50%	50%
Yeshiva University (Einstein) (NY)	31%	N/A	72.7%	21.6%	5.7%	N/A	N/A	48%	52%
Wayne State University (MI)	31%	0.3%	16.8%	12.5%	1.6%	63.2%	2.2%	53%	47%
Emory University (GA)	31%	0.2%	18.3%	7.9%	4.6%	62.9%	2.5%	50%	50%
University of North Carolina–Chapel Hill	31%	N/A	N/A	N/A	N/A	N/A	N/A	52%	48%
Ohio State University	31%	0.4%	19.0%	6.7%	3.3%	69.5%	0.4%	60%	40%
East Carolina University (Brody) (NC)	29%	3.1%	8.5%	14.3%	4.1%	69.6%	0.0%	52%	48%
University of Texas Health Science Center–Houston	29%	0.3%	12.0%	4.1%	12.5%	68.2%	0.0%	55%	45%
University of Cincinnati	29%	0.0%	19.9%	8.0%	0.9%	71.1%	0.0%	57%	43%
SUNY–Syracuse	29%	0.6%	18.1%	9.3%	0.6%	64.0%	7.2%	49%	51%
University of Nevada–Reno	28%	1.8%	20.5%	1.8%	4.0%	71.9%	N/A	51%	49%
Wake Forest University (NC)	27%	1.8%	12.3%	10.1%	3.1%	68.7%	4.0%	54%	46%
University of Arizona	27%	N/A	N/A	N/A	N/A	N/A	N/A	45%	55%
Vanderbilt University (TN)	27%	0.0%	16.5%	8.2%	1.4%	66.2%	4.6%	56%	44%
Southern Illinois University–Springfield	26%	1.4%	9.3%	11.7%	3.8%	73.9%	0.0%	47%	53%
Oklahoma State University	26%	10.8%	6.7%	5.3%	3.2%	71.9%	0.0%	53%	47%
Ohio University	26%	1.4%	8.9%	10.5%	5.0%	74.2%	0.0%	49%	51%
Edward Via Virginia College of Osteopathic Medicine	26%	1.9%	10.5%	13.0%	6.8%	62.3%	0.0%	47%	53%
Medical College of Georgia	26%	N/A	N/A	N/A	N/A	N/A	N/A	56%	44%
University of Virginia	26%	0.4%	18.1%	6.6%	4.5%	65.4%	0.5%	55%	45%
St. Louis University	25%	0.1%	19.8%	2.6%	1.4%	61.7%	2.1%	57%	43%
University of Oklahoma	25%	8.7%	14.6%	1.6%	0.3%	70.3%	0.0%	60%	40%
University of Toledo	25%	0.7%	17.4%	4.4%	2.1%	69.7%	0.3%	56%	44%
Georgetown University (DC)	25%	0.4%	16.0%	6.2%	2.6%	56.4%	1.5%	50%	50%
University of Tennessee Health Science Center	24%	0.7%	8.3%	10.6%	1.3%	71.9%	0.0%	62%	38%
Indiana University–Indianapolis	24%	1.1%	11.7%	5.9%	4.3%	72.7%	1.4%	57%	43%
Lake Erie College of Osteopathic Medicine (PA)	24%	0.1%	16.0%	2.4%	5.6%	75.9%	0.1%	53%	47%
Medical College of Wisconsin	24%	1.4%	14.3%	4.2%	3.9%	71.9%	0.8%	51%	49%
Dartmouth Medical School (NH)	24%	0.0%	17.4%	2.2%	4.1%	63.6%	9.5%	48%	52%
Wright State University (OH)	24%	0.0%	13.7%	7.8%	1.5%	76.3%	0.0%	43%	57%
University of Alabama–Birmingham	23%	1.3%	13.7%	7.0%	1.5%	76.0%	0.0%	60%	40%
University of Wisconsin–Madison	23%	0.5%	14.7%	4.9%	2.9%	77.0%	0.0%	47%	53%
University of Washington	23%	1.5%	15.0%	1.9%	4.2%	71.3%	0.0%	46%	54%
University of Kansas Medical Center	22%	1.4%	10.5%	6.3%	3.5%	70.5%	0.0%	52%	48%
Loyola University Chicago (Stritch)	22%	0.2%	13.0%	4.4%	4.1%	77.6%	0.0%	49%	51%
Medical University of South Carolina	21%	0.5%	6.8%	10.8%	3.1%	74.7%	1.6%	57%	43%
Uniformed Services University of the Health Sciences (Hebert) (MD)	21%	0.9%	13.7%	1.8%	4.6%	73.6%	0.0%	70%	30%
University of Massachusetts–Worcester	20%	0.5%	13.3%	4.8%	1.8%	79.5%	0.0%	45%	55%

	% minority	American Indian	Asian	Black	Hispanic	White	International	Men	Women
University of Vermont	19%	0.2%	13.2%	1.6%	1.9%	63.3%	0.7%	42%	58%
University of Iowa (Carver)	19%	0.5%	7.6%	4.5%	6.8%	74.3%	0.0%	53%	47%
University of Minnesota Medical School	19%	3.7%	9.5%	1.9%	2.4%	80.6%	1.8%	50%	50%
University of Louisville (KY)	19%	0.2%	9.7%	6.4%	0.8%	80.5%	0.0%	58%	42%
Michigan State University College of Osteopathic Medicine	19%	0.6%	13.5%	3.4%	1.5%	80.9%	0.0%	48%	52%
Tulane University (LA)	19%	0.2%	11.5%	5.1%	1.8%	69.5%	1.2%	57%	43%
University of Utah	17%	0.2%	11.4%	1.5%	4.1%	79.3%	0.0%	63%	37%
Creighton University (NE)	17%	1.4%	8.8%	2.6%	6.8%	80.2%	0.2%	53%	47%
University of Kentucky	17%	0.0%	11.1%	4.1%	0.2%	77.0%	3.1%	60%	40%
University of Colorado–Denver	17%	1.5%	8.4%	2.1%	6.4%	78.6%	0.3%	52%	48%
Oregon Health and Science University	17%	1.0%	13.7%	1.6%	1.2%	82.6%	0.0%	45%	55%
A.T. Still University of Health Sciences (Kirksville) (MO)	17%	0.9%	11.8%	1.1%	1.9%	80.2%	1.6%	60%	40%
West Virginia School of Osteopathic Medicine	17%	0.5%	12.7%	1.2%	2.2%	16.6%	0.0%	51%	49%
University of South Carolina	17%	0.0%	10.8%	5.4%	0.3%	83.5%	0.0%	53%	47%
University of Arkansas for Medical Sciences	16%	0.5%	10.7%	4.2%	0.7%	83.9%	0.0%	59%	41%
West Virginia University	15%	0.2%	11.4%	1.2%	1.9%	85.3%	0.0%	59%	41%
University of Missouri–Columbia	14%	0.0%	9.3%	4.7%	1.6%	80.6%	0.0%	51%	49%
East Tennessee State University (Quillen)	14%	0.8%	6.7%	6.3%	0.4%	85.8%	0.0%	50%	50%
University of North Dakota	13%	10.5%	2.4%	0.0%	0.4%	86.7%	0.0%	54%	46%
University of New England College of Osteopathic Medicine (ME)	13%	0.2%	9.0%	1.6%	2.0%	81.8%	0.0%	45%	55%
Mercer University (GA)	13%	0.0%	10.3%	2.5%	1.6%	84.4%	0.0%	53%	47%
University of Nebraska College of Medicine	11%	0.6%	5.0%	2.1%	2.5%	89.3%	0.4%	57%	43%
Pikeville College School of Osteopathic Medicine (KY)	10%	N/A	6.0%	2.3%	1.3%	85.4%	N/A	56%	44%
Eastern Virginia Medical School	6%	N/A	N/A	N/A	N/A	N/A	N/A	50%	50%
University of South Dakota (Sanford)	4%	1.9%	1.9%	0.0%	0.0%	96.2%	0.0%	52%	48%

Which schools turn out the most primary care residents? The fewest?

If you are interested in family practice, general pediatrics, or general internal medicine, you probably want to consider schools that send most of their graduates on to primary care residency programs.

	Average % 2005-2007 graduates entering primary care residencies
West Virginia School of Osteopathic Medicine	84.5%
Michigan State University College of Osteopathic Medicine	83.3%
Pikeville College School of Osteopathic Medicine (KY)	77.0%
U. of N. TX Health Sci. Center (TX Col. of Osteopathic Med.)	76.0%
Lake Erie College of Osteopathic Medicine (PA)	67.0%
Univ. of New England College of Osteopathic Medicine (ME)	65.0%
East Carolina University (Brody) (NC)	60.0%
Edward Via Virginia College of Osteopathic Medicine	60.0%
Nova Southeastern Univ. College of Osteopathic Medicine (FL)	60.0%
University of Nebraska College of Medicine	60.0%
Medical University of South Carolina	58.7%
University of Vermont	58.6%
Touro University College of Osteopathic Medicine (CA)	55.0%
Yeshiva University (Einstein) (NY)	55.0%
Oklahoma State University	53.7%
University of Arkansas for Medical Sciences	53.0%
Loyola University Chicago (Stritch)	52.0%
University of North Carolina–Chapel Hill	52.0%
University of Tennessee Health Science Center	50.3%
Ohio University	50.0%
Wake Forest University (NC)	50.0%
Wright State University (OH)	50.0%
Eastern Virginia Medical School	49.6%
University of Massachusetts–Worcester	49.5%
University of Kansas Medical Center	48.1%
Oregon Health and Science University	48.0%
West Virginia University	48.0%
Michigan State University	47.8%
Florida State University	47.7%
University of Colorado–Denver	47.6%
George Washington University (DC)	47.2%
Temple University (PA)	47.0%
Tufts University (MA)	47.0%
University of South Carolina	46.8%
Mercer University (GA)	46.0%
University of California–Irvine	46.0%
University of Connecticut	46.0%
University of Missouri–Columbia	46.0%
University of New Mexico	46.0%
University of Minnesota Medical School	45.9%
UMDNJ–School of Osteopathic Medicine	45.6%
UMDNJ-Robert Wood Johnson Medical School	45.2%
University of Iowa (Carver)	45.0%
University of Kentucky	45.0%

	Average % 2005-2007 graduates entering primary care residencies
University of Washington	45.0%
Brown University (Alpert) (RI)	44.5%
Ohio State University	44.5%
New York Medical College	44.3%
Harvard University (MA)	44.0%
Rush University (IL)	44.0%
University of California–Los Angeles (Geffen)	44.0%
University of Louisville (KY)	44.0%
Southern Illinois University–Springfield	43.8%
St. Louis University	43.7%
University of North Dakota	43.4%
Baylor College of Medicine (TX)	43.1%
Dartmouth Medical School (NH)	43.1%
University of Maryland	43.0%
University of Nevada–Reno	43.0%
Virginia Commonwealth University	42.6%
University of Arizona	42.5%
University of California–Davis	42.5%
Stony Brook University (NY)	42.2%
University of Chicago (Pritzker)	42.0%
University of Texas Southwestern Medical Center–Dallas	42.0%
University of Toledo	42.0%
University of Missouri–Kansas City	41.9%
East Tennessee State University (Quillen)	41.7%
University of Wisconsin–Madison	41.3%
Duke University (NC)	41.2%
University of Southern California (Keck)	41.0%
University of California–San Diego	40.7%
Texas Tech University Health Sciences Center	40.0%
Washington University in St. Louis	39.8%
Indiana University–Indianapolis	39.5%
University of Miami (Miller) (FL)	39.2%
University of Utah	39.1%
Creighton University (NE)	39.0%
Drexel University (PA)	39.0%
Jefferson Medical College (PA)	39.0%
Medical College of Wisconsin	39.0%
University of Virginia	39.0%
University of Pittsburgh	38.7%
University of Texas Medical Branch–Galveston	38.6%
University of Oklahoma	38.4%
SUNY–Syracuse	38.0%
University of Alabama–Birmingham	38.0%
Texas A&M Health Science Center	37.8%

University of South Florida	37.8%
Emory University (GA)	37.5%
University of California–San Francisco	37.5%
Northeastern Ohio Universities College of Medicine	37.0%
Northwestern University (Feinberg) (IL)	37.0%
Tulane University (LA)	37.0%
University of Pennsylvania	37.0%
Case Western Reserve University (OH)	36.0%
Mayo Medical School (MN)	36.0%
University of Michigan–Ann Arbor	36.0%
University of Rochester (NY)	35.8%
Medical College of Georgia	35.6%
Mount Sinai School of Medicine (NY)	35.6%
New York University	35.4%
Boston University	35.0%
Georgetown University (DC)	35.0%

Johns Hopkins University (MD)	34.9%
Uniformed Services Univ. of the Health Sciences (Hebert) (MD)	34.0%
A.T. Still University of Health Sciences (Kirksville) (MO)	33.3%
University of Cincinnati	33.3%
Howard University (DC)	33.1%
University of Texas Health Science Center–Houston	33.0%
Stanford University (CA)	32.7%
Cornell University (Weill) (NY)	32.6%
University of Florida	32.0%
University at Buffalo–SUNY	31.2%
Columbia University College of Physicians and Surgeons (NY)	30.0%
Vanderbilt University (TN)	30.0%
Wayne State University (MI)	30.0%
University of South Dakota (Sanford)	29.2%
Yale University (CT)	25.4%

Which schools' grads are most likely to stay in state? The least likely?

If you want to stay close to where you study after you graduate, you may want to consider schools whose new doctors choose residencies in-state. Some states also offer incentives to graduates who stay and practice in underserved areas. Doctors in Massachusetts, for instance, can receive as much as $20,000 a year in debt payments if they work at least two years in a Massachusetts community health center.

School	Average % 2006-2007 graduates accepting in-state residencies
Michigan State University College of Osteopathic Medicine	83%
University of Southern California (Keck)	79%
University of California–Davis	78%
University of California–Los Angeles (Geffen)	77%
University of California–San Diego	75%
University of California–Irvine	73%
Ohio University	69%
Mount Sinai School of Medicine (NY)	66%
Stony Brook University (NY)	64%
University of California–San Francisco	64%
University of South Florida	63%
Texas Tech University Health Sciences Center	62%
Wayne State University (MI)	60%
Yeshiva University (Einstein) (NY)	60%
University of Pittsburgh	57%
University of Texas Health Science Center–Houston	57%
New York University	57%
University of Arkansas for Medical Sciences	56%
University of Texas Medical Branch–Galveston	56%
Northeastern Ohio Universities College of Medicine	55%
U. of N. TX Health Sci. Center (TX Col. of Osteopathic Medicine)	54%
Harvard University (MA)	54%
Stanford University (CA)	54%
Texas A&M Health Science Center	53%
University of Massachusetts–Worcester	53%
University of Minnesota Medical School	52%
Baylor College of Medicine (TX)	52%
University of Texas Southwestern Medical Center–Dallas	51%
Oklahoma State University	50%
University of Cincinnati	50%
University of Alabama–Birmingham	49%
Cornell University (Weill) (NY)	48%
Florida State University	48%
Indiana University–Indianapolis	48%
University of Washington	47%
Wright State University (OH)	47%
SUNY–Syracuse	47%
Jefferson Medical College (PA)	46%
Rush University (IL)	46%
West Virginia University	46%
Ohio State University	46%

School	Average % 2006-2007 graduates accepting in-state residencies
Columbia University College of Physicians and Surgeons (NY)	45%
East Carolina University (Brody) (NC)	45%
Temple University (PA)	45%
University of Louisville (KY)	45%
University of Missouri–Columbia	45%
New York Medical College	45%
University of Florida	44%
Touro University College of Osteopathic Medicine (CA)	44%
University of Chicago (Pritzker)	44%
University at Buffalo–SUNY	44%
University of Tennessee Health Science Center	44%
University of Oklahoma	43%
Mayo Medical School (MN)	42%
University of South Carolina	42%
Medical University of South Carolina	41%
University of Kentucky	41%
Drexel University (PA)	40%
Lake Erie College of Osteopathic Medicine (PA)	40%
University of Nebraska College of Medicine	40%
Boston University	40%
Northwestern University (Feinberg) (IL)	39%
Johns Hopkins University (MD)	39%
University of Missouri–Kansas City	39%
UMDNJ–School of Osteopathic Medicine	38%
University of North Carolina–Chapel Hill	38%
East Tennessee State University (Quillen)	38%
University of Kansas Medical Center	38%
Michigan State University	38%
Southern Illinois University–Springfield	38%
University of New Mexico	38%
Medical College of Wisconsin	37%
University of Colorado–Denver	37%
University of Pennsylvania	36%
University of Toledo	36%
West Virginia School of Osteopathic Medicine	35%
Nova Southeastern Univ. College of Osteopathic Medicine (FL)	35%
University of Miami (Miller) (FL)	35%
University of Utah	34%
Case Western Reserve University (OH)	34%
Duke University (NC)	34%
University of Arizona	34%

	Average % 2006-2007 graduates accepting in-state residencies
Eastern Virginia Medical School	33%
University of Rochester (NY)	33%
Oregon Health and Science University	33%
Tufts University (MA)	33%
Tulane University (LA)	33%
Wake Forest University (NC)	32%
University of Wisconsin–Madison	32%
University of Michigan–Ann Arbor	31%
University of Connecticut	31%
Medical College of Georgia	31%
Mercer University (GA)	30%
University of Maryland	30%
Emory University (GA)	29%
Virginia Commonwealth University	29%
Washington University in St. Louis	28%
UMDNJ-Robert Wood Johnson Medical School	28%
St. Louis University	28%
Georgetown University (DC)	27%
University of Iowa (Carver)	27%
Howard University (DC)	27%
University of Virginia	24%
University of South Dakota (Sanford)	24%
Pikeville College School of Osteopathic Medicine (KY)	23%
Vanderbilt University (TN)	22%
Yale University (CT)	22%
University of Vermont	22%
Creighton University (NE)	21%
University of Nevada–Reno	21%
University of North Dakota	19%
George Washington University (DC)	17%
Brown University (Alpert) (RI)	16%
Edward Via Virginia College of Osteopathic Medicine	14%
University of New England College of Osteopathic Medicine (ME)	14%
A.T. Still University of Health Sciences (Kirksville) (MO)	13%
Dartmouth Medical School (NH)	10%

The U.S.News & World Report

Ultimate Medical School Directory

How to use the directory

In the following pages, you'll find in-depth profiles of medical schools fully accredited by the Liaison Committee on Medical Education, plus schools that offer the Doctor of Osteopathy degree accredited by the American Osteopathic Association. The schools are listed alphabetically in two sections: those conferring the M.D. degree, followed by schools of osteopathy.

The data were collected by *U.S. News* from the schools during late 2006 and early 2007. If a medical school did not supply the data requested, or if the data point does not apply to the school, you'll see an N/A, for "not available." Schools that did not return the *U.S. News* questionnaire are listed at the end of the directory.

You may also want to consult the online version of the directory at www.usnews.com/education, which allows you to do a customized search of our database.

ESSENTIAL STATS: In addition to the medical school's address and the year the school was founded, you'll find the following key facts and figures here:

Tuition: for the 2007-2008 academic year.

Enrollment: full-time students during the 2007-2008 academic year.

Specialty ranking: the school's 2009 *U.S. News* ranking in various specialty areas, where applicable (the possible areas are women's health, geriatrics, internal medicine, AIDS, drug/alcohol abuse, rural medicine, pediatrics, and family medicine).

GPA and MCAT: The undergraduate grade point averages and Medical College Admission Test (MCAT) scores shown are for the fall 2007

entering class. The MCAT score is the average of the scores on the verbal, physical sciences, and biological sciences portions of the test.

Acceptance rate: percentage of applicants accepted for the fall 2007 entering class.

U.S. News **ranking:** A school's overall rank indicates where it sits among its peers in the 2009 ranking of medical schools published by *U.S. News* (at www.usnews.com/education) and in its annual guide *America's Best Graduate Schools*. Schools are ranked separately in research and primary care, and the schools in the top 60 are ranked numerically. Schools below the top 60 are listed as "unranked."

ADMISSIONS:

Application website: Many medical schools allow you to complete and submit an application online.

Applicants and acceptees: The acceptance rates for the fall 2007 entering class are broken down by in-state, out-of-state, minority, and international students. The admissions statistics—numbers of applicants and of people interviewed and accepted—are also for the fall 2007 entering class.

Profile of admitted students: Besides the GPA and MCAT scores of fall 2007 entrants, we list the proportion majoring in biological sciences, physical sciences, non-sciences, other health professions, and other disciplines. The percentage who took time off between college and medical school is also shown.

Admission dates and details: We note whether the university uses the American Medical College Application Service (AMCAS), and whether it asks for a second, school-specific application form. Besides key deadlines for applicants to the 2008-2009 first-year class, you'll find information on whether the school has an Early Decision Plan (EDP), whether a personal interview is required for admission, whether admission can be deferred, and what undergraduate coursework is required.

Admissions policy: The text describing admissions policies was written by the schools. *U.S. News* edited the information for style but did not verify it.

FINANCIAL AID:

Tuition and other expenses: for the 2007-2008 academic year. For public schools, we list both in-state and out-of-state tuition.

Financial aid profile: The data on financial aid awards and the percentage of students receiving grants, loans, and scholarships are for the 2007-2008 academic year. The average debt burden of borrowers who graduated in 2006 does not include their undergraduate debt.

STUDENT BODY STATS:
What will your classmates be like? This section supplies the breakdown of male and female students, the in-state enrollments, and the ethnic makeup of the student body during the 2007-2008 academic year (which may not add up to 100 percent due to rounding).

ACADEMIC PROGRAMS:
Besides information on areas of specialization, you can look here for a sense of how early in your training you'll have contact with patients.

Joint degrees awarded: Some medical students pursue a second degree in another university department to marry their interests or gain an edge in the job market. One common joint degree,

the M.D./M.B.A., combines medicine and business. Another, for those interested in research, is the M.D./Ph.D. degree. Other degree combos include the M.D. /J.D. (law) and the M.D./M.P.H. (public health).

Research profile: An indicator of how big a role research plays at the medical school is the amount of grant money the faculty brings in. We list the total amount of National Institutes of Health (NIH) grants awarded to the medical school and affiliated hospitals in fiscal 2007.

CURRICULUM:
The text describing the curriculum was provided by the schools. *U.S. News* edited the text for style but did not verify the information.

FACULTY PROFILE:
Here, you'll find the number of full-time and part-time teaching faculty during fall 2007, as well as information on whether they teach in the basic sciences or in clinical programs. The full-time faculty/student ratio gives some indication of how accessible your professors are likely to be.

SUPPORT SERVICES:
How does the school help students deal with the pressure of medical school?

RESIDENCY PROFILE:
This section provides data on the residency placements of graduates—the most popular residency and specialty programs chosen by the 2006 and 2007 graduates, plus the proportion of graduates who enter into primary care specialties (family practice, general pediatrics, or general internal medicine). The latter figures are three-year average percentages from 2005-2007 and the proportion of 2006-2007 graduates who accepted in-state residencies.

Albany Medical College

- 47 New Scotland Avenue, Albany, NY 12208
- Private
- **Year Founded:** 1839
- **Tuition, 2007-2008:** $42,873
- **Enrollment 2007-2008 academic year:** 566
- **Website:** http://www.amc.edu
- **Specialty ranking:** N/A

3.60	AVERAGE GPA, ENTERING CLASS FALL 2007
10.0	AVERAGE MCAT, ENTERING CLASS FALL 2007
N/A	ACCEPTANCE RATE, ENTERING CLASS FALL 2007
Unranked	2009 U.S. NEWS MEDICAL SCHOOL RANKING (RESEARCH)
Unranked	2009 U.S. NEWS MEDICAL SCHOOL RANKING (PRIMARY CARE)

ADMISSIONS

Admissions phone number: **(518) 262-5521**
Admissions email address: **admissions@mail.amc.edu**
Application website: **N/A**
Acceptance rate: **N/A**
In-state acceptance rate: **N/A**
Out-of-state acceptance rate: **N/A**
Minority acceptance rate: **N/A**
International acceptance rate: **N/A**

Fall 2007 applications and acceptees

	Applied	Interviewed	Accepted	Enrolled
Total:	N/A	N/A	N/A	N/A
In-state:	N/A	N/A	N/A	N/A
Out-of-state:	N/A	N/A	N/A	N/A

Profile of admitted students

Average undergraduate grade point average: **3.60**
MCAT averages (scale: 1-15; writing test: J-T):
  Composite score: **10.0**
  Verbal reasoning score: **10.0**, Physical sciences score: **10.5**, Biological sciences score: **10.9**, Writing score: **N/A**
Proportion with undergraduate majors in: Biological sciences: **N/A**, Physical sciences: **N/A**, Non-sciences: **N/A**, Other health professions: **N/A**, Mixed disciplines and other: **N/A**
Percentage of students not coming directly from college after graduation: **N/A**

Dates and details

The American Medical College Application Service (AMCAS) application is accepted.
School asks for a school-specific application as part of the admissions process.
Oldest MCAT considered for Fall 2009 entry: **2005**
Earliest application date for the 2009-2010 first-year class: **6/1**
Latest application date: **11/15**

Acceptance dates for regular application for the class entering in fall 2009:
  Earliest: **December 1, 2007**
  Latest: **N/A**
The school considers requests for deferred entrance.
Starting month for the class entering in 2009–2010: **August**
The school doesn't have an Early Decision Plan (EDP).
A personal interview is required for admission.

Undergraduate coursework required

Medical school requires undergraduate work in these subjects: biology, organic chemistry, inorganic (general) chemistry, physics.

COSTS AND FINANCIAL AID

Financial aid phone number: **(518) 262-5435**
Tuition, 2007-2008 academic year: **$42,873**
Room and board: **N/A**
Percentage of students receiving financial aid in 2007-08: **82%**
Percentage of students receiving: Loans: **78%**, Grants/scholarships: **33%**, Work-study aid: **16%**
Average medical school debt for the Class of 2006: **$162,151**

STUDENT BODY

Fall 2007 full-time enrollment: **566**
Men: **43%**, Women: **57%**, In-state: **42%**, Minorities: **36%**, American Indian: **N/A**, Asian-American: **N/A**, African-American: **N/A**, Hispanic-American: **N/A**, White: **N/A**, International: **N/A**, Unknown: **N/A**

ACADEMIC PROGRAMS

Program offerings: N/A
Joint degrees awarded: N/A
Total National Institutes of Health (NIH) grants awarded to the medical school and affiliated hospitals: **N/A**

FACULTY PROFILE (FALL 2007)

Total teaching faculty: **N/A (full-time)**, **N/A (part-time)**
Of full-time faculty, those teaching in basic sciences: **N/A**; in clinical programs: **N/A**
Of part-time faculty, those teaching in basic sciences: **N/A**; in clinical programs: **N/A**
Full-time faculty/student ratio: **N/A**

SUPPORT SERVICES

The school offers students these services for dealing with stress: N/A.

RESIDENCY PROFILE

Most popular residency and specialty programs chosen by the 2006 and 2007 M.D. graduating classes: N/A.

WHERE GRADS GO

N/A				

Proportion of 2005-2007 graduates who entered primary care specialties

N/A				

Proportion of 2006-2007 graduates who accepted in-state residencies

Baylor College of Medicine

- 1 Baylor Plaza, Houston, TX 77030
- Private
- Year Founded: 1900
- Tuition, 2007-2008: $12,848
- Enrollment 2007-2008 academic year: 681
- Website: http://www.bcm.edu
- Specialty ranking: family medicine: 17, pediatrics: 5

3.82 AVERAGE GPA, ENTERING CLASS FALL 2007

11.6 AVERAGE MCAT, ENTERING CLASS FALL 2007

6.0% ACCEPTANCE RATE, ENTERING CLASS FALL 2007

13 2009 U.S. NEWS MEDICAL SCHOOL RANKING (RESEARCH)

7 2009 U.S. NEWS MEDICAL SCHOOL RANKING (PRIMARY CARE)

ADMISSIONS

Admissions phone number: **(713) 798-4842**
Admissions email address: **admissions@bcm.tmc.edu**
Application website:
http://public.bcm.edu/admissions/suppapp.htm
Acceptance rate: **6.0%**
In-state acceptance rate: **11.7%**
Out-of-state acceptance rate: **3.4%**
Minority acceptance rate: **6.1%**
International acceptance rate: **3.2%**

Fall 2007 applications and acceptees

	Applied	Interviewed	Accepted	Enrolled
Total:	4,922	751	297	172
In-state:	1,544	394	181	131
Out-of-state:	3,378	357	116	41

Profile of admitted students

Average undergraduate grade point average: **3.82**
MCAT averages (scale: 1-15; writing test: J-T):
   Composite score: **11.6**
   Verbal reasoning score: **11.0**, Physical sciences score:
   11.8, Biological sciences score: **11.9**, Writing score: **P**
Proportion with undergraduate majors in: Biological
   sciences: **42%**, Physical sciences: **28%**, Non-sciences:
   10%, Other health professions: **0%**, Mixed disciplines
   and other: **20%**
Percentage of students not coming directly from college
   after graduation: **10%**

Dates and details

The American Medical College Application Service
   (AMCAS) application is accepted.
School asks for a school-specific application as part of the
   admissions process.
Oldest MCAT considered for Fall 2009 entry: **2004**
Earliest application date for the 2009-2010 first-year class:
   5/1
Latest application date: **11/1**
Acceptance dates for regular application for the class
   entering in fall 2009:

Earliest: **October 16, 2008**
Latest: **June 27, 2009**
The school considers requests for deferred entrance.
Starting month for the class entering in 2009-2010: **July**
The school has an Early Decision Plan (EDP).
A personal interview is required for admission.

Undergraduate coursework required

Medical school requires undergraduate work in these subjects: biology, English, organic chemistry, inorganic (general) chemistry.

ADMISSIONS POLICY

(TEXT PROVIDED BY SCHOOL):
Most applicants accepted have an overall grade-point average of 3.5 or higher. Attention is on the applicant's course
selection, academic challenge imposed by the curriculum,
and the extent to which extracurricular activities and
employment limited the opportunity for high academic
achievement. Applicants are not required to major in a scientific field, and the College of Medicine actively seeks individuals with broad educational backgrounds.

COSTS AND FINANCIAL AID

Financial aid phone number: **(713) 798-4603**
Tuition, 2007-2008 academic year: **$12,848**
Room and board: **$19,718**
Percentage of students receiving financial aid in 2007-08:
   78%
Percentage of students receiving: Loans: **67%**,
   Grants/scholarships: **47%**, Work-study aid: **20%**
Average medical school debt for the Class of 2006:
   $81,329

STUDENT BODY

Fall 2007 full-time enrollment: **681**
Men: **52%**, Women: **48%**, In-state: **86%**, Minorities: **55%**,
   American Indian: **2.1%**, Asian-American: **32.3%**,
   African-American: **7.5%**, Hispanic-American: **12.9%**,
   White: **44.5%**, International: **0.7%**, Unknown: **0.0%**

ACADEMIC PROGRAMS

The school's curriculum frequently gives first-year students substantial contact with patients.

There are opportunities for first- or second-year students to work in community health clinics.

Program offerings: AIDS, drug/alcohol abuse, family medicine, geriatrics, internal medicine, pediatrics, rural medicine, women's health

Joint degrees awarded: M.D./Ph.D., M.D./M.B.A., M.D./M.P.H., M.D./J.D.

Total National Institutes of Health (NIH) grants awarded to the medical school and affiliated hospitals: **$413.1 million**

CURRICULUM

(TEXT PROVIDED BY SCHOOL):

A flexible, integrated curriculum with a solid foundation in the scientific concepts of medicine; a knowledge of core clinical sciences; and the skills and attitudes required to be a capable, compassionate physician and lifelong learner. Basic and clinical sciences are integrated across a curriculum divided into 1.5 years of preclinical courses and 2.5 years of individualized clinical experience.

FACULTY PROFILE (FALL 2007)

Total teaching faculty: **1,832 (full-time)**, **1,762 (part-time)**
Of full-time faculty, those teaching in basic sciences: **15%**; in clinical programs: **85%**

Of part-time faculty, those teaching in basic sciences: **3%**; in clinical programs: **97%**
Full-time faculty/student ratio: **2.7**

SUPPORT SERVICES

The school offers students these services for dealing with stress: expanded-hour gym access, peer counseling, professional counseling, support groups.

RESIDENCY PROFILE

Most popular residency and specialty programs chosen by the 2006 and 2007 M.D. graduating classes: anesthesiology, emergency medicine, family practice, internal medicine, ophthalmology, orthopaedic surgery, otolaryngology, pediatrics, psychiatry, radiology–diagnostic.

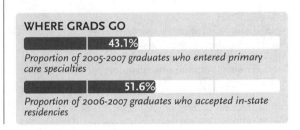

WHERE GRADS GO

43.1%
Proportion of 2005-2007 graduates who entered primary care specialties

51.6%
Proportion of 2006-2007 graduates who accepted in-state residencies

Boston University

- 715 Albany Street, L-103, Boston, MA 02118
- Private
- **Year Founded:** 1848
- **Tuition, 2007-2008:** $43,234
- **Enrollment 2007-2008 academic year:** 674
- **Website:** http://www.bumc.bu.edu
- **Specialty ranking:** drug/alcohol abuse: 17, family medicine: 22, internal medicine: 29, women's health: 15

3.56 AVERAGE GPA, ENTERING CLASS FALL 2007

10.0 AVERAGE MCAT, ENTERING CLASS FALL 2007

4.3% ACCEPTANCE RATE, ENTERING CLASS FALL 2007

43 2009 U.S. NEWS MEDICAL SCHOOL RANKING (RESEARCH)

Unranked 2009 U.S. NEWS MEDICAL SCHOOL RANKING (PRIMARY CARE)

ADMISSIONS

Admissions phone number: **(617) 638-4630**
Admissions email address: **medadms@bu.edu**
Application website:
https://www.bumc.bu.edu/busm/myapplication/shared/signin.aspx
Acceptance rate: **4.3%**
In-state acceptance rate: **11.2%**
Out-of-state acceptance rate: **3.8%**
Minority acceptance rate: **4.7%**
International acceptance rate: **2.7%**

Fall 2007 applications and acceptees

	Applied	Interviewed	Accepted	Enrolled
Total:	11,324	1,011	489	168
In-state:	750	151	84	39
Out-of-state:	10,574	860	405	129

Profile of admitted students

Average undergraduate grade point average: **3.56**
MCAT averages (scale: 1-15; writing test: J-T):
Composite score: **10.0**
Verbal reasoning score: **9.7**, Physical sciences score: **10.5**, Biological sciences score: **10.9**, Writing score: **P**
Proportion with undergraduate majors in: Biological sciences: **45%**, Physical sciences: **21%**, Non-sciences: **12%**, Other health professions: **5%**, Mixed disciplines and other: **17%**
Percentage of students not coming directly from college after graduation: **40%**

Dates and details

The American Medical College Application Service (AMCAS) application is accepted.
School asks for a school-specific application as part of the admissions process.
Oldest MCAT considered for Fall 2009 entry: **2004**
Earliest application date for the 2009-2010 first-year class: **6/1**
Latest application date: **11/1**

Acceptance dates for regular application for the class entering in fall 2009:
Earliest: **January 9, 2008**
Latest: **August 11, 2008**
The school doesn't consider requests for deferred entrance.
Starting month for the class entering in 2009–2010:
August
The school has an Early Decision Plan (EDP).
A personal interview is required for admission.

Undergraduate coursework required

Medical school requires undergraduate work in these subjects: biology, English, organic chemistry, inorganic (general) chemistry, physics, humanities, demonstration of writing skills.

ADMISSIONS POLICY
(TEXT PROVIDED BY SCHOOL):

Boston University School of Medicine draws upon a large and highly qualified applicant pool, with more than 90 applicants for every seat in the entering class. Students represent the full range of geographic, cultural, ethnic, and educational diversity of a pluralistic society. The school believes that diversity contributes to the strength of the experience for everyone.

COSTS AND FINANCIAL AID

Financial aid phone number: **(617) 638-5130**
Tuition, 2007-2008 academic year: **$43,234**
Room and board: **$11,933**
Percentage of students receiving financial aid in 2007-08: **80%**
Percentage of students receiving: Loans: **77%**, Grants/scholarships: **31%**, Work-study aid: **0%**
Average medical school debt for the Class of 2006: **$158,478**

STUDENT BODY

Fall 2007 full-time enrollment: **674**

Men: **45%**, Women: **55%**, In-state: **16%**, Minorities: **47%**,
American Indian: **0.7%**, Asian-American: **27.4%**,
African-American: **10.2%**, Hispanic-American: **8.9%**,
White: **46.7%**, International: **4.3%**, Unknown: **1.6%**

ACADEMIC PROGRAMS

The school's curriculum frequently gives first-year students
substantial contact with patients.

There are opportunities for first- or second-year students to
work in community health clinics.

Program offerings: AIDS, drug/alcohol abuse, family
medicine, geriatrics, internal medicine, pediatrics, rural
medicine, women's health

Joint degrees awarded: M.D./Ph.D., M.D./M.B.A.,
M.D./M.P.H.

Total National Institutes of Health (NIH) grants awarded to
the medical school and affiliated hospitals: **$181.8
million**

CURRICULUM

(TEXT PROVIDED BY SCHOOL):

New curriculum in 2007 offers a maximum of 2.5 lecture
hours per day and early patient contact. The faculty cultivates the skills and perspective necessary to engage in problem-based and team-based learning and to integrate
teamwork with independent study. Clinical training takes
place at Boston Medical Center and community settings, in
work with highly diverse urban and suburban patients.

FACULTY PROFILE (FALL 2007)

Total teaching faculty: **1,400 (full-time)**, **1,246 (part-time)**
Of full-time faculty, those teaching in basic sciences: **11%**;
in clinical programs: **89%**

Of part-time faculty, those teaching in basic sciences: **8%**;
in clinical programs: **92%**
Full-time faculty/student ratio: **2.1**

SUPPORT SERVICES

The school offers students these services for dealing with
stress: expanded-hour gym access, peer counseling, professional counseling, support groups.

RESIDENCY PROFILE

Most popular residency and specialty programs chosen by
the 2006 and 2007 M.D. graduating classes: anesthesiology, emergency medicine, family practice, internal medicine, obstetrics and gynecology, ophthalmology, orthopaedic
surgery, pediatrics, radiology–diagnostic, surgery–general.

WHERE GRADS GO

35.0%

*Proportion of 2005-2007 graduates who entered primary
care specialties*

39.5%

*Proportion of 2006-2007 graduates who accepted in-state
residencies*

Brown University

ALPERT

- 97 Waterman Street, Box G-A213, Providence, RI 02912-9706
- Private
- **Year Founded:** 1764
- **Tuition, 2007-2008:** $41,184
- **Enrollment 2007-2008 academic year:** 372
- **Website:** http://med.brown.edu
- **Specialty ranking:** drug/alcohol abuse: 11

3.66 AVERAGE GPA, ENTERING CLASS FALL 2007

11.7 AVERAGE MCAT, ENTERING CLASS FALL 2007

3.5% ACCEPTANCE RATE, ENTERING CLASS FALL 2007

31 2009 U.S. NEWS MEDICAL SCHOOL RANKING (RESEARCH)

23 2009 U.S. NEWS MEDICAL SCHOOL RANKING (PRIMARY CARE)

ADMISSIONS

Admissions phone number: **(401) 863-2149**
Admissions email address:
  medschool_admissions@brown.edu
Application website:
  http://med.brown.edu/admissions/secondary_forms
Acceptance rate: **3.5%**
In-state acceptance rate: **12.4%**
Out-of-state acceptance rate: **3.3%**
Minority acceptance rate: **3.2%**
International acceptance rate: **1.4%**

Fall 2007 applications and acceptees

	Applied	Interviewed	Accepted	Enrolled
Total:	6,016	229	208	95
In-state:	89	17	11	7
Out-of-state:	5,927	212	197	88

Profile of admitted students

Average undergraduate grade point average: **3.66**
MCAT averages (scale: 1-15; writing test: J-T):
  Composite score: **11.7**
  Verbal reasoning score: **10.8**, Physical sciences score:
  11.6, Biological sciences score: **12.0**, Writing score: **Q**
Proportion with undergraduate majors in: Biological
  sciences: **33%**, Physical sciences: **17%**, Non-sciences:
  42%, Other health professions: **0%**, Mixed disciplines
  and other: **9%**
Percentage of students not coming directly from college
  after graduation: **30%**

Dates and details

The American Medical College Application Service
  (AMCAS) application is accepted.
School asks for a school-specific application as part of the
  admissions process.
Oldest MCAT considered for Fall 2009 entry: **2004**
Earliest application date for the 2009-2010 first-year class:
  6/1
Latest application date: **11/1**

Acceptance dates for regular application for the class
  entering in fall 2009:
  Earliest: **December 1, 2008**
  Latest: **August 15, 2009**
The school considers requests for deferred entrance.
Starting month for the class entering in 2009–2010:
  August
The school doesn't have an Early Decision Plan (EDP).
A personal interview is required for admission.

Undergraduate coursework required

Medical school requires undergraduate work in these subjects: biology, organic chemistry, inorganic (general) chemistry, physics, behavioral science, calculus, social sciences.

ADMISSIONS POLICY

(TEXT PROVIDED BY SCHOOL):
Selection criteria are academic achievement, faculty evaluations, and evidence of maturity, leadership, integrity, and
compassion. Eligible candidates present a minimum cumu-
lative grade-point average of 3.00 (4.00 scale) in undergraduate courses. Applicants must complete baccalaureate
degree requirements before entry into medical school.

COSTS AND FINANCIAL AID

Financial aid phone number: **(401) 863-1142**
Tuition, 2007-2008 academic year: **$41,184**
Room and board: **$16,796**
Percentage of students receiving financial aid in 2007-08:
  75%
Percentage of students receiving: Loans: **73%**,
  Grants/scholarships: **45%**, Work-study aid: **0%**
Average medical school debt for the Class of 2006:
  $112,062

STUDENT BODY

Fall 2007 full-time enrollment: **372**
Men: **45%**, Women: **55%**, In-state: **13%**, Minorities: **43%**,
  American Indian: **0.3%**, Asian-American: **25.5%**,
  African-American: **8.9%**, Hispanic-American: **8.3%**,
  White: **45.7%**, International: **2.7%**, Unknown: **8.6%**

ACADEMIC PROGRAMS

The school's curriculum very frequently gives first-year students substantial contact with patients.

There are opportunities for first- or second-year students to work in community health clinics.

Program offerings: AIDS, drug/alcohol abuse, family medicine, geriatrics, internal medicine, pediatrics, rural medicine, women's health

Joint degrees awarded: M.D./Ph.D., M.D./M.P.H., M.D./M.S.

Total National Institutes of Health (NIH) grants awarded to the medical school and affiliated hospitals: **$118.3 million**

CURRICULUM

(TEXT PROVIDED BY SCHOOL):

Year 1 includes two semesters of Integrated Medical Sciences and Doctoring. Year 2 consists of system-based Pathophysiology with integrated Pharmacology, Pathology, Neurologic Pathophysiology, Epidemiology, and Doctoring. Students in the third and fourth years must complete 50 weeks of clinical clerkships and 30 weeks of electives.

FACULTY PROFILE (FALL 2007)

Total teaching faculty: **707 (full-time), 0 (part-time)**
Of full-time faculty, those teaching in basic sciences: **26%**; in clinical programs: **74%**

Of part-time faculty, those teaching in basic sciences: **N/A;** in clinical programs: **N/A**
Full-time faculty/student ratio: **1.9**

SUPPORT SERVICES

The school offers students these services for dealing with stress: expanded-hour gym access, peer counseling, professional counseling, religious support, support groups.

RESIDENCY PROFILE

Most popular residency and specialty programs chosen by the 2006 and 2007 M.D. graduating classes: emergency medicine, family practice, internal medicine, obstetrics and gynecology, orthopaedic surgery, pediatrics, psychiatry, radiology–diagnostic, surgery–general, internal medicine/pediatrics.

WHERE GRADS GO

44.5%

Proportion of 2005-2007 graduates who entered primary care specialties

16.2%

Proportion of 2006-2007 graduates who accepted in-state residencies

Case Western Reserve University

- 10900 Euclid Avenue, Cleveland, OH 44106
- Private
- Year Founded: 1843
- Tuition, 2007-2008: $43,206
- Enrollment 2007-2008 academic year: 711
- Website: http://casemed.case.edu/
- Specialty ranking: AIDS: 20, family medicine: 13, internal medicine: 25, pediatrics: 13

3.62	AVERAGE GPA, ENTERING CLASS FALL 2007
11.2	AVERAGE MCAT, ENTERING CLASS FALL 2007
7.6%	ACCEPTANCE RATE, ENTERING CLASS FALL 2007
23	2009 U.S. NEWS MEDICAL SCHOOL RANKING (RESEARCH)
51	2009 U.S. NEWS MEDICAL SCHOOL RANKING (PRIMARY CARE)

ADMISSIONS

Admissions phone number: (216) 368-3450
Admissions email address: lina.mehta@case.edu
Application website: N/A
Acceptance rate: 7.6%
In-state acceptance rate: 9.7%
Out-of-state acceptance rate: 7.3%
Minority acceptance rate: 8.3%
International acceptance rate: 5.9%

Fall 2007 applications and acceptees

	Applied	Interviewed	Accepted	Enrolled
Total:	6,077	1,235	462	185
In-state:	797	194	77	40
Out-of-state:	5,280	1,041	385	145

Profile of admitted students

Average undergraduate grade point average: 3.62
MCAT averages (scale: 1-15; writing test: J-T):
 Composite score: 11.2
 Verbal reasoning score: 10.7, Physical sciences score:
 11.5, Biological sciences score: 11.5, Writing score: Q
Proportion with undergraduate majors in: Biological
 sciences: 0%, Physical sciences: 1%, Non-sciences: 0%,
 Other health professions: 0%, Mixed disciplines and
 other: 100%
Percentage of students not coming directly from college
 after graduation: 51%

Dates and details

The American Medical College Application Service
 (AMCAS) application is accepted.
School asks for a school-specific application as part of the
 admissions process.
Oldest MCAT considered for Fall 2009 entry: 2006
Earliest application date for the 2009-2010 first-year class:
 6/1
Latest application date: 11/1
Acceptance dates for regular application for the class
 entering in fall 2009:

Earliest: October 15, 2009
Latest: May 1, 2010
The school considers requests for deferred entrance.
Starting month for the class entering in 2009–2010: July
The school doesn't have an Early Decision Plan (EDP).
A personal interview is required for admission.

Undergraduate coursework required

Medical school requires undergraduate work in these subjects: biology/zoology, English, organic chemistry, inorganic
(general) chemistry, physics.

ADMISSIONS POLICY
(TEXT PROVIDED BY SCHOOL):

The Admissions Committee selects students without regard
to age, national origin, race, religion, sex, or sexual orientation. Although admitted students demonstrate exceptional
academic strength, the candidate's written statements,
extracurricular activities, and letters of recommendation
also weigh heavily in the decision to extend an interview.
The school seeks a diverse student body.

COSTS AND FINANCIAL AID

Financial aid phone number: (216) 368-3666
Tuition, 2007-2008 academic year: $43,206
Room and board: $17,930
Percentage of students receiving financial aid in 2007-08:
 82%
Percentage of students receiving: Loans: 79%,
 Grants/scholarships: 57%, Work-study aid: 0%
Average medical school debt for the Class of 2006:
 $134,100

STUDENT BODY

Fall 2007 full-time enrollment: 711
Men: 55%, Women: 45%, In-state: 41%, Minorities: 38%,
 American Indian: 0.0%, Asian-American: 25.3%,
 African-American: 8.6%, Hispanic-American: 3.1%,
 White: 54.6%, International: 3.9%, Unknown: 4.5%

ACADEMIC PROGRAMS

The school's curriculum very frequently gives first-year students substantial contact with patients.

There are opportunities for first- or second-year students to work in community health clinics.

Program offerings: AIDS, drug/alcohol abuse, family medicine, geriatrics, internal medicine, pediatrics, rural medicine, women's health

Joint degrees awarded: M.D./Ph.D., M.D./M.B.A., M.D./M.P.H., M.D./M.S., M.D./M.A.

Total National Institutes of Health (NIH) grants awarded to the medical school and affiliated hospitals: **$246.4 million**

CURRICULUM

(TEXT PROVIDED BY SCHOOL):

The four-year university program develops physician scholars and leaders in science, patient care, and healthcare policy. The five-year college program develops physician investigators by integrating research training across five years. Both programs focus on scholarship, student-centered, small-group learning, early patient experiences, and research opportunities.î

FACULTY PROFILE (FALL 2007)

Total teaching faculty: **1,984 (full-time)**, **1,883 (part-time)**
Of full-time faculty, those teaching in basic sciences: **20%**; in clinical programs: **80%**

Of part-time faculty, those teaching in basic sciences: **9%**; in clinical programs: **91%**
Full-time faculty/student ratio: **2.8**

SUPPORT SERVICES

The school offers students these services for dealing with stress: expanded-hour gym access, peer counseling, professional counseling, religious support, support groups.

RESIDENCY PROFILE

Most popular residency and specialty programs chosen by the 2006 and 2007 M.D. graduating classes: anesthesiology, emergency medicine, internal medicine, orthopaedic surgery, pediatrics, psychiatry, radiology–diagnostic, surgery–general.

WHERE GRADS GO

36.0%

Proportion of 2005-2007 graduates who entered primary care specialties

34.0%

Proportion of 2006-2007 graduates who accepted in-state residencies

---

Columbia University

COLLEGE OF PHYSICIANS AND SURGEONS

- 630 W. 168th Street, New York, NY 10032
- Private
- Year Founded: 1767
- Tuition, 2007-2008: $45,213
- Enrollment 2007-2008 academic year: 645
- Website: http://www.cumc.columbia.edu/dept/ps
- Specialty ranking: AIDS: 7, drug/alcohol abuse: 2, internal medicine: 10, pediatrics: 10, women's health: 11

3.78 AVERAGE GPA, ENTERING CLASS FALL 2007

11.8 AVERAGE MCAT, ENTERING CLASS FALL 2007

4.1% ACCEPTANCE RATE, ENTERING CLASS FALL 2007

11 2009 U.S. NEWS MEDICAL SCHOOL RANKING (RESEARCH)

58 2009 U.S. NEWS MEDICAL SCHOOL RANKING (PRIMARY CARE)

ADMISSIONS

Admissions phone number: **(212) 305-3595**
Admissions email address: **psadmissions@columbia.edu**
Application website:
   http://www.cumc.columbia.edu/dept/ps
Acceptance rate: **4.1%**
In-state acceptance rate: **N/A**
Out-of-state acceptance rate: **N/A**
Minority acceptance rate: **N/A**
International acceptance rate: **N/A**

Fall 2007 applications and acceptees

	Applied	Interviewed	Accepted	Enrolled
Total:	6,946	1,194	286	155
In-state:	N/A	229	65	47
Out-of-state:	N/A	965	221	108

Profile of admitted students

Average undergraduate grade point average: **3.78**
MCAT averages (scale: 1-15; writing test: J-T):
   Composite score: **11.8**
   Verbal reasoning score: **11.1**, Physical sciences score: **12.1**,
   Biological sciences score: **12.2**, Writing score: **Q**
Proportion with undergraduate majors in: Biological sciences: **37%**, Physical sciences: **25%**, Non-sciences: **26%**, Other health professions: **0%**, Mixed disciplines and other: **12%**
Percentage of students not coming directly from college after graduation: **51%**

Dates and details

The American Medical College Application Service (AMCAS) application is accepted.
School asks for a school-specific application as part of the admissions process.
Oldest MCAT considered for Fall 2009 entry: **2005**
Earliest application date for the 2009-2010 first-year class: **6/1**
Latest application date: **10/15**
Acceptance dates for regular application for the class entering in fall 2009:

   Earliest: **March 1, 2008**
   Latest: **August 25, 2008**
The school considers requests for deferred entrance.
Starting month for the class entering in 2009–2010:
   August
The school doesn't have an Early Decision Plan (EDP).
A personal interview is required for admission.

Undergraduate coursework required

Medical school requires undergraduate work in these subjects: biology, English, organic chemistry, physics, general chemistry.

ADMISSIONS POLICY

(TEXT PROVIDED BY SCHOOL):
For recent classes, the mean grade-point average has been 3.79, and the mean total MCAT score between 35 and 36. Breadth of interests, leadership potential, and participation in extracurricular activities are also looked for. The college seeks diversity of background, geographical and otherwise. No preference is given to state of residence. Members of underrepresented minority groups are encouraged to apply.

COSTS AND FINANCIAL AID

Financial aid phone number: **(212) 305-4100**
Tuition, 2007-2008 academic year: **$45,213**
Room and board: **$11,890**
Percentage of students receiving financial aid in 2007-08: **80%**
Percentage of students receiving: Loans: **67%**, Grants/scholarships: **54%**, Work-study aid: **8%**
Average medical school debt for the Class of 2006: **$120,050**

STUDENT BODY

Fall 2007 full-time enrollment: **645**
Men: **47%**, Women: **53%**, In-state: **31%**, Minorities: **39%**, American Indian: **0.5%**, Asian-American: **17.7%**, African-American: **9.3%**, Hispanic-American: **8.7%**, White: **57.8%**, International: **2.9%**, Unknown: **3.1%**

ACADEMIC PROGRAMS

The school's curriculum very frequently gives first-year students substantial contact with patients.

There are opportunities for first- or second-year students to work in community health clinics.

Program offerings: AIDS, drug/alcohol abuse, family medicine, geriatrics, internal medicine, pediatrics, rural medicine, women's health

Joint degrees awarded: M.D./Ph.D., M.D./M.B.A., M.D./M.P.H.

Total National Institutes of Health (NIH) grants awarded to the medical school and affiliated hospitals: **$362.3 million**

CURRICULUM

(TEXT PROVIDED BY SCHOOL):

The first two years combine basic sciences, introductory clinical experiences, skill-building, and physical diagnosis. The curriculum's depth and strength become evident in Year 3, when students complete clinical clerkships in wide-ranging disciplines in inner-city, suburban, or rural settings. Fourth-year courses re-emphasize the foundation of medical knowledge and critical data appraisal.

FACULTY PROFILE (FALL 2007)

Total teaching faculty: **2,053 (full-time)**, **2,008 (part-time)**
Of full-time faculty, those teaching in basic sciences: **14%**; in clinical programs: **86%**

Of part-time faculty, those teaching in basic sciences: **5%**; in clinical programs: **95%**
Full-time faculty/student ratio: **3.2**

SUPPORT SERVICES

The school offers students these services for dealing with stress: expanded-hour gym access, peer counseling, professional counseling, religious support, support groups.

RESIDENCY PROFILE

Most popular residency and specialty programs chosen by the 2006 and 2007 M.D. graduating classes: anesthesiology, emergency medicine, internal medicine, neurological surgery, orthopaedic surgery, otolaryngology, pediatrics, psychiatry, radiology–diagnostic, surgery–general.

WHERE GRADS GO

30.0%

Proportion of 2005-2007 graduates who entered primary care specialties

45.0%

Proportion of 2006-2007 graduates who accepted in-state residencies

Cornell University

WEILL

- 525 E. 68th Street, New York, NY 10021
- Private
- Year Founded: 1898
- Tuition, 2007-2008: $40,890
- Enrollment 2007-2008 academic year: 410
- Website: http://www.med.cornell.edu
- Specialty ranking: AIDS: 13, drug/alcohol abuse: 18, internal medicine: 15

3.70 AVERAGE GPA, ENTERING CLASS FALL 2007

11.5 AVERAGE MCAT, ENTERING CLASS FALL 2007

4.0% ACCEPTANCE RATE, ENTERING CLASS FALL 2007

18 2009 U.S. NEWS MEDICAL SCHOOL RANKING (RESEARCH)

Unranked 2009 U.S. NEWS MEDICAL SCHOOL RANKING (PRIMARY CARE)

ADMISSIONS

Admissions phone number: (212) 746-1067
Admissions email address: cumc-admissions@med.cornell.edu
Application website:
http://www.med.cornell.edu/education/admissions
Acceptance rate: 4.0%
In-state acceptance rate: 5.0%
Out-of-state acceptance rate: 3.8%
Minority acceptance rate: 4.9%
International acceptance rate: 1.7%

Fall 2007 applications and acceptees

	Applied	Interviewed	Accepted	Enrolled
Total:	5,853	676	237	101
In-state:	1,167	160	58	35
Out-of-state:	4,686	516	179	66

Profile of admitted students

Average undergraduate grade point average: 3.70
MCAT averages (scale: 1-15; writing test: J-T):
Composite score: 11.5
Verbal reasoning score: 11.0, Physical sciences score: 11.6, Biological sciences score: 11.8, Writing score: P
Proportion with undergraduate majors in: Biological sciences: 30%, Physical sciences: 25%, Non-sciences: 23%, Other health professions: 2%, Mixed disciplines and other: 20%
Percentage of students not coming directly from college after graduation: 58%

Dates and details

The American Medical College Application Service (AMCAS) application is accepted.
School asks for a school-specific application as part of the admissions process.
Oldest MCAT considered for Fall 2009 entry: 2005
Earliest application date for the 2009-2010 first-year class: 6/1
Latest application date: 10/15

Acceptance dates for regular application for the class entering in fall 2009:
Earliest: March 1, 2009
Latest: August 28, 2009
The school considers requests for deferred entrance.
Starting month for the class entering in 2009–2010: September
The school has an Early Decision Plan (EDP).
A personal interview is required for admission.

Undergraduate coursework required

Medical school requires undergraduate work in these subjects: biology/zoology, English, organic chemistry, inorganic (general) chemistry, physics.

ADMISSIONS POLICY
(TEXT PROVIDED BY SCHOOL):
Please refer to the website for admissions information.

COSTS AND FINANCIAL AID

Financial aid phone number: (212) 746-1066
Tuition, 2007-2008 academic year: $40,890
Room and board: $10,709
Percentage of students receiving financial aid in 2007-08: 77%
Percentage of students receiving: Loans: 66%, Grants/scholarships: 57%, Work-study aid: 16%
Average medical school debt for the Class of 2006: $98,144

STUDENT BODY

Fall 2007 full-time enrollment: 410
Men: 50%, Women: 50%, In-state: 53%, Minorities: 41%, American Indian: 1.2%, Asian-American: 20.2%, African-American: 10.0%, Hispanic-American: 8.8%, White: 56.1%, International: 1.5%, Unknown: 2.2%

ACADEMIC PROGRAMS

The school's curriculum very frequently gives first-year students substantial contact with patients.

There are opportunities for first- or second-year students to work in community health clinics.

Program offerings: AIDS, drug/alcohol abuse, family medicine, geriatrics, internal medicine, pediatrics, women's health

Joint degrees awarded: M.D./Ph.D., M.D./M.B.A.

Total National Institutes of Health (NIH) grants awarded to the medical school and affiliated hospitals: **$239.7 million**

CURRICULUM
(TEXT PROVIDED BY SCHOOL):
Please see the curriculum section of the website for details.

FACULTY PROFILE (FALL 2007)
Total teaching faculty: **2,183 (full-time)**, **2,061 (part-time)**

Of full-time faculty, those teaching in basic sciences: **12%**; in clinical programs: **88%**

Of part-time faculty, those teaching in basic sciences: **2%**; in clinical programs: **98%**

Full-time faculty/student ratio: **5.3**

SUPPORT SERVICES
The school offers students these services for dealing with stress: professional counseling, religious support, support groups.

RESIDENCY PROFILE
Most popular residency and specialty programs chosen by the 2006 and 2007 M.D. graduating classes: anesthesiology, dermatology, emergency medicine, internal medicine, pediatrics, radiology–diagnostic, surgery–general, urology.

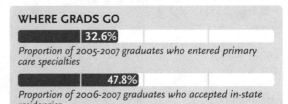

WHERE GRADS GO

32.6%
Proportion of 2005-2007 graduates who entered primary care specialties

47.8%
Proportion of 2006-2007 graduates who accepted in-state residencies

Creighton University

- 2500 California Plaza, Omaha, NE 68178
- Private
- Year Founded: 1878
- Tuition, 2007-2008: $41,778
- Enrollment 2007-2008 academic year: 500
- Website: http://medicine.creighton.edu
- Specialty ranking: N/A

3.67 AVERAGE GPA, ENTERING CLASS FALL 2007

10.0 AVERAGE MCAT, ENTERING CLASS FALL 2007

6.3% ACCEPTANCE RATE, ENTERING CLASS FALL 2007

Unranked 2009 U.S. NEWS MEDICAL SCHOOL RANKING (RESEARCH)

Unranked 2009 U.S. NEWS MEDICAL SCHOOL RANKING (PRIMARY CARE)

ADMISSIONS

Admissions phone number: **(402) 280-2799**
Admissions email address: **medschadm@creighton.edu**
Application website:
http://www2.creighton.edu/medschool/medicine/oma/index.php
Acceptance rate: **6.3%**
In-state acceptance rate: **N/A**
Out-of-state acceptance rate: **N/A**
Minority acceptance rate: **5.9%**
International acceptance rate: **N/A**

Fall 2007 applications and acceptees

	Applied	Interviewed	Accepted	Enrolled
Total:	5,433	593	340	126
In-state:	N/A	N/A	N/A	14
Out-of-state:	N/A	N/A	N/A	112

Profile of admitted students

Average undergraduate grade point average: **3.67**
MCAT averages (scale: 1-15; writing test: J-T):
Composite score: **10.0**
Verbal reasoning score: **9.7**, Physical sciences score: **9.9**,
Biological sciences score: **10.2**, Writing score: **N/A**
Proportion with undergraduate majors in: Biological sciences: **56%**, Physical sciences: **20%**, Non-sciences: **18%**, Other health professions: **2%**, Mixed disciplines and other: **4%**
Percentage of students not coming directly from college after graduation: **10%**

Dates and details

The American Medical College Application Service (AMCAS) application is accepted.
School asks for a school-specific application as part of the admissions process.
Oldest MCAT considered for Fall 2009 entry: **2006**
Earliest application date for the 2009-2010 first-year class: **6/1**
Latest application date: **11/1**

Acceptance dates for regular application for the class entering in fall 2009:
Earliest: **October 15, 2008**
Latest: **N/A**
The school considers requests for deferred entrance.
Starting month for the class entering in 2009–2010: **August**
The school has an Early Decision Plan (EDP).
A personal interview is required for admission.

Undergraduate coursework required

Medical school requires undergraduate work in these subjects: biology, English, organic chemistry, inorganic (general) chemistry, physics.

ADMISSIONS POLICY
(TEXT PROVIDED BY SCHOOL):

Mandatory MCAT and three years of accredited college work. Preference to baccalaureate degree holders. Up to 27 semester hours of credit under the College-Level Examination Program or Advanced Placement. Consideration given to significant humanity service, medical experience, intellectual ability, emotional maturity, honesty, and motivation. Letters of recommendation important. No restrictions on race, religion, sex, age, disability, ethnicity.

COSTS AND FINANCIAL AID

Financial aid phone number: **(402) 280-2666**
Tuition, 2007-2008 academic year: **$41,778**
Room and board: **$13,500**
Percentage of students receiving financial aid in 2007-08: **94%**
Percentage of students receiving: Loans: **88%**, Grants/scholarships: **27%**, Work-study aid: **0%**
Average medical school debt for the Class of 2006: **$155,871**

STUDENT BODY

Fall 2007 full-time enrollment: **500**

Men: 53%, Women: 47%, In-state: 13%, Minorities: 17%, American Indian: 1.4%, Asian-American: 8.8%, African-American: 2.6%, Hispanic-American: 6.8%, White: 80.2%, International: 0.2%, Unknown: N/A

ACADEMIC PROGRAMS

The school's curriculum occasionally gives first-year students substantial contact with patients.

There are opportunities for first- or second-year students to work in community health clinics.

Program offerings: drug/alcohol abuse, family medicine, internal medicine, pediatrics, rural medicine, women's health

Joint degrees awarded: M.D./Ph.D.

Total National Institutes of Health (NIH) grants awarded to the medical school and affiliated hospitals: $11.6 million

CURRICULUM

(TEXT PROVIDED BY SCHOOL):

Integrated curriculum that incorporates basic clinical science with clinical experience. Curriculum integrates ethical and societal issues. Instructional and methodology utilizes case-based, small-group sessions and computer-assisted instruction. A close faculty-student relationship. Competency-based evaluation used in all components. Students graded on pass/fail/honors system.

FACULTY PROFILE (FALL 2007)

Total teaching faculty: 286 (full-time), 17 (part-time)

Of full-time faculty, those teaching in basic sciences: 24%; in clinical programs: 76%

Of part-time faculty, those teaching in basic sciences: 18%; in clinical programs: 82%

Full-time faculty/student ratio: 0.6

SUPPORT SERVICES

The school offers students these services for dealing with stress: expanded-hour gym access, peer counseling, professional counseling, religious support, support groups.

RESIDENCY PROFILE

Most popular residency and specialty programs chosen by the 2006 and 2007 M.D. graduating classes: anesthesiology, emergency medicine, family practice, internal medicine, obstetrics and gynecology, pediatrics, psychiatry, radiology–diagnostic, surgery–general.

WHERE GRADS GO

39.0%

Proportion of 2005-2007 graduates who entered primary care specialties

21.0%

Proportion of 2006-2007 graduates who accepted in-state residencies

Dartmouth Medical School

- 3 Rope Ferry Road, Hanover, NH 03755-1404
- Private
- **Year Founded:** 1797
- **Tuition, 2007-2008:** $40,675
- **Enrollment 2007-2008 academic year:** 316
- **Website:** http://dms.dartmouth.edu
- **Specialty ranking:** rural medicine: 28

3.74 AVERAGE GPA, ENTERING CLASS FALL 2007

11.1 AVERAGE MCAT, ENTERING CLASS FALL 2007

5.6% ACCEPTANCE RATE, ENTERING CLASS FALL 2007

31 2009 U.S. NEWS MEDICAL SCHOOL RANKING (RESEARCH)

13 2009 U.S. NEWS MEDICAL SCHOOL RANKING (PRIMARY CARE)

ADMISSIONS

Admissions phone number: **(603) 650-1505**
Admissions email address:
   dms.admissions@dartmouth.edu
Application website:
   http://dms.dartmouth.edu/admissions/instructions
Acceptance rate: **5.6%**
In-state acceptance rate: **12.1%**
Out-of-state acceptance rate: **5.5%**
Minority acceptance rate: **4.7%**
International acceptance rate: **N/A**

Fall 2007 applications and acceptees

	Applied	Interviewed	Accepted	Enrolled
Total:	4,181	680	233	74
In-state:	66	31	8	5
Out-of-state:	4,115	649	225	69

Profile of admitted students

Average undergraduate grade point average: **3.74**
MCAT averages (scale: 1-15; writing test: J-T):
   Composite score: **11.1**
   Verbal reasoning score: **10.5**, Physical sciences score:
   11.3, Biological sciences score: **11.6**, Writing score: **Q**
Proportion with undergraduate majors in: Biological
   sciences: **56%**, Physical sciences: **19%**, Non-sciences:
   11%, Other health professions: **0%**, Mixed disciplines
   and other: **14%**
Percentage of students not coming directly from college
   after graduation: **N/A**

Dates and details

The American Medical College Application Service
   (AMCAS) application is accepted.
School asks for a school-specific application as part of the
   admissions process.
Oldest MCAT considered for Fall 2009 entry: **2006**
Earliest application date for the 2009-2010 first-year class:
   6/1
Latest application date: **11/1**

Acceptance dates for regular application for the class
   entering in fall 2009:
   Earliest: **October 15, 2008**
   Latest: **August 17, 2009**
The school considers requests for deferred entrance.
Starting month for the class entering in 2009–2010:
   August
The school doesn't have an Early Decision Plan (EDP).
A personal interview is required for admission.

Undergraduate coursework required

Medical school requires undergraduate work in these subjects: biology, organic chemistry, physics, calculus, general
chemistry.

ADMISSIONS POLICY
(TEXT PROVIDED BY SCHOOL):

Admission requirements include: one year (eight semester
hours) each of General Chemistry, Organic Chemistry,
Biology, and Physics. A half-year of Calculus. Facility in
written and spoken English. Equivalent of at least three
years' college work at an American or Canadian post-sec-
ondary institution. A semester of Biochemistry is encouraged but not required. Submission of MCAT scores is
preferred.

COSTS AND FINANCIAL AID

Financial aid phone number: **(603) 650-1919**
Tuition, 2007-2008 academic year: **$40,675**
Room and board: **$9,750**
Percentage of students receiving financial aid in 2007-08:
   80%
Percentage of students receiving: Loans: **80%**,
   Grants/scholarships: **52%**, Work-study aid: **0%**
Average medical school debt for the Class of 2006:
   $110,343

STUDENT BODY

Fall 2007 full-time enrollment: **316**

Men: **48%**, Women: **52%**, In-state: **8%**, Minorities: **24%**,
American Indian: **0.0%**, Asian-American: **17.4%**,
African-American: **2.2%**, Hispanic-American: **4.1%**,
White: **63.6%**, International: **9.5%**, Unknown: **3.2%**

ACADEMIC PROGRAMS

The school's curriculum frequently gives first-year students
substantial contact with patients.
There are opportunities for first- or second-year students to
work in community health clinics.
Program offerings: AIDS, drug/alcohol abuse, family
medicine, geriatrics, internal medicine, pediatrics, rural
medicine, women's health
Joint degrees awarded: M.D./Ph.D., M.D./M.B.A.,
M.D./M.P.H.
Total National Institutes of Health (NIH) grants awarded to
the medical school and affiliated hospitals: **$87.9 million**

CURRICULUM

(TEXT PROVIDED BY SCHOOL):
Year 1: introduction to basic biomedical sciences; work with
community clinicians to begin developing clinical skills.
Year 2: interdisciplinary pathophysiology program; continued clinical study. Year 3: required eight-week clerkships in
the six major clinical disciplines. Year 4: two required four-
week clerkships; advanced subinternship in field of choice;
up to five months of clinical and other electives and four
short courses.

FACULTY PROFILE (FALL 2007)

Total teaching faculty: **842 (full-time)**, **1,194 (part-time)**
Of full-time faculty, those teaching in basic sciences: **11%**;
in clinical programs: **89%**

Of part-time faculty, those teaching in basic sciences: **4%**;
in clinical programs: **96%**
Full-time faculty/student ratio: **2.7**

SUPPORT SERVICES

The school offers students these services for dealing with
stress: expanded-hour gym access, peer counseling, professional counseling, support groups.

RESIDENCY PROFILE

Most popular residency and specialty programs chosen by
the 2006 and 2007 M.D. graduating classes: anesthesiology, internal medicine, obstetrics and gynecology,
orthopaedic surgery, pediatrics, radiology–diagnostic, surgery–general.

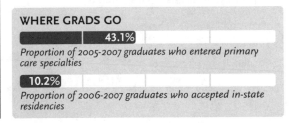

WHERE GRADS GO

43.1%

*Proportion of 2005-2007 graduates who entered primary
care specialties*

10.2%

*Proportion of 2006-2007 graduates who accepted in-state
residencies*

Drexel University

- 2900 Queen Lane, Philadelphia, PA 19129
- Private
- Year Founded: 1848
- Tuition, 2007-2008: $42,030
- Enrollment 2007-2008 academic year: 1,070
- Website: http://www.drexelmed.edu
- Specialty ranking: N/A

3.53 AVERAGE GPA, ENTERING CLASS FALL 2007

10.3 AVERAGE MCAT, ENTERING CLASS FALL 2007

8.8% ACCEPTANCE RATE, ENTERING CLASS FALL 2007

Unranked 2009 U.S. NEWS MEDICAL SCHOOL RANKING (RESEARCH)

Unranked 2009 U.S. NEWS MEDICAL SCHOOL RANKING (PRIMARY CARE)

ADMISSIONS

Admissions phone number: **(215) 991-8202**
Admissions email address: **Medadmis@drexel.edu**
Application website:
  http://www.aamc.org/students/start.htm
Acceptance rate: **8.8%**
In-state acceptance rate: **28.9%**
Out-of-state acceptance rate: **6.6%**
Minority acceptance rate: **5.1%**
International acceptance rate: **7.1%**

Fall 2007 applications and acceptees

	Applied	Interviewed	Accepted	Enrolled
Total:	8,073	1,759	711	280
In-state:	790	391	228	93
Out-of-state:	7,283	1,368	483	187

Profile of admitted students

Average undergraduate grade point average: **3.53**
MCAT averages (scale: 1-15; writing test: J-T):
  Composite score: **10.3**
  Verbal reasoning score: **9.8**, Physical sciences score: **10.2**, Biological sciences score: **10.5**, Writing score: **Q**
Proportion with undergraduate majors in: Biological sciences: **N/A**, Physical sciences: **N/A**, Non-sciences: **N/A**, Other health professions: **N/A**, Mixed disciplines and other: **N/A**
Percentage of students not coming directly from college after graduation: **27%**

Dates and details

The American Medical College Application Service (AMCAS) application is accepted.
School asks for a school-specific application as part of the admissions process.
Oldest MCAT considered for Fall 2009 entry: **2006**
Earliest application date for the 2009-2010 first-year class: **6/1**
Latest application date: **12/15**
Acceptance dates for regular application for the class entering in fall 2009:

Earliest: **October 15, 2008**
Latest: **August 3, 2009**
The school considers requests for deferred entrance.
Starting month for the class entering in 2009–2010: **August**
The school has an Early Decision Plan (EDP).
A personal interview is required for admission.

Undergraduate coursework required

Medical school requires undergraduate work in these subjects: biology, English, organic chemistry, inorganic (general) chemistry, physics, general chemistry.

ADMISSIONS POLICY

(TEXT PROVIDED BY SCHOOL):
Drexel University College of Medicine seeks highly qualified and motivated students who demonstrate the desire, intelligence, integrity, sound motivation, and emotional maturity to become excellent physicians. Because of the school's unique background, nontraditional applicants are encouraged. The school is committed to a diverse student body.

COSTS AND FINANCIAL AID

Financial aid phone number: **(215) 991-8210**
Tuition, 2007-2008 academic year: **$42,030**
Room and board: **$14,960**
Percentage of students receiving financial aid in 2007-08: **61%**
Percentage of students receiving: Loans: **60%**, Grants/scholarships: **23%**, Work-study aid: **17%**
Average medical school debt for the Class of 2006: **$182,684**

STUDENT BODY

Fall 2007 full-time enrollment: **1,070**
Men: **51%**, Women: **49%**, In-state: **30%**, Minorities: **43%**, American Indian: **0.6%**, Asian-American: **34.8%**, African-American: **3.6%**, Hispanic-American: **4.2%**, White: **50.5%**, International: **0.0%**, Unknown: **6.4%**

ACADEMIC PROGRAMS

The school's curriculum frequently gives first-year students substantial contact with patients.

There are opportunities for first- or second-year students to work in community health clinics.

Program offerings: AIDS, drug/alcohol abuse, family medicine, geriatrics, internal medicine, pediatrics, women's health

Joint degrees awarded: M.D./Ph.D., M.D./M.B.A., M.D./M.P.H.

Total National Institutes of Health (NIH) grants awarded to the medical school and affiliated hospitals: **N/A**

CURRICULUM
(TEXT PROVIDED BY SCHOOL):

Medical students are trained to consider each patient's case and needs in a comprehensive integrated manner, taking into account many more factors than the presenting physiological condition. The medical college is dedicated to preparing physician healers

FACULTY PROFILE (FALL 2007)

Total teaching faculty: **569 (full-time)**, **60 (part-time)**
Of full-time faculty, those teaching in basic sciences: **19%**; in clinical programs: **81%**

Of part-time faculty, those teaching in basic sciences: **12%**; in clinical programs: **88%**
Full-time faculty/student ratio: **0.5**

SUPPORT SERVICES

The school offers students these services for dealing with stress: expanded-hour gym access, peer counseling, professional counseling, religious support, support groups.

RESIDENCY PROFILE

Most popular residency and specialty programs chosen by the 2006 and 2007 M.D. graduating classes: anesthesiology, emergency medicine, family practice, internal medicine, obstetrics and gynecology, pediatrics, psychiatry, radiology–diagnostic, surgery–general.

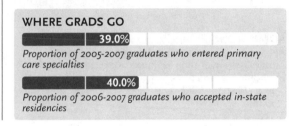

WHERE GRADS GO

39.0%
Proportion of 2005-2007 graduates who entered primary care specialties

40.0%
Proportion of 2006-2007 graduates who accepted in-state residencies

Duke University

- **DUMC, Durham, NC 27710**
- **Private**
- **Year Founded:** 1930
- **Tuition, 2007-2008:** $41,817
- **Enrollment 2007-2008 academic year:** 404
- **Website:** http://dukemed.duke.edu
- **Specialty ranking:** AIDS: 8, drug/alcohol abuse: 18, family medicine: 9, geriatrics: 3, internal medicine: 5, pediatrics: 16, women's health: 11

3.74	AVERAGE GPA, ENTERING CLASS FALL 2007
11.5	AVERAGE MCAT, ENTERING CLASS FALL 2007
3.7%	ACCEPTANCE RATE, ENTERING CLASS FALL 2007
6	2009 U.S. NEWS MEDICAL SCHOOL RANKING (RESEARCH)
41	2009 U.S. NEWS MEDICAL SCHOOL RANKING (PRIMARY CARE)

ADMISSIONS

Admissions phone number: **(919) 684-2985**
Admissions email address: **medadm@mc.duke.edu**
Application website:
　http://dukemed.duke.edu/AdmissionsFinancialAid/index.cfm
Acceptance rate: **3.7%**
In-state acceptance rate: **6.8%**
Out-of-state acceptance rate: **3.4%**
Minority acceptance rate: **6.4%**
International acceptance rate: **1.3%**

Fall 2007 applications and acceptees

	Applied	Interviewed	Accepted	Enrolled
Total:	5,309	739	196	101
In-state:	397	91	27	16
Out-of-state:	4,912	648	169	85

Profile of admitted students

Average undergraduate grade point average: **3.74**
MCAT averages (scale: 1-15; writing test: J-T):
　Composite score: **11.5**
　Verbal reasoning score: **10.7**, Physical sciences score: **11.8**, Biological sciences score: **12.0**, Writing score: **P**
Proportion with undergraduate majors in: Biological sciences: **46%**, Physical sciences: **31%**, Non-sciences: **16%**, Other health professions: **0%**, Mixed disciplines and other: **7%**
Percentage of students not coming directly from college after graduation: **45%**

Dates and details

The American Medical College Application Service (AMCAS) application is accepted.
School asks for a school-specific application as part of the admissions process.
Oldest MCAT considered for Fall 2009 entry: **2004**
Earliest application date for the 2009-2010 first-year class: **6/15**
Latest application date: **1/12**

Acceptance dates for regular application for the class entering in fall 2009:
　Earliest: **January 8, 2008**
　Latest: **December 20, 2008**
The school considers requests for deferred entrance.
Starting month for the class entering in 2009–2010:
　August
The school doesn't have an Early Decision Plan (EDP).
A personal interview is required for admission.

Undergraduate coursework required

Medical school requires undergraduate work in these subjects: biology, English, organic chemistry, inorganic (general) chemistry, physics, mathematics, demonstration of writing skills, calculus, general chemistry.

ADMISSIONS POLICY

(TEXT PROVIDED BY SCHOOL):
Maturity, strong study habits, intelligence, character, integrity, and professionalism are essential qualifications for admission. Beyond these, premedical students should strive for an education that develops abilities to observe critically, think analytically, and work independently.

COSTS AND FINANCIAL AID

Financial aid phone number: **(919) 684-6649**
Tuition, 2007-2008 academic year: **$41,817**
Room and board: **$12,240**
Percentage of students receiving financial aid in 2007-08: **86%**
Percentage of students receiving: Loans: **67%**, Grants/scholarships: **73%**, Work-study aid: **0%**
Average medical school debt for the Class of 2006: **$89,335**

STUDENT BODY

Fall 2007 full-time enrollment: **404**
Men: **52%**, Women: **48%**, In-state: **13%**, Minorities: **50%**, American Indian: **1.5%**, Asian-American: **19.3%**, African-American: **14.9%**, Hispanic-American: **2.2%**, White: **49.0%**, International: **6.9%**, Unknown: **6.2%**

ACADEMIC PROGRAMS

The school's curriculum frequently gives first-year students substantial contact with patients.

There are opportunities for first- or second-year students to work in community health clinics.

Program offerings: AIDS, drug/alcohol abuse, family medicine, geriatrics, internal medicine, pediatrics, rural medicine, women's health

Joint degrees awarded: M.D./Ph.D., M.D./M.B.A., M.D./M.P.H., M.D./J.D., M.D./M.S., M.D./M.A.

Total National Institutes of Health (NIH) grants awarded to the medical school and affiliated hospitals: **$369.4 million**

CURRICULUM

(TEXT PROVIDED BY SCHOOL):
Duke University School of Medicine offers an educational program unlike any other in the country. The basic sciences are taught in one year. The core clerkships are completed in the second year. The third year is devoted to scholarly investigation through one-on-one mentored research or the pursuit of a master's or Ph.D. degree. Elective clinical rotations are fulfilled in the fourth year.

FACULTY PROFILE (FALL 2007)

Total teaching faculty: **1,665 (full-time), 28 (part-time)**
Of full-time faculty, those teaching in basic sciences: **12%**; in clinical programs: **88%**

Of part-time faculty, those teaching in basic sciences: **4%**; in clinical programs: **96%**
Full-time faculty/student ratio: **4.1**

SUPPORT SERVICES

The school offers students these services for dealing with stress: expanded-hour gym access, peer counseling, professional counseling, religious support, support groups.

RESIDENCY PROFILE

Most popular residency and specialty programs chosen by the 2006 and 2007 M.D. graduating classes: anesthesiology, emergency medicine, internal medicine, ophthalmology, orthopaedic surgery, pediatrics, psychiatry, radiology–diagnostic, radiation oncology, surgery–general.

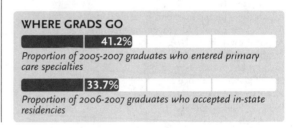

WHERE GRADS GO

41.2%
Proportion of 2005-2007 graduates who entered primary care specialties

33.7%
Proportion of 2006-2007 graduates who accepted in-state residencies

East Carolina University

BRODY

- 600 Moye Boulevard, Greenville, NC 27834
- Public
- **Year Founded:** 1975
- **Tuition, 2007-2008:** In-state: $11,056; Out-of-state: $36,075
- **Enrollment 2007-2008 academic year:** 293
- **Website:** http://www.ecu.edu/bsomadmissions
- **Specialty ranking:** family medicine: 13, rural medicine: 6

3.50	AVERAGE GPA, ENTERING CLASS FALL 2007
9.1	AVERAGE MCAT, ENTERING CLASS FALL 2007
12.9%	ACCEPTANCE RATE, ENTERING CLASS FALL 2007
Unranked	2009 U.S. NEWS MEDICAL SCHOOL RANKING (RESEARCH)
17	2009 U.S. NEWS MEDICAL SCHOOL RANKING (PRIMARY CARE)

ADMISSIONS

Admissions phone number: **(252) 744-2202**
Admissions email address: **somadmissions@ecu.edu**
Application website: **N/A**
Acceptance rate: **12.9%**
In-state acceptance rate: **12.9%**
Out-of-state acceptance rate: **N/A**
Minority acceptance rate: **12.7%**
International acceptance rate: **N/A**

Fall 2007 applications and acceptees

	Applied	Interviewed	Accepted	Enrolled
Total:	815	393	105	73
In-state:	815	393	105	73
Out-of-state:	N/A	N/A	N/A	N/A

Profile of admitted students

Average undergraduate grade point average: **3.50**
MCAT averages (scale: 1-15; writing test: J-T):
  Composite score: **9.1**
  Verbal reasoning score: **8.9**, Physical sciences score: **8.3**,
  Biological sciences score: **9.4**, Writing score: **P**
Proportion with undergraduate majors in: Biological
  sciences: **29%**, Physical sciences: **18%**, Non-sciences:
  12%, Other health professions: **5%**, Mixed disciplines
  and other: **36%**
Percentage of students not coming directly from college
  after graduation: **43%**

Dates and details

The American Medical College Application Service
  (AMCAS) application is accepted.
School asks for a school-specific application as part of the
  admissions process.
Oldest MCAT considered for Fall 2009 entry: **2006**
Earliest application date for the 2009-2010 first-year class:
  6/1
Latest application date: **11/15**
Acceptance dates for regular application for the class
  entering in fall 2009:

Earliest: **October 15, 2008**
Latest: **August 7, 2009**
The school doesn't consider requests for deferred entrance.
Starting month for the class entering in 2009–2010:
  August
The school has an Early Decision Plan (EDP).
A personal interview is required for admission.

Undergraduate coursework required

Medical school requires undergraduate work in these subjects: biology, biology/zoology, English, organic chemistry,
inorganic (general) chemistry, physics.

ADMISSIONS POLICY

(TEXT PROVIDED BY SCHOOL):
Factors encompass the intellectual, personal, and social
development of applicants. A variety of data is used (grades;
MCAT performance or other standardized tests; personal
and professional experiences; evaluations from faculty
members, etc; interviews, etc.). The BSOM is a state-sup-
ported school; very strong preference is given to qualified
residents of North Carolina.

COSTS AND FINANCIAL AID

Financial aid phone number: **(252) 744-2278**
Tuition, 2007-2008 academic year: **In-state: $11,056; Out-
  of-state: $36,075**
Room and board: **$11,019**
Percentage of students receiving financial aid in 2007-08:
  93%
Percentage of students receiving: Loans: **89%**,
  Grants/scholarships: **48%**, Work-study aid: **0%**
Average medical school debt for the Class of 2006: **$81,212**

STUDENT BODY

Fall 2007 full-time enrollment: **293**
Men: **52%**, Women: **48%**, In-state: **100%**, Minorities: **29%**,
  American Indian: **3.1%**, Asian-American: **8.5%**, African-
  American: **14.3%**, Hispanic-American: **4.1%**, White:
  69.6%, International: **0.0%**, Unknown: **0.3%**

ACADEMIC PROGRAMS

The school's curriculum very frequently gives first-year students substantial contact with patients.

There are opportunities for first- or second-year students to work in community health clinics.

Program offerings: drug/alcohol abuse, family medicine, geriatrics, internal medicine, pediatrics, rural medicine, women's health

Joint degrees awarded: M.D./Ph.D., M.D./M.B.A., M.D./M.P.H.

Total National Institutes of Health (NIH) grants awarded to the medical school and affiliated hospitals: **$5.3 million**

CURRICULUM
(TEXT PROVIDED BY SCHOOL):

The curriculum provides a logical integration of basic science and clinical science knowledge over the four-year span. Early experience in patient-care settings is achieved through preceptorships throughout the state and through contact with both standardized and clinical patients in the first two years. Innovative teaching methods are employed.

FACULTY PROFILE (FALL 2007)

Total teaching faculty: **414 (full-time)**, **63 (part-time)**
Of full-time faculty, those teaching in basic sciences: **20%**; in clinical programs: **80%**

Of part-time faculty, those teaching in basic sciences: **14%**; in clinical programs: **86%**
Full-time faculty/student ratio: **1.4**

SUPPORT SERVICES

The school offers students these services for dealing with stress: expanded-hour gym access, peer counseling, professional counseling, religious support, support groups.

RESIDENCY PROFILE

Most popular residency and specialty programs chosen by the 2006 and 2007 M.D. graduating classes: emergency medicine, family practice, internal medicine, internal medicine–pediatrics, obstetrics and gynecology, pediatrics, surgery–general, internal medicine/pediatrics.

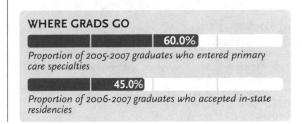

WHERE GRADS GO

60.0%

Proportion of 2005-2007 graduates who entered primary care specialties

45.0%

Proportion of 2006-2007 graduates who accepted in-state residencies

Eastern Virginia Medical School

- 721 Fairfax Avenue, PO Box 1980, Norfolk, VA 23501-1980
- Public
- **Year Founded:** 1973
- **Tuition, 2007-2008:** In-state: $24,204; Out-of-state: $43,400
- **Enrollment 2007-2008 academic year:** 447
- **Website:** http://www.evms.edu
- **Specialty ranking:** N/A

3.49 AVERAGE GPA, ENTERING CLASS FALL 2007

N/A AVERAGE MCAT, ENTERING CLASS FALL 2007

6.2% ACCEPTANCE RATE, ENTERING CLASS FALL 2007

Unranked 2009 U.S. NEWS MEDICAL SCHOOL RANKING (RESEARCH)

Unranked 2009 U.S. NEWS MEDICAL SCHOOL RANKING (PRIMARY CARE)

ADMISSIONS

Admissions phone number: **(757) 446-5812**
Admissions email address: **nanezkf@evms.edu**
Application website: **http://www.evms.edu/admissions**
Acceptance rate: **6.2%**
In-state acceptance rate: **26.5%**
Out-of-state acceptance rate: **2.6%**
Minority acceptance rate: **N/A**
International acceptance rate: **N/A**

Fall 2007 applications and acceptees

	Applied	Interviewed	Accepted	Enrolled
Total:	4,895	624	305	115
In-state:	741	336	196	73
Out-of-state:	4,154	288	109	42

Profile of admitted students

Average undergraduate grade point average: **3.49**
MCAT averages (scale: 1-15; writing test: J-T):
  Composite score: **N/A**
  Verbal reasoning score: **9.9**, Physical sciences score: **9.9**,
  Biological sciences score: **10.3**, Writing score: **N/A**
Proportion with undergraduate majors in: Biological
  sciences: **19%**, Physical sciences: **48%**, Non-sciences:
  33%, Other health professions: **0%**, Mixed disciplines
  and other: **0%**
Percentage of students not coming directly from college
  after graduation: **N/A**

Dates and details

The American Medical College Application Service
  (AMCAS) application is accepted.
School asks for a school-specific application as part of the
  admissions process.
Oldest MCAT considered for Fall 2009 entry: **N/A**
Earliest application date for the 2009-2010 first-year class:
  N/A
Latest application date: **N/A**
Acceptance dates for regular application for the class
  entering in fall 2009:

Earliest: **October 15, 2008**
Latest: **August 10, 2009**
The school considers requests for deferred entrance.
Starting month for the class entering in 2009–2010:
  August
The school has an Early Decision Plan (EDP).
A personal interview is required for admission.

Undergraduate coursework required

Medical school requires undergraduate work in these subjects: biology, organic chemistry, inorganic (general) chemistry, physics.

ADMISSIONS POLICY

(TEXT PROVIDED BY SCHOOL):
EVMS requires academic excellence of those students
admitted to the medical school. Academic ability is gauged
by performance in undergraduate courses and scores on the
MCAT. Applicants must demonstrate an understanding of
the role of the physician and an appreciation for the interactive and caring nature of the practitioner. Preference to
applicants from Virginia, especially Hampton Roads.

COSTS AND FINANCIAL AID

Financial aid phone number: **(757) 446-5814**
Tuition, 2007-2008 academic year: **In-state: $24,204; Out-
  of-state: $43,400**
Room and board: **N/A**
Percentage of students receiving financial aid in 2007-08:
  90%
Percentage of students receiving: Loans: **85%**,
  Grants/scholarships: **66%**, Work-study aid: **9%**
Average medical school debt for the Class of 2006:
  $134,179

STUDENT BODY

Fall 2007 full-time enrollment: **447**
Men: **50%**, Women: **50%**, In-state: **67%**, Minorities: **6%**,
  American Indian: **N/A**, Asian-American: **N/A**, African-
  American: **N/A**, Hispanic-American: **N/A**, White: **N/A**,
  International: **N/A**, Unknown: **N/A**

ACADEMIC PROGRAMS

The school's curriculum very frequently gives first-year students substantial contact with patients.

There are opportunities for first- or second-year students to work in community health clinics.

Program offerings: AIDS, drug/alcohol abuse, family medicine, geriatrics, internal medicine, pediatrics, rural medicine

Joint degrees awarded: M.D./M.P.H.

Total National Institutes of Health (NIH) grants awarded to the medical school and affiliated hospitals: **N/A**

CURRICULUM
(TEXT PROVIDED BY SCHOOL):

Provide a firm foundation in medical sciences and clinical skills; teach medical problem solving using the best available evidence; cultivate independent lifelong learning and scholarship; develop an appreciation for the social and economic responsibilities of the medical profession; encourage self-awareness and communication skills; emphasize human values in the practice of medicine.

FACULTY PROFILE (FALL 2007)

Total teaching faculty: **N/A (full-time)**, **N/A (part-time)**
Of full-time faculty, those teaching in basic sciences: **N/A**; in clinical programs: **N/A**

Of part-time faculty, those teaching in basic sciences: **N/A**; in clinical programs: **N/A**
Full-time faculty/student ratio: **N/A**

SUPPORT SERVICES

The school offers students these services for dealing with stress: expanded-hour gym access, peer counseling, professional counseling, religious support.

RESIDENCY PROFILE

Most popular residency and specialty programs chosen by the 2006 and 2007 M.D. graduating classes: emergency medicine, family practice, internal medicine, obstetrics and gynecology, orthopaedic surgery, pathology–anatomic and clinical, pediatrics, psychiatry, surgery–general.

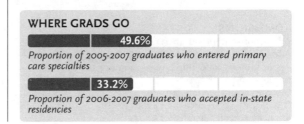

WHERE GRADS GO

49.6%
Proportion of 2005-2007 graduates who entered primary care specialties

33.2%
Proportion of 2006-2007 graduates who accepted in-state residencies

East Tennessee State University

QUILLEN

- PO Box 70694, Johnson City, TN 37614
- Public
- Year Founded: 1974
- Tuition, 2007-2008: In-state: $21,043; Out-of-state: $41,993
- Enrollment 2007-2008 academic year: 240
- Website: http://com.etsu.edu
- Specialty ranking: family medicine: 12, rural medicine: 4

3.64	AVERAGE GPA, ENTERING CLASS FALL 2007
9.4	AVERAGE MCAT, ENTERING CLASS FALL 2007
8.8%	ACCEPTANCE RATE, ENTERING CLASS FALL 2007
Unranked	2009 U.S. NEWS MEDICAL SCHOOL RANKING (RESEARCH)
Unranked	2009 U.S. NEWS MEDICAL SCHOOL RANKING (PRIMARY CARE)

ADMISSIONS

Admissions phone number: **(423) 439-2033**
Admissions email address: **sacom@etsu.edu**
Application website: **http://www.aamc.org**
Acceptance rate: **8.8%**
In-state acceptance rate: **20.0%**
Out-of-state acceptance rate: **1.8%**
Minority acceptance rate: **7.1%**
International acceptance rate: **N/A**

Fall 2007 applications and acceptees

	Applied	Interviewed	Accepted	Enrolled
Total:	1,449	253	127	60
In-state:	555	196	111	55
Out-of-state:	894	57	16	5

Profile of admitted students

Average undergraduate grade point average: **3.64**
MCAT averages (scale: 1-15; writing test: J-T):
   Composite score: **9.4**
   Verbal reasoning score: **9.5**, Physical sciences score: **9.1**,
   Biological sciences score: **9.5**, Writing score: **O**
Proportion with undergraduate majors in: Biological
   sciences: **48%**, Physical sciences: **27%**, Non-sciences:
   15%, Other health professions: **3%**, Mixed disciplines
   and other: **7%**
Percentage of students not coming directly from college
   after graduation: **27%**

Dates and details

The American Medical College Application Service
   (AMCAS) application is accepted.
School asks for a school-specific application as part of the
   admissions process.
Oldest MCAT considered for Fall 2009 entry: **2006**
Earliest application date for the 2009-2010 first-year class:
   6/1
Latest application date: **11/15**
Acceptance dates for regular application for the class
   entering in fall 2009:

Earliest: **October 15, 2008**
   Latest: **N/A**
The school considers requests for deferred entrance.
Starting month for the class entering in 2009–2010:
   August
The school has an Early Decision Plan (EDP).
A personal interview is required for admission.

Undergraduate coursework required

Medical school requires undergraduate work in these subjects: biology/zoology, English, organic chemistry, inorganic
(general) chemistry, physics.

ADMISSIONS POLICY

(TEXT PROVIDED BY SCHOOL):
Quillen COM evaluates applicants on the basis of demonstrated academic achievement, MCAT scores, letters of recommendation, pertinent extracurricular work and research
experience, nonscholastic accomplishment, motivation for
the study and practice of medicine, and interest in a primary care practice in a rural or underserved area. For more
information, please visit the website.

COSTS AND FINANCIAL AID

Financial aid phone number: **(423) 439-2035**
Tuition, 2007-2008 academic year: **In-state: $21,043; Out-
   of-state: $41,993**
Room and board: **$12,325**
Percentage of students receiving financial aid in 2007-08:
   92%
Percentage of students receiving: Loans: **85%**,
   Grants/scholarships: **40%**, Work-study aid: **0%**
Average medical school debt for the Class of 2006:
   $108,073

STUDENT BODY

Fall 2007 full-time enrollment: **240**
Men: **50%**, Women: **50%**, In-state: **91%**, Minorities: **14%**,
   American Indian: **0.8%**, Asian-American: **6.7%**, African-
   American: **6.3%**, Hispanic-American: **0.4%**, White:
   85.8%, International: **0.0%**, Unknown: **0.0%**

ACADEMIC PROGRAMS

The school's curriculum frequently gives first-year students substantial contact with patients.

There are opportunities for first- or second-year students to work in community health clinics.

Program offerings: AIDS, drug/alcohol abuse, family medicine, geriatrics, internal medicine, pediatrics, rural medicine, women's health

Joint degrees awarded: N/A

Total National Institutes of Health (NIH) grants awarded to the medical school and affiliated hospitals: **N/A**

CURRICULUM
(TEXT PROVIDED BY SCHOOL):

The College of Medicine curriculum is designed to assist students in gaining the fundamental knowledge, attitude, skills, and practice principles required to enter residency training while encouraging the acquisition of lifelong habits of intellectual activity, independent thought, critical evaluation, and professionalism. For more information, please visit the Quillen website.

FACULTY PROFILE (FALL 2007)

Total teaching faculty: 257 (full-time), 42 (part-time)
Of full-time faculty, those teaching in basic sciences: 24%; in clinical programs: 76%

Of part-time faculty, those teaching in basic sciences: 2%; in clinical programs: 98%

Full-time faculty/student ratio: 1.1

SUPPORT SERVICES

The school offers students these services for dealing with stress: expanded-hour gym access, peer counseling, professional counseling, religious support.

RESIDENCY PROFILE

Most popular residency and specialty programs chosen by the 2006 and 2007 M.D. graduating classes: anesthesiology, emergency medicine, family practice, internal medicine, obstetrics and gynecology, pathology–anatomic and clinical, pediatrics, psychiatry, radiology–diagnostic, surgery–general.

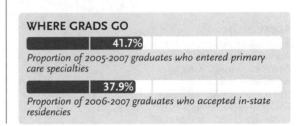

WHERE GRADS GO

41.7%

Proportion of 2005-2007 graduates who entered primary care specialties

37.9%

Proportion of 2006-2007 graduates who accepted in-state residencies

Emory University

- 1648 Pierce Drive, Atlanta, GA 30322-1053
- Private
- Year Founded: 1854
- Tuition, 2007-2008: $39,976
- Enrollment 2007-2008 academic year: 480
- Website: http://www.med.emory.edu
- Specialty ranking: AIDS: 14, internal medicine: 19

3.70 AVERAGE GPA, ENTERING CLASS FALL 2007

11.5 AVERAGE MCAT, ENTERING CLASS FALL 2007

8.4% ACCEPTANCE RATE, ENTERING CLASS FALL 2007

20 2009 U.S. NEWS MEDICAL SCHOOL RANKING (RESEARCH)

48 2009 U.S. NEWS MEDICAL SCHOOL RANKING (PRIMARY CARE)

ADMISSIONS

Admissions phone number: **(404) 727-5660**
Admissions email address: **medadmiss@emory.edu**
Application website: **N/A**
Acceptance rate: **8.4%**
In-state acceptance rate: **16.7%**
Out-of-state acceptance rate: **7.4%**
Minority acceptance rate: **8.6%**
International acceptance rate: **6.1%**

Fall 2007 applications and acceptees

	Applied	Interviewed	Accepted	Enrolled
Total:	4,109	734	344	132
In-state:	413	142	69	42
Out-of-state:	3,696	592	275	90

Profile of admitted students

Average undergraduate grade point average: **3.70**
MCAT averages (scale: 1-15; writing test: J-T):
  Composite score: **11.5**
  Verbal reasoning score: **10.9**, Physical sciences score: **11.6**, Biological sciences score: **11.9**, Writing score: **Q**
Proportion with undergraduate majors in: Biological sciences: **33%**, Physical sciences: **17%**, Non-sciences: **20%**, Other health professions: **0%**, Mixed disciplines and other: **30%**
Percentage of students not coming directly from college after graduation: **24%**

Dates and details

The American Medical College Application Service (AMCAS) application is accepted.
School asks for a school-specific application as part of the admissions process.
Oldest MCAT considered for Fall 2009 entry: **2005**
Earliest application date for the 2009-2010 first-year class: **6/1**
Latest application date: **10/15**
Acceptance dates for regular application for the class entering in fall 2009:

Earliest: **November 1, 2008**
Latest: **March 15, 2009**
The school considers requests for deferred entrance.
Starting month for the class entering in 2009–2010: **July**
The school doesn't have an Early Decision Plan (EDP).
A personal interview is required for admission.

Undergraduate coursework required

Medical school requires undergraduate work in these subjects: biology, English, organic chemistry, inorganic (general) chemistry, physics, humanities, behavioral science, demonstration of writing skills, general chemistry.

ADMISSIONS POLICY

(TEXT PROVIDED BY SCHOOL):
Students are selected on the basis of scholastic achievement and qualifications; no regard to race, sex, sexual orientation, age, disability, creed, veteran status, or national origin. Besides American Medical College Application Service application, all applicants need to have a high level of scholarship; take the MCAT within four years of matriculation; submit Emory supplemental application and fee; submit recommendations; and appear for an interview.

COSTS AND FINANCIAL AID

Financial aid phone number: **(404) 727-6039**
Tuition, 2007-2008 academic year: **$39,976**
Room and board: **$22,020**
Percentage of students receiving financial aid in 2007-08: **87%**
Percentage of students receiving: Loans: **77%**, Grants/scholarships: **66%**, Work-study aid: **0%**
Average medical school debt for the Class of 2006: **$124,138**

STUDENT BODY

Fall 2007 full-time enrollment: **480**
Men: **50%**, Women: **50%**, In-state: **31%**, Minorities: **31%**, American Indian: **0.2%**, Asian-American: **18.3%**, African-American: **7.9%**, Hispanic-American: **4.6%**, White: **62.9%**, International: **2.5%**, Unknown: **3.5%**

ACADEMIC PROGRAMS

The school's curriculum frequently gives first-year students substantial contact with patients.

There are opportunities for first- or second-year students to work in community health clinics.

Program offerings: AIDS, drug/alcohol abuse, family medicine, geriatrics, internal medicine, pediatrics, women's health

Joint degrees awarded: M.D./Ph.D., M.D./M.P.H.

Total National Institutes of Health (NIH) grants awarded to the medical school and affiliated hospitals: **$209.6 million**

CURRICULUM
(TEXT PROVIDED BY SCHOOL):

Emory University has a curriculum based on four phases: Foundations, Applications, Discovery (a supervised project), and Translation. Patient contact is begun during the first month; students enter the Applications phase in March of Year 2. A society system provides for close student/faculty interaction over the entire four years, emphasizing professional development and lifelong learning.

FACULTY PROFILE (FALL 2007)

Total teaching faculty: **1,868 (full-time)**, **185 (part-time)**
Of full-time faculty, those teaching in basic sciences: **9%**; in clinical programs: **91%**

Of part-time faculty, those teaching in basic sciences: **2%**; in clinical programs: **98%**
Full-time faculty/student ratio: **3.9**

SUPPORT SERVICES

The school offers students these services for dealing with stress: expanded-hour gym access, peer counseling, professional counseling, religious support, support groups.

RESIDENCY PROFILE

Most popular residency and specialty programs chosen by the 2006 and 2007 M.D. graduating classes: anesthesiology, emergency medicine, family practice, internal medicine, orthopaedic surgery, pathology–anatomic and clinical, pediatrics, psychiatry, surgery–general.

WHERE GRADS GO

37.5%
Proportion of 2005-2007 graduates who entered primary care specialties

29.1%
Proportion of 2006-2007 graduates who accepted in-state residencies

Florida State University

- 1115 W. Call Street, Tallahassee, FL 32306-4300
- Public
- Year Founded: 2000
- Tuition, 2007-2008: In-state: $19,332; Out-of-state: $52,160
- Enrollment 2007-2008 academic year: 357
- Website: http://www.med.fsu.edu/
- Specialty ranking: N/A

3.62 AVERAGE GPA, ENTERING CLASS FALL 2007

9.4 AVERAGE MCAT, ENTERING CLASS FALL 2007

15.1% ACCEPTANCE RATE, ENTERING CLASS FALL 2007

Unranked 2009 U.S. NEWS MEDICAL SCHOOL RANKING (RESEARCH)

Unranked 2009 U.S. NEWS MEDICAL SCHOOL RANKING (PRIMARY CARE)

ADMISSIONS

Admissions phone number: **(850) 644-7904**
Admissions email address: **medadmissions@med.fsu.edu**
Application website: **N/A**
Acceptance rate: **15.1%**
In-state acceptance rate: **15.1%**
Out-of-state acceptance rate: **N/A**
Minority acceptance rate: **5.0%**
International acceptance rate: **N/A**

Fall 2007 applications and acceptees

	Applied	Interviewed	Accepted	Enrolled
Total:	1,505	365	227	120
In-state:	1,505	365	227	120
Out-of-state:	0	0	0	0

Profile of admitted students

Average undergraduate grade point average: **3.62**
MCAT averages (scale: 1-15; writing test: J-T):
　Composite score: **9.4**
　Verbal reasoning score: **9.4**, Physical sciences score: **9.1**,
　Biological sciences score: **9.6**, Writing score: **P**
Proportion with undergraduate majors in: Biological
　sciences: **55%**, Physical sciences: **23%**, Non-sciences:
　10%, Other health professions: **6%**, Mixed disciplines
　and other: **6%**
Percentage of students not coming directly from college
　after graduation: **10%**

Dates and details

The American Medical College Application Service
　(AMCAS) application is accepted.
School asks for a school-specific application as part of the
　admissions process.
Oldest MCAT considered for Fall 2009 entry: **2006**
Earliest application date for the 2009-2010 first-year class:
　6/1
Latest application date: **12/14**
Acceptance dates for regular application for the class
　entering in fall 2009:
　Earliest: **October 15, 2008**

Latest: **May 29, 2009**
The school considers requests for deferred entrance.
Starting month for the class entering in 2009–2010: **June**
The school has an Early Decision Plan (EDP).
A personal interview is required for admission.

Undergraduate coursework required

Medical school requires undergraduate work in these subjects: biology, English, organic chemistry, inorganic (general) chemistry, physics, biochemistry, mathematics, general
chemistry.

ADMISSIONS POLICY
(TEXT PROVIDED BY SCHOOL):

The College of Medicine seek students, preferably residents
of Florida, who have demonstrated a commitment of service
to others. It encourages applications from traditional and
nontraditional students, as well as students from rural,
inner-city, or other medically underserved areas. An applicant should have completed prerequisite courses in English,
Biology, Chemistry, Organic Chemistry, Physics, and
Biochemistry.

COSTS AND FINANCIAL AID

Financial aid phone number: **(850) 645-7270**
Tuition, 2007-2008 academic year: **In-state: $19,332; Out-
　of-state: $52,160**
Room and board: **$15,910**
Percentage of students receiving financial aid in 2007-08:
　85%
Percentage of students receiving: Loans: **85%**,
　Grants/scholarships: **33%**, Work-study aid: **0%**
Average medical school debt for the Class of 2006:
　$114,543

STUDENT BODY

Fall 2007 full-time enrollment: **357**
Men: **40%**, Women: **60%**, In-state: **100%**, Minorities: **34%**,
　American Indian: **0.8%**, Asian-American: **11.8%**,
　African-American: **12.6%**, Hispanic-American: **9.0%**,
　White: **64.4%**, International: **0.0%**, Unknown: **1.4%**

ACADEMIC PROGRAMS

The school's curriculum very frequently gives first-year students substantial contact with patients.

There are opportunities for first- or second-year students to work in community health clinics.

Program offerings: AIDS, drug/alcohol abuse, family medicine, geriatrics, internal medicine, pediatrics, rural medicine, women's health

Joint degrees awarded: N/A

Total National Institutes of Health (NIH) grants awarded to the medical school and affiliated hospitals: **$2.2 million**

CURRICULUM
(TEXT PROVIDED BY SCHOOL):

In the faculty-scholar model, highly skilled and innovative faculty members present a well-structured continuum of education in biomedical, behavioral, and clinical sciences utilizing problem-based and small-group learning experiences. Community-based clinical education spans the four-year curriculum, providing access to more than 1,200 of the top physicians in Florida at locations across the state.

FACULTY PROFILE (FALL 2007)

Total teaching faculty: **97 (full-time)**, **1,231 (part-time)**
Of full-time faculty, those teaching in basic sciences: **41%**; in clinical programs: **59%**

Of part-time faculty, those teaching in basic sciences: **3%**; in clinical programs: **97%**
Full-time faculty/student ratio: **0.3**

SUPPORT SERVICES

The school offers students these services for dealing with stress: expanded-hour gym access, professional counseling, support groups.

RESIDENCY PROFILE

Most popular residency and specialty programs chosen by the 2006 and 2007 M.D. graduating classes: anesthesiology, emergency medicine, family practice, internal medicine, obstetrics and gynecology, orthopaedic surgery, otolaryngology, pediatrics, radiology–diagnostic, surgery–general.

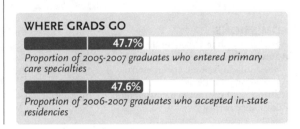

WHERE GRADS GO

47.7%

Proportion of 2005-2007 graduates who entered primary care specialties

47.6%

Proportion of 2006-2007 graduates who accepted in-state residencies

Georgetown University

- 3900 Reservoir Road NW, Med-Dent Building, Washington, DC 20007
- Private
- Year Founded: 1851
- Tuition, 2007-2008: $42,764
- Enrollment 2007-2008 academic year: 779
- Website: http://som.georgetown.edu/index.html
- Specialty ranking: N/A

3.68	AVERAGE GPA, ENTERING CLASS FALL 2007
10.6	AVERAGE MCAT, ENTERING CLASS FALL 2007
3.5%	ACCEPTANCE RATE, ENTERING CLASS FALL 2007
40	2009 U.S. NEWS MEDICAL SCHOOL RANKING (RESEARCH)
Unranked	2009 U.S. NEWS MEDICAL SCHOOL RANKING (PRIMARY CARE)

ADMISSIONS

Admissions phone number: **(202) 687-1154**
Admissions email address:
  medicaladmissions@georgetown.edu
Application website:
  http://som.georgetown.edu/admissions/index.html
Acceptance rate: **3.5%**
In-state acceptance rate: **23.3%**
Out-of-state acceptance rate: **3.4%**
Minority acceptance rate: **N/A**
International acceptance rate: **N/A**

Fall 2007 applications and acceptees

	Applied	Interviewed	Accepted	Enrolled
Total:	10,643	1,236	376	190
In-state:	60	23	14	11
Out-of-state:	10,583	1,213	362	179

Profile of admitted students

Average undergraduate grade point average: **3.68**
MCAT averages (scale: 1-15; writing test: J-T):
  Composite score: **10.6**
  Verbal reasoning score: **10.3**, Physical sciences score: **10.7**, Biological sciences score: **10.8**, Writing score: **N/A**
Proportion with undergraduate majors in: Biological sciences: **60%**, Physical sciences: **16%**, Non-sciences: **20%**, Other health professions: **0%**, Mixed disciplines and other: **4%**
Percentage of students not coming directly from college after graduation: **N/A**

Dates and details

The American Medical College Application Service (AMCAS) application is accepted.
School asks for a school-specific application as part of the admissions process.
Oldest MCAT considered for Fall 2009 entry: **2006**
Earliest application date for the 2009-2010 first-year class: **6/1**
Latest application date: **10/31**

Acceptance dates for regular application for the class entering in fall 2009:
  Earliest: **October 15, 2008**
  Latest: **August 5, 2008**
The school considers requests for deferred entrance.
Starting month for the class entering in 2009-2010:
  August
The school doesn't have an Early Decision Plan (EDP).
A personal interview is required for admission.

Undergraduate coursework required

Medical school requires undergraduate work in these subjects: biology, English, organic chemistry, inorganic (general) chemistry, physics, mathematics.

ADMISSIONS POLICY
(TEXT PROVIDED BY SCHOOL):

Secondary application requirements and procedures are E-mailed to each applicant. A personal essay unique to Georgetown is required for consideration of admission. An applicant must not only present a strong academic profile but also demonstrate well-developed noncognitive qualities. GU selects students on the basis of academic achievement, character, maturity, and motivation.

COSTS AND FINANCIAL AID

Financial aid phone number: **(202) 687-1693**
Tuition, 2007-2008 academic year: **$42,764**
Room and board: **$15,030**
Percentage of students receiving financial aid in 2007-08: **87%**
Percentage of students receiving: Loans: **85%**, Grants/scholarships: **44%**, Work-study aid: **1%**
Average medical school debt for the Class of 2006: **$146,000**

STUDENT BODY

Fall 2007 full-time enrollment: **779**
Men: **50%**, Women: **50%**, In-state: **0%**, Minorities: **25%**, American Indian: **0.4%**, Asian-American: **16.0%**,

African-American: **6.2%**, Hispanic-American: **2.6%**, White: **56.4%**, International: **1.5%**, Unknown: **16.9%**

ACADEMIC PROGRAMS

There are opportunities for first- or second-year students to work in community health clinics.

Program offerings: AIDS, drug/alcohol abuse, family medicine, geriatrics, internal medicine, pediatrics, rural medicine, women's health

Joint degrees awarded: M.D./Ph.D., M.D./M.B.A., M.D./M.S., M.D./M.A.

Total National Institutes of Health (NIH) grants awarded to the medical school and affiliated hospitals: **$190.2 million**

CURRICULUM

(TEXT PROVIDED BY SCHOOL):

The first two years provide students with an early introduction to the patient, as well as to the spiritual and ethical dimensions of medicine. In the third year the student serves clinical rotations conducted by departments at the Medical Center and its affiliates. The fourth year provides the student with supervised responsibility in the clinical management of patients.

FACULTY PROFILE (FALL 2007)

Total teaching faculty: **1,629 (full-time)**, **144 (part-time)**

Of full-time faculty, those teaching in basic sciences: **12%**; in clinical programs: **88%**

Of part-time faculty, those teaching in basic sciences: **45%**; in clinical programs: **55%**

Full-time faculty/student ratio: **2.1**

SUPPORT SERVICES

The school offers students these services for dealing with stress: expanded-hour gym access, professional counseling, religious support, support groups.

RESIDENCY PROFILE

Most popular residency and specialty programs chosen by the 2006 and 2007 M.D. graduating classes: N/A.

WHERE GRADS GO

35.0%

Proportion of 2005-2007 graduates who entered primary care specialties

27.4%

Proportion of 2006-2007 graduates who accepted in-state residencies

George Washington University

- 2300 Eye Street NW, Room 713W, Washington, DC 20037
- Private
- Year Founded: 1821
- Tuition, 2007-2008: $44,615
- Enrollment 2007-2008 academic year: 700
- Website: http://www.gwumc.edu/
- Specialty ranking: N/A

3.55 AVERAGE GPA, ENTERING CLASS FALL 2007

9.6 AVERAGE MCAT, ENTERING CLASS FALL 2007

3.0% ACCEPTANCE RATE, ENTERING CLASS FALL 2007

Unranked 2009 U.S. NEWS MEDICAL SCHOOL RANKING (RESEARCH)

Unranked 2009 U.S. NEWS MEDICAL SCHOOL RANKING (PRIMARY CARE)

ADMISSIONS

Admissions phone number: **(202) 994-3506**
Admissions email address: **medadmit@gwu.edu**
Application website: **http://www.gwumc.edu/edu/admis/**
Acceptance rate: **3.0%**
In-state acceptance rate: **N/A**
Out-of-state acceptance rate: **N/A**
Minority acceptance rate: **N/A**
International acceptance rate: **N/A**

Fall 2007 applications and acceptees

	Applied	Interviewed	Accepted	Enrolled
Total:	10,213	942	302	177
In-state:	N/A	N/A	N/A	6
Out-of-state:	N/A	N/A	N/A	171

Profile of admitted students

Average undergraduate grade point average: **3.55**
MCAT averages (scale: 1-15; writing test: J-T):
  Composite score: **9.6**
  Verbal reasoning score: **9.3**, Physical sciences score: **9.6**,
  Biological sciences score: **10.0**, Writing score: **P**
Proportion with undergraduate majors in: Biological
  sciences: **35%**, Physical sciences: **8%**, Non-sciences: **32%**,
  Other health professions: **3%**, Mixed disciplines and
  other: **23%**
Percentage of students not coming directly from college
  after graduation: **25%**

Dates and details

The American Medical College Application Service
  (AMCAS) application is accepted.
School asks for a school-specific application as part of the
  admissions process.
Oldest MCAT considered for Fall 2009 entry: **2006**
Earliest application date for the 2009-2010 first-year class:
  6/1
Latest application date: **12/1**
Acceptance dates for regular application for the class
  entering in fall 2009:

Earliest: **October 15, 2008**
Latest: **August 5, 2009**
The school considers requests for deferred entrance.
Starting month for the class entering in 2009–2010:
  August
The school has an Early Decision Plan (EDP).
A personal interview is required for admission.

Undergraduate coursework required

Medical school requires undergraduate work in these subjects: biology, biology/zoology, English, organic chemistry,
inorganic (general) chemistry, physics, demonstration of
writing skills, general chemistry.

COSTS AND FINANCIAL AID

Financial aid phone number: **(202) 994-2960**
Tuition, 2007-2008 academic year: **$44,615**
Room and board: **$20,085**
Percentage of students receiving financial aid in 2007-08:
  90%
Percentage of students receiving: Loans: **90%**,
  Grants/scholarships: **40%**, Work-study aid: **0%**
Average medical school debt for the Class of 2006:
  $156,752

STUDENT BODY

Fall 2007 full-time enrollment: **700**
Men: **44%**, Women: **56%**, In-state: **0%**, Minorities: **38%**,
  American Indian: **N/A**, Asian-American: **N/A**, African-
  American: **N/A**, Hispanic-American: **N/A**, White: **N/A**,
  International: **N/A**, Unknown: **N/A**

ACADEMIC PROGRAMS

The school's curriculum very frequently gives first-year
  students substantial contact with patients.
There are opportunities for first- or second-year students to
  work in community health clinics.
Program offerings: AIDS, drug/alcohol abuse, family
  medicine, geriatrics, internal medicine, pediatrics,
  women's health

Joint degrees awarded: M.D./Ph.D., M.D./M.P.H.
Total National Institutes of Health (NIH) grants awarded to
the medical school and affiliated hospitals: **$38.6 million**

FACULTY PROFILE (FALL 2007)

Total teaching faculty: **678 (full-time)**, **1,697 (part-time)**
Of full-time faculty, those teaching in basic sciences: **10%**;
in clinical programs: **90%**
Of part-time faculty, those teaching in basic sciences: **6%**;
in clinical programs: **94%**
Full-time faculty/student ratio: **1.0**

SUPPORT SERVICES

The school offers students these services for dealing with
stress: professional counseling.

RESIDENCY PROFILE

Most popular residency and specialty programs chosen by
the 2006 and 2007 M.D. graduating classes: anesthesiology, emergency medicine, family practice, internal medicine, otolaryngology, pediatrics, psychiatry,
radiology–diagnostic, surgery–general, urology.

WHERE GRADS GO

16.6%

*Proportion of 2005-2007 graduates who entered primary
care specialties*

N/A

*Proportion of 2006-2007 graduates who accepted in-state
residencies*

Harvard University

- 25 Shattuck Street, Boston, MA 02115-6092
- Private
- Year Founded: 1782
- Tuition, 2007-2008: $41,861
- Enrollment 2007-2008 academic year: 758
- Website: http://hms.harvard.edu
- Specialty ranking: AIDS: 3, drug/alcohol abuse: 4, family medicine: 27, geriatrics: 6, internal medicine: 1, pediatrics: 1, women's health: 1

3.81	AVERAGE GPA, ENTERING CLASS FALL 2007
11.9	AVERAGE MCAT, ENTERING CLASS FALL 2007
4.4%	ACCEPTANCE RATE, ENTERING CLASS FALL 2007
1	2009 U.S. NEWS MEDICAL SCHOOL RANKING (RESEARCH)
7	2009 U.S. NEWS MEDICAL SCHOOL RANKING (PRIMARY CARE)

ADMISSIONS

Admissions phone number: **(617) 432-1550**
Admissions email address:
   admissions_office@hms.harvard.edu
Application website:
   http://hms.harvard.edu/admissions/default.asp?page=application
Acceptance rate: **4.4%**
In-state acceptance rate: **N/A**
Out-of-state acceptance rate: **N/A**
Minority acceptance rate: **4.7%**
International acceptance rate: **5.1%**

Fall 2007 applications and acceptees

	Applied	Interviewed	Accepted	Enrolled
Total:	5,482	1,029	240	165
In-state:	N/A	N/A	N/A	N/A
Out-of-state:	N/A	N/A	N/A	N/A

Profile of admitted students

Average undergraduate grade point average: **3.81**
MCAT averages (scale: 1-15; writing test: J-T):
   Composite score: **11.9**
   Verbal reasoning score: **11.1**, Physical sciences score: **12.4**, Biological sciences score: **12.4**, Writing score: **R**
Proportion with undergraduate majors in: Biological sciences: **56%**, Physical sciences: **11%**, Non-sciences: **26%**, Other health professions: **0%**, Mixed disciplines and other: **7%**
Percentage of students not coming directly from college after graduation: **40%**

Dates and details

The American Medical College Application Service (AMCAS) application is accepted.
School asks for a school-specific application as part of the admissions process.
Oldest MCAT considered for Fall 2009 entry: **2005**
Earliest application date for the 2009-2010 first-year class: **N/A**
Latest application date: **N/A**

Acceptance dates for regular application for the class entering in fall 2009:
   Earliest: **N/A**
   Latest: **N/A**
The school considers requests for deferred entrance.
Starting month for the class entering in 2009–2010:
   August
The school doesn't have an Early Decision Plan (EDP).
A personal interview is required for admission.

Undergraduate coursework required

Medical school requires undergraduate work in these subjects: biology, English, organic chemistry, inorganic (general) chemistry, physics, molecular and cell biology, mathematics, demonstration of writing skills, calculus, general chemistry.

ADMISSIONS POLICY
(TEXT PROVIDED BY SCHOOL):

Academic excellence is expected. Committee members consider the entire application, including the essay, extracurricular activities, life experiences, research, community work, and letters of recommendation. HMS looks for evidence of integrity, maturity, humanitarian concerns, leadership potential, and an aptitude for working with people. The 2007 entering class came from 60 different colleges.

COSTS AND FINANCIAL AID

Financial aid phone number: **(617) 432-1575**
Tuition, 2007-2008 academic year: **$41,861**
Room and board: **$11,434**
Percentage of students receiving financial aid in 2007-08: **82%**
Percentage of students receiving: Loans: **79%**, Grants/scholarships: **54%**, Work-study aid: **2%**
Average medical school debt for the Class of 2006: **$106,344**

STUDENT BODY

Fall 2007 full-time enrollment: **758**

Men: **50%**, Women: **50%**, In-state: **N/A**, Minorities: **47%**, American Indian: **1.6%**, Asian-American: **26.4%**, African-American: **11.6%**, Hispanic-American: **7.9%**, White: **41.2%**, International: **6.9%**, Unknown: **4.5%**

ACADEMIC PROGRAMS

The school's curriculum frequently gives first-year students substantial contact with patients.

There are opportunities for first- or second-year students to work in community health clinics.

Program offerings: AIDS, drug/alcohol abuse, family medicine, geriatrics, internal medicine, pediatrics, rural medicine, women's health

Joint degrees awarded: M.D./Ph.D., M.D./M.B.A., M.D./M.P.H.

Total National Institutes of Health (NIH) grants awarded to the medical school and affiliated hospitals: **$1,178.5 million**

CURRICULUM

(TEXT PROVIDED BY SCHOOL):

Harvard Medical School's new integrated curriculum is designed to prepare students for a career in medicine distinguished by a lifelong commitment to service, integrity, and excellence. The program integrates the biological, social, behavioral, and clinical sciences throughout a four-year period.

FACULTY PROFILE (FALL 2007)

Total teaching faculty: **7,656 (full-time)**, **2,830 (part-time)**

Of full-time faculty, those teaching in basic sciences: **5%**; in clinical programs: **95%**

Of part-time faculty, those teaching in basic sciences: **10%**; in clinical programs: **90%**

Full-time faculty/student ratio: **10.1**

SUPPORT SERVICES

The school offers students these services for dealing with stress: expanded-hour gym access, peer counseling, professional counseling, religious support, support groups.

RESIDENCY PROFILE

Most popular residency and specialty programs chosen by the 2006 and 2007 M.D. graduating classes: anesthesiology, emergency medicine, internal medicine, neurology, orthopaedic surgery, pediatrics, psychiatry, radiology–diagnostic, surgery–general.

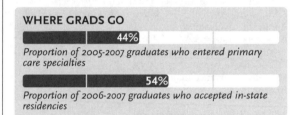

WHERE GRADS GO

44%

Proportion of 2005-2007 graduates who entered primary care specialties

54%

Proportion of 2006-2007 graduates who accepted in-state residencies

Howard University

■ 520 W Street NW, Washington, DC 20059
■ Private
■ Year Founded: 1868
■ Tuition, 2007-2008: $29,846
■ Enrollment 2007-2008 academic year: 469
■ Website: http://www.med.howard.edu
■ Specialty ranking: N/A

3.40 AVERAGE GPA, ENTERING CLASS FALL 2007

8.2 AVERAGE MCAT, ENTERING CLASS FALL 2007

5.8% ACCEPTANCE RATE, ENTERING CLASS FALL 2007

Unranked 2009 U.S. NEWS MEDICAL SCHOOL RANKING (RESEARCH)

Unranked 2009 U.S. NEWS MEDICAL SCHOOL RANKING (PRIMARY CARE)

ADMISSIONS

Admissions phone number: **(202) 806-6279**
Admissions email address: **hucmadmissions@howard.edu**
Application website: **N/A**
Acceptance rate: **5.8%**
In-state acceptance rate: **19.1%**
Out-of-state acceptance rate: **5.7%**
Minority acceptance rate: **7.1%**
International acceptance rate: **3.3%**

Fall 2007 applications and acceptees

	Applied	Interviewed	Accepted	Enrolled
Total:	5,110	363	297	130
In-state:	47	9	9	6
Out-of-state:	5,063	354	288	124

Profile of admitted students

Average undergraduate grade point average: **3.40**
MCAT averages (scale: 1-15; writing test: J-T):
  Composite score: **8.2**
  Verbal reasoning score: **7.8**, Physical sciences score: **8.0**,
  Biological sciences score: **8.7**, Writing score: **O**
Proportion with undergraduate majors in: Biological
  sciences: **64%**, Physical sciences: **14%**, Non-sciences:
  11%, Other health professions: **2%**, Mixed disciplines
  and other: **9%**
Percentage of students not coming directly from college
  after graduation: **65%**

Dates and details

The American Medical College Application Service
  (AMCAS) application is accepted.
School asks for a school-specific application as part of the
  admissions process.
Oldest MCAT considered for Fall 2009 entry: **2005**
Earliest application date for the 2009-2010 first-year class:
  6/1
Latest application date: **12/15**
Acceptance dates for regular application for the class
  entering in fall 2009:

Earliest: **October 15, 2008**
Latest: **July 16, 2009**
The school considers requests for deferred entrance.
Starting month for the class entering in 2009–2010: **July**
The school doesn't have an Early Decision Plan (EDP).
A personal interview is required for admission.

Undergraduate coursework required

Medical school requires undergraduate work in these subjects: biology, English, organic chemistry, inorganic (general) chemistry, physics, mathematics.

ADMISSIONS POLICY
(TEXT PROVIDED BY SCHOOL):

There are no automatic grade-point average or MCAT cutoffs, although a composite MCAT of 21 or better is considered most competitive, as is a GPA of 2.8 or better for
Biology, Chemistry, Physics, and Math. Leadership experience, research experience, and a demonstrated commitment to serve in medically underserved communities are
also considered.

COSTS AND FINANCIAL AID

Financial aid phone number: **(202) 806-6388**
Tuition, 2007-2008 academic year: **$29,846**
Room and board: **$14,340**
Percentage of students receiving financial aid in 2007-08:
  95%
Percentage of students receiving: Loans: **83%**,
  Grants/scholarships: **69%**, Work-study aid: **0%**
Average medical school debt for the Class of 2006:
  $129,136

STUDENT BODY

Fall 2007 full-time enrollment: **469**
Men: **49%**, Women: **51%**, In-state: **8%**, Minorities: **94%**,
  American Indian: **0.2%**, Asian-American: **9.6%**,
  African-American: **71.9%**, Hispanic-American: **2.6%**,
  White: **5.5%**, International: **10.2%**, Unknown: **0.0%**

ACADEMIC PROGRAMS

The school's curriculum occasionally gives first-year students substantial contact with patients.

There are opportunities for first- or second-year students to work in community health clinics.

Program offerings: AIDS, drug/alcohol abuse, family medicine, geriatrics, internal medicine, pediatrics, women's health

Joint degrees awarded: M.D./Ph.D., M.D./M.B.A.

Total National Institutes of Health (NIH) grants awarded to the medical school and affiliated hospitals: **$19.4 million**

CURRICULUM

(TEXT PROVIDED BY SCHOOL):

The first-year courses are Molecules and Cells, Structure and Function, and Medicine and Society. The second year covers six Organ System units, Physical Diagnosis, and Medicine and Society. The third year consists of seven required clinical clerkships. Year 4 includes two required clerkships and six or seven electives. The U.S. Medical Licensing Examination Steps 1 and 2 are required for promotion and graduation.

FACULTY PROFILE (FALL 2007)

Total teaching faculty: **240 (full-time), 239 (part-time)**

Of full-time faculty, those teaching in basic sciences: **32%**; in clinical programs: **68%**

Of part-time faculty, those teaching in basic sciences: **7%**; in clinical programs: **93%**

Full-time faculty/student ratio: **0.5**

SUPPORT SERVICES

The school offers students these services for dealing with stress: professional counseling, religious support, support groups.

RESIDENCY PROFILE

Most popular residency and specialty programs chosen by the 2006 and 2007 M.D. graduating classes: anesthesiology, emergency medicine, family practice, internal medicine, orthopaedic surgery, pediatrics, psychiatry, surgery–general.

WHERE GRADS GO

33.1%

Proportion of 2005-2007 graduates who entered primary care specialties

26.8%

Proportion of 2006-2007 graduates who accepted in-state residencies

Indiana University—Indianapolis

- 1120 South Drive, Indianapolis, IN 46202
- Public
- **Year Founded:** 1903
- **Tuition, 2007-2008:** In-state: $25,904; Out-of-state: $42,894
- **Enrollment 2007-2008 academic year:** 1,175
- **Website:** http://www.medicine.iu.edu
- **Specialty ranking:** rural medicine: 21

3.73 AVERAGE GPA, ENTERING CLASS FALL 2007

10.3 AVERAGE MCAT, ENTERING CLASS FALL 2007

13.5% ACCEPTANCE RATE, ENTERING CLASS FALL 2007

46 2009 U.S. NEWS MEDICAL SCHOOL RANKING (RESEARCH)

26 2009 U.S. NEWS MEDICAL SCHOOL RANKING (PRIMARY CARE)

ADMISSIONS

Admissions phone number: **(317) 274-3772**
Admissions email address: **inmedadm@iupui.edu**
Application website: **http://www.aamc.org/students/amcas**
Acceptance rate: **13.5%**
In-state acceptance rate: **44.4%**
Out-of-state acceptance rate: **5.8%**
Minority acceptance rate: **N/A**
International acceptance rate: **10.2%**

Fall 2007 applications and acceptees

	Applied	Interviewed	Accepted	Enrolled
Total:	3,490	1,003	471	294
In-state:	694	572	308	252
Out-of-state:	2,796	431	163	42

Profile of admitted students

Average undergraduate grade point average: **3.73**
MCAT averages (scale: 1-15; writing test: J-T):
  Composite score: **10.3**
  Verbal reasoning score: **10.2**, Physical sciences score:
  10.2, Biological sciences score: **10.5**, Writing score: **P**
Proportion with undergraduate majors in: Biological
  sciences: **51%**, Physical sciences: **19%**, Non-sciences:
  10%, Other health professions: **1%**, Mixed disciplines
  and other: **18%**
Percentage of students not coming directly from college
  after graduation: **13%**

Dates and details

The American Medical College Application Service
  (AMCAS) application is accepted.
School does not ask for a school-specific application as part
  of the admissions process.
Oldest MCAT considered for Fall 2009 entry: **2005**
Earliest application date for the 2009-2010 first-year class:
  5/1
Latest application date: **12/15**
Acceptance dates for regular application for the class
  entering in fall 2009:
  Earliest: **October 15, 2008**

Latest: **August 15, 2009**
The school considers requests for deferred entrance.
Starting month for the class entering in 2009–2010:
  August
The school has an Early Decision Plan (EDP).
A personal interview is required for admission.

Undergraduate coursework required

Medical school requires undergraduate work in these subjects: biology, organic chemistry, inorganic (general) chemistry, physics, general chemistry.

ADMISSIONS POLICY
(TEXT PROVIDED BY SCHOOL):

The IU School of Medicine admission requirements are
found at the school's website. The school participates in the
American Medical College Application Service and the
early-decision program. Preference is given to applicants
who are Indiana residents. A number of nonresidents are
accepted each year; those with significant ties to the state of
Indiana may be given greater consideration.

COSTS AND FINANCIAL AID

Financial aid phone number: **(317) 274-1967**
Tuition, 2007-2008 academic year: **In-state: $25,904; Out-
of-state: $42,894**
Room and board: **$15,168**
Percentage of students receiving financial aid in 2007-08:
  94%
Percentage of students receiving: Loans: **91%**,
  Grants/scholarships: **34%**, Work-study aid: **1%**
Average medical school debt for the Class of 2006:
  $142,859

STUDENT BODY

Fall 2007 full-time enrollment: **1,175**
Men: **57%**, Women: **43%**, In-state: **88%**, Minorities: **24%**,
  American Indian: **1.1%**, Asian-American: **11.7%**, African-
  American: **5.9%**, Hispanic-American: **4.3%**, White:
  72.7%, International: **1.4%**, Unknown: **3.0%**

ACADEMIC PROGRAMS

The school's curriculum frequently gives first-year students substantial contact with patients.

There are opportunities for first- or second-year students to work in community health clinics.

Program offerings: AIDS, drug/alcohol abuse, family medicine, geriatrics, internal medicine, pediatrics, rural medicine, women's health

Joint degrees awarded: M.D./Ph.D., M.D./M.B.A., M.D./M.P.H., M.D./M.S.W., M.D./M.S., M.D./M.A.

Total National Institutes of Health (NIH) grants awarded to the medical school and affiliated hospitals: **N/A**

CURRICULUM

(TEXT PROVIDED BY SCHOOL):

Indiana's only medical school, the IU School of Medicine is affiliated with Roudebush VA Medical Center, Wishard and Clarian Health hospitals, and Moi University in Kenya. The second-largest medical school in the United States is hosted on nine campuses in Indiana. It features a competency-based curriculum and a relationship-centered care program that fosters human interactions.

FACULTY PROFILE (FALL 2007)

Total teaching faculty: **1,417 (full-time)**, **100 (part-time)**
Of full-time faculty, those teaching in basic sciences: **15%**; in clinical programs: **85%**

Of part-time faculty, those teaching in basic sciences: **9%**; in clinical programs: **91%**
Full-time faculty/student ratio: **1.2**

SUPPORT SERVICES

The school offers students these services for dealing with stress: expanded-hour gym access, peer counseling, professional counseling, religious support, support groups.

RESIDENCY PROFILE

Most popular residency and specialty programs chosen by the 2006 and 2007 M.D. graduating classes: anesthesiology, emergency medicine, family practice, internal medicine, neurology, obstetrics and gynecology, orthopaedic surgery, pediatrics, radiology–diagnostic, surgery–general.

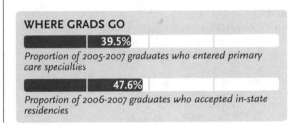

WHERE GRADS GO

39.5%
Proportion of 2005-2007 graduates who entered primary care specialties

47.6%
Proportion of 2006-2007 graduates who accepted in-state residencies

Jefferson Medical College

- 1025 Walnut Street, Room 100, Philadelphia, PA 19107-5083
- Private
- **Year Founded:** 1824
- **Tuition, 2007-2008:** $41,101
- **Enrollment 2007-2008 academic year:** 999
- **Website:** http://www.tju.edu
- **Specialty ranking:** family medicine: 27

3.62 AVERAGE GPA, ENTERING CLASS FALL 2007

10.4 AVERAGE MCAT, ENTERING CLASS FALL 2007

5.9% ACCEPTANCE RATE, ENTERING CLASS FALL 2007

Unranked 2009 U.S. NEWS MEDICAL SCHOOL RANKING (RESEARCH)

Unranked 2009 U.S. NEWS MEDICAL SCHOOL RANKING (PRIMARY CARE)

ADMISSIONS

Admissions phone number: **(215) 955-6983**
Admissions email address: **jmc.admissions@jefferson.edu**
Application website: **http://www.jefferson.edu**
Acceptance rate: **5.9%**
In-state acceptance rate: **13.1%**
Out-of-state acceptance rate: **4.9%**
Minority acceptance rate: **5.9%**
International acceptance rate: **3.6%**

Fall 2007 applications and acceptees

	Applied	Interviewed	Accepted	Enrolled
Total:	8,897	805	521	259
In-state:	1,077	207	141	172
Out-of-state:	7,820	598	380	87

Profile of admitted students

Average undergraduate grade point average: **3.62**
MCAT averages (scale: 1-15; writing test: J-T):
Composite score: **10.4**
Verbal reasoning score: **10.3**, Physical sciences score: **10.3**, Biological sciences score: **10.6**, Writing score: **Q**
Proportion with undergraduate majors in: Biological sciences: **34%**, Physical sciences: **12%**, Non-sciences: **14%**, Other health professions: **1%**, Mixed disciplines and other: **39%**
Percentage of students not coming directly from college after graduation: **51%**

Dates and details

The American Medical College Application Service (AMCAS) application is accepted.
School asks for a school-specific application as part of the admissions process.
Oldest MCAT considered for Fall 2009 entry: **2005**
Earliest application date for the 2009-2010 first-year class: **6/1**
Latest application date: **11/15**
Acceptance dates for regular application for the class entering in fall 2009:

Earliest: **October 15, 2008**
Latest: **August 4, 2009**
The school considers requests for deferred entrance.
Starting month for the class entering in 2009-2010:
August
The school has an Early Decision Plan (EDP).
A personal interview is required for admission.

Undergraduate coursework required

Medical school requires undergraduate work in these subjects: biology, organic chemistry, inorganic (general) chemistry, physics.

ADMISSIONS POLICY

(TEXT PROVIDED BY SCHOOL):
Student selection is made after careful consideration of academic record, letters of recommendation, MCAT scores, and performance in nonacademic areas including motivation, maturity, compassion, dedication, integrity, and commitment. The MCAT is required, as is a bachelor's degree from a university in the United States or Canada.
Preference is given to Pennsylvania and Delaware residents.

COSTS AND FINANCIAL AID

Financial aid phone number: **(215) 955-2867**
Tuition, 2007-2008 academic year: **$41,101**
Room and board: **$15,609**
Percentage of students receiving financial aid in 2007-08: **81%**
Percentage of students receiving: Loans: **77%**, Grants/scholarships: **46%**, Work-study aid: **10%**
Average medical school debt for the Class of 2006: **$153,198**

STUDENT BODY

Fall 2007 full-time enrollment: **999**
Men: **50%**, Women: **50%**, In-state: **50%**, Minorities: **32%**, American Indian: **0.5%**, Asian-American: **22.6%**, African-American: **1.9%**, Hispanic-American: **3.5%**, White: **67.9%**, International: **3.6%**, Unknown: **0.0%**

ACADEMIC PROGRAMS

The school's curriculum frequently gives first-year students substantial contact with patients.

There are opportunities for first- or second-year students to work in community health clinics.

Program offerings: AIDS, drug/alcohol abuse, family medicine, geriatrics, internal medicine, pediatrics, rural medicine, women's health

Joint degrees awarded: M.D./Ph.D., M.D./M.B.A., M.D./M.P.H., M.D./M.H.A.

Total National Institutes of Health (NIH) grants awarded to the medical school and affiliated hospitals: **$70.3 million**

CURRICULUM

(TEXT PROVIDED BY SCHOOL):

Jefferson's curriculum includes two years of basic science followed by two years of clinical instruction, including third-year rotations in Family Practice, Obstetrics/Gynecology, Pediatrics, Psychiatry, Surgery, and Internal Medicine. Fourth year includes 16 weeks of electives; Neurology/Rehabilitation, two subinternships; advanced basic science; and emergency room/advanced clinical skills.

FACULTY PROFILE (FALL 2007)

Total teaching faculty: 2,791 **(full-time)**, 38 **(part-time)**
Of full-time faculty, those teaching in basic sciences: **6%**; in clinical programs: **94%**

Of part-time faculty, those teaching in basic sciences: **3%**; in clinical programs: **97%**
Full-time faculty/student ratio: **2.8**

SUPPORT SERVICES

The school offers students these services for dealing with stress: expanded-hour gym access, peer counseling, professional counseling, religious support, support groups.

RESIDENCY PROFILE

Most popular residency and specialty programs chosen by the 2006 and 2007 M.D. graduating classes: anesthesiology, emergency medicine, family practice, internal medicine, obstetrics and gynecology, ophthalmology, orthopaedic surgery, pediatrics, radiology–diagnostic, surgery–general.

WHERE GRADS GO

39.0%

Proportion of 2005-2007 graduates who entered primary care specialties

46.0%

Proportion of 2006-2007 graduates who accepted in-state residencies

Johns Hopkins University

- 733 N. Broadway, Baltimore, MD 21205
- Private
- Year Founded: 1893
- Tuition, 2007-2008: $40,669
- Enrollment 2007-2008 academic year: 460
- Website: http://www.hopkinsmedicine.org
- Specialty ranking: AIDS: 2, drug/alcohol abuse: 3, geriatrics: 1, internal medicine: 2, pediatrics: 4, women's health: 5

3.85	AVERAGE GPA, ENTERING CLASS FALL 2007
11.8	AVERAGE MCAT, ENTERING CLASS FALL 2007
6.4%	ACCEPTANCE RATE, ENTERING CLASS FALL 2007
2	2009 U.S. NEWS MEDICAL SCHOOL RANKING (RESEARCH)
26	2009 U.S. NEWS MEDICAL SCHOOL RANKING (PRIMARY CARE)

ADMISSIONS

Admissions phone number: **(410) 955-3182**
Admissions email address: **somadmiss@jhmi.edu**
Application website:
  http://www.hopkinsmedicine.org/admissions
Acceptance rate: **6.4%**
In-state acceptance rate: **9.9%**
Out-of-state acceptance rate: **6.1%**
Minority acceptance rate: **5.7%**
International acceptance rate: **6.7%**

Fall 2007 applications and acceptees

	Applied	Interviewed	Accepted	Enrolled
Total:	4,344	774	279	118
In-state:	323	91	32	22
Out-of-state:	4,021	683	247	96

Profile of admitted students

Average undergraduate grade point average: **3.85**
MCAT averages (scale: 1-15; writing test: J-T):
  Composite score: **11.8**
  Verbal reasoning score: **10.9**, Physical sciences score: **12.3**, Biological sciences score: **12.3**, Writing score: **Q**
Proportion with undergraduate majors in: Biological sciences: **57%**, Physical sciences: **24%**, Non-sciences: **11%**, Other health professions: **0%**, Mixed disciplines and other: **8%**
Percentage of students not coming directly from college after graduation: **43%**

Dates and details

The American Medical College Application Service (AMCAS) application is accepted.
School asks for a school-specific application as part of the admissions process.
Oldest MCAT considered for Fall 2009 entry: **2005**
Earliest application date for the 2009-2010 first-year class: **6/1**
Latest application date: **10/15**
Acceptance dates for regular application for the class entering in fall 2009:

Earliest: **October 1, 2008**
Latest: **April 15, 2008**
The school considers requests for deferred entrance.
Starting month for the class entering in 2009–2010: **August**
The school has an Early Decision Plan (EDP).
A personal interview is required for admission.

Undergraduate coursework required

Medical school requires undergraduate work in these subjects: biology, organic chemistry, inorganic (general) chemistry, physics, humanities, behavioral science, calculus, social sciences.

ADMISSIONS POLICY

(TEXT PROVIDED BY SCHOOL):

Attendance at a fully accredited institution is required. If the applicant exclusively studied outside the United States, academic coursework must be supplemented by at least a year of coursework at an accredited U.S. university; bachelor's (B.A. or B.S.) degree is required prior to matriculation. Seven prerequisites to be fulfilled (please refer to the website for complete listing of admissions requirements). MCAT required.

COSTS AND FINANCIAL AID

Financial aid phone number: **(410) 955-1324**
Tuition, 2007-2008 academic year: **$40,669**
Room and board: **$14,906**
Percentage of students receiving financial aid in 2007-08: **78%**
Percentage of students receiving: Loans: **72%**, Grants/scholarships: **57%**, Work-study aid: **16%**
Average medical school debt for the Class of 2006: **$93,753**

STUDENT BODY

Fall 2007 full-time enrollment: **460**
Men: **52%**, Women: **48%**, In-state: **23%**, Minorities: **48%**, American Indian: **0.9%**, Asian-American: **35.0%**, African-American: **8.3%**, Hispanic-American: **4.1%**, White: **48.9%**, International: **2.8%**, Unknown: **0.0%**

ACADEMIC PROGRAMS

The school's curriculum frequently gives first-year students substantial contact with patients.

There are opportunities for first- or second-year students to work in community health clinics.

Program offerings: AIDS, drug/alcohol abuse, family medicine, geriatrics, internal medicine, pediatrics, rural medicine, women's health

Joint degrees awarded: M.D./Ph.D.

Total National Institutes of Health (NIH) grants awarded to the medical school and affiliated hospitals: **$450.8 million**

CURRICULUM

(TEXT PROVIDED BY SCHOOL):

Year 1: Sequential blocks teach Normal Cell Biology, Anatomy, Neuroscience, Metabolism, and Physiology using lecture, lab, and small groups. Year 2 teaches clinical skills and disease, with integrated teaching of Pathology, Pathophysiology, and Pharmacology by organ systems. Years 3 and 4: 50 weeks of nine required clerkships and 30 weeks of elective. Medical humanities course runs longitudinally for four years.

FACULTY PROFILE (FALL 2007)

Total teaching faculty: **2,337 (full-time), 1,268 (part-time)**
Of full-time faculty, those teaching in basic sciences: **8%**; in clinical programs: **92%**

Of part-time faculty, those teaching in basic sciences: **2%**; in clinical programs: **98%**
Full-time faculty/student ratio: **5.1**

SUPPORT SERVICES

The school offers students these services for dealing with stress: expanded-hour gym access, peer counseling, professional counseling, support groups.

RESIDENCY PROFILE

Most popular residency and specialty programs chosen by the 2006 and 2007 M.D. graduating classes: anesthesiology, dermatology, emergency medicine, internal medicine, ophthalmology, orthopaedic surgery, pediatrics, psychiatry, surgery–general.

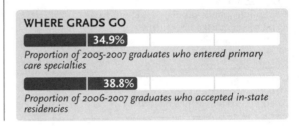

WHERE GRADS GO

34.9%

Proportion of 2005-2007 graduates who entered primary care specialties

38.8%

Proportion of 2006-2007 graduates who accepted in-state residencies

Loyola University Chicago

STRITCH

- 2160 S. First Avenue, Building 120, Maywood, IL 60153
- Private
- **Year Founded:** 1909
- **Tuition, 2007-2008:** $39,215
- **Enrollment 2007-2008 academic year:** 563
- **Website:** http://www.meddean.lumc.edu
- **Specialty ranking:** N/A

3.64 AVERAGE GPA, ENTERING CLASS FALL 2007

9.9 AVERAGE MCAT, ENTERING CLASS FALL 2007

5.0% ACCEPTANCE RATE, ENTERING CLASS FALL 2007

Unranked 2009 U.S. NEWS MEDICAL SCHOOL RANKING (RESEARCH)

54 2009 U.S. NEWS MEDICAL SCHOOL RANKING (PRIMARY CARE)

ADMISSIONS

Admissions phone number: **(708) 216-3229**
Admissions email address: **N/A**
Application website: **N/A**
Acceptance rate: **5.0%**
In-state acceptance rate: **10.8%**
Out-of-state acceptance rate: **3.7%**
Minority acceptance rate: **4.0%**
International acceptance rate: **N/A**

Fall 2007 applications and acceptees

	Applied	Interviewed	Accepted	Enrolled
Total:	5,434	528	269	146
In-state:	979	186	106	70
Out-of-state:	4,455	342	163	76

Profile of admitted students

Average undergraduate grade point average: **3.64**
MCAT averages (scale: 1-15; writing test: J-T):
  Composite score: **9.9**
  Verbal reasoning score: **9.6**, Physical sciences score: **9.9**, Biological sciences score: **10.4**, Writing score: **P**
Proportion with undergraduate majors in: Biological sciences: **42%**, Physical sciences: **12%**, Non-sciences: **16%**, Other health professions: **3%**, Mixed disciplines and other: **26%**
Percentage of students not coming directly from college after graduation: **45%**

Dates and details

The American Medical College Application Service (AMCAS) application is accepted.
School asks for a school-specific application as part of the admissions process.
Oldest MCAT considered for Fall 2009 entry: **2005**
Earliest application date for the 2009-2010 first-year class: **6/1**
Latest application date: **11/15**
Acceptance dates for regular application for the class entering in fall 2009:

Earliest: **October 15, 2008**
Latest: **N/A**
The school considers requests for deferred entrance.
Starting month for the class entering in 2009–2010: **July**
The school doesn't have an Early Decision Plan (EDP).
A personal interview is required for admission.

Undergraduate coursework required

Medical school requires undergraduate work in these subjects: biology/zoology, organic chemistry, inorganic (general) chemistry, physics.

ADMISSIONS POLICY

(TEXT PROVIDED BY SCHOOL):
Applicants capable of succeeding in the rigors of medical education are evaluated on the personal qualifications they can bring to the medical profession. Essential characteristics include interest in lifelong learning, integrity, compassion, ability to assume responsibility, exploration of the medical field, nature of motivation to enter medicine, and involvement in extracurricular activities.

COSTS AND FINANCIAL AID

Financial aid phone number: **(708) 216-3227**
Tuition, 2007-2008 academic year: **$39,215**
Room and board: **$15,725**
Percentage of students receiving financial aid in 2007-08: **93%**
Percentage of students receiving: Loans: **84%**, Grants/scholarships: **73%**, Work-study aid: **0%**
Average medical school debt for the Class of 2006: **$157,299**

STUDENT BODY

Fall 2007 full-time enrollment: **563**
Men: **49%**, Women: **51%**, In-state: **45%**, Minorities: **22%**, American Indian: **0.2%**, Asian-American: **13.0%**, African-American: **4.4%**, Hispanic-American: **4.1%**, White: **77.6%**, International: **0.0%**, Unknown: **0.7%**

ACADEMIC PROGRAMS

The school's curriculum occasionally gives first-year students substantial contact with patients.

There are opportunities for first- or second-year students to work in community health clinics.

Program offerings: AIDS, drug/alcohol abuse, family medicine, geriatrics, internal medicine, pediatrics, women's health

Joint degrees awarded: N/A

Total National Institutes of Health (NIH) grants awarded to the medical school and affiliated hospitals: **$22.6 million**

CURRICULUM

(TEXT PROVIDED BY SCHOOL):

Years 1 and 2 provide instruction in the basic sciences and in developing skills in communicating with patients, taking a history, and performing a physical examination. Years 3 and 4 include required clerkships (Medicine, Surgery, Family Medicine, Obstetrics/Gynecology, Pediatrics, Psychiatry) and electives. Clerkships combine inpatient experience with extensive time in the ambulatory setting.

FACULTY PROFILE (FALL 2007)

Total teaching faculty: **641 (full-time)**, **742 (part-time)**
Of full-time faculty, those teaching in basic sciences: **8%**; in clinical programs: **92%**

Of part-time faculty, those teaching in basic sciences: **4%**; in clinical programs: **96%**
Full-time faculty/student ratio: **1.1**

SUPPORT SERVICES

The school offers students these services for dealing with stress: expanded-hour gym access, peer counseling, professional counseling, religious support, support groups.

RESIDENCY PROFILE

Most popular residency and specialty programs chosen by the 2006 and 2007 M.D. graduating classes: anesthesiology, family practice, internal medicine, obstetrics and gynecology, orthopaedic surgery, pediatrics, surgery–general.

WHERE GRADS GO

52.0%

Proportion of 2005-2007 graduates who entered primary care specialties

N/A

Proportion of 2006-2007 graduates who accepted in-state residencies

Mayo Medical School

■ 200 First Street SW, Rochester, MN 55905
■ Private
■ **Year Founded:** 1972
■ **Tuition, 2007-2008:** $29,700
■ **Enrollment 2007-2008 academic year:** 160
■ **Website:** http://www.mayo.edu/mms/
■ **Specialty ranking:** internal medicine: 15

3.81 AVERAGE GPA, ENTERING CLASS FALL 2007

11.0 AVERAGE MCAT, ENTERING CLASS FALL 2007

1.5% ACCEPTANCE RATE, ENTERING CLASS FALL 2007

23 2009 U.S. NEWS MEDICAL SCHOOL RANKING (RESEARCH)

35 2009 U.S. NEWS MEDICAL SCHOOL RANKING (PRIMARY CARE)

ADMISSIONS
Admissions phone number: **(507) 284-3671**
Admissions email address:
   medschooladmissions@mayo.edu
Application website:
   http://www.aamc.org/stuapps/start.htm
Acceptance rate: **1.5%**
In-state acceptance rate: **3.8%**
Out-of-state acceptance rate: **1.2%**
Minority acceptance rate: **1.6%**
International acceptance rate: **N/A**

Fall 2007 applications and acceptees
	Applied	Interviewed	Accepted	Enrolled
Total:	3,424	242	50	42
In-state:	392	32	15	15
Out-of-state:	3,032	210	35	27

Profile of admitted students
Average undergraduate grade point average: **3.81**
MCAT averages (scale: 1-15; writing test: J-T):
   Composite score: **11.0**
   Verbal reasoning score: **11.2**, Physical sciences score:
   10.9, Biological sciences score: **10.9**, Writing score: **Q**
Proportion with undergraduate majors in: Biological
   sciences: **36%**, Physical sciences: **32%**, Non-sciences:
   10%, Other health professions: **8%**, Mixed disciplines
   and other: **14%**
Percentage of students not coming directly from college
   after graduation: **48%**

Dates and details
The American Medical College Application Service
   (AMCAS) application is accepted.
School does not ask for a school-specific application as part
   of the admissions process.
Oldest MCAT considered for Fall 2009 entry: **2006**
Earliest application date for the 2009-2010 first-year class:
   6/2
Latest application date: **11/3**

Acceptance dates for regular application for the class
   entering in fall 2009:
   Earliest: **October 15, 2008**
   Latest: **July 1, 2009**
The school considers requests for deferred entrance.
Starting month for the class entering in 2009–2010: **July**
The school doesn't have an Early Decision Plan (EDP).
A personal interview is required for admission.

Undergraduate coursework required
Medical school requires undergraduate work in these subjects: biology, organic chemistry, inorganic (general) chemistry, physics, biochemistry.

ADMISSIONS POLICY
(TEXT PROVIDED BY SCHOOL):
Mayo Medical School enrolls students with superior academic credentials, leadership characteristics, and a sincere
desire to commit their lives to service. Recognizing the
strength of diversity, the school encourages individuals with
diverse backgrounds to apply. Equal opportunity and access
are embraced throughout the admissions process.

COSTS AND FINANCIAL AID
Financial aid phone number: **(507) 284-4839**
Tuition, 2007-2008 academic year: **$29,700**
Room and board: **$12,375**
Percentage of students receiving financial aid in 2007-08:
   100%
Percentage of students receiving: Loans: **73%**,
   Grants/scholarships: **100%**, Work-study aid: **0%**
Average medical school debt for the Class of 2006:
   $84,422

STUDENT BODY
Fall 2007 full-time enrollment: **160**
Men: **49%**, Women: **51%**, In-state: **22%**, Minorities: **33%**,
   American Indian: **1.3%**, Asian-American: **11.3%**, African-
   American: **6.3%**, Hispanic-American: **5.6%**, White:
   63.1%, International: **0.0%**, Unknown: **12.5%**

ACADEMIC PROGRAMS

The school's curriculum very frequently gives first-year students substantial contact with patients.

There are opportunities for first- or second-year students to work in community health clinics.

Program offerings: AIDS, drug/alcohol abuse, family medicine, geriatrics, internal medicine, pediatrics, rural medicine, women's health

Joint degrees awarded: M.D./Ph.D., M.D./M.B.A., M.D./M.P.H., M.D./J.D., M.D./M.S.

Total National Institutes of Health (NIH) grants awarded to the medical school and affiliated hospitals: **$188.7 million**

CURRICULUM

(TEXT PROVIDED BY SCHOOL):

Courses occur the first two years in integrated blocks containing a clinical component with experiences related to topics covered in the classroom. Themes of basic science; clinical experiences; leadership; physician and society; principles of pharmacology; and basic and advanced doctoring are represented throughout the curriculum. Selectives engage students in career exploration, shadowing, or volunteer work.

FACULTY PROFILE (FALL 2007)

Total teaching faculty: **2,419 (full-time), 0 (part-time)**

Of full-time faculty, those teaching in basic sciences: **11%**; in clinical programs: **89%**

Of part-time faculty, those teaching in basic sciences: **N/A**; in clinical programs: **N/A**

Full-time faculty/student ratio: **15.1**

SUPPORT SERVICES

The school offers students these services for dealing with stress: expanded-hour gym access, peer counseling, professional counseling, religious support, support groups.

RESIDENCY PROFILE

Most popular residency and specialty programs chosen by the 2006 and 2007 M.D. graduating classes: anesthesiology, emergency medicine, family practice, internal medicine, obstetrics and gynecology, orthopaedic surgery, pediatrics, psychiatry, radiology–diagnostic, surgery–general.

WHERE GRADS GO

36%

Proportion of 2005-2007 graduates who entered primary care specialties

42%

Proportion of 2006-2007 graduates who accepted in-state residencies

Medical College of Georgia

- 1120 15th Street, Augusta, GA 30912-4750
- Public
- Year Founded: 1828
- Tuition, 2007-2008: In-state: $14,297; Out-of-state: $31,723
- Enrollment 2007-2008 academic year: 739
- Website: http://www.mcg.edu/som/index.html
- Specialty ranking: N/A

3.70 AVERAGE GPA, ENTERING CLASS FALL 2007

10.1 AVERAGE MCAT, ENTERING CLASS FALL 2007

13.5% ACCEPTANCE RATE, ENTERING CLASS FALL 2007

Unranked 2009 U.S. NEWS MEDICAL SCHOOL RANKING (RESEARCH)

Unranked 2009 U.S. NEWS MEDICAL SCHOOL RANKING (PRIMARY CARE)

ADMISSIONS

Admissions phone number: **(706) 721-3186**
Admissions email address: **stdadmin@mail.mcg.edu**
Application website: **N/A**
Acceptance rate: **13.5%**
In-state acceptance rate: **N/A**
Out-of-state acceptance rate: **N/A**
Minority acceptance rate: **11.5%**
International acceptance rate: **N/A**

Fall 2007 applications and acceptees

	Applied	Interviewed	Accepted	Enrolled
Total:	2,036	482	274	190
In-state:	N/A	N/A	N/A	N/A
Out-of-state:	N/A	N/A	N/A	N/A

Profile of admitted students

Average undergraduate grade point average: **3.70**
MCAT averages (scale: 1-15; writing test: J-T):
Composite score: **10.1**
Verbal reasoning score: **9.9**, Physical sciences score: **10.1**, Biological sciences score: **10.5**, Writing score: **N/A**
Proportion with undergraduate majors in: Biological sciences: **56%**, Physical sciences: **29%**, Non-sciences: **7%**, Other health professions: **6%**, Mixed disciplines and other: **2%**
Percentage of students not coming directly from college after graduation: **37%**

Dates and details

The American Medical College Application Service (AMCAS) application is accepted.
School asks for a school-specific application as part of the admissions process.
Oldest MCAT considered for Fall 2009 entry: **2006**
Earliest application date for the 2009-2010 first-year class: **6/1**
Latest application date: **11/1**
Acceptance dates for regular application for the class entering in fall 2009:
Earliest: **October 23, 2008**

Latest: **N/A**
The school considers requests for deferred entrance.
Starting month for the class entering in 2009–2010: **August**
The school has an Early Decision Plan (EDP).
A personal interview is required for admission.

Undergraduate coursework required

Medical school requires undergraduate work in these subjects: biology, biology/zoology, English, organic chemistry, inorganic (general) chemistry, physics, molecular and cell biology.

ADMISSIONS POLICY

(TEXT PROVIDED BY SCHOOL):
The Admissions Committee strives to identify and accept applicants who will help meet the healthcare needs of Georgia. It seeks applicants with the academic ability, personal attributes, and interests that produce quality physicians. The Admissions Committee expects applicants to have experiences in the clinical setting. For more, please visit the website.

COSTS AND FINANCIAL AID

Financial aid phone number: **(706) 721-4901**
Tuition, 2007-2008 academic year: **In-state: $14,297; Out-of-state: $31,723**
Room and board: **$3,611**
Percentage of students receiving financial aid in 2007-08: **81%**
Percentage of students receiving: Loans: **77%**, Grants/scholarships: **41%**, Work-study aid: **4%**
Average medical school debt for the Class of 2006: **$93,064**

STUDENT BODY

Fall 2007 full-time enrollment: **739**
Men: **56%**, Women: **44%**, In-state: **99%**, Minorities: **26%**, American Indian: **N/A**, Asian-American: **N/A**, African-American: **N/A**, Hispanic-American: **N/A**, White: **N/A**, International: **N/A**, Unknown: **N/A**

ACADEMIC PROGRAMS

The school's curriculum frequently gives first-year students substantial contact with patients.

There are opportunities for first- or second-year students to work in community health clinics.

Program offerings: AIDS, drug/alcohol abuse, family medicine, geriatrics, internal medicine, pediatrics, rural medicine, women's health

Joint degrees awarded: M.D./Ph.D.

Total National Institutes of Health (NIH) grants awarded to the medical school and affiliated hospitals: **$43.3 million**

CURRICULUM

(TEXT PROVIDED BY SCHOOL):

Year 1: Anatomy, Histology, and Development; Biochemistry; Genetics; Physiology; Neuroscience; Psychology; Essentials of Medicine 1. Year 2: Essentials of Clinical Medicine 2; Microbiology, Pathology, Pharmacology. Year 3: Family Medicine, Medicine, Neurology, Obstetrics/Gynecology, Pediatrics, Psychiatry, Surgery. Year 4: Adult Ambulatory; Critical Care, Emergency Medicine; acting internship; three electives.

FACULTY PROFILE (FALL 2007)

Total teaching faculty: **547 (full-time)**, **59 (part-time)**
Of full-time faculty, those teaching in basic sciences: **12%**; in clinical programs: **88%**

Of part-time faculty, those teaching in basic sciences: **5%**; in clinical programs: **95%**
Full-time faculty/student ratio: **0.7**

SUPPORT SERVICES

The school offers students these services for dealing with stress: expanded-hour gym access, peer counseling, professional counseling, religious support, support groups.

RESIDENCY PROFILE

Most popular residency and specialty programs chosen by the 2006 and 2007 M.D. graduating classes: anesthesiology, emergency medicine, family practice, internal medicine, obstetrics and gynecology, orthopaedic surgery, pediatrics, psychiatry, radiology–diagnostic, surgery–general.

WHERE GRADS GO

35.6%
Proportion of 2005-2007 graduates who entered primary care specialties

30.5%
Proportion of 2006-2007 graduates who accepted in-state residencies

Medical College of Wisconsin

- 8701 Watertown Plank Road, Milwaukee, WI 53226
- Private
- Year Founded: 1893
- Tuition, 2007-2008: $32,515
- Enrollment 2007-2008 academic year: 795
- Website: http://www.mcw.edu/acad/admission
- Specialty ranking: N/A

3.74 AVERAGE GPA, ENTERING CLASS FALL 2007

9.9 AVERAGE MCAT, ENTERING CLASS FALL 2007

6.8% ACCEPTANCE RATE, ENTERING CLASS FALL 2007

52 2009 U.S. NEWS MEDICAL SCHOOL RANKING (RESEARCH)

49 2009 U.S. NEWS MEDICAL SCHOOL RANKING (PRIMARY CARE)

ADMISSIONS

Admissions phone number: **(414) 456-8246**
Admissions email address: **medschool@mcw.edu**
Application website: **N/A**
Acceptance rate: **6.8%**
In-state acceptance rate: **23.2%**
Out-of-state acceptance rate: **5.1%**
Minority acceptance rate: **N/A**
International acceptance rate: **1.1%**

Fall 2007 applications and acceptees

	Applied	Interviewed	Accepted	Enrolled
Total:	6,665	746	453	204
In-state:	612	210	142	85
Out-of-state:	6,053	536	311	119

Profile of admitted students

Average undergraduate grade point average: **3.74**
MCAT averages (scale: 1-15; writing test: J-T):
 Composite score: **9.9**
 Verbal reasoning score: **9.6**, Physical sciences score: **9.8**,
 Biological sciences score: **10.3**, Writing score: **P**
Proportion with undergraduate majors in: Biological
 sciences: **45%**, Physical sciences: **17%**, Non-sciences:
 10%, Other health professions: **0%**, Mixed disciplines
 and other: **29%**
Percentage of students not coming directly from college
 after graduation: **52%**

Dates and details

The American Medical College Application Service
 (AMCAS) application is accepted.
School asks for a school-specific application as part of the
 admissions process.
Oldest MCAT considered for Fall 2009 entry: **2006**
Earliest application date for the 2009-2010 first-year class:
 6/1
Latest application date: **11/1**
Acceptance dates for regular application for the class
 entering in fall 2009:

Earliest: **October 15, 2008**
Latest: **N/A**
The school considers requests for deferred entrance.
Starting month for the class entering in 2009–2010:
 August
The school has an Early Decision Plan (EDP).
A personal interview is required for admission.

Undergraduate coursework required

Medical school requires undergraduate work in these subjects: biology, English, organic chemistry, inorganic (general) chemistry, physics, mathematics.

ADMISSIONS POLICY
(TEXT PROVIDED BY SCHOOL):

The Admissions Committee bases its decisions on a
thoughtful appraisal of each candidate's suitability for the
profession of medicine. Decisions are based upon scholastic
record, MCAT scores, recommendations, involvement in
college and community activities, and the personal interview, as well as by less tangible qualities of personality, character, and maturity.

COSTS AND FINANCIAL AID

Financial aid phone number: **(414) 456-8208**
Tuition, 2007-2008 academic year: **$32,515**
Room and board: **$8,000**
Percentage of students receiving financial aid in 2007-08:
 95%
Percentage of students receiving: Loans: **85%**,
 Grants/scholarships: **62%**, Work-study aid: **0%**
Average medical school debt for the Class of 2006:
 $143,605

STUDENT BODY

Fall 2007 full-time enrollment: **795**
Men: **51%**, Women: **49%**, In-state: **44%**, Minorities: **24%**,
 American Indian: **1.4%**, Asian-American: **14.3%**,
 African-American: **4.2%**, Hispanic-American: **3.9%**,
 White: **71.9%**, International: **0.8%**, Unknown: **3.5%**

ACADEMIC PROGRAMS

The school's curriculum occasionally gives first-year students substantial contact with patients.

There are opportunities for first- or second-year students to work in community health clinics.

Program offerings: family medicine, geriatrics, internal medicine, pediatrics, rural medicine, women's health

Joint degrees awarded: M.D./Ph.D.

Total National Institutes of Health (NIH) grants awarded to the medical school and affiliated hospitals: **$92.4 million**

CURRICULUM
(TEXT PROVIDED BY SCHOOL):

M1/M2 sequenced traditional learning (lecture, labs, dissection) and newer methods (computer aided; small groups; team-based learning; faculty mentor; standardized patients) cover basic sciences and introduction to clinical care to preparation for M3 year. M3/M4 rotations on required/elective clinical services, application of knowledge to patient care, gradual increase in responsibility and autonomy, preparation for internship.

FACULTY PROFILE (FALL 2007)

Total teaching faculty: **1,236 (full-time)**, **59 (part-time)**

Of full-time faculty, those teaching in basic sciences: **9%**; in clinical programs: **91%**

Of part-time faculty, those teaching in basic sciences: **31%**; in clinical programs: **69%**

Full-time faculty/student ratio: **1.6**

SUPPORT SERVICES

The school offers students these services for dealing with stress: expanded-hour gym access, professional counseling, religious support, support groups.

RESIDENCY PROFILE

Most popular residency and specialty programs chosen by the 2006 and 2007 M.D. graduating classes: internal medicine, internal medicine–pediatrics, obstetrics and gynecology, orthopaedic surgery, pediatrics, radiology–diagnostic, surgery–general.

WHERE GRADS GO

39%

Proportion of 2005-2007 graduates who entered primary care specialties

37%

Proportion of 2006-2007 graduates who accepted in-state residencies

Medical University of South Carolina

- 171 Ashley Avenue, Charleston, SC 29425
- Public
- Year Founded: 1824
- Tuition, 2007-2008: In-state: $24,713; Out-of-state: $67,243
- Enrollment 2007-2008 academic year: 620
- Website: http://www2.musc.edu/COM/COM1.shtml
- Specialty ranking: drug/alcohol abuse: 9

3.57	AVERAGE GPA, ENTERING CLASS FALL 2007
9.7	AVERAGE MCAT, ENTERING CLASS FALL 2007
14.4%	ACCEPTANCE RATE, ENTERING CLASS FALL 2007
Unranked	2009 U.S. NEWS MEDICAL SCHOOL RANKING (RESEARCH)
23	2009 U.S. NEWS MEDICAL SCHOOL RANKING (PRIMARY CARE)

ADMISSIONS

Admissions phone number: **(843) 792-2055**
Admissions email address: **taylorwl@musc.edu**
Application website:
   http://www.musc.edu/em/admissions/apply.html
Acceptance rate: **14.4%**
In-state acceptance rate: **38.0%**
Out-of-state acceptance rate: **1.6%**
Minority acceptance rate: **16.1%**
International acceptance rate: **5.6%**

Fall 2007 applications and acceptees

	Applied	Interviewed	Accepted	Enrolled
Total:	1,284	396	185	150
In-state:	453	361	172	140
Out-of-state:	831	35	13	10

Profile of admitted students

Average undergraduate grade point average: **3.57**
MCAT averages (scale: 1-15; writing test: J-T):
   Composite score: **9.7**
   Verbal reasoning score: **9.8**, Physical sciences score: **9.5**,
   Biological sciences score: **9.8**, Writing score: **O**
Proportion with undergraduate majors in: Biological
   sciences: **56%**, Physical sciences: **19%**, Non-sciences:
   14%, Other health professions: **3%**, Mixed disciplines
   and other: **8%**
Percentage of students not coming directly from college
   after graduation: **54%**

Dates and details

The American Medical College Application Service
   (AMCAS) application is accepted.
School asks for a school-specific application as part of the
   admissions process.
Oldest MCAT considered for Fall 2009 entry: **2004**
Earliest application date for the 2009-2010 first-year class:
   6/1
Latest application date: **12/1**
Acceptance dates for regular application for the class
   entering in fall 2009:

Earliest: **November 1, 2008**
Latest: **March 15, 2009**
The school considers requests for deferred entrance.
Starting month for the class entering in 2009–2010:
   August
The school has an Early Decision Plan (EDP).
A personal interview is required for admission.

Undergraduate coursework required

Medical school requires undergraduate work in these subjects: N/A.

ADMISSIONS POLICY

(TEXT PROVIDED BY SCHOOL):
MCAT scores and 90 semester hours of college courses
required. Baccalaureate degree preferred. MCAT by
spring/fall of year prior to admission. South Carolina residency is an admission consideration. Academic background
assessed using grade-point average and MCAT scores.
Those passing the cutoff are invited for interviews.
Noncognitive skills evaluated at interview. Letters of recommendation, leadership, clinical exposure to healthcare also
important.

COSTS AND FINANCIAL AID

Financial aid phone number: **(843) 792-2536**
Tuition, 2007-2008 academic year: **In-state: $24,713; Out-
   of-state: $67,243**
Room and board: **$10,770**
Percentage of students receiving financial aid in 2007-08:
   82%
Percentage of students receiving: Loans: **80%**,
   Grants/scholarships: **25%**, Work-study aid: **3%**
Average medical school debt for the Class of 2006:
   $130,000

STUDENT BODY

Fall 2007 full-time enrollment: **620**
Men: **57%**, Women: **43%**, In-state: **93%**, Minorities: **21%**,
   American Indian: **0.5%**, Asian-American: **6.8%**,

African-American: **10.8%**, Hispanic-American: **3.1%**,
White: **74.7%**, International: **1.6%**, Unknown: **2.6%**

ACADEMIC PROGRAMS

The school's curriculum occasionally gives first-year
students substantial contact with patients.

There are opportunities for first- or second-year students to
work in community health clinics.

Program offerings: AIDS, drug/alcohol abuse, family
medicine, geriatrics, internal medicine, pediatrics, rural
medicine, women's health

Joint degrees awarded: M.D./Ph.D., M.D./M.B.A.,
M.D./M.P.H., M.D./M.H.A.

Total National Institutes of Health (NIH) grants awarded to
the medical school and affiliated hospitals: **$84.0 million**

CURRICULUM

(TEXT PROVIDED BY SCHOOL):

Two years in basic sciences plus a clinical medicine course,
then two years of clinical sciences. Year 3 consists of six
clinical core clerkships and four clinical selectives. Year 4
consists of two core clerkships, an externship, and five electives. Emphasis is placed throughout the curriculum on
basic science concepts, development of clinical knowledge
and skills, and problem-solving skills.

FACULTY PROFILE (FALL 2007)

Total teaching faculty: **1,009 (full-time)**, **144 (part-time)**

Of full-time faculty, those teaching in basic sciences: **16%**;
in clinical programs: **84%**

Of part-time faculty, those teaching in basic sciences: **7%**;
in clinical programs: **93%**

Full-time faculty/student ratio: **1.6**

SUPPORT SERVICES

The school offers students these services for dealing with
stress: expanded-hour gym access, peer counseling, professional counseling, religious support, support groups.

RESIDENCY PROFILE

Most popular residency and specialty programs chosen by
the 2006 and 2007 M.D. graduating classes: anesthesiology, emergency medicine, family practice, internal medicine, obstetrics and gynecology, ophthalmology, orthopaedic
surgery, pediatrics, psychiatry, radiology–diagnostic.

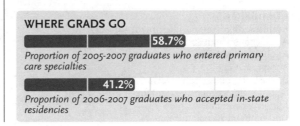

WHERE GRADS GO

58.7%

*Proportion of 2005-2007 graduates who entered primary
care specialties*

41.2%

*Proportion of 2006-2007 graduates who accepted in-state
residencies*

Mercer University

■ 1550 College Street, Macon, GA 31207
■ Private
■ **Year Founded:** 1982
■ **Tuition, 2007-2008:** $35,132
■ **Enrollment 2007-2008 academic year:** 243
■ **Website:** http://medicine.mercer.edu
■ **Specialty ranking:** family medicine: 22, rural medicine: 28

3.52 AVERAGE GPA, ENTERING CLASS FALL 2007

8.5 AVERAGE MCAT, ENTERING CLASS FALL 2007

12.3% ACCEPTANCE RATE, ENTERING CLASS FALL 2007

Unranked 2009 U.S. NEWS MEDICAL SCHOOL RANKING (RESEARCH)

Unranked 2009 U.S. NEWS MEDICAL SCHOOL RANKING (PRIMARY CARE)

ADMISSIONS

Admissions phone number: **(478) 301-2542**
Admissions email address: **admissions@med.mercer.edu**
Application website: **N/A**
Acceptance rate: **12.3%**
In-state acceptance rate: **12.3%**
Out-of-state acceptance rate: **N/A**
Minority acceptance rate: **6.7%**
International acceptance rate: **N/A**

Fall 2007 applications and acceptees

	Applied	Interviewed	Accepted	Enrolled
Total:	732	247	90	63
In-state:	732	247	90	63
Out-of-state:	0	N/A	N/A	N/A

Profile of admitted students

Average undergraduate grade point average: **3.52**
MCAT averages (scale: 1-15; writing test: J-T):
  Composite score: **8.5**
  Verbal reasoning score: **8.9**, Physical sciences score: **8.0**,
  Biological sciences score: **8.6**, Writing score: **N/A**
Proportion with undergraduate majors in: Biological sciences: **48%**, Physical sciences: **19%**, Non-sciences: **8%**, Other health professions: **0%**, Mixed disciplines and other: **25%**
Percentage of students not coming directly from college after graduation: **N/A**

Dates and details

The American Medical College Application Service (AMCAS) application is accepted.
School asks for a school-specific application as part of the admissions process.
Oldest MCAT considered for Fall 2009 entry: **2006**
Earliest application date for the 2009-2010 first-year class: **6/1**
Latest application date: **11/1**
Acceptance dates for regular application for the class entering in fall 2009:

Earliest: **September 1, 2008**
Latest: **March 31, 2009**
The school considers requests for deferred entrance.
Starting month for the class entering in 2009–2010:
  August
The school has an Early Decision Plan (EDP).
A personal interview is required for admission.

Undergraduate coursework required

Medical school requires undergraduate work in these subjects: biology, organic chemistry, inorganic (general) chemistry, physics.

ADMISSIONS POLICY

(TEXT PROVIDED BY SCHOOL):
Georgia residency is a requirement for admission.

COSTS AND FINANCIAL AID

Financial aid phone number: **(478) 301-2853**
Tuition, 2007-2008 academic year: **$35,132**
Room and board: **$13,740**
Percentage of students receiving financial aid in 2007-08: **91%**
Percentage of students receiving: Loans: **88%**, Grants/scholarships: **63%**, Work-study aid: **0%**
Average medical school debt for the Class of 2006: **$147,266**

STUDENT BODY

Fall 2007 full-time enrollment: **243**
Men: **53%**, Women: **47%**, In-state: **100%**, Minorities: **13%**, American Indian: **0.0%**, Asian-American: **10.3%**, African-American: **2.5%**, Hispanic-American: **1.6%**, White: **84.4%**, International: **0.0%**, Unknown: **1.2%**

ACADEMIC PROGRAMS

The school's curriculum frequently gives first-year students substantial contact with patients.
There are opportunities for first- or second-year students to work in community health clinics.

Program offerings: AIDS, drug/alcohol abuse, family medicine, geriatrics, internal medicine, pediatrics, rural medicine, women's health

Joint degrees awarded: N/A

Total National Institutes of Health (NIH) grants awarded to the medical school and affiliated hospitals: **N/A**

CURRICULUM
(TEXT PROVIDED BY SCHOOL):
Please see the website for complete information.

FACULTY PROFILE (FALL 2007)
Total teaching faculty: **218 (full-time)**, **289 (part-time)**
Of full-time faculty, those teaching in basic sciences: **18%**; in clinical programs: **82%**
Of part-time faculty, those teaching in basic sciences: **1%**; in clinical programs: **99%**
Full-time faculty/student ratio: **0.9**

SUPPORT SERVICES
The school offers students these services for dealing with stress: expanded-hour gym access, peer counseling, professional counseling.

RESIDENCY PROFILE
Most popular residency and specialty programs chosen by the 2006 and 2007 M.D. graduating classes: anesthesiology, emergency medicine, family practice, internal medicine, neurology, obstetrics and gynecology, pediatrics, psychiatry, radiology–diagnostic, surgery–general.

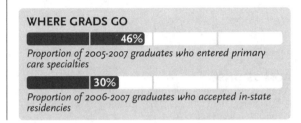

WHERE GRADS GO

46%
Proportion of 2005-2007 graduates who entered primary care specialties

30%
Proportion of 2006-2007 graduates who accepted in-state residencies

Michigan State University

- A110 E. Fee Hall, East Lansing, MI 48824
- Public
- **Year Founded:** 1964
- **Tuition, 2007-2008:** In-state: $28,010; Out-of-state: $60,890
- **Enrollment 2007-2008 academic year:** 494
- **Website:** http://humanmedicine.msu.edu
- **Specialty ranking:** family medicine: 18, rural medicine: 21

3.51	AVERAGE GPA, ENTERING CLASS FALL 2007
9.5	AVERAGE MCAT, ENTERING CLASS FALL 2007
6.3%	ACCEPTANCE RATE, ENTERING CLASS FALL 2007
Unranked	2009 U.S. NEWS MEDICAL SCHOOL RANKING (RESEARCH)
22	2009 U.S. NEWS MEDICAL SCHOOL RANKING (PRIMARY CARE)

ADMISSIONS

Admissions phone number: (517) 353-9620
Admissions email address: **MDadmissions@msu.edu**
Application website: **N/A**
Acceptance rate: **6.3%**
In-state acceptance rate: **15.9%**
Out-of-state acceptance rate: **3.0%**
Minority acceptance rate: **4.5%**
International acceptance rate: **1.6%**

Fall 2007 applications and acceptees

	Applied	Interviewed	Accepted	Enrolled
Total:	4,960	440	310	156
In-state:	1,244	272	198	98
Out-of-state:	3,716	168	112	58

Profile of admitted students

Average undergraduate grade point average: 3.51
MCAT averages (scale: 1-15; writing test: J-T):
  Composite score: 9.5
  Verbal reasoning score: 9.3, Physical sciences score: 9.3, Biological sciences score: 10.0, Writing score: O
Proportion with undergraduate majors in: Biological sciences: 65%, Physical sciences: 18%, Non-sciences: 13%, Other health professions: 0%, Mixed disciplines and other: 4%
Percentage of students not coming directly from college after graduation: 25%

Dates and details

The American Medical College Application Service (AMCAS) application is accepted.
School asks for a school-specific application as part of the admissions process.
Oldest MCAT considered for Fall 2009 entry: **2005**
Earliest application date for the 2009-2010 first-year class: **6/1**
Latest application date: **11/15**
Acceptance dates for regular application for the class entering in fall 2009:
  Earliest: **October 15, 2008**
Latest: **June 15, 2009**
The school considers requests for deferred entrance.
Starting month for the class entering in 2009-2010:
  August
The school has an Early Decision Plan (EDP).
A personal interview is required for admission.

Undergraduate coursework required

Medical school requires undergraduate work in these subjects: biology, English, organic chemistry, inorganic (general) chemistry, physics, humanities, mathematics, social sciences.

ADMISSIONS POLICY

(TEXT PROVIDED BY SCHOOL):
The college seeks an academically competent class that is broadly diverse in personalities, life experiences, and talents and is reflective of rural and urban Michigan. Nonacademic factors are uniquely considered with strong emphasis on medical/clinical experience, problem-solving ability/research, and interpersonal skills. Disadvantaged students are welcome; Michigan residents receive preference.

COSTS AND FINANCIAL AID

Financial aid phone number: (517) 353-5940
Tuition, 2007-2008 academic year: **In-state: $28,010; Out-of-state: $60,890**
Room and board: **$12,456**
Percentage of students receiving financial aid in 2007-08: **92%**
Percentage of students receiving: Loans: **87%**, Grants/scholarships: **64%**, Work-study aid: **0%**
Average medical school debt for the Class of 2006: **$163,390**

STUDENT BODY

Fall 2007 full-time enrollment: **494**
Men: 45%, Women: 55%, In-state: 74%, Minorities: 33%, American Indian: 1.0%, Asian-American: 16.0%, African-American: 9.1%, Hispanic-American: 6.7%, White: 63.2%, International: 1.0%, Unknown: 3.0%

ACADEMIC PROGRAMS

The school's curriculum occasionally gives first-year students substantial contact with patients.

There are opportunities for first- or second-year students to work in community health clinics.

Program offerings: AIDS, drug/alcohol abuse, family medicine, geriatrics, internal medicine, pediatrics, rural medicine, women's health

Joint degrees awarded: M.D./Ph.D., M.D./M.S., M.D./M.A., M.D./M.H.A.

Total National Institutes of Health (NIH) grants awarded to the medical school and affiliated hospitals: **N/A**

CURRICULUM

(TEXT PROVIDED BY SCHOOL):

Curricular format integrates biological, behavioral, and social sciences with a developmental approach to learning; early clinical skills teaching; structured basic science teaching balanced with problem-based learning and clinical correlations; attention to professionalism and special issues in medicine; and a community-integrated approach to clinical training in one of the school's community campuses.

FACULTY PROFILE (FALL 2007)

Total teaching faculty: **593 (full-time), 25 (part-time)**

Of full-time faculty, those teaching in basic sciences: **24%**; in clinical programs: **76%**

Of part-time faculty, those teaching in basic sciences: **32%**; in clinical programs: **68%**

Full-time faculty/student ratio: **1.2**

SUPPORT SERVICES

The school offers students these services for dealing with stress: expanded-hour gym access, professional counseling, support groups.

RESIDENCY PROFILE

Most popular residency and specialty programs chosen by the 2006 and 2007 M.D. graduating classes: anesthesiology, emergency medicine, family practice, internal medicine, obstetrics and gynecology, orthopaedic surgery, pediatrics, psychiatry, surgery–general, transitional year.

WHERE GRADS GO

47.8%

Proportion of 2005-2007 graduates who entered primary care specialties

37.6%

Proportion of 2006-2007 graduates who accepted in-state residencies

Morehouse School of Medicine

- 720 Westview Drive SW, Atlanta, GA 30310
- Private
- Year Founded: 1975
- Tuition, 2007-2008: $33,681
- Enrollment 2007-2008 academic year: 210
- Website: http://www.msm.edu
- Specialty ranking: N/A

N/A AVERAGE GPA, ENTERING CLASS FALL 2007

N/A AVERAGE MCAT, ENTERING CLASS FALL 2007

4.5% ACCEPTANCE RATE, ENTERING CLASS FALL 2007

Unranked 2009 U.S. NEWS MEDICAL SCHOOL RANKING (RESEARCH)

Unranked 2009 U.S. NEWS MEDICAL SCHOOL RANKING (PRIMARY CARE)

ADMISSIONS

Admissions phone number: **(404) 752-1650**
Admissions email address: **mdadmissions@msm.edu**
Application website: **N/A**
Acceptance rate: **4.5%**
In-state acceptance rate: **N/A**
Out-of-state acceptance rate: **N/A**
Minority acceptance rate: **N/A**
International acceptance rate: **N/A**

Fall 2007 applications and acceptees

	Applied	Interviewed	Accepted	Enrolled
Total:	2,973	N/A	134	N/A
In-state:	N/A	N/A	N/A	N/A
Out-of-state:	N/A	N/A	N/A	N/A

Profile of admitted students

Average undergraduate grade point average: **N/A**
MCAT averages (scale: 1-15; writing test: J-T):
Composite score: **N/A**
Verbal reasoning score: **N/A**, Physical sciences score: **N/A**, Biological sciences score: **N/A**, Writing score: **N/A**
Proportion with undergraduate majors in: Biological sciences: **66%**, Physical sciences: **10%**, Non-sciences: **17%**, Other health professions: **5%**, Mixed disciplines and other: **2%**
Percentage of students not coming directly from college after graduation: **30%**

Dates and details

The American Medical College Application Service (AMCAS) application is accepted.
School asks for a school-specific application as part of the admissions process.
Oldest MCAT considered for Fall 2009 entry: **2006**
Earliest application date for the 2009-2010 first-year class: **6/1**
Latest application date: **12/1**
Acceptance dates for regular application for the class entering in fall 2009:

Earliest: **June 1, 2008**
Latest: **December 1, 2008**
The school considers requests for deferred entrance.
Starting month for the class entering in 2009–2010: **July**
The school doesn't have an Early Decision Plan (EDP).
A personal interview is required for admission.

Undergraduate coursework required

Medical school requires undergraduate work in these subjects: biology, English, organic chemistry, physics, mathematics, general chemistry.

ADMISSIONS POLICY

(TEXT PROVIDED BY SCHOOL):

Selection is based on MCAT scores, academic achievement and progress, difficulty and balance of academic program, extracurricular activities. Committee also looks for evidence that applicant will contribute to the advancement of the practice of medicine. Data gathered include letters of recommendation, academic record, supplemental application, and interview.

COSTS AND FINANCIAL AID

Financial aid phone number: **(404) 752-1655**
Tuition, 2007-2008 academic year: **$33,681**
Room and board: **N/A**
Percentage of students receiving financial aid in 2007-08: **100%**
Percentage of students receiving: Loans: **100%**, Grants/scholarships: **77%**, Work-study aid: **0%**
Average medical school debt for the Class of 2006: **$134,930**

STUDENT BODY

Fall 2007 full-time enrollment: **210**
Men: **40%**, Women: **60%**, In-state: **30%**, Minorities: **86%**, American Indian: **N/A**, Asian-American: **5.2%**, African-American: **68.1%**, Hispanic-American: **2.9%**, White: **14.3%**, International: **9.5%**, Unknown: **N/A**

ACADEMIC PROGRAMS

The school's curriculum frequently gives first-year students substantial contact with patients.

There are opportunities for first- or second-year students to work in community health clinics.

Program offerings: drug/alcohol abuse, family medicine, internal medicine, pediatrics, rural medicine

Joint degrees awarded: M.D./Ph.D.

Total National Institutes of Health (NIH) grants awarded to the medical school and affiliated hospitals: **$27.8 million**

CURRICULUM
(TEXT PROVIDED BY SCHOOL):

The MSM M.D. program focuses on primary healthcare. The curriculum includes clinical preceptorships, community service learning opportunities, and clerkships in Surgery, Family Medicine, Maternal and Child Health, Psychiatry, Radiology, Internal Medicine, Pediatrics, Obstetrics/Gynecology, Rural Primary Care, and Ambulatory Medicine, plus five electives.

FACULTY PROFILE (FALL 2007)

Total teaching faculty: **213 (full-time)**, **51 (part-time)**

Of full-time faculty, those teaching in basic sciences: **N/A**; in clinical programs: **N/A**

Of part-time faculty, those teaching in basic sciences: **N/A**; in clinical programs: **N/A**

Full-time faculty/student ratio: **1.0**

SUPPORT SERVICES

The school offers students these services for dealing with stress: expanded-hour gym access, peer counseling, professional counseling, religious support, support groups.

RESIDENCY PROFILE

Most popular residency and specialty programs chosen by the 2006 and 2007 M.D. graduating classes: anesthesiology, emergency medicine, family practice, internal medicine, obstetrics and gynecology, pediatrics, psychiatry, surgery–general, internal medicine/pediatrics.

WHERE GRADS GO

N/A

Proportion of 2005-2007 graduates who entered primary care specialties

N/A

Proportion of 2006-2007 graduates who accepted in-state residencies

Mount Sinai School of Medicine

- 1 Gustave L. Levy Place, PO Box 1475, New York, NY 10029
- Private
- **Year Founded:** 1963
- **Tuition, 2007-2008:** $38,528
- **Enrollment 2007-2008 academic year:** 506
- **Website:** http://www.mssm.edu
- **Specialty ranking:** geriatrics: 2, internal medicine: 25, women's health: 18

3.64	AVERAGE GPA, ENTERING CLASS FALL 2007
11.3	AVERAGE MCAT, ENTERING CLASS FALL 2007
5.7%	ACCEPTANCE RATE, ENTERING CLASS FALL 2007
23	2009 U.S. NEWS MEDICAL SCHOOL RANKING (RESEARCH)
Unranked	2009 U.S. NEWS MEDICAL SCHOOL RANKING (PRIMARY CARE)

ADMISSIONS

Admissions phone number: **(212) 241-6696**
Admissions email address: **admissions@mssm.edu**
Application website: **N/A**
Acceptance rate: **5.7%**
In-state acceptance rate: **7.9%**
Out-of-state acceptance rate: **4.7%**
Minority acceptance rate: **5.8%**
International acceptance rate: **3.2%**

Fall 2007 applications and acceptees

	Applied	Interviewed	Accepted	Enrolled
Total:	6,666	806	379	140
In-state:	2,033	352	161	42
Out-of-state:	4,633	454	218	98

Profile of admitted students

Average undergraduate grade point average: **3.64**
MCAT averages (scale: 1-15; writing test: J-T):
   Composite score: **11.3**
   Verbal reasoning score: **10.7**, Physical sciences score: **11.7**, Biological sciences score: **11.7**, Writing score: **Q**
Proportion with undergraduate majors in: Biological sciences: **44%**, Physical sciences: **19%**, Non-sciences: **37%**, Other health professions: **0%**, Mixed disciplines and other: **0%**
Percentage of students not coming directly from college after graduation: **50%**

Dates and details

The American Medical College Application Service (AMCAS) application is accepted.
School asks for a school-specific application as part of the admissions process.
Oldest MCAT considered for Fall 2009 entry: **2006**
Earliest application date for the 2009-2010 first-year class: **6/5**
Latest application date: **11/1**
Acceptance dates for regular application for the class entering in fall 2009:

Earliest: **November 15, 2008**
   Latest: **August 12, 2009**
The school considers requests for deferred entrance.
Starting month for the class entering in 2009–2010:
   August
The school has an Early Decision Plan (EDP).
A personal interview is required for admission.

Undergraduate coursework required

Medical school requires undergraduate work in these subjects: biology, English, organic chemistry, inorganic (general) chemistry, physics, mathematics.

ADMISSIONS POLICY
(TEXT PROVIDED BY SCHOOL):

Applicants are considered based on qualifications that include intellectual capability and academic achievement; motivation; potential for a career in medicine, service, and leadership; eagerness to shape one's own learning experience; maturity; and conformity to the school's standards of character and health.

COSTS AND FINANCIAL AID

Financial aid phone number: **(212) 241-5245**
Tuition, 2007-2008 academic year: **$38,528**
Room and board: **$15,000**
Percentage of students receiving financial aid in 2007-08: **81%**
Percentage of students receiving: Loans: **77%**, Grants/scholarships: **37%**, Work-study aid: **11%**
Average medical school debt for the Class of 2006: **$136,338**

STUDENT BODY

Fall 2007 full-time enrollment: **506**
Men: **48%**, Women: **52%**, In-state: **33%**, Minorities: **44%**, American Indian: **1.2%**, Asian-American: **20.6%**, African-American: **6.7%**, Hispanic-American: **14.8%**, White: **47.6%**, International: **4.2%**, Unknown: **4.9%**

ACADEMIC PROGRAMS

The school's curriculum frequently gives first-year students substantial contact with patients.

There are opportunities for first- or second-year students to work in community health clinics.

Program offerings: AIDS, drug/alcohol abuse, family medicine, geriatrics, internal medicine, pediatrics, women's health

Joint degrees awarded: M.D./Ph.D., M.D./M.B.A., M.D./M.P.H.

Total National Institutes of Health (NIH) grants awarded to the medical school and affiliated hospitals: **$210.8 million**

CURRICULUM

(TEXT PROVIDED BY SCHOOL):

Mount Sinai School of Medicine offers an innovative curriculum that promotes early patient exposure during the first two years and integration of clinical medicine with the basic sciences throughout all four years. The clinical curriculum is designed to promote self-directed learning, clinical problem solving, and scientific inquiry through diverse and innovative educational offerings.

FACULTY PROFILE (FALL 2007)

Total teaching faculty: 1,077 **(full-time)**, 154 **(part-time)**

Of full-time faculty, those teaching in basic sciences: **27%**; in clinical programs: **73%**

Of part-time faculty, those teaching in basic sciences: **8%**; in clinical programs: **92%**

Full-time faculty/student ratio: **2.1**

SUPPORT SERVICES

The school offers students these services for dealing with stress: expanded-hour gym access, peer counseling, professional counseling, religious support, support groups.

RESIDENCY PROFILE

Most popular residency and specialty programs chosen by the 2006 and 2007 M.D. graduating classes: anesthesiology, emergency medicine, internal medicine, obstetrics and gynecology, pediatrics, psychiatry, surgery–general.

WHERE GRADS GO

35.6%

Proportion of 2005-2007 graduates who entered primary care specialties

66.0%

Proportion of 2006-2007 graduates who accepted in-state residencies

New York Medical College

- Administration Building, Valhalla, NY 10595
- Private
- Year Founded: 1860
- Tuition, 2007-2008: $43,696
- Enrollment 2007-2008 academic year: 786
- Website: http://www.nymc.edu
- Specialty ranking: N/A

3.60 AVERAGE GPA, ENTERING CLASS FALL 2007

10.3 AVERAGE MCAT, ENTERING CLASS FALL 2007

8.0% ACCEPTANCE RATE, ENTERING CLASS FALL 2007

Unranked 2009 U.S. NEWS MEDICAL SCHOOL RANKING (RESEARCH)

Unranked 2009 U.S. NEWS MEDICAL SCHOOL RANKING (PRIMARY CARE)

ADMISSIONS

Admissions phone number: **(914) 594-4507**
Admissions email address: **mdadmit@nymc.edu**
Application website:
   http://www.nymc.edu/admit/medical/info/proced.htm
Acceptance rate: **8.0%**
In-state acceptance rate: **10.6%**
Out-of-state acceptance rate: **7.4%**
Minority acceptance rate: **7.1%**
International acceptance rate: **2.8%**

Fall 2007 applications and acceptees

	Applied	Interviewed	Accepted	Enrolled
Total:	8,319	1,349	669	195
In-state:	1,567	313	166	50
Out-of-state:	6,752	1,036	503	145

Profile of admitted students

Average undergraduate grade point average: 3.60
MCAT averages (scale: 1-15; writing test: J-T):
   Composite score: **10.3**
   Verbal reasoning score: **9.9**, Physical sciences score: **10.3**, Biological sciences score: **10.6**, Writing score: **Q**
Proportion with undergraduate majors in: Biological sciences: **48%**, Physical sciences: **15%**, Non-sciences: **14%**, Other health professions: **1%**, Mixed disciplines and other: **22%**
Percentage of students not coming directly from college after graduation: **62%**

Dates and details

The American Medical College Application Service (AMCAS) application is accepted.
School asks for a school-specific application as part of the admissions process.
Oldest MCAT considered for Fall 2009 entry: **2006**
Earliest application date for the 2009-2010 first-year class: **6/1**
Latest application date: **12/15**
Acceptance dates for regular application for the class entering in fall 2009:

Earliest: **December 15, 2008**
Latest: **August 6, 2009**
The school considers requests for deferred entrance.
Starting month for the class entering in 2009–2010:
   August
The school has an Early Decision Plan (EDP).
A personal interview is required for admission.

Undergraduate coursework required

Medical school requires undergraduate work in these subjects: biology, English, organic chemistry, inorganic (general) chemistry, physics.

ADMISSIONS POLICY

(TEXT PROVIDED BY SCHOOL):
The college admits a diverse class respecting gender, race, and other factors. Students from historically underrepresented backgrounds are actively encouraged to apply. No candidate will be denied admission based on race, color, creed, religion, national or ethnic origin, age, sex, sexual orientation, or disability. Please see the website for details.

COSTS AND FINANCIAL AID

Financial aid phone number: **(914) 594-4491**
Tuition, 2007-2008 academic year: **$43,696**
Room and board: **$18,798**
Percentage of students receiving financial aid in 2007-08: **93%**
Percentage of students receiving: Loans: **91%**, Grants/scholarships: **18%**, Work-study aid: **3%**
Average medical school debt for the Class of 2006: **$168,000**

STUDENT BODY

Fall 2007 full-time enrollment: **786**
Men: **47%**, Women: **53%**, In-state: **32%**, Minorities: **40%**, American Indian: **0.3%**, Asian-American: **37.5%**, African-American: **1.7%**, Hispanic-American: **0.9%**, White: **52.4%**, International: **0.5%**, Unknown: **6.7%**

ACADEMIC PROGRAMS

The school's curriculum frequently gives first-year students substantial contact with patients.

There are opportunities for first- or second-year students to work in community health clinics.

Program offerings: AIDS, drug/alcohol abuse, family medicine, geriatrics, internal medicine, pediatrics, rural medicine, women's health

Joint degrees awarded: M.D./Ph.D., M.D./M.P.H.

Total National Institutes of Health (NIH) grants awarded to the medical school and affiliated hospitals: **$21.7 million**

CURRICULUM
(TEXT PROVIDED BY SCHOOL):

For a description of the New York Medical College School of Medicine curriculum, please visit the website.

FACULTY PROFILE (FALL 2007)

Total teaching faculty: **1,402 (full-time)**, **134 (part-time)**

Of full-time faculty, those teaching in basic sciences: **9%**; in clinical programs: **91%**

Of part-time faculty, those teaching in basic sciences: **3%**; in clinical programs: **97%**

Full-time faculty/student ratio: **1.8**

SUPPORT SERVICES

The school offers students these services for dealing with stress: expanded-hour gym access, professional counseling, religious support, support groups.

RESIDENCY PROFILE

Most popular residency and specialty programs chosen by the 2006 and 2007 M.D. graduating classes: anesthesiology, emergency medicine, family practice, internal medicine, neurology, obstetrics and gynecology, orthopaedic surgery, pediatrics, radiology–diagnostic, surgery–general.

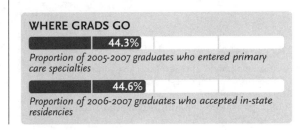

WHERE GRADS GO

44.3%

Proportion of 2005-2007 graduates who entered primary care specialties

44.6%

Proportion of 2006-2007 graduates who accepted in-state residencies

New York University

- 550 First Avenue, New York, NY 10016
- Private
- Year Founded: 1841
- Tuition, 2007-2008: $43,919
- Enrollment 2007-2008 academic year: 670
- Website: http://www.med.nyu.edu/medicaldegree
- Specialty ranking: AIDS: 12, drug/alcohol abuse: 7

3.76 AVERAGE GPA, ENTERING CLASS FALL 2007

11.2 AVERAGE MCAT, ENTERING CLASS FALL 2007

5.7% ACCEPTANCE RATE, ENTERING CLASS FALL 2007

34 2009 U.S. NEWS MEDICAL SCHOOL RANKING (RESEARCH)

Unranked 2009 U.S. NEWS MEDICAL SCHOOL RANKING (PRIMARY CARE)

ADMISSIONS

Admissions phone number: **(212) 263-5290**
Admissions email address: **admissions@med.nyu.edu**
Application website:
   http://www.med.nyu.edu/medicaldegree/admissions
Acceptance rate: **5.7%**
In-state acceptance rate: **8.9%**
Out-of-state acceptance rate: **5.0%**
Minority acceptance rate: **5.4%**
International acceptance rate: **2.9%**

Fall 2007 applications and acceptees

	Applied	Interviewed	Accepted	Enrolled
Total:	7,573	960	435	160
In-state:	1,454	273	129	70
Out-of-state:	6,119	687	306	90

Profile of admitted students

Average undergraduate grade point average: **3.76**
MCAT averages (scale: 1-15; writing test: J-T):
   Composite score: **11.2**
   Verbal reasoning score: **10.5**, Physical sciences score:
   11.5, Biological sciences score: **11.7**, Writing score: **Q**
Proportion with undergraduate majors in: Biological
   sciences: **57%**, Physical sciences: **23%**, Non-sciences:
   16%, Other health professions: **1%**, Mixed disciplines
   and other: **3%**
Percentage of students not coming directly from college
   after graduation: **37%**

Dates and details

The American Medical College Application Service
   (AMCAS) application is accepted.
School asks for a school-specific application as part of the
   admissions process.
Oldest MCAT considered for Fall 2009 entry: **2006**
Earliest application date for the 2009-2010 first-year class:
   6/1
Latest application date: **10/15**
Acceptance dates for regular application for the class
   entering in fall 2009:

   Earliest: **March 1, 2009**
   Latest: **N/A**
The school considers requests for deferred entrance.
Starting month for the class entering in 2009–2010:
   August
The school doesn't have an Early Decision Plan (EDP).
A personal interview is required for admission.

Undergraduate coursework required

Medical school requires undergraduate work in these subjects: biology, English, organic chemistry, inorganic (general) chemistry, physics.

ADMISSIONS POLICY
(TEXT PROVIDED BY SCHOOL):

NYU participates in the American Medical College
Application Service. Applicants must have attended an
accredited college, completing six credits in each of the following: English, Inorganic Chemistry, Organic Chemistry,
Physics, and General Biology or Zoology. The MCAT and
college faculty evaluations are required. Interviews are
granted to applicants who merit serious consideration.
Those who failed in another medical school are ineligible.

COSTS AND FINANCIAL AID

Financial aid phone number: **(212) 263-5286**
Tuition, 2007-2008 academic year: **$43,919**
Room and board: **$10,000**
Percentage of students receiving financial aid in 2007-08:
   69%
Percentage of students receiving: Loans: **66%**,
   Grants/scholarships: **47%**, Work-study aid: **10%**
Average medical school debt for the Class of 2006:
   $112,839

STUDENT BODY

Fall 2007 full-time enrollment: **670**
Men: **51%**, Women: **49%**, In-state: **46%**, Minorities: **35%**,
   American Indian: **0.6%**, Asian-American: **23.4%**,
   African-American: **4.6%**, Hispanic-American: **6.6%**,
   White: **56.6%**, International: **0.4%**, Unknown: **7.8%**

ACADEMIC PROGRAMS

The school's curriculum frequently gives first-year students substantial contact with patients.

There are opportunities for first- or second-year students to work in community health clinics.

Program offerings: AIDS, drug/alcohol abuse, family medicine, geriatrics, internal medicine, pediatrics, rural medicine, women's health

Joint degrees awarded: M.D./Ph.D., M.D./M.P.H.

Total National Institutes of Health (NIH) grants awarded to the medical school and affiliated hospitals: **$143.4 million**

CURRICULUM

(TEXT PROVIDED BY SCHOOL):

NYU's program encourages self-directed learning. The preclinical curriculum is organized into thematic modules with small-group, case-based exercises. The clinical curriculum, with nine core clerkships, stresses interactive, patient-based education; evidence-based problem solving; and spiral learning, building on a strong background in biomedical science and a rich, diverse clinical environment.

FACULTY PROFILE (FALL 2007)

Total teaching faculty: **1,557 (full-time)**, **3,304 (part-time)**
Of full-time faculty, those teaching in basic sciences: **19%**;
in clinical programs: **81%**

Of part-time faculty, those teaching in basic sciences: **6%**;
in clinical programs: **94%**
Full-time faculty/student ratio: **2.3**

SUPPORT SERVICES

The school offers students these services for dealing with stress: expanded-hour gym access, peer counseling, professional counseling, religious support, support groups.

RESIDENCY PROFILE

Most popular residency and specialty programs chosen by the 2006 and 2007 M.D. graduating classes: anesthesiology, emergency medicine, internal medicine, neurology, obstetrics and gynecology, orthopaedic surgery, pediatrics, psychiatry, radiology–diagnostic, surgery–general.

WHERE GRADS GO

35.4%

Proportion of 2005-2007 graduates who entered primary care specialties

56.5%

Proportion of 2006-2007 graduates who accepted in-state residencies

Northeastern Ohio Universities

COLLEGE OF MEDICINE

- 4209 State Route 44, PO Box 95, Rootstown, OH 44272-0095
- Public
- **Year Founded:** 1973
- **Tuition, 2007-2008:** In-state: $28,794; Out-of-state: $55,599
- **Enrollment 2007-2008 academic year:** 455
- **Website:** http://www.neoucom.edu
- **Specialty ranking:** N/A

3.71 AVERAGE GPA, ENTERING CLASS FALL 2007

9.5 AVERAGE MCAT, ENTERING CLASS FALL 2007

10.5% ACCEPTANCE RATE, ENTERING CLASS FALL 2007

Unranked 2009 U.S. NEWS MEDICAL SCHOOL RANKING (RESEARCH)

Unranked 2009 U.S. NEWS MEDICAL SCHOOL RANKING (PRIMARY CARE)

ADMISSIONS

Admissions phone number: **(330) 325-6270**
Admissions email address: **admission@neoucom.edu**
Application website:
http://www.neoucom.edu/students/ADMI
Acceptance rate: **10.5%**
In-state acceptance rate: **23.4%**
Out-of-state acceptance rate: **0.7%**
Minority acceptance rate: **N/A**
International acceptance rate: **N/A**

Fall 2007 applications and acceptees

	Applied	Interviewed	Accepted	Enrolled
Total:	2,400	364	253	120
In-state:	1,040	348	243	119
Out-of-state:	1,360	16	10	1

Profile of admitted students

Average undergraduate grade point average: **3.71**
MCAT averages (scale: 1-15; writing test: J-T):
Composite score: **9.5**
Verbal reasoning score: **9.6**, Physical sciences score: **9.3**, Biological sciences score: **9.6**, Writing score: **P**
Proportion with undergraduate majors in: Biological sciences: **81%**, Physical sciences: **5%**, Non-sciences: **3%**, Other health professions: **6%**, Mixed disciplines and other: **5%**
Percentage of students not coming directly from college after graduation: **17%**

Dates and details

The American Medical College Application Service (AMCAS) application is accepted.
School asks for a school-specific application as part of the admissions process.
Oldest MCAT considered for Fall 2009 entry: **2006**
Earliest application date for the 2009-2010 first-year class: **6/1**
Latest application date: **11/1**
Acceptance dates for regular application for the class entering in fall 2009:

Earliest: **August 1, 2008**
Latest: **November 1, 2008**
The school doesn't consider requests for deferred entrance.
Starting month for the class entering in 2009–2010:
August
The school has an Early Decision Plan (EDP).
A personal interview is required for admission.

Undergraduate coursework required

Medical school requires undergraduate work in these subjects: organic chemistry, physics.

ADMISSIONS POLICY
(TEXT PROVIDED BY SCHOOL):

Candidates must demonstrate the designated skills, abilities, and attributes listed for prospective students on the College of Medicineís website. NEOUCOM is publicly chartered and funded in the state of Ohio, and its charter mandates admission preference to Ohio residents as defined by the Board of Regents. Only U.S. citizens and permanent residents may be considered for admission.

COSTS AND FINANCIAL AID

Financial aid phone number: **(330) 325-6481**
Tuition, 2007-2008 academic year: **In-state: $28,794; Out-of-state: $55,599**
Room and board: **$10,000**
Percentage of students receiving financial aid in 2007-08: **84%**
Percentage of students receiving: Loans: **83%**, Grants/scholarships: **33%**, Work-study aid: **0%**
Average medical school debt for the Class of 2006: **$112,043**

STUDENT BODY

Fall 2007 full-time enrollment: **455**
Men: **49%**, Women: **51%**, In-state: **98%**, Minorities: **40%**, American Indian: **0.4%**, Asian-American: **33.2%**, African-American: **3.7%**, Hispanic-American: **2.4%**, White: **58.2%**, International: **0.0%**, Unknown: **2.0%**

ACADEMIC PROGRAMS

The school's curriculum frequently gives first-year students substantial contact with patients.

There are opportunities for first- or second-year students to work in community health clinics.

Program offerings: AIDS, drug/alcohol abuse, family medicine, geriatrics, internal medicine, pediatrics, rural medicine, women's health

Joint degrees awarded: N/A

Total National Institutes of Health (NIH) grants awarded to the medical school and affiliated hospitals: **$2.5 million**

CURRICULUM

(TEXT PROVIDED BY SCHOOL):

The goal of NEOUCOM's curriculum is to develop and graduate students who demonstrate competence in the knowledge and practice of medicine, exhibit strong communication skills, display a caring attitude, and exhibit professional character, all in the context of the community. These 5 C's guide the expected outcomes for students graduating from the college's program.

FACULTY PROFILE (FALL 2007)

Total teaching faculty: **305 (full-time)**, **1,684 (part-time)**

Of full-time faculty, those teaching in basic sciences: **13%**; in clinical programs: **87%**

Of part-time faculty, those teaching in basic sciences: **7%**; in clinical programs: **93%**

Full-time faculty/student ratio: **0.7**

SUPPORT SERVICES

The school offers students these services for dealing with stress: expanded-hour gym access, peer counseling, professional counseling, support groups.

RESIDENCY PROFILE

Most popular residency and specialty programs chosen by the 2006 and 2007 M.D. graduating classes: emergency medicine, internal medicine, obstetrics and gynecology, pediatrics, surgery–general.

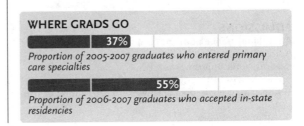

WHERE GRADS GO

37%

Proportion of 2005-2007 graduates who entered primary care specialties

55%

Proportion of 2006-2007 graduates who accepted in-state residencies

Northwestern University

FEINBERG

- 303 E. Chicago Avenue, Morton Building 1-606, Chicago, IL 60611
- Private
- Year Founded: 1859
- Tuition, 2007-2008: $43,140
- Enrollment 2007-2008 academic year: 700
- Website: http://www.feinberg.northwestern.edu
- Specialty ranking: AIDS: 14, internal medicine: 19, pediatrics: 18, women's health: 10

3.71 AVERAGE GPA, ENTERING CLASS FALL 2007

11.4 AVERAGE MCAT, ENTERING CLASS FALL 2007

6.0% ACCEPTANCE RATE, ENTERING CLASS FALL 2007

20 2009 U.S. NEWS MEDICAL SCHOOL RANKING (RESEARCH)

51 2009 U.S. NEWS MEDICAL SCHOOL RANKING (PRIMARY CARE)

ADMISSIONS

Admissions phone number: (312) 503-8206
Admissions email address: med-admissions@northwestern.edu
Application website:
   http://www.medschool.northwestern.edu/admissions/md/
Acceptance rate: 6.0%
In-state acceptance rate: 6.7%
Out-of-state acceptance rate: 5.9%
Minority acceptance rate: N/A
International acceptance rate: N/A

Fall 2007 applications and acceptees

	Applied	Interviewed	Accepted	Enrolled
Total:	7,527	774	454	169
In-state:	961	100	64	39
Out-of-state:	6,566	674	390	130

Profile of admitted students

Average undergraduate grade point average: 3.71
MCAT averages (scale: 1-15; writing test: J-T):
   Composite score: 11.4
   Verbal reasoning score: 10.6, Physical sciences score: 11.8, Biological sciences score: 11.8, Writing score: Q
Proportion with undergraduate majors in: Biological sciences: 45%, Physical sciences: 23%, Non-sciences: 24%, Other health professions: 1%, Mixed disciplines and other: 7%
Percentage of students not coming directly from college after graduation: 19%

Dates and details

The American Medical College Application Service (AMCAS) application is accepted.
School asks for a school-specific application as part of the admissions process.
Oldest MCAT considered for Fall 2009 entry: 2006
Earliest application date for the 2009-2010 first-year class: 6/1
Latest application date: 10/15

Acceptance dates for regular application for the class entering in fall 2009:
   Earliest: November 30, 2008
   Latest: March 1, 2009
The school considers requests for deferred entrance.
Starting month for the class entering in 2009–2010:
   August
The school doesn't have an Early Decision Plan (EDP).
A personal interview is required for admission.

Undergraduate coursework required

Medical school requires undergraduate work in these subjects: biology, English, organic chemistry, inorganic (general) chemistry, physics, humanities, calculus.

ADMISSIONS POLICY

(TEXT PROVIDED BY SCHOOL):
A full year each of Modern Biology, Organic Chemistry, Inorganic Chemistry, General Physics, and English is recommended. The MCAT is required. No preference is given to residents of the state of Illinois. Applications from foreign nationals are welcome; all applicants are required to have completed at least three years of coursework at an accredited U.S. or Canadian college or university.

COSTS AND FINANCIAL AID

Financial aid phone number: (312) 503-8722
Tuition, 2007-2008 academic year: $43,140
Room and board: $12,375
Percentage of students receiving financial aid in 2007-08: 75%
Percentage of students receiving: Loans: 66%, Grants/scholarships: 36%, Work-study aid: 0%
Average medical school debt for the Class of 2006: $150,468

STUDENT BODY

Fall 2007 full-time enrollment: 700
Men: 52%, Women: 48%, In-state: 26%, Minorities: 48%, American Indian: 1.0%, Asian-American: 35.3%,

African-American: **6.4%**, Hispanic-American: **4.9%**,
White: **43.6%**, International: **4.1%**, Unknown: **4.7%**

ACADEMIC PROGRAMS

The school's curriculum frequently gives first-year students substantial contact with patients.

There are opportunities for first- or second-year students to work in community health clinics.

Program offerings: AIDS, drug/alcohol abuse, family medicine, geriatrics, internal medicine, pediatrics, rural medicine, women's health

Joint degrees awarded: M.D./Ph.D., M.D./M.B.A., M.D./M.P.H., M.D./M.A.

Total National Institutes of Health (NIH) grants awarded to the medical school and affiliated hospitals: **$205.9 million**

CURRICULUM

(TEXT PROVIDED BY SCHOOL):

The Feinberg curriculum cultivates leaders who will effect change in their communities and in the profession, and it is designed for independent adult learners. There is one integrated basic science course in each of the first two years, complemented by problem-based learning sessions, labs, and tutorials. Clinical rotations are conducted within a consortium of affiliates, the McGaw Medical Center.

FACULTY PROFILE (FALL 2007)

Total teaching faculty: **1,922 (full-time)**, **220 (part-time)**

Of full-time faculty, those teaching in basic sciences: **7%**; in clinical programs: **93%**

Of part-time faculty, those teaching in basic sciences: **4%**; in clinical programs: **96%**

Full-time faculty/student ratio: **2.7**

SUPPORT SERVICES

The school offers students these services for dealing with stress: professional counseling, religious support, support groups.

RESIDENCY PROFILE

Most popular residency and specialty programs chosen by the 2006 and 2007 M.D. graduating classes: emergency medicine, family practice, internal medicine, obstetrics and gynecology, orthopaedic surgery, pediatrics, psychiatry, radiology–diagnostic, surgery–general, urology.

WHERE GRADS GO

37%

Proportion of 2005-2007 graduates who entered primary care specialties

39%

Proportion of 2006-2007 graduates who accepted in-state residencies

Ohio State University

- 200 Meiling Hall, 370 W. Ninth Avenue, Columbus, OH 43210-1238
- Public
- Year Founded: 1834
- Tuition, 2007-2008: In-state: $27,234; Out-of-state: $33,322
- Enrollment 2007-2008 academic year: 819
- Website: http://medicine.osu.edu
- Specialty ranking: family medicine: 27, internal medicine: 24

3.74	AVERAGE GPA, ENTERING CLASS FALL 2007
11.2	AVERAGE MCAT, ENTERING CLASS FALL 2007
8.7%	ACCEPTANCE RATE, ENTERING CLASS FALL 2007
30	2009 U.S. NEWS MEDICAL SCHOOL RANKING (RESEARCH)
31	2009 U.S. NEWS MEDICAL SCHOOL RANKING (PRIMARY CARE)

ADMISSIONS

Admissions phone number: **(614) 292-7137**
Admissions email address: **medicine@osu.edu**
Application website: **http://www.aamc.org**
Acceptance rate: **8.7%**
In-state acceptance rate: **13.4%**
Out-of-state acceptance rate: **7.2%**
Minority acceptance rate: **6.9%**
International acceptance rate: **0.0%**

Fall 2007 applications and acceptees

	Applied	Interviewed	Accepted	Enrolled
Total:	4,637	708	405	210
In-state:	1,160	279	156	109
Out-of-state:	3,477	429	249	101

Profile of admitted students

Average undergraduate grade point average: **3.74**
MCAT averages (scale: 1-15; writing test: J-T):
  Composite score: **11.2**
  Verbal reasoning score: **10.5**, Physical sciences score: **11.5**, Biological sciences score: **11.6**, Writing score: **O**
Proportion with undergraduate majors in: Biological sciences: **43%**, Physical sciences: **20%**, Non-sciences: **12%**, Other health professions: **2%**, Mixed disciplines and other: **22%**
Percentage of students not coming directly from college after graduation: **31%**

Dates and details

The American Medical College Application Service (AMCAS) application is accepted.
School asks for a school-specific application as part of the admissions process.
Oldest MCAT considered for Fall 2009 entry: **2006**
Earliest application date for the 2009-2010 first-year class: **6/1**
Latest application date: **11/1**
Acceptance dates for regular application for the class entering in fall 2009:
  Earliest: **October 16, 2008**

Latest: **August 10, 2009**
The school considers requests for deferred entrance.
Starting month for the class entering in 2009–2010:
  August
The school has an Early Decision Plan (EDP).
A personal interview is required for admission.

Undergraduate coursework required

Medical school requires undergraduate work in these subjects: biology, biology/zoology, organic chemistry, inorganic (general) chemistry, physics, general chemistry.

ADMISSIONS POLICY

(TEXT PROVIDED BY SCHOOL):

Applicants are evaluated on undergraduate academic performance, MCAT scores, participation in health-related experiences, research, faculty references, personal interview. Competitive applicants demonstrate skills in independent thinking, decision making, active involvement in their community, leadership roles. The college seeks self-motivated, compassionate applicants who embody high ethical standards, honesty, concern for others.

COSTS AND FINANCIAL AID

Financial aid phone number: **(614) 688-4955**
Tuition, 2007-2008 academic year: **In-state: $27,234; Out-of-state: $33,322**
Room and board: **$8,320**
Percentage of students receiving financial aid in 2007-08: **94%**
Percentage of students receiving: Loans: **86%**, Grants/scholarships: **62%**, Work-study aid: **0%**
Average medical school debt for the Class of 2006: **$125,322**

STUDENT BODY

Fall 2007 full-time enrollment: **819**
Men: **60%**, Women: **40%**, In-state: **88%**, Minorities: **31%**, American Indian: **0.4%**, Asian-American: **19.0%**, African-American: **6.7%**, Hispanic-American: **3.3%**, White: **69.5%**, International: **0.4%**, Unknown: **0.7%**

ACADEMIC PROGRAMS

The school's curriculum frequently gives first-year students substantial contact with patients.

There are opportunities for first- or second-year students to work in community health clinics.

Program offerings: AIDS, drug/alcohol abuse, family medicine, geriatrics, internal medicine, pediatrics, rural medicine, women's health

Joint degrees awarded: M.D./Ph.D., M.D./M.B.A., M.D./M.P.H., M.D./J.D., M.D./M.H.A.

Total National Institutes of Health (NIH) grants awarded to the medical school and affiliated hospitals: **$237.8 million**

CURRICULUM

(TEXT PROVIDED BY SCHOOL):

The curriculum prepares students to provide high-quality, patient-centered, evidence-based care with opportunities in research, medical education, and administration. Professionalism, ethical decision making, effective communication, and leadership are priorities. There are two parallel pathways to accommodate different learning styles. Clinical experiences in all specialties are available.

FACULTY PROFILE (FALL 2007)

Total teaching faculty: **2,281 (full-time)**, **1,076 (part-time)**

Of full-time faculty, those teaching in basic sciences: **17%**; in clinical programs: **83%**

Of part-time faculty, those teaching in basic sciences: **15%**; in clinical programs: **85%**

Full-time faculty/student ratio: **2.8**

SUPPORT SERVICES

The school offers students these services for dealing with stress: expanded-hour gym access, professional counseling, support groups.

RESIDENCY PROFILE

Most popular residency and specialty programs chosen by the 2006 and 2007 M.D. graduating classes: anesthesiology, emergency medicine, family practice, internal medicine, obstetrics and gynecology, ophthalmology, orthopaedic surgery, pediatrics, surgery–general.

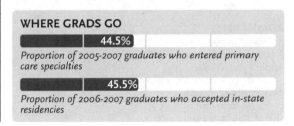

WHERE GRADS GO

44.5%
Proportion of 2005-2007 graduates who entered primary care specialties

45.5%
Proportion of 2006-2007 graduates who accepted in-state residencies

Oregon Health and Science University

- 3181 S.W. Sam Jackson Park Road, L102, Portland, OR 97239-3098
- Public
- Year Founded: 1887
- Tuition, 2007-2008: In-state: $31,538; Out-of-state: $42,353
- Enrollment 2007-2008 academic year: 512
- Website: http://www.ohsu.edu/som
- Specialty ranking: family medicine: 2, rural medicine: 9

3.61 AVERAGE GPA, ENTERING CLASS FALL 2007

10.2 AVERAGE MCAT, ENTERING CLASS FALL 2007

4.8% ACCEPTANCE RATE, ENTERING CLASS FALL 2007

35 2009 U.S. NEWS MEDICAL SCHOOL RANKING (RESEARCH)

2 2009 U.S. NEWS MEDICAL SCHOOL RANKING (PRIMARY CARE)

ADMISSIONS

Admissions phone number: **(503) 494-2998**
Admissions email address: **N/A**
Application website:
   http://www.ohsu.edu/som/dean/md/admissions
Acceptance rate: **4.8%**
In-state acceptance rate: **25.7%**
Out-of-state acceptance rate: **2.9%**
Minority acceptance rate: **3.8%**
International acceptance rate: **N/A**

Fall 2007 applications and acceptees

	Applied	Interviewed	Accepted	Enrolled
Total:	4,455	513	215	118
In-state:	381	209	98	82
Out-of-state:	4,074	304	117	36

Profile of admitted students

Average undergraduate grade point average: **3.61**
MCAT averages (scale: 1-15; writing test: J-T):
   Composite score: **10.2**
   Verbal reasoning score: **10.2**, Physical sciences score: **9.8**, Biological sciences score: **10.7**, Writing score: **P**
Proportion with undergraduate majors in: Biological sciences: **40%**, Physical sciences: **9%**, Non-sciences: **24%**, Other health professions: **3%**, Mixed disciplines and other: **24%**
Percentage of students not coming directly from college after graduation: **75%**

Dates and details

The American Medical College Application Service (AMCAS) application is accepted.
School asks for a school-specific application as part of the admissions process.
Oldest MCAT considered for Fall 2009 entry: **2006**
Earliest application date for the 2009-2010 first-year class: **6/1**
Latest application date: **10/15**
Acceptance dates for regular application for the class entering in fall 2009:

Earliest: **November 1, 2008**
Latest: **August 15, 2009**
The school doesn't consider requests for deferred entrance.
Starting month for the class entering in 2009–2010:
   August
The school doesn't have an Early Decision Plan (EDP).
A personal interview is required for admission.

Undergraduate coursework required

Medical school requires undergraduate work in these subjects: biology, English, organic chemistry, inorganic (general) chemistry, physics, biochemistry, humanities, mathematics, demonstration of writing skills, calculus, social sciences, general chemistry.

ADMISSIONS POLICY
(TEXT PROVIDED BY SCHOOL):

The School of Medicine seeks students who demonstrate academic excellence and readiness for medicine and will contribute to the diversity necessary to enhance the medical education of all students. Applicants are selected on the basis of demonstrated motivation for medicine, humanistic attitudes, and a realistic understanding of the role of the physician in providing healthcare to all communities.

COSTS AND FINANCIAL AID

Financial aid phone number: **(503) 494-7800**
Tuition, 2007-2008 academic year: **In-state: $31,538; Out-of-state: $42,353**
Room and board: **$17,500**
Percentage of students receiving financial aid in 2007-08: **93%**
Percentage of students receiving: Loans: **90%**, Grants/scholarships: **80%**, Work-study aid: **2%**
Average medical school debt for the Class of 2006: **$145,576**

STUDENT BODY

Fall 2007 full-time enrollment: **512**
Men: **45%**, Women: **55%**, In-state: **59%**, Minorities: **17%**, American Indian: **1.0%**, Asian-American: **13.7%**,

African-American: **1.6%**, Hispanic-American: **1.2%**, White: **82.6%**, International: **0.0%**, Unknown: **0.0%**

ACADEMIC PROGRAMS

The school's curriculum very frequently gives first-year students substantial contact with patients.

There are opportunities for first- or second-year students to work in community health clinics.

Program offerings: AIDS, drug/alcohol abuse, family medicine, geriatrics, internal medicine, pediatrics, rural medicine, women's health

Joint degrees awarded: M.D./Ph.D., M.D./M.P.H.

Total National Institutes of Health (NIH) grants awarded to the medical school and affiliated hospitals: **$201.4 million**

CURRICULUM

(TEXT PROVIDED BY SCHOOL):

Highlights: integrated and multidisciplinary courses with clinical relevance; lecture and nonlecture learning balanced in half-day sessions; early and longitudinal clinical preceptorship; experience in a rural or underserved area; performance-based assessment of students utilizing standardized patients.

FACULTY PROFILE (FALL 2007)

Total teaching faculty: **1,616 (full-time)**, **310 (part-time)**
Of full-time faculty, those teaching in basic sciences: **11%**; in clinical programs: **89%**

Of part-time faculty, those teaching in basic sciences: **12%**; in clinical programs: **88%**
Full-time faculty/student ratio: **3.2**

SUPPORT SERVICES

The school offers students these services for dealing with stress: expanded-hour gym access, peer counseling, professional counseling, religious support, support groups.

RESIDENCY PROFILE

Most popular residency and specialty programs chosen by the 2006 and 2007 M.D. graduating classes: anesthesiology, emergency medicine, family practice, internal medicine, obstetrics and gynecology, ophthalmology, pediatrics, psychiatry, radiology–diagnostic, surgery–general.

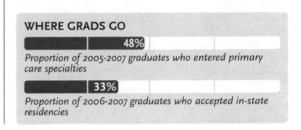

WHERE GRADS GO

48%

Proportion of 2005-2007 graduates who entered primary care specialties

33%

Proportion of 2006-2007 graduates who accepted in-state residencies

Rosalind Franklin

UNIVERSITY OF MEDICINE AND SCIENCE

- 3333 Green Bay Road, North Chicago, IL 60064
- Private
- Year Founded: 1912
- Tuition, 2007-2008: $39,472
- Enrollment 2007-2008 academic year: 757
- Website: http://www.rosalindfranklin.edu
- Specialty ranking: N/A

3.55	AVERAGE GPA, ENTERING CLASS FALL 2007
9.7	AVERAGE MCAT, ENTERING CLASS FALL 2007
5.1%	ACCEPTANCE RATE, ENTERING CLASS FALL 2007
Unranked	2009 U.S. NEWS MEDICAL SCHOOL RANKING (RESEARCH)
Unranked	2009 U.S. NEWS MEDICAL SCHOOL RANKING (PRIMARY CARE)

ADMISSIONS

Admissions phone number: **(847) 578-3204**
Admissions email address:
cms.admissions@rosalindfranklin.edu
Application website:
http://www.rosalindfranklin.edu/admissions/cms
Acceptance rate: **5.1%**
In-state acceptance rate: **14.3%**
Out-of-state acceptance rate: **3.8%**
Minority acceptance rate: **4.0%**
International acceptance rate: **4.2%**

Fall 2007 applications and acceptees

	Applied	Interviewed	Accepted	Enrolled
Total:	9,995	783	509	190
In-state:	1,186	248	170	76
Out-of-state:	8,809	535	339	114

Profile of admitted students

Average undergraduate grade point average: **3.55**
MCAT averages (scale: 1-15; writing test: J-T):
Composite score: **9.7**
Verbal reasoning score: **9.0**, Physical sciences score: **9.9**,
Biological sciences score: **10.3**, Writing score: **P**
Proportion with undergraduate majors in: Biological
sciences: **54%**, Physical sciences: **24%**, Non-sciences:
12%, Other health professions: **3%**, Mixed disciplines
and other: **7%**
Percentage of students not coming directly from college
after graduation: **15%**

Dates and details

The American Medical College Application Service
(AMCAS) application is accepted.
School asks for a school-specific application as part of the
admissions process.
Oldest MCAT considered for Fall 2009 entry: **2006**
Earliest application date for the 2009-2010 first-year class:
6/1
Latest application date: **11/1**

Acceptance dates for regular application for the class
entering in fall 2009:
Earliest: **October 1, 2008**
Latest: **August 1, 2008**
The school considers requests for deferred entrance.
Starting month for the class entering in 2009–2010:
August
The school has an Early Decision Plan (EDP).
A personal interview is required for admission.

Undergraduate coursework required

Medical school requires undergraduate work in these subjects: biology/zoology, organic chemistry, inorganic (general) chemistry, physics.

ADMISSIONS POLICY

(TEXT PROVIDED BY SCHOOL):
The admissions policies are designed to ensure that the
Chicago Medical School matriculates individuals capable of
meeting the needs of current and future patients. All applicants must submit MCAT scores and an application
through the American Medical College Application Service
to initiate the application process. Please see the website for
details on the admissions policies.

COSTS AND FINANCIAL AID

Financial aid phone number: **(847) 578-3217**
Tuition, 2007-2008 academic year: **$39,472**
Room and board: **$14,400**
Percentage of students receiving financial aid in 2007-08:
94%
Percentage of students receiving: Loans: **94%**,
Grants/scholarships: **47%**, Work-study aid: **6%**
Average medical school debt for the Class of 2006:
$169,863

STUDENT BODY

Fall 2007 full-time enrollment: **757**
Men: **54%**, Women: **46%**, In-state: **25%**, Minorities: **48%**,
American Indian: **0.0%**, Asian-American: **41.3%**,

African-American: 5.2%, Hispanic-American: 1.1%, White: 41.5%, International: 0.8%, Unknown: 10.2%

ACADEMIC PROGRAMS

The school's curriculum occasionally gives first-year students substantial contact with patients.

There are opportunities for first- or second-year students to work in community health clinics.

Program offerings: AIDS, drug/alcohol abuse, family medicine, geriatrics, internal medicine, pediatrics, women's health

Joint degrees awarded: M.D./Ph.D., M.D./M.S.

Total National Institutes of Health (NIH) grants awarded to the medical school and affiliated hospitals: **$6.9 million**

CURRICULUM

(TEXT PROVIDED BY SCHOOL):

The CMS competency-based curriculum features a unique interprofessional approach, with interaction among students and practitioners from a broad range of health professions. Medical students have early clinical experiences in the state-of-the-art evaluation and education center, and students are offered a wide variety of clinical opportunities through the multiple hospital affiliates of CMS.

FACULTY PROFILE (FALL 2007)

Total teaching faculty: **N/A (full-time)**, **N/A (part-time)**
Of full-time faculty, those teaching in basic sciences: **N/A**; in clinical programs: **N/A**

Of part-time faculty, those teaching in basic sciences: **N/A**; in clinical programs: **N/A**
Full-time faculty/student ratio: **N/A**

SUPPORT SERVICES

The school offers students these services for dealing with stress: expanded-hour gym access, peer counseling, professional counseling, religious support, support groups.

RESIDENCY PROFILE

Most popular residency and specialty programs chosen by the 2006 and 2007 M.D. graduating classes: anesthesiology, emergency medicine, family practice, internal medicine, obstetrics and gynecology, ophthalmology, pediatrics, physical medicine and rehabilitation, radiology–diagnostic, surgery–general.

WHERE GRADS GO

N/A
Proportion of 2005-2007 graduates who entered primary care specialties

N/A
Proportion of 2006-2007 graduates who accepted in-state residencies

Rush University

- 600 S. Paulina Street, Chicago, IL 60612
- Private
- Year Founded: 1837
- Tuition, 2007-2008: $43,680
- Enrollment 2007-2008 academic year: 536
- Website: http://www.rushu.rush.edu/medcol/
- Specialty ranking: N/A

3.60 AVERAGE GPA, ENTERING CLASS FALL 2007

10.3 AVERAGE MCAT, ENTERING CLASS FALL 2007

4.8% ACCEPTANCE RATE, ENTERING CLASS FALL 2007

Unranked 2009 U.S. NEWS MEDICAL SCHOOL RANKING (RESEARCH)

Unranked 2009 U.S. NEWS MEDICAL SCHOOL RANKING (PRIMARY CARE)

ADMISSIONS

Admissions phone number: **N/A**
Admissions email address: **RMC_Admissions@rush.edu**
Application website: **http://www.aamc.org**
Acceptance rate: **4.8%**
In-state acceptance rate: **14.1%**
Out-of-state acceptance rate: **1.4%**
Minority acceptance rate: **5.2%**
International acceptance rate: **N/A**

Fall 2007 applications and acceptees

	Applied	Interviewed	Accepted	Enrolled
Total:	5,456	392	262	128
In-state:	1,458	285	206	107
Out-of-state:	3,998	107	56	21

Profile of admitted students

Average undergraduate grade point average: **3.60**
MCAT averages (scale: 1-15; writing test: J-T):
   Composite score: **10.3**
   Verbal reasoning score: **9.8**, Physical sciences score: **10.2**, Biological sciences score: **10.4**, Writing score: **P**
Proportion with undergraduate majors in: Biological sciences: **49%**, Physical sciences: **29%**, Non-sciences: **13%**, Other health professions: **5%**, Mixed disciplines and other: **4%**
Percentage of students not coming directly from college after graduation: **N/A**

Dates and details

The American Medical College Application Service (AMCAS) application is accepted.
School asks for a school-specific application as part of the admissions process.
Oldest MCAT considered for Fall 2009 entry: **2007**
Earliest application date for the 2009-2010 first-year class: **N/A**
Latest application date: **11/1**
Acceptance dates for regular application for the class entering in fall 2009:
   Earliest: **November 30, 2008**

Latest: **September 1, 2009**
The school considers requests for deferred entrance.
Starting month for the class entering in 2009–2010:
   September
The school doesn't have an Early Decision Plan (EDP).
A personal interview is required for admission.

Undergraduate coursework required

Medical school requires undergraduate work in these subjects: biology, organic chemistry, inorganic (general) chemistry, physics.

ADMISSIONS POLICY
(TEXT PROVIDED BY SCHOOL):

Admission requirements: U.S. citizen or permanent residency (preference given to Illinois residents); 90 semester hours undergraduate study prior to matriculation, including eight hours each of Biology, Inorganic Chemistry, Organic Chemistry (or four hours of Biochemistry), and Physics; survey courses in the sciences do not qualify; the MCAT exam must be taken by the end of the year preceding the entering class year.

COSTS AND FINANCIAL AID

Financial aid phone number: **(312) 942-6256**
Tuition, 2007-2008 academic year: **$43,680**
Room and board: **$9,340**
Percentage of students receiving financial aid in 2007-08: **88%**
Percentage of students receiving: Loans: **86%**, Grants/scholarships: **59%**, Work-study aid: **6%**
Average medical school debt for the Class of 2006: **$159,701**

STUDENT BODY

Fall 2007 full-time enrollment: **536**
Men: **48%**, Women: **52%**, In-state: **81%**, Minorities: **39%**, American Indian: **1.1%**, Asian-American: **33.2%**, African-American: **2.8%**, Hispanic-American: **2.6%**, White: **59.3%**, International: **0.0%**, Unknown: **0.9%**

ACADEMIC PROGRAMS

The school's curriculum frequently gives first-year students substantial contact with patients.

There are opportunities for first- or second-year students to work in community health clinics.

Program offerings: AIDS, drug/alcohol abuse, family medicine, geriatrics, internal medicine, pediatrics, rural medicine, women's health

Joint degrees awarded: M.D./Ph.D.

Total National Institutes of Health (NIH) grants awarded to the medical school and affiliated hospitals: **$38.0 million**

CURRICULUM
(TEXT PROVIDED BY SCHOOL):

The M1 and M2 years offer a balanced basic science curriculum, with a preceptorship experience and courses in physical diagnosis and communication skills. Students are paired with primary care physicians in outpatient settings throughout the Chicago area. The M3 and M4 years focus on clinical skills, diagnosis, and patient management in core specialty areas and also offer extensive elective experiences.

FACULTY PROFILE (FALL 2007)

Total teaching faculty: **471 (full-time), 199 (part-time)**

Of full-time faculty, those teaching in basic sciences: **22%**; in clinical programs: **78%**

Of part-time faculty, those teaching in basic sciences: **6%**; in clinical programs: **94%**

Full-time faculty/student ratio: **0.9**

SUPPORT SERVICES

The school offers students these services for dealing with stress: expanded-hour gym access, professional counseling, support groups.

RESIDENCY PROFILE

Most popular residency and specialty programs chosen by the 2006 and 2007 M.D. graduating classes: anesthesiology, emergency medicine, family practice, internal medicine, internal medicine–pediatrics, ophthalmology, orthopaedic surgery, pediatrics, psychiatry, surgery–general.

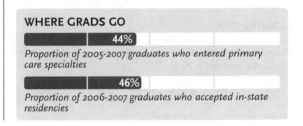

WHERE GRADS GO

44%

Proportion of 2005-2007 graduates who entered primary care specialties

46%

Proportion of 2006-2007 graduates who accepted in-state residencies

Southern Illinois University–Springfield

- 801 N. Rutledge, PO Box 19620, Springfield, IL 62794-9620
- Public
- Year Founded: 1970
- Tuition, 2007-2008: In-state: $23,856; Out-of-state: $66,160
- Enrollment 2007-2008 academic year: 291
- Website: http://www.siumed.edu/
- Specialty ranking: family medicine: 27, rural medicine: 28

3.52	AVERAGE GPA, ENTERING CLASS FALL 2007
9.1	AVERAGE MCAT, ENTERING CLASS FALL 2007
11.2%	ACCEPTANCE RATE, ENTERING CLASS FALL 2007
Unranked	2009 U.S. NEWS MEDICAL SCHOOL RANKING (RESEARCH)
58	2009 U.S. NEWS MEDICAL SCHOOL RANKING (PRIMARY CARE)

ADMISSIONS

Admissions phone number: **(217) 545-6013**
Admissions email address: **admissions@siumed.edu**
Application website: **N/A**
Acceptance rate: **11.2%**
In-state acceptance rate: **13.5%**
Out-of-state acceptance rate: **0.8%**
Minority acceptance rate: **N/A**
International acceptance rate: **N/A**

Fall 2007 applications and acceptees

	Applied	Interviewed	Accepted	Enrolled
Total:	1,380	270	155	72
In-state:	1,134	268	153	72
Out-of-state:	246	2	2	0

Profile of admitted students

Average undergraduate grade point average: **3.52**
MCAT averages (scale: 1-15; writing test: J-T):
  Composite score: **9.1**
  Verbal reasoning score: **9.3**, Physical sciences score: **8.7**,
  Biological sciences score: **9.3**, Writing score: **O**
Proportion with undergraduate majors in: Biological
  sciences: **63%**, Physical sciences: **21%**, Non-sciences:
  12%, Other health professions: **4%**, Mixed disciplines
  and other: **0%**
Percentage of students not coming directly from college
  after graduation: **35%**

Dates and details

The American Medical College Application Service
  (AMCAS) application is accepted.
School asks for a school-specific application as part of the
  admissions process.
Oldest MCAT considered for Fall 2009 entry: **2006**
Earliest application date for the 2009-2010 first-year class:
  6/1
Latest application date: **11/15**
Acceptance dates for regular application for the class
  entering in fall 2009:

Earliest: **December 1, 2008**
Latest: **August 14, 2009**
The school considers requests for deferred entrance.
Starting month for the class entering in 2009–2010:
  August
The school doesn't have an Early Decision Plan (EDP).
A personal interview is required for admission.

Undergraduate coursework required

Medical school requires undergraduate work in these subjects: N/A.

ADMISSIONS POLICY

(TEXT PROVIDED BY SCHOOL):
Applicants need a good foundation in natural and social sciences and humanities; evidence of maturity, integrity, social
awareness, compassion, service, and good interpersonal
skills; and identification with SIU's mission, to help central
and southern Illinois meet its healthcare needs. Accepted
students are from Illinois with preference to residents of
downstate and other underserved areas.

COSTS AND FINANCIAL AID

Financial aid phone number: **(217) 545-2224**
Tuition, 2007-2008 academic year: **In-state: $23,856; Out-
  of-state: $66,160**
Room and board: **$7,560**
Percentage of students receiving financial aid in 2007-08:
  94%
Percentage of students receiving: Loans: **93%**,
  Grants/scholarships: **47%**, Work-study aid: **0%**
Average medical school debt for the Class of 2006:
  $113,724

STUDENT BODY

Fall 2007 full-time enrollment: **291**
Men: **47%**, Women: **53%**, In-state: **100%**, Minorities: **26%**,
  American Indian: **1.4%**, Asian-American: **9.3%**, African-
  American: **11.7%**, Hispanic-American: **3.8%**, White:
  73.9%, International: **0.0%**, Unknown: **0.0%**

ACADEMIC PROGRAMS

The school's curriculum frequently gives first-year students substantial contact with patients.

There are opportunities for first- or second-year students to work in community health clinics.

Program offerings: AIDS, drug/alcohol abuse, family medicine, geriatrics, internal medicine, pediatrics, rural medicine, women's health

Joint degrees awarded: M.D./J.D.

Total National Institutes of Health (NIH) grants awarded to the medical school and affiliated hospitals: **N/A**

CURRICULUM
(TEXT PROVIDED BY SCHOOL):

SIU has been recognized for its innovative teaching and testing techniques, including a competency-based curriculum that emphasizes self-directed learning in small group settings. It includes standardized patients, extensive clinical activities, and substantial study in medical humanities. The goal is for SIU graduates to become humanistic and competent physicians who are lifelong learners.

FACULTY PROFILE (FALL 2007)

Total teaching faculty: **334 (full-time)**, **938 (part-time)**
Of full-time faculty, those teaching in basic sciences: **36%**; in clinical programs: **64%**

Of part-time faculty, those teaching in basic sciences: **20%**; in clinical programs: **80%**
Full-time faculty/student ratio: **1.1**

SUPPORT SERVICES

The school offers students these services for dealing with stress: peer counseling, professional counseling, support groups.

RESIDENCY PROFILE

Most popular residency and specialty programs chosen by the 2006 and 2007 M.D. graduating classes: anesthesiology, emergency medicine, family practice, internal medicine, obstetrics and gynecology, ophthalmology, orthopaedic surgery, pediatrics, radiology–diagnostic, surgery–general.

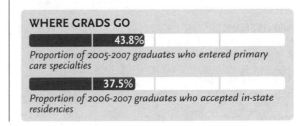

WHERE GRADS GO

43.8%

Proportion of 2005-2007 graduates who entered primary care specialties

37.5%

Proportion of 2006-2007 graduates who accepted in-state residencies

Stanford University

- 300 Pasteur Drive, Suite M121, Stanford, CA 94305
- Private
- **Year Founded:** 1858
- **Tuition, 2007-2008:** $41,760
- **Enrollment 2007-2008 academic year:** 472
- **Website:** http://med.stanford.edu
- **Specialty ranking:** AIDS: 16, geriatrics: 19, internal medicine: 13, pediatrics: 6

3.76 AVERAGE GPA, ENTERING CLASS FALL 2007

11.6 AVERAGE MCAT, ENTERING CLASS FALL 2007

3.3% ACCEPTANCE RATE, ENTERING CLASS FALL 2007

8 2009 U.S. NEWS MEDICAL SCHOOL RANKING (RESEARCH)

58 2009 U.S. NEWS MEDICAL SCHOOL RANKING (PRIMARY CARE)

ADMISSIONS

Admissions phone number: **(650) 723-6861**
Admissions email address: **mdadmissions@stanford.edu**
Application website: **http://www.aamc.org**
Acceptance rate: **3.3%**
In-state acceptance rate: **3.3%**
Out-of-state acceptance rate: **3.3%**
Minority acceptance rate: **3.5%**
International acceptance rate: **3.3%**

Fall 2007 applications and acceptees

	Applied	Interviewed	Accepted	Enrolled
Total:	6,457	585	213	86
In-state:	2,409	207	79	33
Out-of-state:	4,048	378	134	53

Profile of admitted students

Average undergraduate grade point average: **3.76**
MCAT averages (scale: 1-15; writing test: J-T):
Composite score: **11.6**
Verbal reasoning score: **11.0**, Physical sciences score: **12.0**, Biological sciences score: **12.0**, Writing score: **Q**
Proportion with undergraduate majors in: Biological sciences: **30%**, Physical sciences: **40%**, Non-sciences: **6%**, Other health professions: **0%**, Mixed disciplines and other: **24%**
Percentage of students not coming directly from college after graduation: **23%**

Dates and details

The American Medical College Application Service (AMCAS) application is accepted.
School asks for a school-specific application as part of the admissions process.
Oldest MCAT considered for Fall 2009 entry: **2005**
Earliest application date for the 2009-2010 first-year class: **6/1**
Latest application date: **10/15**
Acceptance dates for regular application for the class entering in fall 2009:

Earliest: **December 1, 2008**
Latest: **April 30, 2008**
The school considers requests for deferred entrance.
Starting month for the class entering in 2009–2010:
August
The school has an Early Decision Plan (EDP).
A personal interview is required for admission.

Undergraduate coursework required

Medical school requires undergraduate work in these subjects: biology, organic chemistry, inorganic (general) chemistry, physics.

ADMISSIONS POLICY
(TEXT PROVIDED BY SCHOOL):

The School of Medicine is interested in students whose accomplishments reflect originality, creativity, and independent, critical thinking; a strong humanitarian commitment; and enthusiasm for the basic sciences and humanities. The committee looks at the nature and extent of community service, caring experiences, and academic commitments beyond required coursework. Originality and leadership skills are most valued.

COSTS AND FINANCIAL AID

Financial aid phone number: **(650) 723-6958**
Tuition, 2007-2008 academic year: **$41,760**
Room and board: **$20,700**
Percentage of students receiving financial aid in 2007-08: **80%**
Percentage of students receiving: Loans: **55%**, Grants/scholarships: **71%**, Work-study aid: **11%**
Average medical school debt for the Class of 2006: **$70,235**

STUDENT BODY

Fall 2007 full-time enrollment: **472**
Men: **55%**, Women: **45%**, In-state: **40%**, Minorities: **53%**, American Indian: **0.8%**, Asian-American: **32.4%**, African-American: **4.9%**, Hispanic-American: **14.6%**, White: **43.2%**, International: **4.0%**, Unknown: **0.0%**

ACADEMIC PROGRAMS

The school's curriculum frequently gives first-year students substantial contact with patients.

There are opportunities for first- or second-year students to work in community health clinics.

Program offerings: AIDS, drug/alcohol abuse, family medicine, geriatrics, internal medicine, pediatrics, rural medicine, women's health

Joint degrees awarded: M.D./Ph.D., M.D./M.P.H., M.D./M.S.

Total National Institutes of Health (NIH) grants awarded to the medical school and affiliated hospitals: **N/A**

CURRICULUM
(TEXT PROVIDED BY SCHOOL):

The curriculum equips students to translate laboratory discoveries into life-enhancing therapies throughout their careers. Students receive clinical training early in the education process, get basic science refreshers during the clinical years, and participate in a scholarly concentration in which they can hone their research skills while developing early expertise in a topic that excites them.

FACULTY PROFILE (FALL 2007)

Total teaching faculty: **767 (full-time)**, **32 (part-time)**

Of full-time faculty, those teaching in basic sciences: **13%**; in clinical programs: **87%**

Of part-time faculty, those teaching in basic sciences: **28%**; in clinical programs: **72%**

Full-time faculty/student ratio: **1.6**

SUPPORT SERVICES

The school offers students these services for dealing with stress: expanded-hour gym access, peer counseling, professional counseling, religious support, support groups.

RESIDENCY PROFILE

Most popular residency and specialty programs chosen by the 2006 and 2007 M.D. graduating classes: anesthesiology, emergency medicine, internal medicine, pediatrics, radiology–diagnostic, radiation oncology, surgery–general.

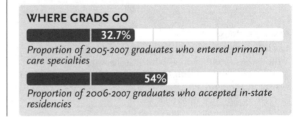

WHERE GRADS GO

32.7%

Proportion of 2005-2007 graduates who entered primary care specialties

54%

Proportion of 2006-2007 graduates who accepted in-state residencies

St. Louis University

■ 1402 S. Grand Boulevard, St. Louis, MO 63104
■ Private
■ Year Founded: 1836
■ Tuition, 2007-2008: $42,783
■ Enrollment 2007-2008 academic year: 698
■ Website: http://medschool.slu.edu
■ Specialty ranking: geriatrics: 14

3.76 AVERAGE GPA, ENTERING CLASS FALL 2007

10.4 AVERAGE MCAT, ENTERING CLASS FALL 2007

9.4% ACCEPTANCE RATE, ENTERING CLASS FALL 2007

Unranked 2009 U.S. NEWS MEDICAL SCHOOL RANKING (RESEARCH)

56 2009 U.S. NEWS MEDICAL SCHOOL RANKING (PRIMARY CARE)

ADMISSIONS

Admissions phone number: **(314) 977-9870**
Admissions email address: **slumd@slu.edu**
Application website: **http://medschool.slu.edu/admissions/**
Acceptance rate: **9.4%**
In-state acceptance rate: **27.8%**
Out-of-state acceptance rate: **7.9%**
Minority acceptance rate: **6.5%**
International acceptance rate: **13.3%**

Fall 2007 applications and acceptees

	Applied	Interviewed	Accepted	Enrolled
Total:	6,370	937	596	181
In-state:	454	110	126	85
Out-of-state:	5,916	827	470	96

Profile of admitted students

Average undergraduate grade point average: **3.76**
MCAT averages (scale: 1-15; writing test: J-T):
  Composite score: **10.4**
  Verbal reasoning score: **10.2**, Physical sciences score: **10.3**, Biological sciences score: **10.7**, Writing score: **P**
Proportion with undergraduate majors in: Biological sciences: **57%**, Physical sciences: **14%**, Non-sciences: **10%**, Other health professions: **1%**, Mixed disciplines and other: **18%**
Percentage of students not coming directly from college after graduation: **38%**

Dates and details

The American Medical College Application Service (AMCAS) application is accepted.
School asks for a school-specific application as part of the admissions process.
Oldest MCAT considered for Fall 2009 entry: **2004**
Earliest application date for the 2009-2010 first-year class: **5/15**
Latest application date: **12/15**
Acceptance dates for regular application for the class entering in fall 2009:
  Earliest: **October 15, 2008**

Latest: **August 6, 2009**
The school considers requests for deferred entrance.
Starting month for the class entering in 2009–2010:
  August
The school has an Early Decision Plan (EDP).
A personal interview is required for admission.

Undergraduate coursework required

Medical school requires undergraduate work in these subjects: biology/zoology, English, organic chemistry, inorganic (general) chemistry, physics, humanities, behavioral science.

ADMISSIONS POLICY
(TEXT PROVIDED BY SCHOOL):

St. Louis University School of Medicine is a private institution that considers national and international applicants. Applicants are encouraged to have achieved a high level of academic performance and to manifest in their personal lives human qualities compatible with a career of service to society. The school strives to recruit, admit, retain, and graduate a diverse student body.

COSTS AND FINANCIAL AID

Financial aid phone number: **(314) 977-9840**
Tuition, 2007-2008 academic year: **$42,783**
Room and board: **$11,988**
Percentage of students receiving financial aid in 2007-08: **80%**
Percentage of students receiving: Loans: **79%**, Grants/scholarships: **25%**, Work-study aid: **0%**
Average medical school debt for the Class of 2006: **$156,722**

STUDENT BODY

Fall 2007 full-time enrollment: **698**
Men: **57%**, Women: **43%**, In-state: **50%**, Minorities: **25%**, American Indian: **0.1%**, Asian-American: **19.8%**, African-American: **2.6%**, Hispanic-American: **1.4%**, White: **61.7%**, International: **2.1%**, Unknown: **12.2%**

ACADEMIC PROGRAMS

The school's curriculum occasionally gives first-year students substantial contact with patients.

There are opportunities for first- or second-year students to work in community health clinics.

Program offerings: AIDS, drug/alcohol abuse, family medicine, geriatrics, internal medicine, pediatrics, rural medicine, women's health

Joint degrees awarded: M.D./Ph.D., M.D./M.B.A., M.D./M.P.H.

Total National Institutes of Health (NIH) grants awarded to the medical school and affiliated hospitals: **$21.0 million**

CURRICULUM

(TEXT PROVIDED BY SCHOOL):

Beyond the essential objective of training competent physicians who are scholars of human biology, the medical school strives to graduate physicians who manifest in their personal and professional lives an appreciation for ethical and professional attitudes that reflect the Jesuit spirit and values and affect the physicians' interactions with patients, colleagues, and society.

FACULTY PROFILE (FALL 2007)

Total teaching faculty: **538 (full-time)**, **1,161 (part-time)**

Of full-time faculty, those teaching in basic sciences: **15%**; in clinical programs: **85%**

Of part-time faculty, those teaching in basic sciences: **0%**; in clinical programs: **100%**

Full-time faculty/student ratio: **0.8**

SUPPORT SERVICES

The school offers students these services for dealing with stress: expanded-hour gym access, professional counseling, religious support, support groups.

RESIDENCY PROFILE

Most popular residency and specialty programs chosen by the 2006 and 2007 M.D. graduating classes: anesthesiology, emergency medicine, family practice, internal medicine, obstetrics and gynecology, ophthalmology, pathology–anatomic and clinical, pediatrics, surgery–general, urology.

WHERE GRADS GO

43.7%

Proportion of 2005-2007 graduates who entered primary care specialties

27.5%

Proportion of 2006-2007 graduates who accepted in-state residencies

Stony Brook University

- Office of Admissions, Health Science Center, L4, Stony Brook, NY 11794-8434
- Public
- Year Founded: 1971
- Tuition, 2007-2008: In-state: $19,890; Out-of-state: $34,590
- Enrollment 2007-2008 academic year: 449
- Website: http://www.stonybrookmedicalcenter.org/ education/som_admissions.cfm
- Specialty ranking: N/A

3.60 AVERAGE GPA, ENTERING CLASS FALL 2007

10.7 AVERAGE MCAT, ENTERING CLASS FALL 2007

8.3% ACCEPTANCE RATE, ENTERING CLASS FALL 2007

55 2009 U.S. NEWS MEDICAL SCHOOL RANKING (RESEARCH)

Unranked 2009 U.S. NEWS MEDICAL SCHOOL RANKING (PRIMARY CARE)

ADMISSIONS

Admissions phone number: **(631) 444-2113**
Admissions email address:
somadmissions@stonybrook.edu
Application website:
http://www.stonybrookmedicalcenter.org/education/som _admissions.cfm
Acceptance rate: **8.3%**
In-state acceptance rate: **12.1%**
Out-of-state acceptance rate: **3.1%**
Minority acceptance rate: **7.4%**
International acceptance rate: **2.0%**

Fall 2007 applications and acceptees

	Applied	Interviewed	Accepted	Enrolled
Total:	3,531	597	292	116
In-state:	2,040	498	246	102
Out-of-state:	1,491	99	46	14

Profile of admitted students

Average undergraduate grade point average: **3.60**
MCAT averages (scale: 1-15; writing test: J-T):
  Composite score: **10.7**
  Verbal reasoning score: **10.0**, Physical sciences score: **11.0**, Biological sciences score: **11.0**, Writing score: **P**
Proportion with undergraduate majors in: Biological sciences: **45%**, Physical sciences: **30%**, Non-sciences: **25%**, Other health professions: **0%**, Mixed disciplines and other: **0%**
Percentage of students not coming directly from college after graduation: **59%**

Dates and details

The American Medical College Application Service (AMCAS) application is accepted.
School asks for a school-specific application as part of the admissions process.
Oldest MCAT considered for Fall 2009 entry: **2004**
Earliest application date for the 2009-2010 first-year class: **7/1**

Latest application date: **12/15**
Acceptance dates for regular application for the class entering in fall 2009:
  Earliest: **October 15, 2008**
  Latest: **August 15, 2009**
The school considers requests for deferred entrance.
Starting month for the class entering in 2009–2010: **August**
The school has an Early Decision Plan (EDP).
A personal interview is required for admission.

Undergraduate coursework required

Medical school requires undergraduate work in these subjects: biology, English, organic chemistry, inorganic (general) chemistry, physics.

ADMISSIONS POLICY

(TEXT PROVIDED BY SCHOOL):
Please refer to the Stony Brook Medical Center website for admissions information.

COSTS AND FINANCIAL AID

Financial aid phone number: **(631) 444-2341**
Tuition, 2007-2008 academic year: **In-state: $19,890; Out-of-state: $34,590**
Room and board: **$22,800**
Percentage of students receiving financial aid in 2007-08: **87%**
Percentage of students receiving: Loans: **80%**, Grants/scholarships: **32%**, Work-study aid: **8%**
Average medical school debt for the Class of 2006: **$130,513**

STUDENT BODY

Fall 2007 full-time enrollment: **449**
Men: **49%**, Women: **51%**, In-state: **96%**, Minorities: **50%**, American Indian: **0.7%**, Asian-American: **36.5%**, African-American: **7.6%**, Hispanic-American: **5.1%**, White: **49.4%**, International: **0.7%**, Unknown: **0.0%**

ACADEMIC PROGRAMS

The school's curriculum frequently gives first-year students substantial contact with patients.

There are opportunities for first- or second-year students to work in community health clinics.

Program offerings: AIDS, drug/alcohol abuse, family medicine, geriatrics, internal medicine, pediatrics, women's health

Joint degrees awarded: M.D./Ph.D., M.D./M.P.H.

Total National Institutes of Health (NIH) grants awarded to the medical school and affiliated hospitals: **$61.5 million**

CURRICULUM
(TEXT PROVIDED BY SCHOOL):
Please refer to the website.

FACULTY PROFILE (FALL 2007)

Total teaching faculty: **536 (full-time), 74 (part-time)**

Of full-time faculty, those teaching in basic sciences: **18%**; in clinical programs: **82%**

Of part-time faculty, those teaching in basic sciences: **0%**; in clinical programs: **100%**

Full-time faculty/student ratio: **1.2**

SUPPORT SERVICES

The school offers students these services for dealing with stress: expanded-hour gym access, peer counseling, professional counseling, religious support, support groups.

RESIDENCY PROFILE

Most popular residency and specialty programs chosen by the 2006 and 2007 M.D. graduating classes: anesthesiology, emergency medicine, family practice, internal medicine, obstetrics and gynecology, pediatrics, psychiatry, radiology–diagnostic, surgery–general.

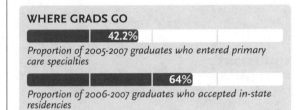

WHERE GRADS GO

42.2%

Proportion of 2005-2007 graduates who entered primary care specialties

64%

Proportion of 2006-2007 graduates who accepted in-state residencies

SUNY–Syracuse

- 766 Irving Avenue, Syracuse, NY 13210
- Public
- Year Founded: 1834
- Tuition, 2007-2008: In-state: $20,850; Out-of-state: $35,550
- Enrollment 2007-2008 academic year: 623
- Website: http://www.upstate.edu/
- Specialty ranking: rural medicine: 28

3.63	AVERAGE GPA, ENTERING CLASS FALL 2007
10.1	AVERAGE MCAT, ENTERING CLASS FALL 2007
8.8%	ACCEPTANCE RATE, ENTERING CLASS FALL 2007
Unranked	2009 U.S. NEWS MEDICAL SCHOOL RANKING (RESEARCH)
Unranked	2009 U.S. NEWS MEDICAL SCHOOL RANKING (PRIMARY CARE)

ADMISSIONS

Admissions phone number: (315) 464-4570
Admissions email address: admiss@upstate.edu
Application website:
  http://www.aamc.org/audienceamcas.htm
Acceptance rate: 8.8%
In-state acceptance rate: 11.4%
Out-of-state acceptance rate: 7.3%
Minority acceptance rate: 6.6%
International acceptance rate: N/A

Fall 2007 applications and acceptees

	Applied	Interviewed	Accepted	Enrolled
Total:	4,508	914	395	160
In-state:	1,587	407	181	78
Out-of-state:	2,921	507	214	82

Profile of admitted students

Average undergraduate grade point average: 3.63
MCAT averages (scale: 1-15; writing test: J-T):
  Composite score: 10.1
  Verbal reasoning score: 9.6, Physical sciences score:
  10.4, Biological sciences score: 10.4, Writing score: P
Proportion with undergraduate majors in: Biological
  sciences: N/A, Physical sciences: N/A, Non-sciences:
  N/A, Other health professions: N/A, Mixed disciplines
  and other: N/A
Percentage of students not coming directly from college
  after graduation: N/A

Dates and details

The American Medical College Application Service
  (AMCAS) application is accepted.
School asks for a school-specific application as part of the
  admissions process.
Oldest MCAT considered for Fall 2009 entry: 2005
Earliest application date for the 2009-2010 first-year class:
  6/1
Latest application date: 11/1
Acceptance dates for regular application for the class
  entering in fall 2009:

Earliest: October 15, 2008
Latest: August 23, 2009
The school considers requests for deferred entrance.
Starting month for the class entering in 2009–2010:
  August
The school has an Early Decision Plan (EDP).
A personal interview is required for admission.

Undergraduate coursework required

Medical school requires undergraduate work in these subjects: biology, biology/zoology, English, organic chemistry,
inorganic (general) chemistry, physics, general chemistry.

ADMISSIONS POLICY

(TEXT PROVIDED BY SCHOOL):

The Admissions Committee considers the following factors
when selecting applicants: academic achievement in the sciences, academic achievement in the humanities and social
sciences, volunteer and clinical experience, communication
skills, meaningful experiences dealing with and relating to
people, character, and motivation for selecting a career in
medicine.

COSTS AND FINANCIAL AID

Financial aid phone number: (315) 464-4329
Tuition, 2007-2008 academic year: In-state: $20,850; Out-
  of-state: $35,550
Room and board: $10,450
Percentage of students receiving financial aid in 2007-08:
  80%
Percentage of students receiving: Loans: 80%,
  Grants/scholarships: 38%, Work-study aid: 5%
Average medical school debt for the Class of 2006:
  $120,442

STUDENT BODY

Fall 2007 full-time enrollment: 623
Men: 49%, Women: 51%, In-state: 86%, Minorities: 29%,
  American Indian: 0.6%, Asian-American: 18.1%,
  African-American: 9.3%, Hispanic-American: 0.6%,
  White: 64.0%, International: 7.2%, Unknown: 0.0%

ACADEMIC PROGRAMS

The school's curriculum occasionally gives first-year students substantial contact with patients.

There are opportunities for first- or second-year students to work in community health clinics.

Program offerings: AIDS, drug/alcohol abuse, family medicine, geriatrics, internal medicine, pediatrics, rural medicine, women's health

Joint degrees awarded: M.D./Ph.D.

Total National Institutes of Health (NIH) grants awarded to the medical school and affiliated hospitals: **N/A**

CURRICULUM
(TEXT PROVIDED BY SCHOOL):

The organ-based curriculum integrates the basic and clinical sciencesówith basic science courses teaching the clinical implications of the materialóand provides clinical experience starting in the first semester. The organ systems approach enables an efficient, in-depth study of major concepts.

FACULTY PROFILE (FALL 2007)

Total teaching faculty: **443 (full-time), 202 (part-time)**
Of full-time faculty, those teaching in basic sciences: **16%**; in clinical programs: **84%**

Of part-time faculty, those teaching in basic sciences: **1%**; in clinical programs: **99%**
Full-time faculty/student ratio: **0.7**

SUPPORT SERVICES

The school offers students these services for dealing with stress: peer counseling, professional counseling, religious support, support groups.

RESIDENCY PROFILE

Most popular residency and specialty programs chosen by the 2006 and 2007 M.D. graduating classes: family practice, internal medicine, pediatrics, psychiatry, transitional year.

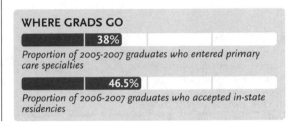

WHERE GRADS GO

38%

Proportion of 2005-2007 graduates who entered primary care specialties

46.5%

Proportion of 2006-2007 graduates who accepted in-state residencies

Temple University

- 3420 N. Broad Street, MRB 102, Philadelphia, PA 19140
- Private
- **Year Founded:** 1901
- **Tuition, 2007-2008:** $38,502
- **Enrollment 2007-2008 academic year:** 707
- **Website:** http://www.temple.edu/medicine
- **Specialty ranking:** N/A

3.64 AVERAGE GPA, ENTERING CLASS FALL 2007

10.2 AVERAGE MCAT, ENTERING CLASS FALL 2007

5.4% ACCEPTANCE RATE, ENTERING CLASS FALL 2007

Unranked 2009 U.S. NEWS MEDICAL SCHOOL RANKING (RESEARCH)

Unranked 2009 U.S. NEWS MEDICAL SCHOOL RANKING (PRIMARY CARE)

ADMISSIONS

Admissions phone number: **(215) 707-3656**
Admissions email address: **medadmissions@temple.edu**
Application website: **http://www.aamc.org**
Acceptance rate: **5.4%**
In-state acceptance rate: **16.8%**
Out-of-state acceptance rate: **4.0%**
Minority acceptance rate: **5.4%**
International acceptance rate: **0.0%**

Fall 2007 applications and acceptees

	Applied	Interviewed	Accepted	Enrolled
Total:	9,890	817	539	178
In-state:	1,110	218	187	77
Out-of-state:	8,780	599	352	101

Profile of admitted students

Average undergraduate grade point average: **3.64**
MCAT averages (scale: 1-15; writing test: J-T):
  Composite score: **10.2**
  Verbal reasoning score: **9.9**, Physical sciences score:
  10.2, Biological sciences score: **10.5**, Writing score: **Q**
Proportion with undergraduate majors in: Biological
  sciences: **40%**, Physical sciences: **18%**, Non-sciences:
  20%, Other health professions: **2%**, Mixed disciplines
  and other: **20%**
Percentage of students not coming directly from college
  after graduation: **46%**

Dates and details

The American Medical College Application Service
  (AMCAS) application is accepted.
School asks for a school-specific application as part of the
  admissions process.
Oldest MCAT considered for Fall 2009 entry: **2006**
Earliest application date for the 2009-2010 first-year class:
  6/1
Latest application date: **12/15**
Acceptance dates for regular application for the class
  entering in fall 2009:
  Earliest: **October 15, 2008**

Latest: **August 8, 2009**
The school considers requests for deferred entrance.
Starting month for the class entering in 2009-2010:
  August
The school has an Early Decision Plan (EDP).
A personal interview is required for admission.

Undergraduate coursework required

Medical school requires undergraduate work in these subjects: biology, organic chemistry, inorganic (general) chemistry, physics, humanities.

ADMISSIONS POLICY
(TEXT PROVIDED BY SCHOOL):

The American Medical College Application Service application and a supplemental application form must be completed. Over 9,000 apply. Fewer than 1,000 are interviewed
for the 180 available positions. Individuals with a variety of
social, ethnic, and scholastic backgrounds, including older
and second-career individuals, make up the diverse student
body. Foreign nationals without permanent resident or
refugee/asylum status are ineligible for consideration.

COSTS AND FINANCIAL AID

Financial aid phone number: **(215) 707-2667**
Tuition, 2007-2008 academic year: **$38,502**
Room and board: **$10,320**
Percentage of students receiving financial aid in 2007-08:
  87%
Percentage of students receiving: Loans: **87%**,
  Grants/scholarships: **33%**, Work-study aid: **11%**
Average medical school debt for the Class of 2006:
  $150,614

STUDENT BODY

Fall 2007 full-time enrollment: **707**
Men: **53%**, Women: **47%**, In-state: **51%**, Minorities: **39%**,
  American Indian: **0.4%**, Asian-American: **23.6%**,
  African-American: **7.4%**, Hispanic-American: **8.1%**,
  White: **56.4%**, International: **0.0%**, Unknown: **4.1%**

ACADEMIC PROGRAMS

The school's curriculum frequently gives first-year students substantial contact with patients.

There are opportunities for first- or second-year students to work in community health clinics.

Program offerings: AIDS, drug/alcohol abuse, family medicine, geriatrics, internal medicine, pediatrics, rural medicine, women's health

Joint degrees awarded: M.D./Ph.D., M.D./M.P.H.

Total National Institutes of Health (NIH) grants awarded to the medical school and affiliated hospitals: **$41.8 million**

CURRICULUM

(TEXT PROVIDED BY SCHOOL):

The curriculum was introduced in August 2005. Years 1 and 2 include a hybrid discipline/systems approach to basic sciences. Clinical instruction utilizes real and standardized patients and programmable mannequins. Year 3 and 4 requirements include Medicine, Surgery, Obstetrics/Gynecology, Family Medicine, Pediatrics, Psychiatry, Neurology, Radiology, and Emergency Medicine. Twenty elective weeks are available.

FACULTY PROFILE (FALL 2007)

Total teaching faculty. **446 (full-time)**, **62 (part-time)**

Of full-time faculty, those teaching in basic sciences: **29%**; in clinical programs: **71%**

Of part-time faculty, those teaching in basic sciences: **10%**; in clinical programs: **90%**

Full-time faculty/student ratio: **0.6**

SUPPORT SERVICES

The school offers students these services for dealing with stress: expanded-hour gym access, peer counseling, professional counseling, support groups.

RESIDENCY PROFILE

Most popular residency and specialty programs chosen by the 2006 and 2007 M.D. graduating classes: anesthesiology, emergency medicine, family practice, internal medicine, obstetrics and gynecology, orthopaedic surgery, pediatrics, surgery–general.

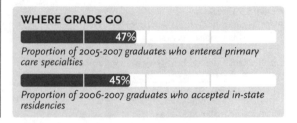

WHERE GRADS GO

47%

Proportion of 2005-2007 graduates who entered primary care specialties

45%

Proportion of 2006-2007 graduates who accepted in-state residencies

Texas A&M Health Science Center

- 147 Joe H. Reynolds Medical Building, College Station, TX 77843-1114
- Public
- Year Founded: 1971
- Tuition, 2007-2008: In-state: $10,682; Out-of-state: $23,782
- Enrollment 2007-2008 academic year: 353
- Website: http://medicine.tamhsc.edu
- Specialty ranking: N/A

3.76 AVERAGE GPA, ENTERING CLASS FALL 2007

9.7 AVERAGE MCAT, ENTERING CLASS FALL 2007

13.6% ACCEPTANCE RATE, ENTERING CLASS FALL 2007

Unranked 2009 U.S. NEWS MEDICAL SCHOOL RANKING (RESEARCH)

Unranked 2009 U.S. NEWS MEDICAL SCHOOL RANKING (PRIMARY CARE)

ADMISSIONS

Admissions phone number: **(979) 845-7743**
Admissions email address:
  admissions@medicine.tamhsc.edu
Application website: **http://www.utsystem.edu/tmdsas/**
Acceptance rate: **13.6%**
In-state acceptance rate: **14.3%**
Out-of-state acceptance rate: **7.5%**
Minority acceptance rate: **13.9%**
International acceptance rate: **0.0%**

Fall 2007 applications and acceptees

	Applied	Interviewed	Accepted	Enrolled
Total:	2,093	726	284	105
In-state:	1,867	673	267	95
Out-of-state:	226	53	17	10

Profile of admitted students

Average undergraduate grade point average: **3.76**
MCAT averages (scale: 1-15; writing test: J-T):
  Composite score: **9.7**
  Verbal reasoning score: **9.0**, Physical sciences score: **10.0**, Biological sciences score: **10.0**, Writing score: **Q**
Proportion with undergraduate majors in: Biological sciences: **68%**, Physical sciences: **10%**, Non-sciences: **7%**, Other health professions: **3%**, Mixed disciplines and other: **12%**
Percentage of students not coming directly from college after graduation: **50%**

Dates and details

The American Medical College Application Service (AMCAS) application is not accepted.
School asks for a school-specific application as part of the admissions process.
Oldest MCAT considered for Fall 2009 entry: **2004**
Earliest application date for the 2009-2010 first-year class: **5/1**
Latest application date: **10/1**
Acceptance dates for regular application for the class entering in fall 2009:

Earliest: **November 15, 2008**
Latest: **August 1, 2009**
The school considers requests for deferred entrance.
Starting month for the class entering in 2009–2010: **August**
The school doesn't have an Early Decision Plan (EDP).
A personal interview is required for admission.

Undergraduate coursework required

Medical school requires undergraduate work in these subjects: biology, biology/zoology, English, organic chemistry, inorganic (general) chemistry, physics, calculus.

ADMISSIONS POLICY

(TEXT PROVIDED BY SCHOOL):
The College of Medicine considers for enrollment individuals who have completed at least 90 credit hours of undergraduate coursework. Ninety percent of the class must be composed of Texas residents. Applicants are screened for interview on academic performance and intellectual capacity, dedication to service, capacity for effective interactions, special life circumstances, and other compelling factors.

COSTS AND FINANCIAL AID

Financial aid phone number: **(979) 845-8854**
Tuition, 2007-2008 academic year: **In-state: $10,682; Out-of-state: $23,782**
Room and board: **$13,000**
Percentage of students receiving financial aid in 2007-08: **84%**
Percentage of students receiving: Loans: **75%**, Grants/scholarships: **74%**, Work-study aid: **0%**
Average medical school debt for the Class of 2006: **$87,961**

STUDENT BODY

Fall 2007 full-time enrollment: **353**
Men: **46%**, Women: **54%**, In-state: **92%**, Minorities: **47%**, American Indian: **0.6%**, Asian-American: **28.3%**, African-American: **3.1%**, Hispanic-American: **9.9%**, White: **53.3%**, International: **0.6%**, Unknown: **4.2%**

ACADEMIC PROGRAMS

The school's curriculum frequently gives first-year students substantial contact with patients.

There are opportunities for first- or second-year students to work in community health clinics.

Program offerings: AIDS, drug/alcohol abuse, family medicine, geriatrics, internal medicine, pediatrics, rural medicine, women's health

Joint degrees awarded: M.D./Ph.D., M.D./M.B.A., M.D./M.P.H.

Total National Institutes of Health (NIH) grants awarded to the medical school and affiliated hospitals: **$8.8 million**

CURRICULUM
(TEXT PROVIDED BY SCHOOL):

The College of Medicine is implementing a new integrated systems-based curriculum that spans all four years of the program. Students will have earlier clinical experiences and increased opportunities for translational research during the clinical clerkships. The third and fourth years consist of the required core clinical clerkships as well as several weeks of selective clerkships.

FACULTY PROFILE (FALL 2007)

Total teaching faculty: **870 (full-time), 53 (part-time)**
Of full-time faculty, those teaching in basic sciences: **7%**; in clinical programs: **93%**

Of part-time faculty, those teaching in basic sciences: **15%**; in clinical programs: **85%**
Full-time faculty/student ratio: **2.5**

SUPPORT SERVICES

The school offers students these services for dealing with stress: expanded-hour gym access, peer counseling, professional counseling, religious support, support groups.

RESIDENCY PROFILE

Most popular residency and specialty programs chosen by the 2006 and 2007 M.D. graduating classes: anesthesiology, emergency medicine, family practice, internal medicine, obstetrics and gynecology, orthopaedic surgery, pediatrics, psychiatry, radiology–diagnostic, surgery–general.

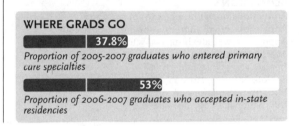

WHERE GRADS GO

37.8%

Proportion of 2005-2007 graduates who entered primary care specialties

53%

Proportion of 2006-2007 graduates who accepted in-state residencies

Texas Tech University

HEALTH SCIENCES CENTER

- 3601 Fourth Street, Lubbock, TX 79430
- Public
- **Year Founded:** 1969
- **Tuition, 2007-2008:** In-state: $11,914; Out-of-state: $25,014
- **Enrollment 2007-2008 academic year:** 571
- **Website:** http://www.ttuhsc.edu/SOM/
- **Specialty ranking:** N/A

3.62	AVERAGE GPA, ENTERING CLASS FALL 2007
9.8	AVERAGE MCAT, ENTERING CLASS FALL 2007
10.3%	ACCEPTANCE RATE, ENTERING CLASS FALL 2007
Unranked	2009 U.S. NEWS MEDICAL SCHOOL RANKING (RESEARCH)
Unranked	2009 U.S. NEWS MEDICAL SCHOOL RANKING (PRIMARY CARE)

ADMISSIONS

Admissions phone number: (806) 743-2297
Admissions email address: **somadm@ttuhsc.edu**
Application website: **http://www.utsystem.edu/tmdsas/**
Acceptance rate: 10.3%
In-state acceptance rate: 11.1%
Out-of-state acceptance rate: 5.1%
Minority acceptance rate: 9.2%
International acceptance rate: 0.0%

Fall 2007 applications and acceptees

	Applied	Interviewed	Accepted	Enrolled
Total:	3,048	743	314	140
In-state:	2,652	705	294	130
Out-of-state:	396	38	20	10

Profile of admitted students

Average undergraduate grade point average: 3.62
MCAT averages (scale: 1-15; writing test: J-T):
  Composite score: 9.8
  Verbal reasoning score: 9.5, Physical sciences score: 9.8,
  Biological sciences score: 10.3, Writing score: R
Proportion with undergraduate majors in: Biological
  sciences: 64%, Physical sciences: 8%, Non-sciences:
  17%, Other health professions: 1%, Mixed disciplines
  and other: 10%
Percentage of students not coming directly from college
  after graduation: 55%

Dates and details

The American Medical College Application Service
  (AMCAS) application is not accepted.
School asks for a school-specific application as part of the
  admissions process.
Oldest MCAT considered for Fall 2009 entry: **2003**
Earliest application date for the 2009-2010 first-year class:
  N/A
Latest application date: **N/A**
Acceptance dates for regular application for the class
  entering in fall 2009:
  Earliest: **November 15, 2008**

Latest: **February 15, 2009**
The school considers requests for deferred entrance.
Starting month for the class entering in 2009–2010:
  August
The school has an Early Decision Plan (EDP).
A personal interview is required for admission.

Undergraduate coursework required

Medical school requires undergraduate work in these subjects: biology, biology/zoology, English, organic chemistry,
inorganic (general) chemistry, physics, mathematics, calculus, general chemistry.

ADMISSIONS POLICY

(TEXT PROVIDED BY SCHOOL):

Three years of study (90 semester hours) in a U.S. or
Canadian accredited college or university are required,
including prerequisite courses. A baccalaureate degree is
highly desirable. The MCAT is a requirement of admission.
Applicants who have high intellectual ability, strong academics, compassion, motivation, the ability to communicate, maturity, and personal integrity are highly considered.

COSTS AND FINANCIAL AID

Financial aid phone number: (806) 743-3025
Tuition, 2007-2008 academic year: **In-state: $11,914; Out-
  of-state: $25,014**
Room and board: **$10,831**
Percentage of students receiving financial aid in 2007-08:
  86%
Percentage of students receiving: Loans: 83%,
  Grants/scholarships: 56%, Work-study aid: 0%
Average medical school debt for the Class of 2006:
  $122,818

STUDENT BODY

Fall 2007 full-time enrollment: 571
Men: 57%, Women: 43%, In-state: 96%, Minorities: 41%,
  American Indian: 0.5%, Asian-American: 25.4%,
  African-American: 3.2%, Hispanic-American: 11.9%,
  White: 55.7%, International: 0.0%, Unknown: 3.3%

ACADEMIC PROGRAMS

The school's curriculum very frequently gives first-year students substantial contact with patients.

There are opportunities for first- or second-year students to work in community health clinics.

Program offerings: AIDS, drug/alcohol abuse, family medicine, geriatrics, internal medicine, pediatrics, rural medicine, women's health

Joint degrees awarded: M.D./Ph.D., M.D./M.B.A.

Total National Institutes of Health (NIH) grants awarded to the medical school and affiliated hospitals: **$4.4 million**

CURRICULUM
(TEXT PROVIDED BY SCHOOL):

Years 1 and 2 contain four interdisciplinary blocks and a yearlong early clinical experience, in which students learn patient care requirements with master clinical teachers and community preceptors. Year 3 has six eight-week clerkships and a yearlong continuity clinic experience; Year 4 has one month in Neurology, two selectives, a subinternship, and four elective months.

FACULTY PROFILE (FALL 2007)

Total teaching faculty: **549 (full-time)**, **42 (part-time)**
Of full-time faculty, those teaching in basic sciences: **12%**; in clinical programs: **88%**

Of part-time faculty, those teaching in basic sciences: **2%**; in clinical programs: **98%**
Full-time faculty/student ratio: **1.0**

SUPPORT SERVICES

The school offers students these services for dealing with stress: expanded-hour gym access, peer counseling, professional counseling, support groups.

RESIDENCY PROFILE

Most popular residency and specialty programs chosen by the 2006 and 2007 M.D. graduating classes: anesthesiology, emergency medicine, family practice, internal medicine, obstetrics and gynecology, ophthalmology, orthopaedic surgery, pediatrics, surgery–general.

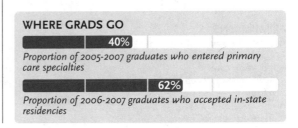

WHERE GRADS GO

40%

Proportion of 2005-2007 graduates who entered primary care specialties

62%

Proportion of 2006-2007 graduates who accepted in-state residencies

Tufts University

- 136 Harrison Avenue, Boston, MA 02111
- Private
- **Year Founded:** 1893
- **Tuition, 2007-2008:** $47,116
- **Enrollment 2007-2008 academic year:** 705
- **Website:** http://www.tufts.edu/med
- **Specialty ranking:** N/A

3.60 AVERAGE GPA, ENTERING CLASS FALL 2007

10.6 AVERAGE MCAT, ENTERING CLASS FALL 2007

7.2% ACCEPTANCE RATE, ENTERING CLASS FALL 2007

46 2009 U.S. NEWS MEDICAL SCHOOL RANKING (RESEARCH)

41 2009 U.S. NEWS MEDICAL SCHOOL RANKING (PRIMARY CARE)

ADMISSIONS

Admissions phone number: **(617) 636-6571**
Admissions email address: **med-admissions@tufts.edu**
Application website:
   http://www.tufts.edu/med/admissions/fye_secondary_app.html
Acceptance rate: **7.2%**
In-state acceptance rate: **17.6%**
Out-of-state acceptance rate: **6.1%**
Minority acceptance rate: **7.1%**
International acceptance rate: **1.1%**

Fall 2007 applications and acceptees

	Applied	Interviewed	Accepted	Enrolled
Total:	6,854	844	493	173
In-state:	630	164	111	51
Out-of-state:	6,224	680	382	122

Profile of admitted students

Average undergraduate grade point average: **3.60**
MCAT averages (scale: 1-15; writing test: J-T):
   Composite score: **10.6**
   Verbal reasoning score: **10.3**, Physical sciences score: **10.7**, Biological sciences score: **10.9**, Writing score: **Q**
Proportion with undergraduate majors in: Biological sciences: **50%**, Physical sciences: **19%**, Non-sciences: **26%**, Other health professions: **2%**, Mixed disciplines and other: **3%**
Percentage of students not coming directly from college after graduation: **62%**

Dates and details

The American Medical College Application Service (AMCAS) application is accepted.
School asks for a school-specific application as part of the admissions process.
Oldest MCAT considered for Fall 2009 entry: **2006**
Earliest application date for the 2009-2010 first-year class: **6/1**

Latest application date: **11/1**
Acceptance dates for regular application for the class entering in fall 2009:
   Earliest: **October 15, 2008**
   Latest: **August 24, 2009**
The school considers requests for deferred entrance.
Starting month for the class entering in 2009–2010: **August**
The school has an Early Decision Plan (EDP).
A personal interview is required for admission.

Undergraduate coursework required

Medical school requires undergraduate work in these subjects: biology, organic chemistry, inorganic (general) chemistry, physics.

ADMISSIONS POLICY
(TEXT PROVIDED BY SCHOOL):

Applicants who apply via the national service (American Medical College Application Service) are requested to complete a school-specific secondary application. All applicants who complete a secondary application are considered for a personal interview based on the qualifications presented on their application. The Admissions Committee meets monthly and admits selected applicants on a rolling basis.

COSTS AND FINANCIAL AID

Financial aid phone number: **(617) 636-6574**
Tuition, 2007-2008 academic year: **$47,116**
Room and board: **$11,088**
Percentage of students receiving financial aid in 2007-08: **79%**
Percentage of students receiving: Loans: **75%**, Grants/scholarships: **20%**, Work-study aid: **1%**
Average medical school debt for the Class of 2006: **$171,686**

STUDENT BODY

Fall 2007 full-time enrollment: **705**

Men: **54%**, Women: **46%**, In-state: **38%**, Minorities: **34%**,
American Indian: **0.6%**, Asian-American: **25.4%**,
African-American: **3.4%**, Hispanic-American: **3.4%**,
White: **64.8%**, International: **0.9%**, Unknown: **1.6%**

ACADEMIC PROGRAMS

The school's curriculum frequently gives first-year students substantial contact with patients.

There are opportunities for first- or second-year students to work in community health clinics.

Program offerings: AIDS, drug/alcohol abuse, family medicine, geriatrics, internal medicine, pediatrics, rural medicine, women's health

Joint degrees awarded: M.D./Ph.D., M.D./M.B.A., M.D./M.P.H.

Total National Institutes of Health (NIH) grants awarded to the medical school and affiliated hospitals: **$86.4 million**

CURRICULUM
(TEXT PROVIDED BY SCHOOL):

Tufts University School of Medicine, a leader in curricular innovation, provides a vibrant, student-centered community for educating physicians to enter any field of medicine. TUSM balances science with the art of medicine and with humanistic professional attitudes needed to competently face the rapid changes in the 21st century.

FACULTY PROFILE (FALL 2007)

Total teaching faculty: **1,531 (full-time)**, **2,485 (part-time)**

Of full-time faculty, those teaching in basic sciences: **7%**;
in clinical programs: **93%**

Of part-time faculty, those teaching in basic sciences: **5%**;
in clinical programs: **95%**

Full-time faculty/student ratio: **2.2**

SUPPORT SERVICES

The school offers students these services for dealing with stress: expanded-hour gym access, peer counseling, professional counseling, religious support, support groups.

RESIDENCY PROFILE

Most popular residency and specialty programs chosen by the 2006 and 2007 M.D. graduating classes: anesthesiology, emergency medicine, family practice, internal medicine, orthopaedic surgery, pediatrics, radiology–diagnostic, surgery–general.

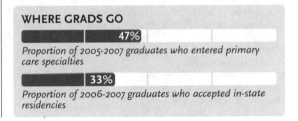

WHERE GRADS GO

47%

Proportion of 2005-2007 graduates who entered primary care specialties

33%

Proportion of 2006-2007 graduates who accepted in-state residencies

Tulane University

■ 1430 Tulane Avenue, SL67, New Orleans, LA 70112-2699
■ Private
■ **Year Founded:** 1834
■ **Tuition, 2007-2008:** $45,080
■ **Enrollment 2007-2008 academic year:** 652
■ **Website:** http://www.mcl.tulane.edu
■ **Specialty ranking:** N/A

3.60 AVERAGE GPA, ENTERING CLASS FALL 2007

10.0 AVERAGE MCAT, ENTERING CLASS FALL 2007

5.1% ACCEPTANCE RATE, ENTERING CLASS FALL 2007

55 2009 U.S. NEWS MEDICAL SCHOOL RANKING (RESEARCH)

Unranked 2009 U.S. NEWS MEDICAL SCHOOL RANKING (PRIMARY CARE)

ADMISSIONS
Admissions phone number: **(504) 988-5331**
Admissions email address: **medsch@tulane.edu**
Application website:
  http://www.som.tulane.edu/admissions/application.pdf
Acceptance rate: **5.1%**
In-state acceptance rate: **14.8%**
Out-of-state acceptance rate: **4.3%**
Minority acceptance rate: **3.5%**
International acceptance rate: **3.1%**

Fall 2007 applications and acceptees

	Applied	Interviewed	Accepted	Enrolled
Total:	6,582	695	335	172
In-state:	473	102	70	36
Out-of-state:	6,109	593	265	136

Profile of admitted students
Average undergraduate grade point average: **3.60**
MCAT averages (scale: 1-15; writing test: J-T):
  Composite score: **10.0**
  Verbal reasoning score: **10.0**, Physical sciences score:
  10.0, Biological sciences score: **10.0**, Writing score: **P**
Proportion with undergraduate majors in: Biological
  sciences: **30%**, Physical sciences: **31%**, Non-sciences:
  18%, Other health professions: **0%**, Mixed disciplines
  and other: **21%**
Percentage of students not coming directly from college
  after graduation: **20%**

Dates and details
The American Medical College Application Service
  (AMCAS) application is accepted.
School asks for a school-specific application as part of the
  admissions process.
Oldest MCAT considered for Fall 2009 entry: **2005**
Earliest application date for the 2009-2010 first-year class:
  6/15
Latest application date: **1/15**
Acceptance dates for regular application for the class
  entering in fall 2009:

Earliest: **October 15, 2008**
Latest: **August 1, 2009**
The school considers requests for deferred entrance.
Starting month for the class entering in 2009–2010:
  August
The school has an Early Decision Plan (EDP).
A personal interview is required for admission.

Undergraduate coursework required
Medical school requires undergraduate work in these subjects: biology, English, organic chemistry, inorganic (general) chemistry, physics, general chemistry.

ADMISSIONS POLICY
(TEXT PROVIDED BY SCHOOL):
All applications are hand screened by the associate or assistant dean for admissions. Approximately 1,000 applicants
are invited for interview. Each applicant is interviewed by
two faculty members and a student. The Admissions
Committee meets weekly, and admissions are granted on a
rolling basis. Tulane strives for a class diverse in talents,
interests, and background.

COSTS AND FINANCIAL AID
Financial aid phone number: **(504) 988-6135**
Tuition, 2007-2008 academic year: **$45,080**
Room and board: **$12,890**
Percentage of students receiving financial aid in 2007-08:
  83%
Percentage of students receiving: Loans: **74%**,
  Grants/scholarships: **38%**, Work-study aid: **0%**
Average medical school debt for the Class of 2006:
  $175,598

STUDENT BODY
Fall 2007 full-time enrollment: **652**
Men: **57%**, Women: **43%**, In-state: **33%**, Minorities: **19%**,
  American Indian: **0.2%**, Asian-American: **11.5%**,
  African-American: **5.1%**, Hispanic-American: **1.8%**,
  White: **69.5%**, International: **1.2%**, Unknown: **10.7%**

ACADEMIC PROGRAMS

The school's curriculum very frequently gives first-year students substantial contact with patients.

There are opportunities for first- or second-year students to work in community health clinics.

Program offerings: AIDS, drug/alcohol abuse, family medicine, geriatrics, internal medicine, pediatrics, rural medicine, women's health

Joint degrees awarded: M.D./Ph.D., M.D./M.B.A., M.D./M.P.H., M.D./J.D., M.D./M.S.

Total National Institutes of Health (NIH) grants awarded to the medical school and affiliated hospitals: **$66.9 million**

CURRICULUM

(TEXT PROVIDED BY SCHOOL):

The four-year curriculum is designed to provide knowledge to care for individuals and populations from varied socioeconomic backgrounds. The curriculum is also designed to ensure scientific literacy and compassionate patient care skills.

FACULTY PROFILE (FALL 2007)

Total teaching faculty: 374 **(full-time)**, 1,110 **(part-time)**
Of full-time faculty, those teaching in basic sciences: **23%**; in clinical programs: **77%**

Of part-time faculty, those teaching in basic sciences: **1%**; in clinical programs: **99%**
Full-time faculty/student ratio: **0.6**

SUPPORT SERVICES

The school offers students these services for dealing with stress: expanded-hour gym access, peer counseling, professional counseling, religious support, support groups.

RESIDENCY PROFILE

Most popular residency and specialty programs chosen by the 2006 and 2007 M.D. graduating classes: anesthesiology, emergency medicine, family practice, internal medicine, obstetrics and gynecology, pediatrics, psychiatry, radiology–diagnostic, surgery–general, internal medicine/pediatrics.

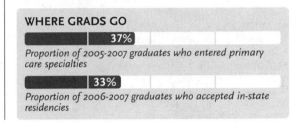

WHERE GRADS GO

37%
Proportion of 2005-2007 graduates who entered primary care specialties

33%
Proportion of 2006-2007 graduates who accepted in-state residencies

UMDNJ

ROBERT WOOD JOHNSON MEDICAL SCHOOL

- 125 Paterson Street, New Brunswick, NJ 08903-0019
- Public
- Year Founded: 1961
- Tuition, 2007-2008: In-state: $26,128; Out-of-state: $39,195
- Enrollment 2007-2008 academic year: 674
- Website: http://rwjms.umdnj.edu
- Specialty ranking: N/A

3.63 AVERAGE GPA, ENTERING CLASS FALL 2007

10.2 AVERAGE MCAT, ENTERING CLASS FALL 2007

10% ACCEPTANCE RATE, ENTERING CLASS FALL 2007

Unranked 2009 U.S. NEWS MEDICAL SCHOOL RANKING (RESEARCH)

58 2009 U.S. NEWS MEDICAL SCHOOL RANKING (PRIMARY CARE)

ADMISSIONS

Admissions phone number: **(732) 235-4576**
Admissions email address: **rwjapadm@umdnj.edu**
Application website: **http://www.aamc.org**
Acceptance rate: **10.0%**
In-state acceptance rate: **23.9%**
Out-of-state acceptance rate: **2.8%**
Minority acceptance rate: **10.1%**
International acceptance rate: **N/A**

Fall 2007 applications and acceptees

	Applied	Interviewed	Accepted	Enrolled
Total:	3,551	515	354	166
In-state:	1,211	418	289	142
Out-of-state:	2,340	97	65	24

Profile of admitted students

Average undergraduate grade point average: **3.63**
MCAT averages (scale: 1-15; writing test: J-T):
  Composite score: **10.2**
  Verbal reasoning score: **9.6**, Physical sciences score: **10.4**, Biological sciences score: **10.7**, Writing score: **P**
Proportion with undergraduate majors in: Biological sciences: **48%**, Physical sciences: **15%**, Non-sciences: **26%**, Other health professions: **1%**, Mixed disciplines and other: **10%**
Percentage of students not coming directly from college after graduation: **54%**

Dates and details

The American Medical College Application Service (AMCAS) application is accepted.
School does not ask for a school-specific application as part of the admissions process.
Oldest MCAT considered for Fall 2009 entry: **2005**
Earliest application date for the 2009-2010 first-year class: **6/1**
Latest application date: **12/1**
Acceptance dates for regular application for the class entering in fall 2009:
  Earliest: **October 15, 2008**

Latest: **August 7, 2009**
The school considers requests for deferred entrance.
Starting month for the class entering in 2009–2010:
  August
The school has an Early Decision Plan (EDP).
A personal interview is required for admission.

Undergraduate coursework required

Medical school requires undergraduate work in these subjects: biology/zoology, English, organic chemistry, inorganic (general) chemistry, physics, mathematics.

ADMISSIONS POLICY

(TEXT PROVIDED BY SCHOOL):

Preference given to New Jersey residents; out-of-state applicants with outstanding credentials are encouraged to apply. Applicants must be U.S. citizens or permanent residents. Selection criteria include academic achievement, MCATs, and nonacademic factors: extracurriculars, motivation, character, humanism, commitment to service, sensitivity to diversity, and qualities conveyed in personal interviews. Interviews by invitation.

COSTS AND FINANCIAL AID

Financial aid phone number: **(732) 235-4689**
Tuition, 2007-2008 academic year: **In-state: $26,128; Out-of-state: $39,195**
Room and board: **$12,294**
Percentage of students receiving financial aid in 2007-08: **86%**
Percentage of students receiving: Loans: **84%**, Grants/scholarships: **47%**, Work-study aid: **7%**
Average medical school debt for the Class of 2006: **$121,096**

STUDENT BODY

Fall 2007 full-time enrollment: **674**
Men: **45%**, Women: **55%**, In-state: **99%**, Minorities: **50%**, American Indian: **0.0%**, Asian-American: **35.3%**, African-American: **9.9%**, Hispanic-American: **4.9%**, White: **45.4%**, International: **0.0%**, Unknown: **4.5%**

ACADEMIC PROGRAMS

The school's curriculum frequently gives first-year students substantial contact with patients.

There are opportunities for first- or second-year students to work in community health clinics.

Program offerings: AIDS, drug/alcohol abuse, family medicine, geriatrics, internal medicine, pediatrics, rural medicine, women's health

Joint degrees awarded: M.D./Ph.D., M.D./M.B.A., M.D./M.P.H., M.D./J.D., M.D./M.S.

Total National Institutes of Health (NIH) grants awarded to the medical school and affiliated hospitals: **$55.5 million**

CURRICULUM

(TEXT PROVIDED BY SCHOOL):

The curriculum fosters graduates who provide ethical, integrated, comprehensive, and culturally sensitive care; it includes health promotion, disease prevention, and medical management. Goals and objectives are organized within six core competencies. Clinical experiences begin early in the first year and are enhanced with standardized patients, objective structured clinical examinations, and individual observation and feedback.

FACULTY PROFILE (FALL 2007)

Total teaching faculty: **934 (full-time), 157 (part-time)**

Of full-time faculty, those teaching in basic sciences: **12%**; in clinical programs: **88%**

Of part-time faculty, those teaching in basic sciences: **11%**; in clinical programs: **89%**

Full-time faculty/student ratio: **1.4**

SUPPORT SERVICES

The school offers students these services for dealing with stress: peer counseling, professional counseling, support groups.

RESIDENCY PROFILE

Most popular residency and specialty programs chosen by the 2006 and 2007 M.D. graduating classes: anesthesiology, emergency medicine, family practice, internal medicine, ophthalmology, orthopaedic surgery, pediatrics, psychiatry, radiology–diagnostic, surgery–general.

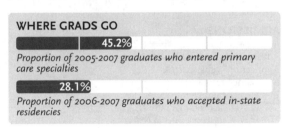

WHERE GRADS GO

45.2%

Proportion of 2005-2007 graduates who entered primary care specialties

28.1%

Proportion of 2006-2007 graduates who accepted in-state residencies

Uniformed Services University

OF THE HEALTH SCIENCES (HEBERT)

- 4301 Jones Bridge Road, Bethesda, MD 20814
- Public
- Year Founded: 1972
- Tuition, 2007-2008: N/A
- Enrollment 2007-2008 academic year: 670
- Website: http://www.usuhs.mil
- Specialty ranking: N/A

3.51 AVERAGE GPA, ENTERING CLASS FALL 2007

9.8 AVERAGE MCAT, ENTERING CLASS FALL 2007

14.7% ACCEPTANCE RATE, ENTERING CLASS FALL 2007

Unranked 2009 U.S. NEWS MEDICAL SCHOOL RANKING (RESEARCH)

Unranked 2009 U.S. NEWS MEDICAL SCHOOL RANKING (PRIMARY CARE)

ADMISSIONS

Admissions phone number: (800) 772-1743
Admissions email address: **admissions@usuhs.mil**
Application website: **N/A**
Acceptance rate: **14.7%**
In-state acceptance rate: **N/A**
Out-of-state acceptance rate: **N/A**
Minority acceptance rate: **9.6%**
International acceptance rate: **N/A**

Fall 2007 applications and acceptees

	Applied	Interviewed	Accepted	Enrolled
Total:	1,908	506	280	170
In-state:	N/A	N/A	N/A	N/A
Out-of-state:	N/A	N/A	N/A	N/A

Profile of admitted students

Average undergraduate grade point average: **3.51**
MCAT averages (scale: 1-15; writing test: J-T):
  Composite score: **9.8**
  Verbal reasoning score: **9.8**, Physical sciences score: **9.5**,
  Biological sciences score: **10.0**, Writing score: **P**
Proportion with undergraduate majors in: Biological sciences: **41%**, Physical sciences: **32%**, Non-sciences: **11%**, Other health professions: **9%**, Mixed disciplines and other: **7%**
Percentage of students not coming directly from college after graduation: **57%**

Dates and details

The American Medical College Application Service (AMCAS) application is accepted.
School asks for a school-specific application as part of the admissions process.
Oldest MCAT considered for Fall 2009 entry: **2006**
Earliest application date for the 2009-2010 first-year class: **6/1**
Latest application date: **11/15**
Acceptance dates for regular application for the class entering in fall 2009:

Earliest: **October 15, 2008**
Latest: **June 15, 2009**
The school considers requests for deferred entrance.
Starting month for the class entering in 2009–2010: **August**
The school doesn't have an Early Decision Plan (EDP).
A personal interview is required for admission.

Undergraduate coursework required

Medical school requires undergraduate work in these subjects: biology, English, organic chemistry, inorganic (general) chemistry, physics, calculus.

ADMISSIONS POLICY
(TEXT PROVIDED BY SCHOOL):

The SOM is a federal institution that does not give any preference to in-state residents. The Admissions Committee evaluates grades, MCATs, clinical work, extracurricular activities, work experience, motivation for military medicine, and interviews. Interviewed applicant must pass a medical examination and security clearance to be eligible to attend the SOM as a commissioned officer.

COSTS AND FINANCIAL AID

Financial aid phone number: **N/A**
Tuition, 2007-2008 academic year: **N/A**
Room and board: **$0**
Percentage of students receiving financial aid in 2007-08: **0%**
Percentage of students receiving: Loans: **0%**, Grants/scholarships: **0%**, Work-study aid: **0%**
Average medical school debt for the Class of 2006: **$0**

STUDENT BODY

Fall 2007 full-time enrollment: **670**
Men: **70%**, Women: **30%**, In-state: **6%**, Minorities: **21%**, American Indian: **0.9%**, Asian-American: **13.7%**, African-American: **1.8%**, Hispanic-American: **4.6%**, White: **73.6%**, International: **0.0%**, Unknown: **5.4%**

ACADEMIC PROGRAMS

The school's curriculum frequently gives first-year students substantial contact with patients.

There are opportunities for first- or second-year students to work in community health clinics.

Program offerings: AIDS, drug/alcohol abuse, family medicine, geriatrics, internal medicine, pediatrics

Joint degrees awarded: M.D./Ph.D.

Total National Institutes of Health (NIH) grants awarded to the medical school and affiliated hospitals: **$34.4 million**

CURRICULUM

(TEXT PROVIDED BY SCHOOL):

The School of Medicine's curriculum is designed to graduate competent, compassionate, dedicated physicians to serve beneficiaries of the military and the public health service. The SOM places emphasis in areas critical to the uniformed physician: Trauma and Emergency Medicine, Infectious Disease and Parasitology, Humanities and Behavioral Sciences, and Principles of Leadership and Teamwork.

FACULTY PROFILE (FALL 2007)

Total teaching faculty: **277 (full-time)**, **1,827 (part-time)**
Of full-time faculty, those teaching in basic sciences: **43%**; in clinical programs: **57%**

Of part-time faculty, those teaching in basic sciences: **4%**; in clinical programs: **96%**
Full-time faculty/student ratio: **0.4**

SUPPORT SERVICES

The school offers students these services for dealing with stress: expanded-hour gym access, professional counseling, religious support, support groups.

RESIDENCY PROFILE

Most popular residency and specialty programs chosen by the 2006 and 2007 M.D. graduating classes: anesthesiology, emergency medicine, family practice, internal medicine, obstetrics and gynecology, pediatrics, psychiatry, surgery–general.

WHERE GRADS GO

34%

Proportion of 2005-2007 graduates who entered primary care specialties

N/A

Proportion of 2006-2007 graduates who accepted in-state residencies

University at Buffalo—SUNY

ADMISSIONS

Admissions phone number: **(716) 829-3466**
Admissions email address: **jjrosso@buffalo.edu**
Application website: **http://www.aamc.org**
Acceptance rate: **8.4%**
In-state acceptance rate: **13.9%**
Out-of-state acceptance rate: **3.7%**
Minority acceptance rate: **N/A**
International acceptance rate: **N/A**

Fall 2007 applications and acceptees

	Applied	Interviewed	Accepted	Enrolled
Total:	3,826	629	322	135
In-state:	1,757	404	245	112
Out-of-state:	2,069	225	77	23

Profile of admitted students

Average undergraduate grade point average: **3.62**
MCAT averages (scale: 1-15; writing test: J-T):
  Composite score: **10.1**
  Verbal reasoning score: **9.6**, Physical sciences score: **10.2**, Biological sciences score: **10.5**, Writing score: **P**
Proportion with undergraduate majors in: Biological sciences: **28%**, Physical sciences: **23%**, Non-sciences: **31%**, Other health professions: **13%**, Mixed disciplines and other: **5%**
Percentage of students not coming directly from college after graduation: **15%**

Dates and details

The American Medical College Application Service (AMCAS) application is accepted.
School asks for a school-specific application as part of the admissions process.
Oldest MCAT considered for Fall 2009 entry: **2005**
Earliest application date for the 2009-2010 first-year class: **6/1**
Latest application date: **11/15**
Acceptance dates for regular application for the class entering in fall 2009:
  Earliest: **October 15, 2008**

Latest: **August 10, 2009**
The school considers requests for deferred entrance.
Starting month for the class entering in 2009–2010:
  August
The school has an Early Decision Plan (EDP).
A personal interview is required for admission.

Undergraduate coursework required

Medical school requires undergraduate work in these subjects: biology, English, organic chemistry, inorganic (general) chemistry, physics.

ADMISSIONS POLICY
(TEXT PROVIDED BY SCHOOL):

Selection is based on scholastic achievement, aptitude, personal qualifications, motivation. College record, MCATs, letters of reference, personal interview provide information. All applicants must be U.S. citizens or permanent residents. Minorities and disadvantaged students are encouraged to apply. In-state residency is not required but is looked upon favorably.

COSTS AND FINANCIAL AID

Financial aid phone number: **(716) 645-2450**
Tuition, 2007-2008 academic year: **In-state: $20,218; Out-of-state: $34,918**
Room and board: **$10,707**
Percentage of students receiving financial aid in 2007-08: **94%**
Percentage of students receiving: Loans: **80%**, Grants/scholarships: **24%**, Work-study aid: **1%**
Average medical school debt for the Class of 2006: **$97,027**

STUDENT BODY

Fall 2007 full-time enrollment: **571**
Men: **47%**, Women: **53%**, In-state: **100%**, Minorities: **33%**, American Indian: **0.5%**, Asian-American: **27.8%**, African-American: **3.2%**, Hispanic-American: **1.1%**, White: **65.0%**, International: **0.0%**, Unknown: **2.5%**

ACADEMIC PROGRAMS

The school's curriculum occasionally gives first-year students substantial contact with patients.

There are opportunities for first- or second-year students to work in community health clinics.

Program offerings: AIDS, drug/alcohol abuse, family medicine, geriatrics, internal medicine, pediatrics, rural medicine

Joint degrees awarded: M.D./Ph.D., M.D./M.B.A., M.D./M.P.H.

Total National Institutes of Health (NIH) grants awarded to the medical school and affiliated hospitals: **$61.1 million**

CURRICULUM
(TEXT PROVIDED BY SCHOOL):

Years 1 and 2 of the medical curriculum begin with an organ-based interdisciplinary core curriculum. Modular lecture sections focus on organs of interest and their diseases. Students also attend small-group, problem-based learning sessions. Students get practical experience in the Clinical Practice of Medicine course. In Years 3 and 4, students rotate in the specialty clinical areas.

FACULTY PROFILE (FALL 2007)

Total teaching faculty: **421 (full-time), 22 (part-time)**

Of full-time faculty, those teaching in basic sciences: **26%**; in clinical programs: **74%**

Of part-time faculty, those teaching in basic sciences: **55%**; in clinical programs: **45%**

Full-time faculty/student ratio: **0.7**

SUPPORT SERVICES

The school offers students these services for dealing with stress: professional counseling, religious support.

RESIDENCY PROFILE

Most popular residency and specialty programs chosen by the 2006 and 2007 M.D. graduating classes: N/A.

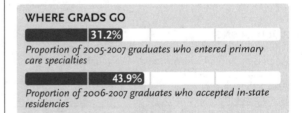

WHERE GRADS GO

31.2%

Proportion of 2005-2007 graduates who entered primary care specialties

43.9%

Proportion of 2006-2007 graduates who accepted in-state residencies

University of Alabama—Birmingham

- **Medical Student Services, VH Suite 100, Birmingham, AL 35294-0019**
- **Public**
- **Year Founded:** 1859
- **Tuition, 2007-2008:** In-state: $17,998; Out-of-state: $45,238
- **Enrollment 2007-2008 academic year:** 716
- **Website:** http://www.uab.edu/uasom/admissions
- **Specialty ranking:** AIDS: 5, geriatrics: 19, internal medicine: 21, pediatrics: 19, rural medicine: 16, women's health: 14

3.71 AVERAGE GPA, ENTERING CLASS FALL 2007

10.0 AVERAGE MCAT, ENTERING CLASS FALL 2007

11.3% ACCEPTANCE RATE, ENTERING CLASS FALL 2007

27 2009 U.S. NEWS MEDICAL SCHOOL RANKING (RESEARCH)

43 2009 U.S. NEWS MEDICAL SCHOOL RANKING (PRIMARY CARE)

ADMISSIONS

Admissions phone number: **(205) 934-2433**
Admissions email address: **medschool@uab.edu**
Application website: **N/A**
Acceptance rate: **11.3%**
In-state acceptance rate: **37.9%**
Out-of-state acceptance rate: **3.6%**
Minority acceptance rate: **8.3%**
International acceptance rate: **N/A**

Fall 2007 applications and acceptees

	Applied	Interviewed	Accepted	Enrolled
Total:	2,055	373	232	176
In-state:	459	254	174	157
Out-of-state:	1,596	119	58	19

Profile of admitted students

Average undergraduate grade point average: **3.71**
MCAT averages (scale: 1-15; writing test: J-T):
  Composite score: **10.0**
  Verbal reasoning score: **9.7**, Physical sciences score: **9.9**, Biological sciences score: **10.3**, Writing score: **P**
Proportion with undergraduate majors in: Biological sciences: **42%**, Physical sciences: **21%**, Non-sciences: **9%**, Other health professions: **3%**, Mixed disciplines and other: **26%**
Percentage of students not coming directly from college after graduation: **10%**

Dates and details

The American Medical College Application Service (AMCAS) application is accepted.
School asks for a school-specific application as part of the admissions process.
Oldest MCAT considered for Fall 2009 entry: **2007**
Earliest application date for the 2009-2010 first-year class: **6/1**
Latest application date: **11/1**
Acceptance dates for regular application for the class entering in fall 2009:

Earliest: **October 15, 2008**
  Latest: **N/A**
The school considers requests for deferred entrance.
Starting month for the class entering in 2009–2010: **July**
The school has an Early Decision Plan (EDP).
A personal interview is required for admission.

Undergraduate coursework required

Medical school requires undergraduate work in these subjects: biology, English, organic chemistry, inorganic (general) chemistry, physics, mathematics, general chemistry.

ADMISSIONS POLICY
(TEXT PROVIDED BY SCHOOL):

The UASOM Admissions Committee is committed to selecting applicants who possess the intelligence, skills, attitudes, and other personal attributes to become excellent physicians and to meet the healthcare needs of Alabama. Other requirements include minimal total MCAT of 24 (latest exam) and other specifics as outlined in Guidelines for the Admissions Cycle on the website.

COSTS AND FINANCIAL AID

Financial aid phone number: **(205) 934-8223**
Tuition, 2007-2008 academic year: **In-state: $17,998; Out-of-state: $45,238**
Room and board: **$10,879**
Percentage of students receiving financial aid in 2007-08: **87%**
Percentage of students receiving: Loans: **76%**, Grants/scholarships: **23%**, Work-study aid: **0%**
Average medical school debt for the Class of 2006: **$110,040**

STUDENT BODY

Fall 2007 full-time enrollment: **716**
Men: **60%**, Women: **40%**, In-state: **93%**, Minorities: **23%**, American Indian: **1.3%**, Asian-American: **13.7%**, African-American: **7.0%**, Hispanic-American: **1.5%**, White: **76.0%**, International: **0.0%**, Unknown: **0.6%**

ACADEMIC PROGRAMS

The school's curriculum frequently gives first-year students substantial contact with patients.

There are opportunities for first- or second-year students to work in community health clinics.

Program offerings: AIDS, drug/alcohol abuse, family medicine, geriatrics, internal medicine, pediatrics, rural medicine, women's health

Joint degrees awarded: M.D./Ph.D., M.D./M.P.H., M.D./M.S.

Total National Institutes of Health (NIH) grants awarded to the medical school and affiliated hospitals: **$180.5 million**

FACULTY PROFILE (FALL 2007)

Total teaching faculty: **1,152 (full-time)**, **43 (part-time)**

Of full-time faculty, those teaching in basic sciences: **21%**; in clinical programs: **79%**

Of part-time faculty, those teaching in basic sciences: **12%**; in clinical programs: **88%**

Full-time faculty/student ratio: **1.6**

SUPPORT SERVICES

The school offers students these services for dealing with stress: expanded-hour gym access, professional counseling, religious support, support groups.

RESIDENCY PROFILE

Most popular residency and specialty programs chosen by the 2006 and 2007 M.D. graduating classes: anesthesiology, emergency medicine, family practice, internal medicine, ophthalmology, orthopaedic surgery, pathology–anatomic and clinical, pediatrics, radiology–diagnostic, surgery–general.

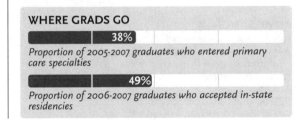

WHERE GRADS GO

38%

Proportion of 2005-2007 graduates who entered primary care specialties

49%

Proportion of 2006-2007 graduates who accepted in-state residencies

University of Arizona

- 1501 N. Campbell Avenue, Tucson, AZ 85724
- Public
- Year Founded: 1967
- Tuition, 2007-2008: $17,736
- Enrollment 2007-2008 academic year: 481
- Website: http://www.medicine.arizona.edu
- Specialty ranking: N/A

3.68 AVERAGE GPA, ENTERING CLASS FALL 2007

9.8 AVERAGE MCAT, ENTERING CLASS FALL 2007

31.7% ACCEPTANCE RATE, ENTERING CLASS FALL 2007

Unranked 2009 U.S. NEWS MEDICAL SCHOOL RANKING (RESEARCH)

62 2009 U.S. NEWS MEDICAL SCHOOL RANKING (PRIMARY CARE)

ADMISSIONS
Admissions phone number: (520) 626-6214
Admissions email address:
   admissions@medicine.arizona.edu
Application website: N/A
Acceptance rate: 31.7%
In-state acceptance rate: 31.4%
Out-of-state acceptance rate: 46.2%
Minority acceptance rate: 32.3%
International acceptance rate: N/A

Fall 2007 applications and acceptees

	Applied	Interviewed	Accepted	Enrolled
Total:	603	603	191	134
In-state:	590	590	185	132
Out-of-state:	13	13	6	2

Profile of admitted students
Average undergraduate grade point average: 3.68
MCAT averages (scale: 1-15; writing test: J-T):
   Composite score: 9.8
   Verbal reasoning score: 9.7, Physical sciences score: 9.6,
   Biological sciences score: 10.0, Writing score: Q
Proportion with undergraduate majors in: Biological
   sciences: N/A, Physical sciences: N/A, Non-sciences:
   N/A, Other health professions: N/A, Mixed disciplines
   and other: N/A
Percentage of students not coming directly from college
   after graduation: N/A

Dates and details
The American Medical College Application Service
   (AMCAS) application is accepted.
School asks for a school-specific application as part of the
   admissions process.
Oldest MCAT considered for Fall 2009 entry: 2005
Earliest application date for the 2009-2010 first-year class:
   6/1
Latest application date: 11/1
Acceptance dates for regular application for the class
   entering in fall 2009:

Earliest: March 2, 2009
   Latest: August 3, 2009
The school considers requests for deferred entrance.
Starting month for the class entering in 2009–2010:
   August
The school doesn't have an Early Decision Plan (EDP).
A personal interview is required for admission.

Undergraduate coursework required
Medical school requires undergraduate work in these subjects: biology/zoology, English, organic chemistry, inorganic
(general) chemistry, physics.

ADMISSIONS POLICY
(TEXT PROVIDED BY SCHOOL):
The College of Medicine admits only Arizona residents and
Western Interstate Commission for Higher Education students. Many factors are considered, including the entire academic record, performance on the MCAT, the applicant's
personal statement, interviews, and letters of recommendation. Applicants are chosen on the basis of their career
goals, motivation, academic ability, integrity, maturity, altruism, communication skills, and leadership abilities.

COSTS AND FINANCIAL AID
Financial aid phone number: (520) 626-7145
Tuition, 2007-2008 academic year: $17,736
Room and board: $9,500
Percentage of students receiving financial aid in 2007-08:
   91%
Percentage of students receiving: Loans: 77%,
   Grants/scholarships: 79%, Work-study aid: 2%
Average medical school debt for the Class of 2006:
   $104,616

STUDENT BODY
Fall 2007 full-time enrollment: 481
Men: 45%, Women: 55%, In-state: 101%, Minorities: 27%,
   American Indian: N/A, Asian-American: N/A, African-
   American: N/A, Hispanic-American: N/A, White: N/A,
   International: N/A, Unknown: N/A

ACADEMIC PROGRAMS

The school's curriculum very frequently gives first-year students substantial contact with patients.

There are opportunities for first- or second-year students to work in community health clinics.

Program offerings: AIDS, drug/alcohol abuse, family medicine, geriatrics, internal medicine, pediatrics, rural medicine, women's health

Joint degrees awarded: M.D./Ph.D., M.D./M.B.A., M.D./M.P.H.

Total National Institutes of Health (NIH) grants awarded to the medical school and affiliated hospitals: **N/A**

CURRICULUM

(TEXT PROVIDED BY SCHOOL):

The University of Arizona College of Medicine has two full, four-year campuses: the original campus in Tucson and a new campus in Phoenix in partnership with Arizona State University. Both provide state-of-the-art, fully integrated, organ-system-based curricula in the first two years and a unified, modern clinical curriculum in the third and fourth years.

FACULTY PROFILE (FALL 2007)

Total teaching faculty: **888 (full-time)**, **37 (part-time)**
Of full-time faculty, those teaching in basic sciences: **11%**; in clinical programs: **89%**

Of part-time faculty, those teaching in basic sciences: **35%**; in clinical programs: **65%**
Full-time faculty/student ratio: **1.8**

SUPPORT SERVICES

The school offers students these services for dealing with stress: expanded-hour gym access, peer counseling, professional counseling, religious support, support groups.

RESIDENCY PROFILE

Most popular residency and specialty programs chosen by the 2006 and 2007 M.D. graduating classes: anesthesiology, emergency medicine, family practice, internal medicine, pediatrics, surgery–general.

WHERE GRADS GO

42.5%

Proportion of 2005-2007 graduates who entered primary care specialties

33.6%

Proportion of 2006-2007 graduates who accepted in-state residencies

University of Arkansas

FOR MEDICAL SCIENCES

- 4301 W. Markham Street, Slot 551, Little Rock, AR 72205
- Public
- **Year Founded:** 1879
- **Tuition, 2007-2008:** In-state: $16,430; Out-of-state: $31,962
- **Enrollment 2007-2008 academic year:** 596
- **Website:** http://www.uams.edu
- **Specialty ranking:** geriatrics: 10

3.62 AVERAGE GPA, ENTERING CLASS FALL 2007

9.8 AVERAGE MCAT, ENTERING CLASS FALL 2007

16.1% ACCEPTANCE RATE, ENTERING CLASS FALL 2007

Unranked 2009 U.S. NEWS MEDICAL SCHOOL RANKING (RESEARCH)

35 2009 U.S. NEWS MEDICAL SCHOOL RANKING (PRIMARY CARE)

ADMISSIONS

Admissions phone number: **(501) 686-5354**
Admissions email address: **southtomg@uams.edu**
Application website: **N/A**
Acceptance rate: **16.1%**
In-state acceptance rate: **43.7%**
Out-of-state acceptance rate: **6.6%**
Minority acceptance rate: **44.4%**
International acceptance rate: **N/A**

Fall 2007 applications and acceptees

	Applied	Interviewed	Accepted	Enrolled
Total:	1,232	402	198	155
In-state:	316	308	138	129
Out-of-state:	916	94	60	26

Profile of admitted students

Average undergraduate grade point average: **3.62**
MCAT averages (scale: 1-15; writing test: J-T):
   Composite score: **9.8**
   Verbal reasoning score: **10.0**, Physical sciences score: **9.4**, Biological sciences score: **9.9**, Writing score: **O**
Proportion with undergraduate majors in: Biological sciences: **56%**, Physical sciences: **25%**, Non-sciences: **15%**, Other health professions: **3%**, Mixed disciplines and other: **1%**
Percentage of students not coming directly from college after graduation: **N/A**

Dates and details

The American Medical College Application Service (AMCAS) application is accepted.
School asks for a school-specific application as part of the admissions process.
Oldest MCAT considered for Fall 2009 entry: **N/A**
Earliest application date for the 2009-2010 first-year class: **N/A**
Latest application date: **N/A**
Acceptance dates for regular application for the class entering in fall 2009:
   Earliest: **N/A**

Latest: **N/A**
The school considers requests for deferred entrance.
Starting month for the class entering in 2009–2010: **N/A**
The school doesn't have an Early Decision Plan (EDP).
A personal interview is required for admission.

Undergraduate coursework required

Medical school requires undergraduate work in these subjects: biology, biology/zoology, English, organic chemistry, inorganic (general) chemistry, physics, mathematics, demonstration of writing skills, calculus, general chemistry.

COSTS AND FINANCIAL AID

Financial aid phone number: **(501) 686-5813**
Tuition, 2007-2008 academic year: **In-state: $16,430; Out-of-state: $31,962**
Room and board: **N/A**
Percentage of students receiving financial aid in 2007-08: **94%**
Percentage of students receiving: Loans: **91%**, Grants/scholarships: **45%**, Work-study aid: **0%**
Average medical school debt for the Class of 2006: **$112,469**

STUDENT BODY

Fall 2007 full-time enrollment: **596**
Men: **59%**, Women: **41%**, In-state: **91%**, Minorities: **16%**, American Indian: **0.5%**, Asian-American: **10.7%**, African-American: **4.2%**, Hispanic-American: **0.7%**, White: **83.9%**, International: **0.0%**, Unknown: **0.0%**

ACADEMIC PROGRAMS

There are opportunities for first- or second-year students to work in community health clinics.
Program offerings: AIDS, drug/alcohol abuse, family medicine, geriatrics, internal medicine, pediatrics, rural medicine, women's health
Joint degrees awarded: M.D./Ph.D., M.D./M.B.A., M.D./M.P.H., M.D./J.D.
Total National Institutes of Health (NIH) grants awarded to the medical school and affiliated hospitals: **N/A**

FACULTY PROFILE (FALL 2007)

Total teaching faculty: **989 (full-time), 150 (part-time)**

Of full-time faculty, those teaching in basic sciences: **12%**; in clinical programs: **88%**

Of part-time faculty, those teaching in basic sciences: **3%**; in clinical programs: **97%**

Full-time faculty/student ratio: **1.7**

SUPPORT SERVICES

The school offers students these services for dealing with stress: expanded-hour gym access, peer counseling, professional counseling, support groups.

RESIDENCY PROFILE

Most popular residency and specialty programs chosen by the 2006 and 2007 M.D. graduating classes: N/A.

WHERE GRADS GO

55.5%

Proportion of 2005-2007 graduates who entered primary care specialties

N/A

Proportion of 2006-2007 graduates who accepted in-state residencies

University of California–Davis

■ 1 Shields Avenue, Davis, CA 95616-8661
■ Public
■ Year Founded: 1966
■ Tuition, 2007-2008: In-state: $25,155; Out-of-state: $37,400
■ Enrollment 2007-2008 academic year: 393
■ Website: http://www.ucdmc.ucdavis.edu
■ Specialty ranking: family medicine: 27

3.62 AVERAGE GPA, ENTERING CLASS FALL 2007

10.3 AVERAGE MCAT, ENTERING CLASS FALL 2007

4.7% ACCEPTANCE RATE, ENTERING CLASS FALL 2007

48 2009 U.S. NEWS MEDICAL SCHOOL RANKING (RESEARCH)

26 2009 U.S. NEWS MEDICAL SCHOOL RANKING (PRIMARY CARE)

ADMISSIONS

Admissions phone number: **(916) 734-4800**
Admissions email address: **medadmisinfo@ucdavis.edu**
Application website: **http://www.ucdmc.ucdavis.edu/ome/admissions/requirements.html**
Acceptance rate: **4.7%**
In-state acceptance rate: **5.7%**
Out-of-state acceptance rate: **1.1%**
Minority acceptance rate: **3.8%**
International acceptance rate: **N/A**

Fall 2007 applications and acceptees

	Applied	Interviewed	Accepted	Enrolled
Total:	4,861	470	229	105
In-state:	3,781	440	217	101
Out-of-state:	1,080	30	12	4

Profile of admitted students

Average undergraduate grade point average: **3.62**
MCAT averages (scale: 1-15; writing test: J-T):
  Composite score: **10.3**
  Verbal reasoning score: **10.8**, Physical sciences score: **10.0**, Biological sciences score: **11.0**, Writing score: **Q**
Proportion with undergraduate majors in: Biological sciences: **52%**, Physical sciences: **21%**, Non-sciences: **26%**, Other health professions: **0%**, Mixed disciplines and other: **1%**
Percentage of students not coming directly from college after graduation: **35%**

Dates and details

The American Medical College Application Service (AMCAS) application is accepted.
School asks for a school-specific application as part of the admissions process.
Oldest MCAT considered for Fall 2009 entry: **N/A**
Earliest application date for the 2009-2010 first-year class: **N/A**
Latest application date: **N/A**
Acceptance dates for regular application for the class entering in fall 2009:
  Earliest: **March 30, 2021**
  Latest: **N/A**
The school considers requests for deferred entrance.
Starting month for the class entering in 2009–2010: **N/A**
The school doesn't have an Early Decision Plan (EDP).
A personal interview is required for admission.

Undergraduate coursework required

Medical school requires undergraduate work in these subjects: biology, English, organic chemistry, inorganic (general) chemistry, physics, molecular and cell biology, biochemistry, mathematics, demonstration of writing skills, calculus, general chemistry.

ADMISSIONS POLICY
(TEXT PROVIDED BY SCHOOL):

The School of Medicine receives an average of 4,000-plus applications annually. Matriculates a class of 93 students with a wide variety of backgrounds. Candidates assessed on grade-point average and MCAT scores, voluntary activities, leadership, personal statement, letters of recommendation, and other criteria. Interviews are offered annually to 400 to 500 applicants. Faculty and students serve on the Admissions Committees and conduct interviews.

COSTS AND FINANCIAL AID

Financial aid phone number: **(916) 734-4120**
Tuition, 2007-2008 academic year: **In-state: $25,155; Out-of-state: $37,400**
Room and board: **$13,978**
Percentage of students receiving financial aid in 2007-08: **93%**
Percentage of students receiving: Loans: **87%**, Grants/scholarships: **92%**, Work-study aid: **0%**
Average medical school debt for the Class of 2006: **$100,178**

STUDENT BODY

Fall 2007 full-time enrollment: **393**
Men: **44%**, Women: **56%**, In-state: **99%**, Minorities: **55%**, American Indian: **0.8%**, Asian-American: **41.0%**,

African-American: 2.5%, Hispanic-American: 10.4%, White: 43.8%, International: 0.3%, Unknown: 1.3%

ACADEMIC PROGRAMS

The school's curriculum occasionally gives first-year students substantial contact with patients.

There are opportunities for first- or second-year students to work in community health clinics.

Program offerings: AIDS, drug/alcohol abuse, family medicine, geriatrics, internal medicine, pediatrics, rural medicine, women's health

Joint degrees awarded: M.D./Ph.D., M.D./M.B.A., M.D./M.P.H., M.D./M.S.

Total National Institutes of Health (NIH) grants awarded to the medical school and affiliated hospitals: **$75.4 million**

CURRICULUM

(TEXT PROVIDED BY SCHOOL):

A four-year curriculum leading to an M.D. degree. The first two years consist of six integrated blocks covering normal structure/function and pathophysiology. The third year is composed of six clinical clerkships. A longitudinal three-year Doctoring course focuses on clinical skills and professionalism. A flexible fourth year allows for electives and community service. Pursuit of research and other degrees is encouraged.

FACULTY PROFILE (FALL 2007)

Total teaching faculty: **624 (full-time), 87 (part-time)**

Of full-time faculty, those teaching in basic sciences: **8%**; in clinical programs: **92%**

Of part-time faculty, those teaching in basic sciences: **15%**; in clinical programs: **85%**

Full-time faculty/student ratio: **1.6**

SUPPORT SERVICES

The school offers students these services for dealing with stress: peer counseling, professional counseling, support groups.

RESIDENCY PROFILE

Most popular residency and specialty programs chosen by the 2006 and 2007 M.D. graduating classes: emergency medicine, family practice–sports medicine, internal medicine, obstetrics and gynecology, ophthalmology, orthopaedic surgery, pediatrics, psychiatry, radiology–diagnostic, surgery–general.

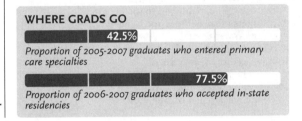

WHERE GRADS GO

42.5%

Proportion of 2005-2007 graduates who entered primary care specialties

77.5%

Proportion of 2006-2007 graduates who accepted in-state residencies

University of California–Irvine

- 252 Irvine Hall, Irvine, CA 92697-3950
- Public
- Year Founded: 1967
- Tuition, 2007-2008: In-state: $24,328; Out-of-state: $36,573
- Enrollment 2007-2008 academic year: 408
- Website: http://www.ucihs.uci.edu
- Specialty ranking: N/A

3.65 AVERAGE GPA, ENTERING CLASS FALL 2007

10.7 AVERAGE MCAT, ENTERING CLASS FALL 2007

6.1% ACCEPTANCE RATE, ENTERING CLASS FALL 2007

43 2009 U.S. NEWS MEDICAL SCHOOL RANKING (RESEARCH)

54 2009 U.S. NEWS MEDICAL SCHOOL RANKING (PRIMARY CARE)

ADMISSIONS

Admissions phone number: **(949) 824-5388**
Admissions email address: **medadmit@uci.edu**
Application website: **N/A**
Acceptance rate: **6.1%**
In-state acceptance rate: **7.2%**
Out-of-state acceptance rate: **0.8%**
Minority acceptance rate: **5.8%**
International acceptance rate: **0.0%**

Fall 2007 applications and acceptees

	Applied	Interviewed	Accepted	Enrolled
Total:	4,536	473	276	104
In-state:	3,749	456	270	101
Out-of-state:	787	17	6	3

Profile of admitted students

Average undergraduate grade point average: **3.65**
MCAT averages (scale: 1-15; writing test: J-T):
   Composite score: **10.7**
   Verbal reasoning score: **10.0**, Physical sciences score: **11.0**, Biological sciences score: **11.0**, Writing score: **Q**
Proportion with undergraduate majors in: Biological sciences: **60%**, Physical sciences: **24%**, Non-sciences: **16%**, Other health professions: **0%**, Mixed disciplines and other: **0%**
Percentage of students not coming directly from college after graduation: **N/A**

Dates and details

The American Medical College Application Service (AMCAS) application is accepted.
School asks for a school-specific application as part of the admissions process.
Oldest MCAT considered for Fall 2009 entry: **2006**
Earliest application date for the 2009-2010 first-year class: **6/1**
Latest application date: **11/1**
Acceptance dates for regular application for the class entering in fall 2009:

Earliest: **November 17, 2008**
Latest: **August 3, 2009**
The school considers requests for deferred entrance.
Starting month for the class entering in 2009–2010: **August**
The school doesn't have an Early Decision Plan (EDP).
A personal interview is required for admission.

Undergraduate coursework required

Medical school requires undergraduate work in these subjects: biology, English, organic chemistry, inorganic (general) chemistry, physics, biochemistry, mathematics, calculus, general chemistry.

ADMISSIONS POLICY

(TEXT PROVIDED BY SCHOOL):
Admissions Committee reviews applicants with academic record and MCAT scores indicating ability to handle rigorous medical school curriculum. Careful consideration is given to those from disadvantaged backgrounds as well as leadership ability, extracurricular activities, and community service. American Medical College Application Service application is used for preliminary screening. Secondary applications may be sent; 500 interviewed.

COSTS AND FINANCIAL AID

Financial aid phone number: **(949) 824-6476**
Tuition, 2007-2008 academic year: **In-state: $24,328; Out-of-state: $36,573**
Room and board: **$13,490**
Percentage of students receiving financial aid in 2007-08: **94%**
Percentage of students receiving: Loans: **83%**, Grants/scholarships: **72%**, Work-study aid: **0%**
Average medical school debt for the Class of 2006: **$90,597**

STUDENT BODY

Fall 2007 full-time enrollment: **408**

Men: **51%**, Women: **49%**, In-state: **100%**, Minorities: **47%**, American Indian: **0.5%**, Asian-American: **35.3%**, African-American: **1.5%**, Hispanic-American: **9.1%**, White: **50.7%**, International: **0.0%**, Unknown: **2.9%**

ACADEMIC PROGRAMS

The school's curriculum frequently gives first-year students substantial contact with patients.

There are opportunities for first- or second-year students to work in community health clinics.

Program offerings: drug/alcohol abuse, family medicine, geriatrics, internal medicine, pediatrics, rural medicine, women's health

Joint degrees awarded: M.D./Ph.D., M.D./M.B.A., M.D./M.S.

Total National Institutes of Health (NIH) grants awarded to the medical school and affiliated hospitals: **$98.9 million**

CURRICULUM

(TEXT PROVIDED BY SCHOOL):

The first two years are devoted to basic science instruction and preclinical experiences. Clinical clerkships and elective rotations are taken during the third and fourth years. The third year is scheduled in six eight-week blocks with one month off during the winter. The fourth year is scheduled in two- and four-week blocks.

FACULTY PROFILE (FALL 2007)

Total teaching faculty: **477 (full-time)**, **82 (part-time)**

Of full-time faculty, those teaching in basic sciences: **13%**; in clinical programs: **87%**

Of part-time faculty, those teaching in basic sciences: **0%**; in clinical programs: **100%**

Full-time faculty/student ratio: **1.2**

SUPPORT SERVICES

The school offers students these services for dealing with stress: expanded-hour gym access, peer counseling, professional counseling, religious support, support groups.

RESIDENCY PROFILE

Most popular residency and specialty programs chosen by the 2006 and 2007 M.D. graduating classes: emergency medicine, family practice, internal medicine, psychiatry.

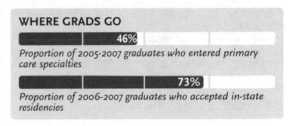

WHERE GRADS GO

46%

Proportion of 2005-2007 graduates who entered primary care specialties

73%

Proportion of 2006-2007 graduates who accepted in-state residencies

University of California–Los Angeles

GEFFEN

- 12-138 CHS, 10833 Le Conte Avenue, Los Angeles, CA 90095-1720
- Public
- Year Founded: 1951
- Tuition, 2007-2008: In-state: $22,551; Out-of-state: $34,796
- Enrollment 2007-2008 academic year: 693
- Website: http://www.medsch.ucla.edu
- Specialty ranking: AIDS: 9, drug/alcohol abuse: 9, family medicine: 18, geriatrics: 4, internal medicine: 12, pediatrics: 19, women's health: 8

3.78 AVERAGE GPA, ENTERING CLASS FALL 2007

11.9 AVERAGE MCAT, ENTERING CLASS FALL 2007

4.0% ACCEPTANCE RATE, ENTERING CLASS FALL 2007

9 2009 U.S. NEWS MEDICAL SCHOOL RANKING (RESEARCH)

12 2009 U.S. NEWS MEDICAL SCHOOL RANKING (PRIMARY CARE)

ADMISSIONS

Admissions phone number: (310) 825-6081
Admissions email address: **somadmiss@mednet.ucla.edu**
Application website:
   http://www.medstudent.ucla.edu/admiss
Acceptance rate: **4.0%**
In-state acceptance rate: **4.7%**
Out-of-state acceptance rate: **2.8%**
Minority acceptance rate: **4.6%**
International acceptance rate: **0.0%**

Fall 2007 applications and acceptees

	Applied	Interviewed	Accepted	Enrolled
Total:	5,822	707	232	121
In-state:	3,604	510	170	102
Out-of-state:	2,218	197	62	19

Profile of admitted students

Average undergraduate grade point average: **3.78**
MCAT averages (scale: 1-15; writing test: J-T):
   Composite score: **11.9**
   Verbal reasoning score: **10.2**, Physical sciences score: **11.7**, Biological sciences score: **11.8**, Writing score: **Q**
Proportion with undergraduate majors in: Biological sciences: **51%**, Physical sciences: **18%**, Non-sciences: **15%**, Other health professions: **2%**, Mixed disciplines and other: **14%**
Percentage of students not coming directly from college after graduation: **0%**

Dates and details

The American Medical College Application Service (AMCAS) application is accepted.
School asks for a school-specific application as part of the admissions process.
Oldest MCAT considered for Fall 2009 entry: **2006**
Earliest application date for the 2009-2010 first-year class: **7/1**
Latest application date: **11/1**
Acceptance dates for regular application for the class entering in fall 2009:

Earliest: **January 1, 2009**
Latest: **July 31, 2009**
The school considers requests for deferred entrance.
Starting month for the class entering in 2009–2010:
   August
The school doesn't have an Early Decision Plan (EDP).
A personal interview is required for admission.

Undergraduate coursework required

Medical school requires undergraduate work in these subjects: biology, English, organic chemistry, inorganic (general) chemistry, physics, mathematics, calculus, general chemistry.

ADMISSIONS POLICY

(TEXT PROVIDED BY SCHOOL):
The School of Medicine seeks future leaders and those who will have distinguished careers in clinical practice, teaching, research, and public service. Preference is given to those who have shown broad training and high achievement and possess, to the greatest degree, those traits of personality and character essential to success in medicine and to the provision of quality, professional, and humane medical care.

COSTS AND FINANCIAL AID

Financial aid phone number: (310) 825-4181
Tuition, 2007-2008 academic year: **In-state: $22,551; Out-of-state: $34,796**
Room and board: $13,780
Percentage of students receiving financial aid in 2007-08: **98%**
Percentage of students receiving: Loans: **91%**, Grants/scholarships: **98%**, Work-study aid: **0%**
Average medical school debt for the Class of 2006: **$86,564**

STUDENT BODY

Fall 2007 full-time enrollment: **693**
Men: **49%**, Women: **51%**, In-state: **94%**, Minorities: **60%**, American Indian: **0.4%**, Asian-American: **39.0%**,

African-American: **8.8%**, Hispanic-American: **11.4%**, White: **35.4%**, International: **0.9%**, Unknown: **4.2%**

ACADEMIC PROGRAMS

The school's curriculum frequently gives first-year students substantial contact with patients.

There are opportunities for first- or second-year students to work in community health clinics.

Program offerings: AIDS, drug/alcohol abuse, family medicine, geriatrics, internal medicine, pediatrics, women's health

Joint degrees awarded: M.D./Ph.D., M.D./M.B.A., M.D./M.P.H., M.D./M.S.

Total National Institutes of Health (NIH) grants awarded to the medical school and affiliated hospitals: **$426.7 million**

CURRICULUM

(TEXT PROVIDED BY SCHOOL):

In the first two years there is an integration of basic, clinical, and social sciences. The third year has clerkships: Inpatient Medicine, Family Medicine, Ambulatory Internal Medicine, Obstetrics/Gynecology, Pediatrics, Psychiatry/Neurology, and Surgery, and three longitudinal courses: Radiology, Doctoring, and Longitudinal Preceptorship. In the senior year there are colleges, with multidisciplinary groups of faculty and students.

FACULTY PROFILE (FALL 2007)

Total teaching faculty: **2,247 (full-time)**, **316 (part-time)**

Of full-time faculty, those teaching in basic sciences: **20%**; in clinical programs: **80%**

Of part-time faculty, those teaching in basic sciences: **28%**; in clinical programs: **72%**

Full-time faculty/student ratio: **3.2**

SUPPORT SERVICES

The school offers students these services for dealing with stress: expanded-hour gym access, professional counseling, religious support, support groups.

RESIDENCY PROFILE

Most popular residency and specialty programs chosen by the 2006 and 2007 M.D. graduating classes: anesthesiology, emergency medicine, family practice, internal medicine, obstetrics and gynecology, orthopaedic surgery, pediatrics, psychiatry, radiology–diagnostic, surgery–general.

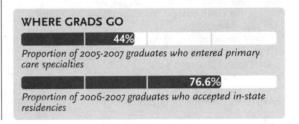

WHERE GRADS GO

44%

Proportion of 2005-2007 graduates who entered primary care specialties

76.6%

Proportion of 2006-2007 graduates who accepted in-state residencies

University of California–San Diego

- 9500 Gilman Drive, La Jolla, CA 92093-0602
- Public
- **Year Founded:** 1965
- **Tuition, 2007-2008:** In-state: $22,959; Out-of-state: $35,204
- **Enrollment 2007-2008 academic year:** 521
- **Website:** http://meded.ucsd.edu/
- **Specialty ranking:** AIDS: 6, drug/alcohol abuse: 13, family medicine: 22, internal medicine: 21

3.75 AVERAGE GPA, ENTERING CLASS FALL 2007

11.0 AVERAGE MCAT, ENTERING CLASS FALL 2007

5.5% ACCEPTANCE RATE, ENTERING CLASS FALL 2007

14 2009 U.S. NEWS MEDICAL SCHOOL RANKING (RESEARCH)

35 2009 U.S. NEWS MEDICAL SCHOOL RANKING (PRIMARY CARE)

ADMISSIONS

Admissions phone number: **(858) 534-3880**
Admissions email address: **somadmissions@ucsd.edu**
Application website:
  http://meded.ucsd.edu/asa/admissions
Acceptance rate: **5.5%**
In-state acceptance rate: **7.1%**
Out-of-state acceptance rate: **2.5%**
Minority acceptance rate: **5.0%**
International acceptance rate: **0.0%**

Fall 2007 applications and acceptees

	Applied	Interviewed	Accepted	Enrolled
Total:	5,500	568	304	134
In-state:	3,632	483	257	123
Out-of-state:	1,868	85	47	11

Profile of admitted students

Average undergraduate grade point average: **3.75**
MCAT averages (scale: 1-15; writing test: J-T):
  Composite score: **11.0**
  Verbal reasoning score: **10.0**, Physical sciences score: **11.3**, Biological sciences score: **11.7**, Writing score: **Q**
Proportion with undergraduate majors in: Biological sciences: **53%**, Physical sciences: **32%**, Non-sciences: **7%**, Other health professions: **1%**, Mixed disciplines and other: **7%**
Percentage of students not coming directly from college after graduation: **27%**

Dates and details

The American Medical College Application Service (AMCAS) application is accepted.
School asks for a school-specific application as part of the admissions process.
Oldest MCAT considered for Fall 2009 entry: **2006**
Earliest application date for the 2009-2010 first-year class: **6/1**
Latest application date: **11/1**
Acceptance dates for regular application for the class entering in fall 2009:

Earliest: **October 15, 2008**
Latest: **August 22, 2009**
The school considers requests for deferred entrance.
Starting month for the class entering in 2009–2010:
  August
The school doesn't have an Early Decision Plan (EDP).
A personal interview is required for admission.

Undergraduate coursework required

Medical school requires undergraduate work in these subjects: biology, organic chemistry, inorganic (general) chemistry, physics, mathematics.

ADMISSIONS POLICY

(TEXT PROVIDED BY SCHOOL):
Please refer to the school catalog.

COSTS AND FINANCIAL AID

Financial aid phone number: **(858) 534-4664**
Tuition, 2007-2008 academic year: **In-state: $22,959; Out-of-state: $35,204**
Room and board: **$12,493**
Percentage of students receiving financial aid in 2007-08: **88%**
Percentage of students receiving: Loans: **81%**, Grants/scholarships: **55%**, Work-study aid: **1%**
Average medical school debt for the Class of 2006: **$79,562**

STUDENT BODY

Fall 2007 full-time enrollment: **521**
Men: **53%**, Women: **47%**, In-state: **92%**, Minorities: **46%**, American Indian: **0.4%**, Asian-American: **41.1%**, African-American: **1.5%**, Hispanic-American: **8.6%**, White: **39.5%**, International: **0.0%**, Unknown: **8.8%**

ACADEMIC PROGRAMS

The school's curriculum frequently gives first-year students substantial contact with patients.
There are opportunities for first- or second-year students to work in community health clinics.

Program offerings: AIDS, drug/alcohol abuse, family medicine, geriatrics, internal medicine, pediatrics, rural medicine, women's health

Joint degrees awarded: M.D./Ph.D., M.D./M.P.H., M.D./M.S.

Total National Institutes of Health (NIH) grants awarded to the medical school and affiliated hospitals: **$293.0 million**

CURRICULUM
(TEXT PROVIDED BY SCHOOL):
Please refer to the catalogís curricular overview on the schoolís website.

FACULTY PROFILE (FALL 2007)
Total teaching faculty: **896 (full-time), 17 (part-time)**
Of full-time faculty, those teaching in basic sciences: **27%**; in clinical programs: **73%**
Of part-time faculty, those teaching in basic sciences: **47%**; in clinical programs: **53%**
Full-time faculty/student ratio: **1.7**

SUPPORT SERVICES
The school offers students these services for dealing with stress: expanded-hour gym access, peer counseling, professional counseling, religious support, support groups.

RESIDENCY PROFILE
Most popular residency and specialty programs chosen by the 2006 and 2007 M.D. graduating classes: anesthesiology, emergency medicine, family practice, internal medicine, obstetrics and gynecology, orthopaedic surgery, pediatrics, psychiatry, radiology–diagnostic, surgery–general.

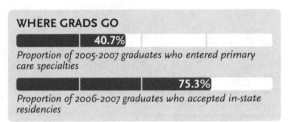

WHERE GRADS GO

40.7%
Proportion of 2005-2007 graduates who entered primary care specialties

75.3%
Proportion of 2006-2007 graduates who accepted in-state residencies

University of California–San Francisco

■ 513 Parnassus Avenue, Room S224,
San Francisco, CA 94143-0410
■ Public
■ Year Founded: 1864
■ Tuition, 2007-2008: In-state: $23,438; Out-of-state: $35,683
■ Enrollment 2007-2008 academic year: 594
■ Website: http://medschool.ucsf.edu/
■ Specialty ranking: AIDS: 1, drug/alcohol abuse: 5, family medicine: 8, geriatrics: 9, internal medicine: 3, pediatrics: 9, women's health: 2

3.73 AVERAGE GPA, ENTERING CLASS FALL 2007

11.4 AVERAGE MCAT, ENTERING CLASS FALL 2007

4.0% ACCEPTANCE RATE, ENTERING CLASS FALL 2007

5 2009 U.S. NEWS MEDICAL SCHOOL RANKING (RESEARCH)

6 2009 U.S. NEWS MEDICAL SCHOOL RANKING (PRIMARY CARE)

ADMISSIONS
Admissions phone number: **(415) 476-4044**
Admissions email address: **admissions@medsch.ucsf.edu**
Application website:
http://medschool.ucsf.edu/admissions/
Acceptance rate: **4.0%**
In-state acceptance rate: **5.0%**
Out-of-state acceptance rate: **3.0%**
Minority acceptance rate: **N/A**
International acceptance rate: **N/A**

Fall 2007 applications and acceptees
	Applied	Interviewed	Accepted	Enrolled
Total:	6,233	529	251	147
In-state:	3,262	N/A	162	117
Out-of-state:	2,971	N/A	89	30

Profile of admitted students
Average undergraduate grade point average: **3.73**
MCAT averages (scale: 1-15; writing test: J-T):
Composite score: **11.4**
Verbal reasoning score: **10.7**, Physical sciences score: **11.6**, Biological sciences score: **11.8**, Writing score: **Q**
Proportion with undergraduate majors in: Biological sciences: **33%**, Physical sciences: **12%**, Non-sciences: **13%**, Other health professions: **N/A**, Mixed disciplines and other: **42%**
Percentage of students not coming directly from college after graduation: **69%**

Dates and details
The American Medical College Application Service (AMCAS) application is accepted.
School asks for a school-specific application as part of the admissions process.
Oldest MCAT considered for Fall 2009 entry: **2006**
Earliest application date for the 2009-2010 first-year class: **6/1**
Latest application date: **10/15**
Acceptance dates for regular application for the class entering in fall 2009:

Earliest: **December 15, 2008**
Latest: **N/A**
The school considers requests for deferred entrance.
Starting month for the class entering in 2009–2010: **September**
The school doesn't have an Early Decision Plan (EDP).
A personal interview is required for admission.

Undergraduate coursework required
Medical school requires undergraduate work in these subjects: biology/zoology, organic chemistry, inorganic (general) chemistry, physics.

ADMISSIONS POLICY
(TEXT PROVIDED BY SCHOOL):
Please refer to the UCSF School of Medicine website for specific details regarding policies, preferences, criteria, selection factors, and procedures.

COSTS AND FINANCIAL AID
Financial aid phone number: **(415) 476-4181**
Tuition, 2007-2008 academic year: **In-state: $23,438; Out-of-state: $35,683**
Room and board: **$18,525**
Percentage of students receiving financial aid in 2007-08: **82%**
Percentage of students receiving: Loans: **79%**, Grants/scholarships: **81%**, Work-study aid: **1%**
Average medical school debt for the Class of 2006: **$85,020**

STUDENT BODY
Fall 2007 full-time enrollment: **594**
Men: **45%**, Women: **55%**, In-state: **94%**, Minorities: **56%**, American Indian: **N/A**, Asian-American: **N/A**, African-American: **N/A**, Hispanic-American: **N/A**, White: **N/A**, International: **N/A**, Unknown: **N/A**

ACADEMIC PROGRAMS
The school's curriculum frequently gives first-year students substantial contact with patients.

There are opportunities for first- or second-year students to work in community health clinics.

Program offerings: AIDS, drug/alcohol abuse, family medicine, geriatrics, internal medicine, pediatrics, rural medicine, women's health

Joint degrees awarded: M.D./Ph.D., M.D./M.P.H., M.D./M.S.

Total National Institutes of Health (NIH) grants awarded to the medical school and affiliated hospitals: **$442.7 million**

CURRICULUM
(TEXT PROVIDED BY SCHOOL):
Please refer to the education section of the UCSF School of Medicine website for details about the curriculum.

FACULTY PROFILE (FALL 2007)
Total teaching faculty: **1,848 (full-time)**, **69 (part-time)**
Of full-time faculty, those teaching in basic sciences: **9%**; in clinical programs: **91%**
Of part-time faculty, those teaching in basic sciences: **16%**; in clinical programs: **84%**
Full-time faculty/student ratio: **3.1**

SUPPORT SERVICES
The school offers students these services for dealing with stress: professional counseling, support groups.

RESIDENCY PROFILE
Most popular residency and specialty programs chosen by the 2006 and 2007 M.D. graduating classes: anesthesiology, dermatology, family practice, internal medicine, obstetrics and gynecology, ophthalmology, pediatrics, psychiatry.

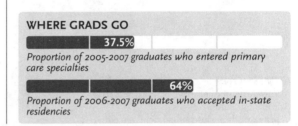

WHERE GRADS GO

37.5%
Proportion of 2005-2007 graduates who entered primary care specialties

64%
Proportion of 2006-2007 graduates who accepted in-state residencies

University of Chicago

PRITZKER

- 5841 S. Maryland Avenue, MC 1000, Chicago, IL 60637-5416
- Private
- Year Founded: 1927
- Tuition, 2007-2008: $38,658
- Enrollment 2007-2008 academic year: 441
- Website: http://pritzker.bsd.uchicago.edu
- Specialty ranking: internal medicine: 15

3.79 AVERAGE GPA, ENTERING CLASS FALL 2007

11.6 AVERAGE MCAT, ENTERING CLASS FALL 2007

3.9% ACCEPTANCE RATE, ENTERING CLASS FALL 2007

16 2009 U.S. NEWS MEDICAL SCHOOL RANKING (RESEARCH)

51 2009 U.S. NEWS MEDICAL SCHOOL RANKING (PRIMARY CARE)

ADMISSIONS

Admissions phone number: (773) 702-1937
Admissions email address:
   pritzkeradmissions@bsd.uchicago.edu
Application website: **N/A**
Acceptance rate: **3.9%**
In-state acceptance rate: **4.9%**
Out-of-state acceptance rate: **3.7%**
Minority acceptance rate: **4.5%**
International acceptance rate: **3.6%**

Fall 2007 applications and acceptees

	Applied	Interviewed	Accepted	Enrolled
Total:	7,787	749	301	112
In-state:	1,000	123	49	31
Out-of-state:	6,787	626	252	81

Profile of admitted students

Average undergraduate grade point average: **3.79**
MCAT averages (scale: 1-15; writing test: J-T):
   Composite score: **11.6**
   Verbal reasoning score: **11.0**, Physical sciences score:
   11.8, Biological sciences score: **11.9**, Writing score: **Q**
Proportion with undergraduate majors in: Biological
   sciences: **48%**, Physical sciences: **21%**, Non-sciences:
   13%, Other health professions: **0%**, Mixed disciplines
   and other: **18%**
Percentage of students not coming directly from college
   after graduation: **43%**

Dates and details

The American Medical College Application Service
   (AMCAS) application is accepted.
School asks for a school-specific application as part of the
   admissions process.
Oldest MCAT considered for Fall 2009 entry: **2006**
Earliest application date for the 2009-2010 first-year class:
   6/15
Latest application date: **10/15**
Acceptance dates for regular application for the class
   entering in fall 2009:

Earliest: **October 15, 2008**
Latest: **N/A**
The school considers requests for deferred entrance.
Starting month for the class entering in 2009–2010:
   August
The school has an Early Decision Plan (EDP).
A personal interview is required for admission.

Undergraduate coursework required

Medical school requires undergraduate work in these subjects: biology, organic chemistry, inorganic (general) chemistry, physics.

ADMISSIONS POLICY

(TEXT PROVIDED BY SCHOOL):
The Pritzker School of Medicine seeks to attract diverse
students of exceptional promise who will become leaders
and innovators in science and medicine for the betterment
of humanity. To that end, over the past four years it has
substantially increased the scholarship dollars available to
students. Candidates who interview with the school spend
the day on campus meeting with students, staff, and faculty.

COSTS AND FINANCIAL AID

Financial aid phone number: **(773) 702-1938**
Tuition, 2007-2008 academic year: **$38,658**
Room and board: **$15,769**
Percentage of students receiving financial aid in 2007-08:
   97%
Percentage of students receiving: Loans: **76%**,
   Grants/scholarships: **79%**, Work-study aid: **1%**
Average medical school debt for the Class of 2006:
   $162,859

STUDENT BODY

Fall 2007 full-time enrollment: **441**
Men: **50%**, Women: **50%**, In-state: **30%**, Minorities: **38%**,
   American Indian: **0.7%**, Asian-American: **22.0%**,
   African-American: **8.4%**, Hispanic-American: **7.0%**,
   White: **53.7%**, International: **3.4%**, Unknown: **4.8%**

ACADEMIC PROGRAMS

The school's curriculum frequently gives first-year students substantial contact with patients.

There are opportunities for first- or second-year students to work in community health clinics.

Program offerings: AIDS, drug/alcohol abuse, family medicine, geriatrics, internal medicine, pediatrics, women's health

Joint degrees awarded: M.D./Ph.D., M.D./M.B.A., M.D./J.D., M.D./M.S.W., M.D./M.S., M.D./M.A., M.D./M.H.A.

Total National Institutes of Health (NIH) grants awarded to the medical school and affiliated hospitals: **$211.7 million**

CURRICULUM

(TEXT PROVIDED BY SCHOOL):

Pritzker's goal is to graduate accomplished physicians who aspire to excellence as outstanding physician-scientists, medical educators, and clinicians. In 2008 the school will launch the Pritzker Initiative: A Curriculum for the 21st Century. The curriculum, built on a foundation of professionalism, will integrate basic and clinical sciences throughout all four years and feature enhanced technology.

FACULTY PROFILE (FALL 2007)

Total teaching faculty: **870 (full-time)**, **111 (part-time)**
Of full-time faculty, those teaching in basic sciences: **14%**; in clinical programs: **86%**

Of part-time faculty, those teaching in basic sciences: **1%**; in clinical programs: **99%**
Full-time faculty/student ratio: **2.0**

SUPPORT SERVICES

The school offers students these services for dealing with stress: expanded-hour gym access, peer counseling, professional counseling, religious support, support groups.

RESIDENCY PROFILE

Most popular residency and specialty programs chosen by the 2006 and 2007 M.D. graduating classes: anesthesiology, emergency medicine, internal medicine, orthopaedic surgery, pediatrics, plastic surgery, psychiatry, radiology–diagnostic, surgery–general, transitional year.

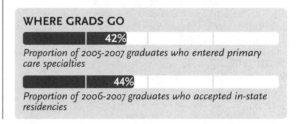

WHERE GRADS GO

42%

Proportion of 2005-2007 graduates who entered primary care specialties

44%

Proportion of 2006-2007 graduates who accepted in-state residencies

University of Cincinnati

- 231 Albert Sabin Way, Cincinnati, OH 45267-0552
- Public
- Year Founded: 1819
- Tuition, 2007-2008: In-state: $28,542; Out-of-state: $47,639
- Enrollment 2007-2008 academic year: 634
- Website: http://www.med.uc.edu
- Specialty ranking: family medicine: 27, pediatrics: 3

3.67 AVERAGE GPA, ENTERING CLASS FALL 2007

10.6 AVERAGE MCAT, ENTERING CLASS FALL 2007

8.2% ACCEPTANCE RATE, ENTERING CLASS FALL 2007

40 2009 U.S. NEWS MEDICAL SCHOOL RANKING (RESEARCH)

62 2009 U.S. NEWS MEDICAL SCHOOL RANKING (PRIMARY CARE)

ADMISSIONS

Admissions phone number: **(513) 558-7314**
Admissions email address: **comadmis@ucmail.uc.edu**
Application website: **http://comdows.uc.edu/MedOneStop/**
Acceptance rate: **8.2%**
In-state acceptance rate: **20.5%**
Out-of-state acceptance rate: **3.4%**
Minority acceptance rate: **N/A**
International acceptance rate: **0.0%**

Fall 2007 applications and acceptees

	Applied	Interviewed	Accepted	Enrolled
Total:	4,237	574	347	161
In-state:	1,185	352	243	121
Out-of-state:	3,052	222	104	40

Profile of admitted students

Average undergraduate grade point average: **3.67**
MCAT averages (scale: 1-15; writing test: J-T):
Composite score: **10.6**
Verbal reasoning score: **10.1**, Physical sciences score: **10.6**, Biological sciences score: **11.0**, Writing score: **O**
Proportion with undergraduate majors in: Biological sciences: **56%**, Physical sciences: **27%**, Non-sciences: **13%**, Other health professions: **3%**, Mixed disciplines and other: **1%**
Percentage of students not coming directly from college after graduation: **47%**

Dates and details

The American Medical College Application Service (AMCAS) application is accepted.
School asks for a school-specific application as part of the admissions process.
Oldest MCAT considered for Fall 2009 entry: **2006**
Earliest application date for the 2009-2010 first-year class: **6/1**
Latest application date: **11/15**
Acceptance dates for regular application for the class entering in fall 2009:
Earliest: **October 15, 2008**

Latest: **August 4, 2008**
The school considers requests for deferred entrance.
Starting month for the class entering in 2009–2010: **August**
The school has an Early Decision Plan (EDP).
A personal interview is required for admission.

Undergraduate coursework required

Medical school requires undergraduate work in these subjects: N/A.

ADMISSIONS POLICY

(TEXT PROVIDED BY SCHOOL):

UCCOM requires the American Medical College Application Service application, an online supplementary application, and letters of recommendation. Applicants are evaluated on a rolling basis for an interview and acceptance using a holistic assessment of their academic record, extracurricular activities, leadership, and other personal qualities. Each applicant can obtain information about his or her progress in the admissions process on the collegeís website.

COSTS AND FINANCIAL AID

Financial aid phone number: **(513) 558-6797**
Tuition, 2007-2008 academic year: **In-state: $28,542;** Out-of-state: **$47,639**
Room and board: **$18,888**
Percentage of students receiving financial aid in 2007-08: **88%**
Percentage of students receiving: Loans: **86%**, Grants/scholarships: **40%**, Work-study aid: **2%**
Average medical school debt for the Class of 2006: **$139,091**

STUDENT BODY

Fall 2007 full-time enrollment: **634**
Men: **57%**, Women: **43%**, In-state: **94%**, Minorities: **29%**, American Indian: **0.0%**, Asian-American: **19.9%**, African-American: **8.0%**, Hispanic-American: **0.9%**, White: **71.1%**, International: **0.0%**, Unknown: **0.0%**

ACADEMIC PROGRAMS

The school's curriculum frequently gives first-year students substantial contact with patients.

There are opportunities for first- or second-year students to work in community health clinics.

Program offerings: AIDS, drug/alcohol abuse, family medicine, geriatrics, internal medicine, pediatrics, rural medicine, women's health

Joint degrees awarded: M.D./Ph.D., M.D./M.B.A., M.D./M.P.H.

Total National Institutes of Health (NIH) grants awarded to the medical school and affiliated hospitals: **$196.5 million**

CURRICULUM

(TEXT PROVIDED BY SCHOOL):

The primary educational mission at the University of Cincinnati College of Medicine is to provide a stimulating learning environment intended to create the undifferentiated M.D. who is ready to excel in his or her chosen residency and who will provide excellent patient care. Please refer to the website for more detailed information on the curriculum.

FACULTY PROFILE (FALL 2007)

Total teaching faculty: **1,416 (full-time)**, **116 (part-time)**
Of full-time faculty, those teaching in basic sciences: **8%**; in clinical programs: **92%**

Of part-time faculty, those teaching in basic sciences: **3%**; in clinical programs: **97%**
Full-time faculty/student ratio: **2.2**

SUPPORT SERVICES

The school offers students these services for dealing with stress: expanded-hour gym access, peer counseling, professional counseling, support groups.

RESIDENCY PROFILE

Most popular residency and specialty programs chosen by the 2006 and 2007 M.D. graduating classes: anesthesiology, emergency medicine, family practice, internal medicine, obstetrics and gynecology, orthopaedic surgery, pediatrics, psychiatry, radiology–diagnostic, surgery–general.

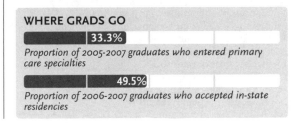

WHERE GRADS GO

33.3%
Proportion of 2005-2007 graduates who entered primary care specialties

49.5%
Proportion of 2006-2007 graduates who accepted in-state residencies

University of Colorado–Denver

- 4200 E. Ninth Avenue, PO Box C290, Denver, CO 80262
- Public
- Year Founded: 1883
- Tuition, 2007-2008: In-state: $24,828; Out-of-state: $48,030
- Enrollment 2007-2008 academic year: 607
- Website: http://www.uchsc.edu/som/admissions
- Specialty ranking: AIDS: 18, family medicine: 6, internal medicine: 29, pediatrics: 11, rural medicine: 18

3.71 AVERAGE GPA, ENTERING CLASS FALL 2007

11.0 AVERAGE MCAT, ENTERING CLASS FALL 2007

9.3% ACCEPTANCE RATE, ENTERING CLASS FALL 2007

27 2009 U.S. NEWS MEDICAL SCHOOL RANKING (RESEARCH)

4 2009 U.S. NEWS MEDICAL SCHOOL RANKING (PRIMARY CARE)

ADMISSIONS

Admissions phone number: (303) 724-8025
Admissions email address: somadmin@uchsc.edu
Application website: http://www.aamc.org
Acceptance rate: 9.3%
In-state acceptance rate: 26.4%
Out-of-state acceptance rate: 5.0%
Minority acceptance rate: 5.8%
International acceptance rate: N/A

Fall 2007 applications and acceptees

	Applied	Interviewed	Accepted	Enrolled
Total:	2,984	572	277	157
In-state:	602	346	159	125
Out-of-state:	2,382	226	118	32

Profile of admitted students

Average undergraduate grade point average: 3.71
MCAT averages (scale: 1-15; writing test: J-T):
  Composite score: 11.0
  Verbal reasoning score: 10.4, Physical sciences score: 10.8, Biological sciences score: 11.1, Writing score: P
Proportion with undergraduate majors in: Biological sciences: 49%, Physical sciences: 21%, Non-sciences: 12%, Other health professions: 0%, Mixed disciplines and other: 19%
Percentage of students not coming directly from college after graduation: 70%

Dates and details

The American Medical College Application Service (AMCAS) application is accepted.
School asks for a school-specific application as part of the admissions process.
Oldest MCAT considered for Fall 2009 entry: 2006
Earliest application date for the 2009-2010 first-year class: 6/1
Latest application date: 11/1
Acceptance dates for regular application for the class entering in fall 2009:
  Earliest: November 16, 2008

Latest: August 7, 2009
The school considers requests for deferred entrance.
Starting month for the class entering in 2009–2010:
  August
The school doesn't have an Early Decision Plan (EDP).
A personal interview is required for admission.

Undergraduate coursework required

Medical school requires undergraduate work in these subjects: biology, English, organic chemistry, inorganic (general) chemistry, physics, mathematics, general chemistry.

ADMISSIONS POLICY

(TEXT PROVIDED BY SCHOOL):
Places are offered to the applicants who are the most highly qualified in terms of intellectual growth and achievement, character, motivation, and maturity. Grades, MCAT scores, recommendations, and personal interviews are assessed. Of the 156 places in the class, the majority are awarded to Colorado residents. Preference is also given to applicants from the western states participating in the Western Interstate Commission for Higher Education program.

COSTS AND FINANCIAL AID

Financial aid phone number: (303) 556-2886
Tuition, 2007-2008 academic year: **In-state: $24,828; Out-of-state: $48,030**
Room and board: $14,500
Percentage of students receiving financial aid in 2007-08: 93%
Percentage of students receiving: Loans: 88%, Grants/scholarships: 73%, Work-study aid: 1%
Average medical school debt for the Class of 2006: $121,327

STUDENT BODY

Fall 2007 full-time enrollment: 607
Men: 52%, Women: 48%, In-state: 89%, Minorities: 17%, American Indian: 1.5%, Asian-American: 8.4%, African-American: 2.1%, Hispanic-American: 6.4%, White: 78.6%, International: 0.3%, Unknown: 2.6%

ACADEMIC PROGRAMS

The school's curriculum frequently gives first-year students substantial contact with patients.

There are opportunities for first- or second-year students to work in community health clinics.

Program offerings: AIDS, drug/alcohol abuse, family medicine, geriatrics, internal medicine, pediatrics, rural medicine, women's health

Joint degrees awarded: M.D./Ph.D., M.D./M.B.A.

Total National Institutes of Health (NIH) grants awarded to the medical school and affiliated hospitals: **$188.3 million**

CURRICULUM

(TEXT PROVIDED BY SCHOOL):

The CU School of Medicine has an innovative curriculum consisting of sequential interdisciplinary blocks that integrate clinical and basic science materials across all four years. The aim is to provide a foundation for further medical education and to equip students for a lifetime of learning, research, clinical care, and community service.

FACULTY PROFILE (FALL 2007)

Total teaching faculty: 1,513 **(full-time)**, 157 **(part-time)**

Of full-time faculty, those teaching in basic sciences: **12%**; in clinical programs: **88%**

Of part-time faculty, those teaching in basic sciences: **10%**; in clinical programs: **90%**

Full-time faculty/student ratio: **2.5**

SUPPORT SERVICES

The school offers students these services for dealing with stress: expanded-hour gym access, peer counseling, professional counseling, support groups.

RESIDENCY PROFILE

Most popular residency and specialty programs chosen by the 2006 and 2007 M.D. graduating classes: anesthesiology, emergency medicine, family practice, internal medicine, obstetrics and gynecology, orthopaedic surgery, pediatrics, psychiatry, radiology–diagnostic, surgery–general.

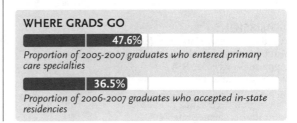

WHERE GRADS GO

47.6%

Proportion of 2005-2007 graduates who entered primary care specialties

36.5%

Proportion of 2006-2007 graduates who accepted in-state residencies

University of Connecticut

- 263 Farmington Avenue, Farmington, CT 06030-1905
- Public
- Year Founded: 1961
- Tuition, 2007-2008: In-state: $26,827; Out-of-state: $49,463
- Enrollment 2007-2008 academic year: 320
- Website: http://medicine.uchc.edu
- Specialty ranking: drug/alcohol abuse: 13

3.65 AVERAGE GPA, ENTERING CLASS FALL 2007

10.0 AVERAGE MCAT, ENTERING CLASS FALL 2007

5.8% ACCEPTANCE RATE, ENTERING CLASS FALL 2007

52 2009 U.S. NEWS MEDICAL SCHOOL RANKING (RESEARCH)

43 2009 U.S. NEWS MEDICAL SCHOOL RANKING (PRIMARY CARE)

ADMISSIONS

Admissions phone number: (860) 679-3874
Admissions email address: sanford@nso1.uchc.edu
Application website: N/A
Acceptance rate: 5.8%
In-state acceptance rate: 30.4%
Out-of-state acceptance rate: 1.8%
Minority acceptance rate: N/A
International acceptance rate: N/A

Fall 2007 applications and acceptees

	Applied	Interviewed	Accepted	Enrolled
Total:	3,042	400	175	81
In-state:	418	240	127	70
Out-of-state:	2,624	160	48	11

Profile of admitted students

Average undergraduate grade point average: 3.65
MCAT averages (scale: 1-15; writing test: J-T):
   Composite score: 10.0
   Verbal reasoning score: 9.8, Physical sciences score: 10.1, Biological sciences score: 10.7, Writing score: Q
Proportion with undergraduate majors in: Biological sciences: 53%, Physical sciences: 12%, Non-sciences: 18%, Other health professions: 1%, Mixed disciplines and other: 16%
Percentage of students not coming directly from college after graduation: 54%

Dates and details

The American Medical College Application Service (AMCAS) application is accepted.
School asks for a school-specific application as part of the admissions process.
Oldest MCAT considered for Fall 2009 entry: 2005
Earliest application date for the 2009-2010 first-year class: 6/1
Latest application date: 12/15
Acceptance dates for regular application for the class entering in fall 2009:

Earliest: June 15, 2008
Latest: August 1, 2009
The school considers requests for deferred entrance.
Starting month for the class entering in 2009–2010:
   August
The school has an Early Decision Plan (EDP).
A personal interview is required for admission.

Undergraduate coursework required

Medical school requires undergraduate work in these subjects: biology, biology/zoology, English, organic chemistry, inorganic (general) chemistry, physics, general chemistry.

ADMISSIONS POLICY

(TEXT PROVIDED BY SCHOOL):
The committee considers the applicant's achievements, ability, motivation, and character. The committee carefully considers the applicant's academic history, MCAT scores, and full range of research, clinical, community service, and extracurricular activities. The School of Medicine has a strong tradition of seeking a very diverse entering class.

COSTS AND FINANCIAL AID

Financial aid phone number: (860) 679-3574
Tuition, 2007-2008 academic year: **In-state: $26,827; Out-of-state: $49,463**
Room and board: N/A
Percentage of students receiving financial aid in 2007-08: 98%
Percentage of students receiving: Loans: 98%, Grants/scholarships: 45%, Work-study aid: 0%
Average medical school debt for the Class of 2006: **$100,000**

STUDENT BODY

Fall 2007 full-time enrollment: 320
Men: 39%, Women: 61%, In-state: 94%, Minorities: 35%, American Indian: 0.9%, Asian-American: 12.2%, African-American: 12.2%, Hispanic-American: 2.5%, White: 63.1%, International: 2.2%, Unknown: 6.9%

ACADEMIC PROGRAMS

The school's curriculum very frequently gives first-year students substantial contact with patients.

There are opportunities for first- or second-year students to work in community health clinics.

Program offerings: AIDS, drug/alcohol abuse, family medicine, geriatrics, internal medicine, pediatrics, rural medicine, women's health

Joint degrees awarded: M.D./Ph.D., M.D./M.B.A., M.D./M.P.H.

Total National Institutes of Health (NIH) grants awarded to the medical school and affiliated hospitals: **N/A**

CURRICULUM

(TEXT PROVIDED BY SCHOOL):

The curriculum consists of four years of instruction divided into three phases. Phase 1 (first two years) covers the core basic science instruction and the foundations of clinical medicine. Phase 2 (the third year) provides the core clinical experiences required of all students. Phase 3 (the fourth year) builds upon the clinical foundation of Phase 2.

FACULTY PROFILE (FALL 2007)

Total teaching faculty: **413 (full-time)**, **113 (part-time)**

Of full-time faculty, those teaching in basic sciences: **34%**; in clinical programs: **66%**

Of part-time faculty, those teaching in basic sciences: **23%**; in clinical programs: **77%**

Full-time faculty/student ratio: **1.3**

SUPPORT SERVICES

The school offers students these services for dealing with stress: peer counseling, professional counseling, support groups.

RESIDENCY PROFILE

Most popular residency and specialty programs chosen by the 2006 and 2007 M.D. graduating classes: anesthesiology, emergency medicine, family practice, internal medicine, obstetrics and gynecology, orthopaedic surgery, pediatrics, radiology–diagnostic, surgery–general.

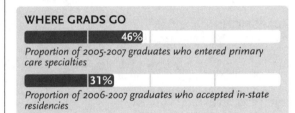

WHERE GRADS GO

46%

Proportion of 2005-2007 graduates who entered primary care specialties

31%

Proportion of 2006-2007 graduates who accepted in-state residencies

University of Florida

■ Box 100215 UFHSC, Gainesville, FL 32610-0215
■ Public
■ **Year Founded:** 1956
■ **Tuition, 2007-2008:** In-state: $23,170; Out-of-state: $51,018
■ **Enrollment 2007-2008 academic year:** 509
■ **Website:** http://www.med.ufl.edu
■ **Specialty ranking:** N/A

3.70	AVERAGE GPA, ENTERING CLASS FALL 2007
10.6	AVERAGE MCAT, ENTERING CLASS FALL 2007
8.2%	ACCEPTANCE RATE, ENTERING CLASS FALL 2007
48	2009 U.S. NEWS MEDICAL SCHOOL RANKING (RESEARCH)
Unranked	2009 U.S. NEWS MEDICAL SCHOOL RANKING (PRIMARY CARE)

ADMISSIONS

Admissions phone number: **(352) 273-7992**
Admissions email address: **robyn@dean.med.ufl.edu**
Application website: **http://www.aamc.org/amcas**
Acceptance rate: **8.2%**
In-state acceptance rate: **13.9%**
Out-of-state acceptance rate: **0.4%**
Minority acceptance rate: **13.2%**
International acceptance rate: **0.0%**

Fall 2007 applications and acceptees

	Applied	Interviewed	Accepted	Enrolled
Total:	2,550	346	208	132
In-state:	1,471	320	204	130
Out-of-state:	1,079	26	4	2

Profile of admitted students

Average undergraduate grade point average: **3.70**
MCAT averages (scale: 1-15; writing test: J-T):
   Composite score: **10.6**
   Verbal reasoning score: **10.0**, Physical sciences score: **10.7**, Biological sciences score: **11.0**, Writing score: **Q**
Proportion with undergraduate majors in: Biological sciences: **47%**, Physical sciences: **10%**, Non-sciences: **35%**, Other health professions: **1%**, Mixed disciplines and other: **7%**
Percentage of students not coming directly from college after graduation: **16%**

Dates and details

The American Medical College Application Service (AMCAS) application is accepted.
School asks for a school-specific application as part of the admissions process.
Oldest MCAT considered for Fall 2009 entry: **2006**
Earliest application date for the 2009-2010 first-year class: **6/5**
Latest application date: **12/1**
Acceptance dates for regular application for the class entering in fall 2009:
   Earliest: **October 15, 2008**

Latest: **August 15, 2009**
The school considers requests for deferred entrance.
Starting month for the class entering in 2009–2010:
   August
The school doesn't have an Early Decision Plan (EDP).
A personal interview is required for admission.

Undergraduate coursework required

Medical school requires undergraduate work in these subjects: biology, organic chemistry, inorganic (general) chemistry, physics, biochemistry, general chemistry.

ADMISSIONS POLICY

(TEXT PROVIDED BY SCHOOL):
Initial selection: grade-point average, MCATs, no cutoffs. Premed course quality, GPA progress, activities affect request for secondary application. Florida residents favored. Interview: Selection is based on academics, motivation, grasp of profession, recommendations; it evaluates personal strengths, service, research. The College of Medicine admits bright, dedicated, interesting people evidencing integrity, conscientiousness, love of learning, compassion.

COSTS AND FINANCIAL AID

Financial aid phone number: **(352) 273-7939**
Tuition, 2007-2008 academic year: **In-state: $23,170; Out-of-state: $51,018**
Room and board: **$9,640**
Percentage of students receiving financial aid in 2007-08: **87%**
Percentage of students receiving: Loans: **78%**, Grants/scholarships: **65%**, Work-study aid: **0%**
Average medical school debt for the Class of 2006: **$109,907**

STUDENT BODY

Fall 2007 full-time enrollment: **509**
Men: **50%**, Women: **50%**, In-state: **97%**, Minorities: **37%**, American Indian: **0.0%**, Asian-American: **0.0%**, African-American: **5.2%**, Hispanic-American: **0.0%**, White: **56.7%**, International: **0.0%**, Unknown: **38.1%**

ACADEMIC PROGRAMS

The school's curriculum very frequently gives first-year students substantial contact with patients.

There are opportunities for first- or second-year students to work in community health clinics.

Program offerings: AIDS, drug/alcohol abuse, family medicine, geriatrics, internal medicine, pediatrics, rural medicine, women's health

Joint degrees awarded: M.D./Ph.D., M.D./M.B.A., M.D./M.P.H., M.D./J.D., M.D./M.S., M.D./M.A.

Total National Institutes of Health (NIH) grants awarded to the medical school and affiliated hospitals: **$91.8 million**

CURRICULUM

(TEXT PROVIDED BY SCHOOL):
Competency-based curriculum emphasizes early development of clinical skills, professionalism, and access to high-quality research track. Competencies provide a set of knowledge, skills, and behaviors that all students must master to graduate. Clinical training is strengthened by the involvement of the urban hospital in Jacksonville, providing students with broad exposure to different types of patients.

FACULTY PROFILE (FALL 2007)

Total teaching faculty: **1,248 (full-time), 129 (part-time)**
Of full-time faculty, those teaching in basic sciences: **13%**; in clinical programs: **87%**

Of part-time faculty, those teaching in basic sciences: **2%**; in clinical programs: **98%**
Full-time faculty/student ratio: **2.5**

SUPPORT SERVICES

The school offers students these services for dealing with stress: expanded-hour gym access, peer counseling, professional counseling, religious support, support groups.

RESIDENCY PROFILE

Most popular residency and specialty programs chosen by the 2006 and 2007 M.D. graduating classes: anesthesiology, emergency medicine, family practice, internal medicine, obstetrics and gynecology, pediatrics, psychiatry, radiology–diagnostic.

WHERE GRADS GO

32%
Proportion of 2005-2007 graduates who entered primary care specialties

44.2%
Proportion of 2006-2007 graduates who accepted in-state residencies

University of Illinois–Chicago

- 1853 W. Polk Street, M/C 784, Chicago, IL 60612
- Public
- **Year Founded:** 1881
- **Tuition, 2007-2008:** In-state: $28,572; Out-of-state: $57,468
- **Enrollment 2007-2008 academic year:** 1,443
- **Website:** http://www.uic.edu/depts/mcam
- **Specialty ranking:** rural medicine: 28

3.58	AVERAGE GPA, ENTERING CLASS FALL 2007
10.1	AVERAGE MCAT, ENTERING CLASS FALL 2007
8.4%	ACCEPTANCE RATE, ENTERING CLASS FALL 2007
55	2009 U.S. NEWS MEDICAL SCHOOL RANKING (RESEARCH)
Unranked	2009 U.S. NEWS MEDICAL SCHOOL RANKING (PRIMARY CARE)

ADMISSIONS

Admissions phone number: **(312) 996-5635**
Admissions email address: **medadmit@uic.edu**
Application website:
  http://www.aamc.org/students/amcas/start.htm
Acceptance rate: **8.4%**
In-state acceptance rate: **21.6%**
Out-of-state acceptance rate: **3.9%**
Minority acceptance rate: **9.1%**
International acceptance rate: **N/A**

Fall 2007 applications and acceptees

	Applied	Interviewed	Accepted	Enrolled
Total:	7,134	846	596	307
In-state:	1,795	547	388	239
Out-of-state:	5,339	299	208	68

Profile of admitted students

Average undergraduate grade point average: **3.58**
MCAT averages (scale: 1-15; writing test: J-T):
  Composite score: **10.1**
  Verbal reasoning score: **N/A**, Physical sciences score:
  N/A, Biological sciences score: **N/A**, Writing score: **N/A**
Proportion with undergraduate majors in: Biological
  sciences: **58%**, Physical sciences: **15%**, Non-sciences:
  25%, Other health professions: **N/A**, Mixed disciplines
  and other: **2%**
Percentage of students not coming directly from college
  after graduation: **20%**

Dates and details

The American Medical College Application Service
  (AMCAS) application is accepted.
School asks for a school-specific application as part of the
  admissions process.
Oldest MCAT considered for Fall 2009 entry: **2006**
Earliest application date for the 2009-2010 first-year class:
  6/2
Latest application date: **11/17**
Acceptance dates for regular application for the class
  entering in fall 2009:

Earliest: **October 15, 2008**
  Latest: **August 17, 2009**
The school considers requests for deferred entrance.
Starting month for the class entering in 2009–2010:
  August
The school has an Early Decision Plan (EDP).
A personal interview is required for admission.

Undergraduate coursework required

Medical school requires undergraduate work in these subjects: biology, organic chemistry, inorganic (general) chemistry, physics, behavioral science, social sciences, general
chemistry.

ADMISSIONS POLICY
(TEXT PROVIDED BY SCHOOL):

Students are selected who demonstrate emotional stability,
maturity, integrity, and the motivation necessary for the successful study and practice of medicine. Students are
selected who will contribute academic, nonacademic, and
socioeconomic diversity to the first-year class. Applicants
must be U.S. citizens or possess a permanent resident visa
when they submit their application to the American
Medical College Application Service.

COSTS AND FINANCIAL AID

Financial aid phone number: **(312) 413-0127**
Tuition, 2007-2008 academic year: **In-state: $28,572; Out-
  of-state: $57,468**
Room and board: **$12,967**
Percentage of students receiving financial aid in 2007-08:
  N/A
Percentage of students receiving: Loans: **N/A**,
  Grants/scholarships: **N/A**, Work-study aid: **N/A**
Average medical school debt for the Class of 2006: **N/A**

STUDENT BODY

Fall 2007 full-time enrollment: **1,443**
Men: **52%**, Women: **48%**, In-state: **74%**, Minorities: **44%**,
  American Indian: **N/A**, Asian-American: **N/A**,

African-American: **N/A**, Hispanic-American: **N/A**, White: **N/A**, International: **N/A**, Unknown: **N/A**

ACADEMIC PROGRAMS

The school's curriculum occasionally gives first-year students substantial contact with patients.

There are opportunities for first- or second-year students to work in community health clinics.

Program offerings: AIDS, drug/alcohol abuse, family medicine, geriatrics, internal medicine, pediatrics, rural medicine, women's health

Joint degrees awarded: M.D./Ph.D., M.D./M.B.A., M.D./M.P.H., M.D./M.H.I., M.D./J.D., M.D./M.S.W., M.D./M.S., M.D./M.A., M.D./M.H.A.

Total National Institutes of Health (NIH) grants awarded to the medical school and affiliated hospitals: **$89.1 million**

CURRICULUM

(TEXT PROVIDED BY SCHOOL):

The curriculum is designed to graduate beginning physicians who have mastered the knowledge, acquired the skills, developed the attitudes, and adopted the professional behavior and commitment to lifelong learning necessary to begin the graduate portion of their study of medicine. It enables students to learn the arts and sciences of medicine that are basic to any career path open to the medical profession.

FACULTY PROFILE (FALL 2007)

Total teaching faculty: **782 (full-time)**, **574 (part-time)**

Of full-time faculty, those teaching in basic sciences: **26%**; in clinical programs: **74%**

Of part-time faculty, those teaching in basic sciences: **4%**; in clinical programs: **96%**

Full-time faculty/student ratio: **0.5**

SUPPORT SERVICES

The school offers students these services for dealing with stress: expanded-hour gym access, peer counseling, professional counseling, religious support, support groups.

RESIDENCY PROFILE

Most popular residency and specialty programs chosen by the 2006 and 2007 M.D. graduating classes: anesthesiology, emergency medicine, family practice, internal medicine, obstetrics and gynecology, pathology–anatomic and clinical, pediatrics, pediatrics–adolescent medicine, radiology–cardiothoracic, surgery–general.

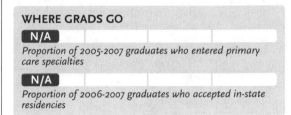

WHERE GRADS GO

N/A

Proportion of 2005-2007 graduates who entered primary care specialties

N/A

Proportion of 2006-2007 graduates who accepted in-state residencies

University of Iowa

CARVER

- 200 CMAB, Iowa City, IA 52242-1101
- Public
- **Year Founded:** 1847
- **Tuition, 2007-2008:** In-state: $25,689; Out-of-state: $41,719
- **Enrollment 2007-2008 academic year:** 576
- **Website:** http://www.medicine.uiowa.edu
- **Specialty ranking:** family medicine: 18, internal medicine: 29, rural medicine: 3

3.71	AVERAGE GPA, ENTERING CLASS FALL 2007
10.5	AVERAGE MCAT, ENTERING CLASS FALL 2007
10.3%	ACCEPTANCE RATE, ENTERING CLASS FALL 2007
31	2009 U.S. NEWS MEDICAL SCHOOL RANKING (RESEARCH)
7	2009 U.S. NEWS MEDICAL SCHOOL RANKING (PRIMARY CARE)

ADMISSIONS

Admissions phone number: **(319) 335-8052**
Admissions email address: **medical-admissions@uiowa.edu**
Application website:
http://www.medicine.uiowa.edu/osac/admissions
Acceptance rate: **10.3%**
In-state acceptance rate: **40.2%**
Out-of-state acceptance rate: **6.7%**
Minority acceptance rate: **7.5%**
International acceptance rate: **N/A**

Fall 2007 applications and acceptees

	Applied	Interviewed	Accepted	Enrolled
Total:	2,956	679	305	148
In-state:	321	260	129	99
Out-of-state:	2,635	419	176	49

Profile of admitted students

Average undergraduate grade point average: **3.71**
MCAT averages (scale: 1-15; writing test: J-T):
  Composite score: **10.5**
  Verbal reasoning score: **10.2**, Physical sciences score: **10.4**, Biological sciences score: **11.0**, Writing score: **P**
Proportion with undergraduate majors in: Biological sciences: **56%**, Physical sciences: **17%**, Non-sciences: **16%**, Other health professions: **0%**, Mixed disciplines and other: **11%**
Percentage of students not coming directly from college after graduation: **39%**

Dates and details

The American Medical College Application Service (AMCAS) application is accepted.
School asks for a school-specific application as part of the admissions process.
Oldest MCAT considered for Fall 2009 entry: **2001**
Earliest application date for the 2009-2010 first-year class: **6/1**
Latest application date: **11/1**

Acceptance dates for regular application for the class entering in fall 2009:
  Earliest: **October 15, 2008**
  Latest: **August 20, 2009**
The school considers requests for deferred entrance.
Starting month for the class entering in 2009-2010:
  August
The school has an Early Decision Plan (EDP).
A personal interview is required for admission.

Undergraduate coursework required

Medical school requires undergraduate work in these subjects: biology, English, organic chemistry, inorganic (general) chemistry, physics, humanities, mathematics, behavioral science, demonstration of writing skills, social sciences, general chemistry.

ADMISSIONS POLICY

(TEXT PROVIDED BY SCHOOL):

Applicants must attain a minimum 2.5 grade-point average; a bachelor's degree before entrance; U.S. citizenship, permanent residency, or asylum. Factors considered: undergraduate academic record; science GPA; MCATs; personal characteristics; on-site interview. Preference given to Iowa residents and outstanding nonresidents. The college is committed to the recruitment, selection, and retention of a diverse student body.

COSTS AND FINANCIAL AID

Financial aid phone number: **(319) 335-8059**
Tuition, 2007-2008 academic year: **In-state: $25,689; Out-of-state: $41,719**
Room and board: **$9,270**
Percentage of students receiving financial aid in 2007-08: **96%**
Percentage of students receiving: Loans: **90%**, Grants/scholarships: **60%**, Work-study aid: **1%**
Average medical school debt for the Class of 2006: **$100,000**

STUDENT BODY

Fall 2007 full-time enrollment: 576

Men: 53%, Women: 47%, In-state: 71%, Minorities: 19%, American Indian: 0.5%, Asian-American: 7.6%, African-American: 4.5%, Hispanic-American: 6.8%, White: 74.3%, International: 0.0%, Unknown: 6.3%

ACADEMIC PROGRAMS

The school's curriculum frequently gives first-year students substantial contact with patients.

There are opportunities for first- or second-year students to work in community health clinics.

Program offerings: AIDS, drug/alcohol abuse, family medicine, geriatrics, internal medicine, pediatrics, rural medicine

Joint degrees awarded: M.D./Ph.D., M.D./M.B.A., M.D./M.P.H., M.D./J.D.

Total National Institutes of Health (NIH) grants awarded to the medical school and affiliated hospitals: **$130.9 million**

CURRICULUM

(TEXT PROVIDED BY SCHOOL):

The college provides a four-year curriculum leading to the M.D. degree. The first four semesters present a core of sciences basic to the study of medicine and introduce students to the foundations of clinical practice. A sequential course introduces students to clinical skills needed to practice medicine. In Years 3 and 4, all students must satisfactorily complete 32 weeks of clerkships.

FACULTY PROFILE (FALL 2007)

Total teaching faculty: **786 (full-time)**, 81 **(part-time)**

Of full-time faculty, those teaching in basic sciences: 10%; in clinical programs: 90%

Of part-time faculty, those teaching in basic sciences: 5%; in clinical programs: 95%

Full-time faculty/student ratio: 1.4

SUPPORT SERVICES

The school offers students these services for dealing with stress: peer counseling, professional counseling, support groups.

RESIDENCY PROFILE

Most popular residency and specialty programs chosen by the 2006 and 2007 M.D. graduating classes: anesthesiology, emergency medicine, family practice, internal medicine, neurology, obstetrics and gynecology, pathology–anatomic and clinical, pediatrics, radiology–diagnostic, surgery–general.

WHERE GRADS GO

45%
Proportion of 2005-2007 graduates who entered primary care specialties

27%
Proportion of 2006-2007 graduates who accepted in-state residencies

University of Kansas Medical Center

- 3901 Rainbow Boulevard, Kansas City, KS 66160
- Public
- **Year Founded:** 1905
- **Tuition, 2007-2008:** In-state: $25,476; Out-of-state: $42,867
- **Enrollment 2007-2008 academic year:** 712
- **Website:** http://www.kumc.edu/som/som.html
- **Specialty ranking:** family medicine: 27, rural medicine: 14

3.69	AVERAGE GPA, ENTERING CLASS FALL 2007
9.5	AVERAGE MCAT, ENTERING CLASS FALL 2007
11.5%	ACCEPTANCE RATE, ENTERING CLASS FALL 2007
Unranked	2009 U.S. NEWS MEDICAL SCHOOL RANKING (RESEARCH)
43	2009 U.S. NEWS MEDICAL SCHOOL RANKING (PRIMARY CARE)

ADMISSIONS

Admissions phone number: **(913) 588-5245**
Admissions email address: **premedinfo@kumc.edu**
Application website: **N/A**
Acceptance rate: **11.5%**
In-state acceptance rate: **40.8%**
Out-of-state acceptance rate: **3.2%**
Minority acceptance rate: **9.2%**
International acceptance rate: **0.0%**

Fall 2007 applications and acceptees

	Applied	Interviewed	Accepted	Enrolled
Total:	1,920	465	221	176
In-state:	424	321	173	153
Out-of-state:	1,496	144	48	23

Profile of admitted students

Average undergraduate grade point average: **3.69**
MCAT averages (scale: 1-15; writing test: J-T):
Composite score: **9.5**
Verbal reasoning score: **9.7**, Physical sciences score: **9.1**,
Biological sciences score: **9.8**, Writing score: **Q**
Proportion with undergraduate majors in: Biological sciences: **58%**, Physical sciences: **19%**, Non-sciences: **9%**, Other health professions: **1%**, Mixed disciplines and other: **14%**
Percentage of students not coming directly from college after graduation: **51%**

Dates and details

The American Medical College Application Service (AMCAS) application is accepted.
School asks for a school-specific application as part of the admissions process.
Oldest MCAT considered for Fall 2009 entry: **2005**
Earliest application date for the 2009-2010 first-year class: **6/2**
Latest application date: **10/15**
Acceptance dates for regular application for the class entering in fall 2009:

Earliest: **October 31, 2008**
Latest: **July 20, 2009**
The school considers requests for deferred entrance.
Starting month for the class entering in 2009–2010: **July**
The school has an Early Decision Plan (EDP).
A personal interview is required for admission.

Undergraduate coursework required

Medical school requires undergraduate work in these subjects: biology, English, organic chemistry, inorganic (general) chemistry, physics, mathematics, general chemistry.

ADMISSIONS POLICY
(TEXT PROVIDED BY SCHOOL):

Qualified Kansas residents receive strong admissions preference; successful nonresident applicants have significant Kansas ties and/or add breadth to the class. Academic performance, personal qualities, motivation for medicine, and commitment to service are assessed through the use of American Medical College Application Service and secondary applications, letters of recommendation, and interviews.

COSTS AND FINANCIAL AID

Financial aid phone number: **(913) 588-5170**
Tuition, 2007-2008 academic year: **In-state: $25,476; Out-of-state: $42,867**
Room and board: **$18,981**
Percentage of students receiving financial aid in 2007-08: **93%**
Percentage of students receiving: Loans: **87%**, Grants/scholarships: **74%**, Work-study aid: **0%**
Average medical school debt for the Class of 2006: **$110,840**

STUDENT BODY

Fall 2007 full-time enrollment: **712**
Men: **52%**, Women: **48%**, In-state: **84%**, Minorities: **22%**, American Indian: **1.4%**, Asian-American: **10.5%**, African-American: **6.3%**, Hispanic-American: **3.5%**, White: **70.5%**, International: **0.0%**, Unknown: **7.7%**

ACADEMIC PROGRAMS

The school's curriculum occasionally gives first-year students substantial contact with patients.

There are opportunities for first- or second-year students to work in community health clinics.

Program offerings: AIDS, drug/alcohol abuse, family medicine, geriatrics, internal medicine, pediatrics, rural medicine, women's health

Joint degrees awarded: M.D./Ph.D., M.D./M.P.H., M.D./M.S., M.D./M.A., M.D./M.H.A.

Total National Institutes of Health (NIH) grants awarded to the medical school and affiliated hospitals: **$49.9 million**

CURRICULUM

(TEXT PROVIDED BY SCHOOL):

The first two years at KUMC consist of required modules integrating core basic science disciplines as well as basic skills and biopsychosocial topics relevant to clinical practice. Years 3 and 4 consist of required clerkships in core clinical disciplines and electives. The curriculum integrates large- and small-group learning and laboratory exercises, and it makes extensive use of technology.

FACULTY PROFILE (FALL 2007)

Total teaching faculty: **538 (full-time), 129 (part-time)**

Of full-time faculty, those teaching in basic sciences: **25%**; in clinical programs: **75%**

Of part-time faculty, those teaching in basic sciences: **10%**; in clinical programs: **90%**

Full-time faculty/student ratio: **0.8**

SUPPORT SERVICES

The school offers students these services for dealing with stress: peer counseling, professional counseling.

RESIDENCY PROFILE

Most popular residency and specialty programs chosen by the 2006 and 2007 M.D. graduating classes: anesthesiology, emergency medicine, family practice, internal medicine, neurology, obstetrics and gynecology, orthopaedic surgery, pediatrics, radiology–diagnostic, surgery–general.

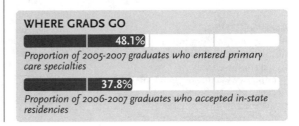

WHERE GRADS GO

48.1%

Proportion of 2005-2007 graduates who entered primary care specialties

37.8%

Proportion of 2006-2007 graduates who accepted in-state residencies

University of Kentucky

- Chandler Medical Center, 800 Rose Street, Lexington, KY 40536
- Public
- **Year Founded:** 1956
- **Tuition, 2007-2008:** In-state: $23,910; Out-of-state: $45,313
- **Enrollment 2007-2008 academic year:** 413
- **Website:** http://www.mc.uky.edu/medicine/
- **Specialty ranking:** N/A

3.65 AVERAGE GPA, ENTERING CLASS FALL 2007

10.1 AVERAGE MCAT, ENTERING CLASS FALL 2007

8.6% ACCEPTANCE RATE, ENTERING CLASS FALL 2007

Unranked 2009 U.S. NEWS MEDICAL SCHOOL RANKING (RESEARCH)

62 2009 U.S. NEWS MEDICAL SCHOOL RANKING (PRIMARY CARE)

ADMISSIONS

Admissions phone number: **(859) 323-6161**
Admissions email address: **kymedap@uky.edu**
Application website:
   http://www.aamc.org/students/amcas/start.htm
Acceptance rate: **8.6%**
In-state acceptance rate: **30.4%**
Out-of-state acceptance rate: **3.2%**
Minority acceptance rate: **N/A**
International acceptance rate: **N/A**

Fall 2007 applications and acceptees

	Applied	Interviewed	Accepted	Enrolled
Total:	2,129	367	184	103
In-state:	425	245	129	80
Out-of-state:	1,704	122	55	23

Profile of admitted students

Average undergraduate grade point average: **3.65**
MCAT averages (scale: 1-15; writing test: J-T):
   Composite score: **10.1**
   Verbal reasoning score: **9.9**, Physical sciences score: **10.1**, Biological sciences score: **10.4**, Writing score: **P**
Proportion with undergraduate majors in: Biological sciences: **49%**, Physical sciences: **23%**, Non-sciences: **13%**, Other health professions: **1%**, Mixed disciplines and other: **14%**
Percentage of students not coming directly from college after graduation: **39%**

Dates and details

The American Medical College Application Service (AMCAS) application is accepted.
School asks for a school-specific application as part of the admissions process.
Oldest MCAT considered for Fall 2009 entry: **2006**
Earliest application date for the 2009-2010 first-year class: **6/1**
Latest application date: **11/1**
Acceptance dates for regular application for the class entering in fall 2009:

Earliest: **October 15, 2008**
Latest: **N/A**
The school considers requests for deferred entrance.
Starting month for the class entering in 2009–2010: **August**
The school has an Early Decision Plan (EDP).
A personal interview is required for admission.

Undergraduate coursework required

Medical school requires undergraduate work in these subjects: biology, English, organic chemistry, inorganic (general) chemistry, physics.

ADMISSIONS POLICY

(TEXT PROVIDED BY SCHOOL):
Preference is given to Kentucky residents. Nonresidents are encouraged to apply. Competitive nonresident applicants should have overall records that compare favorably with average matriculants.

COSTS AND FINANCIAL AID

Financial aid phone number: **(859) 323-5261**
Tuition, 2007-2008 academic year: **In-state: $23,910; Out-of-state: $45,313**
Room and board: **$12,370**
Percentage of students receiving financial aid in 2007-08: **92%**
Percentage of students receiving: Loans: **83%**, Grants/scholarships: **52%**, Work-study aid: **9%**
Average medical school debt for the Class of 2006: **$107,110**

STUDENT BODY

Fall 2007 full-time enrollment: **413**
Men: **60%**, Women: **40%**, In-state: **84%**, Minorities: **17%**, American Indian: **0.0%**, Asian-American: **11.1%**, African-American: **4.1%**, Hispanic-American: **0.2%**, White: **77.0%**, International: **3.1%**, Unknown: **4.4%**

ACADEMIC PROGRAMS

The school's curriculum very frequently gives first-year students substantial contact with patients.

There are opportunities for first- or second-year students to work in community health clinics.

Program offerings: AIDS, drug/alcohol abuse, family medicine, geriatrics, internal medicine, pediatrics, rural medicine, women's health

Joint degrees awarded: M.D./Ph.D., M.D./M.B.A., M.D./M.P.H.

Total National Institutes of Health (NIH) grants awarded to the medical school and affiliated hospitals: **$69.3 million**

CURRICULUM
(TEXT PROVIDED BY SCHOOL):

The curriculum emphasizes early clinical experiences, integration of the basic and clinical sciences, teaching in ambulatory clinic settings, and primary care. The school believes that this curriculum will result in a generation of physicians who will be lifelong learners. The curriculum uses many learning methods, including standardized patients and human patient simulators.

FACULTY PROFILE (FALL 2007)

Total teaching faculty: **717 (full-time)**, **160 (part-time)**
Of full-time faculty, those teaching in basic sciences: **26%**; in clinical programs: **74%**

Of part-time faculty, those teaching in basic sciences: **9%**; in clinical programs: **91%**
Full-time faculty/student ratio: **1.7**

SUPPORT SERVICES

The school offers students these services for dealing with stress: expanded-hour gym access, professional counseling, support groups.

RESIDENCY PROFILE

Most popular residency and specialty programs chosen by the 2006 and 2007 M.D. graduating classes: anesthesiology, emergency medicine, family practice, internal medicine, internal medicine–pediatrics, neurology, obstetrics and gynecology, pediatrics, radiology–diagnostic, surgery–general.

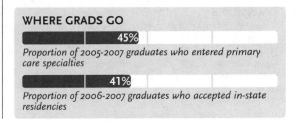

WHERE GRADS GO

45%

Proportion of 2005-2007 graduates who entered primary care specialties

41%

Proportion of 2006-2007 graduates who accepted in-state residencies

University of Louisville

- **Abell Administration Center, H.S.C., Louisville, KY 40202**
- **Public**
- **Year Founded:** 1837
- **Tuition, 2007-2008:** In-state: $23,079; Out-of-state: $43,425
- **Enrollment 2007-2008 academic year:** 595
- **Website:** http://www.louisville.edu
- **Specialty ranking:** N/A

3.65	AVERAGE GPA, ENTERING CLASS FALL 2007
9.7	AVERAGE MCAT, ENTERING CLASS FALL 2007
11.3%	ACCEPTANCE RATE, ENTERING CLASS FALL 2007
Unranked	2009 U.S. NEWS MEDICAL SCHOOL RANKING (RESEARCH)
Unranked	2009 U.S. NEWS MEDICAL SCHOOL RANKING (PRIMARY CARE)

ADMISSIONS

Admissions phone number: **(502) 852-5193**
Admissions email address: **medadm@louisville.edu**
Application website: **http://www.aamc.org**
Acceptance rate: **11.3%**
In-state acceptance rate: **44.4%**
Out-of-state acceptance rate: **3.5%**
Minority acceptance rate: **7.9%**
International acceptance rate: **0.0%**

Fall 2007 applications and acceptees

	Applied	Interviewed	Accepted	Enrolled
Total:	2,179	369	247	148
In-state:	417	276	185	119
Out-of-state:	1,762	93	62	29

Profile of admitted students

Average undergraduate grade point average: **3.65**
MCAT averages (scale: 1-15; writing test: J-T):
  Composite score: **9.7**
  Verbal reasoning score: **9.7**, Physical sciences score: **9.5**,
  Biological sciences score: **9.9**, Writing score: **P**
Proportion with undergraduate majors in: Biological
  sciences: **57%**, Physical sciences: **22%**, Non-sciences:
  14%, Other health professions: **2%**, Mixed disciplines
  and other: **5%**
Percentage of students not coming directly from college
  after graduation: **9%**

Dates and details

The American Medical College Application Service
  (AMCAS) application is accepted.
School asks for a school-specific application as part of the
  admissions process.
Oldest MCAT considered for Fall 2009 entry: **2006**
Earliest application date for the 2009-2010 first-year class:
  6/1
Latest application date: **10/15**
Acceptance dates for regular application for the class
  entering in fall 2009:

Earliest: **October 15, 2008**
Latest: **August 8, 2009**
The school considers requests for deferred entrance.
Starting month for the class entering in 2009–2010:
  August
The school has an Early Decision Plan (EDP).
A personal interview is required for admission.

Undergraduate coursework required

Medical school requires undergraduate work in these subjects: biology, English, organic chemistry, inorganic (general) chemistry, physics, mathematics, calculus, general
chemistry.

ADMISSIONS POLICY

(TEXT PROVIDED BY SCHOOL):

Because the University of Louisville is a state institution,
preference is given to qualified residents of Kentucky.
Applicants are selected on the basis of their individual merits without bias to sex, race, creed, national origin, age, or
handicap. They are chosen on the basis of intellect,
integrity, maturity, and demonstrated sensitivity toward others. Significant weight is given to scored interviews, which
are held at the School of Medicine.

COSTS AND FINANCIAL AID

Financial aid phone number: **(502) 852-5187**
Tuition, 2007-2008 academic year: **In-state: $23,079; Out-
  of-state: $43,425**
Room and board: **$6,618**
Percentage of students receiving financial aid in 2007-08:
  92%
Percentage of students receiving: Loans: **85%**,
  Grants/scholarships: **34%**, Work-study aid: **0%**
Average medical school debt for the Class of 2006:
  $124,604

STUDENT BODY

Fall 2007 full-time enrollment: **595**

Men: 58%, Women: 42%, In-state: 83%, Minorities: 19%,
American Indian: 0.2%, Asian-American: 9.7%,
African-American: 6.4%, Hispanic-American: 0.8%,
White: 80.5%, International: 0.0%, Unknown: 2.4%

ACADEMIC PROGRAMS

The school's curriculum occasionally gives first-year
students substantial contact with patients.

There are opportunities for first- or second-year students to
work in community health clinics.

Program offerings: family medicine, geriatrics, internal
medicine, pediatrics, rural medicine, women's health

Joint degrees awarded: M.D./Ph.D., M.D./M.B.A.,
M.D./M.P.H., M.D./M.A.

Total National Institutes of Health (NIH) grants awarded to
the medical school and affiliated hospitals: $46.6
million

CURRICULUM

(TEXT PROVIDED BY SCHOOL):

The educational program has been developed to provide an
efficiently organized, penetrating presentation of the general topics considered essential for all physicians, yet it has
sufficient flexibility to allow effective development of the
student's individual abilities and interests. The two major
components of this program are the core curriculum and
the preclinical/clinical elective program.

FACULTY PROFILE (FALL 2007)

Total teaching faculty: 710 **(full-time)**, 64 **(part-time)**

Of full-time faculty, those teaching in basic sciences: 15%;
in clinical programs: 85%

Of part-time faculty, those teaching in basic sciences: 8%;
in clinical programs: 92%

Full-time faculty/student ratio: 1.2

SUPPORT SERVICES

The school offers students these services for dealing with
stress: expanded-hour gym access, peer counseling, professional counseling, support groups.

RESIDENCY PROFILE

Most popular residency and specialty programs chosen by
the 2006 and 2007 M.D. graduating classes: anesthesiology, emergency medicine, family practice, internal medicine, orthopaedic surgery, pediatrics, psychiatry,
radiology–diagnostic, surgery–general.

WHERE GRADS GO

44%

*Proportion of 2005-2007 graduates who entered primary
care specialties*

45%

*Proportion of 2006-2007 graduates who accepted in-state
residencies*

University of Maryland

- **655 W. Baltimore Street, Room 14-029, Baltimore, MD 21201-1559**
- **Public**
- **Year Founded:** 1807
- **Tuition, 2007-2008:** In-state: $22,316; Out-of-state: $41,101
- **Enrollment 2007-2008 academic year:** 621
- **Website:** http://medschool.umaryland.edu
- **Specialty ranking:** family medicine: 27

3.67 AVERAGE GPA, ENTERING CLASS FALL 2007

10.4 AVERAGE MCAT, ENTERING CLASS FALL 2007

7.0% ACCEPTANCE RATE, ENTERING CLASS FALL 2007

43 2009 U.S. NEWS MEDICAL SCHOOL RANKING (RESEARCH)

35 2009 U.S. NEWS MEDICAL SCHOOL RANKING (PRIMARY CARE)

ADMISSIONS

Admissions phone number: **(410) 706-7478**
Admissions email address: **mfoxwell@som.umaryland.edu**
Application website: **N/A**
Acceptance rate: **7.0%**
In-state acceptance rate: **25.5%**
Out-of-state acceptance rate: **2.7%**
Minority acceptance rate: **6.9%**
International acceptance rate: **2.1%**

Fall 2007 applications and acceptees

	Applied	Interviewed	Accepted	Enrolled
Total:	4,503	474	317	160
In-state:	864	321	220	129
Out-of-state:	3,639	153	97	31

Profile of admitted students

Average undergraduate grade point average: **3.67**
MCAT averages (scale: 1-15; writing test: J-T):
  Composite score: **10.4**
  Verbal reasoning score: **10.1**, Physical sciences score: **10.5**, Biological sciences score: **10.8**, Writing score: **P**
Proportion with undergraduate majors in: Biological sciences: **52%**, Physical sciences: **20%**, Non-sciences: **19%**, Other health professions: **2%**, Mixed disciplines and other: **7%**
Percentage of students not coming directly from college after graduation: **54%**

Dates and details

The American Medical College Application Service (AMCAS) application is accepted.
School asks for a school-specific application as part of the admissions process.
Oldest MCAT considered for Fall 2009 entry: **2005**
Earliest application date for the 2009-2010 first-year class: **6/1**
Latest application date: **11/1**
Acceptance dates for regular application for the class entering in fall 2009:
  Earliest: **October 15, 2008**

Latest: **N/A**
The school considers requests for deferred entrance.
Starting month for the class entering in 2009-2010: **August**
The school has an Early Decision Plan (EDP).
A personal interview is required for admission.

Undergraduate coursework required

Medical school requires undergraduate work in these subjects: biology/zoology, English, organic chemistry, inorganic (general) chemistry, physics.

ADMISSIONS POLICY

(TEXT PROVIDED BY SCHOOL):
The School of Medicine admits those who possess the ability to successfully complete the academically rigorous curriculum and have personal characteristics that one wants in a personal physician. Close attention is paid to extracurricular activities, life experiences, and letters of recommendation for evidence of maturity, stability, judgment, empathy, intellectual curiosity, leadership, and commitment to excellence.

COSTS AND FINANCIAL AID

Financial aid phone number: **(410) 706-7347**
Tuition, 2007-2008 academic year: **In-state: $22,316; Out-of-state: $41,101**
Room and board: **$18,490**
Percentage of students receiving financial aid in 2007-08: **90%**
Percentage of students receiving: Loans: **82%**, Grants/scholarships: **70%**, Work-study aid: **0%**
Average medical school debt for the Class of 2006: **$112,440**

STUDENT BODY

Fall 2007 full-time enrollment: **621**
Men: **42%**, Women: **58%**, In-state: **81%**, Minorities: **37%**, American Indian: **0.0%**, Asian-American: **22.2%**, African-American: **12.2%**, Hispanic-American: **2.4%**, White: **58.5%**, International: **0.6%**, Unknown: **4.0%**

ACADEMIC PROGRAMS

The school's curriculum frequently gives first-year students substantial contact with patients.

There are opportunities for first- or second-year students to work in community health clinics.

Program offerings: AIDS, drug/alcohol abuse, family medicine, geriatrics, internal medicine, pediatrics, rural medicine

Joint degrees awarded: M.D./Ph.D., M.D./M.P.H., M.D./M.H.I., M.D./M.S.

Total National Institutes of Health (NIH) grants awarded to the medical school and affiliated hospitals: **N/A**

CURRICULUM

(TEXT PROVIDED BY SCHOOL):

The curriculum at the University of Maryland is designed to prepare individuals for academic success during medical school and to help students develop skills and attitudes to be lifelong learners throughout their careers in medicine. Laptops are required for study, lab exercises, and exams. A curriculum description is available on the school-based website.

FACULTY PROFILE (FALL 2007)

Total teaching faculty: **1,220 (full-time)**, **209 (part-time)**

Of full-time faculty, those teaching in basic sciences: **15%**; in clinical programs: **85%**

Of part-time faculty, those teaching in basic sciences: **5%**; in clinical programs: **95%**

Full-time faculty/student ratio: **2.0**

SUPPORT SERVICES

The school offers students these services for dealing with stress: expanded-hour gym access, peer counseling, professional counseling, support groups.

RESIDENCY PROFILE

Most popular residency and specialty programs chosen by the 2006 and 2007 M.D. graduating classes: anesthesiology, emergency medicine, internal medicine, pediatrics, psychiatry, surgery–general.

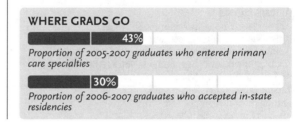

WHERE GRADS GO

43%

Proportion of 2005-2007 graduates who entered primary care specialties

30%

Proportion of 2006-2007 graduates who accepted in-state residencies

University of Massachusetts—Worcester

- 55 Lake Avenue N, Worcester, MA 01655
- Public
- **Year Founded:** 1970
- **Tuition, 2007-2008:** $14,087
- **Enrollment 2007-2008 academic year:** 435
- **Website:** http://www.umassmed.edu
- **Specialty ranking:** N/A

3.59 AVERAGE GPA, ENTERING CLASS FALL 2007

10.5 AVERAGE MCAT, ENTERING CLASS FALL 2007

22.8% ACCEPTANCE RATE, ENTERING CLASS FALL 2007

51 2009 U.S. NEWS MEDICAL SCHOOL RANKING (RESEARCH)

13 2009 U.S. NEWS MEDICAL SCHOOL RANKING (PRIMARY CARE)

ADMISSIONS

Admissions phone number: **(508) 856-2323**
Admissions email address: **admissions@umassmed.edu**
Application website:
http://www.aamc.org/students/amcas/start.htm
Acceptance rate: **22.8%**
In-state acceptance rate: **24.3%**
Out-of-state acceptance rate: **8.1%**
Minority acceptance rate: **N/A**
International acceptance rate: **N/A**

Fall 2007 applications and acceptees

	Applied	Interviewed	Accepted	Enrolled
Total:	803	470	183	103
In-state:	729	451	177	100
Out-of-state:	74	19	6	3

Profile of admitted students

Average undergraduate grade point average: **3.59**
MCAT averages (scale: 1-15; writing test: J-T):
  Composite score: **10.5**
  Verbal reasoning score: **10.3**, Physical sciences score: **10.4**, Biological sciences score: **10.6**, Writing score: **Q**
Proportion with undergraduate majors in: Biological sciences: **29%**, Physical sciences: **23%**, Non-sciences: **38%**, Other health professions: **2%**, Mixed disciplines and other: **8%**
Percentage of students not coming directly from college after graduation: **83%**

Dates and details

The American Medical College Application Service (AMCAS) application is accepted.
School asks for a school-specific application as part of the admissions process.
Oldest MCAT considered for Fall 2009 entry: **2005**
Earliest application date for the 2009-2010 first-year class: **6/1**
Latest application date: **11/1**
Acceptance dates for regular application for the class entering in fall 2009:

Earliest: **October 1, 2008**
Latest: **August 15, 2009**
The school considers requests for deferred entrance.
Starting month for the class entering in 2009–2010:
  August
The school has an Early Decision Plan (EDP).
A personal interview is required for admission.

Undergraduate coursework required

Medical school requires undergraduate work in these subjects: biology, biology/zoology, English, organic chemistry, inorganic (general) chemistry, physics.

ADMISSIONS POLICY

(TEXT PROVIDED BY SCHOOL):
Factors include in-state residency (with the exception of Ph.D./M.D. program); content and breadth of scholastic preparation; service/avocation with people in a helping role; diversity (prior educational/professional experience, social or cultural background); communication/interpersonal skills; professional attributes (altruism, compassion); commitment to primary care; and service to Massachusetts.

COSTS AND FINANCIAL AID

Financial aid phone number: **(508) 856-2265**
Tuition, 2007-2008 academic year: **$14,087**
Room and board: **$12,347**
Percentage of students receiving financial aid in 2007-08: **95%**
Percentage of students receiving: Loans: **93%**, Grants/scholarships: **29%**, Work-study aid: **0%**
Average medical school debt for the Class of 2006: **$110,722**

STUDENT BODY

Fall 2007 full-time enrollment: **435**
Men: **45%**, Women: **55%**, In-state: **98%**, Minorities: **20%**, American Indian: **0.5%**, Asian-American: **13.3%**, African-American: **4.8%**, Hispanic-American: **1.8%**, White: **79.5%**, International: **0.0%**, Unknown: **0.0%**

ACADEMIC PROGRAMS

The school's curriculum very frequently gives first-year students substantial contact with patients.

There are opportunities for first- or second-year students to work in community health clinics.

Program offerings: AIDS, drug/alcohol abuse, family medicine, geriatrics, internal medicine, pediatrics, rural medicine, women's health

Joint degrees awarded: M.D./Ph.D.

Total National Institutes of Health (NIH) grants awarded to the medical school and affiliated hospitals: **N/A**

CURRICULUM
(TEXT PROVIDED BY SCHOOL):

Reflecting the educational goal of training physicians in the full range of medical disciplines with emphasis on practice in the primary care specialties, in the public sector, and in underserved areas of Massachusetts, the curriculum teaches core knowledge, skills, attitudes, and values as the foundation for training the undifferentiated physician.

FACULTY PROFILE (FALL 2007)

Total teaching faculty: **923 (full-time)**, **165 (part-time)**

Of full-time faculty, those teaching in basic sciences: **22%**; in clinical programs: **78%**

Of part-time faculty, those teaching in basic sciences: **10%**; in clinical programs: **90%**

Full-time faculty/student ratio: **2.1**

SUPPORT SERVICES

The school offers students these services for dealing with stress: expanded-hour gym access, peer counseling, professional counseling, religious support, support groups.

RESIDENCY PROFILE

Most popular residency and specialty programs chosen by the 2006 and 2007 M.D. graduating classes: anesthesiology, emergency medicine, family practice, internal medicine, internal medicine–pediatrics, neurology, obstetrics and gynecology, orthopaedic surgery, pediatrics, surgery–general.

WHERE GRADS GO

49.5%

Proportion of 2005-2007 graduates who entered primary care specialties

52.8%

Proportion of 2006-2007 graduates who accepted in-state residencies

University of Miami

MILLER

- 1600 N.W. Tenth Avenue, Miami, FL 33136
- Private
- Year Founded: 1952
- Tuition, 2007-2008: $30,048
- Enrollment 2007-2008 academic year: 681
- Website: http://www.miami.edu/medical-admissions
- Specialty ranking: AIDS: 20

3.68	AVERAGE GPA, ENTERING CLASS FALL 2007
10.4	AVERAGE MCAT, ENTERING CLASS FALL 2007
8.2%	ACCEPTANCE RATE, ENTERING CLASS FALL 2007
52	2009 U.S. NEWS MEDICAL SCHOOL RANKING (RESEARCH)
Unranked	2009 U.S. NEWS MEDICAL SCHOOL RANKING (PRIMARY CARE)

ADMISSIONS

Admissions phone number: (305) 243-6791
Admissions email address: **med.admissions@miami.edu**
Application website: **N/A**
Acceptance rate: **8.2%**
In-state acceptance rate: **15.3%**
Out-of-state acceptance rate: **4.6%**
Minority acceptance rate: **7.2%**
International acceptance rate: **0.0%**

Fall 2007 applications and acceptees

	Applied	Interviewed	Accepted	Enrolled
Total:	4,357	666	358	176
In-state:	1,469	432	225	125
Out-of-state:	2,888	234	133	51

Profile of admitted students

Average undergraduate grade point average: **3.68**
MCAT averages (scale: 1-15; writing test: J-T):
  Composite score: **10.4**
  Verbal reasoning score: **9.9**, Physical sciences score: **10.6**, Biological sciences score: **10.7**, Writing score: **P**
Proportion with undergraduate majors in: Biological sciences: **60%**, Physical sciences: **18%**, Non-sciences: **20%**, Other health professions: **2%**, Mixed disciplines and other: **0%**
Percentage of students not coming directly from college after graduation: **20%**

Dates and details

The American Medical College Application Service (AMCAS) application is accepted.
School asks for a school-specific application as part of the admissions process.
Oldest MCAT considered for Fall 2009 entry: **2005**
Earliest application date for the 2009-2010 first-year class: **6/1**
Latest application date: **12/1**
Acceptance dates for regular application for the class entering in fall 2009:

Earliest: **October 15, 2008**
Latest: **N/A**
The school considers requests for deferred entrance.
Starting month for the class entering in 2009–2010: **August**
The school doesn't have an Early Decision Plan (EDP).
A personal interview is required for admission.

Undergraduate coursework required

Medical school requires undergraduate work in these subjects: biology/zoology, English, organic chemistry, inorganic (general) chemistry, physics.

ADMISSIONS POLICY

(TEXT PROVIDED BY SCHOOL):

The UM Miller School of Medicine participates in the American Medical College Application Service and accepts applications only from U.S. citizens and permanent U.S. residents. Although Florida residents are given preference, since 2001 UM has been recruiting and enrolling non-Floridians in each first-year class. For more information on the application process, please visit the website.

COSTS AND FINANCIAL AID

Financial aid phone number: (305) 243-6211
Tuition, 2007-2008 academic year: $30,048
Room and board: $22,955
Percentage of students receiving financial aid in 2007-08: **87%**
Percentage of students receiving: Loans: **87%**, Grants/scholarships: **40%**, Work-study aid: **0%**
Average medical school debt for the Class of 2006: **$150,607**

STUDENT BODY

Fall 2007 full-time enrollment: **681**
Men: **54%**, Women: **46%**, In-state: **76%**, Minorities: **42%**, American Indian: **0.3%**, Asian-American: **22.3%**, African-American: **6.6%**, Hispanic-American: **12.6%**, White: **55.1%**, International: **0.3%**, Unknown: **2.8%**

ACADEMIC PROGRAMS

The school's curriculum frequently gives first-year students substantial contact with patients.

There are opportunities for first- or second-year students to work in community health clinics.

Program offerings: AIDS, drug/alcohol abuse, family medicine, geriatrics, internal medicine, pediatrics, rural medicine, women's health

Joint degrees awarded: M.D./Ph.D., M.D./M.P.H.

Total National Institutes of Health (NIH) grants awarded to the medical school and affiliated hospitals: **$88.2 million**

CURRICULUM

(TEXT PROVIDED BY SCHOOL):

The curriculum at the University of Miami Miller School of Medicine is designed to develop broadly educated, responsible physicians equipped with the knowledge base, clinical skills, and professional attitudes to provide the very best in patient care.

FACULTY PROFILE (FALL 2007)

Total teaching faculty: **1,280 (full-time), 17 (part-time)**

Of full-time faculty, those teaching in basic sciences: **39%**; in clinical programs: **61%**

Of part-time faculty, those teaching in basic sciences: **35%**; in clinical programs: **65%**

Full-time faculty/student ratio: **1.9**

SUPPORT SERVICES

The school offers students these services for dealing with stress: expanded-hour gym access, professional counseling.

RESIDENCY PROFILE

Most popular residency and specialty programs chosen by the 2006 and 2007 M.D. graduating classes: anesthesiology, emergency medicine, family practice, internal medicine, neurology, obstetrics and gynecology, pediatrics, psychiatry, radiology–diagnostic, surgery–general.

WHERE GRADS GO

39.2%

Proportion of 2005-2007 graduates who entered primary care specialties

34.9%

Proportion of 2006-2007 graduates who accepted in-state residencies

University of Michigan–Ann Arbor

- 1301 Catherine Road, Ann Arbor, MI 48109-0624
- Public
- **Year Founded:** 1848
- **Tuition, 2007-2008:** In-state: $24,755; Out-of-state: $39,119
- **Enrollment 2007-2008 academic year:** 671
- **Website:** http://www.med.umich.edu/medschool/
- **Specialty ranking:** drug/alcohol abuse: 13, family medicine: 7, geriatrics: 5, internal medicine: 7, pediatrics: 11, women's health: 5

3.74 AVERAGE GPA, ENTERING CLASS FALL 2007

11.7 AVERAGE MCAT, ENTERING CLASS FALL 2007

6.8% ACCEPTANCE RATE, ENTERING CLASS FALL 2007

11 2009 U.S. NEWS MEDICAL SCHOOL RANKING (RESEARCH)

17 2009 U.S. NEWS MEDICAL SCHOOL RANKING (PRIMARY CARE)

ADMISSIONS

Admissions phone number: **(734) 764-6317**
Admissions email address: **umichmedadmiss@umich.edu**
Application website: **N/A**
Acceptance rate: **6.8%**
In-state acceptance rate: **9.2%**
Out-of-state acceptance rate: **6.3%**
Minority acceptance rate: **N/A**
International acceptance rate: **N/A**

Fall 2007 applications and acceptees

	Applied	Interviewed	Accepted	Enrolled
Total:	5,735	801	392	170
In-state:	1,076	181	99	75
Out-of-state:	4,659	620	293	95

Profile of admitted students

Average undergraduate grade point average: **3.74**
MCAT averages (scale: 1-15; writing test: J-T):
Composite score: **11.7**
Verbal reasoning score: **11.0**, Physical sciences score: **11.9**, Biological sciences score: **12.2**, Writing score: **Q**
Proportion with undergraduate majors in: Biological sciences: **41%**, Physical sciences: **29%**, Non-sciences: **9%**, Other health professions: **5%**, Mixed disciplines and other: **17%**
Percentage of students not coming directly from college after graduation: **46%**

Dates and details

The American Medical College Application Service (AMCAS) application is accepted.
School asks for a school-specific application as part of the admissions process.
Oldest MCAT considered for Fall 2009 entry: **2005**
Earliest application date for the 2009-2010 first-year class: **6/1**
Latest application date: **11/15**
Acceptance dates for regular application for the class entering in fall 2009:

Earliest: **October 15, 2008**
Latest: **N/A**
The school considers requests for deferred entrance.
Starting month for the class entering in 2009–2010:
August
The school doesn't have an Early Decision Plan (EDP).
A personal interview is required for admission.

Undergraduate coursework required

Medical school requires undergraduate work in these subjects: biology, English, organic chemistry, inorganic (general) chemistry, physics, biochemistry, humanities.

ADMISSIONS POLICY

(TEXT PROVIDED BY SCHOOL):
Each applicant will be considered in the pool of the entire group of applicants and will be assessed on essential attributes and their unique potential to contribute to the educational experience at the Medical School and to the profession of medicine. For detailed information about the admissions process, please visit the website.

COSTS AND FINANCIAL AID

Financial aid phone number: **(734) 763-4147**
Tuition, 2007-2008 academic year: **In-state: $24,755; Out-of-state: $39,119**
Room and board: **$20,052**
Percentage of students receiving financial aid in 2007-08: **84%**
Percentage of students receiving: Loans: **79%**, Grants/scholarships: **61%**, Work-study aid: **0%**
Average medical school debt for the Class of 2006: **$100,373**

STUDENT BODY

Fall 2007 full-time enrollment: **671**
Men: **51%**, Women: **49%**, In-state: **45%**, Minorities: **41%**, American Indian: **1.3%**, Asian-American: **26.2%**, African-American: **8.0%**, Hispanic-American: **5.8%**, White: **55.3%**, International: **0.0%**, Unknown: **3.3%**

ACADEMIC PROGRAMS

The school's curriculum frequently gives first-year students substantial contact with patients.

There are opportunities for first- or second-year students to work in community health clinics.

Program offerings: AIDS, drug/alcohol abuse, family medicine, geriatrics, internal medicine, pediatrics, rural medicine, women's health

Joint degrees awarded: M.D./Ph.D., M.D./M.B.A., M.D./M.P.H., M.D./J.D., M.D./M.S.W., M.D./M.S.

Total National Institutes of Health (NIH) grants awarded to the medical school and affiliated hospitals: **$320.2 million**

CURRICULUM

(TEXT PROVIDED BY SCHOOL):

At the University of Michigan Medical School, medical education begins and ends with patient care. While students will learn about cells, tissues, organ systems, and disease through lectures, labs, and textbooks, it all comes to life through patient interaction. For detailed information about the innovative curriculum, please visit the website.

FACULTY PROFILE (FALL 2007)

Total teaching faculty: **1,669 (full-time)**, **404 (part-time)**

Of full-time faculty, those teaching in basic sciences: **9%**; in clinical programs: **91%**

Of part-time faculty, those teaching in basic sciences: **11%**; in clinical programs: **89%**

Full-time faculty/student ratio: **2.5**

SUPPORT SERVICES

The school offers students these services for dealing with stress: expanded-hour gym access, peer counseling, professional counseling, support groups.

RESIDENCY PROFILE

Most popular residency and specialty programs chosen by the 2006 and 2007 M.D. graduating classes: anesthesiology, emergency medicine, family practice, internal medicine, obstetrics and gynecology, ophthalmology, orthopaedic surgery, otolaryngology, pediatrics, surgery–general.

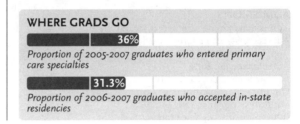

WHERE GRADS GO

36%

Proportion of 2005-2007 graduates who entered primary care specialties

31.3%

Proportion of 2006-2007 graduates who accepted in-state residencies

University of Minnesota

MEDICAL SCHOOL

- 420 Delaware Street SE, MMC 293, Minneapolis, MN 55455
- Public
- Year Founded: 1851
- Tuition, 2007-2008: In-state: $33,109; Out-of-state: $40,423
- Enrollment 2007-2008 academic year: 944
- Website: http://www.med.umn.edu
- Specialty ranking: family medicine: 11, rural medicine: 11

3.69 AVERAGE GPA, ENTERING CLASS FALL 2007

10.4 AVERAGE MCAT, ENTERING CLASS FALL 2007

8.7% ACCEPTANCE RATE, ENTERING CLASS FALL 2007

36 2009 U.S. NEWS MEDICAL SCHOOL RANKING (RESEARCH)

7 2009 U.S. NEWS MEDICAL SCHOOL RANKING (PRIMARY CARE)

ADMISSIONS

Admissions phone number: (612) 625-7977
Admissions email address: meded@umn.edu
Application website: N/A
Acceptance rate: 8.7%
In-state acceptance rate: 21.9%
Out-of-state acceptance rate: 3.6%
Minority acceptance rate: 6.9%
International acceptance rate: 1.7%

Fall 2007 applications and acceptees

	Applied	Interviewed	Accepted	Enrolled
Total:	4,423	580	386	241
In-state:	1,240	403	271	203
Out-of-state:	3,183	177	115	38

Profile of admitted students

Average undergraduate grade point average: 3.69
MCAT averages (scale: 1-15; writing test: J-T):
   Composite score: 10.4
   Verbal reasoning score: 10.2, Physical sciences score: 10.3, Biological sciences score: 10.7, Writing score: P
Proportion with undergraduate majors in: Biological sciences: 47%, Physical sciences: 25%, Non-sciences: 12%, Other health professions: 2%, Mixed disciplines and other: 14%
Percentage of students not coming directly from college after graduation: 52%

Dates and details

The American Medical College Application Service (AMCAS) application is accepted.
School asks for a school-specific application as part of the admissions process.
Oldest MCAT considered for Fall 2009 entry: 2005
Earliest application date for the 2009-2010 first-year class: 6/1
Latest application date: 11/15
Acceptance dates for regular application for the class entering in fall 2009:
   Earliest: October 15, 2008

Latest: May 15, 2009
The school considers requests for deferred entrance.
Starting month for the class entering in 2009–2010:
   August
The school has an Early Decision Plan (EDP).
A personal interview is required for admission.

Undergraduate coursework required

Medical school requires undergraduate work in these subjects: biology, organic chemistry, inorganic (general) chemistry, physics, humanities, demonstration of writing skills, social sciences.

ADMISSIONS POLICY

(TEXT PROVIDED BY SCHOOL):

Those entering in fall 2009 and later will find the prerequisites list shorter. Yet requirements will remain to perform well on the MCAT and to demonstrate the essential qualities of a physician (please see the website). Candidates are evaluated holistically; the school offers several dual-degree programs; the Duluth campus mission is to serve rural and American Indian communities.

COSTS AND FINANCIAL AID

Financial aid phone number: (612) 625-4998
Tuition, 2007-2008 academic year: In-state: $33,109; Out-of-state: $40,423
Room and board: $11,448
Percentage of students receiving financial aid in 2007-08: 94%
Percentage of students receiving: Loans: 80%, Grants/scholarships: 65%, Work-study aid: 1%
Average medical school debt for the Class of 2006: $134,493

STUDENT BODY

Fall 2007 full-time enrollment: 944
Men: 50%, Women: 50%, In-state: 80%, Minorities: 19%, American Indian: 3.7%, Asian-American: 9.5%, African-American: 1.9%, Hispanic-American: 2.4%, White: 80.6%, International: 1.8%, Unknown: 0.0%

ACADEMIC PROGRAMS

The school's curriculum frequently gives first-year students substantial contact with patients.

There are opportunities for first- or second-year students to work in community health clinics.

Program offerings: AIDS, drug/alcohol abuse, family medicine, geriatrics, internal medicine, pediatrics, rural medicine, women's health

Joint degrees awarded: M.D./Ph.D., M.D./M.B.A., M.D./M.P.H., M.D./M.H.I., M.D./J.D., M.D./M.S.

Total National Institutes of Health (NIH) grants awarded to the medical school and affiliated hospitals: **$153.2 million**

CURRICULUM

(TEXT PROVIDED BY SCHOOL):

The school prepares students well for residencies, primary care to specialty, with a comprehensive medical curriculum. Its îFlexible M.D.î allows students to take 3.5 to 6 years to earn an M.D., for one cost. The school is part of MED 2010, an ongoing initiative to move from time-based to competency-defined medical education.

FACULTY PROFILE (FALL 2007)

Total teaching faculty: **1,558 (full-time)**, **31 (part-time)**
Of full-time faculty, those teaching in basic sciences: **12%**; in clinical programs: **88%**

Of part-time faculty, those teaching in basic sciences: **10%**; in clinical programs: **90%**
Full-time faculty/student ratio: **1.7**

SUPPORT SERVICES

The school offers students these services for dealing with stress: peer counseling, professional counseling, support groups.

RESIDENCY PROFILE

Most popular residency and specialty programs chosen by the 2006 and 2007 M.D. graduating classes: anesthesiology, emergency medicine, family practice, internal medicine, obstetrics and gynecology, orthopaedic surgery, pediatrics, radiology–diagnostic, surgery–general, internal medicine/pediatrics.

WHERE GRADS GO

45.9%

Proportion of 2005-2007 graduates who entered primary care specialties

51.9%

Proportion of 2006-2007 graduates who accepted in-state residencies

University of Missouri–Columbia

- 1 Hospital Drive, Columbia, MO 65212
- Public
- **Year Founded:** 1872
- **Tuition, 2007-2008:** In-state: $23,848; Out-of-state: $47,492
- **Enrollment 2007-2008 academic year:** 387
- **Website:** http://som.missouri.edu
- **Specialty ranking:** family medicine: 3, rural medicine: 15

3.77 AVERAGE GPA, ENTERING CLASS FALL 2007

10.3 AVERAGE MCAT, ENTERING CLASS FALL 2007

13.5% ACCEPTANCE RATE, ENTERING CLASS FALL 2007

Unranked 2009 U.S. NEWS MEDICAL SCHOOL RANKING (RESEARCH)

23 2009 U.S. NEWS MEDICAL SCHOOL RANKING (PRIMARY CARE)

ADMISSIONS

Admissions phone number: **(573) 882-8047**
Admissions email address: **eastonm@health.missouri.edu**
Application website: **N/A**
Acceptance rate: **13.5%**
In-state acceptance rate: **33.2%**
Out-of-state acceptance rate: **3.3%**
Minority acceptance rate: **5.3%**
International acceptance rate: **0.0%**

Fall 2007 applications and acceptees

	Applied	Interviewed	Accepted	Enrolled
Total:	1,159	283	156	96
In-state:	395	216	131	91
Out-of-state:	764	67	25	5

Profile of admitted students

Average undergraduate grade point average: **3.77**
MCAT averages (scale: 1-15; writing test: J-T):
Composite score: **10.3**
Verbal reasoning score: **10.2**, Physical sciences score:
10.2, Biological sciences score: **10.5**, Writing score: **N/A**
Proportion with undergraduate majors in: Biological
sciences: **43%**, Physical sciences: **26%**, Non-sciences:
14%, Other health professions: **2%**, Mixed disciplines
and other: **15%**
Percentage of students not coming directly from college
after graduation: **44%**

Dates and details

The American Medical College Application Service
(AMCAS) application is accepted.
School asks for a school-specific application as part of the
admissions process.
Oldest MCAT considered for Fall 2009 entry: **2003**
Earliest application date for the 2009-2010 first-year class:
6/1
Latest application date: **11/1**
Acceptance dates for regular application for the class
entering in fall 2009:
Earliest: **November 15, 2008**

Latest: **August 1, 2009**
The school considers requests for deferred entrance.
Starting month for the class entering in 2009–2010:
August
The school has an Early Decision Plan (EDP).
A personal interview is required for admission.

Undergraduate coursework required

Medical school requires undergraduate work in these subjects: biology, English, organic chemistry, inorganic (general) chemistry, physics, mathematics, demonstration of
writing skills, general chemistry.

ADMISSIONS POLICY

(TEXT PROVIDED BY SCHOOL):

Applicants must have completed at least 90 semester hours
(not including physical education and military science)
from a recognized college or university. Required coursework includes: English Composition or Writing Intensive;
college-level Mathematics; General Biology with lab;
General Chemistry with lab; Organic Chemistry with lab;
and General Physics with lab. The MCAT is required.

COSTS AND FINANCIAL AID

Financial aid phone number: **(573) 882-2923**
Tuition, 2007-2008 academic year: **In-state: $23,848; Out-
of-state: $47,492**
Room and board: **$9,000**
Percentage of students receiving financial aid in 2007-08:
97%
Percentage of students receiving: Loans: **97%**,
Grants/scholarships: **80%**, Work-study aid: **0%**
Average medical school debt for the Class of 2006:
$136,108

STUDENT BODY

Fall 2007 full-time enrollment: **387**
Men: **51%**, Women: **49%**, In-state: **98%**, Minorities: **14%**,
American Indian: **0.0%**, Asian-American: **9.3%**, African-
American: **4.7%**, Hispanic-American: **1.6%**, White:
80.6%, International: **0.0%**, Unknown: **3.9%**

ACADEMIC PROGRAMS

The school's curriculum frequently gives first-year students substantial contact with patients.

There aren't opportunities for first- or second-year students to work in community health clinics.

Program offerings: AIDS, drug/alcohol abuse, family medicine, geriatrics, internal medicine, pediatrics, rural medicine, women's health

Joint degrees awarded: M.D./Ph.D., M.D./M.S.

Total National Institutes of Health (NIH) grants awarded to the medical school and affiliated hospitals: **$23.9 million**

CURRICULUM

(TEXT PROVIDED BY SCHOOL):

The MU School of Medicine pioneered a problem-based teaching method that combines independent learning in small groups with early exposure to patient care. As part of an academic medical center, the school is devoted to improving patient care, education, and research.

FACULTY PROFILE (FALL 2007)

Total teaching faculty: **500 (full-time)**, **106 (part-time)**

Of full-time faculty, those teaching in basic sciences: **20%**; in clinical programs: **80%**

Of part-time faculty, those teaching in basic sciences: **16%**; in clinical programs: **84%**

Full-time faculty/student ratio: **1.3**

SUPPORT SERVICES

The school offers students these services for dealing with stress: expanded-hour gym access, peer counseling, professional counseling, support groups.

RESIDENCY PROFILE

Most popular residency and specialty programs chosen by the 2006 and 2007 M.D. graduating classes: dermatology, emergency medicine, family practice, internal medicine, obstetrics and gynecology, ophthalmology, orthopaedic surgery, pediatrics, surgery–general, urology.

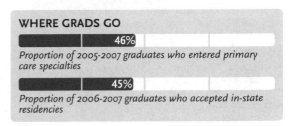

WHERE GRADS GO

46%

Proportion of 2005-2007 graduates who entered primary care specialties

45%

Proportion of 2006-2007 graduates who accepted in-state residencies

University of Missouri–Kansas City

- 2411 Holmes, Kansas City, MO 64108
- Public
- Year Founded: 1971
- Tuition, 2007-2008: In-state: $28,142; Out-of-state: $55,075
- Enrollment 2007-2008 academic year: 401
- Website: http://www.med.umkc.edu
- Specialty ranking: N/A

N/A AVERAGE GPA, ENTERING CLASS FALL 2007

N/A AVERAGE MCAT, ENTERING CLASS FALL 2007

23.1% ACCEPTANCE RATE, ENTERING CLASS FALL 2007

Unranked 2009 U.S. NEWS MEDICAL SCHOOL RANKING (RESEARCH)

Unranked 2009 U.S. NEWS MEDICAL SCHOOL RANKING (PRIMARY CARE)

ADMISSIONS

Admissions phone number: **(816) 235-1208**
Admissions email address: **dehaemersj@umkc.edu**
Application website: **N/A**
Acceptance rate: **23.1%**
In-state acceptance rate: **N/A**
Out-of-state acceptance rate: **N/A**
Minority acceptance rate: **26.3%**
International acceptance rate: **N/A**

Fall 2007 applications and acceptees

	Applied	Interviewed	Accepted	Enrolled
Total:	698	241	161	124
In-state:	N/A	165	113	93
Out-of-state:	N/A	76	48	31

Profile of admitted students

Average undergraduate grade point average: **N/A**
MCAT averages (scale: 1-15; writing test: J-T):
  Composite score: **N/A**
  Verbal reasoning score: **N/A**, Physical sciences score: **N/A**, Biological sciences score: **N/A**, Writing score: **N/A**
Proportion with undergraduate majors in: Biological sciences: **N/A**, Physical sciences: **N/A**, Non-sciences: **N/A**, Other health professions: **N/A**, Mixed disciplines and other: **N/A**
Percentage of students not coming directly from college after graduation: **N/A**

Dates and details

The American Medical College Application Service (AMCAS) application is not accepted.
School asks for a school-specific application as part of the admissions process.
Oldest MCAT considered for Fall 2009 entry: **N/A**
Earliest application date for the 2009-2010 first-year class: **8/1**
Latest application date: **11/15**
Acceptance dates for regular application for the class entering in fall 2009:
  Earliest: **April 1, 2009**

Latest: **N/A**
The school doesn't consider requests for deferred entrance.
Starting month for the class entering in 2009–2010:
  August
The school doesn't have an Early Decision Plan (EDP).
A personal interview is required for admission.

Undergraduate coursework required

Medical school requires undergraduate work in these subjects: N/A.

ADMISSIONS POLICY

(TEXT PROVIDED BY SCHOOL):
Cognitive and noncognitive factors are used in selection. A majority of accepted applicants are in-state residents or from states contiguous to Missouri.

COSTS AND FINANCIAL AID

Financial aid phone number: **(816) 235-1242**
Tuition, 2007-2008 academic year: **In-state: $28,142; Out-of-state: $55,075**
Room and board: **$8,000**
Percentage of students receiving financial aid in 2007-08: **N/A**
Percentage of students receiving: Loans: **N/A**, Grants/scholarships: **N/A**, Work-study aid: **N/A**
Average medical school debt for the Class of 2006: **$107,185**

STUDENT BODY

Fall 2007 full-time enrollment: **401**
Men: **42%**, Women: **58%**, In-state: **81%**, Minorities: **47%**, American Indian: **0.2%**, Asian-American: **38.4%**, African-American: **5.0%**, Hispanic-American: **3.5%**, White: **44.9%**, International: **0.0%**, Unknown: **8.0%**

ACADEMIC PROGRAMS

The school's curriculum very frequently gives first-year students substantial contact with patients.
There are opportunities for first- or second-year students to work in community health clinics.

Program offerings: AIDS, drug/alcohol abuse, family medicine, geriatrics, internal medicine, pediatrics, rural medicine, women's health
Joint degrees awarded: N/A
Total National Institutes of Health (NIH) grants awarded to the medical school and affiliated hospitals: **$6.8 million**

CURRICULUM
(TEXT PROVIDED BY SCHOOL):
In Years 1 and 2 of the six-year baccalaureate-M.D. program, students spend three fourths of their time pursuing undergraduate arts and science courses but one fourth of their time in clinical courses with patient contact. In Years 3 and 4, students study basic science, continue their baccalaureate work, and enroll in clinical rotations including a weekly continuing care clinic. Years 5 and 6 are clinical.

FACULTY PROFILE (FALL 2007)
Total teaching faculty: **647 (full-time), 117 (part-time)**
Of full-time faculty, those teaching in basic sciences: **8%**; in clinical programs: **92%**
Of part-time faculty, those teaching in basic sciences: **3%**; in clinical programs: **97%**
Full-time faculty/student ratio: **1.6**

SUPPORT SERVICES
The school offers students these services for dealing with stress: peer counseling, professional counseling, support groups.

RESIDENCY PROFILE
Most popular residency and specialty programs chosen by the 2006 and 2007 M.D. graduating classes: anesthesiology, emergency medicine, internal medicine, obstetrics and gynecology, ophthalmology, orthopaedic surgery, pediatrics, radiology–diagnostic, surgery–general, internal medicine/pediatrics.

WHERE GRADS GO

41.9%
Proportion of 2005-2007 graduates who entered primary care specialties

38.7%
Proportion of 2006-2007 graduates who accepted in-state residencies

University of Nebraska

COLLEGE OF MEDICINE

- 986585 Nebraska Medical Center, Omaha, NE 68198-6585
- Public
- Year Founded: N/A
- Tuition, 2007-2008: In-state: $24,338; Out-of-state: $53,910
- Enrollment 2007-2008 academic year: 476
- Website: http://www.unmc.edu/UNCOM/
- Specialty ranking: rural medicine: 11

3.73	AVERAGE GPA, ENTERING CLASS FALL 2007
9.7	AVERAGE MCAT, ENTERING CLASS FALL 2007
12.1%	ACCEPTANCE RATE, ENTERING CLASS FALL 2007
Unranked	2009 U.S. NEWS MEDICAL SCHOOL RANKING (RESEARCH)
20	2009 U.S. NEWS MEDICAL SCHOOL RANKING (PRIMARY CARE)

ADMISSIONS

Admissions phone number: **(402) 559-2259**
Admissions email address: **grrogers@unmc.edu**
Application website: **N/A**
Acceptance rate: **12.1%**
In-state acceptance rate: **36.8%**
Out-of-state acceptance rate: **4.5%**
Minority acceptance rate: **4.9%**
International acceptance rate: **8.7%**

Fall 2007 applications and acceptees

	Applied	Interviewed	Accepted	Enrolled
Total:	1,373	408	166	121
In-state:	323	255	119	99
Out-of-state:	1,050	153	47	22

Profile of admitted students

Average undergraduate grade point average: **3.73**
MCAT averages (scale: 1-15; writing test: J-T):
  Composite score: **9.7**
  Verbal reasoning score: **9.7**, Physical sciences score: **9.4**, Biological sciences score: **10.0**, Writing score: **O**
Proportion with undergraduate majors in: Biological sciences: **50%**, Physical sciences: **23%**, Non-sciences: **5%**, Other health professions: **5%**, Mixed disciplines and other: **17%**
Percentage of students not coming directly from college after graduation: **N/A**

Dates and details

The American Medical College Application Service (AMCAS) application is accepted.
School asks for a school-specific application as part of the admissions process.
Oldest MCAT considered for Fall 2009 entry: **2006**
Earliest application date for the 2009-2010 first-year class: **6/1**
Latest application date: **11/1**
Acceptance dates for regular application for the class entering in fall 2009:
  Earliest: **December 1, 2008**

Latest: **March 15, 2009**
The school doesn't consider requests for deferred entrance.
Starting month for the class entering in 2009–2010:
  August
The school has an Early Decision Plan (EDP).
A personal interview is required for admission.

Undergraduate coursework required

Medical school requires undergraduate work in these subjects: biology, English, organic chemistry, inorganic (general) chemistry, physics, biochemistry, humanities, calculus, general chemistry.

COSTS AND FINANCIAL AID

Financial aid phone number: **(402) 559-4199**
Tuition, 2007-2008 academic year: **In-state: $24,338; Out-of-state: $53,910**
Room and board: **$14,400**
Percentage of students receiving financial aid in 2007-08: **98%**
Percentage of students receiving: Loans: **90%**, Grants/scholarships: **60%**, Work-study aid: **0%**
Average medical school debt for the Class of 2006: **$118,669**

STUDENT BODY

Fall 2007 full-time enrollment: **476**
Men: **57%**, Women: **43%**, In-state: **86%**, Minorities: **11%**, American Indian: **0.6%**, Asian-American: **5.0%**, African-American: **2.1%**, Hispanic-American: **2.5%**, White: **89.3%**, International: **0.4%**, Unknown: **0.0%**

ACADEMIC PROGRAMS

The school's curriculum very frequently gives first-year students substantial contact with patients.
There are opportunities for first- or second-year students to work in community health clinics.
Program offerings: AIDS, drug/alcohol abuse, family medicine, geriatrics, internal medicine, pediatrics, rural medicine, women's health
Joint degrees awarded: M.D./Ph.D., M.D./M.P.H.

Total National Institutes of Health (NIH) grants awarded to the medical school and affiliated hospitals: **N/A**

FACULTY PROFILE (FALL 2007)

Total teaching faculty: **565 (full-time)**, **107 (part-time)**

Of full-time faculty, those teaching in basic sciences: **13%**; in clinical programs: **87%**

Of part-time faculty, those teaching in basic sciences: **5%**; in clinical programs: **95%**

Full-time faculty/student ratio: **1.2**

SUPPORT SERVICES

The school offers students these services for dealing with stress: expanded-hour gym access, professional counseling, religious support, support groups.

RESIDENCY PROFILE

Most popular residency and specialty programs chosen by the 2006 and 2007 M.D. graduating classes: anesthesiology, emergency medicine, family practice, internal medicine, obstetrics and gynecology, pediatrics, psychiatry, radiology–diagnostic, surgery–general.

WHERE GRADS GO

60%

Proportion of 2005-2007 graduates who entered primary care specialties

40%

Proportion of 2006-2007 graduates who accepted in-state residencies

University of Nevada–Reno

- Pennington Building, Mailstop 357, Reno, NV 89557-0357
- Public
- Year Founded: 1969
- Tuition, 2007-2008: In-state: $15,077; Out-of-state: $34,933
- Enrollment 2007-2008 academic year: 224
- Website: http://www.medicine.nevada.edu
- Specialty ranking: N/A

3.63 AVERAGE GPA, ENTERING CLASS FALL 2007

10.1 AVERAGE MCAT, ENTERING CLASS FALL 2007

7.8% ACCEPTANCE RATE, ENTERING CLASS FALL 2007

Unranked 2009 U.S. NEWS MEDICAL SCHOOL RANKING (RESEARCH)

Unranked 2009 U.S. NEWS MEDICAL SCHOOL RANKING (PRIMARY CARE)

ADMISSIONS
Admissions phone number: (775) 784-6063
Admissions email address: asa@med.unr.edu
Application website: N/A
Acceptance rate: 7.8%
In-state acceptance rate: 37.0%
Out-of-state acceptance rate: 1.3%
Minority acceptance rate: N/A
International acceptance rate: N/A

Fall 2007 applications and acceptees

	Applied	Interviewed	Accepted	Enrolled
Total:	1,109	238	86	62
In-state:	200	154	74	57
Out-of-state:	909	84	12	5

Profile of admitted students
Average undergraduate grade point average: 3.63
MCAT averages (scale: 1-15; writing test: J-T):
  Composite score: 10.1
  Verbal reasoning score: 9.2, Physical sciences score: 9.3, Biological sciences score: 10.0, Writing score: Q
Proportion with undergraduate majors in: Biological sciences: 53%, Physical sciences: 26%, Non-sciences: 1%, Other health professions: 0%, Mixed disciplines and other: 20%
Percentage of students not coming directly from college after graduation: N/A

Dates and details
The American Medical College Application Service (AMCAS) application is accepted.
School asks for a school-specific application as part of the admissions process.
Oldest MCAT considered for Fall 2009 entry: 2005
Earliest application date for the 2009-2010 first-year class: 6/1
Latest application date: 11/1
Acceptance dates for regular application for the class entering in fall 2009:
  Earliest: January 15, 2009

Latest: April 15, 2009
The school considers requests for deferred entrance.
Starting month for the class entering in 2009–2010:
  August
The school has an Early Decision Plan (EDP).
A personal interview is required for admission.

Undergraduate coursework required
Medical school requires undergraduate work in these subjects: biology, organic chemistry, inorganic (general) chemistry, physics, behavioral science.

ADMISSIONS POLICY
(TEXT PROVIDED BY SCHOOL):
Evaluation is based on: academic performance; MCAT results; nature/depth of scholarly, extracurricular, health-care-related activities; letters of evaluation; and personal interview. First priority is given to residents of Nevada; applicants from Alaska, Idaho, Montana, and Wyoming are also considered. The school is committed to the recruitment, selection, and retention of underrepresented minorities.

COSTS AND FINANCIAL AID
Financial aid phone number: (775) 784-4666
Tuition, 2007-2008 academic year: **In-state: $15,077; Out-of-state: $34,933**
Room and board: $9,540
Percentage of students receiving financial aid in 2007-08: N/A
Percentage of students receiving: Loans: N/A, Grants/scholarships: 81%, Work-study aid: N/A
Average medical school debt for the Class of 2006: $114,760

STUDENT BODY
Fall 2007 full-time enrollment: 224
Men: 51%, Women: 49%, In-state: 90%, Minorities: 28%, American Indian: 1.8%, Asian-American: 20.5%, African-American: 1.8%, Hispanic-American: 4.0%, White: 71.9%, International: N/A, Unknown: N/A

ACADEMIC PROGRAMS

The school's curriculum very frequently gives first-year students substantial contact with patients.

There are opportunities for first- or second-year students to work in community health clinics.

Program offerings: drug/alcohol abuse, family medicine, geriatrics, internal medicine, pediatrics, rural medicine, women's health

Joint degrees awarded: M.D./Ph.D.

Total National Institutes of Health (NIH) grants awarded to the medical school and affiliated hospitals: N/A

CURRICULUM
(TEXT PROVIDED BY SCHOOL):

Curriculum blends traditional coursework with early clinical learning experiences. Introduction of Patient Care (two-year course) exposes students to patient history taking, physical exam, and clinical diagnosis. Clinical Problem Solving (Years 1 and 2) and Clinical Reasoning in Medicine (Year 3) extend this process through patient case management. The four-week Advanced Clinical Experience in Rural Health Care is required.

FACULTY PROFILE (FALL 2007)

Total teaching faculty: 202 (full-time), 75 (part-time)
Of full-time faculty, those teaching in basic sciences: 25%; in clinical programs: 75%

Of part-time faculty, those teaching in basic sciences: 9%; in clinical programs: 91%
Full-time faculty/student ratio: 0.9

SUPPORT SERVICES

The school offers students these services for dealing with stress: peer counseling, professional counseling, support groups.

RESIDENCY PROFILE

Most popular residency and specialty programs chosen by the 2006 and 2007 M.D. graduating classes: anesthesiology, emergency medicine, family practice, internal medicine, orthopaedic surgery, pathology–anatomic and clinical, pediatrics, radiology–diagnostic, surgery–general.

WHERE GRADS GO

43%
Proportion of 2005-2007 graduates who entered primary care specialties

21%
Proportion of 2006-2007 graduates who accepted in-state residencies

University of New Mexico

- Basic Medical Sciences Building, Room 107, Albuquerque, NM 87131
- Public
- **Year Founded:** 1964
- **Tuition, 2007-2008:** In-state: $16,754; Out-of-state: $42,910
- **Enrollment 2007-2008 academic year:** 315
- **Website:** http://hsc.unm.edu/som/
- **Specialty ranking:** family medicine: 9, rural medicine: 2

3.61	AVERAGE GPA, ENTERING CLASS FALL 2007
9.2	AVERAGE MCAT, ENTERING CLASS FALL 2007
8.9%	ACCEPTANCE RATE, ENTERING CLASS FALL 2007
Unranked	2009 U.S. NEWS MEDICAL SCHOOL RANKING (RESEARCH)
31	2009 U.S. NEWS MEDICAL SCHOOL RANKING (PRIMARY CARE)

ADMISSIONS

Admissions phone number: **(505) 272-4766**
Admissions email address:
  somadmissions@salud.unm.edu
Application website: **http://hsc.unm.edu/som/admissions**
Acceptance rate: **8.9%**
In-state acceptance rate: **42.9%**
Out-of-state acceptance rate: **0.7%**
Minority acceptance rate: **8.4%**
International acceptance rate: **N/A**

Fall 2007 applications and acceptees

	Applied	Interviewed	Accepted	Enrolled
Total:	1,093	211	97	75
In-state:	212	190	91	72
Out-of-state:	881	21	6	3

Profile of admitted students

Average undergraduate grade point average: **3.61**
MCAT averages (scale: 1-15; writing test: J-T):
  Composite score: **9.2**
  Verbal reasoning score: **9.0**, Physical sciences score: **8.9**,
  Biological sciences score: **9.8**, Writing score: **N/A**
Proportion with undergraduate majors in: Biological
  sciences: **36%**, Physical sciences: **20%**, Non-sciences:
  15%, Other health professions: **1%**, Mixed disciplines
  and other: **28%**
Percentage of students not coming directly from college
  after graduation: **37%**

Dates and details

The American Medical College Application Service
  (AMCAS) application is accepted.
School asks for a school-specific application as part of the
  admissions process.
Oldest MCAT considered for Fall 2009 entry: **2003**
Earliest application date for the 2009-2010 first-year class:
  6/1
Latest application date: **11/15**
Acceptance dates for regular application for the class
  entering in fall 2009:

Earliest: **March 15, 2009**
  Latest: **N/A**
The school considers requests for deferred entrance.
Starting month for the class entering in 2009–2010:
  August
The school doesn't have an Early Decision Plan (EDP).
A personal interview is required for admission.

Undergraduate coursework required

Medical school requires undergraduate work in these subjects: biology, organic chemistry, inorganic (general) chemistry, physics, biochemistry, general chemistry.

ADMISSIONS POLICY

(TEXT PROVIDED BY SCHOOL):
Selection is based on academic achievement, motivation for
medicine, problem-solving ability, self-appraisal, ability to
relate to people, maturity, breadth of interests and achievement, professional goals, and likelihood of serving the
healthcare needs of the state following postgraduate training. As a state-funded institution, the school primarily
accepts students from New Mexico.

COSTS AND FINANCIAL AID

Financial aid phone number: **(505) 272-8008**
Tuition, 2007-2008 academic year: **In-state: $16,754; Out-
of-state: $42,910**
Room and board: **$10,810**
Percentage of students receiving financial aid in 2007-08:
  89%
Percentage of students receiving: Loans: **83%**,
  Grants/scholarships: **62%**, Work-study aid: **0%**
Average medical school debt for the Class of 2006:
  $94,639

STUDENT BODY

Fall 2007 full-time enrollment: **315**
Men: **47%**, Women: **53%**, In-state: **79%**, Minorities: **40%**,
  American Indian: **3.8%**, Asian-American: **6.7%**, African-
  American: **1.3%**, Hispanic-American: **28.3%**, White:
  58.4%, International: **0.0%**, Unknown: **1.6%**

ACADEMIC PROGRAMS

The school's curriculum very frequently gives first-year students substantial contact with patients.

There are opportunities for first- or second-year students to work in community health clinics.

Program offerings: AIDS, drug/alcohol abuse, family medicine, geriatrics, internal medicine, pediatrics, rural medicine, women's health

Joint degrees awarded: M.D./Ph.D.

Total National Institutes of Health (NIH) grants awarded to the medical school and affiliated hospitals: **$54.0 million**

CURRICULUM

(TEXT PROVIDED BY SCHOOL):

UNM includes problem-based and community-based learning. Phase 1 includes PBL, lectures, labs, and clinical experiences. Phase 2 has experiences in Family Medicine, Internal Medicine, Neurology, Obstetrics/Gynecology, Pediatrics, Psychiatry, and Surgery. Phase 3: one month in a community site, a one-month rotation in intensive care, a one-month subinternship, a one-month interdisciplinary ambulatory care rotation, and various electives.

FACULTY PROFILE (FALL 2007)

Total teaching faculty: **687 (full-time), 151 (part-time)**

Of full-time faculty, those teaching in basic sciences: **10%**; in clinical programs: **90%**

Of part-time faculty, those teaching in basic sciences: **6%**; in clinical programs: **94%**

Full-time faculty/student ratio: **2.2**

SUPPORT SERVICES

The school offers students these services for dealing with stress: expanded-hour gym access, peer counseling, professional counseling, support groups.

RESIDENCY PROFILE

Most popular residency and specialty programs chosen by the 2006 and 2007 M.D. graduating classes: anesthesiology, emergency medicine, family practice, internal medicine, obstetrics and gynecology, pathology–anatomic and clinical, pediatrics, surgery–general.

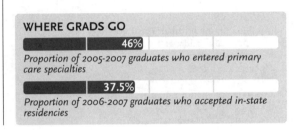

WHERE GRADS GO

46%

Proportion of 2005-2007 graduates who entered primary care specialties

37.5%

Proportion of 2006-2007 graduates who accepted in-state residencies

University of North Carolina–Chapel Hill

- CB #7000, 4030 Bondurant Hall, Chapel Hill, NC 27599-7000
- Public
- Year Founded: 1879
- Tuition, 2007-2008: In-state: $11,919; Out-of-state: $35,585
- Enrollment 2007-2008 academic year: 736
- Website: http://www.med.unc.edu/admit/
- Specialty ranking: AIDS: 10, family medicine: 5, geriatrics: 18, internal medicine: 18, pediatrics: 22, rural medicine: 8, women's health: 9

3.73 AVERAGE GPA, ENTERING CLASS FALL 2007

11.0 AVERAGE MCAT, ENTERING CLASS FALL 2007

5.7% ACCEPTANCE RATE, ENTERING CLASS FALL 2007

19 2009 U.S. NEWS MEDICAL SCHOOL RANKING (RESEARCH)

2 2009 U.S. NEWS MEDICAL SCHOOL RANKING (PRIMARY CARE)

ADMISSIONS

Admissions phone number: **(919) 962-8331**
Admissions email address: **admissions@med.unc.edu**
Application website: **N/A**
Acceptance rate: **5.7%**
In-state acceptance rate: **19.7%**
Out-of-state acceptance rate: **1.5%**
Minority acceptance rate: **5.4%**
International acceptance rate: **3.4%**

Fall 2007 applications and acceptees

	Applied	Interviewed	Accepted	Enrolled
Total:	3,965	556	225	161
In-state:	912	458	180	136
Out-of-state:	3,053	98	45	25

Profile of admitted students

Average undergraduate grade point average: **3.73**
MCAT averages (scale: 1-15; writing test: J-T):
Composite score: **11.0**
Verbal reasoning score: **10.9**, Physical sciences score: **11.0**, Biological sciences score: **11.1**, Writing score: **P**
Proportion with undergraduate majors in: Biological sciences: **44%**, Physical sciences: **23%**, Non-sciences: **22%**, Other health professions: **8%**, Mixed disciplines and other: **3%**
Percentage of students not coming directly from college after graduation: **30%**

Dates and details

The American Medical College Application Service (AMCAS) application is accepted.
School asks for a school-specific application as part of the admissions process.
Oldest MCAT considered for Fall 2009 entry: **2005**
Earliest application date for the 2009-2010 first-year class: **6/1**
Latest application date: **11/15**
Acceptance dates for regular application for the class entering in fall 2009:
Earliest: **October 15, 2008**
Latest: **August 11, 2009**
The school considers requests for deferred entrance.
Starting month for the class entering in 2009–2010: **August**
The school has an Early Decision Plan (EDP).
A personal interview is required for admission.

Undergraduate coursework required

Medical school requires undergraduate work in these subjects: biology, English, organic chemistry, inorganic (general) chemistry, physics, general chemistry.

ADMISSIONS POLICY

(TEXT PROVIDED BY SCHOOL):
The Committee on Admissions evaluates the qualifications of applicants to select those with the greatest potential in the medical field. Preference is given to North Carolina residents. Consideration is given to each candidate's motivation, maturity, leadership, integrity, and personal accomplishments, in addition to the scholastic record. Reapplications are compared to those previously submitted.

COSTS AND FINANCIAL AID

Financial aid phone number: **(919) 962-6117**
Tuition, 2007-2008 academic year: **In-state: $11,919; Out-of-state: $35,585**
Room and board: **$27,052**
Percentage of students receiving financial aid in 2007-08: **89%**
Percentage of students receiving: Loans: **81%**, Grants/scholarships: **82%**, Work-study aid: **0%**
Average medical school debt for the Class of 2006: **$83,475**

STUDENT BODY

Fall 2007 full-time enrollment: **736**
Men: **52%**, Women: **48%**, In-state: **76%**, Minorities: **31%**, American Indian: **N/A**, Asian-American: **N/A**, African-American: **N/A**, Hispanic-American: **N/A**, White: **N/A**, International: **N/A**, Unknown: **N/A**

ACADEMIC PROGRAMS

The school's curriculum frequently gives first-year students substantial contact with patients.

There are opportunities for first- or second-year students to work in community health clinics.

Program offerings: AIDS, drug/alcohol abuse, family medicine, geriatrics, internal medicine, pediatrics, rural medicine, women's health

Joint degrees awarded: M.D./Ph.D.

Total National Institutes of Health (NIH) grants awarded to the medical school and affiliated hospitals: **$210.1 million**

CURRICULUM
(TEXT PROVIDED BY SCHOOL):

UNC School of Medicine is committed to graduating a diverse body of physicians dedicated to public service and leadership in research and patient care. A new curriculum provides an integrated, self-directed approach to learning, with opportunities to explore areas of professional interest, community service, and research. Over 95 percent of students match to one of their three choices of residencies.

FACULTY PROFILE (FALL 2007)

Total teaching faculty: 1,320 **(full-time)**, 139 **(part-time)**

Of full-time faculty, those teaching in basic sciences: **18%**; in clinical programs: **82%**

Of part-time faculty, those teaching in basic sciences: **7%**; in clinical programs: **93%**

Full-time faculty/student ratio: **1.8**

SUPPORT SERVICES

The school offers students these services for dealing with stress: peer counseling, professional counseling, support groups.

RESIDENCY PROFILE

Most popular residency and specialty programs chosen by the 2006 and 2007 M.D. graduating classes: anesthesiology, emergency medicine, family practice, internal medicine, obstetrics and gynecology, pediatrics, psychiatry, surgery–general, urology.

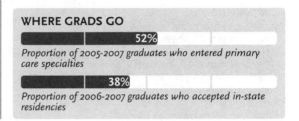

WHERE GRADS GO

52%

Proportion of 2005-2007 graduates who entered primary care specialties

38%

Proportion of 2006-2007 graduates who accepted in-state residencies

University of North Dakota

■ 501 N. Columbia Road, Stop 9037,
   Grand Forks, ND 58202-9037
■ Public
■ Year Founded: 1905
■ Tuition, 2007-2008: In-state: $22,873; Out-of-state: $41,120
■ Enrollment 2007-2008 academic year: 248
■ Website: http://www.med.und.nodak.edu
■ Specialty ranking: family medicine: 27, rural medicine: 5

3.70	AVERAGE GPA, ENTERING CLASS FALL 2007
9.0	AVERAGE MCAT, ENTERING CLASS FALL 2007
28.6%	ACCEPTANCE RATE, ENTERING CLASS FALL 2007
Unranked	2009 U.S. NEWS MEDICAL SCHOOL RANKING (RESEARCH)
Unranked	2009 U.S. NEWS MEDICAL SCHOOL RANKING (PRIMARY CARE)

ADMISSIONS

Admissions phone number: **(701) 777-4221**
Admissions email address: **jdheit@medicine.nodak.edu**
Application website:
   http://www.med.und.nodak.edu/admissions.html
Acceptance rate: **28.6%**
In-state acceptance rate: **41.5%**
Out-of-state acceptance rate: **17.0%**
Minority acceptance rate: **43.3%**
International acceptance rate: **N/A**

Fall 2007 applications and acceptees

	Applied	Interviewed	Accepted	Enrolled
Total:	301	149	86	62
In-state:	142	100	59	46
Out-of-state:	159	49	27	16

Profile of admitted students

Average undergraduate grade point average: **3.70**
MCAT averages (scale: 1-15; writing test: J-T):
   Composite score: **9.0**
   Verbal reasoning score: **8.9**, Physical sciences score: **8.8**,
   Biological sciences score: **9.4**, Writing score: **N**
Proportion with undergraduate majors in: Biological
   sciences: **50%**, Physical sciences: **16%**, Non-sciences:
   21%, Other health professions: **7%**, Mixed disciplines
   and other: **7%**
Percentage of students not coming directly from college
   after graduation: **27%**

Dates and details

The American Medical College Application Service
   (AMCAS) application is not accepted.
School does not ask for a school-specific application as part
   of the admissions process.
Oldest MCAT considered for Fall 2009 entry: **2005**
Earliest application date for the 2009-2010 first-year class:
   7/1
Latest application date: **11/1**
Acceptance dates for regular application for the class
   entering in fall 2009:

Earliest: **January 15, 2009**
Latest: **August 2, 2009**
The school considers requests for deferred entrance.
Starting month for the class entering in 2009–2010:
   August
The school doesn't have an Early Decision Plan (EDP).
A personal interview is required for admission.

Undergraduate coursework required

Medical school requires undergraduate work in these subjects: biology/zoology, English, organic chemistry, inorganic
(general) chemistry, physics, mathematics, behavioral science, general chemistry.

ADMISSIONS POLICY

(TEXT PROVIDED BY SCHOOL):
North Dakota residents and applicants certified by the
Western Interstate Commission for Higher Education
receive preference. Residents of Minnesota and others with
a North Dakota connection also are considered. Enrolled
members of federally recognized tribes, regardless of state
of residency, may apply through the Indians Into Medicine
program. Applicants who have completed an undergraduate
degree and are broadly educated in the sciences and
humanities are preferred.

COSTS AND FINANCIAL AID

Financial aid phone number: **(701) 777-2849**
Tuition, 2007-2008 academic year: **In-state: $22,873; Out-
of-state: $41,120**
Room and board: **$9,104**
Percentage of students receiving financial aid in 2007-08:
   97%
Percentage of students receiving: Loans: **91%**,
   Grants/scholarships: **62%**, Work-study aid: **0%**
Average medical school debt for the Class of 2006:
   $129,975

STUDENT BODY

Fall 2007 full-time enrollment: **248**

Men: **54%**, Women: **46%**, In-state: **82%**, Minorities: **13%**, American Indian: **10.5%**, Asian-American: **2.4%**, African-American: **0.0%**, Hispanic-American: **0.4%**, White: **86.7%**, International: **0.0%**, Unknown: **0.0%**

ACADEMIC PROGRAMS

The school's curriculum frequently gives first-year students substantial contact with patients.

There aren't opportunities for first- or second-year students to work in community health clinics.

Program offerings: AIDS, drug/alcohol abuse, family medicine, geriatrics, internal medicine, pediatrics, rural medicine, women's health

Joint degrees awarded: M.D./Ph.D., M.D./M.P.H., M.D./M.S.

Total National Institutes of Health (NIH) grants awarded to the medical school and affiliated hospitals: **$10.3 million**

CURRICULUM

(TEXT PROVIDED BY SCHOOL):

UNDSMHS is a university-based, community-integrated medical education program. The curriculum for Years 1 and 2 is organized in eight 10-week blocks, using an interdisciplinary case-based and organ systems approach. Years 3 and 4 consist of core clerkships, acting internships, and electives. A limited number of students may complete 28 weeks of Year 3 in a rural community through the ROME Program.

FACULTY PROFILE (FALL 2007)

Total teaching faculty: **137 (full-time)**, **1,347 (part-time)**

Of full-time faculty, those teaching in basic sciences: **53%**; in clinical programs: **47%**

Of part-time faculty, those teaching in basic sciences: **21%**; in clinical programs: **79%**

Full-time faculty/student ratio: **0.6**

SUPPORT SERVICES

The school offers students these services for dealing with stress: expanded-hour gym access, peer counseling, professional counseling, religious support, support groups.

RESIDENCY PROFILE

Most popular residency and specialty programs chosen by the 2006 and 2007 M.D. graduating classes: emergency medicine, family practice, internal medicine, neurology, obstetrics and gynecology, orthopaedic surgery, pathology–anatomic and clinical, pediatrics, radiology–diagnostic, surgery–general.

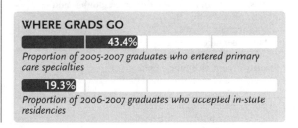

WHERE GRADS GO

43.4%

Proportion of 2005-2007 graduates who entered primary care specialties

19.3%

Proportion of 2006-2007 graduates who accepted in-state residencies

University of Oklahoma

- PO Box 26901, BMSB 357, Oklahoma City, OK 73190
- Public
- **Year Founded:** 1900
- **Tuition, 2007-2008:** In-state: $20,450; Out-of-state: $42,535
- **Enrollment 2007-2008 academic year:** 623
- **Website:** http://www.medicine.ouhsc.edu
- **Specialty ranking:** N/A

3.69	AVERAGE GPA, ENTERING CLASS FALL 2007
9.7	AVERAGE MCAT, ENTERING CLASS FALL 2007
17.2%	ACCEPTANCE RATE, ENTERING CLASS FALL 2007
Unranked	2009 U.S. NEWS MEDICAL SCHOOL RANKING (RESEARCH)
Unranked	2009 U.S. NEWS MEDICAL SCHOOL RANKING (PRIMARY CARE)

ADMISSIONS
Admissions phone number: **(405) 271-2331**
Admissions email address: **adminmed@ouhsc.edu**
Application website: **http://www.aamc.org**
Acceptance rate: **17.2%**
In-state acceptance rate: **43.3%**
Out-of-state acceptance rate: **5.2%**
Minority acceptance rate: **14.5%**
International acceptance rate: **N/A**

Fall 2007 applications and acceptees
	Applied	Interviewed	Accepted	Enrolled
Total:	1,288	299	221	164
In-state:	404	237	175	145
Out-of-state:	884	62	46	19

Profile of admitted students
Average undergraduate grade point average: **3.69**
MCAT averages (scale: 1-15; writing test: J-T):
   Composite score: **9.7**
   Verbal reasoning score: **9.9**, Physical sciences score: **9.5**, Biological sciences score: **9.8**, Writing score: **O**
Proportion with undergraduate majors in: Biological sciences: **62%**, Physical sciences: **18%**, Non-sciences: **12%**, Other health professions: **4%**, Mixed disciplines and other: **4%**
Percentage of students not coming directly from college after graduation: **1%**

Dates and details
The American Medical College Application Service (AMCAS) application is accepted.
School does not ask for a school-specific application as part of the admissions process.
Oldest MCAT considered for Fall 2009 entry: **2007**
Earliest application date for the 2009-2010 first-year class: **6/1**
Latest application date: **10/15**
Acceptance dates for regular application for the class entering in fall 2009:
   Earliest: **October 16, 2008**

Latest: **March 1, 2009**
The school considers requests for deferred entrance.
Starting month for the class entering in 2009–2010:
   August
The school doesn't have an Early Decision Plan (EDP).
A personal interview is required for admission.

Undergraduate coursework required
Medical school requires undergraduate work in these subjects: biology/zoology, English, organic chemistry, inorganic (general) chemistry, physics, molecular and cell biology, humanities, social sciences.

ADMISSIONS POLICY
(TEXT PROVIDED BY SCHOOL):
Acceptance is based on grade-point average, letters of evaluation, and personal interview. Emphasis is placed on self-awareness, self-discipline, empathy, personal competence, social competence, and overall evaluation of character. Nonresidents can occupy 15 percent of class.
The University of Oklahoma College of Medicine does not discriminate on the basis of race, sex, creed, national origin, age, or handicap.

COSTS AND FINANCIAL AID
Financial aid phone number: **(405) 271-2118**
Tuition, 2007-2008 academic year: **In-state: $20,450; Out-of-state: $42,535**
Room and board: **$20,116**
Percentage of students receiving financial aid in 2007-08: **94%**
Percentage of students receiving: Loans: **90%**, Grants/scholarships: **53%**, Work-study aid: **0%**
Average medical school debt for the Class of 2006: **$120,000**

STUDENT BODY
Fall 2007 full-time enrollment: **623**
Men: **60%**, Women: **40%**, In-state: **92%**, Minorities: **25%**, American Indian: **8.7%**, Asian-American: **14.6%**,

African-American: **1.6%**, Hispanic-American: **0.3%**, White: **70.3%**, International: **0.0%**, Unknown: **4.5%**

ACADEMIC PROGRAMS

The school's curriculum frequently gives first-year students substantial contact with patients.

There are opportunities for first- or second-year students to work in community health clinics.

Program offerings: AIDS, drug/alcohol abuse, family medicine, geriatrics, internal medicine, pediatrics, rural medicine, women's health

Joint degrees awarded: M.D./Ph.D., M.D./M.P.H., M.D./M.S., M.D./M.H.A.

Total National Institutes of Health (NIH) grants awarded to the medical school and affiliated hospitals: **$43.4 million**

CURRICULUM

(TEXT PROVIDED BY SCHOOL):

The curriculum consists of two years of basic sciences and two of clinical sciences. The first two years are complemented by a Web-based curriculum. First-year courses provide a strong basic science foundation, and second-year classes form a bridge leading into the clinical portion of the curriculum. The curriculum provides early exposure to patients. The clinical program provides training at two sites.

FACULTY PROFILE (FALL 2007)

Total teaching faculty: **774 (full-time)**, **205 (part-time)**

Of full-time faculty, those teaching in basic sciences: **11%**; in clinical programs: **89%**

Of part-time faculty, those teaching in basic sciences: **1%**; in clinical programs: **99%**

Full-time faculty/student ratio: **1.2**

SUPPORT SERVICES

The school offers students these services for dealing with stress: professional counseling, support groups.

RESIDENCY PROFILE

Most popular residency and specialty programs chosen by the 2006 and 2007 M.D. graduating classes: anesthesiology, family practice, internal medicine, pediatrics, surgery–general, internal medicine/pediatrics.

WHERE GRADS GO

38.4%

Proportion of 2005-2007 graduates who entered primary care specialties

42.7%

Proportion of 2006-2007 graduates who accepted in-state residencies

University of Pennsylvania

- 237 John Morgan Building, 3620 Hamilton Walk, Philadelphia, PA 19104-6055
- Private
- **Year Founded:** 1765
- **Tuition, 2007-2008:** $42,706
- **Enrollment 2007-2008 academic year:** 585
- **Website:** http://www.med.upenn.edu
- **Specialty ranking:** AIDS: 11, drug/alcohol abuse: 6, family medicine: 27, geriatrics: 12, internal medicine: 4, pediatrics: 2, women's health: 3

3.79 AVERAGE GPA, ENTERING CLASS FALL 2007

11.6 AVERAGE MCAT, ENTERING CLASS FALL 2007

4.2% ACCEPTANCE RATE, ENTERING CLASS FALL 2007

4 2009 U.S. NEWS MEDICAL SCHOOL RANKING (RESEARCH)

31 2009 U.S. NEWS MEDICAL SCHOOL RANKING (PRIMARY CARE)

ADMISSIONS

Admissions phone number: (215) 898-8001
Admissions email address: admiss@mail.med.upenn.edu
Application website:
   http://www.med.upenn.edu/admiss/applications.html
Acceptance rate: 4.2%
In-state acceptance rate: 1.0%
Out-of-state acceptance rate: 32.0%
Minority acceptance rate: 4.1%
International acceptance rate: 2.7%

Fall 2007 applications and acceptees

	Applied	Interviewed	Accepted	Enrolled
Total:	5,532	938	234	153
In-state:	4,951	798	48	35
Out-of-state:	581	140	186	118

Profile of admitted students

Average undergraduate grade point average: 3.79
MCAT averages (scale: 1-15; writing test: J-T):
   Composite score: 11.6
   Verbal reasoning score: 10.8, Physical sciences score: 12.0, Biological sciences score: 12.0, Writing score: Q
Proportion with undergraduate majors in: Biological sciences: 51%, Physical sciences: 13%, Non-sciences: 28%, Other health professions: 1%, Mixed disciplines and other: 7%
Percentage of students not coming directly from college after graduation: 50%

Dates and details

The American Medical College Application Service (AMCAS) application is accepted.
School asks for a school-specific application as part of the admissions process.
Oldest MCAT considered for Fall 2009 entry: 2005
Earliest application date for the 2009-2010 first-year class: 6/1
Latest application date: 10/15
Acceptance dates for regular application for the class entering in fall 2009:

Earliest: **March 30, 2009**
Latest: **August 17, 2009**
The school considers requests for deferred entrance.
Starting month for the class entering in 2009-2010: **August**
The school has an Early Decision Plan (EDP).
A personal interview is required for admission.

Undergraduate coursework required

Medical school requires undergraduate work in these subjects: biology, English, organic chemistry, physics, mathematics, general chemistry.

ADMISSIONS POLICY

(TEXT PROVIDED BY SCHOOL):

Selection factors include academic excellence, out-of-class activities, and life experience. Community service, research, letters of recommendation, and leadership are valued. Personal qualities of maturity, integrity, ability to work with others, and humanitarian concerns are sought. Diversity is a part of the school mission. Further information can be obtained at the website.

COSTS AND FINANCIAL AID

Financial aid phone number: (215) 573-3423
Tuition, 2007-2008 academic year: $42,706
Room and board: $17,260
Percentage of students receiving financial aid in 2007-08: 87%
Percentage of students receiving: Loans: 69%, Grants/scholarships: 60%, Work-study aid: 2%
Average medical school debt for the Class of 2006: $116,700

STUDENT BODY

Fall 2007 full-time enrollment: 585
Men: 50%, Women: 50%, In-state: 38%, Minorities: 34%, American Indian: 0.7%, Asian-American: 15.9%, African-American: 9.2%, Hispanic-American: 6.3%, White: 62.9%, International: 1.4%, Unknown: 3.6%

ACADEMIC PROGRAMS

The school's curriculum frequently gives first-year students substantial contact with patients.

There are opportunities for first- or second-year students to work in community health clinics.

Program offerings: AIDS, drug/alcohol abuse, family medicine, geriatrics, internal medicine, pediatrics, rural medicine, women's health

Joint degrees awarded: M.D./Ph.D., M.D./M.B.A., M.D./M.P.H., M.D./J.D., M.D./M.S.

Total National Institutes of Health (NIH) grants awarded to the medical school and affiliated hospitals: **$486.8 million**

CURRICULUM

(TEXT PROVIDED BY SCHOOL):

The curriculum is organized into six modules. Module 1: Core Principles, August to December Year 1. Module 2: Integrative Systems and Diseases, January Year 1 to December Year 2. Module 3: Technology and Practice of Medicine, August Year 1 to December Year 2. Module 4: Required clinical clerkships, January Year 2 to December Year 3. Module 5: Electives and scholarly pursuit, January Year 3 to May Year 4. Module 6: Professionalism and Humanism, August Year 1 to May Year 4.

FACULTY PROFILE (FALL 2007)

Total teaching faculty: **2,158 (full-time), 865 (part-time)**

Of full-time faculty, those teaching in basic sciences: **9%;** in clinical programs: **91%**

Of part-time faculty, those teaching in basic sciences: **10%;** in clinical programs: **90%**

Full-time faculty/student ratio: **3.7**

SUPPORT SERVICES

The school offers students these services for dealing with stress: peer counseling, professional counseling, support groups.

RESIDENCY PROFILE

Most popular residency and specialty programs chosen by the 2006 and 2007 M.D. graduating classes: anesthesiology, dermatology, emergency medicine, family practice, internal medicine, ophthalmology, pediatrics, psychiatry, radiology–diagnostic.

WHERE GRADS GO

37%

Proportion of 2005-2007 graduates who entered primary care specialties

35.5%

Proportion of 2006-2007 graduates who accepted in-state residencies

University of Pittsburgh

- 401 Scaife Hall, Pittsburgh, PA 15261
- Public
- **Year Founded:** 1886
- **Tuition, 2007-2008:** In-state: $35,990; Out-of-state: $39,856
- **Enrollment 2007-2008 academic year:** 582
- **Website:** http://www.medschool.pitt.edu
- **Specialty ranking:** AIDS: 20, geriatrics: 11, internal medicine: 21, pediatrics: 16, women's health: 4

3.70	AVERAGE GPA, ENTERING CLASS FALL 2007
11.4	AVERAGE MCAT, ENTERING CLASS FALL 2007
7.9%	ACCEPTANCE RATE, ENTERING CLASS FALL 2007
14	2009 U.S. NEWS MEDICAL SCHOOL RANKING (RESEARCH)
20	2009 U.S. NEWS MEDICAL SCHOOL RANKING (PRIMARY CARE)

ADMISSIONS

Admissions phone number: **(412) 648-9891**
Admissions email address:
 admissions@medschool.pitt.edu
Application website: **https://admissions.medschool.pitt.edu**
Acceptance rate: **7.9%**
In-state acceptance rate: **10.6%**
Out-of-state acceptance rate: **7.4%**
Minority acceptance rate: **8.6%**
International acceptance rate: **0.0%**

Fall 2007 applications and acceptees

	Applied	Interviewed	Accepted	Enrolled
Total:	5,616	1,229	443	146
In-state:	841	220	89	47
Out-of-state:	4,775	1,009	354	99

Profile of admitted students

Average undergraduate grade point average: **3.70**
MCAT averages (scale: 1-15; writing test: J-T):
 Composite score: **11.4**
 Verbal reasoning score: **10.9**, Physical sciences score: **11.5**, Biological sciences score: **11.8**, Writing score: **P**
Proportion with undergraduate majors in: Biological sciences: **45%**, Physical sciences: **24%**, Non-sciences: **22%**, Other health professions: **0%**, Mixed disciplines and other: **9%**
Percentage of students not coming directly from college after graduation: **59%**

Dates and details

The American Medical College Application Service (AMCAS) application is accepted.
School asks for a school-specific application as part of the admissions process.
Oldest MCAT considered for Fall 2009 entry: **2005**
Earliest application date for the 2009-2010 first-year class: **6/1**
Latest application date: **11/15**
Acceptance dates for regular application for the class entering in fall 2009:

Earliest: **October 15, 2008**
Latest: **August 18, 2009**
The school considers requests for deferred entrance.
Starting month for the class entering in 2009–2010:
 August
The school doesn't have an Early Decision Plan (EDP).
A personal interview is required for admission.

Undergraduate coursework required

Medical school requires undergraduate work in these subjects: biology, English, organic chemistry, inorganic (general) chemistry, physics, general chemistry.

ADMISSIONS POLICY
(TEXT PROVIDED BY SCHOOL):

The University of Pittsburgh School of Medicine is an American Medical College Application Service school. All applicants may complete the secondary application. The school admits on a rolling basis. Pennsylvania residency has minimal effect on admission. The committee seeks to admit a diverse, intellectually talented student body. Applicants should have medical exposure, and extracurricular activities are weighted heavily. Applicants interview with students and faculty.

COSTS AND FINANCIAL AID

Financial aid phone number: **(412) 648-9891**
Tuition, 2007-2008 academic year: **In-state: $35,990; Out-of-state: $39,856**
Room and board: **$14,500**
Percentage of students receiving financial aid in 2007-08: **87%**
Percentage of students receiving: Loans: **72%**, Grants/scholarships: **60%**, Work-study aid: **0%**
Average medical school debt for the Class of 2006: **$135,254**

STUDENT BODY

Fall 2007 full-time enrollment: **582**
Men: **53%**, Women: **47%**, In-state: **30%**, Minorities: **48%**, American Indian: **0.3%**, Asian-American: **33.0%**,

African-American: **9.6%**, Hispanic-American: **4.8%**, White: **51.9%**, International: **0.0%**, Unknown: **0.3%**

ACADEMIC PROGRAMS

The school's curriculum frequently gives first-year students substantial contact with patients.

There are opportunities for first- or second-year students to work in community health clinics.

Program offerings: AIDS, drug/alcohol abuse, family medicine, geriatrics, internal medicine, pediatrics, rural medicine, women's health

Joint degrees awarded: M.D./Ph.D., M.D./M.P.H., M.D./M.A.

Total National Institutes of Health (NIH) grants awarded to the medical school and affiliated hospitals: **$358.3 million**

CURRICULUM

(TEXT PROVIDED BY SCHOOL):

The school seeks to train tomorrow's physician-scientists, academic leaders, and finest practicing physicians. To accomplish these goals, the curriculum combines a strong foundation in basic science with early introduction to patients, small-group learning, and an emphasis on critical thinking and problem solving. Each student participates in a mentored scholarly project.

FACULTY PROFILE (FALL 2007)

Total teaching faculty: **1,981 (full-time)**, **67 (part-time)**

Of full-time faculty, those teaching in basic sciences: **10%**; in clinical programs: **90%**

Of part-time faculty, those teaching in basic sciences: **4%**; in clinical programs: **96%**

Full-time faculty/student ratio: **3.4**

SUPPORT SERVICES

The school offers students these services for dealing with stress: expanded-hour gym access, peer counseling, professional counseling, support groups.

RESIDENCY PROFILE

Most popular residency and specialty programs chosen by the 2006 and 2007 M.D. graduating classes: anesthesiology, emergency medicine, family practice, internal medicine, obstetrics and gynecology, orthopaedic surgery, pediatrics, radiology–diagnostic, surgery–general.

WHERE GRADS GO

38.7%

Proportion of 2005-2007 graduates who entered primary care specialties

57%

Proportion of 2006-2007 graduates who accepted in-state residencies

University of Rochester

- 601 Elmwood Avenue, Box 706, Rochester, NY 14642
- Private
- Year Founded: 1925
- Tuition, 2007-2008: $40,384
- Enrollment 2007-2008 academic year: 414
- Website: http://www.urmc.rochester.edu/smd/
- Specialty ranking: geriatrics: 19, pediatrics: 19

3.63 AVERAGE GPA, ENTERING CLASS FALL 2007

10.6 AVERAGE MCAT, ENTERING CLASS FALL 2007

7.6% ACCEPTANCE RATE, ENTERING CLASS FALL 2007

36 2009 U.S. NEWS MEDICAL SCHOOL RANKING (RESEARCH)

19 2009 U.S. NEWS MEDICAL SCHOOL RANKING (PRIMARY CARE)

ADMISSIONS

Admissions phone number: (585) 275-4542
Admissions email address:
  mdadmish@urmc.rochester.edu
Application website:
  https://admissions.urmc.rochester.edu/studentlogin.cfm
Acceptance rate: **7.6%**
In-state acceptance rate: **10.9%**
Out-of-state acceptance rate: **6.4%**
Minority acceptance rate: **6.9%**
International acceptance rate: **N/A**

Fall 2007 applications and acceptees

	Applied	Interviewed	Accepted	Enrolled
Total:	3,701	724	282	101
In-state:	982	255	107	46
Out-of-state:	2,719	469	175	55

Profile of admitted students

Average undergraduate grade point average: **3.63**
MCAT averages (scale: 1-15; writing test: J-T):
  Composite score: **10.6**
  Verbal reasoning score: **10.0**, Physical sciences score: **10.6**, Biological sciences score: **11.2**, Writing score: **Q**
Proportion with undergraduate majors in: Biological sciences: **43%**, Physical sciences: **18%**, Non-sciences: **8%**, Other health professions: **1%**, Mixed disciplines and other: **30%**
Percentage of students not coming directly from college after graduation: **59%**

Dates and details

The American Medical College Application Service (AMCAS) application is accepted.
School asks for a school-specific application as part of the admissions process.
Oldest MCAT considered for Fall 2009 entry: **2005**
Earliest application date for the 2009-2010 first-year class: **6/1**
Latest application date: **10/15**

Acceptance dates for regular application for the class entering in fall 2009:
  Earliest: **October 15, 2008**
  Latest: **October 8, 2009**
The school considers requests for deferred entrance.
Starting month for the class entering in 2009–2010:
  August
The school doesn't have an Early Decision Plan (EDP).
A personal interview is required for admission.

Undergraduate coursework required

Medical school requires undergraduate work in these subjects: biology, biology/zoology, English, organic chemistry, inorganic (general) chemistry, physics, humanities, demonstration of writing skills, social sciences, general chemistry.

ADMISSIONS POLICY

(TEXT PROVIDED BY SCHOOL):
A strong academic record and good scores on the MCAT are necessary but not sufficient criteria for admission. In addition, the Admissions Committee looks for evidence of scholarship, leadership, community service, integrity, maturity, and excellent interpersonal skills. Rochester seeks students who value human diversity, exhibit a love of learning, and appreciate the science and art of medicine.

COSTS AND FINANCIAL AID

Financial aid phone number: (585) 275-4523
Tuition, 2007-2008 academic year: **$40,384**
Room and board: **$16,000**
Percentage of students receiving financial aid in 2007-08: **90%**
Percentage of students receiving: Loans: **83%**, Grants/scholarships: **45%**, Work-study aid: **22%**
Average medical school debt for the Class of 2006: **$131,881**

STUDENT BODY

Fall 2007 full-time enrollment: **414**
Men: **48%**, Women: **52%**, In-state: **43%**, Minorities: **33%**,

American Indian: **0.5%**, Asian-American: **21.3%**, African-American: **8.2%**, Hispanic-American: **2.9%**, White: **64.5%**, International: **0.0%**, Unknown: **2.7%**

ACADEMIC PROGRAMS

The school's curriculum occasionally gives first-year students substantial contact with patients.

There are opportunities for first- or second-year students to work in community health clinics.

Program offerings: AIDS, drug/alcohol abuse, family medicine, geriatrics, internal medicine, pediatrics, rural medicine, women's health

Joint degrees awarded: M.D./Ph.D., M.D./M.B.A., M.D./M.P.H., M.D./M.S.

Total National Institutes of Health (NIH) grants awarded to the medical school and affiliated hospitals: **$162.0 million**

CURRICULUM

(TEXT PROVIDED BY SCHOOL):

The SMD Double Helix Curriculum weaves together the basic science and clinical strands of medical education through all four years, with enhanced teaching of the scientific principles of biomedical, clinical, and translational research, of information management and data analytic skills, and of the social aspects of health and illness.

FACULTY PROFILE (FALL 2007)

Total teaching faculty: **1,420 (full-time)**, **155 (part-time)**

Of full-time faculty, those teaching in basic sciences: **16%**; in clinical programs: **84%**

Of part-time faculty, those teaching in basic sciences: **10%**; in clinical programs: **90%**

Full-time faculty/student ratio: **3.4**

SUPPORT SERVICES

The school offers students these services for dealing with stress: expanded-hour gym access, peer counseling, professional counseling, religious support, support groups.

RESIDENCY PROFILE

Most popular residency and specialty programs chosen by the 2006 and 2007 M.D. graduating classes: anesthesiology, emergency medicine, internal medicine, neurology, obstetrics and gynecology, orthopaedic surgery, pediatrics, psychiatry, surgery–general.

WHERE GRADS GO

35.8%

Proportion of 2005-2007 graduates who entered primary care specialties

33.2%

Proportion of 2006-2007 graduates who accepted in-state residencies

University of South Carolina

- 311 Garners Ferry Road, Columbia, SC 29208
- Public
- Year Founded: 1974
- Tuition, 2007-2008: In-state: $23,094; Out-of-state: $60,410
- Enrollment 2007-2008 academic year: 315
- Website: http://www.med.sc.edu
- Specialty ranking: N/A

3.66 AVERAGE GPA, ENTERING CLASS FALL 2007

9.5 AVERAGE MCAT, ENTERING CLASS FALL 2007

7.5% ACCEPTANCE RATE, ENTERING CLASS FALL 2007

Unranked 2009 U.S. NEWS MEDICAL SCHOOL RANKING (RESEARCH)

Unranked 2009 U.S. NEWS MEDICAL SCHOOL RANKING (PRIMARY CARE)

ADMISSIONS

Admissions phone number: **(803) 733-3325**
Admissions email address: **jeanette@gw.sc.edu**
Application website: **N/A**
Acceptance rate: **7.5%**
In-state acceptance rate: **26.8%**
Out-of-state acceptance rate: **2.0%**
Minority acceptance rate: **6.4%**
International acceptance rate: **N/A**

Fall 2007 applications and acceptees

	Applied	Interviewed	Accepted	Enrolled
Total:	1,940	336	146	84
In-state:	433	237	116	68
Out-of-state:	1,507	99	30	16

Profile of admitted students

Average undergraduate grade point average: **3.66**
MCAT averages (scale: 1-15; writing test: J-T):
  Composite score: **9.5**
  Verbal reasoning score: **9.7**, Physical sciences score: **8.9**,
  Biological sciences score: **9.8**, Writing score: **O**
Proportion with undergraduate majors in: Biological sciences: **60%**, Physical sciences: **20%**, Non-sciences: **4%**, Other health professions: **5%**, Mixed disciplines and other: **12%**
Percentage of students not coming directly from college after graduation: **11%**

Dates and details

The American Medical College Application Service (AMCAS) application is accepted.
School asks for a school-specific application as part of the admissions process.
Oldest MCAT considered for Fall 2009 entry: **2004**
Earliest application date for the 2009-2010 first-year class: **6/1**
Latest application date: **12/1**
Acceptance dates for regular application for the class entering in fall 2009:
  Earliest: **October 15, 2008**

Latest: **August 3, 2009**
The school considers requests for deferred entrance.
Starting month for the class entering in 2009–2010:
  August
The school has an Early Decision Plan (EDP).
A personal interview is required for admission.

Undergraduate coursework required

Medical school requires undergraduate work in these subjects: biology/zoology, English, organic chemistry, inorganic (general) chemistry.

ADMISSIONS POLICY

(TEXT PROVIDED BY SCHOOL):
The Admissions Committee is composed of members of the basic science and clinical faculty of the School of Medicine and medical students. All aspects of an application are considered. The selection criteria are weighted one third each for (1) MCAT scores and grade-point average, (2) letters of recommendation and work or volunteer experiences, (3)interviews and personal attributes. Preference is given to South Carolina residents for admissions.

COSTS AND FINANCIAL AID

Financial aid phone number: **(803) 733-3135**
Tuition, 2007-2008 academic year: **In-state: $23,094; Out-of-state: $60,410**
Room and board: **$12,210**
Percentage of students receiving financial aid in 2007-08: **93%**
Percentage of students receiving: Loans: **83%**, Grants/scholarships: **42%**, Work-study aid: **0%**
Average medical school debt for the Class of 2006: **$108,000**

STUDENT BODY

Fall 2007 full-time enrollment: **315**
Men: **53%**, Women: **47%**, In-state: **94%**, Minorities: **17%**, American Indian: **0.0%**, Asian-American: **10.8%**, African-American: **5.4%**, Hispanic-American: **0.3%**, White: **83.5%**, International: **0.0%**, Unknown: **0.0%**

ACADEMIC PROGRAMS

The school's curriculum occasionally gives first-year students substantial contact with patients.

There are opportunities for first- or second-year students to work in community health clinics.

Program offerings: family medicine, geriatrics, internal medicine, pediatrics, rural medicine

Joint degrees awarded: M.D./Ph.D., M.D./M.P.H.

Total National Institutes of Health (NIH) grants awarded to the medical school and affiliated hospitals: **$8.5 million**

CURRICULUM

(TEXT PROVIDED BY SCHOOL):

In the first year, students gain an understanding of normal structure and function. In the second year, emphasis is placed on Microbiology, Pathology, and general therapeutic principles. The third year includes eight-week clerkships in Medicine, Surgery, Obstetrics/Gynecology, Psychiatry, Family Medicine, and Pediatrics. The fourth year includes required four-week rotations in Medicine, Surgery, Neurology, and an acting internship.

FACULTY PROFILE (FALL 2007)

Total teaching faculty: **239 (full-time)**, **27 (part-time)**

Of full-time faculty, those teaching in basic sciences: **31%**; in clinical programs: **69%**

Of part-time faculty, those teaching in basic sciences: **19%**; in clinical programs: **81%**

Full-time faculty/student ratio: **0.8**

SUPPORT SERVICES

The school offers students these services for dealing with stress: expanded-hour gym access, peer counseling, professional counseling.

RESIDENCY PROFILE

Most popular residency and specialty programs chosen by the 2006 and 2007 M.D. graduating classes: anesthesiology, emergency medicine, family practice, internal medicine, obstetrics and gynecology, pathology–anatomic and clinical, pediatrics, psychiatry, radiology–diagnostic, surgery–general.

WHERE GRADS GO

46.8%

Proportion of 2005-2007 graduates who entered primary care specialties

41.7%

Proportion of 2006-2007 graduates who accepted in-state residencies

University of South Dakota

SANFORD

- 1400 W. 22nd Street, Sioux Falls, SD 57105
- Public
- Year Founded: 1907
- Tuition, 2007-2008: In-state: $18,436; Out-of-state: $38,409
- Enrollment 2007-2008 academic year: 210
- Website: http://www.usd.edu/med/md
- Specialty ranking: family medicine: 13, rural medicine: 6

3.77 AVERAGE GPA, ENTERING CLASS FALL 2007

9.6 AVERAGE MCAT, ENTERING CLASS FALL 2007

10.1% ACCEPTANCE RATE, ENTERING CLASS FALL 2007

Unranked 2009 U.S. NEWS MEDICAL SCHOOL RANKING (RESEARCH)

Unranked 2009 U.S. NEWS MEDICAL SCHOOL RANKING (PRIMARY CARE)

ADMISSIONS

Admissions phone number: **(605) 677-6886**
Admissions email address: **usdsmsa@usd.edu**
Application website: **N/A**
Acceptance rate: **10.1%**
In-state acceptance rate: **47.5%**
Out-of-state acceptance rate: **1.5%**
Minority acceptance rate: **1.1%**
International acceptance rate: **0.0%**

Fall 2007 applications and acceptees

	Applied	Interviewed	Accepted	Enrolled
Total:	744	169	75	54
In-state:	139	129	66	50
Out-of-state:	605	40	9	4

Profile of admitted students

Average undergraduate grade point average: **3.77**
MCAT averages (scale: 1-15; writing test: J-T):
    Composite score: **9.6**
    Verbal reasoning score: **9.6**, Physical sciences score: **9.4**, Biological sciences score: **9.9**, Writing score: **O**
Proportion with undergraduate majors in: Biological sciences: **56%**, Physical sciences: **17%**, Non-sciences: **9%**, Other health professions: **0%**, Mixed disciplines and other: **18%**
Percentage of students not coming directly from college after graduation: **31%**

Dates and details

The American Medical College Application Service (AMCAS) application is accepted.
School asks for a school-specific application as part of the admissions process.
Oldest MCAT considered for Fall 2009 entry: **2006**
Earliest application date for the 2009-2010 first-year class: **6/1**
Latest application date: **11/15**
Acceptance dates for regular application for the class entering in fall 2009:
    Earliest: **November 18, 2008**

Latest: **March 27, 2009**
The school considers requests for deferred entrance.
Starting month for the class entering in 2009–2010:
    August
The school doesn't have an Early Decision Plan (EDP).
A personal interview is required for admission.

Undergraduate coursework required

Medical school requires undergraduate work in these subjects: biology, organic chemistry, inorganic (general) chemistry, physics, mathematics.

ADMISSIONS POLICY

(TEXT PROVIDED BY SCHOOL):
All accepted applicants are either residents of South Dakota or have very strong ties to the state. All South Dakota resident applicants are granted an interview. Factors considered are academic strength, interest in Family Medicine, interest in practice in South Dakota, motivation, interpersonal skills, a record of service to others and/or leadership experiences, and a demonstrated beginning understanding of the career.

COSTS AND FINANCIAL AID

Financial aid phone number: **(605) 677-5112**
Tuition, 2007-2008 academic year: **In-state: $18,436; Out-of-state: $38,409**
Room and board: **$20,030**
Percentage of students receiving financial aid in 2007-08: **98%**
Percentage of students receiving: Loans: **92%**, Grants/scholarships: **82%**, Work-study aid: **2%**
Average medical school debt for the Class of 2006: **$118,438**

STUDENT BODY

Fall 2007 full-time enrollment: **210**
Men: **52%**, Women: **48%**, In-state: **98%**, Minorities: **4%**, American Indian: **1.9%**, Asian-American: **1.9%**, African-American: **0.0%**, Hispanic-American: **0.0%**, White: **96.2%**, International: **0.0%**, Unknown: **0.0%**

ACADEMIC PROGRAMS

The school's curriculum occasionally gives first-year students substantial contact with patients.

There are opportunities for first- or second-year students to work in community health clinics.

Program offerings: drug/alcohol abuse, family medicine, geriatrics, internal medicine, pediatrics, rural medicine, women's health

Joint degrees awarded: M.D./Ph.D.

Total National Institutes of Health (NIH) grants awarded to the medical school and affiliated hospitals: **$14.2 million**

CURRICULUM

(TEXT PROVIDED BY SCHOOL):

First two years are a blended curriculum of traditional subjects and problem/case-based learning. The third year on two campuses is in block form with 48 weeks in major rotations and three weeks of clinical colloquium. The third campus is based in a multispecialty clinic with students taking all six major rotations all year. The fourth year has 16 required weeks, 22 elective weeks, and six flex weeks.

FACULTY PROFILE (FALL 2007)

Total teaching faculty: **278 (full-time)**, **723 (part-time)**
Of full-time faculty, those teaching in basic sciences: **14%**; in clinical programs: **86%**

Of part-time faculty, those teaching in basic sciences: **0%**; in clinical programs: **100%**
Full-time faculty/student ratio: **1.3**

SUPPORT SERVICES

The school offers students these services for dealing with stress: professional counseling.

RESIDENCY PROFILE

Most popular residency and specialty programs chosen by the 2006 and 2007 M.D. graduating classes: anesthesiology, dermatology, emergency medicine, family practice, internal medicine, obstetrics and gynecology, orthopaedic surgery, pediatrics, surgery–general, transitional year.

WHERE GRADS GO

29.2%

Proportion of 2005-2007 graduates who entered primary care specialties

23.5%

Proportion of 2006-2007 graduates who accepted in-state residencies

University of Southern California

KECK

- 1975 Zonal Avenue, KAM 500, Los Angeles, CA 90033
- Private
- Year Founded: 1895
- Tuition, 2007-2008: $44,240
- Enrollment 2007-2008 academic year: 679
- Website: http://www.usc.edu/keck
- Specialty ranking: N/A

3.64 AVERAGE GPA, ENTERING CLASS FALL 2007

11.1 AVERAGE MCAT, ENTERING CLASS FALL 2007

5.6% ACCEPTANCE RATE, ENTERING CLASS FALL 2007

36 2009 U.S. NEWS MEDICAL SCHOOL RANKING (RESEARCH)

Unranked 2009 U.S. NEWS MEDICAL SCHOOL RANKING (PRIMARY CARE)

ADMISSIONS

Admissions phone number: **(323) 442-2552**
Admissions email address: **medadmit@usc.edu**
Application website: **http://www.usc.edu/keck**
Acceptance rate: **5.6%**
In-state acceptance rate: **6.7%**
Out-of-state acceptance rate: **4.3%**
Minority acceptance rate: **5.1%**
International acceptance rate: **2.3%**

Fall 2007 applications and acceptees

	Applied	Interviewed	Accepted	Enrolled
Total:	6,430	717	362	164
In-state:	3,554	N/A	238	118
Out-of-state:	2,876	N/A	124	46

Profile of admitted students

Average undergraduate grade point average: **3.64**
MCAT averages (scale: 1-15; writing test: J-T):
  Composite score: **11.1**
  Verbal reasoning score: **10.4**, Physical sciences score: **11.4**, Biological sciences score: **11.4**, Writing score: **Q**
Proportion with undergraduate majors in: Biological sciences: **50%**, Physical sciences: **13%**, Non-sciences: **18%**, Other health professions: **1%**, Mixed disciplines and other: **18%**
Percentage of students not coming directly from college after graduation: **N/A**

Dates and details

The American Medical College Application Service (AMCAS) application is accepted.
School asks for a school-specific application as part of the admissions process.
Oldest MCAT considered for Fall 2009 entry: **2007**
Earliest application date for the 2009-2010 first-year class: **7/1**
Latest application date: **11/1**
Acceptance dates for regular application for the class entering in fall 2009:
  Earliest: **October 15, 2008**

Latest: **N/A**
The school considers requests for deferred entrance.
Starting month for the class entering in 2009–2010:
  August
The school has an Early Decision Plan (EDP).
A personal interview is required for admission.

Undergraduate coursework required

Medical school requires undergraduate work in these subjects: biology, organic chemistry, inorganic (general) chemistry, physics, molecular and cell biology, biochemistry, humanities, social sciences, general chemistry.

ADMISSIONS POLICY

(TEXT PROVIDED BY SCHOOL):

The Keck School of Medicine Admissions Committee views the attributes of each applicant holistically, considering the following: performance in college; grade-point average; MCATs; personal characteristics such as communication skills, compassion, empathy, history of leadership, civic service, and a commitment to social justice; interest in teaching, research, or providing patient care to underserved populations.

COSTS AND FINANCIAL AID

Financial aid phone number: **(213) 740-5462**
Tuition, 2007-2008 academic year: **$44,240**
Room and board: **$14,610**
Percentage of students receiving financial aid in 2007-08: **90%**
Percentage of students receiving: Loans: **90%**, Grants/scholarships: **40%**, Work-study aid: **0%**
Average medical school debt for the Class of 2006: **$142,961**

STUDENT BODY

Fall 2007 full-time enrollment: **679**
Men: **51%**, Women: **49%**, In-state: **72%**, Minorities: **38%**, American Indian: **0.3%**, Asian-American: **23.6%**, African-American: **3.2%**, Hispanic-American: **10.6%**, White: **55.7%**, International: **2.1%**, Unknown: **4.6%**

ACADEMIC PROGRAMS

The school's curriculum frequently gives first-year students substantial contact with patients.

There are opportunities for first- or second-year students to work in community health clinics.

Program offerings: AIDS, drug/alcohol abuse, family medicine, geriatrics, internal medicine, pediatrics, rural medicine, women's health

Joint degrees awarded: M.D./Ph.D., M.D./M.B.A., M.D./M.P.H., M.D./M.S.W., M.D./M.S., M.D./M.H.A.

Total National Institutes of Health (NIH) grants awarded to the medical school and affiliated hospitals: $143.7 million

CURRICULUM
(TEXT PROVIDED BY SCHOOL):

Years 1 and 2 integrate basic and clinical sciences and discuss ethical problems, discernment, and action in simulated settings. Year 3 consists of six required clerkships, ethics education by clinical role models, and instruction in core clerkships by ethical standard-bearers. In Year 4, students complete Medicine 2, Neurology, two clerkships, 32 weeks of electives, and retreats on healthcare and the role of M.D.ís in society.

FACULTY PROFILE (FALL 2007)

Total teaching faculty: 1,201 (full-time), 67 (part-time)

Of full-time faculty, those teaching in basic sciences: 12%; in clinical programs: 88%

Of part-time faculty, those teaching in basic sciences: 10%; in clinical programs: 90%

Full-time faculty/student ratio: 1.8

SUPPORT SERVICES

The school offers students these services for dealing with stress: expanded-hour gym access, peer counseling, professional counseling, religious support, support groups.

RESIDENCY PROFILE

Most popular residency and specialty programs chosen by the 2006 and 2007 M.D. graduating classes: anesthesiology, emergency medicine, family practice, internal medicine, obstetrics and gynecology, orthopaedic surgery, pediatrics, psychiatry, radiology–diagnostic, surgery–general.

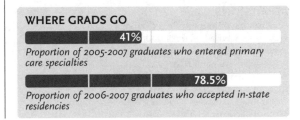

WHERE GRADS GO

41%
Proportion of 2005-2007 graduates who entered primary care specialties

78.5%
Proportion of 2006-2007 graduates who accepted in-state residencies

University of South Florida

- 12901 Bruce B. Downs Boulevard, Box 3, Tampa, FL 33612
- Public
- Year Founded: 1965
- Tuition, 2007-2008: In-state: $21,192; Out-of-state: $53,066
- Enrollment 2007-2008 academic year: 480
- Website: http://www.hsc.usf.edu/medicine/mdadmissions
- Specialty ranking: N/A

3.71 AVERAGE GPA, ENTERING CLASS FALL 2007

9.9 AVERAGE MCAT, ENTERING CLASS FALL 2007

7.4% ACCEPTANCE RATE, ENTERING CLASS FALL 2007

Unranked 2009 U.S. NEWS MEDICAL SCHOOL RANKING (RESEARCH)

Unranked 2009 U.S. NEWS MEDICAL SCHOOL RANKING (PRIMARY CARE)

ADMISSIONS

Admissions phone number: **(813) 974-2229**
Admissions email address: **md-admissions@lyris.hsc.usf.edu**
Application website: **N/A**
Acceptance rate: **7.4%**
In-state acceptance rate: **11.0%**
Out-of-state acceptance rate: **1.5%**
Minority acceptance rate: **7.8%**
International acceptance rate: **N/A**

Fall 2007 applications and acceptees

	Applied	Interviewed	Accepted	Enrolled
Total:	2,649	419	196	120
In-state:	1,639	381	181	110
Out-of-state:	1,010	38	15	10

Profile of admitted students

Average undergraduate grade point average: **3.71**
MCAT averages (scale: 1-15; writing test: J-T):
   Composite score: **9.9**
   Verbal reasoning score: **9.5**, Physical sciences score: **9.8**,
   Biological sciences score: **10.3**, Writing score: **P**
Proportion with undergraduate majors in: Biological sciences: **53%**, Physical sciences: **11%**, Non-sciences: **15%**, Other health professions: **13%**, Mixed disciplines and other: **8%**
Percentage of students not coming directly from college after graduation: **57%**

Dates and details

The American Medical College Application Service (AMCAS) application is accepted.
School asks for a school-specific application as part of the admissions process.
Oldest MCAT considered for Fall 2009 entry: **2006**
Earliest application date for the 2009-2010 first-year class: **6/16**
Latest application date: **12/1**
Acceptance dates for regular application for the class entering in fall 2009:

Earliest: **October 16, 2008**
Latest: **June 15, 2009**
The school considers requests for deferred entrance.
Starting month for the class entering in 2009–2010:
   August
The school has an Early Decision Plan (EDP).
A personal interview is required for admission.

Undergraduate coursework required

Medical school requires undergraduate work in these subjects: biology, English, organic chemistry, inorganic (general) chemistry, physics, mathematics, general chemistry.

ADMISSIONS POLICY
(TEXT PROVIDED BY SCHOOL):
Traditionally accepts Florida students only but now able to take limited, superior, out-of-state applicants. Preference is given to individuals demonstrating outstanding scholarship, leadership skills, and exemplary humanism.

COSTS AND FINANCIAL AID

Financial aid phone number: **(813) 974-2068**
Tuition, 2007-2008 academic year: **In-state: $21,192; Out-of-state: $53,066**
Room and board: **$10,200**
Percentage of students receiving financial aid in 2007-08: **88%**
Percentage of students receiving: Loans: **85%**, Grants/scholarships: **40%**, Work-study aid: **0%**
Average medical school debt for the Class of 2006: **$112,611**

STUDENT BODY

Fall 2007 full-time enrollment: **480**
Men: **47%**, Women: **53%**, In-state: **99%**, Minorities: **40%**, American Indian: **1.0%**, Asian-American: **21.9%**, African-American: **5.8%**, Hispanic-American: **10.8%**, White: **59.0%**, International: **0.0%**, Unknown: **1.5%**

ACADEMIC PROGRAMS

The school's curriculum very frequently gives first-year students substantial contact with patients.

There are opportunities for first- or second-year students to work in community health clinics.

Program offerings: AIDS, drug/alcohol abuse, family medicine, geriatrics, internal medicine, pediatrics, rural medicine, women's health

Joint degrees awarded: M.D./Ph.D., M.D./M.B.A., M.D./M.P.H., M.D./J.D.

Total National Institutes of Health (NIH) grants awarded to the medical school and affiliated hospitals: **$56.7 million**

CURRICULUM

(TEXT PROVIDED BY SCHOOL):

Highly integrated with clinical care, skills testing, and medical professionalism; use of integrated courses at all levels.

FACULTY PROFILE (FALL 2007)

Total teaching faculty: **592 (full-time)**, **43 (part-time)**

Of full-time faculty, those teaching in basic sciences: **26%**; in clinical programs: **74%**

Of part-time faculty, those teaching in basic sciences: **12%**; in clinical programs: **88%**

Full-time faculty/student ratio: **1.2**

SUPPORT SERVICES

The school offers students these services for dealing with stress: expanded-hour gym access, professional counseling, support groups.

RESIDENCY PROFILE

Most popular residency and specialty programs chosen by the 2006 and 2007 M.D. graduating classes: anesthesiology, emergency medicine, family practice, internal medicine, obstetrics and gynecology, pathology–anatomic and clinical, pediatrics, psychiatry, radiology–diagnostic, surgery–general.

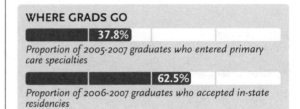

WHERE GRADS GO

37.8%

Proportion of 2005-2007 graduates who entered primary care specialties

62.5%

Proportion of 2006-2007 graduates who accepted in-state residencies

University of Tennessee

HEALTH SCIENCE CENTER

- 62 S. Dunlap, Suite 400 , Memphis, TN 38163
- Public
- Year Founded: 1911
- Tuition, 2007-2008: In-state: $21,095; Out-of-state: $38,935
- Enrollment 2007-2008 academic year: 605
- Website: http://www.utmem.edu/Medicine/
- Specialty ranking: N/A

3.62	AVERAGE GPA, ENTERING CLASS FALL 2007
10.0	AVERAGE MCAT, ENTERING CLASS FALL 2007
17.1%	ACCEPTANCE RATE, ENTERING CLASS FALL 2007
Unranked	2009 U.S. NEWS MEDICAL SCHOOL RANKING (RESEARCH)
62	2009 U.S. NEWS MEDICAL SCHOOL RANKING (PRIMARY CARE)

ADMISSIONS

Admissions phone number: **(901) 448-5559**
Admissions email address: **diharris@utmem.edu**
Application website:
  http://www.utmem.edu/Medicine/Admissions/
Acceptance rate: **17.1%**
In-state acceptance rate: **33.7%**
Out-of-state acceptance rate: **2.8%**
Minority acceptance rate: **16.0%**
International acceptance rate: **0.0%**

Fall 2007 applications and acceptees

	Applied	Interviewed	Accepted	Enrolled
Total:	1,421	488	243	150
In-state:	659	429	222	143
Out-of-state:	762	59	21	7

Profile of admitted students

Average undergraduate grade point average: **3.62**
MCAT averages (scale: 1-15; writing test: J-T):
  Composite score: **10.0**
  Verbal reasoning score: **10.0**, Physical sciences score:
  10.0, Biological sciences score: **10.0**, Writing score: **O**
Proportion with undergraduate majors in: Biological
  sciences: **33%**, Physical sciences: **23%**, Non-sciences:
  13%, Other health professions: **1%**, Mixed disciplines
  and other: **30%**
Percentage of students not coming directly from college
  after graduation: **51%**

Dates and details

The American Medical College Application Service
  (AMCAS) application is accepted.
School asks for a school-specific application as part of the
  admissions process.
Oldest MCAT considered for Fall 2009 entry: **2004**
Earliest application date for the 2009-2010 first-year class:
  6/1
Latest application date: **11/15**

Acceptance dates for regular application for the class
  entering in fall 2009:
  Earliest: **October 15, 2008**
  Latest: **April 15, 2008**
The school considers requests for deferred entrance.
Starting month for the class entering in 2009–2010:
  August
The school doesn't have an Early Decision Plan (EDP).
A personal interview is required for admission.

Undergraduate coursework required

Medical school requires undergraduate work in these subjects: biology, English, organic chemistry, inorganic (general) chemistry, physics.

ADMISSIONS POLICY

(TEXT PROVIDED BY SCHOOL):

The criteria the Committee on Admissions uses in the
selection process are the academic record, MCAT scores,
preprofessional evaluations, and personal interviews. After
review of the American Medical College Application Service
application, a supplemental application will be sent to applicants considered competitive for further review. Both cognitive and noncognitive aspects are considered in applicant
evaluation.

COSTS AND FINANCIAL AID

Financial aid phone number: **(901) 448-5568**
Tuition, 2007-2008 academic year: **In-state: $21,095; Out-
  of-state: $38,935**
Room and board: **$13,251**
Percentage of students receiving financial aid in 2007-08:
  87%
Percentage of students receiving: Loans: **82%**,
  Grants/scholarships: **43%**, Work-study aid: **0%**
Average medical school debt for the Class of 2006:
  $116,936

STUDENT BODY

Fall 2007 full-time enrollment: **605**

Men: **62%**, Women: **38%**, In-state: **97%**, Minorities: **24%**,
American Indian: **0.7%**, Asian-American: **8.3%**, African-American: **10.6%**, Hispanic-American: **1.3%**, White: **71.9%**, International: **0.0%**, Unknown: **7.3%**

ACADEMIC PROGRAMS

The school's curriculum occasionally gives first-year students substantial contact with patients.

There are opportunities for first- or second-year students to work in community health clinics.

Program offerings: family medicine, internal medicine, pediatrics, women's health

Joint degrees awarded: M.D./Ph.D., M.D./M.S.

Total National Institutes of Health (NIH) grants awarded to the medical school and affiliated hospitals: **N/A**

CURRICULUM

(TEXT PROVIDED BY SCHOOL):

The biomedical sciences are taught in an integrated way. Clinical exposure begins in the first semester. The third-year clerkships begin in early May, featuring patient problem-solving and an increasing level of responsibility. The fourth year consists of six clerkships and four electives. Seniors are required to evaluate healthcare delivery, focusing on patient safety and quality improvement.

FACULTY PROFILE (FALL 2007)

Total teaching faculty: **771 (full-time)**, **133 (part-time)**

Of full-time faculty, those teaching in basic sciences: **18%**; in clinical programs: **82%**

Of part-time faculty, those teaching in basic sciences: **2%**; in clinical programs: **98%**

Full-time faculty/student ratio: **1.3**

SUPPORT SERVICES

The school offers students these services for dealing with stress: expanded-hour gym access, peer counseling, professional counseling, religious support, support groups.

RESIDENCY PROFILE

Most popular residency and specialty programs chosen by the 2006 and 2007 M.D. graduating classes: anesthesiology, emergency medicine, family practice, internal medicine, obstetrics and gynecology, orthopaedic surgery, pediatrics, psychiatry, radiology–diagnostic, surgery–general.

WHERE GRADS GO

50.3%

Proportion of 2005-2007 graduates who entered primary care specialties

43.7%

Proportion of 2006-2007 graduates who accepted in-state residencies

University of Texas

HEALTH SCIENCE CENTER–HOUSTON

- 6431 Fannin Street, MSB G. 420, Houston, TX 77030
- Public
- **Year Founded:** 1969
- **Tuition, 2007-2008:** In-state: $12,193; Out-of-state: $25,293
- **Enrollment 2007-2008 academic year:** 877
- **Website:** http://www.med.uth.tmc.edu
- **Specialty ranking:** N/A

3.70	AVERAGE GPA, ENTERING CLASS FALL 2007
10.0	AVERAGE MCAT, ENTERING CLASS FALL 2007
11.5%	ACCEPTANCE RATE, ENTERING CLASS FALL 2007
55	2009 U.S. NEWS MEDICAL SCHOOL RANKING (RESEARCH)
Unranked	2009 U.S. NEWS MEDICAL SCHOOL RANKING (PRIMARY CARE)

ADMISSIONS

Admissions phone number: **(713) 500-5116**
Admissions email address: **msadmissions@uth.tmc.edu**
Application website: **http://www.utsystem.edu/tmdsas**
Acceptance rate: **11.5%**
In-state acceptance rate: **12.9%**
Out-of-state acceptance rate: **4.1%**
Minority acceptance rate: **10.0%**
International acceptance rate: **0.0%**

Fall 2007 applications and acceptees

	Applied	Interviewed	Accepted	Enrolled
Total:	3,683	1,141	422	230
In-state:	3,070	1,044	397	221
Out-of-state:	613	97	25	9

Profile of admitted students

Average undergraduate grade point average: **3.70**
MCAT averages (scale: 1-15; writing test: J-T):
   Composite score: **10.0**
   Verbal reasoning score: **9.8**, Physical sciences score: **9.9**,
   Biological sciences score: **10.3**, Writing score: **P**
Proportion with undergraduate majors in: Biological
   sciences: **41%**, Physical sciences: **26%**, Non-sciences:
   13%, Other health professions: **0%**, Mixed disciplines
   and other: **20%**
Percentage of students not coming directly from college
   after graduation: **8%**

Dates and details

The American Medical College Application Service
   (AMCAS) application is not accepted.
School does not ask for a school-specific application as part
   of the admissions process.
Oldest MCAT considered for Fall 2009 entry: **2002**
Earliest application date for the 2009-2010 first-year class:
   5/1
Latest application date: **10/1**
Acceptance dates for regular application for the class
   entering in fall 2009:
   Earliest: **November 15, 2008**

Latest: **August 13, 2008**
The school doesn't consider requests for deferred entrance.
Starting month for the class entering in 2009–2010:
   August
The school has an Early Decision Plan (EDP).
A personal interview is required for admission.

Undergraduate coursework required

Medical school requires undergraduate work in these subjects: biology, English, organic chemistry, inorganic (general) chemistry, physics.

ADMISSIONS POLICY
(TEXT PROVIDED BY SCHOOL):

Applicants are selected with an emphasis on motivation and
potential for service, especially in the state of Texas.
Emphasis is given to students who have a broad education
and who display intellectual diversity. The applicant's academic record is evaluated with special attention to the subjects taken and the demonstration of a broadly based
comprehensive educational experience.

COSTS AND FINANCIAL AID

Financial aid phone number: **(713) 500-3860**
Tuition, 2007-2008 academic year: **In-state: $12,193; Out-
   of-state: $25,293**
Room and board: **$13,910**
Percentage of students receiving financial aid in 2007-08:
   80%
Percentage of students receiving: Loans: **79%**,
   Grants/scholarships: **44%**, Work-study aid: **0%**
Average medical school debt for the Class of 2006:
   $111,834

STUDENT BODY

Fall 2007 full-time enrollment: **877**
Men: **55%**, Women: **45%**, In-state: **97%**, Minorities: **29%**,
   American Indian: **0.3%**, Asian-American: **12.0%**,
   African-American: **4.1%**, Hispanic-American: **12.5%**,
   White: **68.2%**, International: **0.0%**, Unknown: **2.9%**

ACADEMIC PROGRAMS

The school's curriculum frequently gives first-year students substantial contact with patients.

There are opportunities for first- or second-year students to work in community health clinics.

Program offerings: AIDS, drug/alcohol abuse, family medicine, geriatrics, internal medicine, pediatrics, rural medicine, women's health

Joint degrees awarded: M.D./Ph.D., M.D./M.P.H.

Total National Institutes of Health (NIH) grants awarded to the medical school and affiliated hospitals: **$58.2 million**

CURRICULUM
(TEXT PROVIDED BY SCHOOL):

The first two academic years are divided into four semesters that are devoted to preparing the student for clerkship experiences in the clinical years. The student progresses through a series of clinical clerkships in the major disciplines for the next 12 months. In the remaining year, there are four months of required clerkships and five to seven months of electives.

FACULTY PROFILE (FALL 2007)

Total teaching faculty: **733 (full-time)**, **89 (part-time)**
Of full-time faculty, those teaching in basic sciences: **14%**; in clinical programs: **86%**

Of part-time faculty, those teaching in basic sciences: **2%**; in clinical programs: **98%**
Full-time faculty/student ratio: **0.8**

SUPPORT SERVICES

The school offers students these services for dealing with stress: expanded-hour gym access, peer counseling, professional counseling, religious support, support groups.

RESIDENCY PROFILE

Most popular residency and specialty programs chosen by the 2006 and 2007 M.D. graduating classes: anesthesiology, emergency medicine, family practice, internal medicine, obstetrics and gynecology, orthopaedic surgery, pathology–anatomic and clinical, pediatrics, psychiatry, surgery–general.

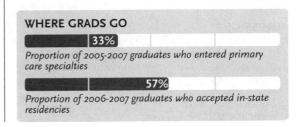

WHERE GRADS GO

33%
Proportion of 2005-2007 graduates who entered primary care specialties

57%
Proportion of 2006-2007 graduates who accepted in-state residencies

University of Texas

MEDICAL BRANCH–GALVESTON

- 301 University Boulevard, Galveston, TX 77555-0133
- Public
- **Year Founded:** 1891
- **Tuition, 2007-2008:** In-state: $12,230; Out-of-state: $25,330
- **Enrollment 2007-2008 academic year:** 882
- **Website:** http://www.utmb.edu/somstudentaffairs
- **Specialty ranking:** N/A

3.78 AVERAGE GPA, ENTERING CLASS FALL 2007

9.7 AVERAGE MCAT, ENTERING CLASS FALL 2007

14.6% ACCEPTANCE RATE, ENTERING CLASS FALL 2007

55 2009 U.S. NEWS MEDICAL SCHOOL RANKING (RESEARCH)

Unranked 2009 U.S. NEWS MEDICAL SCHOOL RANKING (PRIMARY CARE)

ADMISSIONS

Admissions phone number: **(409) 772-6958**
Admissions email address: **lauthoma@utmb.edu**
Application website: **https://www.utsystem.edu/tmdsas**
Acceptance rate: **14.6%**
In-state acceptance rate: **16.5%**
Out-of-state acceptance rate: **5.2%**
Minority acceptance rate: **14.3%**
International acceptance rate: **3.6%**

Fall 2007 applications and acceptees

	Applied	Interviewed	Accepted	Enrolled
Total:	3,642	990	532	227
In-state:	3,043	916	501	218
Out-of-state:	599	74	31	9

Profile of admitted students

Average undergraduate grade point average: **3.78**
MCAT averages (scale: 1-15; writing test: J-T):
 Composite score: **9.7**
 Verbal reasoning score: **9.5**, Physical sciences score: **9.5**,
 Biological sciences score: **10.1**, Writing score: **P**
Proportion with undergraduate majors in: Biological
 sciences: **56%**, Physical sciences: **20%**, Non-sciences:
 14%, Other health professions: **10%**, Mixed disciplines
 and other: **0%**
Percentage of students not coming directly from college
 after graduation: **N/A**

Dates and details

The American Medical College Application Service
 (AMCAS) application is not accepted.
School does not ask for a school-specific application as part
 of the admissions process.
Oldest MCAT considered for Fall 2009 entry: **2003**
Earliest application date for the 2009-2010 first-year class:
 5/1
Latest application date: **10/1**
Acceptance dates for regular application for the class
 entering in fall 2009:
 Earliest: **October 15, 2007**

Latest: **August 18, 2008**
The school considers requests for deferred entrance.
Starting month for the class entering in 2009–2010:
 August
The school doesn't have an Early Decision Plan (EDP).
A personal interview is required for admission.

Undergraduate coursework required

Medical school requires undergraduate work in these subjects: biology, English, organic chemistry, inorganic (general) chemistry, physics, calculus.

ADMISSIONS POLICY

(TEXT PROVIDED BY SCHOOL):
The school receives applications from the Texas Medical
and Dental Schools Application Service. Applications are
computer screened and again screened by the Admissions
Committee. Each applicant is interviewed separately by faculty members, who prepare evaluations to be placed in the
file. Ranking is by a secret ballot; names with the highest
ranks are submitted for the matching.

COSTS AND FINANCIAL AID

Financial aid phone number: **(409) 772-4955**
Tuition, 2007-2008 academic year: **In-state: $12,230; Out-
 of-state: $25,330**
Room and board: **$17,694**
Percentage of students receiving financial aid in 2007-08:
 85%
Percentage of students receiving: Loans: **81%**,
 Grants/scholarships: **49%**, Work-study aid: **3%**
Average medical school debt for the Class of 2006:
 $123,960

STUDENT BODY

Fall 2007 full-time enrollment: **882**
Men: **51%**, Women: **49%**, In-state: **94%**, Minorities: **42%**,
 American Indian: **0.7%**, Asian-American: **16.4%**,
 African-American: **9.4%**, Hispanic-American: **15.5%**,
 White: **53.2%**, International: **0.3%**, Unknown: **4.4%**

ACADEMIC PROGRAMS

The school's curriculum frequently gives first-year students substantial contact with patients.

There are opportunities for first- or second-year students to work in community health clinics.

Program offerings: family medicine, geriatrics, internal medicine, pediatrics, rural medicine, women's health

Joint degrees awarded: M.D./Ph.D.

Total National Institutes of Health (NIH) grants awarded to the medical school and affiliated hospitals: **$100.8 million**

CURRICULUM

(TEXT PROVIDED BY SCHOOL):

The student-centered curriculum at UTMB emphasizes application of basic science to clinical problems, clinical decision making, lifelong learning, and professionalism. It features Year 1 clinical experiences, a Year 3 elective, and heavy use of standardized patients and simulators. Interested students can receive specialized experiences in global health, bilingual medicine, or aerospace medicine.

FACULTY PROFILE (FALL 2007)

Total teaching faculty: **947 (full-time)**, **75 (part-time)**

Of full-time faculty, those teaching in basic sciences: **17%**; in clinical programs: **83%**

Of part-time faculty, those teaching in basic sciences: **8%**; in clinical programs: **92%**

Full-time faculty/student ratio: **1.1**

SUPPORT SERVICES

The school offers students these services for dealing with stress: expanded-hour gym access, professional counseling, religious support, support groups.

RESIDENCY PROFILE

Most popular residency and specialty programs chosen by the 2006 and 2007 M.D. graduating classes: anesthesiology, emergency medicine, family practice, internal medicine, obstetrics and gynecology, pediatrics, psychiatry, surgery–general.

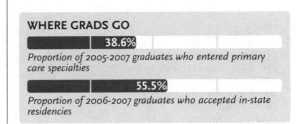

WHERE GRADS GO

38.6%

Proportion of 2005-2007 graduates who entered primary care specialties

55.5%

Proportion of 2006-2007 graduates who accepted in-state residencies

University of Texas

SOUTHWESTERN MEDICAL CENTER–DALLAS

- 5323 Harry Hines Boulevard, Dallas, TX 75390
- Public
- **Year Founded:** 1943
- **Tuition, 2007-2008:** In-state: $12,594; Out-of-state: $25,694
- **Enrollment 2007-2008 academic year:** 909
- **Website:** http://www.utsouthwestern.edu/
- **Specialty ranking:** internal medicine: 11

3.68 AVERAGE GPA, ENTERING CLASS FALL 2007

10.8 AVERAGE MCAT, ENTERING CLASS FALL 2007

12.3% ACCEPTANCE RATE, ENTERING CLASS FALL 2007

22 2009 U.S. NEWS MEDICAL SCHOOL RANKING (RESEARCH)

26 2009 U.S. NEWS MEDICAL SCHOOL RANKING (PRIMARY CARE)

ADMISSIONS

Admissions phone number: **(214) 648-5617**
Admissions email address:
admissions@utsouthwestern.edu
Application website:
http://www.utsouthwestern.edu/medapp
Acceptance rate: **12.3%**
In-state acceptance rate: **12.4%**
Out-of-state acceptance rate: **12.2%**
Minority acceptance rate: **14.3%**
International acceptance rate: **4.1%**

Fall 2007 applications and acceptees

	Applied	Interviewed	Accepted	Enrolled
Total:	3,387	809	418	219
In-state:	2,840	736	351	189
Out-of-state:	547	73	67	30

Profile of admitted students

Average undergraduate grade point average: **3.68**
MCAT averages (scale: 1-15; writing test: J-T):
   Composite score: **10.8**
   Verbal reasoning score: **10.1**, Physical sciences score: **11.0**, Biological sciences score: **11.3**, Writing score: **P**
Proportion with undergraduate majors in: Biological sciences: **40%**, Physical sciences: **25%**, Non-sciences: **10%**, Other health professions: **1%**, Mixed disciplines and other: **24%**
Percentage of students not coming directly from college after graduation: **37%**

Dates and details

The American Medical College Application Service (AMCAS) application is not accepted.
School asks for a school-specific application as part of the admissions process.
Oldest MCAT considered for Fall 2009 entry: **2004**
Earliest application date for the 2009-2010 first-year class: **5/1**
Latest application date: **10/1**

Acceptance dates for regular application for the class entering in fall 2009:
   Earliest: **November 15, 2008**
   Latest: **August 15, 2009**
The school considers requests for deferred entrance.
Starting month for the class entering in 2009–2010:
   August
The school doesn't have an Early Decision Plan (EDP).
A personal interview is required for admission.

Undergraduate coursework required

Medical school requires undergraduate work in these subjects: biology/zoology, English, organic chemistry, inorganic (general) chemistry, physics, calculus.

ADMISSIONS POLICY

(TEXT PROVIDED BY SCHOOL):
Consideration is given to academic performance, curriculum, MCAT scores, recommendations, research, extracurricular activities, socioeconomic background, ethnicity, personal integrity and compassion, English communication, motivation, and other personal qualities. Applicants are evaluated with regard to the school's mission. Personal interview is required. Ninety percent must be Texas residents.

COSTS AND FINANCIAL AID

Financial aid phone number: **(214) 648-3611**
Tuition, 2007-2008 academic year: **In-state: $12,594; Out-of-state: $25,694**
Room and board: **$16,208**
Percentage of students receiving financial aid in 2007-08: **87%**
Percentage of students receiving: Loans: **81%**, Grants/scholarships: **65%**, Work-study aid: **5%**
Average medical school debt for the Class of 2006: **$90,000**

STUDENT BODY

Fall 2007 full-time enrollment: **909**

Men: **54%**, Women: **46%**, In-state: **87%**, Minorities: **50%**, American Indian: **0.4%**, Asian-American: **28.9%**, African-American: **6.5%**, Hispanic-American: **13.5%**, White: **43.9%**, International: **2.2%**, Unknown: **4.5%**

ACADEMIC PROGRAMS

The school's curriculum occasionally gives first-year students substantial contact with patients.

There are opportunities for first- or second-year students to work in community health clinics.

Program offerings: AIDS, drug/alcohol abuse, family medicine, geriatrics, internal medicine, pediatrics, rural medicine, women's health

Joint degrees awarded: M.D./Ph.D., M.D./M.B.A., M.D./M.P.H., M.D./M.S.

Total National Institutes of Health (NIH) grants awarded to the medical school and affiliated hospitals: **$182.7 million**

CURRICULUM

(TEXT PROVIDED BY SCHOOL):

Students study the normal human body, disease processes, and clinical skills in the preclinical years. The clinical years offer direct patient care with rotations in core clerkships. The fourth year includes a medicine subinternship, ambulatory medicine, acute care, and four electives. The curriculum is dynamic and responds to changing requirements for education. Please see the website.

FACULTY PROFILE (FALL 2007)

Total teaching faculty: **1,668 (full-time)**, **241 (part-time)**

Of full-time faculty, those teaching in basic sciences: **16%**; in clinical programs: **84%**

Of part-time faculty, those teaching in basic sciences: **5%**; in clinical programs: **95%**

Full-time faculty/student ratio: **1.8**

SUPPORT SERVICES

The school offers students these services for dealing with stress: expanded-hour gym access, professional counseling, support groups.

RESIDENCY PROFILE

Most popular residency and specialty programs chosen by the 2006 and 2007 M.D. graduating classes: anesthesiology, emergency medicine, family practice, internal medicine, obstetrics and gynecology, pathology–anatomic and clinical, pediatrics, radiology–diagnostic, surgery–general.

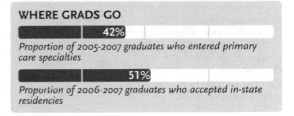

WHERE GRADS GO

42%

Proportion of 2005-2007 graduates who entered primary care specialties

51%

Proportion of 2006-2007 graduates who accepted in-state residencies

University of Toledo

- 3000 Arlington Avenue, Toledo, OH 43614
- Public
- **Year Founded:** 1969
- **Tuition, 2007-2008:** In-state: $24,850; Out-of-state: $53,590
- **Enrollment 2007-2008 academic year:** 614
- **Website:** http://hsc.utoledo.edu
- **Specialty ranking:** N/A

3.58 AVERAGE GPA, ENTERING CLASS FALL 2007

10.0 AVERAGE MCAT, ENTERING CLASS FALL 2007

9.1% ACCEPTANCE RATE, ENTERING CLASS FALL 2007

Unranked 2009 U.S. NEWS MEDICAL SCHOOL RANKING (RESEARCH)

Unranked 2009 U.S. NEWS MEDICAL SCHOOL RANKING (PRIMARY CARE)

ADMISSIONS

Admissions phone number: **(419) 383-4229**
Admissions email address:
medadmissions@utnet.utoledo.edu
Application website:
http://hsc.utoledo.edu/med/admissions/secondary.html
Acceptance rate: **9.1%**
In-state acceptance rate: **17.1%**
Out-of-state acceptance rate: **5.6%**
Minority acceptance rate: **N/A**
International acceptance rate: **N/A**

Fall 2007 applications and acceptees

	Applied	Interviewed	Accepted	Enrolled
Total:	3,369	448	308	165
In-state:	1,030	257	176	109
Out-of-state:	2,339	191	132	56

Profile of admitted students

Average undergraduate grade point average: **3.58**
MCAT averages (scale: 1-15; writing test: J-T):
  Composite score: **10.0**
  Verbal reasoning score: **10.0**, Physical sciences score: **10.0**, Biological sciences score: **10.0**, Writing score: **P**
Proportion with undergraduate majors in: Biological sciences: **63%**, Physical sciences: **12%**, Non-sciences: **13%**, Other health professions: **7%**, Mixed disciplines and other: **5%**
Percentage of students not coming directly from college after graduation: **51%**

Dates and details

The American Medical College Application Service (AMCAS) application is accepted.
School asks for a school-specific application as part of the admissions process.
Oldest MCAT considered for Fall 2009 entry: **2006**
Earliest application date for the 2009-2010 first-year class: **6/15**
Latest application date: **11/1**

Acceptance dates for regular application for the class entering in fall 2009:
  Earliest: **October 15, 2008**
  Latest: **June 1, 2009**
The school considers requests for deferred entrance.
Starting month for the class entering in 2009–2010:
  August
The school has an Early Decision Plan (EDP).
A personal interview is required for admission.

Undergraduate coursework required

Medical school requires undergraduate work in these subjects: biology, English, organic chemistry, inorganic (general) chemistry, physics, mathematics.

ADMISSIONS POLICY

(TEXT PROVIDED BY SCHOOL):
Categories used to assess each candidate include: evaluation of communication and interpersonal skills, commitment to caring for others, community service and leadership, diversity and social awareness, and professionalism.
Requirements include MCAT, bachelor's degree, and a comprehensive command and understanding of English.

COSTS AND FINANCIAL AID

Financial aid phone number: **(419) 383-4232**
Tuition, 2007-2008 academic year: **In-state: $24,850; Out-of-state: $53,590**
Room and board: **N/A**
Percentage of students receiving financial aid in 2007-08: **89%**
Percentage of students receiving: Loans: **86%**, Grants/scholarships: **24%**, Work-study aid: **16%**
Average medical school debt for the Class of 2006: **$128,346**

STUDENT BODY

Fall 2007 full-time enrollment: **614**
Men: **56%**, Women: **44%**, In-state: **90%**, Minorities: **25%**, American Indian: **0.7%**, Asian-American: **17.4%**,

African-American: **4.4%**, Hispanic-American: **2.1%**,
White: **69.7%**, International: **0.3%**, Unknown: **5.4%**

ACADEMIC PROGRAMS

The school's curriculum rarely gives first-year students
substantial contact with patients.

There are opportunities for first- or second-year students to
work in community health clinics.

Program offerings: AIDS, drug/alcohol abuse, family
medicine, geriatrics, internal medicine, pediatrics, rural
medicine, women's health

Joint degrees awarded: M.D./Ph.D., M.D./M.P.H.,
M.D./J.D., M.D./M.S.

Total National Institutes of Health (NIH) grants awarded to
the medical school and affiliated hospitals: **$13.5 million**

FACULTY PROFILE (FALL 2007)

Total teaching faculty: **258 (full-time), 42 (part-time)**

Of full-time faculty, those teaching in basic sciences: **26%**;
in clinical programs: **74%**

Of part-time faculty, those teaching in basic sciences: **24%**;
in clinical programs: **76%**

Full-time faculty/student ratio: **0.4**

SUPPORT SERVICES

The school offers students these services for dealing with
stress: expanded-hour gym access, peer counseling, professional counseling, support groups.

RESIDENCY PROFILE

Most popular residency and specialty programs chosen by
the 2006 and 2007 M.D. graduating classes: anesthesiology, emergency medicine, family practice, internal
medicine, obstetrics and gynecology, orthopaedic surgery,
pathology–anatomic and clinical, pediatrics, radiology–
diagnostic, surgery–general.

WHERE GRADS GO

42%

*Proportion of 2005-2007 graduates who entered primary
care specialties*

35.5%

*Proportion of 2006-2007 graduates who accepted in-state
residencies*

University of Utah

- 30 N. 1900 E, Salt Lake City, UT 84132-2101
- Public
- **Year Founded:** 1941
- **Tuition, 2007-2008:** In-state: $20,693; Out-of-state: $38,529
- **Enrollment 2007-2008 academic year:** 411
- **Website:** http://medicine.utah.edu
- **Specialty ranking:** family medicine: 22, rural medicine: 18

3.64 AVERAGE GPA, ENTERING CLASS FALL 2007

9.7 AVERAGE MCAT, ENTERING CLASS FALL 2007

11.0% ACCEPTANCE RATE, ENTERING CLASS FALL 2007

50 2009 U.S. NEWS MEDICAL SCHOOL RANKING (RESEARCH)

31 2009 U.S. NEWS MEDICAL SCHOOL RANKING (PRIMARY CARE)

ADMISSIONS

Admissions phone number: **(801) 581-7498**
Admissions email address:
  deans.admissions@hsc.utah.edu
Application website: **http://medicine.utah.edu/admissions**
Acceptance rate: **11.0%**
In-state acceptance rate: **21.2%**
Out-of-state acceptance rate: **6.0%**
Minority acceptance rate: **10.4%**
International acceptance rate: **6.6%**

Fall 2007 applications and acceptees

	Applied	Interviewed	Accepted	Enrolled
Total:	1,269	474	139	102
In-state:	416	284	88	76
Out-of-state:	853	190	51	26

Profile of admitted students

Average undergraduate grade point average: **3.64**
MCAT averages (scale: 1-15; writing test: J-T):
  Composite score: **9.7**
  Verbal reasoning score: **9.7**, Physical sciences score: **9.3**,
  Biological sciences score: **10.2**, Writing score: **P**
Proportion with undergraduate majors in: Biological
  sciences: **45%**, Physical sciences: **14%**, Non-sciences:
  16%, Other health professions: **17%**, Mixed disciplines
  and other: **8%**
Percentage of students not coming directly from college
  after graduation: **27%**

Dates and details

The American Medical College Application Service
  (AMCAS) application is accepted.
School asks for a school-specific application as part of the
  admissions process.
Oldest MCAT considered for Fall 2009 entry: **2006**
Earliest application date for the 2009-2010 first-year class:
  5/1
Latest application date: **11/1**
Acceptance dates for regular application for the class
  entering in fall 2009:

Earliest: **October 15, 2008**
Latest: **N/A**
The school considers requests for deferred entrance.
Starting month for the class entering in 2009–2010:
  August
The school doesn't have an Early Decision Plan (EDP).
A personal interview is required for admission.

Undergraduate coursework required

Medical school requires undergraduate work in these subjects: biology, organic chemistry, inorganic (general) chemistry, physics, molecular and cell biology, biochemistry,
humanities, demonstration of writing skills, social sciences.

ADMISSIONS POLICY

(TEXT PROVIDED BY SCHOOL):
The School of Medicine seeks the most capable students for
a balanced but heterogeneous group that excels in the art
and science of medicine. The Admissions Committee is
interested in applicants' motivation for attending medical
school and their understanding of the profession. Ethical
behavior, service, compassion, leadership, and communication skills are important. The school reserves 75 seats for
Utah residents.

COSTS AND FINANCIAL AID

Financial aid phone number: **(801) 581-6474**
Tuition, 2007-2008 academic year: **In-state: $20,693; Out-
  of-state: $38,529**
Room and board: **$8,964**
Percentage of students receiving financial aid in 2007-08:
  86%
Percentage of students receiving: Loans: **86%**,
  Grants/scholarships: **73%**, Work-study aid: **0%**
Average medical school debt for the Class of 2006:
  $123,335

STUDENT BODY

Fall 2007 full-time enrollment: **411**
Men: **63%**, Women: **37%**, In-state: **87%**, Minorities: **17%**,
  American Indian: **0.2%**, Asian-American: **11.4%**,

African-American: **1.5%**, Hispanic-American: **4.1%**,
White: **79.3%**, International: **0.0%**, Unknown: **3.4%**

ACADEMIC PROGRAMS

The school's curriculum occasionally gives first-year
students substantial contact with patients.
There are opportunities for first- or second-year students to
work in community health clinics.
Program offerings: family medicine, geriatrics, internal
medicine, pediatrics, rural medicine, women's health
Joint degrees awarded: M.D./Ph.D., M.D./M.P.H.
Total National Institutes of Health (NIH) grants awarded to
the medical school and affiliated hospitals: **$98.6
million**

CURRICULUM

(TEXT PROVIDED BY SCHOOL):
The first two years include Anatomy, Biochemistry,
Physiology, Microbiology, Genetics, Pharmacology,
Pathology, Organ Systems, and Behavioral Science. The
third year has clerkships in Medicine, Pediatrics, Surgery,
Obstetrics/Gynecology, Psychiatry, and Family Medicine.
The fourth year has courses in Ethics, Healthcare Delivery,
Public Health, and Clinical Neurology, a subinternship, and
electives.

FACULTY PROFILE (FALL 2007)

Total teaching faculty: **1,089 (full-time)**, **314 (part-time)**

Of full-time faculty, those teaching in basic sciences: **18%**;
in clinical programs: **82%**
Of part-time faculty, those teaching in basic sciences: **9%**;
in clinical programs: **91%**
Full-time faculty/student ratio: **2.6**

SUPPORT SERVICES

The school offers students these services for dealing with
stress: peer counseling, professional counseling, support
groups.

RESIDENCY PROFILE

Most popular residency and specialty programs chosen by
the 2006 and 2007 M.D. graduating classes: anesthesiology, emergency medicine, family practice, internal medicine, pediatrics.

WHERE GRADS GO

39.1%

*Proportion of 2005-2007 graduates who entered primary
care specialties*

34.4%

*Proportion of 2006-2007 graduates who accepted in-state
residencies*

University of Vermont

- E-126 Given Building, 89 Beaumont Avenue, Burlington, VT 05405
- Public
- Year Founded: 1822
- Tuition, 2007-2008: In-state: $27,143; Out-of-state: $46,243
- Enrollment 2007-2008 academic year: 431
- Website: https://www.med.uvm.edu/admissions
- Specialty ranking: family medicine: 22, rural medicine: 13

3.70 AVERAGE GPA, ENTERING CLASS FALL 2007

10.2 AVERAGE MCAT, ENTERING CLASS FALL 2007

3.3% ACCEPTANCE RATE, ENTERING CLASS FALL 2007

60 2009 U.S. NEWS MEDICAL SCHOOL RANKING (RESEARCH)

5 2009 U.S. NEWS MEDICAL SCHOOL RANKING (PRIMARY CARE)

ADMISSIONS

Admissions phone number: **(802) 656-2154**
Admissions email address: **medadmissions@uvm.edu**
Application website:
   http://www.aamc.org/students/amcas/application.htm
Acceptance rate: **3.3%**
In-state acceptance rate: **44.3%**
Out-of-state acceptance rate: **2.7%**
Minority acceptance rate: **2.6%**
International acceptance rate: **2.7%**

Fall 2007 applications and acceptees

	Applied	Interviewed	Accepted	Enrolled
Total:	6,127	572	205	112
In-state:	97	77	43	34
Out-of-state:	6,030	495	162	78

Profile of admitted students

Average undergraduate grade point average: **3.70**
MCAT averages (scale: 1-15; writing test: J-T):
   Composite score: **10.2**
   Verbal reasoning score: **9.8**, Physical sciences score: **10.1**, Biological sciences score: **10.5**, Writing score: **Q**
Proportion with undergraduate majors in: Biological sciences: **36%**, Physical sciences: **21%**, Non-sciences: **30%**, Other health professions: **13%**, Mixed disciplines and other: **0%**
Percentage of students not coming directly from college after graduation: **61%**

Dates and details

The American Medical College Application Service (AMCAS) application is accepted.
School asks for a school-specific application as part of the admissions process.
Oldest MCAT considered for Fall 2009 entry: **2005**
Earliest application date for the 2009-2010 first-year class: **6/1**
Latest application date: **11/1**
Acceptance dates for regular application for the class entering in fall 2009:

Earliest: **September 30, 2008**
Latest: **August 3, 2009**
The school considers requests for deferred entrance.
Starting month for the class entering in 2009–2010: **August**
The school has an Early Decision Plan (EDP).
A personal interview is required for admission.

Undergraduate coursework required

Medical school requires undergraduate work in these subjects: biology, organic chemistry, inorganic (general) chemistry, physics, general chemistry.

ADMISSIONS POLICY
(TEXT PROVIDED BY SCHOOL):
The College of Medicine encourages students with a broad and balanced educational background during their undergraduate years. Work must demonstrate intellectual drive, independent thinking, curiosity, and self-discipline. The college seeks in applicants the same humanistic qualities and attitudes it considers essential in a physician: integrity, a respect for otherís choices and rights, compassion, empathy, and personal insight.

COSTS AND FINANCIAL AID
Financial aid phone number: **(802) 656-8293**
Tuition, 2007-2008 academic year: **In-state: $27,143; Out-of-state: $46,243**
Room and board: **$10,564**
Percentage of students receiving financial aid in 2007-08: **92%**
Percentage of students receiving: Loans: **88%**, Grants/scholarships: **58%**, Work-study aid: **0%**
Average medical school debt for the Class of 2006: **$145,409**

STUDENT BODY
Fall 2007 full-time enrollment: **431**
Men: **42%**, Women: **58%**, In-state: **32%**, Minorities: **19%**, American Indian: **0.2%**, Asian-American: **13.2%**,

African-American: **1.6%**, Hispanic-American: **1.9%**, White: **63.3%**, International: **0.7%**, Unknown: **19.0%**

ACADEMIC PROGRAMS

The school's curriculum frequently gives first-year students substantial contact with patients.

There are opportunities for first- or second-year students to work in community health clinics.

Program offerings: AIDS, drug/alcohol abuse, family medicine, geriatrics, internal medicine, pediatrics, rural medicine, women's health

Joint degrees awarded: M.D./Ph.D.

Total National Institutes of Health (NIH) grants awarded to the medical school and affiliated hospitals: **N/A**

CURRICULUM

(TEXT PROVIDED BY SCHOOL):

The curriculum is designed to integrate expanding medical knowledge with a desire for lifelong learning. Courses are designed from well-defined learning objectives, and students are measured to ensure their competency in mastering these objectives. Principles of professionalism and humanism are also integrated throughout all four years.

FACULTY PROFILE (FALL 2007)

Total teaching faculty: **546 (full-time)**, **1,440 (part-time)**

Of full-time faculty, those teaching in basic sciences: **14%**; in clinical programs: **86%**

Of part-time faculty, those teaching in basic sciences: **1%**; in clinical programs: **99%**

Full-time faculty/student ratio: **1.3**

SUPPORT SERVICES

The school offers students these services for dealing with stress: expanded-hour gym access, peer counseling, professional counseling, religious support, support groups.

RESIDENCY PROFILE

Most popular residency and specialty programs chosen by the 2006 and 2007 M.D. graduating classes: emergency medicine, family practice, internal medicine, obstetrics and gynecology, pediatrics, surgery–general.

WHERE GRADS GO

58.6%

Proportion of 2005-2007 graduates who entered primary care specialties

21.7%

Proportion of 2006-2007 graduates who accepted in-state residencies

University of Virginia

- PO Box 800793, McKim Hall, Charlottesville, VA 22908-0793
- Public
- **Year Founded:** 1819
- **Tuition, 2007-2008:** In-state: $31,305; Out-of-state: $41,070
- **Enrollment 2007-2008 academic year:** 558
- **Website:** http://www.healthsystem.virginia.edu/internet/SOM/
- **Specialty ranking:** N/A

3.70 AVERAGE GPA, ENTERING CLASS FALL 2007

11.1 AVERAGE MCAT, ENTERING CLASS FALL 2007

13.0% ACCEPTANCE RATE, ENTERING CLASS FALL 2007

23 2009 U.S. NEWS MEDICAL SCHOOL RANKING (RESEARCH)

35 2009 U.S. NEWS MEDICAL SCHOOL RANKING (PRIMARY CARE)

ADMISSIONS

Admissions phone number: **(434) 924-5571**
Admissions email address: **medsch-adm@virginia.edu**
Application website: **http://www.aamc.org**
Acceptance rate: **13.0%**
In-state acceptance rate: **24.6%**
Out-of-state acceptance rate: **9.9%**
Minority acceptance rate: **13.1%**
International acceptance rate: **9.6%**

Fall 2007 applications and acceptees

	Applied	Interviewed	Accepted	Enrolled
Total:	2,561	534	332	143
In-state:	533	186	131	84
Out-of-state:	2,028	348	201	59

Profile of admitted students

Average undergraduate grade point average: **3.70**
MCAT averages (scale: 1-15; writing test: J-T):
  Composite score: **11.1**
  Verbal reasoning score: **10.7**, Physical sciences score: **11.3**, Biological sciences score: **11.4**, Writing score: **P**
Proportion with undergraduate majors in: Biological sciences: **44%**, Physical sciences: **30%**, Non-sciences: **22%**, Other health professions: **4%**, Mixed disciplines and other: **N/A**
Percentage of students not coming directly from college after graduation: **38%**

Dates and details

The American Medical College Application Service (AMCAS) application is accepted.
School asks for a school-specific application as part of the admissions process.
Oldest MCAT considered for Fall 2009 entry: **2006**
Earliest application date for the 2009-2010 first-year class: **5/1**
Latest application date: **11/1**
Acceptance dates for regular application for the class entering in fall 2009:
  Earliest: **October 15, 2008**

Latest: **August 11, 2008**
The school considers requests for deferred entrance.
Starting month for the class entering in 2009–2010: **August**
The school doesn't have an Early Decision Plan (EDP).
A personal interview is required for admission.

Undergraduate coursework required

Medical school requires undergraduate work in these subjects: biology, organic chemistry, inorganic (general) chemistry, physics.

ADMISSIONS POLICY

(TEXT PROVIDED BY SCHOOL):

The Admissions Committee seeks to admit applicants who will make contributions in clinical care, medical research, or education, and it takes into account academics, MCAT scores, and evidence of a commitment to medicine. Final decisions are based on personal interviews and an overall assessment of the applicant's academic and personal qualities. Approximately 60 percent of the class comes from Virginia.

COSTS AND FINANCIAL AID

Financial aid phone number: **(434) 924-0033**
Tuition, 2007-2008 academic year: **In-state: $31,305; Out-of-state: $41,070**
Room and board: **$18,730**
Percentage of students receiving financial aid in 2007-08: **90%**
Percentage of students receiving: Loans: **85%**, Grants/scholarships: **67%**, Work-study aid: **0%**
Average medical school debt for the Class of 2006: **$112,634**

STUDENT BODY

Fall 2007 full-time enrollment: **558**
Men: **55%**, Women: **45%**, In-state: **59%**, Minorities: **26%**, American Indian: **0.4%**, Asian-American: **18.1%**, African-American: **6.6%**, Hispanic-American: **4.5%**, White: **65.4%**, International: **0.5%**, Unknown: **4.5%**

ACADEMIC PROGRAMS

The school's curriculum frequently gives first-year students substantial contact with patients.

There are opportunities for first- or second-year students to work in community health clinics.

Program offerings: AIDS, drug/alcohol abuse, family medicine, geriatrics, internal medicine, pediatrics, rural medicine, women's health

Joint degrees awarded: M.D./Ph.D., M.D./M.P.H., M.D./M.S., M.D./M.A.

Total National Institutes of Health (NIH) grants awarded to the medical school and affiliated hospitals: **N/A**

CURRICULUM

(TEXT PROVIDED BY SCHOOL):

A new Cells-to-Society curriculum addresses patient care in multiple domains of medicine, especially biomedical science, society, culture, and economics. In Foundations of Medicine and Core Systems, students learn normal human biology; they then apply it to solve clinical cases in small, physician-led groups. A set of core clerkships is followed by a menu of selectives and almost unlimited electives.

FACULTY PROFILE (FALL 2007)

Total teaching faculty: **926 (full-time)**, **115 (part-time)**
Of full-time faculty, those teaching in basic sciences: **21%**; in clinical programs: **79%**

Of part-time faculty, those teaching in basic sciences: **8%**; in clinical programs: **92%**
Full-time faculty/student ratio: **1.7**

SUPPORT SERVICES

The school offers students these services for dealing with stress: expanded-hour gym access, peer counseling, professional counseling, religious support, support groups.

RESIDENCY PROFILE

Most popular residency and specialty programs chosen by the 2006 and 2007 M.D. graduating classes: anesthesiology, emergency medicine, family practice, internal medicine, obstetrics and gynecology, pathology–anatomic and clinical, pediatrics, psychiatry, radiology–diagnostic, surgery–general.

WHERE GRADS GO

39%

Proportion of 2005-2007 graduates who entered primary care specialties

24%

Proportion of 2006-2007 graduates who accepted in-state residencies

University of Washington

- PO Box 356340, Seattle, WA 98195
- Public
- Year Founded: 1946
- Tuition, 2007-2008: In-state: $17,900; Out-of-state: $41,904
- Enrollment 2007-2008 academic year: 826
- Website: http://www.uwmedicine.org
- Specialty ranking: AIDS: 4, drug/alcohol abuse: 8, family medicine: 1, geriatrics: 7, internal medicine: 6, pediatrics: 7, rural medicine: 1, women's health: 7

3.68 AVERAGE GPA, ENTERING CLASS FALL 2007

10.5 AVERAGE MCAT, ENTERING CLASS FALL 2007

5.2% ACCEPTANCE RATE, ENTERING CLASS FALL 2007

6 2009 U.S. NEWS MEDICAL SCHOOL RANKING (RESEARCH)

1 2009 U.S. NEWS MEDICAL SCHOOL RANKING (PRIMARY CARE)

ADMISSIONS

Admissions phone number: **(206) 543-7212**
Admissions email address: **askuwsom@u.washington.edu**
Application website:
   http://depts.washington.edu/mdadmit/secondary
Acceptance rate: **5.2%**
In-state acceptance rate: **18.7%**
Out-of-state acceptance rate: **1.0%**
Minority acceptance rate: **3.1%**
International acceptance rate: **N/A**

Fall 2007 applications and acceptees

	Applied	Interviewed	Accepted	Enrolled
Total:	4,598	838	239	191
In-state:	1,097	732	205	176
Out-of-state:	3,501	106	34	15

Profile of admitted students

Average undergraduate grade point average: **3.68**
MCAT averages (scale: 1-15; writing test: J-T):
   Composite score: **10.5**
   Verbal reasoning score: **10.3**, Physical sciences score: **10.3**, Biological sciences score: **10.9**, Writing score: **Q**
Proportion with undergraduate majors in: Biological sciences: **60%**, Physical sciences: **14%**, Non-sciences: **17%**, Other health professions: **3%**, Mixed disciplines and other: **6%**
Percentage of students not coming directly from college after graduation: **44%**

Dates and details

The American Medical College Application Service (AMCAS) application is accepted.
School asks for a school-specific application as part of the admissions process.
Oldest MCAT considered for Fall 2009 entry: **2006**
Earliest application date for the 2009-2010 first-year class: **6/1**
Latest application date: **11/1**
Acceptance dates for regular application for the class entering in fall 2009:

Earliest: **November 1, 2008**
Latest: **July 1, 2009**
The school considers requests for deferred entrance.
Starting month for the class entering in 2009–2010: **August**
The school doesn't have an Early Decision Plan (EDP).
A personal interview is required for admission.

Undergraduate coursework required

Medical school requires undergraduate work in these subjects: biology, inorganic (general) chemistry, physics, general chemistry.

ADMISSIONS POLICY

(TEXT PROVIDED BY SCHOOL):
Residents of the states of Washington, Wyoming, Alaska, Montana, and Idaho are eligible to apply for the M.D. Others can apply to the M.D./Ph.D. program. Premed science courses are required, as is the MCAT. All must demonstrate ability in their field and in English, basic math, and computing/information technology. A successful interview is an important factor. Recent accepted students had a grade-point average of 3.68, MCAT scores of over 10.3, with a Q in the writing sample.

COSTS AND FINANCIAL AID

Financial aid phone number: **(206) 685-9229**
Tuition, 2007-2008 academic year: **In-state: $17,900; Out-of-state: $41,904**
Room and board: **$14,007**
Percentage of students receiving financial aid in 2007-08: **91%**
Percentage of students receiving: Loans: **83%**, Grants/scholarships: **65%**, Work-study aid: **0%**
Average medical school debt for the Class of 2006: **$97,604**

STUDENT BODY

Fall 2007 full-time enrollment: **826**
Men: **46%**, Women: **54%**, In-state: **88%**, Minorities: **23%**, American Indian: **1.5%**, Asian-American: **15.0%**, African-

American: **1.9%**, Hispanic-American: **4.2%**, White: **71.3%**, International: **0.0%**, Unknown: **6.1%**

ACADEMIC PROGRAMS

The school's curriculum frequently gives first-year students substantial contact with patients.

There are opportunities for first- or second-year students to work in community health clinics.

Program offerings: AIDS, drug/alcohol abuse, family medicine, geriatrics, internal medicine, pediatrics, rural medicine, women's health

Joint degrees awarded: M.D./Ph.D., M.D./M.P.H., M.D./M.H.A.

Total National Institutes of Health (NIH) grants awarded to the medical school and affiliated hospitals: **$579.7 million**

CURRICULUM

(TEXT PROVIDED BY SCHOOL):

The first-year focus on basic sciences uses an organ system approach. Second year adds bedside learning and patient-centered skills. Third and fourth years consist of required and elective clerkships. Features: assignment to small colleges with a clinical mentor; community service pathways in Indian, international, and rural health; and a required research experience with a research mentor.

FACULTY PROFILE (FALL 2007)

Total teaching faculty: **2,047 (full-time)**, **357 (part-time)**

Of full-time faculty, those teaching in basic sciences: **17%**; in clinical programs: **83%**

Of part-time faculty, those teaching in basic sciences: **15%**; in clinical programs: **85%**

Full-time faculty/student ratio: **2.5**

SUPPORT SERVICES

The school offers students these services for dealing with stress: expanded-hour gym access, peer counseling, professional counseling, support groups.

RESIDENCY PROFILE

Most popular residency and specialty programs chosen by the 2006 and 2007 M.D. graduating classes: anesthesiology, emergency medicine, family practice, internal medicine, obstetrics and gynecology, orthopaedic surgery, pediatrics.

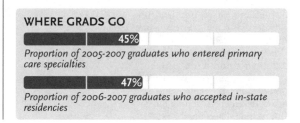

WHERE GRADS GO

45%

Proportion of 2005-2007 graduates who entered primary care specialties

47%

Proportion of 2006-2007 graduates who accepted in-state residencies

University of Wisconsin–Madison

- 750 Highland Avenue, Madison, WI 53705-2221
- Public
- Year Founded: 1848
- Tuition, 2007-2008: In-state: $22,722; Out-of-state: $33,846
- Enrollment 2007-2008 academic year: 614
- Website: http://www.med.wisc.edu/Education
- Specialty ranking: family medicine: 3, internal medicine: 25, rural medicine: 21, women's health: 15

3.76	AVERAGE GPA, ENTERING CLASS FALL 2007
10.4	AVERAGE MCAT, ENTERING CLASS FALL 2007
7.6%	ACCEPTANCE RATE, ENTERING CLASS FALL 2007
27	2009 U.S. NEWS MEDICAL SCHOOL RANKING (RESEARCH)
13	2009 U.S. NEWS MEDICAL SCHOOL RANKING (PRIMARY CARE)

ADMISSIONS

Admissions phone number: **(608) 265-6344**
Admissions email address: **eamenzer@wisc.edu**
Application website:
  http://www.med.wisc.edu/Education/md/admissions
Acceptance rate: **7.6%**
In-state acceptance rate: **23.2%**
Out-of-state acceptance rate: **3.7%**
Minority acceptance rate: **8.6%**
International acceptance rate: **N/A**

Fall 2007 applications and acceptees

	Applied	Interviewed	Accepted	Enrolled
Total:	3,347	626	255	155
In-state:	673	459	156	123
Out-of-state:	2,674	167	99	32

Profile of admitted students

Average undergraduate grade point average: **3.76**
MCAT averages (scale: 1-15; writing test: J-T):
  Composite score: **10.4**
  Verbal reasoning score: **9.8**, Physical sciences score: **10.6**, Biological sciences score: **10.9**, Writing score: **P**
Proportion with undergraduate majors in: Biological sciences: **37%**, Physical sciences: **33%**, Non-sciences: **17%**, Other health professions: **0%**, Mixed disciplines and other: **13%**
Percentage of students not coming directly from college after graduation: **20%**

Dates and details

The American Medical College Application Service (AMCAS) application is accepted.
School asks for a school-specific application as part of the admissions process.
Oldest MCAT considered for Fall 2009 entry: **2005**
Earliest application date for the 2009-2010 first-year class: **6/1**
Latest application date: **11/1**
Acceptance dates for regular application for the class entering in fall 2009:

Earliest: **October 15, 2008**
Latest: **August 15, 2009**
The school considers requests for deferred entrance.
Starting month for the class entering in 2009–2010: **August**
The school has an Early Decision Plan (EDP).
A personal interview is required for admission.

Undergraduate coursework required

Medical school requires undergraduate work in these subjects: biology, biology/zoology, organic chemistry, inorganic (general) chemistry, physics, biochemistry, mathematics, general chemistry.

ADMISSIONS POLICY

(TEXT PROVIDED BY SCHOOL):
The committee considers applicant's undergraduate and graduate academic performance; MCAT scores; extracurricular activities; employment record; personal, educational, and socioeconomic background; response to challenges; and personal character, with reference to honesty and integrity, empathy, maturity, leadership, self-discipline, and emotional stability. Preference is given to residents.

COSTS AND FINANCIAL AID

Financial aid phone number: **(608) 262-3060**
Tuition, 2007-2008 academic year: **In-state: $22,722; Out-of-state: $33,846**
Room and board: **$15,330**
Percentage of students receiving financial aid in 2007-08: **89%**
Percentage of students receiving: Loans: **82%**, Grants/scholarships: **37%**, Work-study aid: **0%**
Average medical school debt for the Class of 2006: **$124,950**

STUDENT BODY

Fall 2007 full-time enrollment: **614**
Men: **47%**, Women: **53%**, In-state: **83%**, Minorities: **23%**, American Indian: **0.5%**, Asian-American: **14.7%**,

African-American: **4.9%**, Hispanic-American: **2.9%**, White: **77.0%**, International: **0.0%**, Unknown: **0.0%**

ACADEMIC PROGRAMS

The school's curriculum frequently gives first-year students substantial contact with patients.

There are opportunities for first- or second-year students to work in community health clinics.

Program offerings: AIDS, drug/alcohol abuse, family medicine, geriatrics, internal medicine, pediatrics, rural medicine, women's health

Joint degrees awarded: M.D./Ph.D., M.D./M.P.H.

Total National Institutes of Health (NIH) grants awarded to the medical school and affiliated hospitals: **$184.0 million**

CURRICULUM

(TEXT PROVIDED BY SCHOOL):

The first-year core curriculum builds a firm base in the sciences fundamental to clinical medicine. In the second year, the courses emphasize organ systems, mechanisms of disease and abnormalities, and therapeutic intervention. Beginning in the third year, clerkships expose students to a wide variety of clinical settings, including outpatient, inpatient, community-based, rural, and inner city.

FACULTY PROFILE (FALL 2007)

Total teaching faculty: **1,024 (full-time)**, **281 (part-time)**

Of full-time faculty, those teaching in basic sciences: **17%**; in clinical programs: **83%**

Of part-time faculty, those teaching in basic sciences: **2%**; in clinical programs: **98%**

Full-time faculty/student ratio: **1.7**

SUPPORT SERVICES

The school offers students these services for dealing with stress: expanded-hour gym access, professional counseling, support groups.

RESIDENCY PROFILE

Most popular residency and specialty programs chosen by the 2006 and 2007 M.D. graduating classes: anesthesiology, emergency medicine, family practice, internal medicine, obstetrics and gynecology, orthopaedic surgery, pediatrics, psychiatry, radiology–diagnostic, surgery–general.

WHERE GRADS GO

41.3%

Proportion of 2005-2007 graduates who entered primary care specialties

31.8%

Proportion of 2006-2007 graduates who accepted in-state residencies

Vanderbilt University

- 21st Avenue S and Garland Avenue, Nashville, TN 37232-2104
- Private
- Year Founded: 1875
- Tuition, 2007-2008: $39,511
- Enrollment 2007-2008 academic year: 417
- Website: http://www.mc.vanderbilt.edu/medschool/
- Specialty ranking: AIDS: 18, geriatrics: 16, internal medicine: 14, pediatrics: 14, women's health: 18

3.80 AVERAGE GPA, ENTERING CLASS FALL 2007

11.5 AVERAGE MCAT, ENTERING CLASS FALL 2007

5.9% ACCEPTANCE RATE, ENTERING CLASS FALL 2007

16 2009 U.S. NEWS MEDICAL SCHOOL RANKING (RESEARCH)

49 2009 U.S. NEWS MEDICAL SCHOOL RANKING (PRIMARY CARE)

ADMISSIONS

Admissions phone number: **(615) 322-2145**
Admissions email address: **N/A**
Application website:
http://www.mc.vanderbilt.edu/medschool/admissions/online_app.php
Acceptance rate: **5.9%**
In-state acceptance rate: **7.2%**
Out-of-state acceptance rate: **5.8%**
Minority acceptance rate: **6.6%**
International acceptance rate: **9.6%**

Fall 2007 applications and acceptees

	Applied	Interviewed	Accepted	Enrolled
Total:	4,787	927	282	105
In-state:	348	55	25	20
Out-of-state:	4,439	872	257	85

Profile of admitted students

Average undergraduate grade point average: **3.80**
MCAT averages (scale: 1-15; writing test: J-T):
  Composite score: **11.5**
  Verbal reasoning score: **10.6**, Physical sciences score: **11.8**, Biological sciences score: **12.0**, Writing score: **Q**
Proportion with undergraduate majors in: Biological sciences: **51%**, Physical sciences: **35%**, Non-sciences: **13%**, Other health professions: **1%**, Mixed disciplines and other: **0%**
Percentage of students not coming directly from college after graduation: **28%**

Dates and details

The American Medical College Application Service (AMCAS) application is accepted.
School asks for a school-specific application as part of the admissions process.
Oldest MCAT considered for Fall 2009 entry: **2005**
Earliest application date for the 2009-2010 first-year class: **6/1**
Latest application date: **1/31**

Acceptance dates for regular application for the class entering in fall 2009:
  Earliest: **October 15, 2008**
  Latest: **April 1, 2009**
The school considers requests for deferred entrance.
Starting month for the class entering in 2009-2010:
  August
The school has an Early Decision Plan (EDP).
A personal interview is required for admission.

Undergraduate coursework required

Medical school requires undergraduate work in these subjects: biology, English, organic chemistry, inorganic (general) chemistry, physics.

ADMISSIONS POLICY

(TEXT PROVIDED BY SCHOOL):
VUSM seeks to admit a diverse group of academically exceptional students whose attributes and accomplishments suggest they will become leaders and scholars in medicine. After initial review of American Medical College Application Service data, 20 percent of applicants are invited to interview and provide secondary essays and recommendations. A faculty-student committee reviews all data in a holistic manner and offers rolling admissions.

COSTS AND FINANCIAL AID

Financial aid phone number: **(615) 343-6310**
Tuition, 2007-2008 academic year: **$39,511**
Room and board: **$10,260**
Percentage of students receiving financial aid in 2007-08: **84%**
Percentage of students receiving: Loans: **69%**, Grants/scholarships: **59%**, Work-study aid: **0%**
Average medical school debt for the Class of 2006: **$110,200**

STUDENT BODY

Fall 2007 full-time enrollment: **417**

Men: 56%, Women: 44%, In-state: 17%, Minorities: 27%, American Indian: 0.0%, Asian-American: 16.5%, African-American: 8.2%, Hispanic-American: 1.4%, White: 66.2%, International: 4.6%, Unknown: 3.1%

ACADEMIC PROGRAMS

The school's curriculum frequently gives first-year students substantial contact with patients.

There are opportunities for first- or second-year students to work in community health clinics.

Program offerings: AIDS, drug/alcohol abuse, family medicine, geriatrics, internal medicine, pediatrics, rural medicine, women's health

Joint degrees awarded: M.D./Ph.D., M.D./M.B.A., M.D./M.P.H., M.D./J.D., M.D./M.S.

Total National Institutes of Health (NIH) grants awarded to the medical school and affiliated hospitals: $285.8 million

CURRICULUM

(TEXT PROVIDED BY SCHOOL):

Vanderbilt's curriculum provides students with the knowledge, skills, and attitudes to become leaders and scholars in medicine. Students build a strong foundation in the biomedical and social sciences while developing clinical competence and a sustainable professional identity. A mentored scholarly project is required, and electives throughout the program allow exploration of individual interests.

FACULTY PROFILE (FALL 2007)

Total teaching faculty: 1,833 (full-time), 71 (part-time)

Of full-time faculty, those teaching in basic sciences: 22%; in clinical programs: 78%

Of part-time faculty, those teaching in basic sciences: 3%; in clinical programs: 97%

Full-time faculty/student ratio: 4.4

SUPPORT SERVICES

The school offers students these services for dealing with stress: expanded-hour gym access, peer counseling, professional counseling, religious support, support groups.

RESIDENCY PROFILE

Most popular residency and specialty programs chosen by the 2006 and 2007 M.D. graduating classes: anesthesiology, dermatology, emergency medicine, internal medicine, obstetrics and gynecology, orthopaedic surgery, pediatrics, psychiatry, radiation oncology, surgery–general.

WHERE GRADS GO

30%

Proportion of 2005-2007 graduates who entered primary care specialties

22%

Proportion of 2006-2007 graduates who accepted in-state residencies

Virginia Commonwealth University

- PO Box 980565, Richmond, VA 23298-0565
- Public
- **Year Founded:** 1838
- **Tuition, 2007-2008:** In-state: $27,502; Out-of-state: $41,004
- **Enrollment 2007-2008 academic year:** 734
- **Website:** http://www.medschool.vcu.edu
- **Specialty ranking:** drug/alcohol abuse: 16, women's health: 18

3.60	AVERAGE GPA, ENTERING CLASS FALL 2007
9.8	AVERAGE MCAT, ENTERING CLASS FALL 2007
7.2%	ACCEPTANCE RATE, ENTERING CLASS FALL 2007
Unranked	2009 U.S. NEWS MEDICAL SCHOOL RANKING (RESEARCH)
Unranked	2009 U.S. NEWS MEDICAL SCHOOL RANKING (PRIMARY CARE)

ADMISSIONS

Admissions phone number: **(804) 828-9629**
Admissions email address: **somume@hsc.vcu.edu**
Application website: **http://www.admissions.som.vcu.edu**
Acceptance rate: **7.2%**
In-state acceptance rate: **26.4%**
Out-of-state acceptance rate: **4.2%**
Minority acceptance rate: **5.9%**
International acceptance rate: **N/A**

Fall 2007 applications and acceptees

	Applied	Interviewed	Accepted	Enrolled
Total:	5,664	734	410	184
In-state:	777	351	205	104
Out-of-state:	4,887	383	205	80

Profile of admitted students

Average undergraduate grade point average: **3.60**
MCAT averages (scale: 1-15; writing test: J-T):
  Composite score: **9.8**
  Verbal reasoning score: **9.5**, Physical sciences score: **9.8**, Biological sciences score: **10.2**, Writing score: **P**
Proportion with undergraduate majors in: Biological sciences: **45%**, Physical sciences: **18%**, Non-sciences: **28%**, Other health professions: **0%**, Mixed disciplines and other: **9%**
Percentage of students not coming directly from college after graduation: **39%**

Dates and details

The American Medical College Application Service (AMCAS) application is accepted.
School asks for a school-specific application as part of the admissions process.
Oldest MCAT considered for Fall 2009 entry: **2005**
Earliest application date for the 2009-2010 first-year class: **6/1**
Latest application date: **10/15**
Acceptance dates for regular application for the class entering in fall 2009:
  Earliest: **October 15, 2008**

Latest: **August 10, 2009**
The school considers requests for deferred entrance.
Starting month for the class entering in 2009–2010:
  August
The school has an Early Decision Plan (EDP).
A personal interview is required for admission.

Undergraduate coursework required

Medical school requires undergraduate work in these subjects: biology, biology/zoology, English, organic chemistry, physics, mathematics, demonstration of writing skills, general chemistry.

ADMISSIONS POLICY

(TEXT PROVIDED BY SCHOOL):
Applicants are selected on the basis of their professionalism and academic skills. Medically related experiences, academic performance, and the interview are important. The school gives preference to residents of Virginia and does not discriminate on the basis of age, race, sex, creed, national origin, or handicap. Applicants must be citizens or permanent residents of the United States or Canada.

COSTS AND FINANCIAL AID

Financial aid phone number: **(804) 828-4006**
Tuition, 2007-2008 academic year: **In-state: $27,502; Out-of-state: $41,004**
Room and board: **$13,400**
Percentage of students receiving financial aid in 2007-08: **95%**
Percentage of students receiving: Loans: **91%**, Grants/scholarships: **41%**, Work-study aid: **0%**
Average medical school debt for the Class of 2006: **$121,056**

STUDENT BODY

Fall 2007 full-time enrollment: **734**
Men: **52%**, Women: **48%**, In-state: **59%**, Minorities: **34%**, American Indian: **0.7%**, Asian-American: **24.9%**, African-American: **7.2%**, Hispanic-American: **1.4%**, White: **58.2%**, International: **0.3%**, Unknown: **7.4%**

ACADEMIC PROGRAMS

The school's curriculum frequently gives first-year students substantial contact with patients.

There are opportunities for first- or second-year students to work in community health clinics.

Program offerings: AIDS, drug/alcohol abuse, family medicine, geriatrics, internal medicine, pediatrics, rural medicine, women's health

Joint degrees awarded: M.D./Ph.D., M.D./M.P.H., M.D./M.H.A.

Total National Institutes of Health (NIH) grants awarded to the medical school and affiliated hospitals: **N/A**

CURRICULUM

(TEXT PROVIDED BY SCHOOL):

The first year focuses on structure and function, and the second year covers pathologic displays in treatment of disease. An M1/M2 longitudinal course provides clinical experience with physicians and small-group instruction on basic clinical medicine. M3 students receive clinical training, rotating through various hospitals and ambulatory services. M4 students choose from a variety of electives.

FACULTY PROFILE (FALL 2007)

Total teaching faculty: **801 (full-time)**, **52 (part-time)**
Of full-time faculty, those teaching in basic sciences: **22%**; in clinical programs: **78%**

Of part-time faculty, those teaching in basic sciences: **48%**; in clinical programs: **52%**
Full-time faculty/student ratio: **1.1**

SUPPORT SERVICES

The school offers students these services for dealing with stress: expanded-hour gym access, peer counseling, professional counseling, religious support, support groups.

RESIDENCY PROFILE

Most popular residency and specialty programs chosen by the 2006 and 2007 M.D. graduating classes: anesthesiology, emergency medicine, family practice, internal medicine, internal medicine–pediatrics, obstetrics and gynecology, pediatrics, physical medicine and rehabilitation, radiology–diagnostic, surgery–general.

WHERE GRADS GO

42.6%

Proportion of 2005-2007 graduates who entered primary care specialties

29%

Proportion of 2006-2007 graduates who accepted in-state residencies

Wake Forest University

- Medical Center Boulevard, Winston-Salem, NC 27157
- Private
- **Year Founded:** 1941
- **Tuition, 2007-2008:** $37,134
- **Enrollment 2007-2008 academic year:** 454
- **Website:** http://www.wfubmc.edu
- **Specialty ranking:** geriatrics: 12, internal medicine: 25, women's health: 18

3.64 AVERAGE GPA, ENTERING CLASS FALL 2007

10.3 AVERAGE MCAT, ENTERING CLASS FALL 2007

3.7% ACCEPTANCE RATE, ENTERING CLASS FALL 2007

42 2009 U.S. NEWS MEDICAL SCHOOL RANKING (RESEARCH)

35 2009 U.S. NEWS MEDICAL SCHOOL RANKING (PRIMARY CARE)

ADMISSIONS
Admissions phone number: **(336) 716-4264**
Admissions email address: **medadmit@wfubmc.edu**
Application website:
   http://www2.wfubmc.edu/graduate/application.html
Acceptance rate: **3.7%**
In-state acceptance rate: **10.8%**
Out-of-state acceptance rate: **2.8%**
Minority acceptance rate: **N/A**
International acceptance rate: **N/A**

Fall 2007 applications and acceptees

	Applied	Interviewed	Accepted	Enrolled
Total:	7,485	501	276	120
In-state:	842	141	91	43
Out-of-state:	6,643	360	185	77

Profile of admitted students
Average undergraduate grade point average: **3.64**
MCAT averages (scale: 1-15; writing test: J-T):
   Composite score: **10.3**
   Verbal reasoning score: **10.3**, Physical sciences score: **10.2**, Biological sciences score: **10.5**, Writing score: **P**
Proportion with undergraduate majors in: Biological sciences: **59%**, Physical sciences: **23%**, Non-sciences: **10%**, Other health professions: **0%**, Mixed disciplines and other: **8%**
Percentage of students not coming directly from college after graduation: **44%**

Dates and details
The American Medical College Application Service (AMCAS) application is accepted.
School asks for a school-specific application as part of the admissions process.
Oldest MCAT considered for Fall 2009 entry: **2005**
Earliest application date for the 2009-2010 first-year class: **6/1**
Latest application date: **11/1**
Acceptance dates for regular application for the class entering in fall 2009:

Earliest: **October 15, 2008**
Latest: **July 28, 2009**
The school considers requests for deferred entrance.
Starting month for the class entering in 2009–2010: **July**
The school has an Early Decision Plan (EDP).
A personal interview is required for admission.

Undergraduate coursework required
Medical school requires undergraduate work in these subjects: biology, biology/zoology, organic chemistry, inorganic (general) chemistry, physics, general chemistry.

ADMISSIONS POLICY
(TEXT PROVIDED BY SCHOOL):
The MCAT scores; grade-point average; personal qualities assessed in the personal interviews. A national pool is considered, so state of residence is inconsequential.

COSTS AND FINANCIAL AID
Financial aid phone number: **(336) 716-2889**
Tuition, 2007-2008 academic year: **$37,134**
Room and board: **$19,326**
Percentage of students receiving financial aid in 2007-08: **92%**
Percentage of students receiving: Loans: **86%**, Grants/scholarships: **68%**, Work-study aid: **0%**
Average medical school debt for the Class of 2006: **$125,852**

STUDENT BODY
Fall 2007 full-time enrollment: **454**
Men: **54%**, Women: **46%**, In-state: **37%**, Minorities: **27%**, American Indian: **1.8%**, Asian-American: **12.3%**, African-American: **10.1%**, Hispanic-American: **3.1%**, White: **68.7%**, International: **4.0%**, Unknown: **0.0%**

ACADEMIC PROGRAMS
The school's curriculum frequently gives first-year students substantial contact with patients.
There are opportunities for first- or second-year students to work in community health clinics.

Program offerings: AIDS, drug/alcohol abuse, family
  medicine, geriatrics, internal medicine, pediatrics, rural
  medicine, women's health
Joint degrees awarded: M.D./Ph.D., M.D./M.B.A.,
  M.D./M.S.
Total National Institutes of Health (NIH) grants awarded to
  the medical school and affiliated hospitals: **N/A**

CURRICULUM
(TEXT PROVIDED BY SCHOOL):
The curriculum is organized to meet the seven goals of the
undergraduate medical education program: the development of proficiency in self-directed and lifelong learning
skills; the acquisition of appropriate core biomedical science
knowledge; clinical skills; problem solving/clinical reasoning skills; interviewing and communication skills, information management skills; and professional attitudes and
behavior.

FACULTY PROFILE (FALL 2007)
Total teaching faculty: **951 (full-time)**, **518 (part-time)**
Of full-time faculty, those teaching in basic sciences: **25%**;
  in clinical programs: **75%**
Of part-time faculty, those teaching in basic sciences: **16%**;
  in clinical programs: **84%**
Full-time faculty/student ratio: **2.1**

SUPPORT SERVICES
The school offers students these services for dealing with
stress: expanded-hour gym access, professional counseling,
religious support.

RESIDENCY PROFILE
Most popular residency and specialty programs chosen by
the 2006 and 2007 M.D. graduating classes: anesthesiology, emergency medicine, family practice, internal medicine, neurology, obstetrics and gynecology, orthopaedic
surgery, pediatrics, radiology–diagnostic, surgery–general.

WHERE GRADS GO

50%
*Proportion of 2005-2007 graduates who entered primary
care specialties*

32%
*Proportion of 2006-2007 graduates who accepted in-state
residencies*

Washington University in St. Louis

- **660 S. Euclid Avenue, St. Louis, MO 63110**
- **Private**
- **Year Founded:** 1891
- **Tuition, 2007-2008:** $43,380
- **Enrollment 2007-2008 academic year:** 591
- **Website:** http://medschool.wustl.edu
- **Specialty ranking:** AIDS: 16, drug/alcohol abuse: 11, internal medicine: 8, pediatrics: 7, women's health: 17

3.88 AVERAGE GPA, ENTERING CLASS FALL 2007

12.5 AVERAGE MCAT, ENTERING CLASS FALL 2007

11.1% ACCEPTANCE RATE, ENTERING CLASS FALL 2007

3 2009 U.S. NEWS MEDICAL SCHOOL RANKING (RESEARCH)

13 2009 U.S. NEWS MEDICAL SCHOOL RANKING (PRIMARY CARE)

ADMISSIONS
Admissions phone number: **(314) 362-6858**
Admissions email address: **wumscoa@wustl.edu**
Application website:
  http://medschool.wustl.edu/admissions/
Acceptance rate: **11.1%**
In-state acceptance rate: **11.2%**
Out-of-state acceptance rate: **11.1%**
Minority acceptance rate: **11.8%**
International acceptance rate: **12.3%**

Fall 2007 applications and acceptees
	Applied	Interviewed	Accepted	Enrolled
Total:	3,062	1,087	339	122
In-state:	143	60	16	9
Out-of-state:	2,919	1,027	323	113

Profile of admitted students
Average undergraduate grade point average: **3.88**
MCAT averages (scale: 1-15; writing test: J-T):
  Composite score: **12.5**
  Verbal reasoning score: **11.7**, Physical sciences score: **12.8**, Biological sciences score: **13.0**, Writing score: **Q**
Proportion with undergraduate majors in: Biological sciences: **40%**, Physical sciences: **40%**, Non-sciences: **15%**, Other health professions: **2%**, Mixed disciplines and other: **3%**
Percentage of students not coming directly from college after graduation: **32%**

Dates and details
The American Medical College Application Service (AMCAS) application is accepted.
School asks for a school-specific application as part of the admissions process.
Oldest MCAT considered for Fall 2009 entry: **2005**
Earliest application date for the 2009-2010 first-year class: **7/1**
Latest application date: **12/1**
Acceptance dates for regular application for the class entering in fall 2009:

Earliest: **November 1, 2008**
Latest: **August 15, 2009**
The school considers requests for deferred entrance.
Starting month for the class entering in 2009–2010:
  August
The school doesn't have an Early Decision Plan (EDP).
A personal interview is required for admission.

Undergraduate coursework required
Medical school requires undergraduate work in these subjects: biology, organic chemistry, inorganic (general) chemistry, physics, mathematics, calculus, general chemistry.

ADMISSIONS POLICY
(TEXT PROVIDED BY SCHOOL):
WUSM seeks to enroll bright, energetic, compassionate students who want to learn to practice medicine at the edge of what is known. The recruitment and selection process seeks to identify people who are personally and academically accomplished and who are energized by interacting with and improving the well-being of others. For more information, please go to the website.

COSTS AND FINANCIAL AID
Financial aid phone number: **(314) 362-6862**
Tuition, 2007-2008 academic year: **$43,380**
Room and board: **$9,428**
Percentage of students receiving financial aid in 2007-08: **90%**
Percentage of students receiving: Loans: **51%**, Grants/scholarships: **73%**, Work-study aid: **0%**
Average medical school debt for the Class of 2006: **$100,975**

STUDENT BODY
Fall 2007 full-time enrollment: **591**
Men: **53%**, Women: **47%**, In-state: **8%**, Minorities: **36%**, American Indian: **0.8%**, Asian-American: **27.1%**, African-American: **4.9%**, Hispanic-American: **3.4%**, White: **57.4%**, International: **3.7%**, Unknown: **2.7%**

ACADEMIC PROGRAMS

The school's curriculum frequently gives first-year students substantial contact with patients.

There are opportunities for first- or second-year students to work in community health clinics.

Program offerings: AIDS, drug/alcohol abuse, family medicine, geriatrics, internal medicine, pediatrics, rural medicine

Joint degrees awarded: M.D./Ph.D., M.D./M.A.

Total National Institutes of Health (NIH) grants awarded to the medical school and affiliated hospitals: **$347.0 million**

CURRICULUM

(TEXT PROVIDED BY SCHOOL):

The Washington University School of Medicine curriculum offers a core experience that presents the principles, methods of investigation, problems, and opportunities in each of the major disciplines of medical science and medical practice. The required elective program helps students decide where major interests lie. For more information, please see the website.

FACULTY PROFILE (FALL 2007)

Total teaching faculty: **1,509 (full-time)**, **88 (part-time)**

Of full-time faculty, those teaching in basic sciences: **10%**; in clinical programs: **90%**

Of part-time faculty, those teaching in basic sciences: **5%**; in clinical programs: **95%**

Full-time faculty/student ratio: **2.6**

SUPPORT SERVICES

The school offers students these services for dealing with stress: expanded-hour gym access, peer counseling, professional counseling, religious support, support groups.

RESIDENCY PROFILE

Most popular residency and specialty programs chosen by the 2006 and 2007 M.D. graduating classes: anesthesiology, emergency medicine, internal medicine, ophthalmology, orthopaedic surgery, pathology–anatomic and clinical, pediatrics, psychiatry, radiology–diagnostic, surgery–general.

WHERE GRADS GO

39.8%

Proportion of 2005-2007 graduates who entered primary care specialties

28.2%

Proportion of 2006-2007 graduates who accepted in-state residencies

Wayne State University

- 540 E. Canfield, Detroit, MI 48201
- Public
- **Year Founded:** 1868
- **Tuition, 2007-2008:** In-state: $28,668; Out-of-state: $56,656
- **Enrollment 2007-2008 academic year:** 1,161
- **Website:** http://www.med.wayne.edu/Admissions
- **Specialty ranking:** N/A

3.57 AVERAGE GPA, ENTERING CLASS FALL 2007

10.1 AVERAGE MCAT, ENTERING CLASS FALL 2007

14.1% ACCEPTANCE RATE, ENTERING CLASS FALL 2007

Unranked 2009 U.S. NEWS MEDICAL SCHOOL RANKING (RESEARCH)

Unranked 2009 U.S. NEWS MEDICAL SCHOOL RANKING (PRIMARY CARE)

ADMISSIONS
Admissions phone number: **(313) 577-1466**
Admissions email address: **admissions@med.wayne.edu**
Application website: **N/A**
Acceptance rate: **14.1%**
In-state acceptance rate: **32.3%**
Out-of-state acceptance rate: **4.4%**
Minority acceptance rate: **9.1%**
International acceptance rate: **6.5%**

Fall 2007 applications and acceptees
	Applied	Interviewed	Accepted	Enrolled
Total:	3,968	919	560	302
In-state:	1,379	653	445	272
Out-of-state:	2,589	266	115	30

Profile of admitted students
Average undergraduate grade point average: **3.57**
MCAT averages (scale: 1-15; writing test: J-T):
  Composite score: **10.1**
  Verbal reasoning score: **9.4**, Physical sciences score: **10.3**, Biological sciences score: **10.6**, Writing score: **O**
Proportion with undergraduate majors in: Biological sciences: **52%**, Physical sciences: **16%**, Non-sciences: **8%**, Other health professions: **4%**, Mixed disciplines and other: **20%**
Percentage of students not coming directly from college after graduation: **27%**

Dates and details
The American Medical College Application Service (AMCAS) application is accepted.
School asks for a school-specific application as part of the admissions process.
Oldest MCAT considered for Fall 2009 entry: **2005**
Earliest application date for the 2009-2010 first-year class: **6/1**
Latest application date: **12/15**
Acceptance dates for regular application for the class entering in fall 2009:

Earliest: **October 22, 2008**
Latest: **N/A**
The school considers requests for deferred entrance.
Starting month for the class entering in 2009–2010:
  August
The school has an Early Decision Plan (EDP).
A personal interview is required for admission.

Undergraduate coursework required
Medical school requires undergraduate work in these subjects: biology, English, organic chemistry, inorganic (general) chemistry, physics.

ADMISSIONS POLICY
(TEXT PROVIDED BY SCHOOL):
The Committee on Admissions will select those applicants who, in its judgment, will make the best students and physicians. Consideration is given to the entire record, grade-point average, MCAT scores, recommendations, and interview results, as these reflect personality, maturity, character, and suitability for medicine. Healthcare experiences such as volunteering or working in hospitals or nursing homes are desirable, as is experience in biomedical research. Special encouragement is given to candidates from medically underserved areas in Michigan.

COSTS AND FINANCIAL AID
Financial aid phone number: **(313) 577-1039**
Tuition, 2007-2008 academic year: **In-state: $28,668; Out-of-state: $56,656**
Room and board: **$13,450**
Percentage of students receiving financial aid in 2007-08: **86%**
Percentage of students receiving: Loans: **84%**, Grants/scholarships: **38%**, Work-study aid: **2%**
Average medical school debt for the Class of 2006: **$129,245**

STUDENT BODY
Fall 2007 full-time enrollment: **1,161**

Men: 53%, Women: 47%, In-state: 90%, Minorities: 31%,
American Indian: 0.3%, Asian-American: 16.8%,
African-American: 12.5%, Hispanic-American: 1.6%,
White: 63.2%, International: 2.2%, Unknown: 3.4%

ACADEMIC PROGRAMS

The school's curriculum occasionally gives first-year
students substantial contact with patients.
There are opportunities for first- or second-year students to
work in community health clinics.
Program offerings: AIDS, drug/alcohol abuse, family
medicine, geriatrics, internal medicine, pediatrics, rural
medicine, women's health
Joint degrees awarded: M.D./Ph.D., M.D./M.S.
Total National Institutes of Health (NIH) grants awarded to
the medical school and affiliated hospitals: **N/A**

CURRICULUM
(TEXT PROVIDED BY SCHOOL):
The four-year Wayne State Medical School program has
158 weeks of basic and clinical science. The Years 1 and 2
curriculum focuses on normal and abnormal structure
and function of the human body. The clinical science
curriculum in Year 3 includes eight required clerkships,
while the Year 4 curriculum has three required courses and
five electives.

FACULTY PROFILE (FALL 2007)
Total teaching faculty: **998 (full-time), 64 (part-time)**

Of full-time faculty, those teaching in basic sciences: **18%**;
in clinical programs: **82%**
Of part-time faculty, those teaching in basic sciences: **6%**;
in clinical programs: **94%**
Full-time faculty/student ratio: **0.9**

SUPPORT SERVICES
The school offers students these services for dealing with
stress: expanded-hour gym access, peer counseling, professional counseling, support groups.

RESIDENCY PROFILE
Most popular residency and specialty programs chosen by
the 2006 and 2007 M.D. graduating classes: anesthesiology, emergency medicine, family practice, internal medicine, obstetrics and gynecology, pediatrics, psychiatry,
radiology–diagnostic, transitional year, internal
medicine/pediatrics.

WHERE GRADS GO

30%

*Proportion of 2005-2007 graduates who entered primary
care specialties*

60%

*Proportion of 2006-2007 graduates who accepted in-state
residencies*

West Virginia University

■ 1 Medical Center Drive , Morgantown, WV 26506-9111
■ Public
■ Year Founded: 1903
■ Tuition, 2007-2008: In-state: $19,204; Out-of-state: $41,866
■ Enrollment 2007-2008 academic year: 421
■ Website: http://www.hsc.wvu.edu/som/students
■ Specialty ranking: rural medicine: 9

3.69 AVERAGE GPA, ENTERING CLASS FALL 2007

9.5 AVERAGE MCAT, ENTERING CLASS FALL 2007

5.6% ACCEPTANCE RATE, ENTERING CLASS FALL 2007

Unranked 2009 U.S. NEWS MEDICAL SCHOOL RANKING (RESEARCH)

56 2009 U.S. NEWS MEDICAL SCHOOL RANKING (PRIMARY CARE)

ADMISSIONS

Admissions phone number: **(304) 293-2408**
Admissions email address: **medadmissions@hsc.wvu.edu**
Application website: **http://www.aamc.org**
Acceptance rate: **5.6%**
In-state acceptance rate: **57.5%**
Out-of-state acceptance rate: **1.5%**
Minority acceptance rate: **5.5%**
International acceptance rate: **N/A**

Fall 2007 applications and acceptees

	Applied	Interviewed	Accepted	Enrolled
Total:	2,878	356	161	108
In-state:	212	138	122	83
Out-of-state:	2,666	218	39	25

Profile of admitted students

Average undergraduate grade point average: **3.69**
MCAT averages (scale: 1-15; writing test: J-T):
  Composite score: **9.5**
  Verbal reasoning score: **9.4**, Physical sciences score: **9.3**,
  Biological sciences score: **9.9**, Writing score: **P**
Proportion with undergraduate majors in: Biological
  sciences: **54%**, Physical sciences: **30%**, Non-sciences:
  7%, Other health professions: **8%**, Mixed disciplines and
  other: **1%**
Percentage of students not coming directly from college
  after graduation: **15%**

Dates and details

The American Medical College Application Service
  (AMCAS) application is accepted.
School asks for a school-specific application as part of the
  admissions process.
Oldest MCAT considered for Fall 2009 entry: **2007**
Earliest application date for the 2009-2010 first-year class:
  6/1
Latest application date: **11/1**
Acceptance dates for regular application for the class
  entering in fall 2009:

Earliest: **October 15, 2008**
Latest: **August 1, 2009**
The school considers requests for deferred entrance.
Starting month for the class entering in 2009–2010:
  August
The school has an Early Decision Plan (EDP).
A personal interview is required for admission.

Undergraduate coursework required

Medical school requires undergraduate work in these subjects: biology/zoology, English, organic chemistry, inorganic (general) chemistry, physics, behavioral science, social sciences, general chemistry.

ADMISSIONS POLICY

(TEXT PROVIDED BY SCHOOL):
Required: American Medical College Application Service application; recent MCAT; three years (90 hours) in U.S. or Canadian college by January for that year's admission. Required, with lab and C grade or better: eight hours each Biology/Zoology, Inorganic Chemistry, Organic Chemistry, Physics; six hours each English and Behavioral/Social Science. Biochemistry and Cell/Molecular Biology recommended. Communication and computer skills, medical experience, and service strongly considered.

COSTS AND FINANCIAL AID

Financial aid phone number: **(304) 293-3706**
Tuition, 2007-2008 academic year: **In-state: $19,204; Out-of-state: $41,866**
Room and board: **$9,080**
Percentage of students receiving financial aid in 2007-08:
  95%
Percentage of students receiving: Loans: **81%**,
  Grants/scholarships: **57%**, Work-study aid: **0%**
Average medical school debt for the Class of 2006:
  $118,962

STUDENT BODY

Fall 2007 full-time enrollment: **421**

Men: 59%, Women: 41%, In-state: 70%, Minorities: 15%, American Indian: 0.2%, Asian-American: 11.4%, African-American: 1.2%, Hispanic-American: 1.9%, White: 85.3%, International: 0.0%, Unknown: 0.0%

ACADEMIC PROGRAMS
The school's curriculum frequently gives first-year students substantial contact with patients.

There are opportunities for first- or second-year students to work in community health clinics.

Program offerings: AIDS, drug/alcohol abuse, family medicine, geriatrics, internal medicine, pediatrics, rural medicine, women's health

Joint degrees awarded: M.D./Ph.D., M.D./M.P.H.

Total National Institutes of Health (NIH) grants awarded to the medical school and affiliated hospitals: **$17.4 million**

CURRICULUM
(TEXT PROVIDED BY SCHOOL):
Competency-based preparation. Basic science courses integrated and blocked. Summer clinical and research externships. Required laptop program. Third-year requirements in Medicine, Surgery, Family Medicine, Pediatrics, Obstetrics/Gynecology, Psychiatry/Neurology. Elective and selective fourth year. Requirements: passage of U.S. Medical Licensing Examination Steps 1 and 2 and WVU SOM Clinical Performance Exam, 100 hours of community service, three months of rural practice.

FACULTY PROFILE (FALL 2007)
Total teaching faculty: **602 (full-time), 107 (part-time)**

Of full-time faculty, those teaching in basic sciences: **12%**; in clinical programs: **88%**

Of part-time faculty, those teaching in basic sciences: **3%**; in clinical programs: **97%**

Full-time faculty/student ratio: **1.4**

SUPPORT SERVICES
The school offers students these services for dealing with stress: expanded-hour gym access, peer counseling, professional counseling, support groups.

RESIDENCY PROFILE
Most popular residency and specialty programs chosen by the 2006 and 2007 M.D. graduating classes: anesthesiology, emergency medicine, family practice, internal medicine, obstetrics and gynecology, pediatrics, psychiatry, radiology–diagnostic, transitional year, internal medicine/pediatrics.

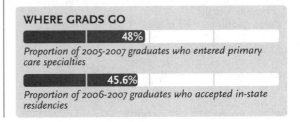

WHERE GRADS GO

48%

Proportion of 2005-2007 graduates who entered primary care specialties

45.6%

Proportion of 2006-2007 graduates who accepted in-state residencies

Wright State University

- PO Box 1751, Dayton, OH 45401-1751
- Public
- Year Founded: 1974
- Tuition, 2007-2008: In-state: $26,393; Out-of-state: $36,461
- Enrollment 2007-2008 academic year: 409
- Website: http://www.med.wright.edu
- Specialty ranking: N/A

3.58 AVERAGE GPA, ENTERING CLASS FALL 2007

9.4 AVERAGE MCAT, ENTERING CLASS FALL 2007

6.8% ACCEPTANCE RATE, ENTERING CLASS FALL 2007

Unranked 2009 U.S. NEWS MEDICAL SCHOOL RANKING (RESEARCH)

Unranked 2009 U.S. NEWS MEDICAL SCHOOL RANKING (PRIMARY CARE)

ADMISSIONS

Admissions phone number: **(937) 775-2934**
Admissions email address: **som_saa@wright.edu**
Application website:
   https://somms2.med.wright.edu/saa/oasys/login.asp
Acceptance rate: **6.8%**
In-state acceptance rate: **18.7%**
Out-of-state acceptance rate: **0.8%**
Minority acceptance rate: **N/A**
International acceptance rate: **N/A**

Fall 2007 applications and acceptees

	Applied	Interviewed	Accepted	Enrolled
Total:	3,237	447	220	100
In-state:	1,080	399	202	92
Out-of-state:	2,157	48	18	8

Profile of admitted students

Average undergraduate grade point average: **3.58**
MCAT averages (scale: 1-15; writing test: J-T):
   Composite score: **9.4**
   Verbal reasoning score: **9.5**, Physical sciences score: **9.1**,
   Biological sciences score: **9.8**, Writing score: **O**
Proportion with undergraduate majors in: Biological
   sciences: **49%**, Physical sciences: **18%**, Non-sciences:
   14%, Other health professions: **0%**, Mixed disciplines
   and other: **19%**
Percentage of students not coming directly from college
   after graduation: **11%**

Dates and details

The American Medical College Application Service
   (AMCAS) application is accepted.
School asks for a school-specific application as part of the
   admissions process.
Oldest MCAT considered for Fall 2009 entry: **2005**
Earliest application date for the 2009-2010 first-year class:
   6/1
Latest application date: **11/15**
Acceptance dates for regular application for the class
   entering in fall 2009:

Earliest: **October 15, 2008**
Latest: **August 1, 2009**
The school considers requests for deferred entrance.
Starting month for the class entering in 2009–2010:
   August
The school has an Early Decision Plan (EDP).
A personal interview is required for admission.

Undergraduate coursework required

Medical school requires undergraduate work in these subjects: biology, English, organic chemistry, inorganic (general) chemistry, physics, mathematics, general chemistry.

ADMISSIONS POLICY

(TEXT PROVIDED BY SCHOOL):
The Admissions Committee reviews applications according
to established policies. Preference is given to Ohio residents. The committee looks for evidence of intellectual ability, dedication to human concerns, communication skills,
maturity, motivation, and potential for medical service in an
underserved area of Ohio.

COSTS AND FINANCIAL AID

Financial aid phone number: **(937) 775-2934**
Tuition, 2007-2008 academic year: **In-state: $26,393; Out-
   of-state: $36,461**
Room and board: **$11,946**
Percentage of students receiving financial aid in 2007-08:
   90%
Percentage of students receiving: Loans: **87%**,
   Grants/scholarships: **40%**, Work-study aid: **4%**
Average medical school debt for the Class of 2006:
   $135,749

STUDENT BODY

Fall 2007 full-time enrollment: **409**
Men: **43%**, Women: **57%**, In-state: **98%**, Minorities: **24%**,
   American Indian: **0.0%**, Asian-American: **13.7%**,
   African-American: **7.8%**, Hispanic-American: **1.5%**,
   White: **76.3%**, International: **0.0%**, Unknown: **0.7%**

ACADEMIC PROGRAMS

The school's curriculum very frequently gives first-year students substantial contact with patients.

There are opportunities for first- or second-year students to work in community health clinics.

Program offerings: AIDS, drug/alcohol abuse, family medicine, geriatrics, internal medicine, pediatrics, rural medicine, women's health

Joint degrees awarded: M.D./Ph.D., M.D./M.B.A., M.D./M.P.H.

Total National Institutes of Health (NIH) grants awarded to the medical school and affiliated hospitals: **N/A**

CURRICULUM

(TEXT PROVIDED BY SCHOOL):

During the first two years, students are taught in an interdisciplinary fashion. Students have patient contact in the first week. In the second year, eight organ systems are taught. Clinically based enrichment electives are offered as immersion experiences in the first two years. In the third year, students are exposed to the basic disciplines of medicine. The fourth year includes mostly electives.

FACULTY PROFILE (FALL 2007)

Total teaching faculty: **358 (full-time)**, **1,255 (part-time)**
Of full-time faculty, those teaching in basic sciences: **12%**; in clinical programs: **88%**

Of part-time faculty, those teaching in basic sciences: **3%**; in clinical programs: **97%**
Full-time faculty/student ratio: **0.9**

SUPPORT SERVICES

The school offers students these services for dealing with stress: professional counseling, support groups.

RESIDENCY PROFILE

Most popular residency and specialty programs chosen by the 2006 and 2007 M.D. graduating classes: anesthesiology, emergency medicine, family practice, internal medicine, obstetrics and gynecology, orthopaedic surgery, pediatrics, psychiatry, surgery–general, internal medicine/pediatrics.

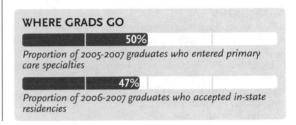

WHERE GRADS GO

50%
Proportion of 2005-2007 graduates who entered primary care specialties

47%
Proportion of 2006-2007 graduates who accepted in-state residencies

Yale University

■ 333 Cedar Street, PO Box 208055, New Haven, CT 06520-8055
■ Private
■ **Year Founded:** 1810
■ **Tuition, 2007-2008:** $40,770
■ **Enrollment 2007-2008 academic year:** 395
■ **Website:** http://info.med.yale.edu/ysm
■ **Specialty ranking:** drug/alcohol abuse: 1, geriatrics: 8, internal medicine: 9, pediatrics: 14, women's health: 11

3.72	AVERAGE GPA, ENTERING CLASS FALL 2007
11.3	AVERAGE MCAT, ENTERING CLASS FALL 2007
5.8%	ACCEPTANCE RATE, ENTERING CLASS FALL 2007
9	2009 U.S. NEWS MEDICAL SCHOOL RANKING (RESEARCH)
Unranked	2009 U.S. NEWS MEDICAL SCHOOL RANKING (PRIMARY CARE)

ADMISSIONS

Admissions phone number: **(203) 785-2643**
Admissions email address: **medical.admissions@yale.edu**
Application website:
http://info.med.yale.edu/education/admissions
Acceptance rate: **5.8%**
In-state acceptance rate: **12.8%**
Out-of-state acceptance rate: **5.4%**
Minority acceptance rate: **6.5%**
International acceptance rate: **6.8%**

Fall 2007 applications and acceptees

	Applied	Interviewed	Accepted	Enrolled
Total:	4,057	998	236	100
In-state:	203	68	26	15
Out-of-state:	3,854	930	210	85

Profile of admitted students

Average undergraduate grade point average: **3.72**
MCAT averages (scale: 1-15; writing test: J-T):
  Composite score: **11.3**
  Verbal reasoning score: **10.6**, Physical sciences score: **11.7**, Biological sciences score: **11.7**, Writing score: **R**
Proportion with undergraduate majors in: Biological sciences: **50%**, Physical sciences: **37%**, Non-sciences: **11%**, Other health professions: **0%**, Mixed disciplines and other: **2%**
Percentage of students not coming directly from college after graduation: **53%**

Dates and details

The American Medical College Application Service (AMCAS) application is accepted.
School asks for a school-specific application as part of the admissions process.
Oldest MCAT considered for Fall 2009 entry: **2005**
Earliest application date for the 2009-2010 first-year class: **6/1**
Latest application date: **10/15**
Acceptance dates for regular application for the class entering in fall 2009:

Earliest: **March 31, 2009**
Latest: **August 31, 2009**
The school considers requests for deferred entrance.
Starting month for the class entering in 2009–2010: **August**
The school has an Early Decision Plan (EDP).
A personal interview is required for admission.

Undergraduate coursework required

Medical school requires undergraduate work in these subjects: biology/zoology, organic chemistry, inorganic (general) chemistry, physics.

ADMISSIONS POLICY

(TEXT PROVIDED BY SCHOOL):
Yale seeks a diverse class of exceptional students who aspire to careers of leadership in the practice of medicine and the biomedical sciences. No rigid cutoffs are used in evaluating candidates. University grades, MCAT scores, medical and research experience, extracurricular activities, and personal qualities are all considered. State of residence and citizenship are not factors.

COSTS AND FINANCIAL AID

Financial aid phone number: **(203) 785-2645**
Tuition, 2007-2008 academic year: **$40,770**
Room and board: **$10,660**
Percentage of students receiving financial aid in 2007-08: **85%**
Percentage of students receiving: Loans: **69%**, Grants/scholarships: **60%**, Work-study aid: **0%**
Average medical school debt for the Class of 2006: **$114,744**

STUDENT BODY

Fall 2007 full-time enrollment: **395**
Men: **47%**, Women: **53%**, In-state: **10%**, Minorities: **37%**, American Indian: **1.0%**, Asian-American: **22.3%**, African-American: **6.8%**, Hispanic-American: **6.6%**, White: **53.9%**, International: **8.4%**, Unknown: **1.0%**

ACADEMIC PROGRAMS

The school's curriculum very frequently gives first-year students substantial contact with patients.

There are opportunities for first- or second-year students to work in community health clinics.

Program offerings: AIDS, drug/alcohol abuse, family medicine, geriatrics, internal medicine, pediatrics, rural medicine, women's health

Joint degrees awarded: M.D./Ph.D., M.D./M.B.A., M.D./M.P.H., M.D./J.D.

Total National Institutes of Health (NIH) grants awarded to the medical school and affiliated hospitals: $320.2 million

CURRICULUM

(TEXT PROVIDED BY SCHOOL):

The core curriculum is divided into preclinical and clinical years. In the preclinical years the scientific basis of health and disease is presented. In the clinical years students rotate through clerkships followed by an Integrative Clinical Medicine course. Complementing the core curriculum are opportunities to explore the leading edge of scientific discovery and learn scientific reasoning.

FACULTY PROFILE (FALL 2007)

Total teaching faculty: 1,063 (full-time), 48 (part-time)

Of full-time faculty, those teaching in basic sciences: 18%; in clinical programs: 82%

Of part-time faculty, those teaching in basic sciences: 2%; in clinical programs: 98%

Full-time faculty/student ratio: 2.7

SUPPORT SERVICES

The school offers students these services for dealing with stress: expanded-hour gym access, peer counseling, professional counseling, religious support, support groups.

RESIDENCY PROFILE

Most popular residency and specialty programs chosen by the 2006 and 2007 M.D. graduating classes: anesthesiology, dermatology, internal medicine, neurological surgery, obstetrics and gynecology, ophthalmology, orthopaedic surgery, pediatrics, psychiatry, radiology–diagnostic.

WHERE GRADS GO

25.4%

Proportion of 2005-2007 graduates who entered primary care specialties

21.9%

Proportion of 2006-2007 graduates who accepted in-state residencies

Yeshiva University

EINSTEIN

- 1300 Morris Park Avenue, Bronx, NY 10461
- Private
- **Year Founded:** 1955
- **Tuition, 2007-2008:** $43,370
- **Enrollment 2007-2008 academic year:** 753
- **Website:** http://www.aecom.yu.edu
- **Specialty ranking:** N/A

3.73 AVERAGE GPA, ENTERING CLASS FALL 2007

10.8 AVERAGE MCAT, ENTERING CLASS FALL 2007

7.3% ACCEPTANCE RATE, ENTERING CLASS FALL 2007

36 2009 U.S. NEWS MEDICAL SCHOOL RANKING (RESEARCH)

26 2009 U.S. NEWS MEDICAL SCHOOL RANKING (PRIMARY CARE)

ADMISSIONS

Admissions phone number: **(718) 430-2106**
Admissions email address: **admissions@aecom.yu.edu**
Application website: **http://www.aecom.yu.edu/home/admissions/Default.htm**
Acceptance rate: **7.3%**
In-state acceptance rate: **11.4%**
Out-of-state acceptance rate: **6.2%**
Minority acceptance rate: **5.5%**
International acceptance rate: **2.3%**

Fall 2007 applications and acceptees

	Applied	Interviewed	Accepted	Enrolled
Total:	7,416	1,446	541	183
In-state:	1,565	423	178	80
Out-of-state:	5,851	1,023	363	103

Profile of admitted students

Average undergraduate grade point average: **3.73**
MCAT averages (scale: 1-15; writing test: J-T):
  Composite score: **10.8**
  Verbal reasoning score: **10.3**, Physical sciences score: **11.0**, Biological sciences score: **11.0**, Writing score: **P**
Proportion with undergraduate majors in: Biological sciences: **45%**, Physical sciences: **21%**, Non-sciences: **26%**, Other health professions: **N/A**, Mixed disciplines and other: **8%**
Percentage of students not coming directly from college after graduation: **27%**

Dates and details

The American Medical College Application Service (AMCAS) application is accepted.
School asks for a school-specific application as part of the admissions process.
Oldest MCAT considered for Fall 2009 entry: **2005**
Earliest application date for the 2009-2010 first-year class: **6/1**
Latest application date: **11/1**
Acceptance dates for regular application for the class entering in fall 2009:

Earliest: **June 1, 2008**
Latest: **November 1, 2008**
The school considers requests for deferred entrance.
Starting month for the class entering in 2009–2010: **August**
The school has an Early Decision Plan (EDP).
A personal interview is required for admission.

Undergraduate coursework required

Medical school requires undergraduate work in these subjects: biology, English, organic chemistry, inorganic (general) chemistry, physics, mathematics.

COSTS AND FINANCIAL AID

Financial aid phone number: **(718) 430-2336**
Tuition, 2007-2008 academic year: **$43,370**
Room and board: **$15,200**
Percentage of students receiving financial aid in 2007-08: **88%**
Percentage of students receiving: Loans: **84%**, Grants/scholarships: **47%**, Work-study aid: **0%**
Average medical school debt for the Class of 2006: **$112,000**

STUDENT BODY

Fall 2007 full-time enrollment: **753**
Men: **48%**, Women: **52%**, In-state: **44%**, Minorities: **31%**, American Indian: **N/A**, Asian-American: **72.7%**, African-American: **21.6%**, Hispanic-American: **5.7%**, White: **N/A**, International: **N/A**, Unknown: **N/A**

ACADEMIC PROGRAMS

The school's curriculum frequently gives first-year students substantial contact with patients.
There are opportunities for first- or second-year students to work in community health clinics.
Program offerings: AIDS, drug/alcohol abuse, family medicine, geriatrics, internal medicine, pediatrics, rural medicine, women's health
Joint degrees awarded: M.D./Ph.D., M.D./M.S.

Total National Institutes of Health (NIH) grants awarded to the medical school and affiliated hospitals: **$178.2 million**

CURRICULUM
(TEXT PROVIDED BY SCHOOL):
The 19-month preclerkship curriculum is devoted primarily to interdisciplinary biomedical science courses. There are also courses in which students interact with patients, learn patient-doctor communication, acquire physical examination and diagnostic skills, study medical ethics, and learn how psychosocial and cultural factors affect patient behavior. Medical Spanish courses offered as electives.

FACULTY PROFILE (FALL 2007)
Total teaching faculty: **2,605 (full-time)**, **315 (part-time)**
Of full-time faculty, those teaching in basic sciences: **14%**; in clinical programs: **86%**
Of part-time faculty, those teaching in basic sciences: **6%**; in clinical programs: **94%**
Full-time faculty/student ratio: **3.5**

SUPPORT SERVICES
The school offers students these services for dealing with stress: expanded-hour gym access, peer counseling, professional counseling, religious support, support groups.

RESIDENCY PROFILE
Most popular residency and specialty programs chosen by the 2006 and 2007 M.D. graduating classes: anesthesiology, emergency medicine, internal medicine, obstetrics and gynecology, ophthalmology, orthopaedic surgery, pathology–anatomic and clinical–selective pathology, pediatrics, radiology–diagnostic, surgery–general.

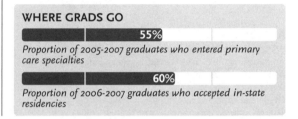

WHERE GRADS GO

55%
Proportion of 2005-2007 graduates who entered primary care specialties

60%
Proportion of 2006-2007 graduates who accepted in-state residencies

A.T. Still University of Health Sciences

KIRKSVILLE

- 800 W. Jefferson Street, Kirksville, MO 63501
- Private
- Year Founded: 1892
- Tuition, 2007-2008: $38,000
- Enrollment 2007-2008 academic year: 697
- Website: http://www.atsu.edu
- Specialty ranking: rural medicine: 28

3.42 AVERAGE GPA, ENTERING CLASS FALL 2007

8.7 AVERAGE MCAT, ENTERING CLASS FALL 2007

12.4% ACCEPTANCE RATE, ENTERING CLASS FALL 2007

Unranked 2009 U.S. NEWS MEDICAL SCHOOL RANKING (RESEARCH)

Unranked 2009 U.S. NEWS MEDICAL SCHOOL RANKING (PRIMARY CARE)

ADMISSIONS

Admissions phone number: (866) 626-2878
Admissions email address: **admissions@atsu.edu**
Application website: **http://www.aacom.org**
Acceptance rate: 12.4%
In-state acceptance rate: 24.5%
Out-of-state acceptance rate: 11.7%
Minority acceptance rate: 10.8%
International acceptance rate: N/A

Fall 2007 applications and acceptees

	Applied	Interviewed	Accepted	Enrolled
Total:	3,103	474	386	172
In-state:	184	43	45	29
Out-of-state:	2,919	431	341	143

Profile of admitted students

Average undergraduate grade point average: 3.42
MCAT averages (scale: 1-15; writing test: J-T):
Composite score: 8.7
Verbal reasoning score: 8.7, Physical sciences score: 8.3,
Biological sciences score: 9.0, Writing score: O
Proportion with undergraduate majors in: Biological
sciences: 47%, Physical sciences: 18%, Non-sciences:
17%, Other health professions: 6%, Mixed disciplines
and other: 12%
Percentage of students not coming directly from college
after graduation: N/A

Dates and details

The American Medical College Application Service
(AMCAS) application is not accepted.
School asks for a school-specific application as part of the
admissions process.
Oldest MCAT considered for Fall 2009 entry: 2005
Earliest application date for the 2009-2010 first-year class:
10/28
Latest application date: 8/2
Acceptance dates for regular application for the class
entering in fall 2009:

Earliest: **March 31, 2007**
Latest: **January 29, 1931**
The school considers requests for deferred entrance.
Starting month for the class entering in 2009–2010:
August
The school has an Early Decision Plan (EDP).
A personal interview is required for admission.

Undergraduate coursework required

Medical school requires undergraduate work in these subjects: biology, English, organic chemistry, inorganic (general) chemistry, physics.

ADMISSIONS POLICY
(TEXT PROVIDED BY SCHOOL):

Admissions Committee screens applicants for academic
achievement, clinical involvement, interpersonal relations,
leadership and service, maturity, motivation, and osteopathic awareness. Those selected are interviewed prior to
acceptance. Applicants are notified as soon as the committee decides on their status. A signed admission agreement
along with a nonrefundable acceptance fee is required.

COSTS AND FINANCIAL AID

Financial aid phone number: (660) 626-2529
Tuition, 2007-2008 academic year: $38,000
Room and board: $10,593
Percentage of students receiving financial aid in 2007-08:
94%
Percentage of students receiving: Loans: 94%,
Grants/scholarships: 16%, Work-study aid: 18%
Average medical school debt for the Class of 2006:
$152,713

STUDENT BODY

Fall 2007 full-time enrollment: 697
Men: 60%, Women: 40%, In-state: 21%, Minorities: 17%,
American Indian: 0.9%, Asian-American: 11.8%,
African-American: 1.1%, Hispanic-American: 1.9%,
White: 80.2%, International: 1.6%, Unknown: 2.6%

ACADEMIC PROGRAMS

The school's curriculum frequently gives first-year students substantial contact with patients.

There are opportunities for first- or second-year students to work in community health clinics.

Program offerings: AIDS, drug/alcohol abuse, family medicine, geriatrics, internal medicine, pediatrics, rural medicine, women's health

Joint degrees awarded: D.O./M.P.H., D.O./M.S., D.O./M.H.A.

Total National Institutes of Health (NIH) grants awarded to the medical school and affiliated hospitals: **$.2 million**

CURRICULUM

(TEXT PROVIDED BY SCHOOL):

The Kirksville College of Osteopathic Medicine has a four-year curriculum that is predominantly disciplined based. The first and second year provide primarily basic science courses and a longitudinal course, designed to teach doctoring skills. Included are communication skills, physical exam skills, history-taking skills, documentation, and the federal Health Insurance Portability and Accountability Act (HIPAA), as well as courses on Ethics, Epidemiology, Community Medicine, and Geriatrics.

FACULTY PROFILE (FALL 2007)

Total teaching faculty: **65 (full-time), 9 (part-time)**

Of full-time faculty, those teaching in basic sciences: **37%**; in clinical programs: **63%**

Of part-time faculty, those teaching in basic sciences: **0%**; in clinical programs: **100%**

Full-time faculty/student ratio: **0.1**

SUPPORT SERVICES

The school offers students these services for dealing with stress: expanded-hour gym access, peer counseling, professional counseling, religious support, support groups.

RESIDENCY PROFILE

Most popular residency and specialty programs chosen by the 2006 and 2007 M.D. graduating classes: anesthesiology, emergency medicine, family practice, internal medicine, obstetrics and gynecology, pediatrics, physical medicine and rehabilitation, radiology–diagnostic, surgery–general, transitional year.

WHERE GRADS GO

33.3%

Proportion of 2005-2007 graduates who entered primary care specialties

13.4%

Proportion of 2006-2007 graduates who accepted in-state residencies

Coll. of Osteopathic Med. of the Pacific

WESTERN UNIVERSITY

- 309 E. Second Street, Pomona, CA 91766-1854
- Private
- Year Founded: 1977
- Tuition, 2007-2008: $39,275
- Enrollment 2007-2008 academic year: 829
- Website: http://www.westernu.edu/comp/home.xml
- Specialty ranking: N/A

3.50	AVERAGE GPA, ENTERING CLASS FALL 2007
9.0	AVERAGE MCAT, ENTERING CLASS FALL 2007
15.6%	ACCEPTANCE RATE, ENTERING CLASS FALL 2007
Unranked	2009 U.S. NEWS MEDICAL SCHOOL RANKING (RESEARCH)
Unranked	2009 U.S. NEWS MEDICAL SCHOOL RANKING (PRIMARY CARE)

ADMISSIONS

Admissions phone number: **(909) 469-5335**
Admissions email address: **admissions@westernu.edu**
Application website: **http://www.aacom.org**
Acceptance rate: **15.6%**
In-state acceptance rate: **20.9%**
Out-of-state acceptance rate: **13.3%**
Minority acceptance rate: **14.8%**
International acceptance rate: **60.0%**

Fall 2007 applications and acceptees

	Applied	Interviewed	Accepted	Enrolled
Total:	3,204	659	501	220
In-state:	969	275	203	125
Out-of-state:	2,235	384	298	95

Profile of admitted students

Average undergraduate grade point average: **3.50**
MCAT averages (scale: 1-15; writing test: J-T):
Composite score: **9.0**
Verbal reasoning score: **8.7**, Physical sciences score: **9.1**,
Biological sciences score: **9.7**, Writing score: **P**
Proportion with undergraduate majors in: Biological
sciences: **50%**, Physical sciences: **15%**, Non-sciences:
13%, Other health professions: **6%**, Mixed disciplines
and other: **16%**
Percentage of students not coming directly from college
after graduation: **7%**

Dates and details

The American Medical College Application Service
(AMCAS) application is not accepted.
School asks for a school-specific application as part of the
admissions process.
Oldest MCAT considered for Fall 2009 entry: **N/A**
Earliest application date for the 2009-2010 first-year class:
N/A
Latest application date: **N/A**
Acceptance dates for regular application for the class
entering in fall 2009:

Earliest: **N/A**
Latest: **N/A**
The school considers requests for deferred entrance.
Starting month for the class entering in 2009–2010: **N/A**
The school doesn't have an Early Decision Plan (EDP).
A personal interview is required for admission.

Undergraduate coursework required

Medical school requires undergraduate work in these subjects: biology/zoology, English, organic chemistry, inorganic
(general) chemistry, physics, behavioral science.

ADMISSIONS POLICY
(TEXT PROVIDED BY SCHOOL):

COMP accepts applications from qualified candidates.
While grades and MCAT scores are important and suggest
future academic success, COMP recognizes that these do
not guarantee success as a physician. Nonacademic criteria
are also important. COMP seeks a diverse and balanced student population. An on-campus interview is required.

COSTS AND FINANCIAL AID

Financial aid phone number: **(909) 469-5350**
Tuition, 2007-2008 academic year: **$39,275**
Room and board: **$11,190**
Percentage of students receiving financial aid in 2007-08:
88%
Percentage of students receiving: Loans: **86%**,
Grants/scholarships: **13%**, Work-study aid: **0%**
Average medical school debt for the Class of 2006:
$164,315

STUDENT BODY

Fall 2007 full-time enrollment: **829**
Men: **50%**, Women: **50%**, In-state: **61%**, Minorities: **45%**,
American Indian: **0.6%**, Asian-American: **39.6%**,
African-American: **1.1%**, Hispanic-American: **4.2%**,
White: **46.6%**, International: **1.6%**, Unknown: **6.4%**

ACADEMIC PROGRAMS

The school's curriculum frequently gives first-year students substantial contact with patients.

There are opportunities for first- or second-year students to work in community health clinics.

Program offerings: AIDS, drug/alcohol abuse, family medicine, geriatrics, internal medicine, pediatrics, rural medicine

Joint degrees awarded: D.O./M.S.

Total National Institutes of Health (NIH) grants awarded to the medical school and affiliated hospitals: **$.6 million**

CURRICULUM

(TEXT PROVIDED BY SCHOOL):

The curriculum is divided into three phases: introduction to the basic sciences; correlated system teaching, incorporating basic and clinical sciences in the study of the organ systems of the body; and clinical experiences.

FACULTY PROFILE (FALL 2007)

Total teaching faculty: **39 (full-time)**, **2 (part-time)**

Of full-time faculty, those teaching in basic sciences: **64%**; in clinical programs: **36%**

Of part-time faculty, those teaching in basic sciences: **0%**; in clinical programs: **100%**

Full-time faculty/student ratio: **N/A**

SUPPORT SERVICES

The school offers students these services for dealing with stress: expanded-hour gym access, peer counseling, professional counseling, religious support, support groups.

RESIDENCY PROFILE

Most popular residency and specialty programs chosen by the 2006 and 2007 M.D. graduating classes: anesthesiology, emergency medicine, family practice, internal medicine, neurology, obstetrics and gynecology, pediatrics, physical medicine and rehabilitation, psychiatry, surgery–general.

WHERE GRADS GO

Proportion of 2005-2007 graduates who entered primary care specialties

Proportion of 2006-2007 graduates who accepted in-state residencies

Edward Via Virginia

COLLEGE OF OSTEOPATHIC MEDICINE

- 2265 Kraft Drive, Blacksburg, VA 24060
- Private
- Year Founded: 2003
- Tuition, 2007-2008: $31,000
- Enrollment 2007-2008 academic year: 617
- Website: http://www.vcom.vt.edu
- Specialty ranking: family medicine: 27, rural medicine: 21

3.53	AVERAGE GPA, ENTERING CLASS FALL 2007
8.0	AVERAGE MCAT, ENTERING CLASS FALL 2007
10.6%	ACCEPTANCE RATE, ENTERING CLASS FALL 2007
Unranked	2009 U.S. NEWS MEDICAL SCHOOL RANKING (RESEARCH)
Unranked	2009 U.S. NEWS MEDICAL SCHOOL RANKING (PRIMARY CARE)

ADMISSIONS

Admissions phone number: **(540) 231-6138**
Admissions email address: **mprice@vcom.vt.edu**
Application website: **http://www.aacom.org**
Acceptance rate: **10.6%**
In-state acceptance rate: **36.3%**
Out-of-state acceptance rate: **7.9%**
Minority acceptance rate: **12.6%**
International acceptance rate: **N/A**

Fall 2007 applications and acceptees

	Applied	Interviewed	Accepted	Enrolled
Total:	2,364	335	250	162
In-state:	223	106	81	56
Out-of-state:	2,141	229	169	106

Profile of admitted students

Average undergraduate grade point average: **3.53**
MCAT averages (scale: 1-15; writing test: J-T):
  Composite score: **8.0**
  Verbal reasoning score: **8.0**, Physical sciences score: **8.0**,
  Biological sciences score: **8.0**, Writing score: **Q**
Proportion with undergraduate majors in: Biological sciences: **56%**, Physical sciences: **15%**, Non-sciences: **11%**, Other health professions: **17%**, Mixed disciplines and other: **1%**
Percentage of students not coming directly from college after graduation: **35%**

Dates and details

The American Medical College Application Service (AMCAS) application is not accepted.
School asks for a school-specific application as part of the admissions process.
Oldest MCAT considered for Fall 2009 entry: **2005**
Earliest application date for the 2009-2010 first-year class: **6/1**
Latest application date: **2/1**
Acceptance dates for regular application for the class entering in fall 2009:
  Earliest: **October 15, 2008**

Latest: **April 1, 2009**
The school considers requests for deferred entrance.
Starting month for the class entering in 2009–2010:
  August
The school has an Early Decision Plan (EDP).
A personal interview is required for admission.

Undergraduate coursework required

Medical school requires undergraduate work in these subjects: biology, English, organic chemistry, physics, demonstration of writing skills, general chemistry.

ADMISSIONS POLICY

(TEXT PROVIDED BY SCHOOL):
Basic requirements: undergraduate degree including eight semester hours each of Biology, General Chemistry, and Organic Chemistry and six hours each of Physics, English, and additional science, with minimum grade-point average of 2.75, and a recent MCAT score no earlier than April 2005. Preference is given to candidates who fulfill the collegeís mission (Appalachian, rural, minority, mission-minded) and have scores near the college average (GPA of 3.5, total MCAT score of 24).

COSTS AND FINANCIAL AID

Financial aid phone number: **(540) 231-6021**
Tuition, 2007-2008 academic year: **$31,000**
Room and board: **$25,300**
Percentage of students receiving financial aid in 2007-08: **95%**
Percentage of students receiving: Loans: **91%**, Grants/scholarships: **21%**, Work-study aid: **0%**
Average medical school debt for the Class of 2006: **N/A**

STUDENT BODY

Fall 2007 full-time enrollment: **617**
Men: **47%**, Women: **53%**, In-state: **37%**, Minorities: **26%**, American Indian: **1.9%**, Asian-American: **10.5%**, African-American: **13.0%**, Hispanic-American: **6.8%**, White: **62.3%**, International: **0.0%**, Unknown: **5.6%**

ACADEMIC PROGRAMS

The school's curriculum frequently gives first-year students substantial contact with patients.

There are opportunities for first- or second-year students to work in community health clinics.

Program offerings: drug/alcohol abuse, family medicine, geriatrics, internal medicine, pediatrics, rural medicine, women's health

Joint degrees awarded: D.O./Ph.D., D.O./M.B.A., D.O./M.P.H., D.O./M.S.

Total National Institutes of Health (NIH) grants awarded to the medical school and affiliated hospitals: **$.9 million**

CURRICULUM

(TEXT PROVIDED BY SCHOOL):

The curriculum at VCOM is innovative and modern. The faculty recognizes that students learn in a number of ways. Students generally assimilate a knowledge base through instruction, reading, and experience. VCOM developed a hybrid curriculum consisting of lectures, computerized case tutorials, laboratory experiences, clinical skills laboratories, and clinical experiences throughout the four years.

FACULTY PROFILE (FALL 2007)

Total teaching faculty: **42 (full-time)**, **594 (part-time)**

Of full-time faculty, those teaching in basic sciences: **48%**; in clinical programs: **52%**

Of part-time faculty, those teaching in basic sciences: **1%**; in clinical programs: **99%**

Full-time faculty/student ratio: **0.1**

SUPPORT SERVICES

The school offers students these services for dealing with stress: expanded-hour gym access, peer counseling, professional counseling, religious support, support groups.

RESIDENCY PROFILE

Most popular residency and specialty programs chosen by the 2006 and 2007 M.D. graduating classes: anesthesiology, emergency medicine, family practice, internal medicine, obstetrics and gynecology, orthopaedic surgery, radiology–diagnostic, surgery–general.

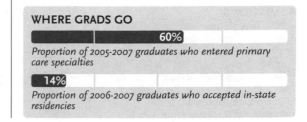

WHERE GRADS GO

60%

Proportion of 2005-2007 graduates who entered primary care specialties

14%

Proportion of 2006-2007 graduates who accepted in-state residencies

Lake Erie College of Osteopathic Med.

- 1858 W. Grandview Boulevard, Erie, PA 16509
- Private
- **Year Founded:** 1992
- **Tuition, 2007-2008:** $25,950
- **Enrollment 2007-2008 academic year:** 1,567
- **Website:** http://www.lecom.edu
- **Specialty ranking:** N/A

3.40 AVERAGE GPA, ENTERING CLASS FALL 2007

8.7 AVERAGE MCAT, ENTERING CLASS FALL 2007

11.5% ACCEPTANCE RATE, ENTERING CLASS FALL 2007

Unranked 2009 U.S. NEWS MEDICAL SCHOOL RANKING (RESEARCH)

Unranked 2009 U.S. NEWS MEDICAL SCHOOL RANKING (PRIMARY CARE)

ADMISSIONS

Admissions phone number: **(814) 866-6641**
Admissions email address: **admissions@lecom.edu**
Application website: **http://www.aacom.org**
Acceptance rate: **11.5%**
In-state acceptance rate: **34.1%**
Out-of-state acceptance rate: **7.8%**
Minority acceptance rate: **11.2%**
International acceptance rate: **100.0%**

Fall 2007 applications and acceptees

	Applied	Interviewed	Accepted	Enrolled
Total:	6,623	1,484	762	421
In-state:	940	418	321	173
Out-of-state:	5,683	1,066	441	248

Profile of admitted students

Average undergraduate grade point average: 3.40
MCAT averages (scale: 1-15; writing test: J-T):
  Composite score: **8.7**
  Verbal reasoning score: **9.0**, Physical sciences score: **8.2**,
  Biological sciences score: **9.0**, Writing score: **O**
Proportion with undergraduate majors in: Biological
  sciences: **68%**, Physical sciences: **6%**, Non-sciences:
  15%, Other health professions: **6%**, Mixed disciplines
  and other: **5%**
Percentage of students not coming directly from college
  after graduation: **14%**

Dates and details

The American Medical College Application Service
  (AMCAS) application is not accepted.
School asks for a school-specific application as part of the
  admissions process.
Oldest MCAT considered for Fall 2009 entry: **2006**
Earliest application date for the 2009-2010 first-year class:
  6/1
Latest application date: **4/1**
Acceptance dates for regular application for the class
  entering in fall 2009:

Earliest: **September 1, 2008**
Latest: **July 30, 2009**
The school considers requests for deferred entrance.
Starting month for the class entering in 2009–2010:
  August
The school doesn't have an Early Decision Plan (EDP).
A personal interview is required for admission.

Undergraduate coursework required

Medical school requires undergraduate work in these subjects: biology, English, organic chemistry, inorganic (general) chemistry, physics, molecular and cell biology,
humanities, mathematics, behavioral science, demonstration of writing skills, social sciences, general chemistry.

ADMISSIONS POLICY

(TEXT PROVIDED BY SCHOOL):

LECOM seeks students who will excel in academics, clinical
care, research, and community service. Successful candidates have grade-point averages of 3.3 or higher and total
MCATs of 24 or higher. LECOM requires a D.O. recommendation showing the applicant has awareness of osteopathic medicine. Working with a physician prepares
students for the required interview. LECOM sets no limits
on out-of-state resident admissions.

COSTS AND FINANCIAL AID

Financial aid phone number: **(814) 866-6641**
Tuition, 2007-2008 academic year: **$25,950**
Room and board: **$11,550**
Percentage of students receiving financial aid in 2007-08:
  92%
Percentage of students receiving: Loans: **90%**,
  Grants/scholarships: **25%**, Work-study aid: **N/A**
Average medical school debt for the Class of 2006:
  $159,000

STUDENT BODY

Fall 2007 full-time enrollment: **1,567**

Men: **53%**, Women: **47%**, In-state: **36%**, Minorities: **24%**,
American Indian: **0.1%**, Asian-American: **16.0%**,
African-American: **2.4%**, Hispanic-American: **5.6%**,
White: **75.9%**, International: **0.1%**, Unknown: **0.0%**

ACADEMIC PROGRAMS

The school's curriculum occasionally gives first-year
students substantial contact with patients.

There are opportunities for first- or second-year students to
work in community health clinics.

Program offerings: AIDS, drug/alcohol abuse, family
medicine, geriatrics, internal medicine, pediatrics, rural
medicine, women's health

Joint degrees awarded: D.O./M.S.

Total National Institutes of Health (NIH) grants awarded to
the medical school and affiliated hospitals: **N/A**

CURRICULUM

(TEXT PROVIDED BY SCHOOL):

LECOM offers more student-centered learning pathways
than any other medical school. The new Primary Care
Scholars pathway provides a condensed three-year track to
becoming a family physician. LECOM students also choose
from traditional lecture and discussion; small-group, problem-based learning; and an independent study curriculum.
LECOM offers clinical training at 100-plus affiliated hospitals and clinics.

FACULTY PROFILE (FALL 2007)

Total teaching faculty: **110 (full-time)**, **1,675 (part-time)**

Of full-time faculty, those teaching in basic sciences: **46%**;
in clinical programs: **54%**

Of part-time faculty, those teaching in basic sciences: **2%**;
in clinical programs: **98%**

Full-time faculty/student ratio: **0.1**

SUPPORT SERVICES

The school offers students these services for dealing with
stress: expanded-hour gym access, peer counseling, professional counseling, religious support, support groups.

RESIDENCY PROFILE

Most popular residency and specialty programs chosen by
the 2006 and 2007 M.D. graduating classes: anesthesiology, emergency medicine, family practice, internal
medicine, obstetrics and gynecology, orthopaedic surgery,
pediatrics, radiology–diagnostic, surgery–general,
transitional year.

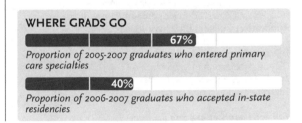

WHERE GRADS GO

67%

*Proportion of 2005-2007 graduates who entered primary
care specialties*

40%

*Proportion of 2006-2007 graduates who accepted in-state
residencies*

Michigan State University

COLLEGE OF OSTEOPATHIC MEDICINE

- A308 E. Fee Hall, East Lansing, MI 48824
- Public
- **Year Founded:** 1969
- **Tuition, 2007-2008:** In-state: $28,025; Out-of-state: $60,905
- **Enrollment 2007-2008 academic year:** 787
- **Website:** http://www.com.msu.edu
- **Specialty ranking:** family medicine: 13

3.55	AVERAGE GPA, ENTERING CLASS FALL 2007
8.7	AVERAGE MCAT, ENTERING CLASS FALL 2007
11.0%	ACCEPTANCE RATE, ENTERING CLASS FALL 2007
Unranked	2009 U.S. NEWS MEDICAL SCHOOL RANKING (RESEARCH)
7	2009 U.S. NEWS MEDICAL SCHOOL RANKING (PRIMARY CARE)

ADMISSIONS

Admissions phone number: **(517) 353-7740**
Admissions email address: **comadm@com.msu.edu**
Application website: **http://www.aacom.org**
Acceptance rate: **11.0%**
In-state acceptance rate: **37.3%**
Out-of-state acceptance rate: **2.2%**
Minority acceptance rate: **6.6%**
International acceptance rate: **N/A**

Fall 2007 applications and acceptees

	Applied	Interviewed	Accepted	Enrolled
Total:	3,017	432	331	211
In-state:	753	376	281	195
Out-of-state:	2,264	56	50	16

Profile of admitted students

Average undergraduate grade point average: **3.55**
MCAT averages (scale: 1-15; writing test: J-T):
   Composite score: **8.7**
   Verbal reasoning score: **8.5**, Physical sciences score: **8.4**,
   Biological sciences score: **9.1**, Writing score: **O**
Proportion with undergraduate majors in: Biological sciences: **58%**, Physical sciences: **4%**, Non-sciences: **11%**, Other health professions: **11%**, Mixed disciplines and other: **16%**
Percentage of students not coming directly from college after graduation: **18%**

Dates and details

The American Medical College Application Service (AMCAS) application is not accepted.
School asks for a school-specific application as part of the admissions process.
Oldest MCAT considered for Fall 2009 entry: **2005**
Earliest application date for the 2009-2010 first-year class: **6/1**
Latest application date: **12/1**
Acceptance dates for regular application for the class entering in fall 2009:

Earliest: **September 15, 2008**
Latest: **June 15, 2009**
The school considers requests for deferred entrance.
Starting month for the class entering in 2009–2010: **July**
The school doesn't have an Early Decision Plan (EDP).
A personal interview isn't required for admission.

Undergraduate coursework required

Medical school requires undergraduate work in these subjects: biology, biology/zoology, English, organic chemistry, inorganic (general) chemistry, physics, biochemistry, behavioral science, general chemistry.

ADMISSIONS POLICY

(TEXT PROVIDED BY SCHOOL):

Minimum to receive a secondary application: 2.7 science and overall grade-point average, total MCAT score of 18 (minimum 4 verbal, 5 physical sciences, and 6 biologic sciences). Application review is 60 percent academic and 40 percent nonacademic. Final evaluation: academic ability, level/type of coursework, MCAT scores, academic honors, commitment to service, breadth of experiences, communication, leadership, collaboration, problem solving, critical thinking.

COSTS AND FINANCIAL AID

Financial aid phone number: **(517) 353-5188**
Tuition, 2007-2008 academic year: **In-state: $28,025; Out-of-state: $60,905**
Room and board: **$14,484**
Percentage of students receiving financial aid in 2007-08: **92%**
Percentage of students receiving: Loans: **88%**, Grants/scholarships: **72%**, Work-study aid: **0%**
Average medical school debt for the Class of 2006: **$156,045**

STUDENT BODY

Fall 2007 full-time enrollment: **787**

Men: 48%, Women: 52%, In-state: 90%, Minorities: 19%, American Indian: 0.6%, Asian-American: 13.5%, African-American: 3.4%, Hispanic-American: 1.5%, White: 80.9%, International: 0.0%, Unknown: 0.0%

ACADEMIC PROGRAMS
The school's curriculum frequently gives first-year students substantial contact with patients.

There are opportunities for first- or second-year students to work in community health clinics.

Program offerings: AIDS, drug/alcohol abuse, family medicine, geriatrics, internal medicine, pediatrics, rural medicine, women's health

Joint degrees awarded: D.O./Ph.D., D.O./M.B.A., D.O./M.P.H., D.O./M.S.

Total National Institutes of Health (NIH) grants awarded to the medical school and affiliated hospitals: **$4.9 million**

CURRICULUM
(TEXT PROVIDED BY SCHOOL):
The college is dedicated to assisting in meeting the ever growing public demand for physicians who can provide comprehensive and continuing health care to all members of the family. While the educational program of MSUCOM is geared to the training of primary care physicians, the curricula are also designed to meet the continuing need for medical specialists and teacher-investigators.

FACULTY PROFILE (FALL 2007)
Total teaching faculty: 213 (full-time), 26 (part-time)

Of full-time faculty, those teaching in basic sciences: 29%; in clinical programs: 71%
Of part-time faculty, those teaching in basic sciences: 12%; in clinical programs: 88%
Full-time faculty/student ratio: 0.3

SUPPORT SERVICES
The school offers students these services for dealing with stress: expanded-hour gym access, peer counseling, professional counseling, religious support, support groups.

RESIDENCY PROFILE
Most popular residency and specialty programs chosen by the 2006 and 2007 M.D. graduating classes: emergency medicine, family practice, internal medicine, neurology, ophthalmology, pediatrics, physical medicine and rehabilitation, psychiatry, radiology–diagnostic, surgery–general.

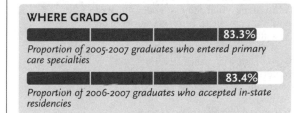

WHERE GRADS GO

83.3%
Proportion of 2005-2007 graduates who entered primary care specialties

83.4%
Proportion of 2006-2007 graduates who accepted in-state residencies

New York College of Osteopathic Med.

- Old Westbury, Northern Boulevard, Long Island, NY 11568
- Private
- **Year Founded:** 1977
- **Tuition, 2007-2008:** $38,965
- **Enrollment 2007-2008 academic year:** 1,202
- **Website:** http://www.nyit.edu
- **Specialty ranking:** N/A

N/A	AVERAGE GPA, ENTERING CLASS FALL 2007
N/A	AVERAGE MCAT, ENTERING CLASS FALL 2007
11.8%	ACCEPTANCE RATE, ENTERING CLASS FALL 2007
Unranked	2009 U.S. NEWS MEDICAL SCHOOL RANKING (RESEARCH)
Unranked	2009 U.S. NEWS MEDICAL SCHOOL RANKING (PRIMARY CARE)

ADMISSIONS
Admissions phone number: **(516) 686-3747**
Admissions email address: **rzaika@nyit.edu**
Application website: **http://www.aacom.org**
Acceptance rate: **11.8%**
In-state acceptance rate: **55.0%**
Out-of-state acceptance rate: **1.9%**
Minority acceptance rate: **N/A**
International acceptance rate: **N/A**

Fall 2007 applications and acceptees
	Applied	Interviewed	Accepted	Enrolled
Total:	4,436	540	523	295
In-state:	825	469	454	254
Out-of-state:	3,611	71	69	41

Profile of admitted students
Average undergraduate grade point average: **N/A**
MCAT averages (scale: 1-15; writing test: J-T):
   Composite score: **N/A**
   Verbal reasoning score: **N/A**, Physical sciences score:
   N/A, Biological sciences score: **N/A**, Writing score: **N/A**
Proportion with undergraduate majors in: Biological
   sciences: **N/A**, Physical sciences: **N/A**, Non-sciences:
   N/A, Other health professions: **N/A**, Mixed disciplines
   and other: **N/A**
Percentage of students not coming directly from college
   after graduation: **23%**

Dates and details
The American Medical College Application Service
   (AMCAS) application is not accepted.
School asks for a school-specific application as part of the
   admissions process.
Oldest MCAT considered for Fall 2009 entry: **2005**
Earliest application date for the 2009-2010 first-year class:
   5/1
Latest application date: **2/1**
Acceptance dates for regular application for the class
   entering in fall 2009:

Earliest: **December 1, 2008**
Latest: **August 20, 2009**
The school considers requests for deferred entrance.
Starting month for the class entering in 2009-2010:
   August
The school doesn't have an Early Decision Plan (EDP).
A personal interview is required for admission.

Undergraduate coursework required
Medical school requires undergraduate work in these subjects: biology, biology/zoology, English, organic chemistry,
inorganic (general) chemistry, physics.

ADMISSIONS POLICY
(TEXT PROVIDED BY SCHOOL):
A percentage of applicants are selected for mandatory interviews. An Admissions Committee meets to determine
which applicants will be accepted. Factors include grade-
point average, MCAT scores, interview score, assessment of
required courses, letters of reference, and applicable experience.

COSTS AND FINANCIAL AID
Financial aid phone number: **(516) 686-7960**
Tuition, 2007-2008 academic year: **$38,965**
Room and board: **$21,000**
Percentage of students receiving financial aid in 2007-08:
   95%
Percentage of students receiving: Loans: **92%**,
   Grants/scholarships: **34%**, Work-study aid: **N/A**
Average medical school debt for the Class of 2006:
   $158,600

STUDENT BODY
Fall 2007 full-time enrollment: **1,202**
Men: **47%**, Women: **53%**, In-state: **85%**, Minorities: **N/A**,
   American Indian: **N/A**, Asian-American: **N/A**, African-
   American: **N/A**, Hispanic-American: **N/A**, White: **N/A**,
   International: **N/A**, Unknown: **N/A**

ACADEMIC PROGRAMS

The school's curriculum frequently gives first-year students substantial contact with patients.

There are opportunities for first- or second-year students to work in community health clinics.

Program offerings: drug/alcohol abuse, family medicine, geriatrics, internal medicine, pediatrics, rural medicine, women's health

Joint degrees awarded: D.O./M.B.A., D.O./M.S.

Total National Institutes of Health (NIH) grants awarded to the medical school and affiliated hospitals: **N/A**

CURRICULUM

(TEXT PROVIDED BY SCHOOL):

Two curricular tracks are offered: 1) an integrated systems-based curriculum consisting of three ongoing threads–(a) molecular/cellular basis, (b) structural/functional basis, (c) clinical practice of osteopathic medicine; 2) a problem-based learning track, whose cornerstone is small-group, case-based learning. In both tracks, Years 3 and 4 consist of required/elective rotations at affiliated clinical sites.

FACULTY PROFILE (FALL 2007)

Total teaching faculty: **N/A (full-time)**, **N/A (part-time)**
Of full-time faculty, those teaching in basic sciences: **N/A**; in clinical programs: **N/A**

Of part-time faculty, those teaching in basic sciences: **N/A**; in clinical programs: **N/A**
Full-time faculty/student ratio: **N/A**

SUPPORT SERVICES

The school offers students these services for dealing with stress: expanded-hour gym access, peer counseling, professional counseling.

RESIDENCY PROFILE

Most popular residency and specialty programs chosen by the 2006 and 2007 M.D. graduating classes: anesthesiology, emergency medicine, family practice, internal medicine, obstetrics and gynecology, pediatrics, physical medicine and rehabilitation, psychiatry, surgery–general, internal medicine/emergency medicine.

WHERE GRADS GO

N/A

Proportion of 2005-2007 graduates who entered primary care specialties

N/A

Proportion of 2006-2007 graduates who accepted in-state residencies

Nova Southeastern University

COLLEGE OF OSTEOPATHIC MEDICINE

- 3200 S. University Drive, Fort Lauderdale, FL 33328
- Private
- **Year Founded:** 1981
- **Tuition, 2007-2008:** $28,580
- **Enrollment 2007-2008 academic year:** 916
- **Website:** http://medicine.nova.edu
- **Specialty ranking:** N/A

3.48 AVERAGE GPA, ENTERING CLASS FALL 2007

8.3 AVERAGE MCAT, ENTERING CLASS FALL 2007

17.4% ACCEPTANCE RATE, ENTERING CLASS FALL 2007

Unranked 2009 U.S. NEWS MEDICAL SCHOOL RANKING (RESEARCH)

Unranked 2009 U.S. NEWS MEDICAL SCHOOL RANKING (PRIMARY CARE)

ADMISSIONS

Admissions phone number: **(954) 262-1101**
Admissions email address: **rachwein@nsu.nova.edu**
Application website: **http://hpd.nova.edu/**
Acceptance rate: **17.4%**
In-state acceptance rate: **31.0%**
Out-of-state acceptance rate: **13.0%**
Minority acceptance rate: **N/A**
International acceptance rate: **N/A**

Fall 2007 applications and acceptees

	Applied	Interviewed	Accepted	Enrolled
Total:	2,102	481	366	228
In-state:	516	203	160	138
Out-of-state:	1,586	278	206	90

Profile of admitted students

Average undergraduate grade point average: **3.48**
MCAT averages (scale: 1-15; writing test: J-T):
　Composite score: **8.3**
　Verbal reasoning score: **8.3**, Physical sciences score: **8.2**,
　Biological sciences score: **8.6**, Writing score: **M**
Proportion with undergraduate majors in: Biological
　sciences: **25%**, Physical sciences: **12%**, Non-sciences:
　13%, Other health professions: **23%**, Mixed disciplines
　and other: **28%**
Percentage of students not coming directly from college
　after graduation: **5%**

Dates and details

The American Medical College Application Service
　(AMCAS) application is not accepted.
School asks for a school-specific application as part of the
　admissions process.
Oldest MCAT considered for Fall 2009 entry: **2006**
Earliest application date for the 2009-2010 first-year class:
　6/4
Latest application date: **1/15**
Acceptance dates for regular application for the class
　entering in fall 2009:
　Earliest: **September 22, 2008**

Latest: **May 31, 2009**
The school considers requests for deferred entrance.
Starting month for the class entering in 2009–2010:
　August
The school doesn't have an Early Decision Plan (EDP).
A personal interview is required for admission.

Undergraduate coursework required

Medical school requires undergraduate work in these subjects: biology, English, organic chemistry, inorganic (general) chemistry, physics.

ADMISSIONS POLICY

(TEXT PROVIDED BY SCHOOL):

Prefer bachelor's but at least 90 semester hours.
Prerequisites: eight semester hours each of Biology,
Chemistry, Organic Chemistry, Physics; three semester
hours each of English Composition and Literature; MCAT;
letter from preprofessional committee or three professors in
science and liberal arts; letter from osteopathic physician;
personal interview for invited applicants. 3,500 applicants,
230 admitted. Florida residents eligible for reduced tuition.

COSTS AND FINANCIAL AID

Financial aid phone number: **(954) 262-3380**
Tuition, 2007-2008 academic year: **$28,580**
Room and board: **$17,050**
Percentage of students receiving financial aid in 2007-08:
　94%
Percentage of students receiving: Loans: **88%**,
　Grants/scholarships: **N/A**, Work-study aid: **1%**
Average medical school debt for the Class of 2006:
　$154,676

STUDENT BODY

Fall 2007 full-time enrollment: **916**
Men: **50%**, Women: **50%**, In-state: **49%**, Minorities: **33%**,
　American Indian: **0.8%**, Asian-American: **18.2%**,
　African-American: **3.5%**, Hispanic-American: **10.9%**,
　White: **61.2%**, International: **1.1%**, Unknown: **4.3%**

ACADEMIC PROGRAMS
The school's curriculum frequently gives first-year students substantial contact with patients.

There are opportunities for first- or second-year students to work in community health clinics.

Program offerings: AIDS, drug/alcohol abuse, family medicine, geriatrics, internal medicine, pediatrics, rural medicine, women's health

Joint degrees awarded: D.O./M.B.A., D.O./M.P.H., D.O./M.H.I.

Total National Institutes of Health (NIH) grants awarded to the medical school and affiliated hospitals: **$.6 million**

CURRICULUM
(TEXT PROVIDED BY SCHOOL):
The curriculum emphasizes primary care, interdisciplinary collaboration, and a holistic and osteopathic approach to care. Students are in clinical settings in their first semester. Clinical exposure continues into the second year in interactions with standardized and real patients in clinical settings. The clinical program features three months in rural settings providing care to medically underserved.

FACULTY PROFILE (FALL 2007)
Total teaching faculty: **103 (full-time)**, **883 (part-time)**

Of full-time faculty, those teaching in basic sciences: **29%**; in clinical programs: **71%**

Of part-time faculty, those teaching in basic sciences: **0%**; in clinical programs: **100%**

Full-time faculty/student ratio: **0.1**

SUPPORT SERVICES
The school offers students these services for dealing with stress: peer counseling, professional counseling.

RESIDENCY PROFILE
Most popular residency and specialty programs chosen by the 2006 and 2007 M.D. graduating classes: anesthesiology, dermatology, emergency medicine, family practice, internal medicine, obstetrics and gynecology, pediatrics, radiology–diagnostic, surgery–general, transitional year.

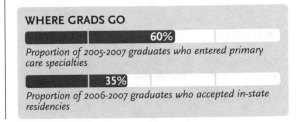

WHERE GRADS GO

60%

Proportion of 2005-2007 graduates who entered primary care specialties

35%

Proportion of 2006-2007 graduates who accepted in-state residencies

Ohio University

- **Grosvenor and Irvine Halls, Athens, OH 45701**
- **Public**
- **Year Founded:** 1975
- **Tuition, 2007-2008:** In-state: $25,476; Out-of-state: $35,809
- **Enrollment 2007-2008 academic year:** 438
- **Website:** http://www.oucom.ohiou.edu
- **Specialty ranking:** rural medicine: 21

3.57	AVERAGE GPA, ENTERING CLASS FALL 2007
8.4	AVERAGE MCAT, ENTERING CLASS FALL 2007
4.8%	ACCEPTANCE RATE, ENTERING CLASS FALL 2007
Unranked	2009 U.S. NEWS MEDICAL SCHOOL RANKING (RESEARCH)
Unranked	2009 U.S. NEWS MEDICAL SCHOOL RANKING (PRIMARY CARE)

ADMISSIONS

Admissions phone number: **(740) 593-4313**
Admissions email address: **admissions@oucom.ohiou.edu**
Application website: **http://www.aacom.org**
Acceptance rate: **4.8%**
In-state acceptance rate: **26.2%**
Out-of-state acceptance rate: **0.9%**
Minority acceptance rate: **3.0%**
International acceptance rate: **0.0%**

Fall 2007 applications and acceptees

	Applied	Interviewed	Accepted	Enrolled
Total:	3,173	217	152	108
In-state:	489	181	128	94
Out-of-state:	2,684	36	24	14

Profile of admitted students

Average undergraduate grade point average: **3.57**
MCAT averages (scale: 1-15; writing test: J-T):
  Composite score: **8.4**
  Verbal reasoning score: **8.4**, Physical sciences score: **7.5**,
  Biological sciences score: **8.4**, Writing score: **O**
Proportion with undergraduate majors in: Biological
  sciences: **70%**, Physical sciences: **14%**, Non-sciences:
  6%, Other health professions: **6%**, Mixed disciplines
  and other: **4%**
Percentage of students not coming directly from college
  after graduation: **43%**

Dates and details

The American Medical College Application Service
  (AMCAS) application is not accepted.
School asks for a school-specific application as part of the
  admissions process.
Oldest MCAT considered for Fall 2009 entry: **2006**
Earliest application date for the 2009-2010 first-year class:
  6/1
Latest application date: **2/1**
Acceptance dates for regular application for the class
  entering in fall 2009:
  Earliest: **August 1, 2008**

Latest: **August 1, 2009**
The school considers requests for deferred entrance.
Starting month for the class entering in 2009–2010:
  August
The school doesn't have an Early Decision Plan (EDP).
A personal interview is required for admission.

Undergraduate coursework required

Medical school requires undergraduate work in these subjects: biology, biology/zoology, English, organic chemistry,
inorganic (general) chemistry, physics, behavioral science,
social sciences, general chemistry.

ADMISSIONS POLICY

(TEXT PROVIDED BY SCHOOL):
Superior academic performance and strong MCAT scores;
dedication to humane medical care delivery; motivation for
osteopathic medicine; excellent communication skills; four-
year baccalaureate degree preferred; letters of recommendation. Must be U.S. citizen or hold permanent visa.
Additional information available at the website.

COSTS AND FINANCIAL AID

Financial aid phone number: **(740) 593-2158**
Tuition, 2007-2008 academic year: **In-state: $25,476; Out-
of-state: $35,809**
Room and board: **$10,071**
Percentage of students receiving financial aid in 2007-08:
  92%
Percentage of students receiving: Loans: **90%**,
  Grants/scholarships: **30%**, Work-study aid: **2%**
Average medical school debt for the Class of 2006:
  $143,771

STUDENT BODY

Fall 2007 full-time enrollment: **438**
Men: **49%**, Women: **51%**, In-state: **98%**, Minorities: **26%**,
  American Indian: **1.4%**, Asian-American: **8.9%**, African-
  American: **10.5%**, Hispanic-American: **5.0%**, White:
  74.2%, International: **0.0%**, Unknown: **0.0%**

ACADEMIC PROGRAMS

The school's curriculum very frequently gives first-year students substantial contact with patients.

There are opportunities for first- or second-year students to work in community health clinics.

Program offerings: AIDS, drug/alcohol abuse, family medicine, geriatrics, internal medicine, pediatrics, rural medicine, women's health

Joint degrees awarded: D.O./Ph.D., D.O./M.B.A., D.O./M.P.H., D.O./M.S.W., D.O./M.S., D.O./M.A., D.O./M.H.A.

Total National Institutes of Health (NIH) grants awarded to the medical school and affiliated hospitals: **$.5 million**

CURRICULUM

(TEXT PROVIDED BY SCHOOL):

Student empowerment and clinical relevance form the basis of OUCOMís two tracks of study. Years 1 and 2 integrate clinical, biomedical, and social medicine fundamentals and include patient interaction. Years 3 and 4 involve clinical rotations in the schoolís hospital system with didactic components in medicine, ethics, and law. Please see the website for details.î

FACULTY PROFILE (FALL 2007)

Total teaching faculty: **85 (full-time), 1,111 (part-time)**
Of full-time faculty, those teaching in basic sciences: **46%**; in clinical programs: **54%**

Of part-time faculty, those teaching in basic sciences: **3%**; in clinical programs: **97%**
Full-time faculty/student ratio: **0.2**

SUPPORT SERVICES

The school offers students these services for dealing with stress: expanded-hour gym access, peer counseling, professional counseling, religious support, support groups.

RESIDENCY PROFILE

Most popular residency and specialty programs chosen by the 2006 and 2007 M.D. graduating classes: anesthesiology, emergency medicine, family practice, internal medicine, obstetrics and gynecology, orthopaedic surgery, pediatrics, physical medicine and rehabilitation, psychiatry, surgery–general.

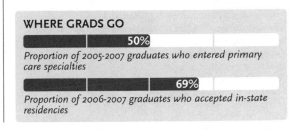

WHERE GRADS GO

50%

Proportion of 2005-2007 graduates who entered primary care specialties

69%

Proportion of 2006-2007 graduates who accepted in-state residencies

Oklahoma State University

- 1111 W. 17th Street, Tulsa, OK 74107-1898
- Public
- Year Founded: 1972
- Tuition, 2007-2008: In-state: $18,325; Out-of-state: $34,686
- Enrollment 2007-2008 academic year: 342
- Website: http://healthsciences.okstate.edu
- Specialty ranking: rural medicine: 16

3.64 AVERAGE GPA, ENTERING CLASS FALL 2007

8.7 AVERAGE MCAT, ENTERING CLASS FALL 2007

22.4% ACCEPTANCE RATE, ENTERING CLASS FALL 2007

Unranked 2009 U.S. NEWS MEDICAL SCHOOL RANKING (RESEARCH)

Unranked 2009 U.S. NEWS MEDICAL SCHOOL RANKING (PRIMARY CARE)

ADMISSIONS

Admissions phone number: **(918) 561-8421**
Admissions email address: **sarah.quinten@okstate.edu**
Application website: **http://www.aacom.org**
Acceptance rate: **22.4%**
In-state acceptance rate: **39.0%**
Out-of-state acceptance rate: **9.1%**
Minority acceptance rate: **N/A**
International acceptance rate: **N/A**

Fall 2007 applications and acceptees

	Applied	Interviewed	Accepted	Enrolled
Total:	518	213	116	88
In-state:	231	178	90	73
Out-of-state:	287	35	26	15

Profile of admitted students

Average undergraduate grade point average: **3.64**
MCAT averages (scale: 1-15; writing test: J-T):
Composite score: **8.7**
Verbal reasoning score: **9.1**, Physical sciences score: **8.1**,
Biological sciences score: **8.8**, Writing score: **O**
Proportion with undergraduate majors in: Biological
sciences: **51%**, Physical sciences: **15%**, Non-sciences:
10%, Other health professions: **0%**, Mixed disciplines
and other: **24%**
Percentage of students not coming directly from college
after graduation: **31%**

Dates and details

The American Medical College Application Service
(AMCAS) application is not accepted.
School asks for a school-specific application as part of the
admissions process.
Oldest MCAT considered for Fall 2009 entry: **2006**
Earliest application date for the 2009-2010 first-year class:
6/1
Latest application date: **2/1**
Acceptance dates for regular application for the class
entering in fall 2009:
Earliest: **October 1, 2008**

Latest: **August 1, 2009**
The school considers requests for deferred entrance.
Starting month for the class entering in 2009–2010:
August
The school doesn't have an Early Decision Plan (EDP).
A personal interview is required for admission.

Undergraduate coursework required

Medical school requires undergraduate work in these subjects: biology, biology/zoology, English, organic chemistry,
inorganic (general) chemistry, physics, molecular and cell
biology, biochemistry, general chemistry.

ADMISSIONS POLICY
(TEXT PROVIDED BY SCHOOL):

Scholarship, aptitude, motivation, academic achievement,
evaluations from preprofessional committees and osteopathic physicians, MCAT results, on-campus interview, and
motivation to be osteopathic physician are factors.
Preference to Oklahoma applicants. Qualified minority students actively recruited.

COSTS AND FINANCIAL AID

Financial aid phone number: **(918) 561-1228**
Tuition, 2007-2008 academic year: **In-state: $18,325; Out-
of-state: $34,686**
Room and board: **$7,300**
Percentage of students receiving financial aid in 2007-08:
96%
Percentage of students receiving: Loans: **90%**,
Grants/scholarships: **42%**, Work-study aid: **23%**
Average medical school debt for the Class of 2006:
$142,791

STUDENT BODY

Fall 2007 full-time enrollment: **342**
Men: **53%**, Women: **47%**, In-state: **90%**, Minorities: **26%**,
American Indian: **10.8%**, Asian-American: **6.7%**,
African-American: **5.3%**, Hispanic-American: **3.2%**,
White: **71.9%**, International: **0.0%**, Unknown: **2.0%**

ACADEMIC PROGRAMS

The school's curriculum occasionally gives first-year students substantial contact with patients.

There are opportunities for first- or second-year students to work in community health clinics.

Program offerings: AIDS, drug/alcohol abuse, family medicine, geriatrics, internal medicine, pediatrics, rural medicine, women's health

Joint degrees awarded: D.O./Ph.D., D.O./M.B.A., D.O./M.S.

Total National Institutes of Health (NIH) grants awarded to the medical school and affiliated hospitals: **$1.1 million**

FACULTY PROFILE (FALL 2007)

Total teaching faculty: **107 (full-time)**, **578 (part-time)**

Of full-time faculty, those teaching in basic sciences: **32%**; in clinical programs: **68%**

Of part-time faculty, those teaching in basic sciences: **5%**; in clinical programs: **95%**

Full-time faculty/student ratio: **0.3**

SUPPORT SERVICES

The school offers students these services for dealing with stress: expanded-hour gym access, peer counseling, professional counseling, religious support, support groups.

RESIDENCY PROFILE

Most popular residency and specialty programs chosen by the 2006 and 2007 M.D. graduating classes: anesthesiology, emergency medicine, family practice, internal medicine, obstetrics and gynecology, orthopaedic surgery, pediatrics, psychiatry, radiology–diagnostic, surgery–general.

WHERE GRADS GO

53.7%

Proportion of 2005-2007 graduates who entered primary care specialties

50.3%

Proportion of 2006-2007 graduates who accepted in-state residencies

Pikeville College

SCHOOL OF OSTEOPATHIC MEDICINE

- **147 Sycamore Street, Pikeville, KY 41501**
- **Private**
- **Year Founded:** 1997
- **Tuition, 2007-2008:** $31,745
- **Enrollment 2007-2008 academic year:** 301
- **Website:** http://www.pc.edu
- **Specialty ranking:** rural medicine: 21

3.30 AVERAGE GPA, ENTERING CLASS FALL 2007

7.3 AVERAGE MCAT, ENTERING CLASS FALL 2007

14.7% ACCEPTANCE RATE, ENTERING CLASS FALL 2007

Unranked 2009 U.S. NEWS MEDICAL SCHOOL RANKING (RESEARCH)

Unranked 2009 U.S. NEWS MEDICAL SCHOOL RANKING (PRIMARY CARE)

ADMISSIONS

Admissions phone number: **(606) 218-5400**
Admissions email address: **ahamilto@pc.edu**
Application website: **http://www.aacom.org**
Acceptance rate: **14.7%**
In-state acceptance rate: **60.8%**
Out-of-state acceptance rate: **8.2%**
Minority acceptance rate: **3.8%**
International acceptance rate: **0.0%**

Fall 2007 applications and acceptees

	Applied	Interviewed	Accepted	Enrolled
Total:	638	129	94	76
In-state:	79	65	48	40
Out-of-state:	559	64	46	36

Profile of admitted students

Average undergraduate grade point average: **3.30**
MCAT averages (scale: 1-15; writing test: J-T):
Composite score: **7.3**
Verbal reasoning score: **7.6**, Physical sciences score: **7.0**,
Biological sciences score: **7.4**, Writing score: **O**
Proportion with undergraduate majors in: Biological sciences: **59%**, Physical sciences: **9%**, Non-sciences: **9%**, Other health professions: **9%**, Mixed disciplines and other: **14%**
Percentage of students not coming directly from college after graduation: **33%**

Dates and details

The American Medical College Application Service (AMCAS) application is not accepted.
School asks for a school-specific application as part of the admissions process.
Oldest MCAT considered for Fall 2009 entry: **2005**
Earliest application date for the 2009-2010 first-year class: **6/1**
Latest application date: **2/1**
Acceptance dates for regular application for the class entering in fall 2009:
Earliest: **November 1, 2008**

Latest: **August 1, 2009**
The school considers requests for deferred entrance.
Starting month for the class entering in 2009–2010:
August
The school doesn't have an Early Decision Plan (EDP).
A personal interview is required for admission.

Undergraduate coursework required

Medical school requires undergraduate work in these subjects: biology, biology/zoology, English, organic chemistry, inorganic (general) chemistry, physics, general chemistry.

ADMISSIONS POLICY
(TEXT PROVIDED BY SCHOOL):

Applicants to the college are considered on their intellectual ability, scholastic achievement, commitment, suitability to succeed in the study of osteopathic medicine, and ability to help achieve the mission of the school.

COSTS AND FINANCIAL AID

Financial aid phone number: **(606) 218-5407**
Tuition, 2007-2008 academic year: **$31,745**
Room and board: **N/A**
Percentage of students receiving financial aid in 2007-08: **98%**
Percentage of students receiving: Loans: **98%**, Grants/scholarships: **72%**, Work-study aid: **N/A**
Average medical school debt for the Class of 2006: **$136,000**

STUDENT BODY

Fall 2007 full-time enrollment: **301**
Men: **56%**, Women: **44%**, In-state: **51%**, Minorities: **10%**, American Indian: **N/A**, Asian-American: **6.0%**, African-American: **2.3%**, Hispanic-American: **1.3%**, White: **85.4%**, International: **N/A**, Unknown: **5.0%**

ACADEMIC PROGRAMS

The school's curriculum occasionally gives first-year students substantial contact with patients.

There are opportunities for first- or second-year students to work in community health clinics.

Program offerings: AIDS, drug/alcohol abuse, family medicine, geriatrics, internal medicine, pediatrics, rural medicine, women's health

Joint degrees awarded: N/A

Total National Institutes of Health (NIH) grants awarded to the medical school and affiliated hospitals: **N/A**

CURRICULUM
(TEXT PROVIDED BY SCHOOL):
The methods of instruction in the first and second years: didactic lecture and lab; problem-based learning; computer-based case studies; primary care office interactions; scientific paper review and presentation; essay production. In the third and fourth years: clinical rotations; clinical conferences; computer-based case studies.

FACULTY PROFILE (FALL 2007)
Total teaching faculty: **28 (full-time)**, **757 (part-time)**

Of full-time faculty, those teaching in basic sciences: **57%**; in clinical programs: **43%**

Of part-time faculty, those teaching in basic sciences: **N/A**; in clinical programs: **100%**

Full-time faculty/student ratio: **0.1**

SUPPORT SERVICES
The school offers students these services for dealing with stress: peer counseling, professional counseling, religious support, support groups.

RESIDENCY PROFILE
Most popular residency and specialty programs chosen by the 2006 and 2007 M.D. graduating classes: anesthesiology, emergency medicine, family practice, internal medicine, obstetrics and gynecology, pediatrics, psychiatry, radiology–diagnostic, surgery–general.

WHERE GRADS GO

77%

Proportion of 2005-2007 graduates who entered primary care specialties

23%

Proportion of 2006-2007 graduates who accepted in-state residencies

Touro University

COLLEGE OF OSTEOPATHIC MEDICINE

- 1310 Johnson Lane, Vallejo, CA 94592
- Private
- Year Founded: 1997
- Tuition, 2007-2008: $35,800
- Enrollment 2007-2008 academic year: 540
- Website: http://www.tu.edu
- Specialty ranking: N/A

3.35 AVERAGE GPA, ENTERING CLASS FALL 2007

9.0 AVERAGE MCAT, ENTERING CLASS FALL 2007

6.9% ACCEPTANCE RATE, ENTERING CLASS FALL 2007

Unranked 2009 U.S. NEWS MEDICAL SCHOOL RANKING (RESEARCH)

Unranked 2009 U.S. NEWS MEDICAL SCHOOL RANKING (PRIMARY CARE)

ADMISSIONS

Admissions phone number: **(707) 638-5270**
Admissions email address: **haight@touro.edu**
Application website: **N/A**
Acceptance rate: **6.9%**
In-state acceptance rate: **N/A**
Out-of-state acceptance rate: **N/A**
Minority acceptance rate: **N/A**
International acceptance rate: **N/A**

Fall 2007 applications and acceptees

	Applied	Interviewed	Accepted	Enrolled
Total:	3,080	425	212	135
In-state:	N/A	N/A	N/A	N/A
Out-of-state:	N/A	N/A	N/A	N/A

Profile of admitted students

Average undergraduate grade point average: **3.35**
MCAT averages (scale: 1-15; writing test: J-T):
  Composite score: **9.0**
  Verbal reasoning score: **8.9**, Physical sciences score: **8.8**,
  Biological sciences score: **9.4**, Writing score: **Q**
Proportion with undergraduate majors in: Biological
  sciences: **66%**, Physical sciences: **29%**, Non-sciences:
  5%, Other health professions: **0%**, Mixed disciplines and
  other: **0%**
Percentage of students not coming directly from college
  after graduation: **33%**

Dates and details

The American Medical College Application Service
  (AMCAS) application is not accepted.
School asks for a school-specific application as part of the
  admissions process.
Oldest MCAT considered for Fall 2009 entry: **2005**
Earliest application date for the 2009-2010 first-year class:
  5/15
Latest application date: **4/1**
Acceptance dates for regular application for the class
  entering in fall 2009:
  Earliest: **October 1, 2008**

Latest: **June 30, 2009**
The school considers requests for deferred entrance.
Starting month for the class entering in 2009–2010:
  August
The school doesn't have an Early Decision Plan (EDP).
A personal interview is required for admission.

Undergraduate coursework required

Medical school requires undergraduate work in these subjects: biology, English, organic chemistry, inorganic (general) chemistry, physics, behavioral science.

ADMISSIONS POLICY

(TEXT PROVIDED BY SCHOOL):
TUCOM has no mandate to enroll any particular percentage
of in-state residents. Complete the primary application with
the American Association of Colleges of Osteopathic
Medicine Application Service. TUCOM's code number is
618. Qualified candidates will be instructed to complete the
secondary application process. TUCOM requires a letter of
recommendation from a preprofessional advisory committee or two letters from science faculty, as well as a letter
from a physician.

COSTS AND FINANCIAL AID

Financial aid phone number: **(707) 638-5280**
Tuition, 2007-2008 academic year: **$35,800**
Room and board: **$14,798**
Percentage of students receiving financial aid in 2007-08:
  93%
Percentage of students receiving: Loans: **90%**,
  Grants/scholarships: **18%**, Work-study aid: **10%**
Average medical school debt for the Class of 2006:
  $145,200

STUDENT BODY

Fall 2007 full-time enrollment: **540**
Men: **N/A**, Women: **N/A**, In-state: **N/A**, Minorities: **N/A**,
  American Indian: **N/A**, Asian-American: **N/A**, African-
  American: **N/A**, Hispanic-American: **N/A**, White: **N/A**,
  International: **N/A**, Unknown: **100.0%**

ACADEMIC PROGRAMS

The school's curriculum occasionally gives first-year students substantial contact with patients.

There are opportunities for first- or second-year students to work in community health clinics.

Program offerings: AIDS, drug/alcohol abuse, family medicine, geriatrics, internal medicine, pediatrics, rural medicine

Joint degrees awarded: D.O./M.P.H.

Total National Institutes of Health (NIH) grants awarded to the medical school and affiliated hospitals: **N/A**

CURRICULUM
(TEXT PROVIDED BY SCHOOL):

TUCOM students take courses in all subject areas one would expect any physician to master. The schoolís goal is to prepare students for the realities of medicine as it currently exists, as well as how it is likely to be in the future. Practice in problem solving is part of the daily classroom clinical experience as Touro strives to deliver a curriculum consistent with emerging directions of healthcare.

FACULTY PROFILE (FALL 2007)

Total teaching faculty: **58 (full-time)**, **6 (part-time)**
Of full-time faculty, those teaching in basic sciences: **53%**;
in clinical programs: **47%**

Of part-time faculty, those teaching in basic sciences: **0%**;
in clinical programs: **100%**
Full-time faculty/student ratio: **0.1**

SUPPORT SERVICES

The school offers students these services for dealing with stress: expanded-hour gym access, peer counseling, professional counseling, religious support, support groups.

RESIDENCY PROFILE

Most popular residency and specialty programs chosen by the 2006 and 2007 M.D. graduating classes: emergency medicine–sports medicine, family practice, internal medicine, pediatrics.

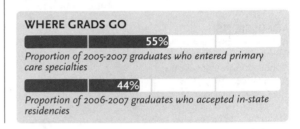

WHERE GRADS GO

55%

Proportion of 2005-2007 graduates who entered primary care specialties

44%

Proportion of 2006-2007 graduates who accepted in-state residencies

UMDNJ

SCHOOL OF OSTEOPATHIC MEDICINE

- 1 Medical Center Drive, Stratford, NJ 08084-1501
- Public
- Year Founded: 1977
- Tuition, 2007-2008: In-state: $25,783; Out-of-state: $38,850
- Enrollment 2007-2008 academic year: 413
- Website: http://som.umdnj.edu
- Specialty ranking: geriatrics: 15

3.47 AVERAGE GPA, ENTERING CLASS FALL 2007

8.9 AVERAGE MCAT, ENTERING CLASS FALL 2007

5.5% ACCEPTANCE RATE, ENTERING CLASS FALL 2007

Unranked 2009 U.S. NEWS MEDICAL SCHOOL RANKING (RESEARCH)

Unranked 2009 U.S. NEWS MEDICAL SCHOOL RANKING (PRIMARY CARE)

ADMISSIONS

Admissions phone number: **(856) 566-7050**
Admissions email address: **somadm@umdnj.edu**
Application website: **N/A**
Acceptance rate: **5.5%**
In-state acceptance rate: **24.7%**
Out-of-state acceptance rate: **2.0%**
Minority acceptance rate: **3.7%**
International acceptance rate: **N/A**

Fall 2007 applications and acceptees

	Applied	Interviewed	Accepted	Enrolled
Total:	3,386	389	186	108
In-state:	522	201	129	86
Out-of-state:	2,864	188	57	22

Profile of admitted students

Average undergraduate grade point average: **3.47**
MCAT averages (scale: 1-15; writing test: J-T):
  Composite score: **8.9**
  Verbal reasoning score: **8.6**, Physical sciences score: **8.8**,
  Biological sciences score: **9.3**, Writing score: **P**
Proportion with undergraduate majors in: Biological sciences: **44%**, Physical sciences: **8%**, Non-sciences: **13%**, Other health professions: **13%**, Mixed disciplines and other: **22%**
Percentage of students not coming directly from college after graduation: **65%**

Dates and details

The American Medical College Application Service (AMCAS) application is not accepted.
School asks for a school-specific application as part of the admissions process.
Oldest MCAT considered for Fall 2009 entry: **2002**
Earliest application date for the 2009-2010 first-year class: **6/2**
Latest application date: **2/1**
Acceptance dates for regular application for the class entering in fall 2009:

Earliest: **September 19, 2008**
Latest: **August 4, 2009**
The school considers requests for deferred entrance.
Starting month for the class entering in 2009–2010:
  August
The school doesn't have an Early Decision Plan (EDP).
A personal interview is required for admission.

Undergraduate coursework required

Medical school requires undergraduate work in these subjects: biology, English, organic chemistry, inorganic (general) chemistry, physics, mathematics, behavioral science.

ADMISSIONS POLICY
(TEXT PROVIDED BY SCHOOL):

Applicants must submit MCAT scores and premedical committee letter. Accepted students must have baccalaureate degree upon matriculation to UMDNJSOM. Applicants may complete online application through the American Association of Colleges of Osteopathic Medicine Application Service, and it must be submitted between June 1 of that year and February 1 of the year of desired admission. Must be U.S. citizen or permanent resident at time of application. Out-of-state students encouraged to apply.

COSTS AND FINANCIAL AID

Financial aid phone number: **(856) 566-6008**
Tuition, 2007-2008 academic year: **In-state: $25,783; Out-of-state: $38,850**
Room and board: **$13,650**
Percentage of students receiving financial aid in 2007-08: **N/A**
Percentage of students receiving: Loans: **N/A**, Grants/scholarships: **N/A**, Work-study aid: **N/A**
Average medical school debt for the Class of 2006: **$118,039**

STUDENT BODY

Fall 2007 full-time enrollment: **413**

Men: 41%, Women: 59%, In-state: 99%, Minorities: 47%, American Indian: 0.0%, Asian-American: 19.9%, African-American: 19.4%, Hispanic-American: 8.0%, White: 50.6%, International: 0.2%, Unknown: 1.9%

ACADEMIC PROGRAMS

The school's curriculum frequently gives first-year students substantial contact with patients.

There are opportunities for first- or second-year students to work in community health clinics.

Program offerings: AIDS, drug/alcohol abuse, family medicine, geriatrics, internal medicine, pediatrics, rural medicine, women's health

Joint degrees awarded: D.O./Ph.D., D.O./M.B.A., D.O./M.P.H., D.O./J.D., D.O./M.S.

Total National Institutes of Health (NIH) grants awarded to the medical school and affiliated hospitals: **$3.6 million**

CURRICULUM

(TEXT PROVIDED BY SCHOOL):

Curriculum combines case-based learning, small groups, cultural competency, and interdisciplinary training. Clinical Education Center used for interpersonal, communications, ethics, palliative care, and physical diagnosis. Formative, summative assessment of learning. Students have regular input into curricular process. Osteopathic manipulation is integrated. Problem-based learning also offered.

FACULTY PROFILE (FALL 2007)

Total teaching faculty: **168 (full-time)**, **29 (part-time)**

Of full-time faculty, those teaching in basic sciences: **17%**; in clinical programs: **83%**

Of part-time faculty, those teaching in basic sciences: **14%**; in clinical programs: **86%**

Full-time faculty/student ratio: **0.4**

SUPPORT SERVICES

The school offers students these services for dealing with stress: expanded-hour gym access, professional counseling.

RESIDENCY PROFILE

Most popular residency and specialty programs chosen by the 2006 and 2007 M.D. graduating classes: emergency medicine, family practice, internal medicine, obstetrics and gynecology, orthopaedic surgery, pediatrics, psychiatry, surgery–general, transitional year, internal medicine/emergency medicine.

WHERE GRADS GO

45.6%

Proportion of 2005-2007 graduates who entered primary care specialties

38.1%

Proportion of 2006-2007 graduates who accepted in-state residencies

University of New England

COLLEGE OF OSTEOPATHIC MEDICINE

- 11 Hills Beach Road, Biddeford, ME 04005
- Private
- Year Founded: 1978
- Tuition, 2007-2008: $39,520
- Enrollment 2007-2008 academic year: 501
- Website: http://www.une.edu/com/
- Specialty ranking: N/A

3.41 AVERAGE GPA, ENTERING CLASS FALL 2007

8.5 AVERAGE MCAT, ENTERING CLASS FALL 2007

7.1% ACCEPTANCE RATE, ENTERING CLASS FALL 2007

Unranked 2009 U.S. NEWS MEDICAL SCHOOL RANKING (RESEARCH)

Unranked 2009 U.S. NEWS MEDICAL SCHOOL RANKING (PRIMARY CARE)

ADMISSIONS

Admissions phone number: **(800) 477-4863**
Admissions email address: **unecomadmissions@une.edu**
Application website: **https://aacomas.aacom.org**
Acceptance rate: **7.1%**
In-state acceptance rate: **46.7%**
Out-of-state acceptance rate: **6.4%**
Minority acceptance rate: **1.0%**
International acceptance rate: **N/A**

Fall 2007 applications and acceptees

	Applied	Interviewed	Accepted	Enrolled
Total:	3,250	356	232	124
In-state:	60	39	28	24
Out-of-state:	3,190	317	204	100

Profile of admitted students

Average undergraduate grade point average: **3.41**
MCAT averages (scale: 1-15; writing test: J-T):
  Composite score: **8.5**
  Verbal reasoning score: **8.8**, Physical sciences score: **8.0**,
  Biological sciences score: **8.8**, Writing score: **Q**
Proportion with undergraduate majors in: Biological
  sciences: **51%**, Physical sciences: **14%**, Non-sciences:
  21%, Other health professions: **2%**, Mixed disciplines
  and other: **12%**
Percentage of students not coming directly from college
  after graduation: **77%**

Dates and details

The American Medical College Application Service
  (AMCAS) application is not accepted.
School asks for a school-specific application as part of the
  admissions process.
Oldest MCAT considered for Fall 2009 entry: **2006**
Earliest application date for the 2009-2010 first-year class:
  5/15
Latest application date: **2/1**
Acceptance dates for regular application for the class
  entering in fall 2009:
  Earliest: **October 1, 2008**

Latest: **August 8, 2009**
The school considers requests for deferred entrance.
Starting month for the class entering in 2009–2010:
  August
The school doesn't have an Early Decision Plan (EDP).
A personal interview is required for admission.

Undergraduate coursework required

Medical school requires undergraduate work in these subjects: biology, biology/zoology, English, organic chemistry,
inorganic (general) chemistry, physics, biochemistry, general chemistry.

ADMISSIONS POLICY

(TEXT PROVIDED BY SCHOOL):
Academic record and scholastic ability; exposure to and
experience in healthcare and human services; leadership,
community service and/or research experience; interest in
practicing primary care, practicing in New England, and/or
working in underserved communities; and the maturity and
desire to work collaboratively with classmates, faculty,
healthcare providers, and patients.

COSTS AND FINANCIAL AID

Financial aid phone number: **(207) 283-0171**
Tuition, 2007-2008 academic year: **$39,520**
Room and board: **$11,500**
Percentage of students receiving financial aid in 2007-08:
  91%
Percentage of students receiving: Loans: **89%**,
  Grants/scholarships: **29%**, Work-study aid: **0%**
Average medical school debt for the Class of 2006:
  $180,730

STUDENT BODY

Fall 2007 full-time enrollment: **501**
Men: **45%**, Women: **55%**, In-state: **20%**, Minorities: **13%**,
  American Indian: **0.2%**, Asian-American: **9.0%**,
  African-American: **1.6%**, Hispanic-American: **2.0%**,
  White: **81.8%**, International: **0.0%**, Unknown: **5.4%**

ACADEMIC PROGRAMS

The school's curriculum occasionally gives first-year students substantial contact with patients.

There are opportunities for first- or second-year students to work in community health clinics.

Program offerings: AIDS, drug/alcohol abuse, family medicine, geriatrics, internal medicine, pediatrics, rural medicine, women's health

Joint degrees awarded: D.O./M.P.H.

Total National Institutes of Health (NIH) grants awarded to the medical school and affiliated hospitals: **N/A**

CURRICULUM

(TEXT PROVIDED BY SCHOOL):

Please see the collegeís website.

FACULTY PROFILE (FALL 2007)

Total teaching faculty: **54 (full-time), 464 (part-time)**

Of full-time faculty, those teaching in basic sciences: **30%**; in clinical programs: **70%**

Of part-time faculty, those teaching in basic sciences: **2%**; in clinical programs: **98%**

Full-time faculty/student ratio: **0.1**

SUPPORT SERVICES

The school offers students these services for dealing with stress: expanded-hour gym access, professional counseling.

RESIDENCY PROFILE

Most popular residency and specialty programs chosen by the 2006 and 2007 M.D. graduating classes: emergency medicine, family practice, internal medicine, obstetrics and gynecology, pediatrics, physical medicine and rehabilitation, psychiatry, surgery–general, transitional year.

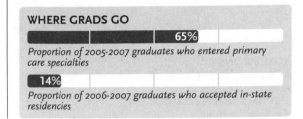

WHERE GRADS GO

65%

Proportion of 2005-2007 graduates who entered primary care specialties

14%

Proportion of 2006-2007 graduates who accepted in-state residencies

U. of North Texas Health Sci. Center

TEXAS COL. OF OSTEOPATHIC MEDICINE

- 3500 Camp Bowie Boulevard, Fort Worth, TX 76107-2699
- Public
- **Year Founded:** 1966
- **Tuition, 2007-2008:** In-state: $13,950; Out-of-state: $29,700
- **Enrollment 2007-2008 academic year:** 593
- **Website:** http://www.hsc.unt.edu
- **Specialty ranking:** family medicine: 27, rural medicine: 21

3.56 AVERAGE GPA, ENTERING CLASS FALL 2007

9.1 AVERAGE MCAT, ENTERING CLASS FALL 2007

20.1% ACCEPTANCE RATE, ENTERING CLASS FALL 2007

Unranked 2009 U.S. NEWS MEDICAL SCHOOL RANKING (RESEARCH)

Unranked 2009 U.S. NEWS MEDICAL SCHOOL RANKING (PRIMARY CARE)

ADMISSIONS

Admissions phone number: **(800) 535-8266**
Admissions email address:
   TCOMAdmissions@hsc.unt.edu
Application website:
   http://www.hsc.unt.edu/education/tcom/Admissions.cf m
Acceptance rate: **20.1%**
In-state acceptance rate: **20.6%**
Out-of-state acceptance rate: **15.9%**
Minority acceptance rate: **19.8%**
International acceptance rate: **20.0%**

Fall 2007 applications and acceptees

	Applied	Interviewed	Accepted	Enrolled
Total:	1,966	619	395	165
In-state:	1,739	574	359	153
Out-of-state:	227	45	36	12

Profile of admitted students

Average undergraduate grade point average: **3.56**
MCAT averages (scale: 1-15; writing test: J-T):
   Composite score: **9.1**
   Verbal reasoning score: **9.0**, Physical sciences score: **8.8**, Biological sciences score: **9.5**, Writing score: **O**
Proportion with undergraduate majors in: Biological sciences: **55%**, Physical sciences: **11%**, Non-sciences: **6%**, Other health professions: **10%**, Mixed disciplines and other: **18%**
Percentage of students not coming directly from college after graduation: **5%**

Dates and details

The American Medical College Application Service (AMCAS) application is not accepted.
School asks for a school-specific application as part of the admissions process.
Oldest MCAT considered for Fall 2009 entry: **2004**
Earliest application date for the 2009-2010 first-year class: **5/1**
Latest application date: **10/1**

Acceptance dates for regular application for the class entering in fall 2009:
   Earliest: **October 1, 2008**
   Latest: **July 15, 2009**
The school considers requests for deferred entrance.
Starting month for the class entering in 2009–2010: **July**
The school has an Early Decision Plan (EDP).
A personal interview is required for admission.

Undergraduate coursework required

Medical school requires undergraduate work in these subjects: biology, biology/zoology, English, organic chemistry, inorganic (general) chemistry, physics, mathematics, demonstration of writing skills, calculus, general chemistry.

ADMISSIONS POLICY

(TEXT PROVIDED BY SCHOOL):

Applicants are evaluated on a variety of characteristics such as performance in coursework, test scores, motivation, socioeconomic background, interview scores, letters of evaluation, and ability to contribute to the diversity of the class. Only selected applicants are invited to campus for interviews. At least 90 percent of the incoming class must be from the Texas resident applicant pool.

COSTS AND FINANCIAL AID

Financial aid phone number: **(800) 346-8266**
Tuition, 2007-2008 academic year: **In-state: $13,950; Out-of-state: $29,700**
Room and board: **$14,070**
Percentage of students receiving financial aid in 2007-08: **96%**
Percentage of students receiving: Loans: **92%**, Grants/scholarships: **65%**, Work-study aid: **2%**
Average medical school debt for the Class of 2006: **$114,000**

STUDENT BODY

Fall 2007 full-time enrollment: **593**
Men: **50%**, Women: **50%**, In-state: **95%**, Minorities: **40%**, American Indian: **0.5%**, Asian-American: **27.2%**,

African-American: 2.7%, Hispanic-American: 9.9%, White: 57.8%, International: 0.5%, Unknown: 1.3%

ACADEMIC PROGRAMS

The school's curriculum frequently gives first-year students substantial contact with patients.

There are opportunities for first- or second-year students to work in community health clinics.

Program offerings: AIDS, drug/alcohol abuse, family medicine, geriatrics, internal medicine, pediatrics, rural medicine, women's health

Joint degrees awarded: D.O./Ph.D., D.O./M.P.H., D.O./M.S.

Total National Institutes of Health (NIH) grants awarded to the medical school and affiliated hospitals: **$16.0 million**

CURRICULUM
(TEXT PROVIDED BY SCHOOL):

The TCOM curriculum is a hybrid model that includes early student clinical exposure and application-based learning theory. Using interactive clinical learning sessions, students receive the best of case-based, problem-based, systems-based, and traditional medical education curricula.

FACULTY PROFILE (FALL 2007)

Total teaching faculty: **314 (full-time)**, **13 (part-time)**
Of full-time faculty, those teaching in basic sciences: **23%**; in clinical programs: **77%**

Of part-time faculty, those teaching in basic sciences: **8%**; in clinical programs: **92%**
Full-time faculty/student ratio: **0.5**

SUPPORT SERVICES

The school offers students these services for dealing with stress: expanded-hour gym access, peer counseling, professional counseling, religious support, support groups.

RESIDENCY PROFILE

Most popular residency and specialty programs chosen by the 2006 and 2007 M.D. graduating classes: anesthesiology, emergency medicine, family practice, internal medicine, obstetrics and gynecology, orthopaedic surgery, pathology–anatomic and clinical, pediatrics, surgery–general.

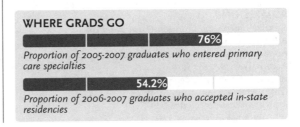

WHERE GRADS GO

76%
Proportion of 2005-2007 graduates who entered primary care specialties

54.2%
Proportion of 2006-2007 graduates who accepted in-state residencies

West Virginia School

OF OSTEOPATHIC MEDICINE

- 400 N. Lee Street, Lewisburg, WV 24901
- Public
- Year Founded: 1972
- Tuition, 2007-2008: In-state: $20,030; Out-of-state: $49,273
- Enrollment 2007-2008 academic year: 598
- Website: http://www.wvsom.edu
- Specialty ranking: family medicine: 18, rural medicine: 18

3.44 AVERAGE GPA, ENTERING CLASS FALL 2007

7.8 AVERAGE MCAT, ENTERING CLASS FALL 2007

18.7% ACCEPTANCE RATE, ENTERING CLASS FALL 2007

Unranked 2009 U.S. NEWS MEDICAL SCHOOL RANKING (RESEARCH)

43 2009 U.S. NEWS MEDICAL SCHOOL RANKING (PRIMARY CARE)

ADMISSIONS

Admissions phone number: (800) 356-7836
Admissions email address: admissions@wvsom.edu
Application website: http://www.aacom.org
Acceptance rate: 18.7%
In-state acceptance rate: 45.6%
Out-of-state acceptance rate: 17.3%
Minority acceptance rate: N/A
International acceptance rate: N/A

Fall 2007 applications and acceptees

	Applied	Interviewed	Accepted	Enrolled
Total:	2,770	601	518	198
In-state:	136	84	62	53
Out-of-state:	2,634	517	456	145

Profile of admitted students

Average undergraduate grade point average: 3.44
MCAT averages (scale: 1-15; writing test: J-T):
  Composite score: 7.8
  Verbal reasoning score: 8.1, Physical sciences score: 7.4,
  Biological sciences score: 8.0, Writing score: M
Proportion with undergraduate majors in: Biological
  sciences: 58%, Physical sciences: 20%, Non-sciences:
  6%, Other health professions: 7%, Mixed disciplines and
  other: 9%
Percentage of students not coming directly from college
  after graduation: 42%

Dates and details

The American Medical College Application Service
  (AMCAS) application is not accepted.
School asks for a school-specific application as part of the
  admissions process.
Oldest MCAT considered for Fall 2009 entry: 2006
Earliest application date for the 2009-2010 first-year class:
  6/1
Latest application date: 2/15
Acceptance dates for regular application for the class
  entering in fall 2009:
  Earliest: September 1, 2008

Latest: May 1, 2009
The school considers requests for deferred entrance.
Starting month for the class entering in 2009–2010:
  August
The school doesn't have an Early Decision Plan (EDP).
A personal interview is required for admission.

Undergraduate coursework required

Medical school requires undergraduate work in these subjects: biology/zoology, English, organic chemistry, inorganic
(general) chemistry, physics.

ADMISSIONS POLICY

(TEXT PROVIDED BY SCHOOL):
Students are the key to WVSOM's commitment to improving healthcare. The Admissions Committee strives to fill
each class with students motivated toward primary care in
rural communities, seeking students who share the school's
commitment to rural healthcare. The committee also evaluates aptitude, maturity, ability to relate to people, motivation
for osteopathic medicine, personal conduct, and scholarship.

COSTS AND FINANCIAL AID

Financial aid phone number: (800) 356-7836
Tuition, 2007-2008 academic year: **In-state: $20,030; Out-
  of-state: $49,273**
Room and board: N/A
Percentage of students receiving financial aid in 2007-08:
  98%
Percentage of students receiving: Loans: 96%,
  Grants/scholarships: 16%, Work-study aid: 8%
Average medical school debt for the Class of 2006:
  $158,372

STUDENT BODY

Fall 2007 full-time enrollment: 598
Men: 51%, Women: 49%, In-state: 36%, Minorities: 17%,
  American Indian: 0.5%, Asian-American: 12.7%,
  African-American: 1.2%, Hispanic-American: 2.2%,
  White: 16.6%, International: 0.0%, Unknown: 66.9%

ACADEMIC PROGRAMS

The school's curriculum frequently gives first-year students substantial contact with patients.

There are opportunities for first- or second-year students to work in community health clinics.

Program offerings: AIDS, drug/alcohol abuse, family medicine, geriatrics, internal medicine, pediatrics, rural medicine, women's health

Joint degrees awarded: N/A

Total National Institutes of Health (NIH) grants awarded to the medical school and affiliated hospitals: **$.0 million**

CURRICULUM

(TEXT PROVIDED BY SCHOOL):

WVSOM provides dual learning methods for students: a systems-based track and problem-based learning. Extensive clinical contact is available throughout the program. Objective structured clinical evaluations and extensive use of robotics are components of both tracks. The clinical years are identical for both tracks and utilize clinician preceptors throughout the state as well as clinical settings outside of West Virginia.

FACULTY PROFILE (FALL 2007)

Total teaching faculty: 57 **(full-time)**, 104 **(part-time)**
Of full-time faculty, those teaching in basic sciences: **49%**; in clinical programs: **51%**

Of part-time faculty, those teaching in basic sciences: **0%** in clinical programs: **100%**
Full-time faculty/student ratio: **0.1**

SUPPORT SERVICES

The school offers students these services for dealing with stress: expanded-hour gym access, peer counseling, professional counseling, religious support, support groups.

RESIDENCY PROFILE

Most popular residency and specialty programs chosen by the 2006 and 2007 M.D. graduating classes: anesthesiology, family practice, internal medicine, obstetrics and gynecology, pediatrics, physical medicine and rehabilitation, radiology–diagnostic, surgery–general, transitional year.

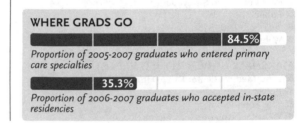

WHERE GRADS GO

84.5%

Proportion of 2005-2007 graduates who entered primary care specialties

35.3%

Proportion of 2006-2007 graduates who accepted in-state residencies

Additional Schools

Basic contact information for those schools that did not respond to the U.S. News survey is provided below.

LOMA LINDA UNIVERSITY
- Loma Linda, CA 92350
- Private
- Website: http://www.llu.edu

LSU SCHOOL OF MEDICINE–NEW ORLEANS
- Admissions Office, 1901 Perdido Street, New Orleans, LA 70112-1393
- Public
- Year Founded: 1941
- Website: http://www.medschool.lsuhsc.edu

LSU SCHOOL OF MEDICINE–SHREVEPORT
- P.O. Box 33932, Shreveport, LA 71130-3932
- Public
- Year Founded: 1969
- Website: http://www.sh.lsuhsc.edu/index.html

MARSHALL UNIVERSITY (EDWARDS)
- 1600 Medical Center Drive, Huntington, WV 25701-3655
- Public
- Year Founded: 1977
- Website: http://musom.marshall.edu

MEHARRY MEDICAL COLLEGE
- 1005 D.B. Todd Jr. Boulevard, Nashville, TN 37208
- Private
- Year Founded: 1876
- Website: http://www.mmc.edu

PENNSYLVANIA STATE UNIVERSITY COLLEGE OF MEDICINE
- 500 University Drive, Hershey, PA 17033
- Public
- Year Founded: 1967
- Website: http://www.hmc.psu.edu

SUNY–DOWNSTATE MEDICAL CENTER
- 450 Clarkson Avenue, Box 60, Brooklyn, NY 11203
- Public
- Year Founded: 1860
- Website: http://www.hscbklyn.edu

UMDNJ–NEW JERSEY MEDICAL SCHOOL
- 185 S. Orange Ave., PO Box 1709, Newark, NJ 07101-1709
- Public
- Year Founded: 1954
- Website: http://www.njms.umdnj.edu

UNIVERSITY OF HAWAII–MANOA (BURNS)
- 651 Ilalo Street, Honolulu, HI 96813
- Public
- Year Founded: 1967
- Website: http://jabsom.hawaii.edu

UNIVERSITY OF MISSISSIPPI
- 2500 N. State Street, Jackson, MS 39216-4505
- Public
- Year Founded: 1903
- Website: http://www.umc.edu

UNIVERSITY OF SOUTH ALABAMA
- 307 University Boulevard, 170 CSAB, Mobile, AL 36688
- Public
- Website: http://southmed.usouthal.edu/library

UNIVERSITY OF TEXAS HEALTH SCIENCE CENTER–SAN ANTONIO
- 7703 Floyd Curl Drive, San Antonio, TX 78229-3900
- Public
- Website: http://www.uthscsa.edu

ARIZONA COLLEGE OF OSTEOPATHIC MEDICINE (MIDWESTERN UNIVERSITY)
- 19555 N. 59th Avenue, Glendale, AZ 85308
- Private
- Year Founded: 1995
- Website: http://www.midwestern.edu

CHICAGO COLLEGE OF OSTEOPATHIC MEDICINE
- 555 31st Street, Downers Grove, IL 60515
- Private
- Year Founded: 1900
- Website: http://www.midwestern.edu

DES MOINES UNIVERSITY OSTEOPATHIC MEDICAL CENTER
- 3200 Grand Avenue, Des Moines, IA 50312
- Private
- Year Founded: 1898
- Website: http://www.dmu.edu

PHILADELPHIA COLLEGE OF OSTEOPATHIC MEDICINE
- 4170 City Avenue, Philadelphia, PA 19131
- Private
- Year Founded: 1899
- Website: http://www.pcom.edu

KANSAS CITY UNIVERSITY OF MEDICINE AND BIOSCIENCES
- 1750 Independence Avenue, Kansas City, MO 64106-1453
- Private
- Year Founded: 1916
- Website: http://www.kcumb.edu

Resources for Late Starters

Postbaccalaureate programs for nonscientists

What if you come late to your decision to apply to med school and have little or no science background? Here are several highly regarded postbaccalaureate programs designed to help career-changers make their dreams come true. They offer all the science courses you'll need as well as advice and support when it comes time to apply to medical school; students who successfully complete the coursework are "sponsored" by the program, meaning the program vouches for their readiness to go on. (For a complete list of postbac premed programs, go to www.aamc.org/postbac.) Once you complete a program, it usually takes another year to apply to medical school, unless the program has "linkage" with one or more medical schools—an arrangement that allows qualified students to go directly to those med schools when they complete the postbac program.

BRYN MAWR COLLEGE

Canwyll House

101 North Merion Avenue

Bryn Mawr, PA 19010-2899

(610) 526-7350

Website: www.brynmawr.edu/postbac

Year started: 1972

Description: One-year program. Full-time, days only. Three courses per semester. Each usually has a laboratory. Classes are predominantly postbac classes although some are open to undergrads.

Enrollment: 76

Admissions requirements: Minimum

undergraduate GPA of 3.0; standardized testing required. Interview required for competitive applicants.

Acceptance rate: 60%

Average MCAT score of those who apply to medical school: 31.5

Acceptance rate into medical school in 2003: 100% (over past 5 years: 99%)

Tuition: $17,280; $1,550 per summer session

Financial aid: (610) 526-5267

Linkage with: Brown University School of Medicine, Dartmouth Medical College, Drexel University College of Medicine, George Washington University School of Medicine, Jefferson Medical College, SUNY at Downstate College of Medicine, SUNY Stony Brook School of Medicine, Health Sciences Center, Temple University School of Medicine, University of Rochester School of Medicine

COLUMBIA UNIVERSITY

Lewisohn Hall, Room 408

Mail Code 4101

2780 Broadway

New York, NY 10027

(212) 854-2772

Website: www.columbia.edu/cu/gs/postbacc

Year started: 1955

Description: Two-year program. Full-time or part-time, days or evenings. General chemistry prerequisite for both bio and organic chemistry. Minimum 120 hours of clinical volunteer work; 18–20 hours research volunteer work required. Postbac students are mixed with undergrad premed students.

Enrollment: 427

Admissions requirements: Minimum undergraduate GPA of 3.0; standardized testing, if taken, must be submitted. Interview not required.

Acceptance rate into program: 50–60%

Average MCAT score of those sponsored: 31

Acceptance rate into medical school of those sponsored in 2001 (last year available): 92%

Tuition: Around $10,000 per year ($1,146 per credit; need 20 credits to get certificate). Full program is 38 credits: $37,088.

Financial aid: (212) 854-7040

Linkage with: Ben Gurion University of the Negev; Brown University School of Medicine; Jefferson Medical College of Thomas Jefferson University; Drexel University College of Medicine; National University of Ireland, University College, Cork; New York Medical College; SUNY Brooklyn School of Medicine; SUNY Stony Brook School of Medicine; Temple University School of Medicine; Trinity College–Dublin; UMDNJ–New Jersey Medical School

GOUCHER COLLEGE

Postbaccalaureate Premedical Program

1021 Dulaney Valley Road

Baltimore, MD 21204-2794

(800) 414-3437

Website: www.goucher.edu/postbac

Year started: 1980

Description: One-year program. Full-time, days only. Classes separate from undergrads. Three courses per semester; intensive general chemistry over the summer. Volunteer work required.

Enrollment: 25–30

Admissions requirements: Standardized testing required. Interview required.

Acceptance rate into program: 20–30%

Average MCAT score of those sponsored: 32

Acceptance rate into medical school for those sponsored in 2003: 100%

Tuition: $720 per credit. The typical curriculum consists of eight courses, bringing total tuition to $24,480.

Financial aid: (410) 337-6430

Linkage with: Brown Medical School, George Washington University School of Medicine, Drexel University School of Medicine, SUNY Stony Brook School of Medicine, Temple University School of Medicine, Tulane University School of Medicine, University of Pittsburgh School of Medicine

HARVARD UNIVERSITY

Health Careers Program

Harvard University Extension School

51 Brattle Street

Cambridge, MA 02138

(617) 495-2926

Website: www.extension.harvard.edu/hcp

Year started: 1980

Description: Two-year program, part-time evenings only. Postbac students are separated from undergrad premed students. Standard load is two courses per term. Students expected to find patient-contact work, either paid or volunteer.

Enrollment: 200 plus

Admissions requirements: Minimum undergraduate GPA of 2.7, no standardized test required. No interview required.

Acceptance rate into program: 90%

Average MCAT score of those sponsored: 32

Acceptance rate into medical school for those sponsored in 2003: 89%

Tuition: $800 per course

Financial aid: (617) 495-4293

JOHNS HOPKINS UNIVERSITY

3400 North Charles Street

Wyman Park Building, Suite G-05

Baltimore, MD 21218

(410) 516-7748

Website: www.jhu.edu/postbac

Description: One-year program. Full-time, days only. Four or five courses with no more than two lab science courses each semester. Students participate in a "journal club" and "mini-medical school" to learn about and discuss contemporary medical/health care issues. Students engage in a wide choice of clinical activities, including medical tutorials with medical school faculty, structured hospital internships and volunteer programs, and volunteer work in the community. Postbac students are mixed in with undergrad premed students.

Enrollment: 25–30

Admissions requirements: Minimum undergraduate GPA of 3.0 plus; standardized testing (SAT, ACT, or GRE) required. Interview required.

Acceptance rate into program: 19%

Average MCAT Score of medical school applicants: approximately 31

Acceptance rate into medical school of applicants in 2003: 100%

Tuition: $26,930

Financial aid: (410) 516-4688

Linkage with: George Washington University School of Medicine, UMDNJ–Robert Wood Johnson Medical School, and University of Rochester

MILLS COLLEGE

5000 MacArthur Boulevard

Oakland, CA 94613

(510) 430-2317

Website: www.mills.edu/academics/graduate/pmc_gr

Year started: 1979

Description: One- or two-year program. Full-time or part-time, days only. Students take two or three courses per semester. Volunteer work not required, but encouraged. Postbac students are separated from undergrad premed students.

Enrollment: 60

Admissions requirements: Minimum undergraduate GPA of 3.0; standardized testing required. No interview required.

Acceptance rate into program: Varies considerably from year to year; approximately 75%

Average MCAT score of those sponsored: 31

Acceptance rate into medical school for those sponsored in 2003: 87.5%

Tuition: $15,000–$25,000 per year, depending on number of courses

Financial aid: Need to respond on application; Mills College will not discuss aid over the phone.

Linkage with: Tulane University Medical School

SCRIPPS COLLEGE W.M. KECK SCIENCE CENTER

925 N. Mills Avenue

Claremont, CA 91711-5916

(909) 621-8764

Website: www.scrippscollege.edu/academics/postbac/index/php

Year started: 1994

Description: One- or two-year program. Full-time or part-time, days only. Postbac students are mixed with undergrad premed students. Students in the one-year program take three or four courses per semester and two summer courses each summer. Students in the two-year program take two courses per semester and are required to work at least 20 hours a week. Internships and volunteer work required.

Enrollment: 60

Admissions requirements: Minimum undergraduate GPA of 3.0; standardized testing required. Interview required.

Acceptance rate into program: 27%

Average MCAT score of those sponsored: 31.2

Acceptance rate into medical school for those sponsored in 2003: 100%

Tuition: $20,000–$26,000 per year, depending on number of courses

Financial aid: (909) 621-8275

Linkage with: University of Pittsburgh School of Medicine, Drexel University School of Medicine, George Washington School of Medicine, Temple University School of Medicine, Western University School of Medicine, College of Osteopathic Medicine of the Pacific

TUFTS UNIVERSITY

419 Boston Ave. Dowling Hall

Medford, MA 02155

(617) 627-2321

Website: http://studentservices.tufts.edu/postbac

Year started: 1988

Description: 11 to 20 months depending on student. Full-time, days only. Two laboratory science courses per semester and other electives available. Volunteer or paid part-time work recommended. Postbac students are mixed in with undergrad premed students.

Enrollment: 40

Admissions requirements: Minimum undergraduate GPA of 3.0; standardized testing required. No interview required.

Acceptance rate into program: 30–40%

Average MCAT score of those sponsored: 30–31

Acceptance rate into medical school of those sponsored in 2003: 90%

Tuition: $24,500 for the program

Financial aid: Once admitted, students can discuss it with counselors.

Linkage with: Tufts University School of Medicine and University of New England College of Osteopathic Medicine

UNIVERSITY OF PENNSYLVANIA

3440 Market Street, Suite 100

College of General Studies

Philadelphia, PA 19104-3335

(215) 898-7326

Website: www.sas.upenn.edu/CGS/postbac/premed

Year started: 1977

Description: One- or two-year program. Full-time or part-time, days, or evenings. Postbac students are separated from undergrad premed students.

Enrollment: 50–70

Admissions requirements: Minimum undergraduate GPA of 3.0; standardized testing required. Interview required.

Acceptance rate into program: N/A

Average MCAT score of those sponsored: N/A

Acceptance rate into medical school of those sponsored in 2003: 100%

Tuition: $12,000 per academic year

Financial aid: www.sfs.upenn.edu/home

Linkage with: George Washington University School of Medicine, Jefferson Medical College, Drexel University College of Medicine, Temple University School of Medicine, UMDNJ–Robert Wood Johnson School of Medicine, University of Pittsburgh School of Medicine

Overseas Options
Foreign medical schools that welcome Americans

If you don't get into an American medical school, one possible alternate route is a foreign or "offshore" school that accepts a significant number of U.S. applicants (see Chapter 6, page 55). Before you make a choice, be sure you know what you're getting into: Visit the school, find out what kind of program it offers and how many Americans attend, how students do on the United States Medical Licensing Examination (USMLE), and how many end up with residencies in the States. Below is a sampling of programs that accept Americans.

AMERICAN UNIVERSITY OF THE CARIBBEAN SCHOOL OF MEDICINE

Jordan Road

Cupecoy

St. Maarten, N.A.

Admissions: Medical Education Information Office

901 Ponce de Leon Boulevard, Suite 201

Coral Gables, Florida 33134

(866) 372-2282

Website: www.aucmed.edu

Year founded: 1978. AUC offers basic medical sciences in St. Maarten and clinical rotations at affiliated hospitals in the U.S., U.K., and Ireland. Graduates include more than 3,500 licensed physicians practicing in the U.S. Semesters begin in January, May, and September.

Enrollment: 380 in basic sciences; 235 in clinical sciences (May 2004)

Percentage of U.S. citizens (or permanent residents): 88.4

Admissions information: Entering class 2003: average GPA: 3.1; average MCAT: 22

Acceptance rate: 51%

Language: Courses taught in English

Pass rate on USMLE Step 1: N/A

Percentage of first-year residency placements in U.S.: 81.5% (110 of 135 graduates)

Tuition: $12,000 per semester (semesters 1–4); $13,000 per semester thereafter

Financial aid: (305) 446-0600, ext. 22 or 23

BEN-GURION UNIVERSITY OF THE NEGEV

Beer Sheva, Israel

M.D. Program in International Health and Medicine in collaboration with Columbia University Medical Center

Admissions: 630 W. 168th Street, PH15E-1512

New York, New York 10032

(212) 305-9587

Website: http://cpmcnet.columbia.edu/dept/bgcu-md

Year founded: 1996

Enrollment: Average entering class size is 30; currently 123 students in the four-year program.

Percentage of U.S. citizens: 66%

Admissions information: Average undergraduate GPA of 3.4 ; average MCAT score: 27. Interview is required.

Acceptance rate: 46%

Language: courses taught in English

Pass rate on USMLE Step 1: more than 95% for U.S. students

Percentage of first-year residency placements in U.S.: 100% in 2004

Tuition: $27,200 (2005–2006)

Financial aid: American students may use Stafford and alternative loans; and after the first semester, all students may apply for limited scholarships based on financial need.

Average attrition rate: About 4%

ROSS UNIVERSITY SCHOOL OF MEDICINE

Dominica, West Indies

Admissions: 499 Thornall St, 10th Floor
Edison, NJ 08837

(732) 978-5300

Website: www.rossmed.edu

Year founded: 1978

Enrollment: 2,500 plus

Percentage of U.S. citizens: 93%

Admissions information: Mean undergraduate GPA of 3.25; MCAT score: N/A (though now required). Interview is required.

Acceptance rate: Approximately 55%

Language: Courses taught in English

Pass rate on USMLE Step 1: 88% for 2002 first-time test takers; 94% for first- and second-time test takers.

Percentage of first-year residency placements in U.S.: 64.2% through the match; 16.3% prematch; 19.5% outside the match. Typically, 96% of eligible graduates achieve a residency position in the States.

Tuition: $12,950 per semester

Financial aid: (732) 978-5300

Average attrition: 17%

ST. GEORGE'S UNIVERSITY MEDICAL SCHOOL

Grenada, West Indies

Admissions: The North American Correspondent c/o University Services, Ltd.

1 East Main Street Bay Shore, NY 11706

(800) 899-6337, ext. 280 or (631) 665-8500

Website: www.sgu.edu

Year founded: 1976

Enrollment: 2,349

Percentage of U.S. citizens: 75%

Admissions information: average undergraduate GPA for the 2003 entering class of 3.3; MCAT Score: 24. Interview required

Language: Courses taught in English

Pass rate on USMLE Step 1: 90%

Percentage of first-year residency placements in U.S.: 99% of those eligible U.S. graduates who applied obtained residency positions in 650 hospitals throughout 50 states.

Tuition: Around $19,000 per semester

Financial aid: 1-631-665-8500, ext. 232

TECHNION-ISRAEL INSTITUTE OF TECHNOLOGY

The Technion American Medical Students (TEAMS) Program

12th Efron St., P.O. Box 9649

Haifa, 31096, Israel

011-972-829-5248

Website: http://teams.technion.ac.il

Year founded: 1983

Enrollment: 60 Americans

Percentage of U.S. citizens: 100% in the TEAMS program (U.S. citizens make up 10–15% of Technion student body).

Admissions information: Average GPA of above 3.4 and average MCAT score of 24 are required Interview is required.

Acceptance rate into program: 70%

Language: Courses taught in English

Pass rate on USMLE Step 1: 98%

Percentage of first-year residency placements in U.S.: 100%

Tuition: $22,000 per academic year

Financial aid: Federal and private

Attrition rate: Less than 1 percent

TEL AVIV UNIVERSITY SACKLER SCHOOL OF MEDICINE

New York State/American Program

Ramat Aviv Israel

Admissions: 17 E. 62nd Street

New York, NY 10021

(212) 688-8811

Website: www.tau.ac.il/medicine

Year founded: 1976

Enrollment: 300

Percentage of U.S. citizens: 100%

Admissions information: Minimum undergraduate GPA of 3.0. MCAT score: minimum of 8 on each section. Interview required.

Acceptance rate: 50%

Language: Courses are taught in English.

Pass rate on USMLE Step 1: 98%

Percentage of first-year residency placements in U.S.: 100%

Tuition: $22,000

Financial aid: Federal Stafford loan and several private loans

UNIVERSIDAD AUTÓNOMA DE GUADALAJARA

Av. Patria # 1201, Lomas del Valle, 3a. Sección

Guadalajara, Jalisco, México C.P. 44100

Admissions: 110 Gallery Circle, San Antonio, TX 78258

(210) 366-1611

(800) 531-5494

Website: www.uag.mx/medicine/default.html

Year founded: 1935

Enrollment: 4,000 plus

Percentage of U.S. citizens: 20%

Admissions information: Average GPA of 2.9; MCAT: 24. Interview required.

Acceptance rate: 33%

Language: Lectures and some labs taught in English for only the first two years, then Spanish.

Pass rate on USMLE Step 1: 82%

Percentage of first-year residency placements in U.S.: 92%

Tuition: $17,580

Financial aid: Yes

Alphabetical Index of Schools

Index of Schools by State

Georgia

Emory University, 134
Medical College of Georgia, 156
Mercer University, 162
Morehouse School of Medicine, 166

Iowa

University of Iowa (Carver), 240

Illinois

Loyola University Chicago (Stritch), 152
Northwestern University (Feinberg), 176
Rosalind Franklin University of Medicine and Science, 182
Rush University, 184
Southern Illinois University–Springfield, 186
University of Chicago (Pritzker), 228
University of Illinois–Chicago, 238

Indiana

Indiana University–Indianapolis, 146

Kansas

University of Kansas Medical Center, 242

Kentucky

Pikesville College School of Osteopathic Medicine, 344
University of Kentucky, 244
University of Louisville, 246

Louisiana

Tulane University, 204

Massachusetts

Boston University, 110
Harvard University, 142
Tufts University, 202
University of Massachusetts–Worcester, 250

Maryland

Johns Hopkins University, 150
Uniformed Services University of the Health Sciences (Herbert), 208
University of Maryland, 248

Maine

University of New England College of Osteopathic Medicine, 350

Michigan

Michigan State University, 164
Michigan State University College of Osteopathic Medicine, 334
University of Michigan–Ann Arbor, 254
Wayne State University, 316

Minnesota

Mayo Medical School, 154
University of Minnesota Medical School, 256

Missouri

A.T. Still University of Health Sciences (Kirksville), 326
St. Louis University, 190
University of Missouri–Columbia, 258
University of Missouri–Kansas City, 260
Washington University in St. Louis, 314

Nebraska

Creighton University, 120
University of Nebraska College of Medicine, 262

Nevada

University of Nevada–Reno, 264

New Hampshire

Dartmouth Medical School, 122

New Jersey

UMDNJ–Robert Wood Johnson Medical School, 206

UMDNJ–School of Osteopathic Medicine, 348

New Mexico

University of New Mexico, 266

New York

Albany Medical College, 106
Columbia University College of Physicians and Surgeons, 116
Cornell University (Weill), 118
Mount Sinai School of Medicine, 168
New York College of Osteopathic Medicine, 336
New York Medical College, 170
New York University, 172
Stony Brook University, 192
SUNY–Syracuse, 194
University at Buffalo–SUNY, 210
University of Rochester, 278
Yeshiva University (Einstein), 324

North Carolina

Duke University, 126
East Carolina University (Brody), 128
University of North Carolina–Chapel Hill, 268
Wake Forest University, 312

North Dakota

University of North Dakota, 270

Ohio

Case Western Reserve University, 114
Northeastern Ohio Universities College of Medicine, 174
Ohio State University, 178
Ohio University, 340
University of Cincinnati, 230
University of Toledo, 296
Wright State University, 320

Oklahoma

Oklahoma State University, 342
University of Oklahoma, 272

About the Authors & Editors

Founded in 1933, Washington, D.C.–based *U.S.News & World Report* delivers a unique brand of weekly magazine journalism to its 12.2 million readers. In 1983, *U.S. News* began its exclusive annual rankings of American colleges and universities. The *U.S. News* education franchise is second to none, with its annual college and graduate school rankings among the most eagerly anticipated magazine issues in the country.

Josh Fischman, the book's lead writer and editor, covers health and science for *U.S. News & World Report*. Previously, he was editor-in-chief at *Earth*, deputy news editor at *Science*, and a senior editor at *Discover*. He has also cowritten the children's book *101 Things Every Kid Should Know about Dinosaurs*. He has won the Blakeslee Award for excellence in medical reporting from the American Heart Association.

Anne McGrath, editor, is a deputy editor at *U.S.News & World Report*, where she covers health. Previously, she was managing editor of "America's Best Colleges" and "America's Best Graduate Schools," the two *U.S. News* annual publications featuring rankings of the country's colleges and universities.

Robert Morse is the director of data research at *U.S.News & World Report*. He is in charge of the research, data collection, methodologies, and survey design for the annual "America's Best Colleges" rankings and the "America's Best Graduate Schools" rankings.

Brian Kelly is the executive editor of *U.S.News & World Report*. As the magazine's No. 2 editor, he oversees the weekly magazine, the website, and a series of newsstand books. He is a former editor at the *Washington Post* and the author of three books.

Other writers who contributed chapters or passages to the book are **Ulrich Boser, Kristin Davis, Justin Ewers, Helen Fields, Dan Gilgoff, Vicky Hallett, Cory Hatch, Bernadine Healy, Caroline Hsu, Katy Kelly, Carolyn Kleiner Butler, Samantha Levine, Marianne Szegedy-Maszak, Stacy Schultz, Nancy Shute, Rachel K. Sobel**, and **Amanda Spake**. The work involved in producing the directory and *U.S. News* Insider's Index was handled by **Sam Flanigan**. Thanks to **David Griffin** for his work in designing the book and to **Sara Sklaroff** for project editing. Thanks as well to **James Bock** for his copyediting assistance and to members of the *U.S. News* **factchecking team** for making sure we got it right.

Get Over 200 Puzzles!

The Best Sudoku Puzzles Presented by Will Shortz

Inside this special edition you'll find over 200 new sudoku puzzles for every skill level! Whether you're a beginner or expert, there are grids inside that will excite and entertain you.

Plus, you'll also find the latest tips to solving sudoku from Will Shortz, *The New York Times* crossword editor and NPR puzzlemaster. Just pick a grid and start "Sudoku-ing"!

- 🖊 **The newest tips for solving sudoku**
- 🖊 **Large grids for easy play**
- 🖊 **Step-by-step instructions for beginners**
- 🖊 **200 easy-to-expert puzzles, plus 20 bonus puzzles**

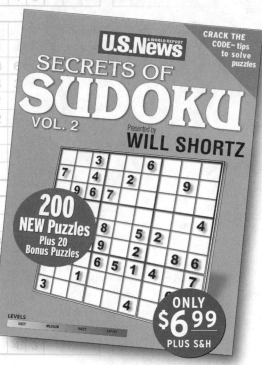